(Continued on back endsheets)

Early Modern Russian Writers, Late Seventeenth and Eighteenth Centuries

Early Modern Russian Writers, Late Seventeenth and Eighteenth Centuries

Edited by
Marcus C. Levitt
University of Southern California

A Bruccoli Clark Layman Book
Gale Research Inc.
Detroit, Washington, D.C., London

The paper used in this publication meets the minimum requirements
of American National Standard for Information Sciences—Permanence
Paper for Printed Library Materials, ANSI Z39.48-1984. ∞ ™

Library of Congress Cataloging-in-Publication Data
Early modern Russian writers: late seventeenth and eighteenth centuries / edited by Marcus C. Levitt.
    p. cm. – (Dictionary of literary biography; v. 150)
"A Bruccoli Clark Layman book."
Includes bibliographical references and index.
ISBN 0-8103-5711-9 (alk. paper)
    1. Russian literature – To 1700 – Bio-bibliography. 2. Russian literature – 18th century –
Bio-bibliography. 3. Authors, Russian – Biography – Dictionaries. I. Levitt, Marcus C., 1954–
II. Series.
Z2500.E17 1995
[PG2991.2]
891.709'001 – dc20   95-1711
[B]   CIP

10 9 8 7 6 5 4 3 2 1

Contents

Contents

Plan of the Series

. . . Almost the most prodigious asset of a country, and perhaps its most precious possession, is its native literary product – when that product is fine and noble and enduring.

Mark Twain*

The advisory board, the editors, and the publisher of the *Dictionary of Literary Biography* are joined in endorsing Mark Twain's declaration. The literature of a nation provides an inexhaustible resource of permanent worth. We intend to make literature and its creators better understood and more accessible to students and the reading public, while satisfying the standards of teachers and scholars.

To meet these requirements, *literary biography* has been construed in terms of the author's achievement. The most important thing about a writer is his writing. Accordingly, the entries in *DLB* are career biographies, tracing the development of the author's canon and the evolution of his reputation.

The purpose of *DLB* is not only to provide reliable information in a convenient format but also to place the figures in the larger perspective of literary history and to offer appraisals of their accomplishments by qualified scholars.

The publication plan for *DLB* resulted from two years of preparation. The project was proposed to Bruccoli Clark by Frederick C. Ruffner, president of the Gale Research Company, in November 1975. After specimen entries were prepared and typeset, an advisory board was formed to refine the entry format and develop the series rationale. In meetings held during 1976, the publisher, series editors, and advisory board approved the scheme for a comprehensive biographical dictionary of persons who contributed to North American literature. Editorial work on the first volume began in January 1977, and it was published in 1978. In order to make *DLB* more than a reference tool and to compile volumes that individually have claim to status as literary history, it was decided to organize vol-

From an unpublished section of Mark Twain's autobiography, copyright by the Mark Twain Company

umes by topic, period, or genre. Each of these free-standing volumes provides a biographical-bibliographical guide and overview for a particular area of literature. We are convinced that this organization – as opposed to a single alphabet method – constitutes a valuable innovation in the presentation of reference material. The volume plan necessarily requires many decisions for the placement and treatment of authors who might properly be included in two or three volumes. In some instances a major figure will be included in separate volumes, but with different entries emphasizing the aspect of his career appropriate to each volume. Ernest Hemingway, for example, is represented in *American Writers in Paris, 1920–1939* by an entry focusing on his expatriate apprenticeship; he is also in *American Novelists, 1910–1945* with an entry surveying his entire career. Each volume includes a cumulative index of the subject authors and articles. Comprehensive indexes to the entire series are planned.

With volume ten in 1982 it was decided to enlarge the scope of *DLB*. By the end of 1986 twenty-one volumes treating British literature had been published, and volumes for Commonwealth and Modern European literature were in progress. The series has been further augmented by the *DLB Yearbooks* (since 1981) which update published entries and add new entries to keep the *DLB* current with contemporary activity. There have also been *DLB Documentary Series* volumes which provide biographical and critical source materials for figures whose work is judged to have particular interest for students. One of these companion volumes is entirely devoted to Tennessee Williams.

We define literature as the *intellectual commerce of a nation*: not merely as belles lettres but as that ample and complex process by which ideas are generated, shaped, and transmitted. *DLB* entries are not limited to "creative writers" but extend to other figures who in their time and in their way influenced the mind of a people. Thus the series encompasses historians, journalists, publishers, and screenwriters. By this means readers of *DLB* may be aided to perceive literature not as cult scripture in the keeping of intellectual high priests but firmly positioned at the center of a nation's life.

DLB includes the major writers appropriate to each volume and those standing in the ranks immediately behind them. Scholarly and critical counsel has been sought in deciding which minor figures to include and how full their entries should be. Wherever possible, useful references are made to figures who do not warrant separate entries.

Each *DLB* volume has a volume editor responsible for planning the volume, selecting the figures for inclusion, and assigning the entries. Volume editors are also responsible for preparing, where appropriate, appendices surveying the major periodicals and literary and intellectual movements for their volumes, as well as lists of further readings. Work on the series as a whole is coordinated at the Bruccoli Clark Layman editorial center in Columbia, South Carolina, where the editorial staff is responsible for accuracy of the published volumes.

One feature that distinguishes *DLB* is the illustration policy – its concern with the iconography of literature. Just as an author is influenced by his surroundings, so is the reader's understanding of the author enhanced by a knowledge of his environment. Therefore *DLB* volumes include not only drawings, paintings, and photographs of authors, often depicting them at various stages in their careers, but also illustrations of their families and places where they lived. Title pages are regularly reproduced in facsimile along with dust jackets for modern authors. The dust jackets are a special feature of *DLB* because they often document better than anything else the way in which an author's work was perceived in its own time. Specimens of the writers' manuscripts are included when feasible.

Samuel Johnson rightly decreed that "The chief glory of every people arises from its authors." The purpose of the *Dictionary of Literary Biography* is to compile literary history in the surest way available to us – by accurate and comprehensive treatment of the lives and work of those who contributed to it.

The *DLB* Advisory Board

Introduction

The forty-nine career biographies included in this volume span the period in which Russia was transformed from an essentially medieval, feudal culture into a modern, secularized, European empire. Because of the Mongol invasion of the mid thirteenth century, Russia's "Dark Ages" lasted far longer than in the West; her isolation was extended by the despotic princes of Moscow – Basil I (1389–1425); Basil II (1425–1462, with interruptions); Ivan III (1462–1505); Basil III (1505–1533); and Ivan IV (the Terrible, 1533–1584) – who both threw off "the Tatar yoke" and forced such independent centers of old Russian culture as Novgorod under their control. The ebullient ages of Renaissance and Reformation in the West had virtually no effect on Russia. Russia's attempts under the rulers of Muscovy to maintain its high-medieval religious culture and to shut out the rest of the world – what has been called the "monasticization" of Russia – reached its apogee in the later sixteenth century under Ivan the Terrible, who enforced xenophobic, antisecular cultural policies and by the end of his reign had forcibly curtailed Russia's already-modest contacts with the West. Russia's long isolation was sundered, brutally, by the "Time of Troubles" (1603–1613), a violent decade of foreign invasion and chaotic political interregnum which finally ended with the election of the Romanov dynasty – the dynasty that was to rule Russia until the Revolution of 1917.

While from that time Russia's political development as an increasingly powerful centralized state continued unabated, culturally the nation underwent a prolonged period of transition and often-painful change. Russia's sudden, frequently violent exposure to the West – first via invasion, then via her own policies of expansion and conquest – came during an age of religious war and ideological conflict, and her need to modernize, if only to compete with her more sophisticated ideological opponents, was traumatic. On the one hand it led to the great schism within the Russian Orthodox church. The schism, which became final in 1666, was a kind of Russian Reformation in reverse: a protest against modern rationalist reformism in the name of preserving, not reforming, church practice. On the

other hand, it culminated in the epochal westernizing reforms of Peter the Great (1682–1725). With Peter, Russia consciously abandoned the medieval world of *Slavia Orthodoxa* – that common Slavic culture embracing Russia and her southern and eastern Slavic neighbors which was based on a shared religion (Eastern Orthodoxy), language, and literary heritage (primarily religious texts in the Church Slavonic language) – and shifted its cultural sights to western Europe and the cultural stream that flowed from classical Greece and Rome via Renaissance Italy to the France of Louis XIV.

During the period covered in this volume the phenomenon commonly referred to as literature underwent such radical, fundamental change – in its subject matter, in those who produced and consumed it, in its status and existence as a social institution, in its aesthetic and ideological values, in its means of dissemination, and even in its linguistic medium – that it is problematic to speak of a continuous literary tradition at all in any usual sense without significant qualifications. The boundaries of "early modern" Russian literature, its beginning and end, as well as the relevance of such borrowed concepts as classicism, sentimentalism, and the baroque, remain the subject of substantial scholarly debate. The question of their relevance depends in large part on how even such basic terms as *modern* and *literature* are defined and to what extent Western period labels (as definitions of literary, stylistic, philosophical, and chronological phenomena) are deemed applicable to Russian cultural realities.

The birth of modern, European-oriented "Russian literature" is often ascribed to the immediate post-Petrine period, in particular to the reform of Russian versification. Vasilii Trediakovsky's *New and Brief Method for Composing Russian Verse* of 1735 and Mikhail Lomonosov's "Letter on the Rules of Russian Versification" of 1739 established a new syllabotonic system of versification (combining long and short syllables into regular metric feet). Just as Peter I had put an end to medieval Muscovite culture by founding his new capital of Saint Petersburg, his "window to the West," and by mandating new styles of dress and establishing a new calendar and new civil alphabet, Trediakovsky and his generation felt that they were founding a "new" literature. Certainly there is much to support this view. They began to establish for the first time a high poetic tradition in the Russian vernacular tongue, written by people who were not of the clergy, and gave public sanction to such new secular literary pursuits as romantic love and satire. Writing ceased to be the exclusive domain of monks and clerics and began its migration through the institutions of modern society: salon, academy, theater, and literary journal. Yet scholars of recent decades have come increasingly to appreciate the continuities between the "new" literature and not only that of the immediately preceding Petrine period but also the later-seventeenth-century tradition. The myth of a sharp break between "old" and "new" Russian literature – an extension of the mythical opposition between old and new Russia promulgated by Peter the Great that later generations of Russians accepted as undisputed truth – obscures the long period of development and many continuities which linked them.

Increasing attention has been paid to the "transitional" literature of the later seventeenth century, whose heterogeneous and disparate nature testifies not only to strong medieval elements but also to unmistakable European influences. Complex social changes, including the emergence of a new aristocracy as well as a rudimentary urban middle class of merchants, artisans, and petty bureaucrats, created new audiences for secular literature and the first signs of a fissure between highbrow literature, centered at the court and in certain monastic centers, and anonymous "popular" or "democratic" writing. The anonymous lowbrow prose tales of the later seventeenth century and Petrine period that circulated in manuscript display a hodgepodge of medieval, oral folkloric, and (mostly second- or thirdhand) Western sources, both in language and theme. This tradition continued in the eighteenth century in the flourishing trade in *lubki* (chapbooks and broadsides) and contributed to the great popularity of translated (or, rather, adapted) novels after midcentury. "Medieval" and mixed types of popular literature – which should be thought of as separate modes of literature's social and cultural existence rather than chronological categories – continued to exist in Russia together with the highbrow literature that followed more up-to-date European styles and trends.

While popular literature was frequently anonymous and slow to separate itself from older literary modes, the emergence of the notion of authorship in the modern sense (and hence of having a

"literary biography") was connected with the new trends at first imported from Russia's eastern and southern Slavic neighbors. Of crucial interest for the tradition of high literature was the seventeenth-century "Russian Baroque" represented by Simeon Polotsky and his followers. While in fundamental ways unlike the baroque in the West, the philosophical and religious roots of which lay in the Counter-Reformation and which represented in global terms a reaction against Renaissance humanism, in Russia the baroque, as the Russian scholar Dmitrii Likhachev has argued, functioned in terms of Russia's cultural development as a simultaneous Renaissance and baroque, insofar as it served to introduce modern literary values into Russia. Like Byzantine Christian writings at the time of Russia's conversion to Christianity, the new type of literature was transplanted into Russia, although as Likhachev has argued, Western influence should not be seen as the cause of cultural reform but as the result of long-standing gradual developments within medieval Russian literature.

The union of Ukraine with the Russian Empire in 1654 brought contemporary Western trends (primarily via the Polish, Ukrainian, Byelorussian, and Latin languages) into Russia's backyard as Moscow struggled to compete with Kiev's modern, sophisticated educational and intellectual accomplishments. With the influence of bookmen from the Kiev religious academies, such as Polotsky, who came to Moscow in 1664, came an interest in the modern editing of church texts (which spurred the schism) and the study of rhetoric and poetics in the Jesuit scholastic school tradition; these practices now became part of the Orthodox educational curriculum in Russia as well. Polotsky took part in the council that condemned the Old Believers as heretics, set up the first printing press independent of the patriarchate, helped plan what would become under Peter the first institution of higher learning in Russia, the Slavonic-Greek-Latin Academy, and wrote the first "school dramas" and panegyric odes for the Russian court; he became what some scholars have argued was Russia's first professional court poet. School drama, which combined elements of the medieval mystery play with more modern baroque allegory, became popular at court during the last part of the reign of Czar Alexis I (1645–1676), although his successor, Fedor III (1676–1682), discontinued the practice. It was revived later in the century and endured in Russia until about the time a classicist theater began to develop in the late 1740s.

With the Jesuit school tradition the late-Renaissance neo-Aristotelian hierarchy of genres began to supersede the largely unself-conscious and informal literary system of medieval Russia; this change may be taken as one of the basic markers of modern literary consciousness in Russia. Although the process was one of modernization, it is important to keep in mind that the literary traditions being assimilated were already centuries old in Europe and that it was to take Russia more than a century and a half to close the chronological gap – and almost two hundred years before Europe was to recognize Russian literature as a full-fledged member of the literary fraternity. Notably, the Aristotelian hierarchy was almost exclusively a hierarchy of poetry – something almost completely lacking in Russia at that time (with the possible exceptions of oral folk poetry, the Orthodox liturgy, traditions of oral religious verse, or of medieval "poetic prose," about which there is considerable scholarly debate). While there were earlier precedents in writing verse, it was not until Polotsky introduced his regular syllabic verse into Muscovy that poetry was codified into a formal literary system. During what might be called the "early modern" period covered in this volume, the "classical" hierarchical system of genres underwent three basic transmutations in Russia before it was finally dethroned in the nineteenth century: the seventeenth-century baroque; mid-eighteenth-century Russian classicism; and the sentimentalism of the later eighteenth and early nineteenth century. The notion of hierarchy was increasingly discredited in the nineteenth century, first by Romanticism and later by the rise of Russian realist prose.

A crucial figure who bridged the seventeenth- and eighteenth-century literary traditions was the Ukrainian clergyman Feofan Prokopovich. Brought to Saint Petersburg from Kiev by Peter, he helped engineer the reform that turned the Orthodox church into an arm of the secular state and also defended Peter's enlightened but absolutist rule. Since Polotsky, the new literature had served the interests of the Europeanized Russian court, providing panegyrical poetry, speeches, and sermons for religious holidays as well as dynastic and political events. However, the fact that most of Polotsky's estimated eighty thousand lines of poetry – almost all but his *Psaltir tsaria i proroka Davida* (Psalter of King David the Prophet, 1680) – remained in manuscript served to curtail sharply its influence and impede the creation of a poetic tradition. Prokopovich's sermons confirmed literature's role not only as celebration of state power but as obedient partner in advancing the cause of Petrine reform, and with him literature began to move out of the intimate circle of the czar's family, its primary arena for Polotsky, who had been tutor to Czarevna Sofia and her siblings, and out into the public sphere.

The period of Peter I's rule has been called the most unliterary in Russian history, a situation due both to the utilitarian pathos of the age and to the perplexing linguistic situation. Late-seventeenth-century baroque writers had written in the Church Slavonic language, though Prokopovich had introduced a "hybrid" variety into his sermons that incorporated elements of the "unliterary" Russian vernacular. Church Slavonic had been introduced into Russia in the tenth century together with Christianity and had served as virtually the only literary language the country had ever known; Russian, while spoken, practically never served as a written medium. As part of his wholesale rejection of all aspects of medieval culture, Peter demanded a new "simple" and comprehensible written language in vernacular Russian and devised a new "civil script" in which to write and print it. Peter wanted the language primarily in order to import Western technology into Russia more easily, but creating a modern literary vehicle out of a vacuum was a task with which Russian writers struggled for the next hundred years, culminating in the achievements of Nikolai Karamzin and Aleksandr Pushkin. After Prokopovich, Russian literature (that is, literature in Russian) remained associated with the Petrine mission of service to the state but ceased to be the exclusive domain of churchmen, although Prokopovich's homiletic legacy was continued by a distinguished tradition of church orators (such as Metropolitan Platon, whose meteoric career began as the court preacher for Catherine II) who wrote not in Church Slavonic but in the new literary tongue (referred to as "Slaveno-Russian" at mid century).

Peter's successors Empresses Anne (1730–1740) and Elizabeth (1741–1762), and later Catherine the Great (1762–1796), invited architects, artists, sculptors, and artisans from all over Europe to transform Saint Petersburg (founded by Peter in 1703 in swampland) into the capital of a mighty Europeanized Russian Empire. They presided over a flowering of a brilliant imperial court culture which featured lavish ceremonials, often including fireworks and sumptuous masquerade balls, which utilized the services of musicians, dancers, singers, pyrotechnicians, painters, architects, and writers. In the 1730s and 1740s odes, orations, and other oral ceremonial genres were written on order in German and in Russian by members of the new Academy of Sciences (founded just after Peter's death in 1726) and by academicians such as Trediakovsky and Lomonosov, in their early years members of Prokopovich's "learned guard." Under Anna, German was the language of preference at court, but after the death of this despotic and unpopular empress French became established as the main language of polite society, which it remained until well into the nineteenth century. Peter I's successors ushered in a century of aristocratic culture, as the Russian gentry became increasingly powerful at the expense of the enserfed peasantry; the compulsory service obligations imposed under Peter's "Table of Ranks" were abolished during the short reign of Peter III in 1762, and the gentry's rights and privileges reached an apogee with Catherine's Charter to the Nobility of 1785. The spread of modern, Europeanized education, coupled with increased financial means and leisure time, helped to create an aristocratic "intelligentsia," which, although still tied to the court in many ways, began to address the needs and interests of its class. While the syllabic verse satires of Prince Antiokh Kantemir had been a rather isolated achievement, in the 1750s and 1760s Russian literary life began to coalesce into trends and groupings, centered in such institutions as the First Cadet Corps, founded in 1732, and Moscow University, founded with Lomonosov's urging in 1755. A national theater was established in 1756 under the direction of Aleksandr Sumarokov, who wrote Russia's first tragedies, comedies, operas, and ballets and who edited one of the first private literary journals. Whereas it has been calculated that during the first quarter of the century only three works of belles lettres had been published (.2 percent of the total output of books), during 1725–1755 the number was up to 8 percent (71 titles), and in 1756–1775 up to 17 percent (482 titles). These numbers testify not only to the highly elitist nature of literary culture of the time in Russia, which was still overwhelmingly illiterate, but also, in relative terms, to the rapid expansion of Russian literature. It should be kept in mind that the majority of written texts circulated in manuscript and that the commercial book trade was just beginning to take its first shaky steps.

A fundamental impulse behind Russian classicism, which predominated from the 1730s to the 1770s, was to establish and normalize literary practice, to establish the rules for the new literary language (for example, Lomonosov's 1748 *Rhetoric* and his *Rossiiskaia grammatika,* 1755) for poetic genres (Sumarokov's *Dve epistoly,* 1748), as well as for versi-

fication. Its ideological mission was to propagate the ideals of enlightened absolutism, although the two halves of this equation – enlightenment ideals of social justice and rule under law, on the one hand, and the unchecked power of the throne, on the other – came into increasing conflict. Eighteenth-century poets such as Sumarokov struggled to harmonize their social ideals with the vagaries of patronage; it was not until the first third of the next century that a Russian reading public capable of making a writer financially self-supporting emerged. The reign of Catherine II dramatizes the problem. Catherine came to the throne declaring her liberal and enlightened intentions (in part to offset the fact that she had deposed her husband Peter III). In her famous *Nakaz* (Instruction) prepared for the Legislative Commission of 1767, she advertised the ideas of Cesare Beccaria (who opposed capital punishment) and Montesquieu and did more than anyone else to establish the ideals of free speech and rule based on law in Russia; it was she who encouraged the publication of the so-called satirical journals of 1769–1774, granted the right to establish private presses in 1783, and patronized a whole string of writers from Denis Diderot and Voltaire to Aleksandr Sumarokov and Gavriil Derzhavin. Yet it was also Catherine who tried to suppress the independence of Russian letters after the bloody peasant rebellion led by Emelian Pugachev in 1774, and it was she who seemed to do a complete about-face after the outbreak of the French Revolution. Her "enlightened" reign concluded with the arrest and exile of Aleksandr Radishchev and Nikolai Novikov, among others, the persecution of the Masons, the revocation of the free-press law, and the institution of an oppressive censorship.

Muscovite baroque literature as well as Saint Petersburg classicism had shifted the focus of Russian letters from the medieval God-centered universe onto the modern secular state centered in the person of the emperor or empress. The fact that Russia had bypassed the traditions of Renaissance humanism, which championed the value of the individual, also served to emphasize the "service mentality" of early modern Russian literature. However, by the later eighteenth century certain factors furthered the independence and diversification of Russian letters. The first and most obvious was political: disenchantment with Catherine led to varying degrees of opposition (in such leading writers as Denis Fonvizin, Vasilii Kapnist, Novikov, Radishchev), sharpened by the empress's cultivation of her "own" official court poet, Vasilii Petrov (who, together with the sycophantic Vasilii Ruban, helped give the entire eighteenth-century tradition a bad name among later generations). Another was institutional: new educational establishments (Moscow University, the spread of secondary schools), presses, specialized journals, theaters, and scholarly and amateur associations all created support for literary activity independent of the court. A third factor was social: literature was no longer a peculiar and suspect activity but part of every educated Russian's heritage and education; it provided models for modern manners and came to serve, among other things, as an aid or even prerequisite to advancement in governmental service.

Indeed the majority of Russian writers in the eighteenth century were state servitors first and writers second; for many writing was thought of as a kind of state service. With time literary groupings came to reflect social differentiation within the aristocracy. By the end of the century, under the pressure of events, Russian literature largely retreated from the political arena and became primarily a noble pastime, reflecting the tastes of various aristocratic cliques and circles; satiric mock epics, obscene verse, and "unprofessional" salon genres became popular (the latter two remaining primarily in manuscript). Growing interest in Freemasonry and writing on Masonic themes (which had made their appearance as early as the 1750s) also reflected a move toward aristocratic introspection.

At the same time, high literature soon ceased to be the exclusive domain of the Russian gentry. European "bourgeois drama" (of Diderot, Beaumarchais, and others) made itself felt in the comedies and comic translation-adaptions of the V. I. Lukin group. It is risky, however, mechanically to apply Western concepts of class development to the still-preindustrial and largely feudal eighteenth-century Russia; Russian scholars often fall back on the somewhat nebulous label *raznochintsy* (people of varied ranks) to mask the lack of a basic social history of the period. Theater was one possible venue for attracting an audience that was not exclusively gentry; another more obvious one was the translated novel, which from the 1760s became the most prevalent and best-selling kind of nonreligious reading matter in Russia. The popular seventeenth-century and Petrine tales (which had circulated in manuscript), translated European novels (such as those of Abbé Prévost), popular miscellanies, and song collections made the fortunes of commercial chapbook publishers, who created a precedent for the nascent bourgeois commercial book-publishing

industry of the 1830s. There were also attempts at Russian novels, like Fedor Emin's multivolume sentimental works à la Samuel Richardson and Jean-Jacques Rousseau and those of Mikhail Chulkov. Notably, the classicist hierarchy of genres was a hierarchy of poetry alone, and writers like Sumarokov and Mikhail Kheraskov disdained the novel.

Sentimentalism, which cultivated the middle poetic registers of the classicist hierarchy (the elegy and idyll rather than ode or epic), is also sometimes described as "Pre-Romanticism," which places emphasis on the hierarchy's eventual dissolution and its displacement by a new aesthetic. Sentimentalists turned to new models – German and English rather than French, Jakob Lenz and Edward Young rather than Voltaire – and to new genres: prose forms (the prose idyll, travel notes, the essay) gained new prominence. The main audience for Russian literature was no longer the empress and her court but the salon and informal literary associations, and the language for literature was increasingly based on the spoken tongue of "polite society" (which had only begun to emerge as a cultural reality, although linguistic reformers since the 1730s had alluded to it as a source of literary norms). While still aristocratic in many ways, the ideals of polite society promoted an egalitarianism of culture and taste that broadened the social base for highbrow Russian letters.

Because of the marked dualism of Russian culture, Russian literary movements tend to bifurcate: hence Avvakum and Polotsky, for all their differences, may be viewed as two poles of the Russian baroque, and Sumarokov and Lomonosov as two poles of classicism. Similarly, Russian sentimentalism may be seen to have had a second, opposing strain. As opposed to Karamzin's emphasis on taste and culture and his "polite," ameliorative approach to social ills, in his *Puteshestvie iz Peterburga v Moskvu* (Journey from Saint Petersburg to Moscow, 1970) Radishchev combined an emotive, sentimentalist manner (arguably even an attack on the impotence of sentiment) with an outspoken denunciation of the evils of serfdom, censorship, and political corruption, expressed in a purposefully jolting, archaic style. "Russia's first philosophe," Radishchev decried Catherine's failure to live up to her enlightenment ideals, and for this Catherine had him arrested and sent into exile. If Russian literature's "service mentality" remained, it now began in part to distance itself from the throne and dedicate itself rather to the good of Russian society. This commitment to serve the good of society was one of the eighteenth century's most potent legacies to the Russian intelligentsia (and to the revolutionary movements) of the nineteenth.

By early in that century Russian literature had diversified into various factions and groupings, which simultaneously represented trends that looked backward to the eighteenth century and those that looked forward; hence several members of the "Beseda" group are represented in this volume of *Early Modern Russian Writers,* while their rivals, the early Romantics of "Arzamas," will appear in the next. Opposed to the Karamzinian "innovators" (to use Iury Tynianov's convenient terms), the "archaists" of Beseda (Admiral Shishkov and his followers) advocated a return to national political, religious, and linguistic roots, in this case the high Slaveno-Russian tradition of Lomonosov, indicating that the eighteenth-century tradition had already undergone a process of canonization (even though it was soon to be overthrown by Romantic critics of the 1820s). While such a division is convenient, it may also be misleading; it should be emphasized that sentimentalism was a direct offshoot of classicism (which, it has been argued, never existed in "pure" form in Russia anyway), and there were arguably more elements linking "archaists" and "innovators" than separating them. Furthermore, many of the groups of the next literary generation of the 1810s and 1820s – the Decembrists or the proto-Slavophile "Liubomudry," for example – were both strongly tied to the "archaic" eighteenth century and seen by the later tradition as its progenitors.

Just as it has proved difficult to pinpoint the beginnings of early modern literature in Russia, so too its end is vague; once again the way terms are defined will determine the verdict. Epochal political events like the French Revolution, Catherine's repressions (which ended with her death in 1796), and the Napoleonic invasion of 1812, which marked a major watershed in national self-consciousness, could all serve as endpoints. In Russian intellectual history the failed Decembrist coup of 1825 marks the death knell for Enlightenment thought in Russia, a failure which led in the next generation (in the historian Nicholas Riasanovsky's phrase) to the "parting of the ways" between educated Russian society and government. This was also, one may argue, the true divide between the eighteenth and nineteenth centuries in Russian literary culture, marking the demise of classicism and the victory of Romanticism, to use the terms current in literary debates of the time. In Russian critical consciousness, this was the moment when it was decided with

horror that "we have no literature," and that Russian literature had to create itself anew, from scratch, when it was discovered that (to paraphrase the famous nineteenth-century critic Vissarion Belinsky) the old idols had feet of clay and that new monuments had yet to be found to replace them. The political failure of Enlightenment ideals led to the discrediting of practically the entire earlier literary and aesthetic tradition, which, with the exception of certain works and figures, was largely forgotten. This was also the date after which Russian literature began to be legally independent (as far as it could be under an autocracy) as well as potentially remunerative, as the patronage system and salon groupings gave way to literary parties and the interests of a new bourgeois-style reading public.

Medieval Slavic literature had been resolutely anonymous, even more so than medieval literature in the West. The Orthodox tradition of *kenotic* humility (based on the notion of Jesus's voluntary *kenosis,* or "emptying" of earthly passions) encouraged suppression of any marks of individual biography, and little is known about those few names the old tradition did preserve. The gradual emergence of literary biography as a cultural phenomenon may also be seen as a signpost of a modern post-Renaissance literary consciousness. Paradoxically, the *Zhitie protopopa Avvakuma* (Life of the Archpriest Avvakum), by the schismatic priest Avvakum, who perished at the stake in 1682, was simultaneously the swan song of medieval Russian culture and a unique example of "modern" Russian autobiography. Despite the new complex picture of human psychology presented in the *Zhitie protopopa Avvakuma* and its macaronic blending of Church Slavonic and the Russian vernacular – which make Avvakum in the opinion of some scholars a baroque writer *malgré lui* – Avvakum rejected the exalted view of the modern poet's calling promoted by Simeon Polotsky and his followers. Both shared a faith in the potentially divine nature of the Word (as Logos), an exalted view of the power of writing which characterizes Russian literature of all periods. However, Avvakum denounced an interest in rhetoric and philosophy as heretical. He condemned Polotsky's quasi-Protestant rationalist idea that writing could be considered as a "good work," a notion that presented a potential challenge to the traditional Orthodox emphasis on the primacy of faith. With the rise of the baroque, the center of literary attention shifted from religious ideals per se to their incarnation in the state and the czar, and, as Stephen Baehr has shown in his 1991 book, literature's function changed from praising God's immortality to immortalizing the fame of the "earthly God." Together with this, and especially as Russian literature moved more clearly into the secular sphere, the poet's own glory – as Iurii Lotman (1986) puts it, his "right to a biography," to be remembered by posterity – emerged as a new cultural value, the worldly counterpart to the desire for an afterlife. This Horatian idea of *exegi monumentum,* of the writer erecting an immortal monument unto himself via his works, which had entered European literary consciousness with the Renaissance, was to have a long and fertile afterlife in Russian poetry and culture.

At the same time, the precise shape and content of literary biography conforms to each era's changing conception of both literature and biography. Eighteenth-century poets in Russia were still largely poets without "biographies" in the current sense of the word; that is, they usually revealed little about their private lives. In general almost no direct testimony from them survives, apart from the sporadic information that can be inferred from their works or letters. The historian is often left, on the one hand, with mere lists of the official positions and ranks enjoyed – which underscores the reigning view of literature as a branch of state service – and, on the other, with a body of most often unreliable anecdotal material. This paucity of information is due in large part to the consistent distinction Russian classicism drew between the everyday, material world in its "base" manifestations and the absolute and immutable laws of nature, the distance maintained between life and art. "Low reality" was relegated to base genres like the comedy or fable or left outside art's purview. Hence, as Irina Reyfman writes in *Vasilii Trediakovsky: The Fool of the "New" Russian Literature* (1990), "the literature of Russian Classicism was impersonal in principle. In an ode, tragedy, or fable the author was totally irrelevant. The author spoke on behalf of eternal truths, and no one was interested in a particular author's personality."

On the other hand, if medieval literature had been anonymous out of religious humility, the rise of a modern literary scene was marked by exaggerated literary egos and personal antagonisms to what seems an excessive degree. The dark side of the belief in literature's laws as absolute was that relatively minor literary disagreements were often magnified into nasty polemics of a highly personal nature. At issue was a writer's authority and his "right to a biography." As Avvakum had feared, to be a writer of the modern type necessarily involved self-promotion, which he felt to be bordering on blas-

phemy. For Russian classicists, self-creation could be a prime virtue, as in Kheraskov's praise of Sumarokov – he "sam soboi dostig Permesskikh tokov" (reached Hippocrene's sources all by himself) – or a cardinal sin, exemplified by the endless complaints about amateurism and graphomania, faults from which Catherine the Great particularly suffered as a writer. Given the absence of literary critics and the limited, somewhat artificial nature of literary production, dissemination, and reception under a system of patronage, there were few control mechanisms to help decide such questions. Hence eighteenth-century Russian writing tended to be markedly metaliterary, taking the burden of criticism upon itself, most often in the form of satire and parody. Thus, satire and parody may often serve as sources of biographical data, insofar as they deal with deviations from the ideal of the perfect, impersonal self.

Classicism's preference for the absolute rule over individual idiosyncrasy and the marked "impersonality" of a writer's creations tended to disassociate a specific author from a specific text and even to separate a writer's name from his own creations. "Biography" became a rather impersonalized construction. Hence such ubiquitous references to writers as "the Russian Malherbe" (Lomonosov), "the Russian Racine" (Sumarokov), and so on, as G. A. Gukovsky noted in 1929, did not basically refer to the similarities of those author's works to those of the European writers in question, or even to any particular or personal qualities of their own writing but were rather meant as marks of their fame and allusions to the analogous places they deserved to occupy in the history of Russian letters. A landmark of this sort of classicist approach to biography was Novikov's *Opyt istoricheskogo slovaria o rossiiskikh pisateliakh* (Attempt at a Historical Dictionary of Russian Writers, 1772), reportedly compiled with Sumarokov's assistance. Russian literature was to acquire its own canon of literary biography.

The large body of anecdotal information about writers' lives testifies to the strong tendency in the eighteenth and early nineteenth century to "mythologize" its writers and to create pseudo-biographies that in many cases eclipsed the actual circumstances of writers' lives and creations. Irina Reyfman analyzes a central myth of the age, that of the Hero-Creator (a role the later tradition conferred on Lomonosov) and his alter ego the Fool (whose lot fell to Trediakovsky). The remarkable vitality of this myth, which survived well into the nineteenth century as a part of Russian cultural consciousness, derived in large measure from the overarching influence of the larger myth of Peter the Great as creator of a "new nation," and the almost apocalyptic significance Russians assigned to modernization. The enduring Russian "medieval" value system explored in the works of the Russian scholars Iurii Lotman and Boris Uspensky assigned all things either a radically positive or negative assessment and hence constantly generated dual images (New/Old, Hero/Fool). Such was the force of this scheme that the third member of the mid-century poetic triumvirate, the influential Aleksandr Sumarokov, largely disappeared from view.

The mythogenic spirit of early modern Russian letters, however, has yet to be studied in full, nor has the full panoply of literary biographical types been catalogued. Such a gallery would no doubt include the Pedant, Bohemian, and Fop (*Petimetr*, from the French "petit-maitre") of the mid-century, as well as the rich cast from Russian comedies and satiric journals, such as Catherine the Great as Babushka (Grandma) or Denis Fonvizin as Starodum (Wise Old Man, one of a whole series of enlightened landowner types such as Pravdoliubov, "truth lover," Dobroliubov, "lover of good," and others, who also had their negative counterparts). In addition, there were the many roles specifically reserved for (bad) poets such as the Boaster, Tippler, the Sycophantic Court Versifier, the dishonest and uncultured Grub Street Scribbler, and so on. In this gallery may also be included Barkov as personification of iconoclast pornographer, Bogdanovich as carefree sentimentalist bohemian, Khemnitser as absent-minded fabulist à la Jean de la Fontaine, images which commonly eclipsed the actual facts of their writers' lives. Then there were writers, such as Chulkov, Emin, and the little-known K. A. Kondratovich, who purposefully mystified (and parodied) the classicist biographical expectations of their audience. The mythologizing process continued, and even intensified, in the first third of the nineteenth century, when an entire anecdotal literature could be generated around such types as the hapless Count Khvostov. Finally, there was the heroic figure of the Political Martyr, personified by Novikov and especially by Radishchev – one of the most potent legacies of the late eighteenth century to the subsequent literary (and revolutionary) tradition. In all of these cases, literary reputation attained to the status of literary fact, blurring the borders between history and legend, literature and biography, documentary and fictional truth.

It was Derzhavin's remarkable ability to play his own stylized, individual self off against the "offi-cial" odic persona in his poems that amazed contemporaries; notably, almost alone among major eighteenth-century poets, Derzhavin compiled autobiographical commentaries to his poetry. Derzhavin's irony within the highest classicist genre, the ode, signaled the movement's maturity (as well as its decline) and marked the transition from classicism to sentimentalism, which were not by any means so clearly disassociated in the minds of their practitioners as they may seem to modern scholars. The sentimentalism of Karamzin and Mikhail Murav'ev transformed the terms of a writer's literary biography. The rationalist doctrine of imitating classical models gave way to a new emphasis on the individual, irrepeatable, emotional sides of human experience. However, paradoxically, the sentimentalist pose was at the same time no less based on a poetics of imitation and the literary conceit: the models merely changed. Karamzin's memorable phrase from his *Letters of a Russian Traveller* is representative: "For me spring would not be so memorable in its beauties had not Thomson and Kleist described to me all its beauties." The personal is filtered through the sensibility of the ideal other (hence Karamzin is also known as "the Russian Sterne"). Whereas Russian classicists often defined themselves by opposition (Trediakovsky versus Lomonosov versus Sumarokov), the sentimentalist literary stance was "conjunctive," and the act of writing an act of coauthorship. Solipsistic almost by definition and consciously rejecting the ill-humored polemics of Russian classicists, sentimentalism was expressly uncritical as it erected its own "temple of Russian literature." Not until the Romantic era, when the idols of the eighteenth century were violently overthrown, did a writer's personal life become merged with his literary persona and actual works, and a poet's life come to be judged as even more important than his writing (as in the case of George Gordon, Lord Byron, who was immensely popular in Russia). In this as in so many other areas, the career of Aleksandr Pushkin, whose biography was to be indissolubly intertwined with his poetry, both consolidated and transcended the traditions of early modern Russian literature and heralded the beginning of Russian literature's Golden Age.

Marcus C. Levitt
University of Southern California

Note on Bibliography

Publishers of books have been cited whenever possible, but in many cases they are not listed in standard bibliographies or other sources and have been impossible to identify. Separate publications of brief occasional works such as odes have sometimes been omitted from the list of the subject's works; in such cases the opening rubrics begin with "SE-LECTED BOOKS."

For more detailed bibliographical information on eighteenth and early nineteenth century editions of Russian works (including the occasional publications mentioned above), the reader is referred to *Svodnyi katalog russkoj knigi XVIII veka: 1725–1800* (1962–1967); its additional volume, *Dopolneniia, razyskivaemye izdaniia, utochneniia* (1975); and also *Istoriia russkoi literarury XVIII veka: Bibliograficheskii ukazatel'* (1968), edited by P. N. Berkov, V. P. Stepanov, and Iu. V. Stennik. For writers whose careers run into the nineteenth century, see *Istoriia russkoi literarury XIX veka: Bibliograficheskii ukazatel'* (1962), edited by K. D. Muratova. The latter two works also include bibliographies of secondary materials published in Russia on individual writers, as well as bibliographies of their individual letters published in Russian journals (not included in the bibliographies in this volume). These bibliographical works were the basis for much of the information given in the individual bibliographies in this volume. Incompleteness of citations (including ellipses in titles) indicate lacunae in the available bibliographical sources, although wherever possible information has been added, corrected, and updated, and listings of Western scholarship and translations added. Likewise, the use of brackets in the *Svodnyi katalog* has been retained, indicating conjectural data. Also useful to researchers is volume one of the *Slovar' russkikh pisatelei XVIII veka (A - I)* (1988), which cites archival sources; further volumes are forthcoming.

The specialist searching for publications of specific authors in eighteenth-century journals is also referred to A. N. Neustroev's *Istoricheskoe rozyskanie o russkikh povremennykh izdaniiakh i sbornikakh za 1703–1802 gg., bibliograficheski i v khronologicheskom poriadka opisanykh* (1874), which includes valuable information on journals and chronological listings of their contents and to the same author's *Ukazatel' k russkim povremennym izdaniiam i sbornikam za 1703–1802 g.g. i k istoricheskomu rozyskaniiu o nikh* (1898; reprinted, 1963), whose alphabetical listings include authors, title words, subjects, and genres. Also useful for data on journals and newspapers is *Russkaia periodicheskaia pechat' (1702–1894): Spravochnik* (1959) edited by A. G. Dement'eva, A. V. Zapadov, and M. S. Cherepakhova.

Abbreviations

Abbreviations in the bibliographies have mostly been avoided, except for a few items, for example, "Gos." instead of Gosudarstvennyi/oe/aia. "E. i. v." in eighteenth-century book titles stands for "eia [ee]" or "ego imperatorskogo velichestva" [her or his imperial highness]. "Tipografiia" and "(Gos.) Izdatel'stvo" have been eliminated from the bibliographical entries, except where an integral part of the name (hence "Tipografiia Shnora" is given as "Shnor," but "Tipograficheskaia kompaniia" remains, and "Gosudarstvennoe izdatel'stvo khudozhestvennoi literatury" becomes "Khudozhestvennaia literatura"). "Imperatorskaia Akademiia nauk" and "Akademiia nauk SSSR" have likewise been shortened to "Akademiia nauk," and "Imp(eratorskii)" also eliminated from "Moskovskii universitet" and other organizations. Further, in the case of those who leased the Moscow University typography in the eighteenth century, we have only listed the name of the lessee (hence not "Universitetskaia tipografiia u Ridigera i Klaudiia" or "u N. Novikova," but simply "Ridiger & Klaudii" or "N. Novikov").

Note on Dates, Names, and Transliteration

Dates of birth and death and all other dates referred to in the articles in this volume are given in Old Style, that is, according to the Julian calendar in use in Russia until 1918; to convert to the Gregorian calendar (New Style), add eleven days.

The Library of Congress system of transliteration with the diacritical marks omitted is used in this volume, with two exceptions. Commonly accepted spellings of personal and place-names are often used (e.g., Maria rather than Mariia, and Archangel rather than Arkhangel'sk), as well as certain well-known figures (e.g., Fyodor Dostoyevsky and Leo Tolstoy), and soft signs are omitted (e.g., Kazan rather than Kazan'). Surnames ending in "-skii" are given as "-sky" (for example, Trediakovsky rather than Trediakovskii). Russianized versions of foreign names have been retained for easier bibliographic reference (hence Veitbrekht and Shnor rather than Weitbrecht and Schnoor). In lists of translated works we have included in parentheses the Russianized spellings of authors' names where they significantly diverge from the original, for example, d'Aubeuf (d'Obef).

A few words should be said about names of writers from the clergy which often have several variants (church name and title, given name and surname, place name) and their alphabetization. This volume follows scholarly usage and common practice rather than imposing strict consistency: hence Archpriest Avvakum keeps his title where others do not, and some figures are alphabetized by their second name — which in some cases indicates place of origin rather than surname, as with Dimitrii Rostovsky (of Rostov) or Simeon Polotsky (of Polotsk) — while others are listed by their clerical name (Avvakum, Gedeon, and Platon).

Acknowledgments

This book was produced by Bruccoli Clark Layman, Inc. Karen L. Rood is the senior editor for the *Dictionary of Literary Biography* series. Sam Bruce was the in-house editor.

Production coordinator is James W. Hipp. Photography editor is Bruce Andrew Bowlin. Photographic copy work was performed by Joseph M. Bruccoli. Layout and graphics supervisor is Penney L. Haughton. Copyediting supervisor is Denise W. Edwards. Typesetting supervisor is Kathleen M. Flanagan. Systems manager is George F. Dodge. Julie E. Frick and Laura S. Pleicones are editorial associates. The production staff includes Phyllis A. Avant, Ann M. Cheschi, Melody W. Clegg, Patricia Coate, Brigitte B. de Guzman, Joyce Fowler, Laurel M. Gladden, Stephanie C. Hatchell, Kathy Lawler Merlette, Jeff Miller, Pamela D. Norton, Delores I. Plastow, Patricia F. Salisbury, Emily Sharpe, and William L. Thomas, Jr.

Walter W. Ross and Robert S. McConnell did library research. They were assisted by the following librarians at the Thomas Cooper Library of the University of South Carolina: Linda Holderfield and the interlibrary-loan staff; reference-department head Virginia Weathers; reference librarians Marilee Birchfield, Stefanie Buck, Cathy Eckman, Rebecca Feind, Jill Holman, Karen Joseph, Jean Rhyne, Kwamine Washington, and Connie Widney; circulation-department head Caroline Taylor; and acquisitions-searching supervisor David Haggard.

The editor wishes to thank Harold Segel, Natal'ia Dmitrievna Kochetkova, Alexander Levitsky, Irina Reyfman, and Mark Altshuller for their advice and encouragement in planning this volume. The following people helped the editor in translating articles from Russian and in other aspects of preparing this volume for publication: Jim Dochterman, Thea Durfee, Christopher Gilman, John Kachur, Susan Kechekian, Mark Konecny, Karen Myers, Amy Obrist, Anne-Marie Olbrechts, Galina Pastur, Walt Richmond, Susan Ryan, and Alice Taylor. Thanks also to the curators at the Museum of the Pushkin House (Institute of Russian Literature) in Saint Petersburg for their help in gathering many of the gravure portraits reproduced in this volume. A trip by the editor to consult with contributors in Russia and gather illustrations was funded by a Collaborative Travel Grant from the International Research and Exchange Organization (IREX). Thanks also to the University of Southern California, the Department of Slavic Languages and Literatures, the Dean's Office (Division of Humanities), and the Thematic Option Program, for their support at various stages of this project.

Early Modern Russian Writers, Late Seventeenth and Eighteenth Centuries

Dictionary of Literary Biography

Aleksandr Onisimovich Ablesimov
(27 August 1742 - 1783)

Elena Dmitrievna Kukushkina
Institute of Russian Literature (Pushkin House), Saint Petersburg

BOOKS: *Skazki* (Saint Petersburg: [Morskoi kadetskii korpus], 1769);
Komicheskaia opera, Mel'nik, koldun, obmanshchik i svat (Moscow: Moskovskii universitet, [1779]); translated by Lindsey Hughes as "The Miller Who Was Wizard, Cheat, and Matchmaker," *Russian Literature Triquarterly*, 20 (1987): 21–49;
Dialog Stranniki, na otkrytie novogo Petrovskogo teatra (Moscow: N. Novikov, 1780);
Shchastie po zhereb'iu (Moscow: N. Novikov, 1780);
Sochineniia. Polnoe sobranie sochinenii russkikh avtorov (Saint Petersburg: A. Smirdin, 1849).

OTHER: *Razkashchik zabavnykh basen, sluzhashchikh k chteniiu v skuchnoe vremia, ili kogda komy delat' nechevo*, nos. 1–52, edited by Ablesimov, (1781);
"Komicheskaia opera A. O. Ablesimova 'Pokhod s nepremennykh kvartir,' " edited by Pavel N. Berkov, in *Teatral'noe nasledstvo* (Moscow: Iskusstvo, 1956), pp. 189–224.

Aleksandr Onisimovich Ablesimov was a typical representative of those eighteenth-century Russian writers who, although members of the gentry, were of meager means and who occupied posts in state service. His works greatly influenced the development of Russian literature by bringing everyday peasant life into its purview and by making peasants full-fledged heroes of literary works. In an age when all traces of Russianness were disappearing beneath powdered wigs, cuffs, and farthingales, Ablesimov, with his extremely popular comic opera *Mel'nik, koldun, obmanshchik i svat* ([1779]; translated as "The Miller Who Was Wizard, Cheat, and Matchmaker," 1987), charted a fruitful path for Russian dramaturgy by depicting simple people engaged in everyday activities. In this work Ablesimov refused to imitate Western European comedies with traditional comic characters and subjects, creating instead an original musical and dramatic work that would remain popular for about a hundred years and serve as the forefather of Russian vaudeville.

Aleksandr Onisimovich Ablesimov was born on 27 August 1742 in the Galichsky district of the Kostroma province. According to several sources the Ablesimovs were distant relatives of the Sumarokov family, which was likewise descended from Kostroma nobility. Ablesimov spent his childhood at the family estate. His education, received at home, was extremely limited. All of his life Ablesimov's literary foes were to ridicule him because he did not know a single foreign language.

According to the custom of the day Ablesimov had been enlisted for military service and registered with the herald master's department while still a child. In 1756, at the poet Aleksandr Sumarokov's request, Ablesimov was assigned to Sumarokov as a copyist for the newly organized Russian theater which he directed. His two years of work at the theater and contact with Sumarokov greatly influenced both Ablesimov's literary tastes and the course of his later life. Transcribing Sumarokov's works kindled Ablesimov's own desire to write, and Sumarokov soon began calling him his "chernil'nyi synok" (little inky son).

In 1758 Ablesimov began actual military service as a soldier in the artillery corps, and in the next year he was promoted to the rank of *podpraporshchik* (underensign). At the same time he maintained his contact with Sumarokov, and in 1759 he published his first poems in his journal *Trudoliubivaia pchela* (The Industrious Bee), in the June and September issues. These were an elegy about betrayal by a lover, "Sokrylisia moi drazhaishie utekhi" (My Dearest Pleasures Are Gone); a satirical epigraph, "Pod'iachii zdes' zaryt" (A clerk is buried here); and six epigrams. Nikolai Novikov later mistakenly included the epigrams in the second edition (1787) of Sumarokov's complete collected works.

From 1760 to 1762 Ablesimov took part in the Seven Years' War, serving in the rank of sergeant. During these years he acquired the nickname Onisimych (a shortened, affectionate version of his patronymic, Onisimovich). In 1765 Ablesimov was appointed *furmeister*, that is, commander of a brigade, and a year later he was discharged from military service with the rank of ensign. He was sent to work in the Commission for Composing a New Law Code, and his association with the young literati Mikhail Popov, Vasilii Maikov, and Nikolai Novikov, all of whom fulfilled various secretarial duties connected with keeping the protocols of the commission's sessions, played a decisive role in Ablesimov's further career in literature.

During his work for the commission Ablesimov also prepared for publication twelve tales in verse, which were collected in 1769 as *Skazki i basni* (Fairy Tales and Fables). At Ablesimov's request, Novikov announced the sale of the new edition in his popular satiric journal *Truten'* (The Drone). Ablesimov's tales were expressive satiric pictures of the reality of his time. In them Ablesimov tells of how lies trample the truth; ironically relates the story of an old man who marries a young girl; and meditates upon the thought that human beings, though considering themselves the crown of creation, nevertheless have – like all living beings – their own imperfections. In the same year Ablesimov also published several satirical poems and articles in *Truten'*, both anonymously and under the pseudonym "Azazez Azezezov." In imitation of Sumarokov's satires and fables, he ridicules dandies, spendthrifts, braggarts, and bribe-taking clerks. In the journal Ablesimov also attacks his literary rival Vasilii Lukin. The conflict with Lukin apparently arose because of a certain comedy which Ablesimov had written and presented to the new director of the Russian theater, Lukin's close associate Ivan Elagin; it was returned after a year with a rejection. Two of Ablesimov's satiric poems, "Igrok, sdelavshiisia pistsom" (The Gambler Turned Scribe) and "Styd khuliteliu'" (Shame on the Defamer), were directed at Lukin, who had given the negative assessment of Ablesimov's comedy.

In 1770 Ablesimov again entered military service. He participated in the campaigns against the Turks in Georgia and in the siege of the Turkish-held fortress of Poti, serving as adjutant to Gen.-Maj. Aleksei Sukhotin. In 1772 Ablesimov left the army with the rank of captain and took up residence in Moscow, where he served as a minor official in the "Uprava blagochiniia" (Board of Decorum), that is, the administration of the city police.

Ablesimov continued to compose satiric verse and earned the reputation in society of a man with a sharp tongue. According to tradition, once, as guests were dispersing, an officer, annoyed by Ablesimov's slowness in bringing a carriage, complained about him to a lady standing nearby and asked that she pass along his grievances to Ablesimov's superior, Moscow police chief Nikolai Arkharov. The woman allegedly replied with a smile, "No I won't, not for anything, or Ablesimov will bring forth a couplet instead of a carriage!"

By the end of 1771 Ablesimov had composed three comedies – one five-act and two one-acts – and a comic opera in verse. In his *Opyt istoricheskogo slovaria o rossiiskikh pisateliakh* (Attempt at a Historical Dictionary of Russian Writers, 1772) Novikov writes that these were "vse oni dovol'no khoroshi, a nekotorye iavleniia i pokhvaly zasluzhivaiut, ibo v nikh mnogo soli, ostroty i zabavnykh shutok" (all quite good and several scenes even deserve praise because they are full of salt, sharp humor, and entertaining gags). The comedy in five acts, called *Pod'iacheskaia pirushka* (The Clerk's Little Feast), has not survived, nor is there information about its ever having been staged.

Ablesimov's employer, Arkharov, was tolerant of his subordinate's literary inclinations, but his coworkers ridiculed Ablesimov and called him a *piit* (an archaic and condescending word for poet). When it was learned that he had written an opera and that it was being prepared for production, they began to call him the "police department's Sumarokov." Ablesimov brought his comic opera *Mel'nik, koldun, obmanshchik i svat* to read to Arkharov. The listeners approved of his work, but according to tradition, Arkharov warned the beginning playwright to be careful: "The public – that's a big deal. It's rich in praise, but twice as rich in abuse. I am afraid for you." To which Ablesimov allegedly answered, "No, my *Mel'nik* will not die."

Mel'nik was first presented on 20 January 1779 in Moscow, in the Medoks Theater with the renowned actor Aleksei Ozhogin in the leading role. It sustained twenty-two consecutive performances, something almost unheard of on the Russian stage of that time. Then it was produced in Saint Petersburg at the court theater. There the actor Anton Krutitsky, who was playing the role of the miller, was invited to the empress's box after the first act and showered with praise; on the following day Catherine sent him a gold watch. The opera was then presented in Knipper's Theater and ran for twenty-seven consecutive performances. According to the author of the *Dramaticheskii slovar'* (Theatrical Dictionary, 1787), the play was well received not only by Russians but also by foreigners. "It was probably the first Russian opera to have had such an ecstatic reception and such applause." It was said that Ablesimov's coworkers and acquaintances who had formerly been cynical about his literary pursuits were amazed upon seeing *Mel'nik* performed and inquired whether or not it was really he, Aleksandr Onisimovich, who had written it. And Ablesimov (so the story goes), growing red in the face and starting to hiccup, answered, "I!"

Contemporaries considered the Russianness of *Mel'nik* the reason for its unprecedented success. In his journal titled the *Spectator* (1792) Petr A. Plavil'shchikov posed the question of why the opera, with all of its weakness of composition and "failure to adhere to Aristotle's rules," had nonetheless sustained more than two hundred performances, while Molière's *Le Misanthrope* (1666) had never been able to bring in a full house. His answer was, "*Mel'nik* is ours, and *Misanthrope* is not!" However, though contemporaries considered *Mel'nik* a completely original comedy of Russian manners, recent research reveals that the opera's overall concept — in which a sorcerer brings about young lovers' happiness through deceptions — may have been borrowed from Jean-Jacques Rousseau's opera *Le Devin du village* (The Village Soothsayer, 1752), which may have been performed at the Smol'ny Institute in Saint Petersburg in 1775.

Other factors contributed to the success of *Mel'nik*. First was that the music for the opera, based on Russian folk songs and written by M. Sokolovsky, the talented conductor of the Moscow Theater, and second was that the main role of the miller Faddei was always played by well-known actors. The primary reason for the opera's success, however, was Ablesimov's libretto. As noted, its composition and cast of characters did not fit into the operatic stereotype that had become established in Russia by that time. The specific setting of the play and its detailed descriptions of the lives and occupations of its characters immerse the audience in the atmosphere of everyday peasant life. The opera also cleverly plays upon peasants' belief in *zagovornye* and *prislushlivye slova* (charms and magic spells), and these things make the traditional love conflict seem new. The miller Faddei adeptly uses his reputation as a sorcerer to bring about a happy ending for the lovers Filimon and Aniuta — not without some profit for himself, of course.

The opera utilizes many sorts of popular folk songs and melodies: *protiazhnye* (drawn-out refrains), lyrical and comic songs, dance tunes, and *chastushki* (short lyrics, usually of four lines, often comic and satiric). Ablesimov also presented peasant customs onstage: *gadanie o suzhenom* (guessing of one's intended) and *devich'i posidelki* (young maidens' get-togethers). The play's connections with folk culture also express themselves in a specific kind of open attitude toward the audience. For example, the audience laughs along with the sly miller at the old men who, despite all their constant squabbling over who their son-in-law will be, never realize that they both have the same man in mind. The intrigue, based on Faddei's trickery, is also resolved in the peasant spirit, by means of a riddle. Filimon turns out to be both a nobleman and a peasant at the same time, since he is an *odnodvorets*. The *odnodvortsy* were a special caste in eighteenth-century Russia, descendants of members of the minor service class such as Cossacks, *streltsy*, and *pushkari* (old types of soldiers), who in the sixteenth and seventeenth centuries had settled in the eastern and southern borders of the Muscovite state to defend it against the Tatars; they were not serfs and were permitted to own land.

Another of Ablesimov's innovations was in his departure from the usual manner of depicting comic characters; his heroes are multidimensional. Aleksei Merzliakov, analyzing the opera for the periodical *Vestnik Evropy* in 1817, by which time it had been performed successfully for half a century, noted that the feelings and complaints of Fetin'ia, a former house serf, make her an object of entertainment, but not in a derisive sense; her situation is presented, instead, in a touching manner. He found Ablesimov's characters "simple but not stupid to the point of disgusting us" and "not overblown beyond their station," as in other comedies depicting peasants.

At the same time, Ablesimov's literary manner, which was generally appreciated by lower-class audiences for its everyday realism, aroused perplexity and even protest among some of the nobility. One of the spectators of the court production of the play wrote a letter to Catherine stating that Ablesimov's opera was offensive to persons of high society and that its success among the masses must arouse indignation. In "Satira I" (Satire I, 1780) Vasilii Kapnist called Ablesimov "Obvesimov" (Cheater, one who gives short weight) and placed him in an "oslinyi sobor" (congress of asses), that is, group of bad writers of asinine works. An anonymous "Oda pokhval'naia avtoru 'Mel'nika'" (Laudatory Ode to the Author of "Mel'nik"), apparently written by Dmitrii Gorchakov, made fun of the vulgar language used by the opera's characters and condemned the enactment of folk rituals and the singing of folk songs in the theater. The poet Nikolai Nikolev also dedicated a few ironic lines to *Mel'nik*, comparing

Ablesimov to Molière and noting acidly that the quantity of spectators at the Medoks Theater production of the play exceeded their quality.

Nevertheless, *Mel'nik* continued to enjoy success. It remained the unsurpassed example of Russian musical comedy and a standard in Moscow and Saint Petersburg until the middle of the nineteenth century. It was first produced with the music of Mikhail Sokolovsky, then with a score by Evstignei Fomin, and still later with an arrangement by an anonymous composer. When the opera was staged in the Aleksandrinsky Theater in Saint Petersburg in 1847 it was already perceived by reviewers as a "bibliographical rarity" and an "archaeological reminiscence," but it nevertheless continued to attract popular interest.

In the eighteenth century the success of *Mel'nik* inspired many imitations, including the anonymous opera *Vecherinki, ili Gadai, gadai, devitsa, otgadyvaia, krasnaia* (Get-togethers, or Guess, Guess, Maiden, Guess Right, Blush, 1788), *Nevesta pod fatoiu, ili Meshchanskaia svad'ba* (The Bride Beneath the Veil, or The Vulgar Wedding, 1791), and Ivan Iukin's *Koldun, vorozheia i svakha* (Wizard, Fortune-teller, and Matchmaker, 1789), the basic plot and composition of which were taken from Ablesimov's work. The characters in these operas stayed within the boundaries of fixed comic conventions, and they did not enjoy much success.

For some time Iakov Kniazhnin's comic opera *Sbitenshchik* (The Seller of *Sbiten'*, 1783 – *sbiten'* is a hot drink made with honey and spices), which was also widely popular, eclipsed the success of *Mel'nik*. Arguments over the comparative worth of these two works were widespread. Petr Plavil'shchikov's *Mel'nik i sbitenshchik – soperniki* (Miller and Sbitenshchik – Rivals, 1789) even brought the heroes of the two operas together into one comic intrigue.

Emboldened by the success of *Mel'nik*, Ablesimov brought a second comic opera to the theater the same year, his *Shchastie po zhereb'iu* (Happiness by Lot, 1780). Its plot is based on the humiliation of rival suitors by a clever soldier. This opera, however, was not a success.

In 1780 Ablesimov was commissioned by the directors of the new Petrovsky Theater in Moscow to compose the allegorical *Dialog Stranniki* (Dialogue: Wanderers) in honor of the theater's opening. This one-act comic sketch, in which Apollo, Mercury, the muse Thalia, a satyr, and Momus (dressed as a peasant) all take part, is written in lively language and burlesque style. The idea of the play is that satire must be driven out of the comic theater because attempts to correct human failings are futile.

Soon, following Novikov's example and with his financial support, Ablesimov founded the journal *Razkashchik zabavnykh basen, sluzhashchikh k chteniiu v skuchnoe vremia, ili kogda delat' nechevo* (Teller of Funny Tales, Serving for Reading Matter When you are Bored or When There is Nothing To Do, 1781). The journal came out in small weekly *listy* (sheets). Ablesimov mostly published his own compositions, some of which had been included in the book *Skazki*, but also included poems by other authors. In several issues Ablesimov published the correspondence of Bernard de Fontenelle and Edward Young, taken from Jean de Sales's *De la philosophie de la nature* (1766). In number 49 of his journal Ablesimov included his response to the anonymous satiric "Oda pokhval'naia avtoru 'Mel'nika' " (Laudatory Ode to the Author of "Mel'nik," 1781). He cleverly and accurately portrays the argument of the poets "pro Feba" (concerning the muses) and presents their harsh verdict:

> . . . А Мельника издатель
> И в роде оном то ж Разкащика писатель
> Не смели бы возвесть и око на Парнас!

> (And neither the publisher of the Miller
> Nor – in the same line – the writer of Razkashchik
> Should dare raise even an eye to Parnassus!)

Ablesimov counted himself among the *nepyshnye* (unpretentious) writers, who explain their own position in the debate:

> Ответствовать на то они сочли излишним.
> Мысль та: што ссору лишь чрез это заведут,
> И в распри многие войдут,
> То не тщеславяся никак своим уменьем,
> Предприняли сносить все што ни есть с терпеньем.

> (To reply to that they considered unnecessary.
> The idea was this: that this would only lead to quarreling,
> And many would join in recriminations,
> And so, without becoming all haughty about their abilities,
> They decided to bear whatever would come with patience.)

Like Novikov, Ablesimov included letters from readers in his journal. Some of these advised him to be more discreet, because his jokes "seem[ed] too salty to many." Ablesimov was forced to cease publication of *Razkashchik* after only one year, due to what he said was the constant faultfinding of his ill-wishers. He explained the deficiencies of the journal by referring to his modest material and social position, emphasizing the problem of authorial impoverishment, a note first sounded in Russian journalism by Mikhail Chulkov.

In 1782 Ablesimov once again tested his strength in the theater. On 7 June his comic opera in three acts called *Pok'hod s nepremennykh kvartir* (Expedition from Permanent Quarters), with music (performed) by Ekkel', premiered. Despite its traditional comic plot, which hinges on trickery, the play accurately portrays everyday life in the army, which Ablesimov knew firsthand. The cast of characters is made up of officers, depicted in a highly unflattering manner as gamblers and braggarts, and soldiers, depicted as brave and honest men. Their hard life in the army is described in songs included in the text of the opera. According to *Dramaticheskii slovar'* (Theatrical Dictionary, 1787), Ablesimov's opera was fairly well received by the public. Its text has not been preserved intact – its third act is missing – and it was not published until 1956.

Ablesimov died in poverty in 1783. According to legend, he had spent all of his resources on the education of his only daughter and left as her only inheritance the three-legged table at which he had composed all of his works. His grave site was soon forgotten.

Several facets of Ablesimov's biography probably figured in Nikolai Polevoi's comedy *Pervoe predstavlenie 'Mel'nika – kolduna, obmanshchika i svata'* (The First Performance of "Miller – Wizard, Cheat, and Matchmaker," 1842), but it would be a mistake to consider them reliable. In this play Sumarokov decides to marry his ward, Anna Ivanovna, to a writer; the rival suitors are Sumarokov's nephew, "khodiachaia rifma" (walking rhyme) Zhukov, and Ablesimov, who gains the victory after the success of *Mel'nik*. Some ten years earlier, in reviewing one of the many publications of *Mel'nik*, Polevoi provided what may be an appropriate epigraph for the writer when he wrote in *Moskovskii telegraf* (The Moscow Telegraph) in 1831 that "some sixty years ago the genius of true comedy flew through Russia and its wing snagged on the head of one writer.... This writer was Ablesimov, and the fruit of this momentary inspiration was the opera, or better, the vaudeville 'Mel'nik – koldun, obmanshchik i svat.' "

References:

Abram A. Gozenpud, "A. O. Ablesimov," in *Stikhotvornaia komediia, komicheskaia opera, vodevil' kontsa XVII–nachala XIX veka*, volume 1, Biblioteka poeta, Bol'shaia seriia (Leningrad: Sovetskii pisatel', 1990), pp. 676–679;

Gozenpud, *Muzykal'nyi teatr v Rossii ot istokov do Glinki* (Leningrad: Gos. muzykal'noe izdatel'stvo, 1959);

Ia-v [Aleksei A. Iartsev], " 'Chernil'nyi synok' Sumarokova i ego bessmertnoe detishche," *Novosti dnia,* 27 August 1891, p. 3;

Vasilii V. Kastorsky, "A. O. Ablesimov," in his *Pisateli kostromichi XVIII–XIX vekov* (Kostroma, 1858), pp. 134–144;

Efim G. Kholodov and others, eds., *Ot istokov do kontsa XVIII veka,* volume 1 of their *Istoriia russkogo dramaticheskogo teatra* (Moscow: Iskusstvo, 1977);

F. K. [Fedor A. Koni], " 'Mel'nik – koldun, obmanshchik i svat' v Aleskandrinskom teatre," *Repertuar i panteon,* 11, section 2 (1847): 61–64;

Georgii K. Kryzhitsky, "Vliianie Russo na Ablesimova," *Izvestiia Otdeleniia russkogo iazyka i slovesnosti,* 22, no. 2 (1918): 58–64;

Elena D. Kukushkina, "Komicheskaia opera XVIII veka," in *Istoriia russkoi dramaturgii: XVII–pervaia polovina XIX veka* (Leningrad: Nauka, 1982), pp. 163–180;

Leonid Maikov, "Ablesimov, A. O.," in *Russkii biograficheskii slovar',* volume 1 (Saint Petersburg, 1896), pp. 11–12;

Mikhail Makarov, "Ablesimov," *Repetuar russkogo teatra,* 2, no. 12, section 3 (1841): 20–23;

Aleksei F. Merzliakov, "Razbor opery 'Mel'nika,' " *Vestnik Evropy,* 92, no. 6 (1817): 113–126;

Vasilii N. Osokin, "Onisimych," in his *Rasskazy o pisateliakh i khudozhnikakh kostromichakh* (Kostroma: Knizhnoe izdatel'stvo, 1961), pp. 5–30;

Nikolai A. Polevoi, "Komicheskaia opera 'Mel'nik, koldun, obmanshchik i svat.' Sochinennaia A. Ablesimovym. Saint Petersburg, 1831," *Moskovskii telegraf,* 38, no. 8 (1831): 551–553;

Nikolai M. Tupikov, "Satira na Ablesimova," *Ezhegodnik imperatorskikh teatrov,* supplement 2 (1893–1894): 141–146;

V. E. Vasilev, M. G. Gillel'son, and N. G. Zakharenko, eds., *Russkaia epigramma vtoroi poloviny XVII–nachala XX veka* (Leningrad: Sovetskii pisatel', 1975);

Semen A. Vengerov, "Ablesimov, A. O.," in *Kritiko-biograficheskii slovar' russkikh pisatelei i uchenykh,* volume 1 (Saint Petersburg: Semenovskaia tipografiia, 1889), pp. 11–18.

Archpriest Avvakum (Petrovich)

(1620? – April 1682)

Marcia A. Morris
Georgetown University

BOOKS: *Zhitie protopopa Avvakuma im samim napisannoe,* edited by Nikolai S. Tikhonravov (Saint Petersburg: Tovarishchestvo Obshchestvennaia Pol'za, 1861); republished as *Zhitie protopopa Avvakuma im samim napisannoe i drugie sochineniia,* edited by Nikolai K. Gudzii (Moscow: Khudozhestvennaia literatura, 1960); translated by Jane Harrison and Hope Mirrlees as *The Life of the Archpriest Avvakum By Himself* (London: Hogarth Press, 1924); translated by Helen Iswolsky as "The Life of the Archpriest Avvakum," in *A Treasury of Russian Spirituality,* edited by G. P. Fedotov (New York: Harper & Row, 1965), pp. 137–181; translated by Kenneth N. Brostrom as *The Life Written by Himself* (Ann Arbor: University of Michigan Press, 1979);

Pamiatniki istorii staroobriadchestva XVII veka (Leningrad: Akademiia Nauk, 1927) – includes the *Zhitie* redactions A, B, and C; the *Kniga besed; Kniga tolkovanii i nravouchenii, Kniga oblichenii ili evangelie vechnoe;*

Zhizneopisanie Avvakuma i Epifaniia: Issledovanie i teksty, edited by Andrei N. Robinson (Moscow: Akademiia nauk, 1963);

Pustozerskii sbornik: Avtografy sochinenii Avvakuma i Epifaniia, edited by Natalia S. Demkova and others (Leningrad: Nauka, 1975);

Pustozerskaia proza (Moscow: Moskovskii rabochii, 1989).

Archpriest Avvakum Petrovich should be numbered among the most commanding, self-assured, and influential figures of seventeenth-century Russian culture. By conviction a profoundly conservative man, he came to be associated, contrary to his own intentions, with much that was new in Russian life. In his most widely read work, the *Zhitie protopopa Avvakuma im samim napisannoe* (1861; translated as *The Life of the Archpriest Avvakum By Himself,* 1924), composed between 1669 and 1675, he passionately championed the liturgical and scrip-tural practices that had been cultivated for centuries on Russian Orthodox soil. He was militant in his rejection of compromise with foreign innovations, whether imported from the West or from the Greek Orthodox world, and, by his own example of martyrdom, he did much to encourage the division in the Russian Orthodox church known as the Schism. At the same time, through his *Zhitie protopopa Avvakuma,* he introduced a great many novelties of both form and content into the traditional medieval genre of the saint's life. Because of these innovations, Russian scholars have argued that the work should be read as an incipient novel.

Avvakum was born in 1620 (possibly 1621) in Grigorovo, a town to the southeast of Nizhnii Novgorod. His father, Petr, was the local parish priest and was, in Avvakum's words, "given to hard drink." His mother, Mariia, a devout and pious woman, eventually took the veil as Sister Marfa. At least three, and probably four, other sons were born to the couple; Gerasim, Koz'ma, and Evfimii are known by name. In the *Zhitie protopopa Avvakuma* Avvakum mentions that two of his brothers died in Moscow in the plague of 1654, but he elsewhere notes that Gerasim and Koz'ma were alive in 1666, which implies that Evfimii and an unnamed fourth brother were the plague victims. At some point in the 1630s Avvakum's father died, leaving the family in difficulties.

In 1638 Avvakum married Anastasiia Markovna, the daughter of the town blacksmith. A loyal helpmate, Anastasiia was to follow Avvakum into exile, watch two of her children die of starvation, and be imprisoned herself.

Avvakum entered the diaconate in 1642, and two years later he was promoted to the priesthood. He most probably lived and served in the town of Lopatishchi for ten years, from 1642 to 1652, a period during which he was threatened by intermittent bouts of hostility from his parishioners because of the strict moral code that he preached. During a particularly violent outbreak in 1647, he was forced

8

Portrait of Archpriest Avvakum dating from the late seventeenth or early eighteenth century (from Dm. Zhukov, Russkie pisateli XVII veka, *1972)*

to flee the town and reside in Moscow for a brief period.

Avvakum's journey to Moscow brings into focus that which motivated him and his countrymen. Since the interregnum following the reign of the last of the Riurik dynasty, known as the Time of Troubles (1598–1613), Russia had been struggling with questions of self-identity. The central Russian lands had earlier been unified under the hegemony of Moscow, and the Stoglav Council of 1551 had codified and affirmed many features of Russian ecclesiastical practice. Russians were beginning to take a noticeable pride in their standing as citizens of an increasingly powerful and self-confident autocracy. Accordingly, a subtle sense of Russia's special destiny was growing. The chaos that descended on the country during the Troubles must, therefore, have come as a profound shock. Muscovy was invaded by Western powers, and Moscow was briefly

held by the Poles. For a time the threat of a Roman Catholic czar seemed very real.

Although Russia finally freed herself from usurpers and foreign armies and elected a new czar, Mikhail Romanov, an abiding distrust of unfamiliar, Western ways remained as a legacy of the Troubles. Under the first Romanovs the Russian people saw their destiny as firmly anchored in the Greek Orthodox world. Yet, as Ukrainian and Belarusian territories previously held by the Poles were gradually incorporated into the empire, it became clear that Russian church practices differed in small but noticeable ways from those of other Orthodox lands. A process for correcting the scribal errors that had accrued in ecclesiastical books was initiated. At the same time, many members of the clergy felt that the church needed to be renewed. Old Russia had always been mindful of the imminence of the end of the world, and the year 1666, because of its obvious associations with the number of the apocalyptic beast in the Book of Revelation, aroused new fears. As the fateful year approached, there was a marked increase in interest in spiritual revival.

The atmosphere of ardor and spiritual devotion that permeated certain circles of Russian society at this time did much to facilitate the birth of the Zealots of the Ancient Piety, sometimes called the Bogoliubtsy (Lovers of God), a movement led primarily by "white" or parish clergy. The fundamentalist Zealots, who numbered Avvakum among their members, advocated a strict moral code. It was Avvakum's unremitting attempts to apply this code to the daily lives of his parishioners that led to his being temporarily driven out of Lopatishchi.

Avvakum's appearance in Moscow in 1647 coincided with the arrival of Ivan Neronov, a fundamentalist cleric who had worked in the Nizhnii Novgorod area and who was known for sermons preached in a simple, understandable vernacular. Neronov, who advocated *edinoglasie,* or choral singing in one voice, as a means to achieve a deep state of meditation conducive to communion with God, became a close confidant of Czar Aleksei Mikhailovich. Avvakum and Neronov held many views in common, and after Neronov was arrested for his defense of the old religion in 1653, they would become even closer.

Iosif, the presiding patriarch of the Russian church, died in 1652. Aleksei Mikhailovich's first choice for a successor was his confessor, Stefan Vonifat'ev, but when Vonifat'ev declined the honor, the czar turned to Nikon (born Nikita Minich), who since 1649 had been metropolitan of Novgorod. Both Vonifat'ev and Nikon had the support of the Zealots, and initially Nikon advanced the fundamentalist program. This was an exciting time for Avvakum, who, living in Moscow again, had become an intimate of the czar himself. At about this time he was elevated to archpriest, the highest position open to the white clergy, and was sent to supervise a parish in Iurievets-on-the-Volga.

Unfortunately for the Zealots of the Ancient Piety, Nikon soon unfolded a powerful agenda of his own. He was determined to elevate the power of the church over that of the state and, in pursuit of these ambitions, sought the blessings of non-Russian, Orthodox churchmen. He undertook a series of reforms designed to bring Russian liturgical practices into strict conformity with contemporary Greek usage and in February 1653 issued a new Psalter which omitted the traditional instruction for forming the sign of the cross with two fingers. Two

weeks later he proscribed the old practices, insisting, among other things, that the sign of the cross must be made with three fingers. His ill-considered reforms profoundly shocked both the Zealots of the Ancient Piety and a large segment of Russian society, who were unconvinced of the wisdom of adopting the practices of nations that had long since succumbed to the domination of the Ottoman Empire.

Avvakum, who had left Iurievets and was again in Moscow, immediately reacted against Nikon's innovations. In August 1653 he was arrested for insubordination and placed in chains. Nikon sentenced him to be defrocked and exiled to distant Eniseisk, but Czar Aleksei intervened. Avvakum was allowed to retain his priestly office and was sent to Tobolsk. Upon his arrival in December, he was warmly welcomed by Simeon, the archbishop of Tobolsk and Siberia. The new church books had not yet been introduced in Tobolsk, and, as Avvakum and Simeon shared many views, it looked for a time as though Avvakum would find a congenial exile in the Siberian city.

The year 1654 brought a series of misfortunes, however. The plague ravaged Moscow, and as much as one half of the city's population is said to have perished. A solar eclipse that occurred at the same time led to an outbreak of apocalyptic fears, and there was a short-lived uprising against Nikon. Concurrently Simeon left Tobolsk for the church council that would eventually legalize the Nikonian reforms. Avvakum began to have serious disagreements with Ivan Struna, the archbishop's deputy, which led to the archpriest savagely beating the deputy in church. News of the two men's enmity reached Nikon, who, while the czar was away leading his troops in battle against the Poles and Swedes, had a freer field of action than previously. Accordingly, in 1655 he reiterated his earlier sentence of exile to Eniseisk and forbade Avvakum to say the liturgy.

Avvakum and his family had barely settled in Eniseisk when the order came to join an expedition to Dauriia, far to the east. In July 1656 the family set out on what was to be a horrific journey. Afanasii Pashkov, the leader of the company, was a brutal man who flogged Avvakum and showed no mercy toward his family. After pushing on throughout the summer and fall of 1656, the travelers reached Bratsk, where Avvakum was imprisoned for the winter. The party managed to reach Lake Irgen by fall 1657, and in June 1658 they finally arrived at Nerchinsk.

While Avvakum and his family were being subjected to cold, hunger, and the rigors of travel in the trackless Siberian wilderness, Czar Aleksei was becoming increasingly disenchanted with the archpriest's main persecutor, Nikon. Leading Russia's campaign against the Poles and Swedes had equipped Aleksei with a sense of his own strength and autocratic power. On his return to Moscow he was determined to reassert the authority of the state over the Orthodox church. In 1658 Nikon, incensed by the czar's new views, abandoned his ecclesiastical responsibilities and retired to the Voskresensky Monastery. Confident that he would be recalled by Aleksei, he found himself, instead, languishing in a self-inflicted exile. The situation would not be resolved until 1666 when a church council attended by the patriarchs of Alexandria and Antioch officially deposed him. In the meantime the czar took over effective control of the church.

In 1661 Avvakum was recalled to European Russia. He had suffered egregiously in Siberia, and two of his children had perished from hunger. Furthermore, Afanasii Pashkov, his official escort during the journey out of European Russia, refused Avvakum permission to join his Cossacks on the return trip. Avvakum, accompanied by family and household members, made his long journey back to Tobolsk in 1663. From there he continued to Moscow, where he preached against the Nikonian reforms between February and August 1664.

At first Avvakum was optimistic that his views would find an audience. Nikon was still in exile in his monastery, and Czar Aleksei Mikhailovich had not yet come to a final decision regarding his innovations. The czarina, Maria Miloslavskaia, was favorably inclined toward the intractable archpriest, and two influential and wealthy sisters, Feodosiia Morozova and Evdokiia Urusova, became his spiritual daughters. Avvakum also met on a fairly regular if informal basis with Fedor Rtishchev, one of the czar's intimates and a man known to favor the assimilation of many elements of Western learning into the larger body of old Muscovite traditions.

Sometime in early 1664 Avvakum sent the czar the first of his extant petitions, ostensibly a request for the abrogation of Nikon's reforms. This petition, the manuscript of which has survived in Avvakum's own hand, was highly unusual in both tone and narrative structure. Normally seventeenth-century petitions were written to a standard pattern: an opening protocol was followed by the main section, in which an allegation or request was voiced, and a closing protocol completed the document. The stance invariably adopted by writers of petitions has been referred to as "upward allocution," meaning that the rhetoric employed recog-

The church in Grigorovo, Avvakum's birthplace

nized the petitioner's humble status vis-à-vis his audience. In his first petition, however, Avvakum adopted a fairly neutral style, one that carefully preserved his own dignity. Even more noteworthy is the fact that Avvakum framed his petition so as to give voice to two separate themes: the first concerned with the sufferings he had undergone at the hands of Pashkov and the second dealing with the discord that was rending his beloved church. Finally, the petition was accompanied by a zapiska (note), which concentrated on Avvakum's personal travails.

Much has been made of the idiosyncracies of Avvakum's first petition. The fact that its subject was of a spiritual rather than material nature is certainly striking, as is its author's refusal to sound an obsequious note. The inclusion of autobiographical material also served to individualize the work. Several schools of thought exist regarding Avvakum's intentions in this petition. On the one hand, the strong emphasis on recounting the petitioner's life experiences could be seen to prefigure the approach taken in the *Zhitie protopopa Avvakuma,* Avvakum's most celebrated work. Concrete events are narrated in order to make a broader and, ultimately, more abstract, spiritual point. On the other hand, although the thrust of these autobiographical incidents is to paint Avvakum's persecutor, Pashkov, as an inhuman monster, the archpriest asks the czar not to punish Pashkov but rather to try to save him. The rhetoric of the Christian economy of salvation is quite marked and may, in fact, have been intended to outweigh the actual accounting of personal affliction. Finally, regardless of the function that the autobiographical *zapiska* was expected to serve, an appended note was not entirely unprecedented in texts of the period – they were affixed to works documenting business transactions, for example.

Avvakum's petition had unfortunate and probably unforeseen consequences for the archpriest and his family. Aleksei Mikhailovich had transferred his affections from Nikon to Simeon Polotsky, a scholar of Belarusian extraction. Polotsky, who was appointed tutor to the czar's children, brought a wealth of learning to Moscow. He cultivated Western forms in the arts, promoting among other things syllabic verse forms, drama, and baroque, polyphonic music. Perhaps even more significant, he shared Aleksei Mikhailovich's belief in the primacy of the czar over the patriarch. Although his views on such questions differed markedly from Nikon's, they were equally remote from the outlook advanced by Avvakum and the other Zealots of the Ancient Piety. The czar's fondness for Polotsky was consonant with his decision to adopt a more Western path, a determination that dismayed the fundamentalists. The insistent and annoying edge in Avvakum's petition, a document which, of course, argued against Polotsky, persuaded the czar to rid himself of the archpriest. He exiled Avvakum to Pustozersk, in the barren north.

On 29 August 1664 Avvakum departed with his family for his new place of exile. During his trek he had opportunity to write another petition requesting an investigation into charges of sodomy against a Greek prelate. Sometime in the late autumn he petitioned a third time that he and his family be allowed to stay in Mezen, where the climate was less harsh. This request was presumably granted, since Avvakum spent the next eighteen months in the settlement.

Avvakum's second and third petitions were more traditional than the first, at least in content. One voiced an allegation of wrongdoing and re-

quested redress, while the other asked for a personal favor. Their style, however, was again fairly neutral and avoided upward allocution. Avvakum's language at this point included few colloquialisms, the relative abundance of which would strongly distinguish both the *Zhitie protopopa Avvakuma* and later petitions. In 1665 Avvakum penned yet another petition requesting more food and better supplies for himself and the other exiles in Mezen.

In 1666 the archpriest was recalled to Moscow, this time to attend a church council to discuss both Nikon and the Old Belief. He arrived in March, and the meeting was convened in April. The council condemned Nikon, which was a victory of sorts for Avvakum, but affirmed the legality of the Nikonian reforms and stressed the need to unify the church, endorsing a suppression of the Old Belief. On 13 May Avvakum disputed doctrine with the Russian bishops and laid out his views. Because of his intransigence on this occasion, he was defrocked in the Cathedral of the Assumption in the Kremlin, and, together with his coreligionist, Deacon Fedor, he was anathematized.

The church council in the meantime continued its work, convening for a second session that lasted from December 1666 through summer 1667. During this second sitting prelates from other, non-Russian branches of Orthodoxy made up almost half of the council. The old faith was laid under official interdict, and Avvakum was imprisoned in the Pafnutiev Monastery outside Moscow. Czar Aleksei still retained a degree of feeling for the archpriest, however, and sent Ivan Neronov (who had by now relented in his fury against the Nikonian innovations) and Polotsky to urge him to recant. Avvakum remained adamant and in August 1667 was sent to Pustozersk together with three like-minded companions, Nikifor, Lazar, and Epifanii, the latter two of whom had had their hands mutilated and their tongues cut out. This time the archpriest reached his sterile, tundra-surrounded place of exile. Shortly after Avvakum's arrival, Deacon Fedor also joined the group.

During their first years in Pustozersk, the five leaders of the Old Belief enjoyed a relatively large degree of freedom. They lived in the private homes of the settlement's inhabitants and were in regular communication with supporters and family members. The most important contact was Avvakum's wife, who remained in Mezen. Anastasiia Markovna served as a rallying point for other members of the old faith and conveyed messages to her exiled husband.

From the time of their arrival in late 1667, the exiles engaged in lively polemics. Since the Old Belief had lost all formal connection with the mainstream Orthodox church, and there were no longer any official authorities on religious belief to whom the Old Believers could turn, Avvakum and his companions engaged in theoretical discussions to determine doctrine. Questions regarding Christ's humanity and the nature of the Trinity were actively debated. Many of these disputations are recorded and discussed in Avvakum's *Kniga besed* (Book of Colloquies), *Kniga tolkovanii i nravouchenii* (Book of Exegesis and Moral Admonition), and *Kniga oblichenii ili evangelie vechnoe* (Book of Accusations or the Eternal Gospel).

During his years in Pustozersk, Avvakum petitioned Aleksei Mikhailovich three more times. In his fourth petition Avvakum requested the czar's forgiveness and asked for more flour. He also begged that his sons be allowed to join their mother in Mezen. His fifth petition entreated the czar to seek reconciliation between himself and the Old Belief. His final petition to Aleksei attacked the Nikonites and, again, appealed for mercy and forgiveness. In this period Avvakum also wrote many letters and epistles to his supporters. These were frequently smuggled out of Pustozersk by sympathetic guards. He often appended *zapiski,* which sometimes contained autobiographical material and sometimes detailed the lives of his fellow exiles.

Outside the small world of Pustozersk the affairs of the Old Believers were taking a serious turn. The venerable Solovki Monastery had resolutely refused to submit to liturgical innovations. In 1668 the government, tired of humoring the Old Believers, laid siege to the monastery. In the same year a popular rebellion led by Sten'ka Razin broke out, and insurgents ravaged the Volga River area. Since many of Razin's men followed the old faith, the government feared an alliance between them and Solovki. The Old Believer community of Moscow was suspected of acting as liaison between the two groups of rebels, and its repression was summarily ordered. As if to compound the Muscovites' misfortunes, Maria Miloslavskaia, Czar Aleksei's first wife, died in 1669, and Feodosiia Morozova, who had by this time become an important source of strength and support for the Moscow Old Believers, lost her protectress. Morozova was summoned to Aleksei's second wedding and ordered to participate in the new rituals. She refused, leading to her arrest and the full-scale persecution of the Moscow Old Believer community.

The authorities now decided that the time had come to put an end to the activities of the Pustozersk exiles. In 1670 Ivan Elagin was dispatched with instructions to shut away Avvakum's wife and sons in underground log prisons. After accomplishing his mission, he traveled to Pustozersk and did the same to Avvakum, Fedor, Epifanii, and Lazar (Nikifor had died by this time). Fedor, Epifanii, and Lazar had the remains of their tongues cut out and parts of their right hands amputated. Avvakum was spared physical mutilation. Although the exiles' living conditions had become gruesome, they persisted in their literary work.

Most important, Avvakum began sometime between 1669 and 1672 to write the *Zhitie protopopa Avvakuma im samim napisannoe.* Unquestionably one of the outstanding works of Russian literature, the *Zhitie protopopa Avvakuma* is unique in many respects. It may be seen as one of the first examples of modern Russian autobiography, describing Avvakum's travails from his birth through his incarceration (and imminent martyrdom) in Pustozersk, and yet at the same time it resembles a traditional saint's life, in large part as an assertion of the righteousness of the Old Believers' cause. It is thus both a work of abstract theology and a graphic portrait of dreadful human suffering. As with the later novels of Leo Tolstoy and Fyodor Dostoyevsky, the agonies of this life are often invested with sublime allegorical and transcendent meanings. The generic dualism of the *Zhitie protopopa Avvakuma* corresponds to the author's psychology, which alternates between the humility of a confession and a bellicose rage against those who persecute the true faith and a righteous pride that allows Avvakum to elevate himself to the rank of a saint. On a stylistic level, these oppositions correspond to the work's oscillation between high style Church Slavonic, the traditional language of the saint's life and of prayer, and the lowest subliterary Russian vernacular, which Avvakum virtually introduced into Russian letters, at least with such literary power.

Avvakum continued writing the *Zhitie protopopa Avvakuma* for many years and made many amendments to it. Numerous manuscript versions of the *Zhitie protopopa Avvakuma* survive, but all can be traced to four discrete redactions: the Prianishnikov (referred to by the name of the manuscript collection in the Lenin Library Archives in which the manuscript was found) and redactions A, B, and C. The autographs of redactions A and C have been preserved in collections that came to light in 1912 and 1966 respectively, and versions of both in hands other than Avvakum's as well as copies of redaction B were discovered somewhat earlier. The Prianishnikov redaction was not uncovered until the early 1950s. The first attempt to work out the

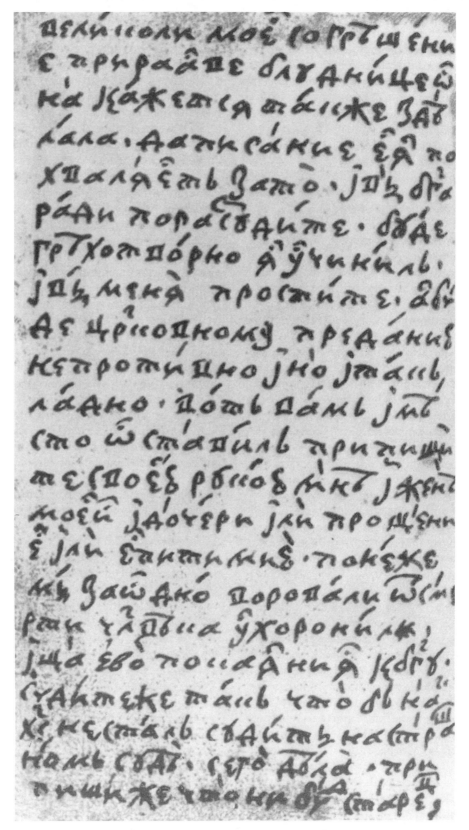

Page from a manuscript of Avvakum's Redaction A of Zhitie protopopa Avvakuma, *the only extant copy of this version in his own hand (Saint Petersburg, Biblioteka Akademii nauk, Sobranie Druzhinina, no. 746)*

relationship between the known redactions yielded the order A, B, C (the Prianishnikov redaction was not yet available). Version A is a fairly long and detailed manuscript, and scholars assumed that Avvakum made it shorter and more effective in the B redaction. C is longer than either of the other two manuscripts and supposedly represented a further development in light of new thoughts and events in Avvakum's life. The logic of first shortening and then lengthening the work seemed suspect to the Soviet scholar Natal'ia S. Demkova, however, and she proceeded to conduct a careful analysis of all three texts as well as of the recently discovered Prianishnikov version. She came to the conclusion that the order of writing should begin with the Prianishnikov redaction (composed sometime between 1669 and 1672), which was followed by B (dating from the first half of 1672), A (the first half of 1673), and C (1675).

Although quibbling over the order of composition of different variants of the *Zhitie protopopa Avvakuma* may seem at first glance rather arcane, it is actually of the utmost importance. The sequence established by Demkova provides a coherent picture of the evolution of the text and, by extension, of its author's intentions and meaning. The Prianishnikov manuscript includes a whole series of episodes in Avvakum's life that are not mentioned in any other version. Redaction C is highly didactic and contains theological material not found in the others. B and A, if read in this order, reveal a steady progression away from the autobiographical "realism" of the first (Prianishnikov) version and toward the schematization typical of a saint's life that can be discerned in the final (C) rendering.

The chronology thus established is vital to understanding the dialogue that has developed in the critical literature about the *Zhitie protopopa Avvakuma*. The basic question posed is whether the work should most properly be read as a product of medieval Russian spirituality or as a harbinger of trends in modern Russian literature. Western scholars are more inclined to take the former view, while Russian scholars have argued forcibly for the latter. Each side concedes at least some of the points made by the other.

A basic issue addressed by most scholars of the *Zhitie protopopa Avvakuma* is its hybrid language. Large portions of the work, especially those that address theological concerns, are composed in Church Slavonic, the official ecclesiastical language. Other sections, particularly those in which the author describes his travels in Siberia, are written in a lively vernacular Russian. Relating autobiographical material, Avvakum avails himself of an abundance of expletives, diminutives, and words deriving from everyday life and thus creates the impression of engaging his reader in an animated chat. Conversational interpolations of this sort are not entirely unprecedented in the literature of the late sixteenth and seventeenth centuries, but they are more sustained, consistent, and artistically satisfying in the *Zhitie protopopa Avvakuma*.

Some scholars have suggested that ultimately there can be no contradiction between the registers of language employed by Avvakum. The higher, more formal type of language used in theological discussions is representative of the order of the eternal, heavenly kingdom of God, while lower, more conversational forms reflect daily life in the profane world. By juxtaposing them Avvakum shows that the two poles, sacred and profane, exist as points on a single continuum. There are, in other words, no absolute or insurmountable barriers that would prohibit merging the heavenly order with the earthly. The fact that with each new version of the *Zhitie protopopa Avvakuma* Avvakum expanded the role of Church Slavonic would seem to point to an unspoken intention to make the work reflect the immediacy of God and the omnipresence of his truth.

Although the *Zhitie protopopa Avvakuma* was circulated only in manuscript copies and was essentially lost to the literary tradition for almost two hundred years, once it had been published by Nikolai S. Tikhonravov in 1861, it exercised an immediate and almost electric effect on nineteenth-century writers. Tolstoy, Dostoyevsky, Nikolai Leskov, and Ivan Turgenev, to mention only the most prominent, were struck by its tremendous power as a document of human suffering, as a testament to Avvakum's towering faith, and as a novelistic combination of theological and human dimensions of reality.

Looked at from a broadly literary context, the *Zhitie protopopa Avvakuma* could reasonably be said to presage the arrival in Russia of the baroque aesthetic. It is highly unlikely that Avvakum himself would have approved of such a conclusion. Reflections of the "high" baroque were clearly evidenced in the relatively secularized works of Avvakum's enemy, Polotsky, and Avvakum inveighed bitterly against baroque trends in icon painting. Nevertheless, ignoring authorial intentions and looking to the actual literary work, it is reasonable to view Avvakum's mixture of high and low styles as an example of the baroque predilection for contrast. The structuring of the *Zhitie protopopa Avvakuma* also reveals certain affinities with baroque strategies. The *Zhitie protopopa Avvakuma* takes shape as a series of separate vignettes or novellas that are bound to each other by virtue of sharing the same hero. Particularly in the earlier redactions, the narrative has much in common with a travelogue, and in all versions narration is first-person. While the *Zhitie protopopa Avvakuma* could hardly be said to constitute a picaresque (a favorite genre of German baroque writers), the compositional strategies Avvakum adopts are highly suggestive. Finally, if Avvakum attempts to reconcile the earthly and heavenly orders in the *Zhitie protopopa Avvakuma,* a reading that seems quite convincing, then this aspect of the work is also consonant with baroque culture. Particularly in Germany, the yearning to bring the flesh into communion with the spirit and the temporal order into communion with the eternal was highly characteristic of the baroque.

Discussions of the affinity of the *Zhitie protopopa Avvakuma* with baroque poetics leave an important facet of the work unexplained, however. Avvakum explicitly calls his work a "life," and many of its compositional features support reading it as an example of hagiography. Although, for example, the microstructure of the text is episodic, the macrostructure reflects the traditional tripartite division characteristic of a saint's life. An introductory segment, in this case an exposition on various teachings of the Pseudo-Dionysios, is followed by the body of the work, which recounts the actual events of the saint's life. A brief conclusion follows that, of necessity, omits the details of the saint's death but, nevertheless, foresees it (Avvakum predicts his own martyrdom). A study of the extant redactions of the *Zhitie protopopa Avvakuma* suggests that Avvakum's intention was to write a hagiographic work: with each successive redaction, hagiographic elements become more common.

Ultimately, the *Zhitie protopopa Avvakuma* should probably be read from two complementary perspectives, and one is unquestionably the religious. The *Zhitie protopopa Avvakuma* was intended as an exemplary life, a document to teach and strengthen the Old Believer community for the hard times and martyrdom that were to come. The claims of scholars interested in the work's purely literary merits must also be admitted, however. Andreas Angyal's 1961 book on the Slavic baroque may provide a way of harmonizing both positions. He posits the existence of a gothic-baroque period, a time during which baroque artistic devices mixed and blended with medieval, religious ones. A favorite device of gothic-baroque literature was antithesis, which was used to accent both the radiance of

eternity and the transitoriness of everyday life. Avvakum's *Zhitie protopopa Avvakuma* seems to fit into Angyal's theoretical framework well, and the recognition of both its religious and its literary significance is crucial to a full understanding of its nature as a transitional work embodying all the complexity of the seventeenth century.

The community for which Avvakum wrote his *Zhitie protopopa Avvakuma* suffered a series of severe blows during the years of the work's composition and revision, a fact that may explain many of the changes and additions the archpriest made to his text. In November 1675 Morozova and her sister Urusova starved to death in Borovsk, their place of detention. The loss of his spiritual children affected Avvakum painfully. Furthermore, in early 1676 Solovki was betrayed by an insider and fell to the czar's troops. A week later Czar Aleksei died, an event which the Old Believers lost no time in interpreting as just retribution for his persecutions. Meanwhile, in Pustozersk the exiles continued discussions among themselves concerning questions of dogma. The polemics between Avvakum and Deacon Fedor took on an increasingly bitter tone, and a split in the Old Believer leadership began to develop.

In 1676 Avvakum wrote a petition to the new czar, Fedor Alekseevich, in which he expressed his desire to destroy the enemies of the Old Belief and asserted that Czar Aleksei Mikhailovich was most certainly burning in hell, a statement which did not endear him to the young ruler. Moreover, in 1681 an extremist Old Believers' plot was uncovered in Moscow. Patriarch Ioakim, well out of patience with the controversy, called a new council in 1682 to deal with the Old Belief. The Pustozersk exiles were condemned to be burned to death, and in April 1682 Avvakum attained the crown of martyrdom he had predicted for himself in the *Zhitie protopopa Avvakuma.* Avvakum actively embraced this martyrdom and may have set a precedent for the actions of the estimated twenty thousand Old Believers who shut themselves up in churches and burned themselves to death during the 1670s and 1680s.

References:

Andreas (Endre) Angyal, *Die slavische Barockwelt* (Leipzig: E. A. Seemann, 1961);

Jostein Børtnes, "Dissimilar Similarities: Imitatio Christi in the Life of Archpriest Avvakum," *Canadian-American Slavic Studies,* 13 (1979): 224–229;

Børtnes, *Visions of Glory* (N.p.: Humanities Press International, 1988);

Kenneth N. Brostrom, "Further Remarks on the Life of the Archpriest Avvakum," in *The Archpriest Avvakum: The Life Written by Himself,* edited by Brostrom (Ann Arbor: University of Michigan Press, 1979), pp. 147–207;

V. A. Chernov, "Na kakom iazyke pisal Avvakum?," *Trudy Otdela Drevnerusskoi Literatury,* 42 (1989): 369–373;

Anatolii S. Demin, "Chelobitnye Avvakuma i odna iz neissledovannykh traditsii delovoi pis'mennosti XVII v.," *Trudy Otdela Drevnerusskoi Literatury,* 25 (1969): 220–231;

Demin, "Nabliudeniia nad peizazhem v Zhitii protopopa Avvakuma," *Trudy Otdela Drevnerusskoi Literatury,* 22 (1966): 402–406;

Natal'ia S. Demkova, "Izuchenie khudozhestvennoi struktury Zhitiia Avvakuma: Printsip kontrastnosti izobrazheniia," in *Puti izucheniia drevnerusskoi literatury i pis'mennosti,* edited by Dmitrii S. Likhachev and Nadezhda F. Droblenkova (Leningrad: Nauka, 1970), pp. 100–108;

Demkova, "K voprosu ob istokakh avtobiograficheskogo povestvovaniia v Zhitii Avvakuma," *Trudy Otdela Drevnerusskoi Literatury,* 24 (1968): 228–232;

Demkova, "Tvorcheskaia istoriia Zhitiia protopopa Avvakuma," *Trudy Otdela Drevnerusskoi Literatury,* 25 (1969): 197–219;

Demkova, *Zhitie protopopa Avvakuma: Tvorcheskaia istoriia proizvedeniia* (Leningrad: Leningradskii universitet, 1974);

Bruce T. Holl, "Avvakum and the Genesis of Siberian Literature," in *Between Heaven and Hell: The Myth of Siberia in Russian Culture,* edited by Galya Diment and Yuri Slezkine (New York: St. Martin's Press, 1993), pp. 33–45;

Priscilla Hart Hunt, "The Autobiography of the Archpriest Avvakum: The Outer Limits of the Narrative Icon," Ph.D. dissertation, Stanford University, 1979;

Hunt, "A Penitential Journey: The Life of the Archpriest Avvakum and the Kenotic Tradition," *Canadian-American Slavic Studies,* 25 (1991): 201–224;

Dmitrii S. Likhachev, *Chelovek v literature drevnei Rusi,* revised edition (Moscow: Nauka, 1970);

Likhachev and Aleksandr M. Panchenko, *Smekhovoi mir drevnei Rusi* (Leningrad, 1976); revised as *Smekh v drevnei Rusi,* with N. V. Ponyrko (Leningrad: Nauka, 1984);

Panchenko, "Avvakum kak novator," *Russkaia literatura,* 4 (1982): 142–152;

Pierre Pascal, *Avvakum et les débuts du raskol* (Paris: Centre d'etudes russes "Istina," 1938);

Mary Foster Peabody, "Traditional and Individualist Aspects of the Petitions of the Archpriest Avvakum," Ph.D. dissertation, University of California, Berkeley, 1991;

Andrei N. Robinson, "Tvorchestvo Avvakuma v istoriko-funktsional'nom osveshchenii," in *Russkaia literatura v istoriko-Funktsional' num osveshchenii,* edited by N. V. Os'makov and others (Moscow: Nauka, 1979), pp. 98–181;

Anthony Stokes, "Literature of the Seventeenth Century," in *Early Russian Literature,* edited by John Fennell and Stokes (Berkeley: University of California Press, 1974), pp. 207–268;

Viktor V. Vinogradov, "O zadachakh stilistiki: nabliudeniia nad stilem *Zhitiia protopopa Avvakuma,*" *Russkaia rech',* 1 (1925): 195–293; translated as "On the Tasks of Stylistics: Observations Regarding the Style of the Archpriest Avvakum," in *The Archpriest Avvakum: The Life Written by Himself,* edited by Brostrom (Ann Arbor: University of Michigan Press, 1979), pp. 117–147;

Serge Zenkovsky, "The Old Believer Avvakum: His Writings," *Indiana Slavic Studies,* 1 (1956): 1–51;

Zenkovsky, *Russkoe staroobriadchestvo* (Munich: Wilhelm Fink, 1970).

Papers:

The main manuscript redactions of Avvakum's *Zhitie protopoga Avvakuma im samim napisannoe* are: "Redaction A," the autograph of which is at the Library of the Academy of Sciences (Saint Petersburg), Sobranie Druzhinina, no. 746; "Redaction B," whose autograph has not survived, but which exists in many copies, for example, at the State Historical Museum (Moscow), muzeinoe sobranie, no. 2582; "Redaction C," whose autograph is preserved in the Institute of Russian Literature (Saint Petersburg), Drevnekhranilishche, op. 24, no. 43, and which exists in a number of later, less accurate copies; and the "Prianishnikov" redaction, which exists in one (not autograph) copy at the Lenin Library, Moscow, Sobranie G. M. Prianishnikova, fond 242, no. 61.

Ivan Semenovich Barkov
(1732 – 1768)

Andrei Zorin
Russian State Humanitarian University, Moscow

BOOKS: *Oda na vseradostnyi den' rozhedeniia ego velichestva blagochestiveishego gosudariia Petra Fedorovicha, imperatora i samoderzhtsa rossiiskogo* (Saint Petersburg, 1762);

Sochineniia i perevody (Saint Petersburg, 1872).

Editions: *Devich'ia igrushka,* edited by Valerii Sazhen (Saint Petersburg: Biblioteka "Zvezdy," 1992);

Devich'ia igrushka, ili Sochineniia gospodina Barkova, edited by A. Zorin and N. Sapov (Moscow: Ladomir, 1992).

OTHER: "Sokrashchennaia rossiiskaia istoria," in G. Kuras, *Sokrashchennaia Rossiiskaia istoriia, soderzhashchaia vse dostopamiatnye v svete sluchai* (Saint Petersburg: Akademiia nauk, 1762), pp. 357–390;

A. D. Kantemir, *Satiry i drugie stikhotvornye sochineniia,* edited, with an introductory essay, by Barkov (Saint Petersburg: Akademiia nauk, 1762);

Lodovico Lazzaroni, *Mir geroev, dramma na muzyke,* translated by Barkov (Saint Petersburg: Akademiia nauk, 1762);

Horace, *Satiry, ili Besedy s primechaniiami,* translated by Barkov (Saint Petersburg: Akademiia nauk, 1763);

Phaedrus, *Nravouchitel'nye basni s Ezopova obraztsa sochinennyia,* translated by Barkov (Saint Petersburg: Akademiia nauk, 1764) – includes Barkov's translation of Dionysius Cato (Psevdo-Katon), "Dvustrochnye stikhi o blagonravii k synu";

Ludovic Golberg, *Sokrashchenie universal'noi istorii,* translated by Barkov (Saint Petersburg, 1766);

"Letopis' Nesterova s prodolzhateliami po Kenigsbergskomu spisku, do 1206 goda," edited by Barkov, in *Biblioteka rossiiskaia istoricheskaia,* volume 1 (Saint Petersburg: Akademiia nauk, 1767);

Perevody s latinskogo i shvedskogo iazykov: Sluchivshiiasia vo vremena imp. Marka Avreliia rimskago i

Ivan Semenovich Barkov

Karolusa 12 shvedskago, translated by Barkov (Saint Petersburg: M. O[vchinnikov], 1786).

Ivan Semenovich Barkov was a translator, poet, editor, and publisher for the Academy of Sciences and a participant in the literary debates of the 1750s and 1760s. He prepared the first edition of Antiokh Kantemir's satires in Russia as well as translations of Horace and Phaedrus. Barkov's main historical and literary reputation, however, rests on his authorship of a series of poetic works of obscene content. By the end of the eighteenth century virtually every collection of verse "not meant for print" was attributed exclusively to him, a circumstance which laid the basis for a special kind of myth that pictured Barkov as the author of almost all obscene Russian poetry. Later, even into the twentieth century, almost all popular indecent verse was attributed to him. The poem "Luka Mudishchev," for example, composed in the last third of the nineteenth century, gained particular notoriety and was consistently associated in the public consciousness, and even in the popular press, with Barkov's name.

Barkov was born in 1732 into the family of a priest. Beginning in 1744 he studied at the Aleksandr Nevsky seminary in Saint Petersburg, where he took courses in grammar and poetics. In 1748 he was examined by Mikhailo Lomonosov, who noted Barkov's "keen understanding," and was sent to study at the Academy of Sciences' gymnasium. Barkov's further academic and service career involved a continuing series of punishments – primarily as a result of his drinking binges – and pardons, which were accompanied by the academy's repeated attempts to reform its gifted young student.

In 1750 Barkov was subjected to physical punishment for "absence without leave and other loathsome actions." In 1751 he caused a scandal in the home of Prof. S. Krasheninnikov, and, while being held in custody for riotous behavior, he denounced the professor for alleged knowledge of crimes against the state. After an inquiry revealed that the charge lacked any basis, Barkov was released by the secret chancellery, which declared that he was "liable to cruel punishment, but [that] in consideration of his young age and in hopes that he will make up for his bad actions by good successes in the sciences, he is released from such punishment, but if henceforth, he, Barkov, is found to be [in a state of] drunkenness or [caught] in any other foul deeds, then he will be severely punished and sent into permanent service as a sailor." Later that year Barkov's status as a student was revoked, and he was assigned to the academy's press as an apprentice to a typesetter, although he was allowed to continue to attend classes. New punishments were imposed on Barkov in 1752 "for drunkenness and fighting during the nocturnal hour," and in 1753 he was once put under guard "for gross impertinences." Nevertheless, in the same year his petition to be made a copyist in the academy chancellery was approved, and in 1755 Barkov found himself ordered to recopy several manuscripts for Lomonosov. The renowned scientist and poet had Barkov make faircopies of his *Rossiiskaia grammatika* (Russian Grammar, 1755) and of several of his historical and other works and also had him make a copy of one of the versions of Nestor's thirteenth-century chronicle, the *Povest' vremennykh let* (Tale of Bygone Years),

also known as the *Iznachal'naia letopis'* (Primary Chronicle).

In 1756 Barkov was assigned to manage the written affairs of G. K. Razumovsky, president of the academy, but in January 1757 he was discharged from those duties "for drunkenness and disorderliness." In 1758 he disappeared from another job for several weeks and was only found with the help of the police. Despite such behavior, he received work translating and editing several books, probably with Lomonosov's intercession. Among other things, in 1758 he worked on *Perevody s latinskogo i shvedskogo iazykov* (Translations from the Latin and Swedish Languages, 1786), which was not published until after his death.

On 10 February 1762 Barkov published his *Oda na vseradostnyi den' rozhdeniia ego velichestva blagochestiveishego gosudariia Petra Fedorovicha, imperatora i samoderzhtsa rossiikogo* (Ode on the Joyous Birthday of His Majesty the Most Pious Sovereign Peter Fedorovich, Emperor and Autocrat of Russia), dedicated to the emperor who had just ascended to the throne; this was Barkov's only original poetic work published during his lifetime. On 13 February Razumovsky issued an order making Barkov an academy translator; the document noted Barkov's "excellent experience and knowledge" in language and literature as well as his promise "to correct his behavior completely." The year 1762 was the peak of Barkov's official literary activity. For the festivities connected with ending the war with Prussia he translated (from German) Lodovico Lazzaroni's "World of the Heroes," and in the same year he prepared A. D. Kantemir's satires for publication (a project financed by I. I. Taubert, an official at the academy chancellery). In editing the satires Barkov followed accepted eighteenth-century practice and significantly modernized their language, in particular excluding obsolescent and vulgar expressions. In the "Zhitie kniazia Antiokha Dmitrievicha Kantemira" (Life of Prince Antiokh Dmitrievich Kantemir), which Barkov wrote for this edition, he relied primarily on the preface to the French edition of the satires written by Abbott Guasco. Barkov continued his work in history with the publication of *Sokrashchenie universal'noi istorii* (Abridged Universal History), a condensed translation of Ludovic Golberg's opus, and he also prepared for publication the so-called Köningsberg copy of Nestor's chronicles. This latter work was sharply censured by A. L. Shletzer (Schlöser), who in his critique did not fail to mention that Barkov, "beyond his lack of scholarly qualifications, had this weakness as well – he was often not in a sober state."

Translations of Latin poetry held an important place in Barkov's career. In 1763 he published Horace's satires, together with N. N. Popovsky's translation of the "Epistle to the Pisos." In a foreword written in verse and dedicated to Count G. G. Orlov, Barkov asserts his preference for the Horatian type of "satire of vices" (that is, rather than of particular persons). Another dedicatory piece to Orlov has survived in manuscript, and the oral tradition holds that Orlov was Barkov's patron and benefactor. In 1764 Barkov's translation of Phaedrus's fables was published, with Latin originals printed on facing pages; he excluded a series of fables because of their "improper content." Barkov also translated a series of moralistic couplets by Dionysius Cato which were included in the edition as a supplement. Barkov used regular iambic hexameter verse to translate both the fables and the couplets and demonstrated his undeniable expertise in doing so; on the whole Barkov's Latin translations testify to a rather high level of verse technique. Barkov was also entrusted with editing several books for the academy's press, including George Buffon's *Natural History* (1789–1808), an edition of Aesop, *Ezopovy i drugiia basni* (1766), and Andrei Lyzlov's *Skifskaia istoriia* (1776). In 1766 Barkov was permanently let go by the academy, and after two years — a period of Barkov's life about which nothing is known — he died.

The dearth of biographical information about Barkov is partly relieved by a wealth of anecdotal material. The oral tradition commonly focuses on several traits of Barkov's character: his predilection for drink and drunken brawls, his poverty, and his sarcasm and wit. There are also anecdotes concerning Barkov's special position in contemporary literary polemics, in particular his closeness to Lomonosov and his critical attitude toward Aleksandr Sumarokov, who characterized Lomonosov and Barkov as "scholarly drunkards"; in *Table-talk* (1835–1836) Aleksandr Pushkin records the tradition that "no one was able to enrage Sumarokov like Barkov." In the opinions of literary historians these anecdotes generally accord with history. Several polemical literary works commonly attributed to Barkov include two attacks on Vasilii Trediakovsky — "Satira na samokhvala" (Satire on a Braggart) and "Nadgrobnaia nadpis'" (Gravestone Epitaph) — and a defense of Lomonosov in the polemic surrounding his "Gimn borode" (Hymn to the Beard): "Pronessia slukh: khotiat kogo-to budto szhech'" (There is a rumor they want to burn someone at the stake).

Several satires on contemporary Russian poets reportedly appeared in Moscow in 1753 under pseudonyms associated with Barkov, suggesting that the poet wrote many polemical works, though most have not survived. It is possible that one of these was the obscene tragedy "Durnosov i Farnos" (Uglynose and Farnos [the hero of an obscene *lubok*, or chapbook]), which parodies Sumarokov's tragedy "Sinav i Truvor." Sumarokov's responding epigram "Na sochinenie tragedii *Durakov*" (On the Composition of the Tragedy *Fools*) characterizes Barkov as "iazvitel'nyi zlodei" (a caustic villain), a "predatel' istinnyi i p'ianitsa do smerti" (true traitor and drunkard unto death), but at the same time recognizes his knowledge of philology and of Latin and Russian.

Barkov's obscene poetry — the so-called barkovshchina — was compiled in manuscript collections that circulated under his name. The earliest surviving examples are dated to the late 1770s, postdating Barkov's death by about a decade. These collections of "Barkov's works," which traditionally bore the title *Devich'ia igrushka* (Maiden's Plaything), overtly bring together works by various authors. In the foreword usually affixed to these collections, entitled "Prinoshenie Belinde" (An Offering to Belinda), it is noted that "In presenting this book to you, incomparable Belinda, I do not seek your favor for myself alone, but for many, since I am not the sole author of the works found here, and did not alone collect them." These collections include works attributed to Mikhail Chulkov, A. V. Olsuf'ev, F. D. Dmitriev-Manonov, possibly Sumarokov, and others. With a great degree of certainty the "Oda Priapu" (Ode to Priapus), the long poem "Na pobedu Priapovoi dshcheri" (To the Victory of Priapus's Daughter), and the tragedy "Durnosov i Farnos" are attributed to Barkov. It is apparent, however, that Barkov's contribution to *Devich'ia igrushka* was more substantial. In his *Attempt at a Historical Dictionary of Russian Writers* (1772) Nikolai Novikov asserts that Barkov had written "mnozhestvo tselykh i melkikh stikhotvorenii v chest' Vakkha i Afrodity" (a great quantity of large and small poems in honor of Bacchus and Aphrodite). Testimony about "burleskakh, koikh on vystupil v svet mnozhestvo" (burlesques, of which he circulated many), also comes from the "Information About Several Russian Writers," which was published in Leipzig during Barkov's life and written by either I. A. Dmitrevsky or V. I. Lukin. Nonetheless, it is not possible to determine which texts in *Devich'ia igrushka* definitely belong to Barkov. The tradition that developed of attributing the entire collection – and indeed all obscene Russian verse – to Barkov clearly reflects processes of literary mythologizing.

The indisputable connection between Barkov's poetic practice as a literary polemicist and his obscene verse at times has led some critics to see the entire corpus of so-called Barkoviana as fundamentally a parody. Thus the Soviet scholar Georgii P. Makogonenko characterizes Barkov's work as a "conscious and rigorously thought-out attack on the entire poetic system of Russian classicism." However, the place of parody in the overall poetic system of *Devich'ia igrushka* is rather limited. The authors of Barkoviana resorted to using most of the then-existing canonical genres of classicism in order to make literary those types of composition and language that existed beyond the bounds of the permissible. They used the language of *matershchina* (cursing) and copulation not so much to discredit Sumarokovian tragedy or the Lomonosovian ode or the folk song as to take advantage of the stylistic repertoire they offered in order to speak about the unspeakable. A parodic effect arises and is at times purposefully created, but the authors' main goal is to generate, with the help of an already-developed poetic technique, an integral and all-embracing literary inferno, a world in which the mythological figures of Priapus and Venus reign supreme.

For the eighteenth and early nineteenth centuries Barkoviana, although it was considered separate from the main body of Russian literature, was not juxtaposed against that literature as something inimical. The author of "Nachricht von einigen russischen Schriftstellern," (Information About Several Russian Writers, 1768) speaks of Barkov's "hale and hearty, merry turn of mind" and only complains a little about the fact that in his works "in some places decency is offended." In his *Opyt irstoricheskogo slovaria o rossiiskikh pisateliakh* (Attempt at a Historical Dictionary of Russian Writers, 1772) Novikov notes Barkov's "gay and carefree manner" and says that "a great many praise [his satiric works] for their wit." Allusions to Barkovian poems may be found in the works of many poets of the later eighteenth and early nineteenth centuries, including those of Derzhavin. Even such a writer as Nikolai Karamzin, who hardly approved of any kind of indecency, gave Barkov a far-from-annihilating (if somewhat skeptical) evaluation in his *Panteon rossiiskikh avtorov* (Pantheon of Russian Writers, 1801). "Barkov was born with a gift, of course," he wrote, "but one should note that this sort of wittiness does not lead to the same kind of fame which is the goal and reward for the genuine poet."

With time, Barkov's image grew ever more separate from historical and literary reality and accrued new mythological dimensions. In the poem "Ten' Barkova" (Barkov's Ghost), which has been attributed to Pushkin, Barkov appears in the role of a kind of god of fertility, one who demands worship and glorification and who comes to the aid of his loyal followers at moments of masculine difficulty. In the second half of the nineteenth century a new image was created of Barkov as a poet and alcoholic tormented by his milieu, who dissipated his talent in taverns. In the Soviet period Barkov was consistently turned into a fighter against czarism, a rebel against the social and literary establishment. In more recent decades Barkov's image has become that of an eccentric and innovator and creator of poetic *smekhovaia kul'tura* (culture of laughter), a notion made popular by Mikhail M. Bakhtin in his work on the French writer François Rabelais and related to Russian culture by such modern scholars as D. S. Likhachev and A. M. Panchenko. In Barkov's case the process of mythologizing was further complicated by the fact that his obscene poetry remained unpublished, and its very corpus of texts not even approximately established. The publication and serious study of Barkov's poetry and of Barkoviana has essentially only begun in the 1990s.

Bibliography:

Anthony G. Cross, " 'The Notorious Barkov': An Annotated Bibliography," *Study Group on Eighteenth Century Russia Newsletter,* no. 2 (1972): 41–52.

References:

Pavel N. Berkov, *Lomonosov i literaturnaia polemika ego vremeni, 1750–1765* (Moscow & Leningrad: Akademia nauk, 1936);

Berkov, "Rannie russkie perevodchiki Goratsiia," *Izvestiia Akademii nauk SSSR, Otdel obshchestvennykh nauk,* no. 10 (1935): 1053–1055;

P. A. Efremov, *Materialy dlia istorii russkoi literatury* (Saint Petersburg, 1867);

Aleksei A. Iliushin, "Iarost' pravednykh," *Literaturnoe obozrenie,* no. 11 (1991): 7–14;

Elena S. Kuliabko, *Zamechatel'nye pitomtsy akademicheskogo universiteta* (Leningrad: Nauka, 1977);

Kuliabko and N. V. Sokolova, "Barkov – uchenik Lomonosova," in *Lomonosov: Sbornik statei i materialov,* edited by A. I. Andreeva and L. B.

Modzalevskogo (Moscow & Leningrad: Akademiia nauk, 1965), pp. 190–216;

Georgii P. Makogonenko, "Vrag parnasskikh uz," *Russkaia literatura,* 4 (1964): 136–148;

Galina N. Moiseeva, "Barkov i izdanie satir Kantemira," *Russkaia literatura,* 2 (1967): 102–115;

Moiseeva, "Iz istorii russkogo literaturnogo iazyka XVIII veka," in *Poetika i stilistika russkoi literatury* (Leningrad: Nauka, 1971), pp. 69–73;

Moiseeva, "K istorii literaturno-obshchestvennoi polemiki XVIII veka," in *Iskusstvo slova* (Moscow: Nauka, 1973), pp. 56–64;

Moiseeva, "Sochineniia Barkova po russkoi istorii," in *Stranitsy po istorii russkoi literatury* (Moscow, 1971);

Aleksandr A. Morozov, "Russkaia stikhotvornaia parodiia," in *Russkaia stikhotvornaia parodiia XVIII–nachala XX veka,* Biblioteka poeta, Bol'shaia seriia (Leningrad: Sovetskii pisatel', 1987), pp. 5–88;

N. Sapov, "Ivan Barkov: biograficheskii ocherk," in Barkov's *Devich'ia igrushka, ili Sochineniia gospodina Barkova* (Moscow: Ladomir, 1992), pp. 17–36;

P. E. Shegolev, "Poema Pushkina 'Monakh,' " *Krasnyi arkhiv,* 6, no. 31 (1928): 160–175;

V. P. Stepanov, "Barkov (Borkov), Ivan Semenovich," in *Slovar' russkikh pisatelei XVIII veka,* volume 1 (Leningrad: Nauka, 1988), pp. 57–62;

Semen A. Vengerov, "Barkov, I. S.," in *Kritiko-bibliograficheskii slovar' russkikh pisatelei i uchenykh,* volume 2 (Saint Petersburg, 1891), pp. 148–154;

A. L. Zorin, "Barkov i barkoviana (Predvaritel'nye zamechaniia)," *Literaturnoe obozrenie,* no. 11 (1991): 19–21;

Zorin, "Ivan Barkov – istoriia kul'turnogo mifa," in Barkov's *Devich'ia igrushka, ili sochineniia gospodina Barkova,* edited by Zorin and Sapov (Moscow: Ladomir, 1992), pp. 5–16;

Zorin and Sapov, "Obzor rukopisnykh sbornikov barkoviany," in Barkov's *Devich'ia igrushka, ili Sochineniia gospodina Barkova,* edited by Zorin and Sapov (Moscow: Ladomir, 1992), pp. 369–381.

Semen Sergeevich Bobrov

(1763? – 22 March 1810)

Mark G. Altshuller
University of Pittsburgh

BOOKS: *Drammaticheskaia pesn' na konchinu Ekateriny II v trekh iavleniiakh* ([Saint Petersburg: Artillereiskii kadetskii korpus, 1769]);

Oda rossiiskomu admiralu i raznykh ordenov kavaleru Vasil'iu Iakovlevichu Chichagovu, na sluchai slavnago otrazheniia shvedskago flota u Revelia maiia 2 dnia 1790 goda ([Saint Petersburg, 1790]);

Slava rossiiskikh iroev, oznamenovavshikh sebia v techenie 1788 po 1792 god. Pobednaia pesn' . . . Na sluchai torzhestva mira s Portoiu 1793 goda sentiabria 2 dnia (Saint Petersburg: Vil'kovsky, [1793]);

Tavrida, ili Moi letnyi den' v Tavricheskom Khersonise. Lyriko-epicheskoe pesnotvorenie (Nikolaev: Chernomorskaia admiralteiskaia tipografiia, 1798);

Rassvet polnochi, ili sozertsanie slavy, torzhestva i mudrosti porfironosnykh, branonosnykh i mirnykh geniev Rossii s posledovaniem didakticheskikh, eroticheskikh i drugikh raznogo roda v stikhakh i proze opytov, 4 volumes (Saint Petersburg, 1804);

Rossy v bure, ili Groznaia noch' na iaponskikh vodakh (Saint Petersburg, 1807);

Na sluchai vyrosshei vetki na monumente Rumiantseva-Zadunaiskogo (Saint Petersburg, 1807);

Drevniaia noch' Vselennoi, ili stranstvuiushchyi slepets, 2 volumes (Saint Petersburg, 1807–1809);

Parenie ventsenosnogo geniia Rossii s polunoshchnykh predelov k zapadnym 15 Marta 1808 (Saint Petersburg: Glazunov, 1808);

Drevnii rossiiskii plavetel', ili opyt kratkogo deepisaniia o prezhnikh morskikh pokhodakh Rossiian (Saint Petersburg: Morskaia, 1812).

SELECTED PERIODICAL PUBLICATION – UNCOLLECTED: "Proisshestvie v tsartve tenei, ili sud'bina rossiiskogo iazyka 1805 goda, Noiabria dnia, Sanktpeterburg," edited by Iurii M. Lotman and Boris Uspensky, *Uchenye zapiski Tartuskogo gos. universiteta, 358,*

Semen Sergeevich Bobrov

Trudy po russkoi i slavianskoi filologii, 24 (1975): 255–322.

Semen Sergeevich Bobrov played a notable role in the history of Russian poetry at the turn of the nineteenth century. His verses, which were heavy and awkward yet full of unique majesty and strength, elicited ardent praise from some and furious and witty jibes from others. Defenders and devotees of Bobrov's poetry advocated a serious, difficult, high literary style. Among contemporaries of the poet these included Aleksandr Radishchev and Gavriil Derzhavin, and in the next generation Vilgelm Kiukhel'beker, Aleksandr Griboedov, and the mature Aleksandr Pushkin. Among his bitter detractors were the followers of Nikolai Karamzin and proponents of the *legkii slog* (light style): Konstantin Batiushkov, Petr Viazemsky, and the young Pushkin. Intense, difficult to understand, and full of meditative thought, Bobrov's lyrics helped begin the tradition of Russian philosophical verse, that of Fedor Tiutchev, Evgenii Baratynsky, Konstantin Sluchevsky and others. Bobrov also wrote the first and one of the only descriptive poems in Russian literature, *Tavrida, ili Moi letnyi den' v Tavricheskom Khersonise* (Tauride, or My Summer Day in the Tauric Chersonese, 1798 – Tauride is the Greek name for the Crimea).

Semen Sergeevich Bobrov was most likely born in 1763 (or 1765) into the family of a priest in the city of Iaroslavl or nearby. In his autobiographical poem "Vykladka zhizni bestalannogo Vorbaba" (Exposition of the Life of the Untalented Vorbab, 1804 – "Vorbab" being an obvious anagram for Bobrov) – the future poet says he left home at the age of nine. In all likelihood his family sent him to a theological seminary, as was accepted practice in priestly families. In 1780 he entered the gymnasium of Moscow University, and he became a student at the university in 1782.

The activities of Nikolai Novikov, the celebrated Russian writer, publisher, and journalist, were closely tied to the university, where he had transferred his publishing activities in 1779. The most active Russian Freemasons could also be found at Moscow University. One of Freemasonry's leaders and founders in Russia, Johann Schwartz, gave lectures both at the university and in his own home. Mikhail Kheraskov, one of the greatest Russian writers of the eighteenth century and a prominent Mason, was director and curator of the university, which was the center for much of his creative activity. Bobrov's talent and worldview undoubtedly took shape under the influence of these outstanding personalities. He tried his strength in poetry from an early age: "Chut' nachal um moi rastsvetat' . . . / Ia s bozhestvom stikhov stolknulsia" (Hardly had my mind begun to bloom . . . / I encountered the divinity of verse).

Under the aegis of Schwartz the Sobranie universitetskikh pitomtsev (Assembly of University Alumni) opened in March 1781. Its purpose was the "education of the mind and taste, . . . reading and discussion of literary experiences, . . . and exercises in philanthropy." In November 1782 Schwartz organized the Druzheskoe uchenoe obshchestvo (Friendly Scientific Society) and a translators' seminar, which included at first six and later as many as thirty students, with the backing of the Masons. Bobrov was a member of all of these associations, and it is highly likely that the Masons helped support him during his years of residence at the university. Bobrov immersed himself in the works of writers and philosophers popular in Masonic circles, in-

cluding Jacob Boehme, Louis-Claude de Saint-Martin, John Bunyan, Friedrich Klopstock, Johann Gottfried von Herder, and others. He was able to read them firsthand since he became proficient in Latin, French, German, and English. In his service record he later emphasized his knowledge of French and English. The latter is especially interesting, for at the turn of the century English was not popular in Russia, and few knew the language; even later, Russian translations of English literature were commonly done from French intermediaries. Bobrov was an admirer of English poetry and knew well the works of John Milton, James Thomson, and the Ossianic poems published by James Macpherson from 1760 to 1763. His acquaintance with the works of Edward Young turned out to be especially important for him.

Bobrov's public activity as a poet began in the journal *Pokoiashchiisia Trudoliubets* (The Reposing Work Lover), which was published by the Assembly of University Alumni and saturated with Masonic ideas. The journal published Bobrov's poems about the end of the world, the frailty of existence, and the essence of life and death. His verses depict cosmic pictures of planets floating through the heavenly firmament, which the imagination of the poet perceives as mere spheres destined to perish in the flames of the Last Judgment. These works, like much of Bobrov's later poetry, were written under the obvious influence of Young's nocturnal graveyard poetry, in particular his poem "The Last Day."

Bobrov graduated from the university in 1785, but it was not until 1787 that he found a position in Saint Petersburg (at the Heraldry Office of the Senate). He joined the Saint Petersburg Masonic Obshchestvo druzei slovensnykh nauk (Society of Friends of the Literary Sciences), which was closely connected to the Friendly Scientific Society. The head of the organization was Mikhail Antonovsky, graduate of Moscow University. The Friends of the Literary Sciences published the journal *Beseduiushchii Grazhdanin* (The Conversing Citizen), to which Bobrov began to contribute regularly.

Bobrov's poetry published in *Beseduiushchii Grazhdanin* developed themes already seen in his early works and were characteristic both of gloomy and mystical Masonic attitudes and of pre-Romantic and early Romantic poetry. These themes included death, the frailty of being, the all-destroying march of time, and eschatological expectation. In two lines of his ode "Sud'ba mira" (Fate of the World) Bobrov brilliantly succeeds in communicating the fragility and doom, not only of our world, but of the entire macrocosm:

Падут миры с осей великих,
шары с своих стряхнутся мест.

(Worlds fall from their mighty axes,
Spheres are shaken from their places.)

The poems published in *Beseduiushchii Grazhdanin* probably brought Bobrov some literary fame. The author of an anonymous manuscript notebook apparently written in 1793 refers to Bobrov as "quite an excellent poet."

However, Bobrov's career was soon to undergo significant changes. The last years of Catherine the Great's reign were marked by her anxiety, due on one hand to the growing strength of the French Revolution and on the other to the legal claim to the Russian throne on the part of her son, Pavel Petrovich, the future emperor Paul I. In 1790 Radishchev published his *Puteshestvie iz Peterburga v Moskvu* (Journey from Saint Petersburg to Moscow). The frightened empress considered the book completely seditious and had the author placed under arrest; he was quickly tried and sentenced to death but then sent into Siberian exile. There is good reason to think that Bobrov had become acquainted with Radishchev, who was an active member of the Society of Friends of the Literary Sciences and participant in *Beseduiushchii Grazhdanin;* there is also evidence that Radishchev liked Bobrov's work a great deal.

According to the authoritative testimony of one member of the society, Sergei Tuchkov, after Radishchev's arrest suspicion of complicity fell upon all participants in the society, and "a large portion of its members were deprived of their positions and ordered to leave Petersburg under various pretexts and circumstances." Bobrov quit the city in 1791 or early 1792. It is possible that he may also have been frightened by the persecution of the Moscow Masons who had had ties with Pavel Petrovich. Investigations and interrogations began in April 1792 and concluded in August with the sentencing of Novikov to fifteen years in the Schusselburg fortress. By this time Bobrov had become a translator in the field office of Adm. Nikolai Mordvinov, the president of the Black Sea Admiralty Governing Board. This liberal and enlightened grandee may have helped Bobrov at this critical time in his life. Preserved in Mordvinov's archive are manuscripts of several poems Bobrov dedicated to him, and Bobrov also dedicated the first edition of *Tavrida* to the admiral. He traveled a great deal on official business, accompanying Mordvinov to Nikolaev, Kherson, Odessa, Kerch, and Taganrog.

ТАВРИДА,

ИЛИ

МОЙ ЛѢТНІЙ ДЕНЬ

ВЪ ТАВРИЧЕСКОМЪ ХЕРСОНИСѢ.

Лирико – Эпическое пѣснотвореніе

Сочиненное

Капитаномъ

Семеномъ Бобровымъ.

НИКОЛАЕВЪ,
въ Черноморской Адмиралтейской Типографіи,
1798 года.

Title page for Bobrov's Tavrida, *the first descriptive poem in Russian literature*

After 1791 the poet's name disappeared from the pages of Russian literary journals. In 1804 a reviewer of Bobrov's recently published four-volume works noted: "unfortunately for lovers of poetry, this poet has been silent for a long time." The existence of later published works, however, reveals that Bobrov continued to write a great deal. Having found himself on the shores of the Black Sea, in regions where traces of ancient civilization still lingered, the highly cultured poet felt a living connection between the past and present when visiting the ruins of Kherson, or while he was sailing in the waters through which the mythical Jason had made his way in search of the Golden Fleece, or while meditating upon Orestes, who had found his long-lost sister Iphigenia on the shores of distant Tauride. Similar classical reminiscences fill Bobrov's poems from this time – for example, "Stansy na ucherezhdenie korabel'nykh i shturmanskikh uchilischch pri admiralteistvakh 1798 goda" (Stanzas on the Establishment of Naval and Navigational Schools Attached to the Admiralties in 1798), "K korabliu 74-pushechnomu, spushchennimu 1794 goda v Khersone" (To the Ship with Seventy-four Cannons, Launched in 1794 in Kherson), and others.

An especially interesting poem written during the time Bobrov spent in the south was his "Ballada. Mogila Ovidiia, slavnogo liubimtsa muz" (Ballad. The Grave of Ovid, Glorious Favorite of the Muses). In this long poem Bobrov contemplates the frailty of everything of this earth, the inexorable march of time, and how both czars and ordinary mortals turn to dust. It is noteworthy that Bobrov compares his fate with that of the great Roman poet Ovid, banished from the capital by Emperor Augustus (much as Pushkin would later, during his exile of 1820–1826, compare himself to the Roman poet), suggesting that Bobrov's departure from Saint Petersburg was mandatory.

In 1798 Russia's first descriptive poem, Bobrov's *Tavrida,* was published in Nikolaev, where the poet was then serving. In the foreword a dedication to Mordvinov, Bobrov persuasively defends the superiority of blank over rhymed verse, basing his arguments on Young's *Conjectures on Original Composition* (1759). While the poem emulates the blank verse of Young's *Night Thoughts on Life, Death, and Immortality* (1742–1746), *Tavrida* was also strongly influenced by Thomson's poem *The Seasons* (1726–1730), although Bobrov expresses nature philosophy and pantheistic ideas more strongly. Bobrov's God permeates all of nature, which appears in the poem as a kind of threatening and spiritualized elemental force. Critics praised the poem: the *Zhurnal rossiiskoi slovesnosti* (Journal of Russian Literature) in 1805 called it "a creation of genius" and ranked it with the works of Mikhail Lomonosov and Derzhavin.

In 1799 Bobrov quit his post, probably in order to return to Saint Petersburg (Catherine the Great had died in 1796). By this time he had already attained the rank of collegiate assessor, the equivalent of a major or lieutenant captain in naval service; he referred to himself as a captain on the title page of *Tavrida.* In 1800 Bobrov became a translator in the admiralty at Saint Petersburg, and after 1806 he also served on the commission to create a new law code.

Service did not interfere with Bobrov's creative activity. At the turn of the century he composed a whole series of poems devoted to reflections on the rapid passage of time, the change of generations, and the fate of nations – these poems include "K novostoletiiu XIX" (To the New Nineteenth Century); "Stoletniaia pesn', ili torzhestvo os'mogonadesiat' veka Rossii" (Century Song, or Celebration of Russia's Eighteenth Century); "Zapros novomu veku" (Questioning the New Age); and "Predchuvstvennyi otzyv veka" (Premonitory Judg-

ment of the Age). Bobrov was not immune to Enlightenment enthusiasm for the successes of science. At the same time, however, he was always conscious of the restricted potential of human reason. Even Sir Isaac Newton, who "almost reached the secret limits of nature," had become lost in God's unknowable world and went insane with horror:

И вдруг, увы!--как человек,
Нашел себя в ужасной бездне
И в ту ж минуту меж великих
Двух бесконечностей безмерных.

(And suddenly, alas!--as a man
He found himself in a horrible abyss
And at that very moment between two
Great unmeasurable infinities.)

Thus, philosophical meditations of the Enlightenment were combined in Bobrov's work with eschatological motifs characteristic of Masonic poetry, with its emphasis on the catastrophic, fragile, transient, and sinful nature of human life. At the same time, the most important quality of Bobrov's poetics was a living, almost physical perception of the movement of time; he "hears" its approaching footsteps. For Bobrov, "Begut vekov kolesa s shumom" (the wheels of the ages turn noisily), and "iunyi vek v zarnitse / Iz bezdny vechnosti letit: / Zvuchit os' pylka v kolesnitse" (the young century at dawn / Flies from out of eternity's abyss: / The avid axis creaks in the chariot).

In one of his best poems, "Noch'" (Night), Bobrov comments on the murder of Czar Paul I. The new century, "creaking on copper door pins," has brought with it an evil night similar to the last night of Julius Caesar, as the sovereign of "half the planet," falls under dagger blows. Bobrov could not speak openly about the czar's murder in print because of censorship, but in a surviving manuscript copy of the poem the murdered man refers to himself as the father of Alexander I – clearly a reference to the regicide. The same subject is found in the poem "Glas vozrozhdennoi Ol'gi k synu Sviatoslavliu" (The Voice of Reborn Olga to Her Son Sviatoslav), where a transparent allegory unfolds: as the soul of the dead Sviatoslav (Paul I), who has perished as a result of a conspiracy, leaves for the spirit world, his mother, Olga (Catherine), appeals to her grandson (Alexander I). Amid the intense, ominous images of these poems, sympathy shines through for an emperor who had been a protector of the Masons and who had fallen victim to a cruel conspiracy.

In 1804 Bobrov's collected works, titled *Rassvet polnochi, ili sozertsanie slavy, torzhestva i mudrosti porfironosnykh, branonosnykh i mirnykh geniev Rossii s posledovaniem didakticheskikh, eroticheskikh i drugikh raznogo roda v stikhakh i proze opytov* (The Dawn of Midnight, or the Contemplation of Glory, Triumph, and Wisdom of Russia's Porphyry-Bearing, Martial, and Peaceful Geniuses, Followed by Experiments in Verse and Prose, Didactic, Erotic, and of Various Other Sorts), were published in four volumes. Its appearance consolidated Bobrov's literary reputation, and in 1807 he became a member of the Vol'noe obshchestvo liubitelei slovesnosti, nauk i khudozhestv (Free Society of Lovers of Literature, Science, and Art). Although he almost never attended its meetings, Bobrov regularly published in journals connected to the society: *Severnyi vestnik* (The Northern Herald), *Litsei* (Lycée), and *Taliia* (Thalia). With his "cosmism," philosophical searching, linguistic complexity, and deliberate "inarticulateness," Bobrov's position was close to that of the most influential poet members of the society, Ivan Pnin and Aleksandr Vostokov.

In his outlook and his approach to literature Bobrov was able to accept neither the Enlightenment position of Karamzin and his followers nor their advocacy of a light, transparent style oriented on the conversational speech of the salon. Bobrov's poems are awkward, ponderous, and full of archaic phrases that are deliberately difficult to pronounce. In November 1805 Bobrov entered the struggle against the Karamzinists with his polemical work "Proisshestvie v tsarstve tenei, ili sud'bina rossiiskogo iazyka" (An Incident in the Kingdom of Shadows, or the Fate of the Russian Language), in which he supported the position of the "archaist" Aleksandr Shishkov and spoke out against Karamzin's "new style" and its partisans.

This work, though unpublished until its rediscovery in 1975, did not remain a secret from Bobrov's literary opponents. In the first decade of the nineteenth century the poet's clumsy verses made him a favorite target of the Karamzinists. He was nicknamed "Bibrus" (from the Latin *bibere*, to drink), presumably in reference to his predilection for strong spirits. In many epigrams, satiric poems, and mocking rejoinders Bobrov was bluntly called a drunkard, as in the anecdote, "I dropped by the poet Bibrus's, but only found vodka on the table and no bread in the house." Batiushkov even suggested that Bobrov's labored poems were engendered by his constant inebriation: "Kak trudno Bibrisu so slavoiu uzhit'sia! / On p'et, chtoby pisat' i pishet, chtob napit'sia!" (How hard it is for Bibrus

РАЗСВѢТЪ ПОЛНОЧИ

или

СОЗЕРЦАНІЕ

СЛАВЫ, ТОРЖЕСТВА И МУДРОСТИ ПОРФИРОНОСНЫХЪ, БРАНОНОСНЫХЪ И МИРНЫХЪ

ГЕНІЕВЪ РОССІИ

съ послѣдованіемъ

Дидактическихъ, Эротическихъ и другихъ разнаго рода въ стихахъ и прозѣ

опытовъ

Семена Боброва.

ВЪ САНКТ-ПЕТЕРБУРГѢ,
Въ Типографіи Ив. Глазунова 1804 года.

Title page for Bobrov's 1804 collected works

to get used to fame! / He drinks in order to write, and writes in order to drink!). His critics mocked the incomprehensibility and obscurity of Bobrov's poetic language, as in Viazemsky's verses: "Net spora, chto Bibris bogov iazykom pel: / Iz smertnykh bo nikto ego ne razumel" (There's no question Bibrus sang in the language of the gods: / Hence no one on earth could understand him).

The things the Karamzin circle mocked were considered virtues by the archaists, who advocated a high, solemn style. Radishchev mentioned Bobrov's name with praise in the 1790s, and Shishkov, the head of the literary association Beseda liubitelei rossiiskogo slova (Colloquy of Lovers of the Russian Word), followed his work with a great deal of attention. While serving in the Admiralty College, Bobrov was under the direct supervision of Shishkov and on his instructions worked on a history of the Russian navy. Derzhavin, the most influential poet of the era, referred to Bobrov's work with respect and praise. Ivan Levitsky, in his *Kurs rossiiskoi slovesnosti* (Course in Russian Literature, 1812), proposes the division of all Russian lyric poetry into three types, defined by the works of Lomonosov, Derzhavin, and Bobrov.

The last decade of Bobrov's life was dedicated to the creation of his monumental poem "Drevniaia noch' Vselennoi, ili stranstvuiushchii slepets" (Ancient Night of the Universe, or the Wandering Blind Man). The work is a philosophical allegory, telling the story of a soul's travels in search of God. The foundations of various philosophical systems are set forth during the course of this search, until the restless soul finds truth in Christianity; the allegory refers to mankind but is also a history of the strivings and delusions of the author. The poem includes descriptions of cosmic horrors and catastrophes that are characteristic of Bobrov's eschatological consciousness. The work demonstrates Bobrov's continuing belief that complicated and unexpected ideas demand complicated syntactical constructions, unexpected word usage, and combinations of high-style archaisms with everyday speech. These qualities, however, made the poem rather inaccessible to readers, and it did not sell well. The author, who underwrote the publication, took a large loss. This grandiose production of over six hundred pages, unique in Russian poetry, has never been analyzed by literary scholars and still awaits detailed study.

To this period belongs an important episode in Bobrov's literary activity. During the 1790s the Moscow publisher Semen Selivanovsky had established a publishing house and press in Nikolaev at the suggestion of Admiral Mordvinov. There he became acquainted with and befriended Bobrov; *Tavrida* was printed at his press. In September 1806 Selivanovsky proposed that Bobrov prepare a translation of poems attributed to the legendary Gaelic warrior Ossian (later exposed as forgeries written by James Macpherson). A complete and solid translation by Ermil Kostrov had come out in 1792, but the experienced publisher and bookseller apparently took into account the recent success of Vladislav Ozerov's tragedy *Fingal* (staged on 8 December 1805), based on motifs from Ossian, and he decided a new edition of the poems would prove popular. No one could have been better suited for this job than Bobrov. First of all, he knew English superbly, whereas Kostrov had based his translation on Le Tourneur's French version. More important, the spirit of Bobrov's writing was compatible with Ossian's intense imagery full of cruelty, tragedy, and gloom. The new edition might have become a remarkable event in the history of early Russian romanticism, but unfortunately, apparently

because of Bobrov's illness and death, or because of his difficult family circumstances, the proposed work was never realized.

Bobrov's health deteriorated. For a long time he suffered from tuberculosis, probably along with the effects of alcoholism, both common ailments among *raznochintsy* (nonaristocratic) Russian intellectuals. In a short note written between 1803 and 1807, perhaps to N. I. Gnedich, he wrote: "From the start of new year it is apparent that there will be grief; I congratulate you, but myself am sick with coughing. Sem. Bobrov." Even though Bobrov was promoted to the rank of court counselor on 31 December 1806, poverty overcame him. After agreeing to do the Ossian translation, Bobrov asked Selivanovsky to purchase the English original for twenty rubles, since, he said, "extreme need" hampered him in "the purchase of this item." Bobrov's last book, *Drevnii rossiiskii plavatel'* (The Ancient Russian Sailor, 1812), was published posthumously "out of consideration for the poverty of the family which was . . . left behind." It is likely that alcoholism intensified and aggravated Bobrov's sickness. He died of tuberculosis on 22 March 1810.

References:

Mark G. Altshuller, "Poeticheskaia traditsiia Radishcheva v literaturnoi zhizni nachala XIX veka. Radishchev i Bobrov," *XVIII vek,* 12 (1977): 114–124;

Altshuller, "S. S. Bobrov i russkaia poezia kontsa XVIII–nachala XIX v.," *XVIII vek,* 6 (1964): 224–246;

Altshuller, "Semen Bobrov and Edward Young," *Russian Literature Triquarterly,* 21 (1988): 129–140;

S. Brailovsky, "Semen Sergeevich Bobrov. Istoriko-literaturnyi ocherk," *Izvestiia Istoriko-filologicheskogo instituta kn. Bezborodko v Nezhine,* 15 (1895): 1–39;

Iurii D. Levin, "Angliiskaia poeziia i literatura russkogo sentimentalizma," in *Ot klassitsizma k romantizmu: Iz istorii mezhdunarodnykh sviazei russkoi literatury* (Leningrad: Nauka, 1970), pp. 262–267;

Levin, *Vospriiatie Angliiskoi literatury v Rossii* (Leningrad: Nauka, 1990);

Iurii M. Lotman and Boris A. Uspensky, "Spory o iazyke v nachale XIX v. kak fakt russkoi kul'tury," *Uchenye zapiski Tartuskogo gos. universiteta, 358, Trudy po russkoi i slavianskoi filologii,* 24 (1975): 168–254;

Ivan N. Rozanov, *Russkaia lirika,* volume 1 (Moscow, 1914), pp. 376–393.

Ippolit Fedorovich Bogdanovich

(circa 23 December 1743 – 6 January 1803)

Thomas Barran
Brooklyn College, City University of New York

BOOKS: *Oda . . . imp. Petru Feodorovichu . . . na vseradostneishee vosshestvie na prestol* (Moscow: Moskovskii universitet, [1762]);

Oda na den' tezoimenitstva . . . imp. Petra Feodorovicha . . . i e. i. v. blagovernago gosudaria tsesarevicha i velikogo kniazia Pavla Petrovicha (Moscow: Moskovskii universitet, 1762);

Oda . . . imp. Ekaterine Alekseevne . . . izbavitel'nitse i materi otechestva na vseradostneishee eia prishestvie v prestol'nyi grad Moskvu (Moscow: Moskovskii universitet, [1762]);

Oda vsemilostiveishei gosudaryne Ekaterine Alekseevne . . . na novoi 1763 god . . . (Moscow: Moskovskii universitet, [1763]);

Suguboe blazhenstvo (Saint Petersburg: [Sukhoputnyi kadetskii korpus], 1765);

Lira, ili Sobranie raznykh v stikhakh sochinenii i perevodov, nekotorago muz liubitelia (Saint Petersburg: Akademiia nauk, 1773);

Gimn na brakosochetanie ikh imp. vysochestv gosudaria tsesarevicha i velikago kniazia Pavla Petrovicha i blagovernoi gosudaryni velikoi kniagini Marii Feodorovny, proizshedshee v 26 den' sentiabria 1776 goda, prinosimyi v znak userdneishago blagogoveniia (Saint Petersburg: Akademiia nauk, 1776);

Stans: Na torzhestvo piatidesiatiletniago iubileia Sankpeterburgskoi imp. Akademii nauk ([Saint Petersburg: Akademiia nauk, 1776]);

Istoricheskoe izobrazhenie Rossii, volume 1 (Saint Petersburg: Akademiia nauk, 1777);

Dushin'kiny pokhozhdeniia, skaska v stikhakh, [book 1] (Moscow: Universitetskaia tipografiia, 1778);

Dushin'ka: Drevniaia povest' v vol'nykh stikhakh, edited by A. A. Rzhevsky (Saint Petersburg: Veitbrekht, 1783); revised as *Dushen'ka. Drevniaia povest' v vol'nykh stikhakh* (Saint Petersburg: Korpus chuzhestrannykh edinovertsov, 1794; revised again, Moscow: Rudiger & Klaudi, 1799); translated by Harold B. Segel, in *The Literature of Eighteenth-Century Russia,* volume 2, edited by Segel (New York: Dutton, 1967), pp. 180–238;

Ippolit Fedorovich Bogdanovich

Radost' Dushin'ki, liricheskaia komediia, posleduemaia baletom, v odnom deistvii (Saint Petersburg: Akademiia nauk, 1786);

Slaviane, drama v trekh deistviiakh, s khorom i baletom v kontse predstavleniia (Saint Petersburg: Akademiia nauk, 1788);

Pesn': Eia imp. velichestvu, velikoi gosudaryne Ekaterine Alekseevne . . . Na mir s Shvetsieiu (Saint Petersburg: Gornoe uchilishche, [1790]);

Dobromysl: Starinnaia povest' v stikhakh (Moscow, 1805);

Bereg: Otryvok, naidennyi v bumagakh pokoinogo Sochinitelia D . . . ki (Saint Petersburg, 1812).

Editions: *Sobranie sochinenii i perevodov,* edited by Platon Beketov (6 volumes, Moscow, 1809–1810; 4 volumes, Moscow, 1818–1819);

Sochineniia, 2 volumes (Saint Petersburg: A. Smirdin, 1848);

Stikhotvoreniia i poemy, edited by I. Z. Serman, Biblioteka poeta, bol'shaia seriia (Leningrad: Sovetskii pisatel', 1957).

OTHER: Voltaire (Vol'ter), "Na razrushenie Lissabona," translated by Bogdanovich, *Nevinnoe uprazhnenie,* 4 (April 1763): 173–183;

Voltaire, *Naina, ili Pobezhdennoe predrassuzhdenie* (Saint Petersburg: Sukhoputnyi kadetskii korpus, 1766; revised edition, Moscow: Kompaniia tipograficheskaia, 1788);

Anonymous, *Malaia voina, opisannia maiorom v sluzhbe korolia Prusskogo,* translated by Bogdanovich (Saint Petersburg: Sukhoputnyi kadetskii korpus, 1766);

Charles Castel Saint-Pierre (Sen-P'er), *Sokrashchenie, sdelannoe Zhan Zhakom Ruso, Zhenevskim grazhdaninom, iz proekta o vechnom mire,* translated by Bogdanovich (Saint Petersburg: Akademiia nauk, 1771);

René Aubert Vertot d'Aubeuf (Verto d'Obef), *Istoriia o byvshikh peremenakh v Rimskoi respublike,* 3 volumes, translated by Bogdanovich (Saint Petersburg: Akademiia nauk, 1771–1775);

Ruskiia poslovitsy, sobrannyia Ippolitom Bogdanovichem, 3 volumes, edited by Bogdanovich (Saint Petersburg: Akademiia nauk, 1785).

Ippolit Fedorovich Bogdanovich – poet, translator, playwright, and journalist during the reign of Catherine the Great – earned an enduring place in Russian literary history with his long verse tale *Dushin'ka* (1783; revised as *Dushen'ka,* 1794). The light tone and playful eroticism of *Dushen'ka* entranced generations of Russian readers and started a vogue for light poetry that continued well past Aleksandr Pushkin's time. This poem brought Bogdanovich such fame that his admirers created a posthumous image of him as a carefree, mercurial bohemian, thus inventing a poet who corresponds to the poem. While this personality had its attractions, it obscured the details of an active service career and intellectual life during Catherine's reign.

Bogdanovich, the son of an impoverished nobleman, was born around 23 December 1743 in a little village in Ukraine called Perevolochna. Parents in the Russian nobility often started their children on their service careers at an early age, and at the age of ten Bogdanovich was sent to Moscow to take his first steps in a career as a civil servant, enrolling as a junker in the Justice College. Although the requirements for mandatory military or civil

service had moderated considerably since Peter I had instituted them at the beginning of the eighteenth century and would be done away with completely by Peter III in February 1762, at midcentury most male children of the nobility faced a service obligation of twenty-five years. Early enrollment carried the combined advantages of providing education and getting the required years of service out of the way at a younger age. The Justice College functioned as one of the government *kollegiia* that would be reformed into ministries in the nineteenth century.

Bogdanovich left some autobiographical notes in which he describes his early education. He relates that he had little interest in his proposed service career but that in school he excelled in mathematics, music, and poetry. At the age of fourteen, he composed several concertos of religious music that were well received, and at fifteen he was producing poetry that gained him the favor of Prince Mikhail Dashkov, as well as of the influential writer and educator Mikhail Kheraskov. Through Dashkov, Bogdanovich received a release from his duties at the Justice College in order to attend Moscow University, which had recently begun its operations. He lived in Kheraskov's house while attending the university. On 29 October 1761 Bogdanovich received the position of overseer of classes at Moscow University, gained the rank of ensign, and joined the Navaginskoi regiment. During his university years he wrote poetry on philosophical themes, which he published in the university periodicals, primarily *Poleznoe uveselenie* (Useful Amusement).

Nikolai Karamzin, in his article "O Bogdanoviche i ego sochineniiakh" (On Bogdanovich and His Works), first published in *Vestnik Evropy* (European Herald) in 1803, portrays a personality that corresponds to the tone of Bogdanovich's light poetry. He provides a fanciful version of Bogdanovich's meeting with Kheraskov, claiming that at the age of fifteen, the bashful young man approached the director of the Moscow Theater and told him that he wanted to be an actor. Kheraskov explained that an actor's career would be unseemly for a nobleman; then he enrolled Bogdanovich in the university and let the young writer reside in his house. Karamzin insists that he heard this anecdote from Kheraskov himself, but it presents an oversimplified, if not entirely apocryphal, version of a talented provincial youth's search for protection and patronage.

Bogdanovich had the good fortune of having chosen patrons who sided with Catherine when she deposed her husband and ascended the Russian throne in the summer of 1762. After the coup Field

Marshal Prince Nikita Trubetskoi named him to a commission organized to design ornamental gates for Catherine's triumphal procession through Moscow. The following year, through the agency of Princess Ekaterina Romanovna Dashkova, Bogdanovich gained an appointment to the College of War, then to the staff of Gen. Petr Panin. Dashkova, Catherine's closest female friend and wife of Bogdanovich's protector, stayed at her side during the coup and remained one of the most influential court personalities during the first years of Catherine's reign. When the court came to Moscow for Catherine's official coronation ceremonies and triumphal festivities, Dashkova enlisted local talent to participate in a short-lived periodical entitled *Nevinnoe upriazhnenie* (Innocent Exercises).

Dashkova invited Bogdanovich to contribute a translation of Voltaire's *Poème sur le désastre de Lisbonne* (1756), which had recently gained some notoriety in Moscow literary circles. A year earlier Johann Reichel, a professor at Moscow University and later a leading figure in Russian Freemasonry, had published four issues of a periodical entitled *Sobranie luchshikh sochinenii k rasprostraneniiu znaniia i k proizvedeniiu udovol'stviia* (Collection of the Best Writings for the Dissemination of Knowledge and Production of Enjoyment). In one of the issues Reichel published his Russian translations of Jean-Jacques Rousseau's *Lettre à Voltaire sur la Providence* (Letter to Voltaire on Providence, 1756), accompanied by a lengthy preface in which the translator took Voltaire to task for voicing his pessimism and his loss of faith in Divine Providence. Rousseau's open letter responding to Voltaire's poem contained an eloquent defense of Divine Providence, thus attracting many Russian admirers who had been put off by Rousseau's other works.

Catherine and Dashkova, however, had adopted Voltaire as the presiding genius of the new reign. Catherine began a correspondence with him as soon as she ascended the throne, while Dashkova had occasion to visit him during her travels in France. During the 1760s Catherine's court embraced rationalism and skepticism and called for the merciless examination of all received wisdom. Voltaire's attacks, which spared no sacred cows, corresponded to the prevailing intellectual spirit of the new regime. By translating a key statement of Voltaire's philosophy in one of the first official publications of Catherine's reign, Bogdanovich became in effect one of the poetic voices of the new order.

Once the court went back to Saint Petersburg, the periodical closed, and Bogdanovich had to seek other employment in the new regime. Through the considerable influence of Dashkova, in May 1763 he received an appointment to Gen. P. I. Panin's staff as a translator. He remained in Moscow for slightly less than a year in this capacity, during which time he finished translating an anonymous French book on guerrilla warfare. When Panin traveled to Saint Petersburg to join the staff of his younger brother, Nikita, Bogdanovich went with him to work as a translator in the Foreign College.

Nikita Panin had enormous influence during the first years of Catherine II's reign, chiefly in the formulation of her foreign policy. Among his many responsibilities, Panin held the position of tutor to Catherine's son, Grand Duke Pavel Petrovich, the presumptive heir to the imperial throne. Bogdanovich's acquaintance with Panin gave him some access to the grand duke, and in 1765 he composed a philosophical poem, *Suguboe blazhenstvo* (A Special Felicity), which he dedicated to the grand duke. This poem may represent an idealistic attempt at contributing to the education of the prince, or it may have been a strategy for attracting the attention of a powerful potential patron. Bogdanovich drew on the philosophical poems of Alexander Pope and Voltaire for inspiration, but he used as his immediate model a poem of Kheraskov's written in 1761 entitled "Plody nauk" (The Fruits of Learning), which was also dedicated to Pavel Petrovich. Bogdanovich, in fact, conducts a poetic dialogue with his early patron, disputing with him on several points.

Both "Plody nauk" and "Suguboe blazhenstvo" give poetic expression to the concept of natural law. For over a century thinkers in Western Europe had been developing theories about the contractual basis of civil society, according to which humanity left the state of nature and voluntarily organized political structures based on reciprocal or mutual obligations. While no consensus emerged in their writings as to whether the state of nature was benevolent or harsh, or whether the primal pact was absolutist or democratic in character, the philosophers who wrote on natural law did much to dismantle the theological justifications for government and to provide a theoretical basis for insisting that a ruler's legitimacy must depend on his or her fulfillment of obligations according to a social contract.

Kheraskov and Bogdanovich both depict the origins of civil society in their poems and present progress in the arts and sciences as more than adequate compensation for the surrender of natural freedoms. Both poems constitute defenses of learning, yet each accounts for its value to civilization in a different way. Kheraskov envisions life in the state of nature as did Thomas Hobbes in his memorable formulation: "solitary, poor, nasty, brutish and short." He glorifies the cultural heroes and legislators who pulled humanity out of this condition. Bogdanovich seems to regard natural life as John Locke and Rousseau described it: as a condition of mindless, static felicity where each individual enjoys total autonomy. Perfectibility alone pulls Bogdanovich's human out of the natural state, with progress in the arts and sciences contributing additional benefits. Thus Bogdanovich's debate with his patron concerned their differing views on the origins of civil society. Both, however, emphatically defended the benefits of progress in the arts and sciences and stressed the necessity of the monarch's protection of these pursuits.

In 1766 Bogdanovich received an appointment as secretary to Prince Belosel'sky, the Russian ambassador to the Saxon court in Dresden, where he spent two and a half years. His exposure to the artistic riches of that city emerged later in the lovingly detailed visual descriptions in his poem *Dushen'ka*. Returning to Saint Petersburg in 1768, he continued to serve Nikita Panin in the Foreign College during the years of Panin's greatest influence.

In the early 1770s Bogdanovich completed and had published two translations of French works as part of his work for the Foreign Office. The first of these was Rousseau's summary of the political writings of Charles Castel Saint-Pierre, another René Aubert Vertot d'Aubeuf's history of the Roman Republic. A collection of Bogdanovich's early poetry, entitled *Lira,* was published in 1773; it included several poems published in the previous twelve years, with most of them reworked and shortened, as well as Bogdanovich's translation of the concluding section of Voltaire's poem on the Lisbon earthquake, as well as an abridgment of "Suguboe blazhenstvo," which he entitled "Blazhenstvo narodov." Apart from this compilation, Bogdanovich's work for the Foreign College constituted his sole occupation until 1775, when he branched out into journalism and resumed his own literary work. His *Istoricheskoe izobrazhenie Rossii* (Historical Depiction of Russia) was published in 1777. In this work Bogdanovich followed the methods of Vertot and produced less a detailed and researched chronicle of Russian history than an inspiring narrative glorifying the virtues and deeds of past heroes and intended to effect moral and patriotic edification. Shortly thereafter he began work on *Dushen'ka,* the poem which would earn him lasting fame.

ДУШИНЬКА.

ДРЕВНЯЯ ПОВѢСТЬ

ВЪ ВОЛЬНЫХЪ СТИХАХЪ

ВЪ САНКТПЕТЕРБУРГѢ,
печатана въ вольной типографіи у Вейтбрехта,
1783 года.

Title page for the first complete edition of Bogdanovich's Dushen'ka, *the work for which he is primarily remembered*

Dushen'ka, a Russian diminutive for *dusha* (soul), serves as a Russianization of the name Psyche. Bogdanovich based his long poem on the mythical tale of Psyche and Cupid that first appeared in Ovid's *Metamorphoses* (circa A.D. 8) and was also used by Lucius Apulieus in his second-century prose work of the same title, popularly known as *The Golden Ass.* A Russian translation of the latter work appeared in 1778, the year that Bogdanovich published the first book of *Dushen'ka.* The French fabulist Jean de La Fontaine also treated the story in a *conte,* which he titled *Les amours de Psyché et de Cupidon* (The Loves of Psyche and Cupid, 1669). La Fontaine's tale enjoyed considerable popularity in Russia, as evidenced by two Russian translations of the work, one by F. Dmitriev-Mamonov, which appeared in 1769, the other by E. I. Kostrov, which appeared in 1780.

According to Bogdanovich's version of the tale of Cupid and Psyche, Venus becomes enraged when mortals begin devoting their attention to Psyche's beauty while neglecting to worship that of the goddess of love. She orders her son, Cupid, to punish Psyche by making her ugly and marrying her to an undesirable spouse. Cupid, however, falls in love with Psyche and takes her to his dwelling as his wife, though she is never permitted to look at him. Succumbing to the evil counsel of her envious sisters, Psyche takes a lantern and a dagger to look at Cupid and to kill him if he is indeed the monster her sisters have described. When she beholds Cupid asleep, some of the wax from her lamp spills on his thigh and burns him. He awakens and banishes her from his palace. In order to expiate her sin and appease the wrath of Venus, Psyche performs several dangerous labors, the last of which involves carrying a pot of soot from Hades. When she peeks into the pot, some of the soot escapes and blackens her face. Convinced that she is ugly and outcast, she hides in a cave, where Cupid finds her and forgives her. Venus's wrath is appeased. Psyche's beauty returns. The couple enjoys married life.

Bogdanovich presents the poetic equivalent of a rococo painting with elements of Russian folklore, such as a hat that makes its wearer invisible, skillfully and unobtrusively added. Bogdanovich's poem was not a translation but a free improvisation upon an established plot. Where Apuleius and La Fontaine tell their stories in prose, Bogdanovich renders his in rhymed iambic lines of varying length, the meter that Aleksandr Sumarokov used in his fables. Ivan Khemnitzer also used this meter in the fables he was writing at the same time, as did the most famous Russian fabulist, Ivan Krylov. In Bogdanovich's day this verse form already had associations with Russian oral folklore and provides only one of many folkloric touches Bogdanovich uses in his tale. Although the action of *Dushen'ka* takes place in the realm of classical myth, Bogdanovich includes details from Russian folklore and peasant life, as if to suggest that Russian folk mythology springs from the same sources as the Greek tales and myths and that therefore the two can comfortably appear in the same poem.

Bogdanovich's poem marks a complete break with the serious poetry of its time. It presents neither philosophical instruction nor coded or idealized references to current events or personalities. *Dushen'ka* also breaks with contemporary categories of satire, comedy, and travesty. Bogdanovich constructed his poem on the clever interweaving of thematic oppositions: superficial versus inner beauty, appearances versus essences, and mutability versus permanence. The poet utilizes this thematic material according to an internal, aesthetic logic with little reference to topical, moral, or historical themes outside the text. It is true that the poem has a moral, the lesson presumably learned by the heroine as a result of her ordeals, which is announced by Zeus at the end:

Закон времен творит прекрасный вид худым,
Наружный блеск в очах преходит так, как дым,
Но красоту души ничто не изменяет,
Он единая всегда и всех пленяет.

(The law of time robs good looks of their glory,
Like smoke, external gloss is transitory,
But beauty that is in the soul will never pall,
It and only it at all times conquers all.)

This moral does not provide the justification for the poem's existence, however; on the contrary, it is belied by the poem's love of seductive surfaces, abundant descriptions of lush locales, and detailed attention to the heroine's physical charms.

Dushen'ka had a tremendous impact both on Bogdanovich's reputation and on the subsequent development of Russian poetry. The poem became so well known that it had the retroactive effect of creating a biographical myth about Bogdanovich, forming a personality for the poet that corresponds to the nature of the poem, but this persona does not agree with the biographical facts. Bogdanovich adopted an authorial pose in the preface to *Dushen'ka* that may have provided the impetus for the rewriting of his biography. He claims to have composed the work in his spare time for his own entertainment, and that the positive reactions of those who read it persuaded him to have it published.

This stylized modesty alone, however, could not have imparted to Bogdanovich the reputation of bohemian nonchalance that later generations accepted. Its main source was Karamzin's essay "On Bogdanovich and His Works," which gives a memorable portrait of the poet at work on his masterpiece. Karamzin insists that the character of the writer can always be found in his works and provides a description of Bogdanovich's poetic temperament that corresponds to the lighthearted tone of *Dushen'ka*: "He lived at the time on Vasil'evsky Island, in a quiet isolated little home, devoting his time to music and verse in happy insouciance and freedom; he had a pleasant circle of acquaintances; he loved to go out on occasion, but he loved even more to return to where the muse awaited him with new ideas and colors." However charming Karamzin's account of Bogdanovich may be, it does not correspond at all to what is known of Bogdanovich's career in the civil service or as an editor and publisher.

Bogdanovich published the first part of *Dushen'ka* in 1778 and published the entire work in

1783. He continued to work in the Foreign College under Nikita Panin until 1780, when he moved to the newly established Saint Petersburg Archive. Bogdanovich's posts were not sinecures. Not only did he continue his service career, but he also worked in journalism. In 1775 and 1776 Bogdanovich edited the Saint Petersburg *Sobranie novostei* (Collected News), and he edited the *Sankt-Peterburgskie vedomosti* (Saint Petersburg News) from 1776 to 1782, that is, during the entire time he composed *Dushen'ka*. At the time *Sankt-Peterburgskie vedomosti* functioned as the official periodical of the Saint Petersburg Academy of Sciences, and Bogdanovich lost his position with the paper when a group within the academy called the "akademicheskaia konferentsiia" (academic conference) complained about Bogdanovich's choice of articles. Bogdanovich resented this incident bitterly and referred to it in his autobiographical notes as a slander against him. Juggling a career in the state service with the editorship of major periodicals, wrangling with hostile opponents, and writing poetry in whatever time he had left over — such a picture hardly accords with Karamzin's idyllic portrayal of Bogdanovich as a carefree Bohemian enjoying a semirural retreat on Saint Petersburg's Vasilevsky Island.

Critics of the Soviet period made some progress in looking behind the poetic persona that grew up around Bogdanovich. They found it problematic, however, that a poet who maintained some political involvements and seemed to participate in the aims of the Enlightenment would suddenly turn to "art for art's sake" in a poem like *Dushen'ka*, which has no political or social message. They explained *Dushen'ka* as an attempt to escape what they considered to be the grim political reversals of Catherine's reign in the late 1770s: the breakup of Nikita Panin's system of Northern Alliances and his loss of influence, the ascendancy of Grigory Potemkin, Catherine's expansionist adventures against the Ottoman Empire, and her increasing repression of Russians. Bogdanovich, in the view of these critics, retreated into the world of pure art and abandoned his former activities as a politically engaged writer. This approach does not stand up to close scrutiny, however; Bogdanovich continued his combination of literary activity and state service, looking for patronage and protection from whomever happened to be in power.

The biographical legend that grew up around Bogdanovich had considerable appeal for Aleksandr Pushkin. The lighthearted, spontaneous, companionable, easily distracted nature of the poet, as Karamzin described him, contributed to Pushkin's own creative persona. Bogdanovich bequeathed another legacy to Pushkin. Before *Dushen'ka,* feminine characters in literature had appeared either as idealizations (in the higher genres) or as vulgar creatures of instinct (in comedies and travesties). In spite of Pushkin's identifying Bogdanovich's verse as one of the sins of his youth in chapter 3 of Pushkin's *Evgenii Onegin* (1833), its heroine Tat'iana could not have appeared in Russian literature without the precedent of *Dushen'ka*. Like Tat'iana, Dushen'ka captivates the narrator of her poem who describes both her attractions and flaws lovingly. In *Evgenii Onegin* Pushkin addresses Tat'iana as his muse, much as Bogdanovich invokes Dushen'ka at the beginning of his poem. Bogdanovich's example cleared the ground for Pushkin's portrayal of a feminine subject who experiences erotic passions, makes mistakes, acts on her own judgment (even if it means risking disgrace), and finally emerges from her experiences into mature womanhood.

Bogdanovich continued to produce literary works after the success of *Dushen'ka;* none, unfortunately, came up to the quality of his masterpiece. *Dushen'ka* delighted Catherine II, and through her intercession the Academy of Sciences, whose new director was Bogdanovich's literary associate Princess Dashkova, purchased the entire printing of both *Dushen'ka* and Bogdanovich's *Istoricheskoe izobrazhenie Rossii* (1777). For three years following the appearance of *Dushen'ka* Catherine encouraged further productions from Bogdanovich. He in turn praised her lavishly in poetry he published in the journal *Sobesednik liubitelei rossiiskogo slova* (Interlocutor of Friends of the Russian Word). In 1785 his edition of Russian proverbs, *Ruskiia poslovitsy, sobrannyia Ippolitom Bogdanovichem* (Russian Proverbs Collected by Ippolit Bogdanovich), was published. In 1786 he adapted *Dushin'ka* for the stage as *Radost' – Dushin'ki* (Dushen'ka's Joy), a work commissioned by Catherine and in return for which she awarded Bogdanovich a valuable snuffbox and paid off his outstanding debts. The monarch presented him with another snuffbox at the work's premiere at the court theater. In 1787 Bogdanovich produced a drama entitled *Slaviane* (The Slavs), for which the empress rewarded him with a ring.

By 1788 the senate conferred on Bogdanovich the chairmanship of the State Archive, where he worked until his retirement. His literary activity dwindled during his final years of service, although he did participate in the compilation of the Russian Academy's dictionary. His final years were marred by frustration and poverty. He retired from state service in 1795, apparently having accumulated no money or property, and went to live on his brother's estate in Sumi. While there he fell in love with and proposed marriage to one of his distant relations. As the girl was quite young, his relatives objected, and Bogdanovich left his brother's home. He moved to Kursk, where he barely subsisted on his small pension and had to sell his library to make ends meet. At the accession of Alexander I, Bogdanovich sent the new czar an ode composed in his honor. He apparently was trying to resume work with the Russian Academy when he fell ill in 1802. He died early the following year.

Biography:

Dmitrii D. Iazykov, *I. F. Bogdanovich: Biograficheskii ocherk* (Moscow, 1903).

References:

Richard L. Chapple, "A Note on Sources of the Erotic in Ippolit Bogdanovich's *Dushen'ka*," *Festschrift für Nikola R. Pribic,* edited by Josip Matesic and Erwin Wedel (Neuried: Hieronymus, 1983), pp. 87–93;

Grigorii Gennadi, "Ippolit Fedorovich Bogdanovich," *Russkaia poeziia: Sobranie proizvedenii russkikh poetov chast'iu v polnom sostave, chast'iu v izvlecheniiakh, s vazhneishimi kritiko-biograficheskimi stat'iami, biograficheskimi primechaniiami i portretami,* volume 1, edited by S. A. Vengerov (Saint Petersburg: A. E. Vineke, 1897), pp. 552–554;

Andrew T. Griffin, "Linguistic Elements of Humor: The Poetry of Grammar and the Grammar of Poetry in Ippolit Bogdanovich's *Dushen'ka*," *Proceedings of the Kentucky Foreign Language Conference: Slavic Section,* 3 (1985): 66–74;

Nikolai Karamzin, "O Bogdanovich i ego sochineniiakh," *Izbrannye sochineniia,* volume 2, edited by Georgii P. Makogonenko (Leningrad, 1964), pp. 198–226;

Liubov I. Kulakova, "Bogdanovich," *Istoriia russkoi literatury,* volume 4, part 2, edited by G. A. Gukovsky and V. A. Desnitsky (Moscow & Leningrad: Akademiia nauk, 1947), pp. 342–352;

Aleksandr Nezelenov, "Bogdanovich i ego *Dushen'ka*," in *Russkaia poeziia: Sobranie proizvedenii russkikh poetov chast'iu v polnom sostave, chast'iu v izvlecheniiakh, s vazhneishimi kritiko-biograficheskimi stat'iami, biograficheskimi primechaniiami i portretami,* volume 1, edited by Vengerov (Saint Petersburg: A. E. Vineke, 1897), pp. 554–556;

Il'ia Z. Serman, "I. F. Bogdanovich – zhurnalist i kritik," *XVIII vek,* 4 (1959): 85–103;

A. L. Slonimsky, *"Dushen'ka" Bogdanovicha: Istoriko-literaturnyi ocherk* (Saint Petersburg, 1903);

Mikhail I. Sukhomlinov, "I. F. Bogdanovich," *Istoriia Rossiiskoi Akademii,* volume 7 (Saint Petersburg: Akademia nauk, 1885), pp. 43–54.

Andrei Timofeevich Bolotov

(7 October 1738 – 3 October 1833)

Thomas Newlin
Oberlin College

BOOKS: *Detskaia filosofiia, ili Nravouchitel'nyia razgovory mezhdu odnoiu gospozheiu i eia det'mi, sochinennye dlia pospeshestvovaniia istinnoi pol'ze molodykh liudei,* 2 volumes (volume 1, Moscow: Universitetskaia tipografiia, 1776; volume 2, Moscow: N. Novikov, 1779);

Chuvstvovaniia khristianina, pri nachale i kontse kazhdago dnia v nedele, otnosiashchiiasia k samomu sebe i k Bogu. Sochinenie odnogo rossianina (Moscow: N. Novikov, 1781);

Neshchastnyia siroty, dramma v trekh deistviiakh. Sochinena v Bogoroditske, 1780 gode (Moscow: N. Novikov, 1781);

Putivoditel' k istinnomu chelovecheskomu schastiiu, ili Opyt nravouchitel'nykh i otchasti filosoficheskikh razsuzhdenii o blagopoluchii chelovecheskoi zhizni i o sredstvakh k priobretenii onago, 3 volumes (Moscow: N. Novikov, 1784);

Kratkiia i na opytnosti osnovannyia zamechaniia o elektritsizme i o sposobnosti elektricheskikh makhin k pomoganiiu ot raznyx boleznei . . . (Saint Petersburg: Akademiia nauk, 1803).

Editions: *Zhizn' i prikliucheniia Andreia Bolotova, opisannyia samim im dlia svoikh potomkov, 1738–1796,* 4 volumes, edited by M. I. Semevsky (Saint Petersburg: V. Golovin, 1870–1873); further installments published in *Russkaia starina,* 62 (April–June 1888): 535–576; 64 (October–December 1889): 23–30; and 84 (August 1895): 135–155;

Pamiatnik protekshikh vremian ili kratkiia istoricheskiia zapiski o byvshykh proisshestviiakh i o nosivshikhsia v narode slukhakh — liubopytnyia i dostopamiatnyia deianiia i anekdoty Gosudaria Imperatora Pavla Pervago (Moscow: V. Islen'ev, 1875);

Izobrazheniia i opisaniia raznykh porod iablok i grush, rodiashchikhsia v Dvoreninovskikh, a otchasti i v drugikh sadakh. Risovany i opisany Andreem Bolotovym v Dvoreninove s 1797 po 1801 god, in *Plodovodstvo v Rossii: Materialy i izsledovaniia,* volume 3, Ministerstvo Zemledeliia i Gosudarstvennykh Imushchestv, Departament Zemledeliia (Saint Petersburg, 1900);

Izbrannye sochineniia po agronomii, plodovodstvu, lesovodstvu, botanike, edited by I. M. Poliakov and A. P. Berdyshev (Moscow: Moskovskoe obshchestvo ispytatelei prirody, 1952);

Izbrannye trudy (Moscow: Agropromizdat, 1988);

Izbrannoe, edited by A. K. Demikhovskii (Pskov: POIPKRO, 1993) — includes Bolotov's *Chestokhval* (1779), *Pis'ma o krasotakh prirody* (1795), and *Zhivopisatel' natury* (1788–1798).

OTHER: Adam Beuvius, *Genrietta, ili Gusarkoe pokhishchenie . . . ,* 3 volumes, translated by Bolotov (Moscow: N. Novikov, 1782);

Johann Melchior Goeze, *Ionna Melkhiora Getsena razsuzhdeniia o nachale i kontse nyneshniago i o sostoianii budushchago mira,* translated by Bolotov (Moscow: N. Novikov, 1783);

Nicolas Le Camus de Mézieres, *Aaba, ili torzhestvo nevinnosti,* translated by Bolotov (Moscow: N. Novikov, 1788);

Zhizn' i strannyia prikiucheniia umershago v 1788 godu Karla Eduarda, predententa Velikobritanskoi, Frantsuzskoi i Irlandskoi korony, translated by Bolotov (Moscow: Kh. Ridiger and Kh. Klaudi, 1794);

"Pesn' k vezdesushchemu," *Priiatnoe i poleznoe preprovozhdenie vremeni,* 11 (1796): 269–271;

"Utrenee raspolozhenie dukha," *Priiatnoe i poleznoe preprovozhdenie vremeni,* 13 (1797): 271–272;

"Okanchivaiushchaiasia zima," *Priiatnoe i poleznoe preprovozhdenie vremeni,* 13 (1797): 289–298;

"Vremia sozrevaniia plodov," *Priiatnoe i poleznoe preprovozhdenie vremeni,* 15 (1797): 385–398, 401–409;

Russkaia poeziia. Sobranie proizvedenii russkikh poetov, edited by S. A. Vengerov (Saint Petersburg: A. E. Vineke, 1897) — includes volume 1 of "Oda iskusstvu uveseliat'sia krasotami prirody" (1793) and a segment of "Vzdokh

*Andrei Timofeevich Bolotov at his desk; a portrait by his son Paul that
was published in Bolotov's* Zhizn' i prikliucheniia Andreia
Bolotova, opisannyia samim im dlia svoikh potomkov,
1738–1796 *(1870–1873)*

blagodarnyi ko Tvortsu" (1793), section 5, pp. 59–66;

"Iz neizdannogo literaturnogo naslediia Bolotova," edited by I. Morozov and A. Kucherov, *Literaturnoe nasledstvo,* 9–10 (1933): 166–221 — includes excerpts from Bolotov's manuscript works: "Opyt nravouchitel'nym sochineniiam" (1764); "Mysli i bespristrastnyia suzhdeniia o romanakh kak original'nykh rossiiskikh tak i perevedennykh s inostrannykh iazykov" (1791); "Sovremennik ili zapiski dlia potomstva" (1795); "65-oi god moei zhizni ili podrobnoe opisanie vsego proiskhodivshego so mnoiu s 7 chisla oktiabria 1802 goda" (1802); and "Rassuzhdenie o sravnitel'noi vygodnosti krepostnogo i vol'nonaemnogo truda" (circa 1812);

"Diuzhina soten vzdokhov, chuvstvovanii i myslei khristianskikh," in *Rossiiskii arkhiv* (Moscow, 1992), pp. 471–536.

Andrei Timofeevich Bolotov stands out as the most prolific writer that Russia has ever produced, penning, by one estimate, the equivalent of some 350 volumes of written material — memoirs, diaries, letters, poems, plays, criticism, and translations, as well as a vast array of other works of literary, philosophical, religious, didactic, scientific, agricultural, and historical natures — over the course of his long and quietly astonishing career. During his lifetime Bolotov achieved a modest measure of recognition as a writer on agricultural and horticultural issues; he is best known today, however, for his massive *Zhizn' i prikliucheniia Andreia Bolotova, opisannyia samim im dlia svoikh potomkov, 1738–1796* (The Life and Adventures of Andrei Bolotov, Written by Himself for His Descendants, 1738–1796 [1870–1873]). Because only a relatively small portion of what he wrote found its way into print — the memoirs, for instance, were not published until almost forty years after his death in 1833 – Bolotov, despite his phenomenal productivity and his considerable originality as a writer, ended up having virtually no influence on the development of Russian belle-lettres. Hence literary scholars, with a few notable exceptions, have all but ignored him, and his name goes unmentioned in most standard histories of Russian literature. Even his memoirs, which constitute one of the great masterpieces of late-eighteenth- and early-nineteenth-century autobiography, have to this day achieved only a circumscribed sort of fame and remain, as Viktor Shklovsky put it, "more renowned than known" – that is, they have more of a reputation (above all regarding their immense length) than an actual readership.

The only son of Timofei Petrovich Bolotov, a regimental commander in the Russian army, and Mavra Stepanovna Bolotova (née Bakeeva), Andrei Bolotov was born on 7 October 1738 at Dvorianinovo, his family's small estate in northwestern Tula province. He spent much of his childhood being trundled about the western reaches of the Russian empire from one encampment to another, and, like many noble children of the time, he received a haphazard and uneven education at the hands of various Russian, French, and German tutors. Despite the frequently horrendous quality of the instruction he was given, by his early teens he had managed to acquire a good command of French and German and had developed what would prove a lifelong passion for books and learning. Following his father's death in 1750 and his mother's death in 1752 Bolotov returned to Dvorianinovo, where he lived in solitary splendor for more than a year and a half, busying himself by practicing drawing and geometry, building mock fortifications in his garden, and reading religious tracts such as Stefan Iavorsky's *Kamen' very* (Rock of Faith, 1728).

Already at this young age he had begun to show an almost manic impulse to set pen to paper: for lack of anything better to do he made a manuscript duplicate of his favorite work, a Russian translation of François Fénelon's *Télémaque* (1699), and he stayed up late into the night copying out sections of the *Chet'i minei* (Lives of the Saints) into a special notebook. He grew so used to this carefree rural *vita contemplativa* that it was only with great reluctance that he reported to his late father's regiment in the winter of 1754–1755 to begin his service, which was then required of all noblemen. Over the next few years he took part in several campaigns in the Seven Years' War, and, although he never had to fire a single shot at anyone, he developed an almost Tolstoyan disgust at the senseless carnage that he saw all around him and increasingly came to detest the "shumnaia i bespokoinaia voennaia zhizn'" (noisy and turbulent military life) that he was forced to lead. Instead of carousing with his fellow officers Bolotov spent all his spare time reading, studying, and translating: he read Russian translations of John Barclay's *Argenis* and René Lesage's *Gil Blas* (1715–1735); he memorized Aleksandr Sumarokov's tragedy *Khorev* (1747) and practiced declaiming passages from it as he traveled on horseback; and when on marches he kept in his pocket a German translation of Antoine-François Prévost's *Le Philosophe anglais, ou Histoire de Cleveland* (The English Philosopher, or The Story of Cleveland, 1731), which he would read whenever his regiment stopped.

After enduring several years of this military vagabondage Bolotov was pulled from his regiment in 1758 to serve as a translator at army staff headquarters in Russian-occupied Königsberg. His duties there, though intermittently demanding, allowed him considerable free time to enjoy the cultural life of the city and to pursue his growing intellectual interests. He read widely and voraciously, first plowing through scores of German novels, which he credited with having a highly salutary effect on his moral and intellectual development, and then moving on to more-weighty philosophical, religious, and moral-didactic fare. Particularly crucial in the formation of his quietist Weltanschauung was his discovery of Christian August Crusius's new philosophy, which he studied privately with a local professor, as well as the aesthetic theories of Johann Georg Sulzer, from whom he learned "iskusstvo uveseliat'sia krasotamy natury" (the art of enjoying the beauties of nature).

Most important for his literary development, it was in Königsberg that Bolotov discovered the pleasures of letter writing. In the summer of 1760 he developed a close friendship with Nikolai Eremeevich Tulub'ev, a lieutenant in the Russian navy several years his senior. When Tulub'ev was reassigned to another city that autumn, the two began sending each other lengthy epistles. Allowing as it did for unfettered expatiation within an intimately enclosed space, the familiar letter proved ideally suited to Bolotov's talents and temperament as a writer. Indeed, although his friend would die at sea within a year, Bolotov continued to use the epistolary form for much of what he wrote over the course of his long life, regardless of whether a real addressee existed or not.

Early in 1762 the newly crowned czar, Peter III, in an unexpected gesture of goodwill, issued a proclamation releasing the nobility from obligatory service. Bolotov, who felt increasingly constrained by his bureaucratic duties in Königsberg and wanted nothing more than to return to his estate in Tula and live out his life in pastoral solitude, became one of the first noblemen to take advantage of this offer. He retired from service with almost indecent alacrity that summer at the age of twenty-three. He arrived back at Dvorianinovo on 3 September 1762, overjoyed at being able to ensconce himself at last among his books and flowers and to begin cultivating his garden in earnest. In short order Bolotov produced a book-length collection of philosophical and didactic ruminations (many of them in epistolary form) that he bound together in a manuscript he titled "Opyt nravouchitel'nym sochineniiam" (Exercises in Moral-Didactic Composition). He also became closely involved in the day-to-day management of his estate and in 1766 began corresponding with the Free Economic Society, a newly established organization devoted to the improvement of Russian agriculture. Over the course of the next several decades he would write dozens of pieces for publication in the journal, *Trudy vol'nogo ekonomicheskogo obshchestva* (Proceedings of the Free Economic Society). He continued to work in a literary and moral-didactic vein as well. In the latter half of the 1760s he penned pointedly satiric pieces – later included in a 1791 manuscript volume titled "Zabavy zhivushchago v derevne" (Amusements of a Country Dweller) – in which he lambasted the ignorance and superficiality of the provincial nobility – and he began composing a curious self-help manual titled *Putivoditel' k istinnomu chelovecheskomu schastiiu* (Guide to True Happiness), which he completed in 1772 and published in 1784.

He also forged ahead with a two-volume pedagogical work titled *Detskaia filosofiia* (Children's Philosophy, 1776, 1779), modeled after Madame de Beaumont's *Le Magasin des enfants* (Children's Magazine, 1761–1764) and consisting of a series of edifying dialogues between a mother and her two children. He had originally undertaken this project sometime in 1763 or 1764, when he first began looking for a wife; and when he married the fourteen-year-old Aleksandra Mikhailovna Kaverina in July 1764, he evidently had high hopes of being able to shape her character in accordance with his own idealized notions of womanhood. It soon became distressingly clear to him, however, that his young bride was a singularly resistant pupil: she expressed no interest whatsoever in his various intellectual and horticultural pursuits and even remained unimpressed – to Bolotov's profound astonishment – by

his much-prized stereopticon. Although less than satisfactory on a personal level, the marriage resulted in four daughters and one son, as well as several other children who died in infancy. Hence Bolotov eventually had ample opportunity to make use of his pedagogical opus. He appears to have particularly succeeded in molding his son, Pavel, who ended up sharing virtually all his interests and enthusiasms and whom Bolotov at various points characterized as "drugoi ia" (another me).

In 1774 Bolotov accepted an offer to serve as bailiff on the Crown estate of Kiiasovka, located a relatively short distance from Dvorianinovo, and then a year later moved on to a more prestigious and better-paid post at the larger but more distant estate of Bogoroditsk in southeastern Tula province, where he remained for twenty-two years before finally retiring to Dvorianinovo in 1797. Although in his memoirs he complains about the heavy burden that his official duties placed on him, it is evident that he usually had more than enough time to engage in his own private pursuits – in fact, some of his most productive years as a writer were during this period. In 1778, having become increasingly disgruntled with the Free Economic Society, which he felt had not adequately rewarded his efforts on its behalf, Bolotov came to an agreement with the Moscow printer Kh. Ridiger to publish his own agricultural journal, titled *Sel'skoi zhitel'* (Country Dweller), for the sum of two hundred rubles a year. Although financial troubles on Ridiger's part forced Bolotov to discontinue the journal after only one year, he was able to resurrect it a short while later under substantially more lucrative terms, as a result of his having met Nikolai Novikov, the new proprietor of the University Press, in September 1779. Starting in 1780 and continuing for ten years, Bolotov's journal, now titled *Ekonomicheskii magazin* (Economic Magazine), was published weekly as a supplement to the newspaper *Moskovskie vedomosti* (Moscow News). The forty volumes of the journal are an unrivaled compendium of information on eighteenth-century rural life and contain thousands of detailed articles covering all facets of agriculture, horticulture, landscaping, kitchen gardening, and medicine, as well as countless tidbits of homespun advice on everything from making whitewash to curing diarrhea and bad breath.

Although Bolotov warily rebuffed Novikov's repeated attempts to draw him into the Masonic brotherhood, the two nevertheless became fairly good friends, and Novikov undertook to publish some of Bolotov's literary and moral-didactic efforts over the course of the next decade. These included the second part of his *Detskaia filosofiia* (Children's Philosophy); his *Chuvstvovaniia khristianina, pri nachale i kontse kazhdago dnia v nedele, otnosiashchiiasia k samomu sebe i k Bogu* (A Christian's Sentiments Relating to God and to Himself at the Beginning and End of Each Day of the Week, 1781), 134 copies of which were confiscated from Moscow bookstores in 1787 as part of a roundup ordered by Catherine II of unsanctioned religious literature; the three-part *Putivoditel' k istinnomu chelovecheskomu schastiiu*; and a derivative three-act play titled *Neshchastnyia siroty* (The Unfortunate Orphans, 1781), which Bolotov had written for a children's theater that he had started at Bogoroditsk. Novikov also published several of Bolotov's translations of German and French works.

Despite his immense enthusiasm as a writer, throughout his life Bolotov remained oddly ambivalent about the whole business of being published. The preponderance of what he penned remained in manuscript, and when he did venture to publish he always did so anonymously. Even as the editor of the agricultural journals, he was careful to protect his identity. His brief foray into literary criticism in the early 1790s provides a particularly telling example of his self-effacing – and ultimately self-defeating – diffidence about going public. In January 1790, inspired perhaps by the receipt of a large package of French novels from Ridiger, Bolotov decided "pisat' kritiku na vse te knigi, kotoryia mne prochityvat' sluchalos', i kritiku osobago roda, a ne takuiu, kakaia inymi pishetsia, no polezneishuiu" (to write criticism on all the books that [he] happened to read, and criticism of a special sort, and not the kind that others write, but rather of a much more useful nature). He soon produced several manuscript volumes of highly opinionated and hard-hitting essays that he titled "Mysli i bespristrastnyia suzhdeniia o romanakh kak original'nykh, rossiiskikh tak i perevedennykh s inostrannykh iazykov" (Thoughts and Dispassionate Judgments on Novels, Both Originally in Russian and Translated from Various Foreign Languages). Although certain of these judgments were anything but dispassionate, and although he tended (not altogether surprising, given his own habits as a writer) to equate length with literary worth, on the whole the essays, had they been made available to the public, would indeed have made an important contribution to the literary polemics of the time. Among other things, Bolotov repeatedly demanded "naturalness" both of plot and style and issued what was perhaps the first appeal for a truly Russian novel, a novel "v kotorom by vse soobrazhalos' s rossiiskimi

nravami, obstoiatel' stvami i obyknoveniiami" (in which everything would be in accordance with Russian manners, circumstances, and customs). It was not until the 1930s, however, that a selection of essays from the one surviving volume of this ill-fated project was finally published in the journal *Literaturnoe nasledstvo*.

Of a more clearly private nature were Bolotov's efforts in verse. Although he had experimented with writing poetry in Königsberg as a young man, it was not until much later that his lyric impulse emerged in earnest. In the summer of 1791 he was overcome with a sudden burst of poetic inspiration while riding home one day in his carriage, and over the course of the next three decades Bolotov produced a substantial body of poetry, most of it either of a religious or what he called "naturological" nature. Bolotov himself took a properly modest view of his own limited poetic talents and referred to his efforts with self-deprecating good humor as his "tananakan'e" – which might be translated roughly as "tumteetummery." Because he had difficulty coming up with proper rhymes and even meters, he composed his lyrics in blank verse and to the tunes of various popular songs, usually either while walking in his garden or riding in a carriage or sleigh. Many of the poems, in fact, are expressly performatory in nature and were intended to be ritualistically sung or chanted at morning or eventide in the privacy of the garden. Typically, the poems are addressed either to an individual (usually God or Bolotov himself), or to some abstraction, place, or thing: Dvorianinovo, various flowers and trees in Bolotov's gardens, nightingales, fog, spring mornings, the dew on spring mornings, spring evenings, grass settees, watch stands, cups of tea, and so on. Although some of the poems show a certain quirky originality, by and large their artistic merit is low; only a handful have been published to date.

Bolotov's most enduring literary achievement, his *Zhizn' i prikliucheniia Andreia Bolotova, opisannyia samim im dlia svoikh potomkov,* was likewise a private production; it was written, as the title indicates, for his family and descendants and not intended for public perusal. He began the project on 24 January 1789 at Bogoroditsk and continued to work on it for some three decades after he returned to Dvorianinovo in 1797. Composed as a series of letters to an unnamed "Dear Friend," the memoirs constitute one of the few – and one of the most sustained – exercises in epistolary autobiography ever undertaken in any language. Of the thirty-seven manuscript volumes that Bolotov completed, and which cover his life from his birth in 1738 up until the early 1800s, twenty-nine were eventually published in the early 1870s as a supplement to the journal *Russkaia starina;* in printed form they fill four volumes, comprising almost five thousand densely printed columns. Although the *Russkaia starina* edition of the memoirs still remains the fullest version available, it is by no means complete. The journal's editor, M. I. Semevsky, felt that the many poems that Bolotov included were "meaningless" and summarily excised most of them from the published text. Also cut were letters that Pavel Bolotov had written to his father in the 1790s, as well as several examples of Bolotov's correspondence with the Free Economic Society. Three parts (35–37), covering Bolotov's life from the second half of 1799 up to the end of 1802, are extant in manuscript form; approximately half of part 35 was published in *Russkaia starina* between 1889 and 1895.

Domestic censorship also took its toll: the latter half of letter 134, comprising some twenty-five manuscript pages, for example, appears to have been torn out by a family member, so that Bolotov's narrative breaks off at midsentence in tantalizing Gothic-novel fashion: "Vskore za sim sluchilos' u nas v dome odno osoblivoe, strannoe i takoe proizshestvie . . . " (Soon afterward a particularly terrible incident occurred in our household that . . .). Another much more substantial gap (parts 30–34, covering the years 1796–1799) likewise appears to have been the result of domestic interference.

Although neither confessional nor even particularly introspective, the memoirs provide a remarkably nuanced psychological portrait of their author and are written in a full-bodied, richly modulated style that is variously comic and elegiac, caustic and sentimental, pompous and spontaneous, elevated and earthy. A chronicle both of Bolotov's life and of his age, the memoirs are monumental in their exhaustive detail and in their sweep. They are a tale of day-to-day existence told against the vast background of contemporary history. Throughout his career Bolotov showed a healthily ironic detachment from his age and assiduously maintained a position at the periphery of fame, power, and great events. Philosophically, the memoirs both emanate from and reflect this position. Commenting on his decision to begin composing his *Zhizn' i prikliucheniia Andreia Bolotova, opisannyia samim im dlia svoikh potomkov,* Bolotov made the following telling remark in his preface to the work: "obstoiatel'stvo chto zhizn' moia ne takova slavna, chtob stoila opisaniia i chto v techenie onoi ne sluchilos' so mnoiu nikakikh chrezvychainykh, redkikh i osoblivago

primechaniia dostoinykh proisshestvii, ni malo ne meshaet opisat' mne Zhizn' svoiu" (the fact that my life is not so illustrious as to be worth describing, and that during the course of it nothing happened to me that was extraordinary, unusual, or worthy of special notice, in no way prevents me from describing it). At first such a statement may seem self-contradictory, or, at best, self-evident; yet implicit here is a belief that it is the ordinary, overlooked, small events of daily life – life's transient "chatter," to use Aleksandr Pushkin's term – that are interesting and that are the true stuff of history.

After retiring to Dvorianinovo in 1797 with the rank of collegiate assessor, Bolotov refused all subsequent offers to take up an official post, preferring instead to enjoy the freedom and quiet of his beloved country home and to devote himself to his many literary, horticultural, and scientific projects. Over the next thirty-five years he ventured forth from Dvorianinovo only a handful of times, most notably in 1803, when he spent ten months in Saint Petersburg settling a boundary dispute. During his stay there he was feted lavishly by the Free Economic Society, with whom he had resumed his on-again-off-again correspondence, and he was granted an audience with the great poet and soon-to-be-deposed Minister of Justice Gavriil Derzhavin – a meeting that he describes with colorful and splendidly bristling invective in one of his letters to his son, Pavel. Although he gradually went blind and deaf in his last years, Bolotov remained spry and indefatigable well into his eighties, and at his granddaughter's wedding in 1821 he reportedly danced all the younger revelers off their feet. Bolotov died in his son's arms on 3 October 1833 at Dvorianinovo, four days before his ninety-fifth birthday.

Bibliographies:

S. A. Vengerov, *Kritiko-biograficheskii slovar' russkikh pisatelei i uchenykh* (Saint Petersburg, 1897), pp. 106–122;

A. T. Bolotov: Bibliograficheskii ukazatel' (Moscow: Tsentral'naia nauchnaia sel'sko-khoziaistvennaia biblioteka VASKhNIL, 1984).

Biographies:

John H. Brown, "A Provincial Landowner: A. T. Bolotov (1738–1833)," Ph.D. dissertation, Princeton University, 1976;

A. P. Berdyshev, *Andrei Bolotov – vydaiushchiisia deiatel' nauki i kul'tury, 1738–1822* (Moscow: Nauka, 1988).

References:

Aleksandr Blok, "Bolotov i Novikov," in his *Sobranie sochinenii,* volume 11 (Leningrad: Izdatel'stvo pisatelei, 1934), pp. 7–80;

M. P. Bolotov, "A. T. Bolotov (1737–1833)," *Russkaia starina,* 8 (November 1873): 738–753;

Aleksandr Konstantinovich Demikhovskii, "A. T. Bolotov – dramaturg," in Bolotov, *Izbrannoe* (Pskov: POIPKRO, 1993), pp. 5–23;

Demikhovskii, "A. T. Bolotov – poet i filosof prirody," in Bolotov, *Izbrannoe,* pp. 125–132;

A. Kucherov, "Bolotov – literaturnyi kritik," *Literaturnoe nasledstvo,* 9–10 (1933): 191–193;

I. Morozov, "Bolotov-publitsist," in *Literaturnoe nasledstvo,* 9–10 (1933): 153–165;

Thomas Newlin, "The Voice in the Garden: Andrei Bolotov and the Anxieties of Russian Pastoral, 1738–1833," Ph.D. dissertation, Columbia University, 1994;

E. P. Privalova, "A. T. Bolotov i teatr dlia detei," *XVIII vek,* 3 (1958): 242–261;

James L. Rice, "The Bolotov Papers and Andrei Timofeevich Bolotov, Himself," *Russian Review,* 35 (Spring 1976): 125–154;

Rice, "The Memoirs of A. T. Bolotov and Russian Literary History," in *Russian Literature in the Age of Catherine the Great,* edited by A. G. Cross (Oxford: Meeuws, 1976), pp. 17–43;

Ekaterina Shchepkina, "A. T. Bolotov," in S. A. Vengerov, *Kritiko-biograficheskii slovar' russkikh pisatelei i uchenykh,* volume 5 (Saint Petersburg, 1897), pp. 90–106;

Shchepkina, *Starinnye pomeshchiki na sluzhbe i doma: Iz semeinoi khroniki (1578–1762)* (Saint Petersburg, 1890);

Viktor Shklovsky, "Kratkaia i dostovernaia povest' o dvorianine Bolotove," *Krasnaia nov',* 12 (December 1928): 97–186.

Papers:

The vast corpus of manuscript works left by Bolotov is scattered among the manuscript divisions of the following institutions: Academy of Sciences Library, Saint Petersburg, fond 69; Saltykov-Shchedrin Library, Saint Petersburg, fond 89; Institute of Russian Literature (Pushkinskii Dom), Saint Petersburg, fond 537; Lenin Library, Moscow, fond 178; State Historical Museum, Moscow, fond 349. For detailed listings and descriptions of Bolotov's manuscripts, consult John H. Brown and S. A. Vengerov.

Catherine II (Ekaterina Alekseevna), "The Great," Empress of Russia

(21 April 1729 – 5 November 1796)

John T. Alexander
University of Kansas

BOOKS: *O vremia! Komediia v trekh deistviiakh. Sochinena v Iaroslavle vo vremia chumy* (Saint Petersburg: [Senate, 1772]; revised edition, Saint Petersburg: Akademiia nauk, 1786); French translation by M. Leclerc as *O temps! o moeurs!* (Paris: F. Didot, 1826);

Gospozha Vestnikova s sem'eiu komediia v odnom deistvii. Sochinena v Iaroslavle (Saint Petersburg: Senatskaia tipografiia, [1774]);

Imianiny gospozhi Varchalkinoi komediia v piati deistviiakh. Sochinena v Iaroslavle (Saint Petersburg: Senatskaia tipografiia, [1774]);

Taina protivo-nelepogo obshchestva (Anti-absurde), otkrytaia ne prichastnym onomu, translated from French by A. B. Khrapovitsky (Saint Petersburg: Veitbrekht i Shnor, 1759 [1780]);

Skazka o tsareviche Khlore ([Saint Petersburg: Akademiia nauk, 1781]);

Raz-go-vor i raz-ska-zy ([Saint Petersburg: Akademiia nauk, 1782]; enlarged, 1782);

Skazka o tsareviche Fevee ([Saint Petersburg: Akademiia nauk, 1783]);

Komediia Obmanshchik ([Saint Petersburg: Akademiia nauk, 1785]);

Komediia Obol'shchennyi ([Saint Petersburg: Akademiia nauk, 1785]);

Peredniaia znatnogo boiarina (Saint Petersburg: Akademiia nauk, 1786);

Vol'noe, no slaboe perelozhenie iz Shakespira, komediia Vot kakovo imet' korzinu i bel'e (Saint Petersburg: Akademiia nauk, 1786);

Komediia Shaman sibirskoi (Saint Petersburg: Akademiia nauk, 1786);

Novgorodskoi bogatyr' Boeslaevich opera komicheskaia, sostavlena iz skazki, pesnei ruskikh i inykh sochinenii (Saint Petersburg: Akademiia nauk, 1786);

Opera komicheskaia Fevei, sostavlena iz slov skaski, pesnei ruskikh i inykh sochinenii (Saint Petersburg: Akademiia nauk, 1786; revised edition, with

Catherine II (anonymous portrait, circa 1766; private collection)

music, Saint Petersburg: Gornoe uchilishche, 1789);

Podrazhanie Shakespiru, istoricheskoe predstavlenie bez sokhraneniia featral'nykh obyknovennykh pravil, iz zhizni Riurika (Saint Petersburg: Akademiia nauk, 1786; revised edition, with notes by Ivan Boltin, Saint Petersburg: Imperatorskaia tipografiia, 1792);

Opera komicheskaia Khrabroi i smeloi vitiaz' Akhrideich' (Saint Petersburg: Akademiia nauk, 1787);

43

Sravnitel'nye slovari vsekh iazykov i narechii, sobrannye desnitseiu vsevysochaishei osoby, volume 1, edited by Peter Simon Pallas (Saint Petersburg, 1787);

Komediia. Razstroennaia sem'ia ostorozhkami i podozreniiami (Saint Petersburg: Akademiia nauk, 1788);

Skazka o Gorebogatyre Kosometoviche i Opera komicheskaia iz slov skaski sostavlennaia (Saint Petersburg: Gornoe uchilishche, 1789);

Fedul s det'mi (Saint Petersburg: Imperatorskaia tipografiia, 1790);

Mémoires de l'impératrice Catherine II (London: Trübner, 1859); translated into Russian as *Zapiski imperatritsy Ekateriny II* (London: Trübner, 1859).

Editions: *Sochineniia,* 3 volumes (Saint Petersburg: A. Smirdin, 1849–1850);

Izbrannyia sochineniia (Saint Petersburg: A. S. Suvorin, 1890);

Sochineniia, edited by V. F. Solntsev, 3 volumes (Saint Petersburg: E. Evdokimov, 1893);

Sochineniia, edited by A. I. Vvedensky (Saint Petersburg: A. F. Marks, 1893);

Izbrannyia sochineniia (Saint Petersburg: I. Glazunov, 1894);

Sochineniia imperatritsy Ekateriny II na osnovanii podlinnykh rukopisei i s ob"iasnitel'ny primechaniiami, 11 volumes, edited by A. N. Pypin (Saint Petersburg: Akademiia nauk, 1901–1907);

Sochineniia Ekateriny II, edited by V. K. Bylinin and M. P. Odessky (Moscow: Sovremennik, 1990);

Sochineniia Ekateriny II, edited by O. N. Mikhailov (Moscow: Sovetskaia Rossiia, 1990).

Editions in English: *Ivan Czarowitz, Or the Rose Without Prickles, That Stings Not* (London: Robinson, 1768);

The Antidote: or an Enquiry into the Merits of a Book Entitled a Journey into Siberia, translated by Maria Johnson (London, 1772);

Memoirs of the Empress Catherine II, Written by Herself with a Preface by Alexander Herzen (New York: Appleton, 1859; London: Trübner, 1859);

Memoirs of Catherine the Great, translated by Katharine Anthony (New York: Knopf, 1927);

Correspondence of Catherine the Great when Grand-Duchess, with Sir Charles Hanbury-Williams and Letters from Count Poniatowski, edited and translated by the Earl of Ilchester and Mrs. Langford-Brooke (London: Butterworth, 1928);

Documents of Catherine the Great: The Correspondence with Voltaire and the Instruction of 1767 in the En-

glish Text of 1768, edited by W. F. Reddaway, translated by Michael Tatischeff (Cambridge: Cambridge University Press, 1931);

Memoirs of Catherine the Great, edited by Dominique Maroger, translated by Moura Budberg (New York: Macmillan, 1955);

Memoirs of Catherine the Great, edited by Maroger, translated by Budberg (London: Hamilton, 1955);

Memoirs of Catherine the Great, translated by Lowell Bair (New York: Bantam, 1957).

BOOKS EDITED: *Nakaz Komissii o sostavlenii proekta novago ulozheniia* (Moscow: Senate, [1767]); (Moscow: Moskovskii universitet, 1767) – parallel German and Russian texts; published as *Nakaz ... dannyi Komissii o sochinenii proekta novago ulozheniia* (Saint Petersburg: Akademiia nauk, 1770); enlarged, 1776; edited by N. D. Chechulin (Saint Petersburg, 1907); translated by Michael Tatischeff as *The Grand Instructions to the Commissioners Appointed to Frame a New Code of Laws for the Russian Empire ...* (London: Jeffreys, 1768);

Obriad upravleniia Kommissii o sochinenii proekta novago ulozheniia ([Moscow: Senate, 1767]; Moscow: Moskovskii universitet, 1767) – parallel German and Russian texts;

Dopolnenie k bol'shomu Nakazu. Glava XXI (Saint Petersburg: Senate, [1768]);

Dopolnenie k bol'shomu Nakazu. Glava XXII (Saint Petersburg: Senate, [1768]);

Nachertanie o privedenii k okonchaniiu Kommissii o sostavlenii proekta novago ulozheniia (Saint Petersburg: Senate, [1768]);

Antidote, ou examen du mauvais livre ... intitulé: Voyage en Sibérie fait ... en 1761, 2 volumes ([Saint Petersburg, 1770]); translated by Maria Johnson as *The Antidote: or an Enquiry into the Merits of a Book Entitled a Journey into Siberia* (London: Printed for S. Leacroft, 1772);

Rossiiskaia azbuka dlia obucheniia iunoshestva chteniiu, napechatannaia dlia obshchestvennykh shkol po vysochaishemu poveleniiu (Saint Petersburg: Akademiia nauk, [1781]);

Vybornye rossiiskie poslovitsy ([Saint Petersburg: Akademiia nauk, 1783]);

Zapiski kasatel'no rossiiskoi istorii, 6 volumes (Saint Petersburg: Imperatorskaia tipografiia, 1787–1794);

Recueil des piéces données au Théâtre de l'Hermitage, 4 volumes (Saint Petersburg: Gornoe uchilishche, 1788); published as *Théâtre de l'Hermitage de Catherine II* (Paris: Gide, 1799);

translated into Russian by P. Pel'skii as *Ermitazhnyi teatr, v kotorom sobrany piesy, igrannye v Ermitazhe imp. Ekateriny II, sochinennye samoiu eiu i osobami, sostavliavshimi ee obshchestvo* (Moscow: Senate, 1802); abridged as *Ermitazhnyi teatr, ili sobranie teatral'nykh sochinenii Ekateriny II* (Moscow: Universitetskaia tipografiia, 1802);
Rodoslovnik kniazei velikikh i udel'nykh roda Riurika (Saint Petersburg: Imperatorskaia tipografiia, 1793).

OTHER: Jean-François Marmontel, *Velizer,* translated by Catherine II and others (Moscow: Moskovskii universitet, 1768);
"Vorositel' " [erroneously known as "Nevesta nevidimka"], in *Rossiiskii featr,* volume 12 (Saint Petersburg: Akademiia nauk, 1786), pp. 2–50;
"Nachal'noe upravlenie Olega, podrazhanie Shakespiru bez sokhraneniia featral'nykh obyknovennykh pravil," in *Rossiiskii featr,* volume 14 (Saint Petersburg: Akademiia nauk, 1787), pp. 167–248;
"Nedorazumeniia," in *Rossiiskii featr,* volume 31 (Saint Petersburg: Akademiia nauk, 1789), pp. 153–318.

It is difficult to define Catherine the Great's place in literature because a long and controversial career made her into a "world-historical" figure who still seems larger than life. In ruling the immense Russian Empire as absolute sovereign or autocratrix for more than three decades of territorial, economic, and cultural expansion (1762–1796), she has been lauded for a multitude of virtues and achievements and damned for as many vices and disasters. Officially idolized throughout Russia's imperial era before the revolutions of 1917, Catherine was subsequently reviled or ignored in what used to be known as the Soviet Union. In the last few years, by contrast, her good repute has been largely reclaimed, and a series of popular historical studies has been initiated in Russia on "the golden century of Catherine the Great." In the West, scholars have recently heralded Catherine's resurgence by accenting her contributions to the Russian theater and her general patronage of literature and culture.

If most scholars agree on Catherine's significance as a patron of literature and culture in general, there is less consensus as to the intrinsic literary value of her own writings. First, there are complex questions about the authorship of many of her compositions. She obviously received much help in producing her Russian plays and comic operas.

Catherine in a Preobrazhensky guards' uniform, which she wore during the coup that brought her to the throne (engraving by Zh. B. Fossoier after a 1762 portrait by Eriksen)

Some of her fiction was in effect written by committee, whereas all of it was published anonymously, and the authorship or editorship of certain pieces (especially journalistic items) is still disputed. Another problem in establishing Catherine's literary reputation is that in the process of ruling she wrote, dictated, edited, or signed thousands of letters, many of which were probably drafted by others. How many of these should be termed literary or how they should be linked to her biography is problematic. Presumably many other letters remain unpublished, and varied standards have been utilized in determining the texts of the thousands that have been published. These are some of the major reasons no authoritative scholarly biography has been published in any language.

Little is known about the readership for her literary output, however defined, inside or outside

Russia. The sizes of the printings of only a few works are known, but the fact that several were quickly reissued suggests there was some demand for them. Versions of her so-called memoirs have been more widely read by people around the world than anything else she wrote. But it is doubtful whether she ever intended her sporadic, unfinished autobiography, which she composed in at least seven distinct drafts over a period of some forty years, to be published at all. There are many differences and contradictions among the drafts, none of which deals directly with the period of her reign. Most are character sketches and personal statements, not a recounting of public events. Ironically, this most famous of her writings was first published in London by Russian radicals bent on embarrassing the Romanov dynasty and the imperial Russian government. Although Catherine's memoirs are usually admired for their racy style, psychological appeal, and historical value, they may be appraised as her most significant literary achievement — artfully structured — and a prime reason for her enduring fame or notoriety. Their repeated republication in Russia and translation into many other languages suggest widespread appreciation.

In fact, graphomania appears to have been one of Catherine's earliest and most durable passions — a primary ingredient of her strategy for literally inventing herself and literarily assuring her immortality. A recent psychological portrait by Peter Petschauer contends that "she remained susceptible into maturity to humiliation and questioning and used pen and paper to ward off what she saw as attempts to embarrass her. She upstaged before she could be upstaged." She had much to invent, for she was not born to immediate greatness in her native land. With the birth name Sophia Augusta Fredericka, she entered the world on 21 April 1729 in the Pomeranian town of Stettin; she was the first child of a minor German aristocrat who was a Prussian general and official, Prince Christian August of tiny Anhalt-Zerbst, and his penurious but well-connected and ambitious wife, Princess Johanna Elizabeth of Holstein-Gottorp. Sophia apparently endured a relatively uneventful youth that included a traditional education at home by tutors and fairly frequent visits to larger German courts.

From her French Huguenot governess, Elizabeth Cardel, she learned French, and she memorized many lines from the classic French dramas of Jean Racine, Moliére, and Pierre Corneille. Manifesting an independent spirit and tomboyish taste for physical games, young Fike, or Figchen, as she was called, began reading eagerly, if indiscrimi-

nately, by age ten. Reading became a lifelong passion and the key to her self-education. Evidently she wrote little but, like her mother, loved to talk and learned to ingratiate herself via conversation, capitalizing on a ready wit, high spirits, and close observation. Indeed she became one of the world's great conversationalists, holding her own with people from diverse cultures and stations in life.

Young Sophia's marriage into the Russian imperial family was arranged by Empress Elizabeth and her own mother with the eager mediation of King Frederick II of Prussia. Her spouse was a cousin, Karl Peter Ulrich of Holstein, who was a grandson of Peter the Great and who might have succeeded to the Swedish throne had not his Russian aunt, the childless Elizabeth, brought him to Russia and named him heir apparent as Grand Duke Peter Fedorovich. Sophia had met him at least once before she went to Russia, and their similar background and ages were among the reasons that she was chosen as his consort. Mother and daughter arrived in Russia in February 1744; Sophia's conversion to Orthodoxy with the new name of Ekaterina Alekseevna was followed by her official betrothal in June 1744. Despite the bridegroom's weak health and near death from smallpox, Elizabeth's acute need for a male heir dictated that the wedding take place in Saint Petersburg on 21 August 1745.

During Catherine's first years in Russia she mastered the spoken language (she spelled badly in French, German, and Russian, sometimes mangling Russian grammar), memorized the Orthodox service, and established many long-lived friendships at court. She saw some of the country via Elizabeth's frequent trips and restless moves from palace to palace. Repelled by her immature and boorish husband and bored by court routine, she renewed her love of reading. For the Swedish envoy Count Adolf Gyllenborg, with whom she shared an interest in Voltaire's works, she even penned a self-appraisal entitled "Portrait of a Fifteen-Year-Old Philosopher," which has not survived. She continued to enjoy lighter works, such as a French version of Joanot Martorell and Marti Joan de Galba's picaresque romance, *Tiran le Blanc* (1490). Most of her reading was in French, it seems; she was enthralled by the wit of Madame de Sévigné's account of French court life and may have used it as a model for her own writing. She also enjoyed the scandalous memoirs of Pierre de Bourdeilles, Abbé de Brantôme, and Hardouin de Beaumont de Péréfixe's life of Henry IV of France, who became a favorite hero.

Intellectual pursuits took second place to the necessity to produce a male heir, however, a ticklish

Catherine's Coronation in the Assumption Cathedral of the Kremlin, in September 1762; painting by Felice Torelli

task in view of Peter's probable sterility and impotence. After several miscarriages Catherine finally succeeded with the birth of Pavel Petrovich (whose probable father was Sergei Saltykov) in September 1754. Her marital duty acquitted and the baby taken away by Elizabeth, Catherine enjoyed greater personal freedom, and with Elizabeth's manifestly declining health, she started planning for a future reign with or without Peter. Her plunge deeper into court politics brought her into close contact with the new British envoy, Sir Charles Hanbury-Williams, and his refined young Polish protégé, Count Stanislaus August Poniatowski. In working with Hanbury-Williams, Poniatowski, and Chancellor Aleksei Bestuzhev-Riumin to counter other political factions maneuvering for power, Catherine began writing steadily (mainly in French). At Hanbury-Williams's suggestion she drafted the first version of what would become known as her memoirs. By then she was already reading voraciously and judiciously. She plowed through four volumes of Pierre Bayle's *Dictionnairre historique et critique* (Historical and Critical Dictionary, 1697–1706), Voltaire's his-

torical works, the *Annals* of Tacitus, and Charles de Montesquieu's *De l'esprit des lois* (Spirit of the Laws, 1748). She also read books in Russian, starting with dictionaries and conversation handbooks and extending to Baronius's ecclesiastical annals and various descriptions of regions and cities. Later her interests broadened to include a five-volume history of voyages and the first volumes of Denis Diderot and Jean Le Rond d'Alembert's *Encyclopédie* (1751–1780). On friendly terms with Ivan Shuvalov, Elizabeth's young favorite who was a great Francophile with broad interests in the arts and sciences, Catherine had open access to his well-stocked library and continued her intensive self-education. She conversed with some well-educated foreigners, too, such as the English scholar Daniel Dumaresque.

Hanbury-Williams lent her money, advised her on court politics, and recommended that she read English plays. Playgoing was in high fashion with Elizabeth's vigorous patronage, and Catherine and Peter patronized a small theater at their suburban estate of Oranienbaum. The consorts lived more and more separate lives, which allowed Catherine to have an extended affair with Poniatowski that in 1757 produced a daughter, Anna Petrovna, who lived just sixteen months. Stung by this loss along with Poniatowski's expulsion from Petersburg and Bestuzhev-Riumin's arrest and exile for alleged treason, Catherine found herself dangerously isolated at a time when Elizabeth's death appeared imminent. She began a new liaison with Colonel Grigorii Orlov, a dashing military hero with excellent connections among the Guards regiments of the capital. When Elizabeth died on 25 December 1761, Peter III was proclaimed without incident; Catherine was pregnant with Orlov's child and in no position to oppose the new emperor, whom she scarcely saw over the six months of his fateful reign. Such seclusion enabled her to give birth to a son named Aleksei Grigor'evich (later given the surname Bobrinskoi) on 11 April 1762.

She recovered just in time to oust Peter III in the palace coup of 28–29 June 1762. Proclaimed Empress Catherine II, she was widowed a week later by the murder of Peter III by her partisans. She would rule for more than thirty-four years, and though she was offered the honorific title of "The Great" many times beginning in 1762, she apparently never explicitly accepted it.

While Horace Walpole denounced her as "This Fury of the North" and "This northern Athaliah" (after the biblical queen of Judah who seized the throne and tried to exterminate the house of David before she was overthrown and murdered), an admiring portrait appeared in the English press (*The Court Magazine* [London], August 1762) barely a month after the coup, which asserted that "Her majesty excels in every accomplishment that adds grace and beauty to one sex, and is acquainted with most of the sciences that are useful and ornamental in the other: she has long been the delight of the people over whom she now reigns; she has studied their genius, and will make their good her principal care." The early appearance of such praise abroad and its republication even in the English provincial press hints at Catherine's proficiency in publicizing her enlightened cultural program, which would defend her reputation from the charges of usurpation and murder that had accompanied her accession.

Crowned in Moscow on 22 September 1762, Catherine II stayed in the old capital nine months while consolidating her regime. At first she felt insecure, for there were serious doubts about her legitimacy and competence to rule, but her industrious ways won respect at home and abroad. Her government's initial program stressed peace abroad and mild domestic reform while she deftly cultivated such French philosophes as Voltaire and Diderot, whose library she purchased and who made a much-publicized visit to Saint Petersburg in 1773–1774. She disapproved of Rousseau's works, however, and in 1763 banned the sale of his treatise on education, *Émile,* probably because of its radical interpretation of religion, although most of his works later appeared in Russian translations. She patronized the arts, especially the theater, her coronation festivities including a huge public masquerade, *Minerva Triumphant,* organized by Aleksandr Sumarokov, Mikhail Kheraskov, and the actor Fedor Volkov.

Her style of rule drew much from Montesquieu and from German cameralist writers; hence she strove to know her huge realm better by extensive travels and to create a climate for moderate reform. Except for her extensive correspondence she had little time for literary preoccupations in these early years of her reign, but she encouraged others to take up literary pursuits, particularly her secretary and editorial assistant, Ivan Elagin, who headed a circle of playwrights that included Denis Fonvizin and Vladimir Lukin. She also financed the publication of the works of Sumarokov, perhaps the best-known Russian playwright of the era. Several of her state secretaries, Adam Olsuf'ev and Grigorii Teplov in particular, were well-educated and well-read and interested in literature. In 1766 she hired a young Moscow teacher, translator, and aspiring poet, Vasilii Petrov, to work for her personal chancery. He later became known as her "pocket" poet and wrote odes on many ceremonial occasions. If she had hoped he might become a new Lomonosov, her patronage did not shield him from much jealous criticism and even disdain. Her patronage of Gavriil Derzhavin in the late 1770s and 1780s has generally been viewed as better founded and more deserved, although it is sometimes attributed to her vanity in being depicted by the poet as "Felitsa" (Felicity).

In preparing for the opening in the summer of 1767 of the Legislative Commission in Moscow, a huge representative public assembly that was supposed to assist in framing a new national law code, Catherine made a much-publicized voyage down the Volga River from Tver' to Kazan and Simbirsk, during which she participated in a group translation (published in Moscow in 1768) of Marmontel's new dramatized political tract, *Belisarius;* she translated chapter nine, on absolutism. As guidelines for the Legislative Commission she had compiled her *Nakaz Komissii o sostavlenii proekta novago ulozheniia*

Catherine's Hermitage Theater in Saint Petersburg

(1767), also known as the *Bol'shoi nakaz* (Great Instruction), largely based on Montesquieu; the work was soon translated into English, Italian, Greek, Swedish, Dutch, Polish, and Romanian. The Academy of Sciences issued a sumptuous quadralingual edition in Russian, French, German, and Latin in 1770, but it was overpriced and sold poorly. Repeatedly reissued in Russia, the *Bol'shoi nakaz* was also praised abroad, where Voltaire called it "the finest monument of the age" and Frederick II sounded the theme of sexual politics: "a masculine, nervous performance, and worthy of a great man." This became Catherine's best-known statement of political and social principles.

War with Turkey in 1768 led to postponement of the Legislative Commission's plenary sessions, and though subcommissions continued to meet for several years, no full-blown law code ever emerged. Catherine maintained the political initiative, however, by covertly sponsoring a batch of satiric journals in 1769–1774, led by *Vsiakaia vsiachina* (All Sorts of Things). Modeled after Joseph Addison and Richard Steele's *The Spectator* (1711–1712), the Russian periodicals were printed on government presses and were not subjected to censorship. None of the contributions was signed, so it has been almost impossible to determine authorship and whether Catherine herself contributed. The genre throve on controversy, of course, and the empress appreciated general satire and even attacks on individuals, but she may have been bothered by the journalistic free-for-all that ensued. It is now generally admitted that she did not close down any of the journals; most of them failed for commercial reasons. Moreover, their polemics do not break down into a simple progressive society versus reactionary government rubric, and Catherine continued to patronize several publishing initiatives of Nikolai Novikov, a young nationalistic noble entrepreneur who had published several of the satiric journals. Many of these periodicals were republished in book form, and their satiric attacks on gallomania, parental tyranny, noble selfishness, and abuse of enserfed peasants were all within the ethical parameters established by the Legislative Commission.

In November 1768 Catherine founded the Sobranie staraiushcheesia o perevode inostrannykh knig (Society for the Translation of Foreign Books) with two thousand rubles of seed money. This organization sponsored 112 translations before it merged with the new Russian Academy of Letters in 1783, by which time another 129 were ready for publication. Its selection of titles was varied, ranging from classics by Livy, Tacitus, Homer, and Cicero to works by European authors such as Pierre Corneille, Voltaire, and Montesquieu; recent history and jurisprudence by William Robertson, David Hume, and Sir William Blackstone; and English fiction and satire by Henry Fielding and Jonathan Swift. Despite her partiality for English literature, Catherine did not read English, making use of German and French translations of English works.

Such translations were only a tiny part of the substantial increase in the number of books and titles published during Catherine's reign, a trend capped by her legalization of privately owned presses in 1783 – an innovation probably motivated as much by commercial calculations as by political tolerance or liberalism. The annual average of Russian-language books increased from between 150 and 160 in the 1760s to 373 in the early 1790s. As a dominant category of Russian-language titles, belles lettres expanded from 17 percent in 1756–1775 to 30 percent in 1787, an expansion that Catherine had encouraged and to which she had personally contributed. She also built up a large court library divided into foreign and Russian holdings. By the end of the eighteenth century it comprised more than forty-four thousand volumes, with about four thousand of these in Russian. The Russian book trade grew to several times its original size during this period, particularly in Saint Petersburg and Moscow.

Although the general level of literacy in this period seems to have grown only modestly, the theater may have bridged some of the gap between the elite literacy and popular illiteracy. Indeed, some commentators have maintained that a virtual theatricalization of court and noble society took shape during Catherine's reign.

While Catherine was being crowned in Moscow she had left directions in Saint Petersburg to build an Opera House in the Winter Palace in the new neoclassical style that she favored. Designed and supervised by architects Jean-Baptist Michel Vallen de la Mothe and Georg Friedrich Felten, the Opera House was hastily built near Catherine's private apartments. It comprised a large parterre and four tiers of boxes embellished by elaborate plasterwork and paintings by twenty-seven artists. A multitude of candles and four chandeliers illuminated the gilt decorations of this splendid hall – one of the most remarkable interiors anywhere in the city. A German visitor who saw it in 1777 thought it compared favorably with the Berlin opera house and noted that it presented ballets, French musical comedies, Italian operas, and "once per week, except during days of fasting, Russian tragedies and comedies." Its first production was staged on 28 December 1763. Besides attending performances in the Winter Palace, in several of which her son Pavel Petrovich acted, Catherine patronized presentations by the resident German, French, and Italian troupes.

The series of Catherine's comedies that were staged and published anonymously from 1772 onward may be seen as part of her general effort to mold a climate of public opinion facilitating moderate social and intellectual change. The titles of *O vremia!* (O Time!), *Imianiny gospozhi Varchalkinoi* (Mrs. Grumbler's Nameday, 1774), and *Gospozha Vestnikova s sem'eiu* (Mrs. Newsmonger and Her Family, 1774), as well as the leading characters of the former – Khanzhakhina (Mrs. Hypocrite), Vestnikova (Mrs. Newsmonger), and Chudikhina (Mrs. Astounded) – show that the satire was aimed at such foibles as gossiping, miserliness, parental tyranny, and false religiosity. Several were set in noble houses of Moscow, a city and milieu that Catherine found retrograde, as dramatized by the terrible plague of 1770–1771. She took her revenge on Moscow by pretending that these comedies had been composed in Iaroslavl during the plague of 1772, a bit of deliberate obfuscation that scarcely concealed her horror over the Moscow "Plague Riot" of September 1771 that had resulted in the murder of Archbishop Amvrosii.

To her literary friend Friedrich Melchior Grimm, however, she explained her motivation for writing for the stage more simply: first, to amuse herself, and second, to elevate the national theater, which, lacking new plays, was somewhat neglected. About her plays she admitted to Voltaire: "The author has many deficiencies; he doesn't know the theater; the intrigues of his plays are weak. But you can't say the same about the characters: they are restrained and are taken from nature, which he has before his eyes. Besides, he has comic sallies; he makes you laugh; his morals are pure, he knows the common folk." *O vremia!* was hardly original, for Catherine adapted it from Christian Fürchtegott Gellert's *Die Betschwester* (1745), Russifying some characters while adding others barely mentioned in the original and cutting some scenes. While the U.S. scholar Simon Karlinsky has praised her comedies for their daring critique of the manners of the nobility, others have faulted her portrayal of servants as lacking individuality and credibility while serving a Greek-chorus function.

In 1780 Catherine published an attack in French on Freemasonry, but the Russian translation by her secretary, Aleksandr Khrapovitsky, bore the date of 1759 ostensibly for tactical reasons: *Taina protivo-nelepogo obshchestva (Anti-absurde), otkrytaia ne prichastnym onomu* (The Secret of the Anti-Absurd Society Revealed by One not Privy to It). This was followed a few years later by three additional satiric plays attacking Freemasonry: *Komediia Obmanshchik* (The Deceiver, 1785), *Komediia Obol'shchennyi* (The Deluded, 1785), and *Komediia Shaman sibirskoi* (The Siberian Shaman, 1786). The first two ridiculed the visit to Saint Petersburg in 1779 of "Count Cagliostro," the assumed name of adventurer Giuseppe Balsamo. All were translated into German and published in Saint Petersburg and were later issued independently in Germany. These were more skits than plays, and their humor is simple. They may have had some role, however, in helping Catherine to recover from the severe depression she suffered after the sudden death in 1784 of her favorite, Lanskoi, and to cope with some of her worries over reports of widespread famine in the south, her anguish over the oft-postponed Tauride Tour of 1787, and the threat of renewed war with the Turks.

The centrality of the theater in the life of Catherine's court was reaffirmed in the 1780s when, because of the growth of the imperial family, she directed that the Opera House in the Winter Palace be converted into living quarters, but first the old facility had to be carefully disassembled because of its artistic importance. Catherine commissioned Giacomo Antonio Quarenghi to design a new court theater, which would supersede the Malyi Theater in Pavel Petrovich's palace quarters (perhaps a minor indication of the rivalry worsening between mother and son). Conceived as an amphitheater *al' antica*, its walls and columns were faced with artificial marble. Enough was constructed for the first production to be mounted on 16 November 1785, and thereafter plays were offered once or twice per week. The exterior was finally finished in 1789. Catherine and her close friends wrote various plays and skits, many of them in French, for this small court theater.

In these same years she dabbled in philological matters, sponsoring the collection of a core vocabulary in more than two hundred languages and dialects, including materials from American Indian languages and dialects that she obtained through the help of Lafayette and George Washington. In sending such materials to Lafayette for transmission to Russia, Washington in a letter of 10 January 1788 applauded the enterprise: "I heartily wish the attempt of that singular great character, the empress of Russia, to form a universal Dictionary, may be attended with the merited success." Catherine turned the material over to Peter Simon Pallas, who edited *Sravnitel'nye slovari vsekh iazykov i narechii, sobrannye desnitseiu vsevysochaishei osoby* (Comparative Dictionaries of All Languages and Dialects Collected by the Hand of a Most August Person), which was published in 1787. It apparently had little direct impact at the time but has recently been acclaimed as a pioneering venture in comparative linguistics. Although other recent commentators have derided Catherine's amateurish attempts to find Russian or Slavic roots for words found far afield, perhaps she deserves credit for her boldness in undertaking such a daunting task.

She also contributed to a new journal, *Sobesednik liubitelei rossiiskago slova* (Interlocutor of Lovers of the Russian Word), her compilations on Russian history (originally intended for the education of her grandsons, these were some of the first historical works in Russian compiled specifically for children) and a question-and-answer feature entitled "Byli i nebylitsy" (Facts and Fancies). Like her supposed satiric journalism of the late 1760s, the latter has been the subject of much dispute. The liberal-radical interpretation of "Byli i nebylitsy" as a political statement now seems exaggerated and dogmatic. Her historical works appear naive and blatantly nationalistic. Along with the foundation of the Russian Academy in 1783, Catherine's contributions to *Sobesednik liubitelei rossiiskago slova* may be seen as part of a campaign to cultivate Russian national consciousness and self-esteem.

Catherine had long patronized writings in Russian and particularly favored comedies as useful psychological exercises, advising her friend Princess Ekaterina Dashkova to write one as a way of dispelling an attack of depression. The empress was assisted in her playwriting by her secretaries and sometimes her young favorites. She made no great claims for her playwriting, which she also classified as useful therapy. Her efforts on behalf of the theater elicited considerable response; a collection of plays in Russian issued by the Academy of Sciences, *Rossiiskii featr* (Russian Theater, 1786–1794), includes some two hundred titles. She wrote (or collaborated on) libretti for comic operas in the late 1780s: *Opera komicheskaia Fevei* (The Comic Opera, Fevei, 1786), four acts, music by Pashkevich; *Novgorodskoi bogatyr' Boeslaevich* (Boeslaevich, the Knight of Novgorod, 1786), four acts, music by Fomin; *Opera komicheskaia Khrabroi i smeloi vitiaz' Akhrideich'* (The Comic Opera, The Brave and Bold Knight Akhrideich, 1787), five acts, music by Wanzura; *Skazka o Gorebogatyre Kosometoviche i Opera komicheskaia iz slov skaski sostavlennaia* (Tale of the Doleful Knight Kosometovich, 1789), five acts, music by Soler and Pashkevich; and *Fedul s det'mi* (Fedul and His Children, 1790), one act, music by Martin Soler and Pashkevich. These productions were luxuriously staged, and some employed hundreds of extras.

If it were not for the supposed reactionary character of the last decade of Catherine's reign, usually attributed to her rejection of the French Revolution and concerns over Russian succession, her contributions to and patronage of Russian literature would be unanimously praised. But liberal, radical, and Soviet Communist commentators have tended to blame her for this reactionary period, which they sometimes see as beginning much earlier, linked to the Pugachev rebellion of 1773–1774. This view now seems to be unduly dogmatic and monolithic, based on unrealistic assumptions about the bases of Catherine's political authority and her cultural aspirations. More-recent scholarship contends that Catherine felt more confident after the crises of the early 1770s and that her reign does not divide neatly into liberal and reactionary halves.

As an absolute monarch Catherine rejected the antiaristocratic concepts of the French Revolution, and she was understandably worried about its impact on interstate relations in Europe and on Russian domestic affairs. Her rejection of these principles may have been exacerbated by her own advancing age and, perhaps, by greater doubts about her earlier ideals about liberty and enlightenment as motive forces in human affairs. Some commentators have also contended that she received more militantly conservative advice from new advisers and favorites, such as Platon Zubov. It should also be remembered that Russia was at war for most of her reign after 1787, a fact that probably also aggravated the empress's conservative tendencies. The arrests of Aleksandr Radishchev and Novikov in 1790 and 1792, for example, were bound up with wartime fears and Catherine's deepening apprehensions of seditious repercussions from revolutionary France.

In the legislative sphere Catherine's reaction in literary matters was epitomized a month before her death in the proclamation of Russia's first full-blown system of censorship. Like many enactments, this one was easier to announce than to implement, and its main practical effects were felt during the militantly conservative reign of her son, Paul I (1796–1801). Most of the restrictions were abolished by Catherine's grandson Alexander I after 1801. In any event, her broadening of the concept of freedom of expression in Russia could not be undone by such a brief bout of reaction.

Often called the only intellectual to sit on the Russian throne, Catherine wrote in a variety of genres and was amazingly prolific. Whatever the merits of her original works, Catherine's efforts cer-

Catherine II in later years; engraving after a portrait by Johann Lampi

tainly assisted the flowering of Russian literary culture and intellectual life and helped to publicize both abroad.

Letters:

Perepiska rossiiskoi imperatritsy Ekateriny II i gospodina Vol'tera, prodolzhavshaiasia s 1763 po 1778 god, translated by Ivan Fabian (Moscow: Garii, 1803);

Pis'ma i bumagi imperatritsy Ekateriny II khraniashchiiasia v Imperatorskoi publichnoi biblioteke, edited by Afanasii F. Bychkov (Saint Petersburg, 1873);

Ekaterina II v perepiske s Grimmom, 3 volumes, edited by Iakov K. Grot (Saint Petersburg: Akademiia nauk, 1879–1889);

"Imperatritsa Ekaterina II v eia neizdannykh ili izdannykh ne vpolne pis'makh k I. G. Tsimmermannu," *Russkaia starina,* 44 (1887): 239–320;

Les lettres de Catherine II au prince de Ligne (1780–1796), edited by Princess Charles de Ligne (Brussels & Paris: G. van Oest, 1924);

Lettres d'amour de Catherine à Potemkine: Correspondance inedite, edited by Georges Oudard (Paris: Calmann-Levy, 1934);

Les plus belles lettres de Catherine II, edited by Oudard (Paris: Calman-Levy, 1962);

Vol'ter i Ekaterina II, edited by V. V. Chuiko (Saint Petersburg: Novosti, 1882); translated and edited by A. Lentin as *Voltaire and Catherine the Great: Selected Correspondence* (Cambridge: Oriental Research Partners, 1974).

Bibliography:

David R. Egan and Melinda A. Egan, *Russian Autocrats from Ivan the Great to the Fall of the Romanov Dynasty: An Annotated Bibliography of English Language Sources to 1985* (Metuchen, N. J.: Scarecrow Press, 1987).

Biographies:

Aleksandr G. Brikner, *Istoriia Ekateriny Vtoroi* (Saint Petersburg, 1885);

Vasilii A. Bil'basov, *Istoriia Ekateriny Vtoroi,* third edition, volumes 1, 2, and 12 (Berlin: F. Gottgeimer, 1900);

John T. Alexander, *Catherine the Great: Life and Legend* (New York: Oxford University Press, 1989);

Isabel De Madariaga, *Catherine the Great: A Short History* (New Haven: Yale University Press, 1990).

References:

John T. Alexander, "Catherine the Great and the Foundation of the Russian Academy," *Study Group on Eighteenth-Century Russia Newsletter,* 13 (1985): 16–24;

Alexander, "The Theater of Catherine the Great's Court," *Touchstone: The Magazine of the Tennessee Humanities Council,* 17 (1991): 11–13;

John H. Appleby, "Daniel Dumaresq, D.D., F.R.S. (1712–1805) as a Promoter of Anglo-Russian Science and Culture," *Notes and Records of the Royal Society of London,* 44 (1990): 25–50;

A. Chebyshev, "Istochnik komedii imperatritsy Ekateriny 'O, vremia!'," *Russkaia starina,* 2 (1907): 389–409;

Wilfrid-Rene Chetteoui, *Cagliostro et Catherine II: La Satire impériale contre le Mage* (Paris: Editions des Champs-Elysées, 1947);

Anthony G. Cross, "The Eighteenth-Century Russian Theatre through British Eyes," *Studies on Voltaire and the Eighteenth Century,* 219 (1983): 225–240;

Cross, "A Royal Blue-Stocking: Catherine the Great's Early Reputation in England as an Authoress," in *Gorski vijenac: A Garland of Essays offered to Professor Elizabeth Mary Hill,* edited by Robert Auty, L. R. Lewitter, and Alexis P. Vlasto (Cambridge: Modern Humanities Research Association, 1970), pp. 85–99;

Cross, " 'S anglinskago': Books of English Origin in Russian Translation in Late Eighteenth-Century Russia," *Oxford Slavonic Papers,* 19 (1986): 62–87;

I. M. Dadykin, "Zhurnal'naia deiatel'nost' Ekateriny II," in *Imperatritsa Ekateriny II: Sbornik istoricheskikh statei,* edited by A. Turtsevich (Vil'na, 1904), pp. 351–388;

Isabel De Madariaga, "Catherine II et la littérature," in *Histoire de la Littérature russe,* volume 1, edited by Efim Etkind, Georges Nivat, Ilya Serman, and V. Strada (Paris: Fayard, 1992), pp. 656–669;

De Madariaga, *Russia in the Age of Catherine the Great* (London: Weidenfeld & Nicholson / New Haven: Yale University Press, 1981);

Hedwig Fleischhacker, *Mit Feder und Zepter: Katharina II. als Autorin* (Stuttgart: Deutsche Verlags-Anstalt, 1978);

David M. Griffiths, "To Live Forever: Catherine II, Voltaire, and the Pursuit of Immortality," in *Russia and the World of the Eighteenth Century,* edited by Roger Bartlett and others (Columbus, Ohio: Slavica, 1988), pp. 446–468;

Iakov K. Grot, "Filologicheskie zaniatiia Ekateriny II," *Russkii arkhiv,* 4 (1877): 425–442;

Grigorii A. Gukovskii, "The Empress as Writer," in *Catherine the Great: A Profile,* edited by Marc Raeff (New York: Hill & Wang, 1972), pp. 64–89;

Charles Hyart, "Le Théâtre de l'Hermitage et Catherine II," *Revue de Littérature Comparée,* 61 (January–March 1987): 81–103;

W. Gareth Jones, "Biography in Eighteenth-Century Russia," *Oxford Slavonic Papers,* 22 (1989): 58–80;

Aleksandr B. Kamensky, "Catherine the Great," *Soviet Studies in History,* 30 (Fall 1991): 30–65;

Kamensky, *"Pod seniiu Ekateriny": Vtoraia polovina XVIII veka* (Saint Petersburg: Lenizdat, 1992);

Simon Karlinsky, *Russian Drama from Its Beginnings to the Age of Pushkin* (Berkeley: University of California, 1985);

Mary Ritchie Key, *Catherine the Great's Linguistic Contribution* (Carbondale, Ill.: Linguistic Research, 1980);

O. E. Kornilovich, "'Zapiski' imperatritsy Ekateriny II," *Zhurnal ministerstva narodnago prosveshcheniia,* 37 (1911): 37–74;

Gary Marker, *Publishing, Printing, and the Origins of Intellectual Life in Russia, 1700–1800* (Princeton: Princeton University Press, 1985);

O. A. Omel'chenko, *"Zakonnaia monarkhii" Ekateriny II: Prosveshchennyi Absoliutizm v Rossii* (Moscow: Izdanie avtora, 1993);

K. A. Papmehl, *Freedom of Expression in Eighteenth Century Russia* (The Hague: Martinus Nijhoff, 1971);

Peter Petschauer, "Learning to Reject the Feminine: Catherine II's Youth in a Large German Household," *Journal of Psychohistory,* 17 (Winter 1990): 267–288;

Boris B. Piotrovsky, ed., *Ermitazh: Istoriia stroitel'stva i arkhitektura zdanii* (Leningrad: Stroizdat, 1989);

Marshall S. Shatz, "The Noble Landowner in Russian Comic Operas of the Time of Catherine the Great: The Patriarchal Image," *Canadian Slavic Studies,* 3 (Spring 1969): 22–38;

Ernest J. Simmons, "Catherine the Great and Shakespeare," *PMLA,* 47 (September 1932): 790–806;

Vasilii V. Sipovskii, "Ekaterina II i russkaia bytovaia komediia eia epokhi," in *Istoriia russkogo teatra,* volume 1, edited by V. V. Kallash and N. E. Efros (Moscow: Kn-vo Ob"nedineniie, 1914), pp. 317–340;

M. Sokolov, "Literaturnaia deiatel'nost' imperatritsy Ekateriny II," in *Imperatritsa Ekateriny II: Sbornik istoricheskikh statei,* edited by A. Turtsevich (Vil'na: A. G. Syrkina, 1904), pp. 315–350;

Iurii V. Stennik, "Dramaturgiia russkogo klassitsizma: Komediia," in *Istoriia russkoi dramaturgii XVII-pervaia polovina XIX veka,* edited by Iu. K. Gerasimov, Iurii Lotman, and F. Ia. Priima (Leningrad: Nauka, 1982), pp. 109–162;

V. P. Stepanov, "Ekaterina II," in *Slovar' russkikh pisatelei XVIII veka,* volume 1 (Leningrad: Nauka, 1988), pp. 291–302;

Michael Von Herzen, "Catherine II: Editor of *Vsiakaia Vsiachina?* A Reappraisal," *Russian Review,* 38 (July 1979): 283–297;

David J. Welsh, *Russian Comedy 1765–1823* (The Hague: Mouton, 1966).

Mikhail Dmitrievich Chulkov
(1743? – 14 October 1792)

David Gasperetti
University of Notre Dame

BOOKS: *Peresmeshnik, ili Slavenskie skazki*, 4 volumes (Saint Petersburg: Akademiia nauk, 1766–1768); revised edition, 5 volumes (Moscow: Ponomarev, 1789);

Kratkoi mifologicheskoi leksikon (Saint Petersburg: Akademiia nauk, 1767);

Plachevnoe padenie stikhotvortsev. Satiricheskaia poema ([Saint Petersburg: Morskoi kadetskii korpus, 1769]);

Prigozhaia povarikha, ili Pokhozhdenie razvratnoi zhenshchiny, volume 1 (Saint Petersburg: [Morskoi kadetskii korpus], 1770); translated by Harold B. Segel as "The Comely Cook, or The Adventures of a Debauched Woman," in *The Literature of Eighteenth-Century Russia*, volume 2, edited by Segel (New York: Dutton, 1967), pp. 26–68;

I. Plachevnoe padenie stikhotvortsev satiricheskaia poema. II. Stikhi na kacheli. III. Stikhi na semik. IV. Na maslenitsu ([Saint Petersburg: Morskoi kadetskii korpus, 1775]);

Istoricheskoe opisanie rossiiskoi kommertsii pri vsekh portakh i granitsakh ot drevnikh vremian do nyne nastoiashchago i vsekh preimushchestvennykh uzakonenii po onoi gosudaria imp. Petra Velikgo i nyne blagopoluchno tsarstvuiushchei gosudaryni imp. Ekateriny Velikiia, 7 volumes (Saint Petersburg: Akademiia nauk, 1781–1788);

Istoriia krataia rossiiskoi torgovli (Moscow: Ponomarev, 1788);

Nastavlenie neobkhodimonuzhnoe dlia rossiiskikh kuptsov, a bolee dlia molodykh liudei (Moscow: [Ponomarev, 1788]);

Slovar' uchrezhdennykh v Rossii iarmarok, izdannyi dlia obrashchaiushchikhsia v torgovle (Moscow: Ponomarev, 1788);

Sel'skii lechebnik, ili Slovar' vrachevaniia boleznei, byvaemykh v rode chelovecheskom, takzhe v rode skotskom, konskom, i ptits domashnikh sobrannyi iz pechatnykh sochinenii, 7 parts (Moscow: Ponomarev, 1789–1805);

Slovar' iuridicheskii ili Svod rossiiskikh uzakonenii, vremiannykh uchrezdenii, suda i raspravy. Chast' pervaia po azbuchnomu poriadky; chast' vtoraia po starshinstvu godov, mesiatsov i chisl ot Ulozheniia, ili s 7157 goda, 2 volumes (Moscow: V. Okorokova, 1792).

OTHER: *I to i sio*, nos. 1–52 (January 1769–December 1769), edited by Chulkov;

Vasilii Trediakovsky, *Pokhozhdenie Akhillesovo pod imenem Pirry do Troianskoi osady*, adapted by Chulkov (Saint Petersburg: Sukhoputnyi kadetskii korpus, 1769);

Parnasskii shchepetil'nik, (May 1770–December 1770), edited by Chulkov;

Sobranie raznykh pesen, compiled by Chulkov, volume 1 (Saint Petersburg: Akademiia nauk, 1770); volumes 2–4 (Saint Petersburg: Morskoi kadetskii korpus, 1771–1774); revised as *Novoe i polnoe sobranie rossiiskikh pesen; soderzhashchee v sebe pesni liubovnye, pastusheskie, shutlivye, prostonarodnye, khoral'nye, svadebnye, sviatochnye, s prisovokupleniem pesen iz raznykh rossiiskikh oper i komedii*, 6 volumes (Moscow: N. Novikov, 1780–1781);

Slovar' ruskikh sueverii, compiled by Chulkov (Saint Petersburg: Shnor, 1782); revised as *Abevega ruskikh sueverii idolopoklonnicheskikh zhertvoprinoshenii svadebnykh prostonarodnykh obriadov koldovstva, shemanstva i proch* (Moscow: F. Gippius, 1786);

"Nastavlenie maloletnomu synu moemu, vstupaiushchemu v sluzhbu," in *Zapiski ekonomicheskie, dlia vsegdashnego ispolneniia v derevniakh prikashchiku, izbrannye Mikhailom Chulkovym iz sochiniaemogo im Slovaria zemledeliia, skotovodstva i domostroitel'stva*, second edition (Moscow: Ponomarev, 1790), pp. 165–171;

"Kak khochesh' nazovi," *Literaturnoe nasledstvo*, no. 9–10 (1933): 226–242.

Mikhail Dmitrievich Chulkov

Active during the high point of Russian classicism, Mikhail Dmitrievich Chulkov left his mark on a broad range of undertakings. Before his literary career began, he was involved in the opening act of the modern era of Russian drama, performing several roles in plays written by Aleksandr Sumarokov, the founder of the first permanent theater in Russia. When he took up the pen in the mid 1760s, Chulkov contributed engaging works in many genres, along the way producing several firsts in the annals of Russian literature. In 1769 he wrote "Stikhi na kacheli" (Verses on a Ferris Wheel, 1775) initiating the genre of the low burlesque poem in Russia, and his *Prigozhaia povarikha, ili Pokhozhdenie razvratnoi zhenshchiny* (1770; translated as "The Comely Cook, or The Adventures of a Debauched Woman," 1967), stands near the beginning of the Russian tradition of the memoir novel and remains unrivaled as the supreme parody of the literary aesthetic of its day. At the end of the 1760s, when the empress

Catherine inaugurated a series of satiric literary journals with her *Vsiakaia vsiachina* (All Sorts and Sundries), Chulkov joined the fray as the founder and editor of *I to i sio* (Both This and That) in 1769 and *Parnasskii shcheptil'nik* (The Trinket Dealer of Parnassus) in 1770. Moreover, Chulkov led the way in tapping the fertile reservoir of folk culture as a prominent source of inspiration for belles lettres. From his collections of songs and myths to his use of proverbs in his original compositions, he helped to break down the barriers between "high" and "low" culture.

Although Chulkov wrote during the era of Russian classicism and practiced most of its prescribed genres, he remained a loner throughout his literary career. Refusing to take sides in the major literary debates of his time or to align himself with a particular school, Chulkov most often struck an attitude of whimsical detachment. In almost everything he wrote, satire and parody became the lenses

56

through which he viewed his contemporaries. Sometimes, as in his journalism, this approach was simply an extension of the classicist penchant for various forms of satire. Given his interest in folk culture, however, it often was generated by a carnivalesque attitude toward life. Using the lusty, mocking sense of humor symbolized by the popular carnival, Chulkov frequently undercut the seriousness and didacticism that underpinned Russian classicism. In the eighteenth-century Russian carnival, life's everyday hierarchies and limits were overturned and abolished; the lowly folk became the masters as laws, rules, and inhibitions were temporarily suspended. Always more interested in literary targets than social ones, Chulkov focused the antiauthoritarian impulses of the popular subculture against the high-mindedness of his fellow writers to create a series of memorable parodies.

Even though Chulkov was well known to his contemporaries, little is known about his life, especially the early years. No biographer chose to write about him, and Chulkov was reticent about the subject. He was born around 1743, but his place of birth is not known. The earliest substantive biographical information about Chulkov dates from the mid to late 1750s, when he was a student at Moscow University. The university had two gymnasiums, one for nobles and one for *raznochintsy* (people of various ranks), a group that embraced all classes except for the highest (the nobility) and lowest (the peasantry). Chulkov studied at the gymnasium for *raznochintsy* roughly between 1756 and 1758. Given the social dynamics of the mid eighteenth century as well as the commercial motif that pervades most of Chulkov's work, he most likely came from a merchant family or the clergy. Whatever his origins, Chulkov did not complete his studies at the gymnasium and, with his nonnoble birth, found it difficult, at least for quite some time, to find his niche in life.

In 1761 Chulkov relocated from Moscow to Saint Petersburg to become active in the court theater, a move that may have been prompted by experience gained as a student at the gymnasium. The ardent classicist Mikhail Kheraskov had established a theatrical school at the newly founded university, and it appears that students from the gymnasiums took part in it. Whatever the motivation for Chulkov's move, evidence suggests that he served a humble apprenticeship before making his appearance on the stage. Piecing together information from several sources, including *I to i sio,* John Garrard concludes in his *Mixail Čulkov: An Introduction to His Prose and Verse* (1970) that Chulkov worked as a hairdresser for the troupe. After serving in this capacity for an unknown length of time, he apparently had the opportunity to perform onstage. From the scant evidence available, it seems as though Chulkov had roles in about half a dozen plays. These works include Sumarokov's *Pustynnik* (The Hermit; performed 1757; published 1769) and *Semira* (performed 1757; published 1768), Russian versions of Molière's *George Dandin* (1668) and *L'Amour médecin* (1665), and an unknown French play by Phillipe Destouches. In all cases Chulkov had supporting roles at best, which most likely explains the paucity of information about his acting career. Whatever his successes or disappointments, Chulkov received permission to leave the court theater in 1765 and abruptly closed that chapter of his life.

One positive outcome of Chulkov's shortlived theatrical experience was his play, *Kak khochesh' nazovi* (Call It What You Will), a one-act comedy that was performed frequently in the latter part of the eighteenth century but not actually published until 1933. The plot centers on the fate of the star-crossed lovers Polyeuctus and Euthymia and the bumbling of Euthymia's meddling parents. Both mother and father have chosen different suitors for their daughter and spend much of the play arguing over which young man will win Euthymia's hand. As frequently happens in French farce, a crafty servant, Kir'iak in this case, breaks the deadlock and facilitates the engagement of the true lovers. He manages this feat by encouraging the two other suitors to act like such idiots that the parents choose Polyeuctus by default, allowing everything to end happily.

Written in prose and divided into fourteen scenes, *Kak khochesh' nazovi* exhibits little if any real wit and not much action. Chulkov touches upon such stock themes of the Russian Enlightenment as the importance of reason and the customs of bygone days. The humor of the play resides in the oftenvulgar squabbles of the parents, and in Kir'iak's crude manipulation of the two suitors Euthymia has rejected. The only truly interesting moments of *Kak khochesh' nazovi* are provided by the first glimpse of what would become the trademark of Chulkov's career, namely a fondness for folklore, especially proverbs.

Chulkov's request to retire from the court theater was no doubt motivated by changes in his personal life. At about this time he married Anna Gavrilovna Batalina, and in 1766 their son, Vladimir, was born. One month after asking to terminate employment with the court theater, Chulkov was registered as a court lackey, drawing a salary of forty rubles per year. Garrard speculates that Chulkov's responsibilities to his family precipitated this move to a steadier, if less colorful, source of income. Whatever his reasons, Chulkov held this post for over a year until some time in 1766, when he was granted the position of court quartermaster. Just how long Chulkov served at court is not known. In 1766 he made his debut as an author with the publication of the first two parts of *Peresmeshnik, ili Slavenskie skazki* (The Mocker, or Slavic Tales, 1766–1768). Whether he continued to work outside the field of literature during the next five years is not known. It is certain, however, that between 1766 and 1770 Chulkov enjoyed a brief, yet prolific, career as author, journalist, and publisher, and it is not until the year 1772 that he can be identified with a position outside of belles lettres.

Together with the fifth part, which was not published until 1789, *Peresmeshnik* consists of a series of tales divided into one hundred nights. The stories are told by two narrators, a young man named Ladon and a renegade monk whose name is never revealed. Staying at the house of Alenona, a young girl who has just lost both her parents, Ladon and the monk offer to tell her stories as a way of relieving her grief. The conglomeration of tales they offer reveals a wide array of sources, both foreign (*Arabian Nights,* Greek adventure novels, the medieval chivalric romance, French heroic literature) and native (folklore and manuscript tales). Given the lack of an overriding narrational authority in *Peresmeshnik* and the eclectic nature of its tales, which range from the didactic to the risqué, Garrard likens the work to Geoffrey Chaucer's *Canterbury Tales* (circa 1375–1400) and Giovanni Boccaccio's *Decameron* (1351–1353).

Over the course of the five parts of *Peresmeshnik* Ladon dominates Alenona's attention. He narrates more than two-thirds of the work, whereas the monk, after establishing his identity in the frame story that opens the novel, does not get to tell his first tale until the middle of part two. Ladon's stories are written in a heroic vein. Set in Russia before the founding of Kiev, this part of *Peresmeshnik* takes as its point of origin the mythological Slavic kingdom of Vineta, allegedly located where Saint Petersburg would one day stand. The kingdom is ruled by Nravoblag ("Noble Manner"; Chulkov makes extensive use of high-minded "speaking names" in this section of *Peresmeshnik*), a truly progressive monarch who has not only fought against Greece and Rome and conquered many neighboring peoples, but who also makes the peace and prosperity of his subjects his prime concern. As the enlightened despot so sought after by eighteenth-century intellectuals, Nravoblag uses his strength and reason to secure the "abundance and tranquility of the state." This philosopher's dream is shattered, however, when Prince Siloslav ("Strong Slav") sets out on a quest to recover his beloved Prelepa ("Most Fair"), who has been abducted by evil spirits. There follows an extended narrative of Siloslav's adventures, which in turn, according to the rules of the genre, generates a series of equally heroic interpolated tales. Ladon's storytelling abounds with magic, monsters, and intrigue, with emphasis always focused on the role of love, especially the sorrowful plight of separated lovers. Chulkov adds a classicist touch to this mélange as his nobly born characters move through an idealized world full of classical statuary and the active intervention of gods and goddesses, both classical and Slavic.

When the renegade monk finally gets to take over the role of storyteller, *Peresmeshnik* begins to live up to its name. The most outstanding feature of this part of Chulkov's collection is the consistent application of irony in one form or another. Although it would be going too far to say that the monk's tales always function as well-focused parody, they do have the whimsical, antiofficial tone that characterizes the carnivalesque literary subculture. The tales told by the monk are much more down-to-earth than the high-minded adventures related by Ladon. His stories are set in contemporary Russia and revolve around characters of modest social background. Moreover, in this section of *Peresmeshnik* Chulkov uses humor to focus on the less-than-heroic side of human nature. The monk recites stories about the ignorance of the provincial clergy, the social-climbing machinations of a roguish student, and the benign intervention of playful devils in the affairs of humankind. Whereas Ladon's tales are a virtual primer of virtue and self-sacrifice, the characters in the monk's stories are almost always out for themselves, whether in pursuit of a fortune or the attentions of a beautiful woman. The monk's narrative manner frequently undermines the conventions of serious literature, from the concept of authorial omniscience to the moralistic digression.

Because of its dual nature, this early example of Russian prose fiction managed to make important contributions to two divergent literary trends. On the one hand, Chulkov's narrative enriched the artistic possibilities of Russian classicism. His implementation of a Slavic pantheon helped Russian literature break out of the narrow confines of an imported classical mythology. Basing some of his mythology on accepted Slavic deities and creating the rest, Chulkov offered a native alternative that Russian writers would utilize well into the nineteenth century. On the other hand, the ironic, roguish side of *Peresmeshnik* set the course for an even more independent direction for Russian literature, one that would often stand in opposition to the appropriated culture of classicism. Chulkov's frequent use of folklore and Russian manuscript tales canonized this material in the nascent prose culture of late-eighteenth-century Russia. Denounced as unworthy of serious consideration by Russia's literary elite, this fund of material played a central role not only in *Peresmeshnik* but in Chulkov's other literary endeavors as well. By charting his own course and, more specifically, playfully ridiculing the didactic commonplaces of official literature, Chulkov facilitated the establishment of a truly native aesthetic for Russian prose fiction.

Published just one year after the first two volumes of *Peresmeshnik,* Chulkov's *Kratkoi mifologicheskoi leksikon* (A Brief Mythological Lexicon, 1767) served as a commentary on his eclectic novel. Containing a dual mythology, both classical (Greek and Roman) and Slavic, this work gives readers the background of the deities that play so prominent a role in his first publication. While the intellectuals of the age, including Chulkov, often looked down on folk customs as a sign of ignorance and superstition, and even though it was common knowledge that the mythology in *Kratkoi mifologicheskoi leksikon* was partially fabricated, writers from Gavriil Derzhavin and Aleksandr Radishchev through Aleksandr Pushkin were inspired by its contents.

With a printing of six hundred copies, the sales history of *Kratkoi mifologicheskoi leksikon* points out the dilemma faced by eighteenth-century Russian writers in general and Chulkov in particular. Chulkov had agreed to pay the Academy of Sciences ninety-four rubles to cover the cost of printing the dictionary, but as of 1770, three years after its publication, he had failed to settle accounts. Chulkov's inability to pay this debt implies how difficult his financial circumstances really were, and the academy's threat to liquidate its losses by confiscating a presumably large number of still-unsold copies underscores just how small the reading public was in the early part of Catherine's reign. Caught between economic necessity and the meager commercial appeal of literature, it is no wonder that Chulkov would cut short his quest for fame and fortune as a man of letters after only four or five years.

Pokhozhdenie Akhillesovo pod imenem Pirry do Troianskoi osady (The Adventures of Achilles under the Name of Pyrrha before the Siege of Troy, 1769)

continues the type of heroic narrative represented by Ladon's stories in *Peresmeshnik.* This novel, which Chulkov lifted almost intact from Vasilii Trediakovsky's verse drama *Deidamiia* (1775), recounts an episode from Greek myth, the period of Achilles' youth when he was disguised as a girl to foil the prognostication of his death at the walls of Troy. Chulkov's treatment of this episode concentrates on the love triangle formed between Achilles, his true love Deidamiia, and the vengeful Navpliia, whom Achilles rejects. In telling this tale, Chulkov relies heavily on the conventions of heroic fiction: fate constantly intervenes in the young lovers' lives, often with unwanted results; the rhetoric is elevated and emotion filled; and the plot is advanced through such commonplaces of the genre as falsely interpreted letters, mysterious voices from above, prophetic dreams, and the slander of a scorned lover. Characters frequently express their deepest, most troubling thoughts via pathetic monologues and laments, and even Achilles is described as a sensitive hero who proves his purity of heart with ready tears, fainting, and passionate speeches.

Though published twice in the eighteenth century, *Pokhozhdenie Akhillesovo pod imenem Pirry do Troianskoi osady* has been virtually ignored by critics, most likely for two reasons. First, as Chulkov's least original work, it reveals little about his unique abilities and literary outlook. Second, with its emphasis on the sentimental-heroic tradition, it seems like a dead end, and a plagiarized one at that, in Chulkov's development as a writer.

Chulkov's experience as the driving force behind two literary journals, the weekly *I to i sio* from January to December 1769 and the monthly *Parnasskii shchepetil'nik* from May to December 1770, reveals both sides of his professional persona. On the one hand, Chulkov marched in perfect cadence with the spirit of the times, which in this instance was being led by Catherine the Great. In January 1769 Catherine initiated a series of satiric literary journals with *Vsiakaia vsiachina.* Before the month was out Chulkov began publishing *I to i sio,* thus making it the first such journal to come out after Catherine's effort. From the title on page 1 to the letters, essays, stories, and satires written by Chulkov (with sizable contributions by Sumarokov and Mikhail Popov), this eight-page weekly followed the lead set by Catherine to offer readers a wide array of informative and critical material. On the other hand, Chulkov loved to play the role of the mischievous rebel. Eschewing both the satire of universal vices (greed or ignorance, for example) favored by Catherine and the more pointed critique of social institutions exhibited in Nikolai Novikov's journals, Chulkov made good-natured mockery of his fellow writers the cornerstone of *I to i sio*. Moreover, Chulkov also broke from the classicist fold in his frequent use of folklore. In *I to i sio* he published an abridged version of his dictionary of Slavic mythology, and both his journals contain many sayings, riddles, prognostications, and proverbs culled from the world of the simple folk.

Chulkov opens *I to i sio* with the commercial motif that would preoccupy him throughout his literary career, if not his entire adult life. In week one he proclaims that "vsiakaia veshch' svoiu imeet tsenu" (everything has its price) and exhorts readers to buy his journal because "iz blagodarnosti shubu ne sosh'esh" (you can not sew a fur coat out of gratitude). For Chulkov, everything, even the inspiration of Parnassus, has its price. He openly attacked the system of literary patronage that encouraged writers to prostitute themselves, and in the burlesque poem "Stikhi na kacheli" he mockingly provides a price list for various genres, including the standard-bearer of Russian classicism, the ode. Moreover, in many instances the motif of money takes on a personal cast. Chulkov never made his literary career into a profitable undertaking, a fact that made him openly bitter. In *I to i sio* he laments that hairdressers and tailors earn more than writers and decries the fate that makes a scoundrel and thief happier, richer, and more satisfied than he is. In particular Chulkov kindled a special dislike for what he considered the self-aggrandizing approach to writing exhibited by his chief literary rival, Fedor Emin. Having published six novels between 1763 and 1766, Emin dominated the early years of modern Russian prose fiction. While Emin defended his novels on the altruistic grounds that the information they contained provided a service to society, Chulkov portrayed their author as a charlatan and liar. In a "Conversation of the Dead" in week 36 of *I to i sio* a character named Zloiazychnik (Evil Tongue) is forced to drink from the river of oblivion so that he will tell the truth about himself. Far from singing his praises, this character, who clearly represents Emin, openly admits that he has fabricated his biography and taken up the calling of novelist solely for the money.

Although the issue of money plays a prominent role in Chulkov's periodicals, the real core of these works consists of a particularly Chulkovian brand of lighthearted humor. In fact, the mockery of the prevailing literary aesthetic that informs *I to i sio,* especially its three burlesque poems — *Stikhi na kacheli* (Verses on a Ferris Wheel, 1775); *Stikhi na semik* (Verses on Semik, 1775), first published in the issue for week 22; and *Plachevnoe padenie stikhotvortsev* (The Poets' Sad Downfall, 1775), first published as a supplement to weeks 51–52 — was quite innovative and marked the emergence of parody as the dominant discourse in a major work of Russian literature. In week 28 Chulkov takes aim at the loftiest target of all by publishing a parody of the fictitious letters of praise that Catherine employed in *Vsiaknia vsiachina,* and in *Plachevnoe padenie stikhotvortsev* he portrays Emin as a warrior-poet who appears on Parnassus and wins for himself the unanimous censure of its inhabitants until Jupiter finally banishes him from the sacred mountain for good. The eminent poets of Russian classicism also come in for their fair share of criticism, especially in *Stikhi na kacheli.* Here the first-person poet-narrator tries his hand at various verse genres, only to fail and in the process poke fun at those who turn them out. After a mock invocation of the Muse, the poet proceeds to undermine the hyperbole and pomposity of the triumphant ode as practiced by Mikhail Lomonosov, the saccharine clichés of the love lyric, the self-assured didacticism of Vasilii Maikov's fables, and the fairy-tale world of the pastoral. In his final and perhaps most characteristic cut at the classicist aesthetic, Chulkov has his would-be poet succeed only when he decides to describe a most commonplace occurrence: a carnival. The description of the holiday revelry that forms the second part of *Stikhi na kacheli* represents the type of subject matter that authors such as Sumarokov would have found unworthy of a poet.

The depiction of a popular festival is just one example of an extensive use of folk culture that constituted Chulkov's boldest move in *I to i sio.* In several instances Chulkov broke new ground: the list of fifteen common Russian riddles that appears in *Parnasskii shchepetil'nik* is the first of its kind in Russian literature, and the seventy proverbs spread throughout *I to i sio* represent in both quantity and quality a striking literary innovation. By comparing the proverbs in *I to i sio* with later collections by such prominent classicists as Catherine the Great and Ippolit Bogdanovich, it is readily apparent that Chulkov left his examples in their natural, rough-hewn state. Given this quality, critics believe that Chulkov collected his proverbs directly from their source — the merchants, tradesmen, lackeys, and peasants who made up the lower ranks of society. No doubt the free-spirited, often coarse authenticity of the Russian proverb was just what Chulkov was looking for because it complemented his love of parody so well. As Garrard points out, proverbs such as "zerkalo ne vinovato, koli rozha kriva" (The mirror is not at fault if your mug is crooked) fit right into Chulkov's notion of burlesquing the inflated rhetoric of classicism with the directness and at times even vulgarity of a much more popular approach to literature.

In his second satiric journal, *Parnasskii shchepetil'nik,* Chulkov touched on many of the same topics that made up the core of *I to i sio.* For example, from May through July he offered a whimsically mocking auction of excess poets. Concluding that Parnassus has too many poets, Apollo commissions Chulkov to sell off the superfluous ones. Chulkov gladly assumes the role of auctioneer and in the playful spirit that marks his brand of humor even agrees to sell off his own work. Without directly alluding to any of his contemporaries, he auctions the excess poets by genre: a dull, pedestrian dramatic poet goes for one ruble, eight grivna, and a haughty, yet totally obscure, lyric poet who sells his serfs for pocket money is given away for free. Despite his return to the theme of unworthy poets, however, Chulkov has no illusions. In keeping with his oft-stated philosophy that literature can neither reform nor improve society, he knows that his parodies will not change the behavior of his fellow writers. For Chulkov, literature was not a tool for social engineering, but rather a means of providing entertainment, mostly via laughter. In both journals that is precisely what he emphasized.

Even when taken together, both of Chulkov's journals were rather short-lived. Like their editor, they were something of an anomaly for the time, and it is difficult to trace what effect they had on the contemporary literary scene. Yet it is precisely in their uniqueness that *I to i sio* and *Parnasskii shchepetil'nik* stand out. The list of firsts achieved by these two journals is indeed impressive. Chulkov's pioneering use of the commercial motif, first broached in *Peresmeshnik,* reaches fruition in *I to i sio.* He can also lay claim to being the first Russian writer to use parody in a substantial manner, and to his *Stikhi na kacheli* belongs the title of the first low burlesque in Russian literature. Moreover, as Aleksandr V. Zapadov writes, Chulkov's journals prove that he is one of Russia's first ethnographers. The use of sayings, riddles, and proverbs in *I to i sio* and *Parnasskii shchepetil'nik* is truly ahead of its time.

Chulkov's final original literary work, *Prigozhaia povarikha* is narrated in the first person by a young woman named Martona. Widowed at the age of nineteen when her soldier husband dies on the battlefield of Poltava, the protagonist must fend for herself. Without taking much time to mourn her husband or lament her fate, she allows herself to be recruited as a prostitute into a Kievan bordello. She revels in the attention and monetary benefits that come her way and even hires a servant. After this brief introduction, Martona's life becomes a whirlwind of comic reversals as the feisty heroine experiences the vagaries of fate. Martona leads the classic rogue's life, from swearing eternal allegiance to one lover and abandoning him when she meets another who is richer or more handsome to enjoying the blessings bestowed on her by a smiling Fate, only to be stripped of all worldly possessions as luck runs against her. Lying, stealing, and cajoling, she struggles against the representatives of wealth, authority, and propriety to find a secure niche for herself. Whether duping an eighty-year-old retired colonel or being cast out on the road by the irate wife of one of her lovers, Martona recounts her life story in a whimsical manner. No matter how dark a given episode might seem, she finds a way to overcome the barriers and prejudices of official society comically and by the end of the novel is rewarded with the inheritance of a landed estate.

As with *Peresmeshnik* and *I to i sio,* there are two sides to *Prigozhaia povarikha.* On the one hand, the use of a beleaguered first-person female narrator places Chulkov's novel firmly in the tradition of West European prose fiction established by writers such as Pierre Marivaux, Daniel Defoe, and Samuel Richardson. In fact, given Martona's status as a prostitute, *Prigozhaia povarikha* is often referred to as the Russian version of Defoe's *Moll Flanders* (1722). Moreover, Chulkov's strategic use of time and space, the broad manner in which he portrays the classes of society, and the complex, rounded nature of his heroine qualify as milestones in the tradition of Russian prose fiction that brought it closer to literary practice in the West. In *Prigozhaia povarikha* Chulkov takes great care to give a plausible motivation for his characters' actions, works subplots smoothly into the overall texture of the novel, and moves beyond the classicist penchant for ridiculing "vulgar reality." Through Martona's unflinching, straightforward recitation of events, Chulkov develops motifs and explores types of experience formerly deemed improper by the reigning literary aesthetic.

Despite the many ways in which *Prigozhaia povarikha* reflects the beginning of a sophisticated, or at least circumspect, tradition of prose fiction in Russia, Chulkov's real inspiration resides in his use of carnival subculture. From the plotline to the heroine to the novel's rhetoric, a carnivalesque sense of humor serves as the dynamic force behind *Prigozhaia povarikha.* Resembling the pauper crowned king at the carnival, Martona ascends the ranks of polite society until at the novel's end she has attained the lofty position of landowner. Usurping the roles of society lady, philosopher, and landowner, she tries on each given station in life as though it were a change of clothes, parades about in it until her interest wanes, and then discards it for another. In the language she uses, Martona betrays a carnivalesque disregard for morality, authority, and truth. Far from condemning her life, à la Moll Flanders, Martona sums up her philosophy with the saying "stoit tol'ko otdat' sebe porokam, to onye zavsegda budut kazat'sia priiatnee i milee dobrodeteli" (Just give yourself up to vice, and it will always seem more pleasant and nicer than virtue). For her the world is a wonderful pageant full of ups and downs that are to be enjoyed to the fullest. Whether it be an erotic or comically ambiguous proverb or the most unconventional of philosophical monologues, Martona's view of the world consistently inverts the hierarchy of values that forms the core of official society. By so smoothly and completely incorporating the carnivalesque subculture into *Prigozhaia povarikha,* Chulkov created a minor masterpiece of Russian prose fiction.

Comprising about eight hundred songs in its original version, Chulkov's *Sobranie raznykh pesen* (A Collection of Various Songs, 1770–1774) was expanded to include over twelve hundred entries in its third and largest edition (1780–1781). As an extension of the tradition of manuscript songbooks, Chulkov's anthology includes authentic folk songs as well as songs written by such well-known eighteenth-century literary figures as Popov, Lomonosov, and Sumarokov. In compiling this work, Chulkov apparently drew from manuscript collections gathered from various regions of the empire and may have located some of the ritual folk songs on his own. The folkloric material in the anthology includes historical songs, soldiers' songs, and songs on Russian customs, morals, and life. Irked by the unauthorized alterations made in one of his lyrics, Sumarokov castigated Chulkov in the introduction to his play *Dimitrii Samozvanets* (Dimitrii the Pretender, 1771) for tampering with his work without permission. While it does not seem that Chulkov intended to undermine the credibility of the literary entries in his anthology, at least one critic has noted that the clichéd poetic devices of such works are at a decided disadvantage when juxtaposed with the simplicity and raw energy of the authentic folk creations in the collection.

As the many editions (four in Chulkov's lifetime) of *Sobranie raznykh pesen* indicate, it was quite popular in its day. The first printed anthology of folk songs directed at a broad audience, it inspired a series of similar works by such well-known figures as Novikov, Popov, and Ivan Dmitriev. Moreover, the influence of this collection is evident in the attention it received from both admirers and detractors. Matvei Komarov incorporated songs from it into Russia's first best-selling novel, *Van'ka Kain* (1779), and in 1786 Archbishop Platon denounced the anthology for what he considered its tendency to delude and inflame the minds of readers. By the early nineteenth century *Sobranie raznykh pesen* had become part of the freewheeling *lubok* (chapbook) industry. In the commercialized world of *lubok,* where editions were mass-produced for barely literate readers, Chulkov's collection underwent many of the same changes of which Sumarokov had complained decades earlier. The title of the anthology was frequently altered, and the songs were often distorted to such a degree that they bore little resemblance to the works in the original collection. However, publishers' interest in making this work available to the common people testifies to the popularity of the songs it contained.

Discouraged by his inability to achieve financial security in the world of letters, Chulkov suspended his literary pursuits around 1770 and entered government service. In 1772 he is listed as working first in the Senate and then in the Department of Commerce at the fourteenth, or lowest, grade in the table of ranks. Despite starting at the bottom, he found government service a slow but steady way of attaining the wealth and status that had eluded him earlier. For the next twenty years, to the time of his death, Chulkov used two means to advance his personal and professional life: he wrote practical works (including a history of Russian commerce, dictionaries of jurisprudence and fairs, and an introduction to bookkeeping), and he successfully sought the aid of rich patrons. His *Slovar' russkikh sueverii* (Dictionary of Russian Superstitions, 1782), which returns to the subject of Slavic mythology but with greater emphasis on the ritualistic life of the folk, as well as his son's college education, were financed by the rich merchant Mikhail Golikov. An even greater honor was bestowed upon Chulkov when he received a gold snuffbox trimmed in diamonds from Catherine upon presenting her with a copy of his history of Russian commerce. If Chulkov noticed the irony in the situation, in light of his attack twenty years earlier on poets who received such gifts for the writing of odes and tragedies, he did not show it. Throughout the 1780s he had the support of a wealthy patron for each of his publications.

Chulkov explains his theory for success in "Nastavlenie maloletnomu synu moemu vstupaiushchemu v sluzhbu" (Instruction to My Young Son About to Enter the Service, 1785). In this didactic work Chulkov counsels his son to show respect for all who are highborn and to lead a life that is dedicated to God and country. Gone is the carnivalesque mocking of privilege and power, replaced by a thoroughgoing respect and appreciation for the hierarchies of officialdom. Apparently this formula worked for its author. In 1783 he had accumulated enough wealth to buy an estate called Kovkino in Moscow province, and by 1790 he had risen to the seventh rank in the civil service. Much like the characters in his literary works, but without the scheming, trickery, and lawlessness, Chulkov the *raznochinets,* who started out as a wig dresser, had risen to become an affluent member of society.

Three years before his death Chulkov returned to the calling of literature. In 1789 he published the third and final edition of *Peresmeshnik,* to which he had added a fifth part. In the new material Chulkov resolved plotlines begun in the first four parts and ended the work with three new stories: "Gor'kaia uchast" (A Bitter Lot), "Prianichnaia moneta" (Gingerbread Money), and "Dragotsennaia shchuka" (The Precious Pike). They mark a noticeable departure from the mockery and fantasy informing the rest of *Peresmeshnik.* Virtually devoid of humor and focusing on the grimmer aspects of late-eighteenth-century Russian society, these three stories take a serious, and at times cynical, look at such topics as greed, corruption, and the nearly subhuman living conditions of the peasantry. They would have fit nicely into one of Novikov's periodicals and may have been inspired or suggested by Chulkov's colleague Radishchev, who was known for his highly developed social consciousness. Author of the revolutionary *Puteshestvie iz Peterburga v Moskvu* (Journey from Petersburg to Moscow, 1790), Radishchev worked in the Department of Commerce starting in 1777 and seems to have collaborated with Chulkov on several official projects.

Chulkov's later approach to literature is best exemplified by "Gor'kaia uchast," the bleakest of the three stories concluding *Peresmeshnik.* In this tale Chulkov focuses on the misery and cruelty attending the typical peasant life of his central character, Sysoi Fofanov. The story begins with a brief description of the hardships of Fofanov's youth – his meager diet of bread and water; his barefoot, ragged existence; and his failure as a farmer despite all his efforts. Later in life Fofanov is exploited by the "cannibals" of the village, those rich enough to lend money to peasants, who then become virtual slaves. Falling into this predicament, Fofanov is sent off to the army to fulfill the village's recruiting allotment. Despite serving valorously, he returns home with little but the clothes on his back and minus his right arm, which was lost in combat. When he arrives at the family home on Christmas Day, he is met by a ghastly sight: his father has been hung from a crossbeam in the middle of the yard; his mother lies dead in the house, her head crushed by an ax; his four-year-old brother has been burned to death in the oven; and his infant sister has had her throat slashed. The story ends with three attempts to explain this horrendous scene, each one revealing a different yet equally depressing aspect of Russian society. The local peasants display their superstitious nature by claiming the *domovoi* (house spirit) wreaked this havoc; the authorities are so indifferent they only get around to their investigation six weeks later, well after all the victims have been buried; and the haughty "learned people" of the age come up with an explanation as implausible as it is condescending, without ever having actually visited the murder site. Ironically, eighteenth-century Russia's premier literary jester closed his career on the humorless, even accusatory, note sounded by "Gor'kaia uchast" and its two companion stories.

Chulkov's importance in Russian literary history lies precisely in his originality. While it can be said that he had no immediate successors, it would be false to say that he had no influence on the Russian literary tradition. Through his many innovations in Russian literature – the first low burlesque poem; the first mythological dictionary; the first memoir novel; and the first printed collection of folk songs designed for a broad audience – he opened up areas of literary explorations that had previously been closed or unexamined. In a general sense, Chulkov is also a major figure in the history of modern Russian literature for the way in which he combined an interest in parody and the carnivalesque subculture. The irreverent humor of Pushkin's "Ruslan and Liudmila" (1817–1820) and "Gavriiliada" (1821), the use of puppet theater and folklore in the works of Nikolai Gogol, and the young Fyodor Dostoyevsky's transformations of the journalistic clichés of the 1840s all reveal a parodic turn of mind based on raw materials supplied by a carnivalized subculture. To claim that Chulkov directly influenced these major nineteenth-century authors would be going too far. To say that he was one of the first Russian writers to explore this literary orientation, however, would be an accurate assessment of his career and would more than justify his place in the annals of Russian literature.

References:

John G. Garrard, *Mixail Čulkov: An Introduction to His Prose and Verse* (The Hague: Mouton, 1970);

Garrard, "Narrative Technique in Chulkov's *Prigozhaia povarikha*," *Slavic Review,* 27 (December 1968): 554–563;

Garrard, "The Portrayal of Reality in the Prose Fiction of M. D. Chulkov," *Slavonic and East European Review,* 48 (January 1970): 16–26;

David Gasperetti, "The Carnivalesque Spirit of the Eighteenth-Century Russian Novel," *Russian Review,* 52 (April 1993): 166–183;

J. D. Goodliffe, "Some Comments on Narrative Prose Fiction in Eighteenth-Century Russian Literature with Special Reference to Chulkov," *Melbourne Slavonic Studies,* no. 5–6 (1971): 124–136;

Alexander Levitsky, "Mikhail Chulkov's *The Comely Cook:* The Symmetry of a Hoax," *Russian Literature Triquarterly,* no. 21 (1988): 97–115;

E. Mechnikova, "Na zare russkogo romana," *Golos minuvshego* (June 1914): 5–40;

V. S. Nechaeva, "Russkii bytovoi roman XVIII veka. M. D. Chulkov," *Uchenye zapiski instituta iazyka i literatury, RANION,* 2 (1928): 5–41;

Felix J. Oinas, "The Transformation of Folklore into Literature," in *Literature,* volume 2 of *American Contributions to the Eighth International Congress of Slavists,* edited by Victor Terras (Columbus, Ohio: Slavica, 1978), pp. 570–604;

P. A. Orlov, "Real'no-bytovye romany M. D. Chulkova i ego satiriko-bytovye povesti," *Uchenye zapiski Riazanskogo pedagogicheskogo instituta,* no. 8 (1949): 60–97;

Il'ia Z. Serman, "Stanovlenie i razvitie romana v russkoi literature serediny XVIII veka," in *Iz istorii russkikh literaturnykh otnoshenii XVIII–XX vv,* edited by S. V. Kastorsky (Moscow & Leningrad: Akademiia nauk, institut russkoi literatury, 1959), pp. 82–95;

Viktor Shklovsky, *Chulkov i Levshin* (Leningrad: Izdatel'stvo pisatelei, 1933);

V. P. Stepanov, "Chulkov i 'fol'klornoe' napravlenie v literature," in *Russkaia literatura i fol'klor (XI–XVIII vv.),* edited by V. G. Bazanov (Leningrad: Nauka, 1970), pp. 226–247;

Jurij Striedter, *Der Schelmenroman in Russland* (Berlin: Otto Harrassowitz, 1961), pp. 58–120;

Irwin R. Titunik, "Mikhail Chulkov's 'Double-Talk' Narrative (Skazka o rozhdenii taftianoi mushki) (The Tale of the Origin of the Taffeta Beauty Patch)," *Canadian-American Slavic Studies,* 9 (Spring 1975): 30–42;

Aleksandr V. Zapadov, "Zhurnal M. D. Chulkova *I to i s'o* i ego literaturnoe okruzhenie," *XVIII vek,* 2 (1940): 95–141.

Ekaterina Romanovna Dashkova

(17 March 1743 – 4 January 1810)

A. Woronzoff-Dashkoff
Smith College

BOOKS: *Rech', govorennaia pri otkrytii Imp. Rossiiskoi akademii oktiabria 21 dnia 1783 goda predsedatelem sei Akademii kniagineiu Ekaterinoio Dashkovoiu, eia imp. velichestva stats-damoiu, Imp. Akademii nauk direktorom . . . Stokgol'mskoi Korolevskoi akademii nauk i Sanktpeterburgskago Vol'nago ekonomicheskogo obshchestva chlenom* (Saint Petersburg: Akademii nauk, 1783);

Toisiôkov, Komediia v piati deistviiakh (Saint Petersburg: Akademiia Nauk, 1786);

Zapiski pokazyvaiushchii sravnitel'noe sostoianie Akademii v posledstvie desiatiletnee ([Saint Petersburg: Akademiia Nauk, 1793]);

Memoirs of the Princess Daschkaw, 2 volumes, translated and edited by Martha Wilmot Bradford (London: H. Colburn, 1840); translated by Blagosvetlov as *Zapiski kniagini E. R. Dashkovoi* (London: Trübner, 1859); translated by G. E. Blagosvetlov as *Vospominaniia kniagini E. R. Dashkovoi* (Leipzig: E. L. Kasprovich, 1876); another version published as "Bumagi kniagini E. R. Dashkovoi (urozhdennoi Vorontsovoi)," in *Arkhiv kniazia Vorontsova,* volume 21 edited by Petr Bartenev (Moscow: Got'e, 1881), pp. 1–365; translated by Kyril Fitzlyon as *The Memoirs of Princess Dashkov* (London: Calder, 1958).

Edition: *Literaturnye sochineniia,* edited by G. N. Moiseeva (Moscow: Pravda, 1990).

SELECTED PERIODICAL PUBLICATIONS – UNCOLLECTED: "Nadpis' k portretu Ekateriny II," *Sobesednik liubitelei rossiiskogo slova,* 1, no. 1 (1783): 14;

"O smysle slova 'vospitanie,'" *Sobesednik liubitelei rossiiskogo slova,* 1, no. 2 (1783): 12–28.

Ekaterina Romanovna Dashkova; engraving after a portrait by D. Levitsky

Writer, autobiographer, journalist, and public figure, Princess Ekaterina Romanovna Dashkova was one of the first women in Europe to hold governmental office. In 1783 she was appointed director of the Saint Petersburg Academy of Sciences and founded and became president of the Russian Academy. Because of her education, travel abroad, and writings she became a leading figure in the introduction of eighteenth-century Russian culture to the West, while passing on aspects of the French Enlightenment to Russia.

An eminent woman of letters in eighteenth-century Russia, Dashkova was exceptional, mostly because the choices available to her were more representative of a man's life. She was born Ekaterina Romanovna Vorontsova in Saint Petersburg into wealth and privilege – the Empress Elizabeth was her godmother, and Peter III, whom she subsequently helped dethrone, was her godfather. Brought up in the home of her uncle the chancellor M. I. Vorontsov, she received an excellent education: she learned French, Russian, German, and Italian (English was acquired later); read Voltaire, Charles Montesquieu, Pierre Bayle, Nicholas Boileau, and Claude Helvétius; and in 1758 met the future empress, Catherine the Great. Dashkova's awakening to freedom and to the potential for change was inspired and sanctioned by Catherine, in whom Dashkova thought she had discovered an ideal, a female model for self-creation and individual achievement with whom she could work and cooperate in the public arena. Her youthful enthusiasm for the grand duchess was given voice in the short, panegyric poem "Nadpis' k portretu Ekateriny II" (Inscription to a Portrait of Catherine II, 1783), published in the first issue of Dashkova's journal *Sobesednik liubitelei rossiiskogo slova* (Interlocutor of Lovers of the Russian Word).

In 1759 she married Prince M. I. Dashkov, with whom she would have three children: Anastassiia (1760–1831), Mikhail (1761–1762), and Pavel (1763–1807). At nineteen she played an important role in the palace revolution of 28 June 1762 that brought Catherine to the throne. After a falling out with Catherine, in part caused by Dashkova's disapproval of the monarch's policies and personal life, the subsequent peaks and valleys of Dashkova's life describe a pattern of exile and return. The years 1765–1767, following the death of her husband in 1764, were spent primarily in Moscow and on her estate, Troitskoe. Later she chose to live abroad (1770–1771, 1775–1782) and traveled in Germany, France, England, Italy, Switzerland, and Holland. She became a prominent figure in the intellectual circles of eighteenth-century Europe, meeting and corresponding with Denis Diderot, Voltaire, Abbé Reynal, Benjamin Franklin, Adam Smith, and William Robertson, the Scottish historian and then principal of Edinburgh University. Thus, in letters to Robertson regarding her son's curriculum, Dashkova expressed her views on education. These were later published in her autobiography along with comments concerning the inadequacy of her own upbringing. Dashkova also elaborated her ideas in the article "O smysle slova 'vospitanie'" (On the Meaning of the Word "Education," 1783), which appeared in *Sobesednik,* and in a letter to C. Wilmot published in 1806 in *Drug prosveshcheniia* (Friend of Enlightenment).

Indeed, Dashkova considered education and the dissemination of enlightened ideas to be her lifework, and she is associated with several leading institutes of higher learning. In 1771 she was one of the organizers of the Vol'noe Rossiiskoe sobranie (Free Russian Society), under whose auspices she published several articles, including "Obshchestvo dolzhno delat' blagopoluchie svoikh chlenov" (Society is Responsible for the Well-being of its Members, 1774). Upon Dashkova's return from Europe in 1783, Catherine appointed her head of the Academy of Sciences. Dashkova was keenly aware of her exceptional position and of the fact that she was a woman temporarily in a position of power. She was also a member of the Saint Petersburg Economic Society, as well as the Royal Irish, Berlin, and Stockholm Academies. On Franklin's nomination she became the first woman member of the Philadelphia (now American) Philosophical Society. Although publicly she claimed that "God himself, by creating me a woman, had exempted me from accepting the employment of a Director of the Academy of Sciences," she headed it successfully for eleven years. At the academy she demonstrated great administrative and organizational skills, participating fully in its scholarly, pedagogical, and publishing activities. She oversaw research projects, instituted courses and public lectures, and initiated the publication of Mikhail Lomonosov's complete works. Moreover, it was upon her recommendation that the Russian Academy was founded. Based on the French model, its mandate included "the celebration of the Russian language," along with the normalization of grammar, syntax, and pronunciation. During her tenure as president, the Russian Academy's greatest achievement was perhaps the six-volume *Slovar' Akademii Rossiiskoi* (Russian Academy Dictionary, 1789–1794). An accomplishment praised by Nikolai Karamzin and Aleksandr Pushkin, it was composed under Dashkova's supervision. She also contributed definitions, especially for words dealing with morality, politics, and government.

Her own writings appeared in various journals, often under the pseudonym "Rossiianka," and since she published anonymously, many still lack positive attribution. They include translations of Helvétius, David Hume, and Voltaire, as well as articles on education, agriculture, travel, memory, and the pernicious influence of French. She also wrote aphorisms, verse, travelogues, and plays. Some have ascribed *Narodnoe igrishche* (Country Celebration, 1774) to her, while her *Svad'ba Fabiana, ili Alchnost' k bogatstvu nakazana* (Fabian's Wedding, or the Desire for Riches Punished, 1799) has not survived. The satiric five-act comedy *Toisiôkov* was published in 1786 and collected in *Rossiiskii featr* (Russian Theater), a series edited and compiled by Dashkova from 1786 to 1794. The play pits the indecisive and Oblomov-like landowner Toisiokov against his aunt, the purposeful and resolute Reshimova. Dashkova's other writings include occasional papers, speeches, and an extensive epistolary output.

Dashkova was also one of the first women in Russia to become extensively involved in journalism. She assisted in the publication of *Nevinnoe uprazhnenie* (Innocent Exercise, 1763) and as head of the two academies founded the scholarly journals *Sobesednik,* published from 1783 to 1784, and *Novye ezhemesiachnye sochineniia* (New Monthly Compositions), published from 1786 to 1796. Actively participating in the work of these journals, she was able to attract and encourage some leading literary figures such as Gavriil Derzhavin, Denis Fonvizin, Iakov Kniazhnin, and Vasilii Kapnist. In fact, Dashkova arranged to have Derzhavin's groundbreaking "Ode to Felitsa" published anonymously and without the poet's knowledge in the first issue of *Sobesednik.* Fortunately, Catherine was delighted with the poem, and Derzhavin's future was assured.

Two events led to Dashkova's resignation from the academy. The first was the "retirement" of her lifelong friend and favorite brother, A. R. Vorontsov, which came at least partially in response to the arrest of his protégé, Aleksandr Radishchev, for the publication of his *Puteshestvie iz S. Peterburga v Mosku* (Journey from St. Petersburg to Moscow, 1790). The second was the posthumous publication in 1793 of Iakov Kniazhnin's tragedy *Vadim Novgorodskii* at the academy's expense. The play's republican sentiments infuriated Catherine, since its appearance coincided with the executions of Louis XVI and Marie Antoinette. Dashkova bore the full brunt of Catherine's anger. Hurt by this reprimand, she requested and was granted a two-year leave of absence. Two years later Catherine was dead, and Paul I exiled Dashkova to the north of Russia for her participation in the overthrow of his father, Peter III.

Later, when Dashkova was once again invited to head the Russian Academy, she refused. Rather, she chose to affirm her own, individual voice by returning to the public arena through the agency of her autobiography – "Mon histoire," written 1804–1805 in French and first published in English as *Memoirs of the Princess Dashkaw* (1840), and later in Russian as *Zapiski kniagini E. R. Dashkovoi* (1859). When Dashkova returned from exile in the north, she was visited by two Anglo-Irish sisters, Catherine and Martha Wilmot. Fascinated by stories and anecdotes of life in the court of Catherine II, Martha persuaded a seemingly reluctant Dashkova to record her experiences in autobiographical form. As Dashkova wrote, Martha copied the manu-

Dashkova in exile; engraving by A. Varren

script and Catherine undertook an English translation. In 1807 Catherine left for home, taking with her one copy of the *Memoirs.* Afterward, when Martha was also planning to depart, hostilities broke out between Russia and England, and the authorities were informed that she was carrying important secret documents. In point of fact, Martha had the original copy of the *Memoirs,* Dashkova's correspondence with Catherine II, and some other papers. Arrested and interrogated for five days, Martha became frightened and burned the manuscript. With the original destroyed, only two copies of the *Memoirs* remained: Catherine's copy in England and another in Russia among Dashkova's papers and documents. Dashkova's copy was a draft version that in all likelihood was not meant for publication, and it did not contain some of the later additions and notes. After her death the draft copy existed only in manuscript versions in Russia and was well known by Pushkin.

Meanwhile the highly altered version of the English copy of the *Memoirs* possessed by Martha Wilmot (now Mrs. Martha Bradford) was published in 1840. It served as the basis for a Russian-language edition (1859) and for succeeding translations back into French (1859, 1966), German (1857, 1918), and Czech (1911). Excerpts also appeared in various Russian journals such as *Moskvitianin* (The Muscovite) in 1842, *Sovremennik* (Contemporary) in 1845, *Otechestvennye zapiski* (Notes of the Fatherland) in 1859, and *Russkaia starina* (Russian Antiquity) in 1873–1874. The original was donated to the British Museum Library. Dashkova's original French copy appeared in print only in 1881 when Petr Bartenev published it in volume twenty-one of the *Arkhiv kniazia Vorontsova,* and several Russian translations were based on this version. To date, the fullest, most complete rendering of the *Memoirs* remains Kyril Fitzlyon's 1958 English-language translation from the British Museum copy.

Mon histoire is Dashkova's best-known work. Completed five years before her death at the age of sixty-two, it presents an older woman's final assessment of her career and family life, while focusing on the revolution of 1762, her travels, and her work as head of the academies. Most studies have considered the biographical and historical components of the *Memoirs* rather than questions of narrative design or the author's individual, subjective vision. More recently there has been a growing interest in the questions of gender, mask, and self-definition in this autobiographical work. Dashkova inscribed her life as a series of disguises based on sexual differentiation – from the daring and adventurous to the ordinary and expected, from dreams of escape and deliverance to the reality of alienation and exile. Her tragedy, as expressed in the *Memoirs,* was that she could not realize her dreams and desires within the accepted norms of eighteenth-century female behavior. But just as the donning of an officer's uniform empowered Dashkova and lent authority to her actions during the coup d'état of 1762, so too her *Memoirs* were an assertive step back into the public arena – a type of rhetorical cross-dressing. As a result, the work isolates, clarifies, and establishes patterns of relationship and identity for its author as well as for other women.

Although publicly successful and at the center of Russia's political, cultural, and literary life during the second half of the eighteenth century, Dashkova's private life was deeply tragic. She sought the friendship and companionship of other women but was bitterly disappointed, especially by Catherine II. Widowed early, she outlived her son

and disowned her daughter. Dashkova's last years were spent alone, as she tended to the affairs of her estate far from family and friends. She died in Moscow on 4 January 1810 and was buried in Troitskoe. Her funeral was attended by only a few people.

Bibliographies:

Ekaterina Romanova Dashkova (1743–1810): Katalog knizhnoi vystavki (Saint Petersburg: Biblioteka Rossiiskoi Akademii Nauk, 1993);

E. S. Alexandrova, "E. R. Dashkova v 'Russkom arkhive': Bibliografiia," in *Mezhdunarodnaia konferentsiia Vorontsovy – Dva veka v istorii Rossii: K 250-letiiu E. R. Dashkovoi* (Saint Petersburg: Rossiiskaia Akademiia nauk and Biblioteka Rossiiskoi Akademii nauk, 1993), pp. 37–50.

Biographies:

E. Taigny, *Catherine II et la princesse Daschkoff* (Paris: Paetz, 1860);

D. I. Ilovaisky, *E. R. Dashkova* (Moscow: Vasil'ev, 1884);

A. A. Suvorin, *Kniaginia E. R. Dashkova,* volume 1 (Saint Petersburg: A. S. Suvorin, 1888);

V. V. Ogarkov, *E. R. Daskova: Ee zhizn' i obshchestvennaia deiatel'nost'* (Saint Petersburg: Shtein, 1893);

H. Montgomery Hyde, *The Empress Catherine and Princess Dashkov* (London: Chapman & Hall, 1935);

Gunther Schlegelberger, *Die Fürstin Daschkowa: Eine biographische Studie zur Geschichte Katarinas II* (Berlin: Junter & Dünnhaupt, 1935);

L. Ia. Lozinskaia, *Vo glave dvukh akademii* (Moscow: Nauka, 1978).

References:

A. G. Cross, *"By the Banks of the Thames": Russians in Eighteenth-Century Britain* (Newtonville, Mass., 1980);

Eufrosina Dvoichenko-Markoff, "Benjamin Franklin, the American Philosophical Society and the Russian Academy of Sciences," *Proceedings of the American Philosophical Society,* 3 (August 1947): 250–257;

Barbara Heldt, *Terrible Perfection: Women and Russian Literature* (Bloomington: Indiana University Press, 1987);

A. I. Herzen, "Kniaginia Ekaterina Romanovna Dashkova," in his *Polnoe sobranie sochinenii,* volume 12 (Moscow: Akademia nauk, 1957), pp. 361–422;

V. V. Kolominov and M. Sh. Fainshtein, *Khram muz slovesnykh: Iz istorii Rossiiskoi Akademii* (Leningrad: Nauka, 1986);

O. Kornilovich-Zubasheva, "Kniaginia E. R. Dashkova za cheteniem Kastera," *Sbornik statei po istorii posviashchennykh S. F. Platonovu* (1922; Würzburg: Jal, 1978), pp. 355–370;

R. A. Longmire, "Princess Dashkova and the Intellectual Life of Eighteenth Century Russia," M.A. thesis, University of London, 1955;

Luc Mailloux, "La princesse Daschkoff et la France," *Revue d'historie diplomatique,* 1 (1981): 5–25;

E. L. Rudnitskaia, ed., *Spravochnyi tom k zapiskam E. R. Dashkovoi, Ekateriny i I. V. Lopukhina* (Moscow: Nauka, 1992);

M. F. Shugarov, "Miss Vil'mot i kniaginia Dashkova," *Russkii arkhiv,* 3, no. 1 (1880): 150–217;

G. A. Tishkin, "E. R. Dashkova i uchebnaia deiatel'nost' v Petersburgskoi Akademii Nauk," in *Ocherki po istorii Leningradskogo universiteta* (Leningrad: Leningradskii universitet, 1989);

Martha and Catherine Wilmot, *The Russian Journals of Martha and Catherine Wilmot, 1803–1808,* edited by the Marchioness of Londonderry and H. Montgomery Hyde (London: Macmillan, 1934);

A. Woronzoff-Dashkoff, "Additions and Notes in Princess Dashkova's *Mon histoire*," *Study Group on Eighteenth-Century Russia Newsletter,* 19 (September 1991): 15–21;

Woronzoff-Dashkoff, "Disguise and Gender in Princess Dashkova's Memoirs," *Canadian Slavonic Papers,* 32 (March 1991): 61–74.

Gavriil Romanovich Derzhavin
(3 July 1743 – 9 July 1816)

Alexander Levitsky
Brown University

BOOKS: *Izobrazhenie Felitsy* ([Saint Petersburg], n.d.);

Oda k premudroi kirgizkaisatskoi tsarevne Felitse, pisannaia nekotorym tatarskim Murzoiu (Saint Petersburg, n.d.);

Oda na panikhidu v Katolitskoi tserkve, byvshuiu v Sanktpeterburge, po pokoinnom korole frantsuzskom Liudovike XVI marta 16 dnia 1793 goda, soprovozhdennuiu muzykoiu g. Sartiia (N.p., n.d.);

Rech govorennaia, 1786 goda v den' vysokotorzhestvennago korovaniia na vserossiiskii prestol, velikiia gosudaryni Ekateriny Alekseevny II, to est', 22 chisla sentiabria; pri otkrytii v namestnicheskom gorode Tambove glavnago narodnago uchilishcha v sobranii vsego pritom byvshago znamenitago obshchestva, Poseiannom Petrom Zakhar'inym (N.p., n.d.);

Oda na vseradostnoe brakosochetanie ikh imperatorskogo vysochestva. Sochinennaia potomkom Atilly, zhitelem reki Ra (Saint Petersburg: [Akademiia nauk], 1773);

Ody perevedennyia i sochinennyia pri gore Chitalagae 1774 goda ([Saint Petersburg: Akademiia nauk, 1776]);

Pis'mo eia imp. velichestvu, v kotorom prinositsia blagodarnost' ot poluchivshago eia milosti kolezhskago sovetnika Derzhavina ([Saint Petersburg: Akademiia nauk, 1777]);

Prolog na otkrytie v Tambove teatra i narodnago uchilishcha. Predstavlen v den' tezoimenitstva eia imp. velichestva noiabria 24 dnia 1786 goda (Saint Petersburg: [Akademiia nauk], 1787);

Rech, govorennaia v 22 den' sentiabria 1786 goda pri otkrytii v Tambove glavnago narodnago uchilishcha Kozlovskoi okrugi sela Nikol'skago chto na Surene, odnodvortsem Petrom Mikhailovym synom Zakhar'inym i v tom zhe godu perevedena v Sanktpeterburge na raznye inostrannye iazyki (Tambov: Vol'naia tipografiia, 1788);

Torzhestvo vosshestviia na prestol e. i. v. Ekateriny Vtoryia, otpravlennoe v Tambove 1786 goda, iiunia 28 dnia (Tambov: Vol'naia tipografiia, 1788);

Gavriil Romanovich Derzhavin

Osen' v sele Zubrilovke 1788 v noiabre ([Tambov: Vol'naia tipografiia, 1788]);

Oda na vysochaishee v S. Peterburg pribytie k torzhestvu o mire s korolem Shvedskim imperatritsy Ekateriny II 1790 goda avgusta 15 dnia ([Saint Petersburg: Akademiia nauk, 1790]);

Pesn' domu liubiashchemu nauki i khudozhestva v novyi god (Saint Petersburg: [Akademiia nauk, 1791]);

Pesn' liricheskaia Rossu po vziatii Izmaila ([Saint Petersburg: Akademiia nauk, 1791)];

Khory (N.p., [1791]);

Pamiatnik geroiiu. 28 iiunia 1791 ([Saint Petersburg, 1791]; republished, with French and German prose translations ([Riga], 1791);

K Kalliope v 31 den' oktiabria 1792 goda (Saint Petersburg: I. K. Shnor, 1792);

Oda Bog ([Moscow: Okorokov, circa 1792]);

Opisanie prazdnestva, byvshago po sluchaiu vziatiia Izmaila, u ego svetlosti gospodina general-fel'dmarshala i velikogo kniazia Grigoriia Aleksandrovicha Potemkina-Tavricheskogo, v prisutstvii eia imp. velichestva i ikh imp. vysochestv, v Peterburge, v dome ego bliz' Konnoi gvardii, 1791 goda aprelia 28 dnia (Saint Petersburg: I. K. Shnor, 1792);

Prazdnik vospitanits Obshchestva blagorodnykh devits, Bessmertie dushi i Molitva (Saint Petersburg: Gos. meditsinskaia kollegiia, 1792);

Videnie Murzy. Der Traum des Mursa (Saint Petersburg: I. K. Shnor, 1793) – includes parallel German translation by August von Kotzebue;

Pesn' e. i. v. Ekaterine II, na pobedy grafa Suvorova Rymnikskago 1794 goda (Saint Petersburg: Korpus chuzhestrannykh edinovertsev, 1794);

Oda na rozhdenie e. i. v. velikago kniazia Mikhaila Pavlovicha, 1798 goda genvaria 28 dnia (Saint Petersburg: Imperatorskaia tipografiia, 1798);

Sochineniia (Moscow: Ridiger i Klaudii, 1798);

Oda na pobedy frantsuzov v Italii, fel'dmarshalom grafom Suvorovym Rymnikskim 1799 godu ([Saint Petersburg: Imperatorskaia tipografiia, 1799]);

Perekhod v Shveitsarii chrez Al'piiskie gory, rossiiskikh imperatorskikh voisk, pod predvoditel'stvom generalissima; 1799 godu (Saint Petersburg: Imperatorskaia tipografiia, 1800);

Stikhi Elene Aleksandrovne Naryshkinoi ([Saint Petersburg, 1800]);

Anakreonticheskiia pesni (Saint Petersburg, 1804);

Sochineniia, 4 volumes (Saint Petersburg: I. K. Shnor, 1808; enlarged edition, 5 volumes, Saint Petersburg: Plavil'shchikov, 1808–1816);

Irod i Mariamna: Tragediia v piati deistviiakh (Saint Petersburg, 1809).

Editions: *Lira Derzhavina ili izbrannye ego stikhotvoreniia* (Moscow, 1817);

Sochineniia, 4 volumes (Saint Petersburg: A. S. Smirdin, 1831);

Ob"isneniia na sochineniia Derzhavina, im samim diktovannye rodnoi ego plemiannitse E. N. L'vovoi v 1809 godu . . ., 4 volumes (Saint Petersburg: F. N. L'vov, 1834);

Sochineniia, 4 volumes (Saint Petersburg, 1843);

Sochineniia (Saint Petersburg: D. P. Shtukin, 1845);

Sochineniia, 2 volumes (Saint Petersburg: A. Smirdin, 1847);

Temnyi. Tragediia v piati deistviiakh (Saint Petersburg, 1852);

Zapiski (1743–1812), edited by P. I. Bartenev (Moscow: Russkaia beseda, 1860);

Sochineniia, 9 volumes, edited by Iakov K. Grot (Saint Petersburg: Akademiia nauk, 1864–1883; 7 volumes, Saint Petersburg, 1868–1878);

Izbrannye sochineniia, edited by L. Polivanov (Moscow, 1884; revised edition, Moscow: G. O. Nemirovsky, 1894);

Sochineniia, 4 volumes, edited by Grot (Saint Petersburg: N. O. Mertts, 1895);

Stikhotvoreniia, edited by R. V. Ivanov-Razumnik (Saint Petersburg, 1911);

Stikhotvoreniia, edited by G. A. Gukovsky, Biblioteka poeta, bol'shaia seriia (Leningrad: Izdate'stvo pisatelei v Leningrade, 1933);

Stikhotvoreniia, edited by Gukovsky, Biblioteka poeta, malaia seriia (Moscow: Sovetskii pisatel', 1935);

Stikhotvoreniia, edited by D. D. Blagoi, Biblioteka poeta, bol'shaia seriia (Leningrad: Sovetskii pisatel', 1957);

Stikhotvoreniia, edited by A. Ia. Kucherov (Moscow: Khudozhestvennaia literatura, 1958);

Stikhotvoreniia, edited by V. P. Druzin, Biblioteka poeta, malaia seriia (Moscow & Leningrad: Sovetskii pisatel', 1963);

Almazna sypletsia gora (Moscow: Sovetskaia Rossiia, 1972);

Anakreonticheskiia pesni, edited by G. P. Makogonenko, G. N. Ionin, and E. N. Petrova, Literaturnye pamiatniki (Moscow: Nauka, 1986);

Sochineniia, edited by V. P. Stepanov and Makogonenko (Leningrad: Khudozhestvennaia literatura, 1987).

Gavriil Romanovich Derzhavin was probably the greatest Russian poet of the eighteenth century. His poetic achievement was seen by contemporaries as the crowning jewel of an entire epoch, one that stretched from the reforms of Peter I to the Napoleonic era. Translations of his work into many languages ensured him an international recognition never before achieved by a Russian poet. Just before his death, Derzhavin sat in on the final exam of a rising young star, Aleksandr Pushkin, barely in his teens at the time. Upon hearing Pushkin's verses dedicated to the lycée at Tsarskoe Selo, from which he was graduating, the old bard, overcome by emotion, is reported to have shed tears of approval. This incident is usually treated in the history of Russian literature as a sign of the transition between two literary epochs in Russia – between the eighteenth century and the so-called golden age of Rus-

*Drawing and manuscript text by A. N. Olenin (1795) for Derzhavin's
1782 ode "Felitsa" (Pushkin House Museum)*

sian literature. While problems of periodization in literary history are rarely resolved to everyone's satisfaction, there is ample justification to refer to an Age of Derzhavin.

According to Derzhavin's autobiographical *Zapiski* (1743–1812) (Notes [1743–1812], 1860), as an infant Derzhavin saw a comet flashing across the night sky during the winter of 1744, raised his index finger to the sky, and uttered his first word: "Bog" (God). The anecdote clearly implies a connection between the incident and one of Derzhavin's most famous poems, the ode "Bog." Throughout his career, odes were to be Derzhavin's principal mode of poetic expression. Odes served him for purposes of career advancement; they established his fame as a poet; toward the end of his life they served him as a testing ground to prove himself as a literary theoretician; and, perhaps most important, they provided him with a means of expressing his deepest spiritual and intellectual concerns. Paradoxically, Derzhavin's work may be seen both as a culmination of Russian classicism, for which the ode was the central genre, as well as pointing the way toward Romanticism by breaking down generic distinctions so central to classicism. His poetry is notoriously hard to classify and has been labeled at various times as baroque, classicist, pre-Romantic, sentimentalist, and Romantic – indicative perhaps of the fact that great poetry transcends simple labels.

Derzhavin's first nineteen years of life, before his move to Saint Petersburg, were unremarkable. He was born in Kazan' on 3 July 1743 to noble but impoverished parents; his father made a career in the army but retired when Derzhavin was eleven. Derzhavin's education, received at home and later in the local gymnasium, was at best rudimentary and became the source of his continual failings to master the nuances of Russian grammar, a weakness he was able to turn into a stylistic strength in his verse. His early studies in Kazan' and Orenburg did, however, provide him with knowledge of religious literature (the Psalter in particular), German, and draftsmanship.

In 1762 Derzhavin traveled to Saint Petersburg, where he was enrolled in the Preobrazhensky Guard Regiment. Shortly afterward, dressed in the uniform of this regiment and riding a white horse, Catherine II assumed the Russian throne in a palace coup. This event left a permanent impression on Derzhavin; in his fertile imagination he deemed himself an active participant in the rise to power of this attractive monarch. Derzhavin's adult life and most productive years as a poet were closely connected to Catherine, soon to be called the Great, and it was with her that Derzhavin's own greatness became associated. However, it took almost two decades for his career, both in the service and as a poet, to begin its rise. His promotions in the army did not come about nearly as rapidly as he wished, and, despite the fact that he was of gentry background, he had to begin his service as any peasant soldier would — as an enlisted man. To alleviate his boredom, he occasionally courted women, drank, and played cards. He also began to read a great deal and compose simple poetry and soldier songs, many of which became popular among his friends. In order to help himself financially, Derzhavin took to composing letters on behalf of other men less skilled at writing. He became so adroit at letter writing that one of his clients, P. V. Nekliudov, had a proposal for marriage accepted on the basis of love letters composed by Derzhavin.

In this way eleven years of military service passed, punctuated by frequent transfers between Moscow and Saint Petersburg. Although these were relatively uneventful years from the perspective of career making, they were not dull: Derzhavin was nearly killed by a wild boar, came close to being bankrupted by gambling debts, was once imprisoned on false charges, and narrowly escaped the plague of 1770. He had left Moscow for Saint Petersburg just at the time that the pestilence first broke out and was forcibly quarantined by the Saint Petersburg health authorities for two weeks. As part of their quarantine efforts, the authorities burned all of Derzhavin's possessions, including a trunk containing manuscripts of his poetry and literary essays. If for scholars this episode represents a great literary loss, for Derzhavin it was another obstacle to his ambitions, and one which left him destitute. Advancement in the ranks was his central concern at the time, and, as he bitterly laments in his *Zapiski,* another decade passed before he was promoted to ensign.

Derzhavin longed for a chance to prove himself. Finally, in 1773, an opportunity arose, when he enlisted in Gen. Aleksandr Bibikov's campaign to suppress the peasant rebellion led by Pugachev. For the first time in his life, Derzhavin was entrusted with what he described as interesting and important work, gathering intelligence under orders from the top command. He fulfilled his commissions with alacrity and was soon promoted to lieutenant. Having worked on several occasions with Bibikov, although in minor capacities, Derzhavin grew attached to the old man and, upon the general's death, composed an ode that was included in Derzhavin's first published collection of poetry, the *Ody perevedennyia i sochinennyia pri gore Chitalagae 1774 goda* (Odes Translated and Composed at the Chitalagai Mountain in 1774), published in 1776. The translated odes were by Frederick II and were probably influenced by Vasilii Maikov's earlier translation into Russian verse, published in 1767, and based in turn on a prose version by Bibikov.

Though still dependent on earlier Russian poetry, and often bombastic and extravagant in its imagery, the entire collection displays some of the features that mark Derzhavin's mature work. The first of these was his uncanny ability to assume a lyrical persona fully attuned to the highly placed addressees of his odes. Although in real life Derzhavin had not been much more than an orderly for Bibikov, in his ode to the general it appears as if he had been Bibikov's closest confidant and friend.

Derzhavin's need for associating his persona with that of the object of his veneration was so pronounced that it led the poet in other works of this first collection into some risky rhetorical positions. For example, in his ode "Na velikost'" (To Greatness) Derzhavin attempts to associate the image of the poet with the incarnation of Greatness (personified as a goddess standing amidst his verses) by having himself "vozlegshi na tvoikh persiakh" (rest on her breasts). While it is true that his readers only learned explicitly at the end of the poem that for the poet the epitome of Greatness was Catherine II, the allusion made the preceding image potentially awkward.

Another device that marks this early set of odes is evident in the collection's title. Nearness to a

A nineteenth-century engraving of Derzhavin's estate in Saint Petersburg

mountaintop, introduced into Russian odes as a strictly rhetorical figure by Mikhail Lomonosov, becomes for Derzhavin a concrete physical setting. His first set of odes was written at Chitalagai, and his last was to be composed, for the most part, literally on the slopes overlooking the river, at his summer residence, Zvanka, thus actualizing Lomonosov's hyperbolic trope.

Of course, Derzhavin had to attend to military matters, as well as poetry, at Chitalagai. After Bibikov's death Gen. Petr Panin assumed command. Derzhavin's devotion and loyalty to Catherine's cause were beyond reproach, but while he continued to serve with enthusiasm, he did not always completely obey his superiors' orders and took it upon himself to improve upon them as he saw fit, even if at times it meant going over their heads. Such was the case with a superior officer's failure, as he saw it, to fortify Saratov properly. Derzhavin dispatched a letter to the empress, pleading the need to remedy the situation; he did not mention his own failure to be present at Saratov – contrary to specific orders – during an attack by the rebels. Despite the fact that Derzhavin had legitimate reasons (at least from his point of view) for his act of insubordination, it so enraged Panin that he was ready to hang Pugachev and Derzhavin together and in fact began court-martial proceedings against Derzhavin. Only a note from Catherine, re-

sponding in part to Derzhavin's earlier letter, saved him from potentially severe punishment. Derzhavin did not learn until later of Catherine's intercession on his behalf. Recent research has shown some striking similarities between Derzhavin's involvement in the Pugachev campaign and the story of Grinev, protagonist of Pushkin's historical novel *Kapitanskaia dochka* (The Captain's Daughter, 1836), and it is possible that Derzhavin was a prototype for the character.

Another intercession of Catherine on behalf of Derzhavin occurred on 15 February 1777, when he was given a civil-service post as collegiate adviser in the state's highest administration body, the Senate, in addition to receiving a large tract of land in Belarus along with three hundred serfs. These were part of the widespread rewards meted out after Pugachev's final defeat, although for Derzhavin they were less than those for which he had hoped (and petitioned). Nevertheless, after years of bitter waiting, he could now begin to feel a part of the elite of the capital, especially after he gained the patronage of the influential Prince A. Viazemsky. In appreciation of Catherine's gift, Derzhavin wrote and published *Pis'mo eia imp. velichestvu, v kotorom prinositsia blagodarnost' ot poluchivshago eia milosti kolezhskago sovetnika Derzhavina* (A Letter to Her Imperial Majesty, in Which Gratitude is Offered from Collegiate Adviser Derzhavin, Who Received Her Beneficence, 1777), of dubious literary merit.

Now having sufficient means, Derzhavin turned his thoughts to matrimony and soon found himself a bride in Catherine Bastidon, daughter of a former associate of Peter II and Grand Duke Pavel Petrovich's nurse. Derzhavin, usually self-confident and able to write love letters on behalf of others, was so entranced by this young woman (only seventeen when they met) that he could not muster enough courage to ask her for a dance during a ball. He had to beg Petr Kirilov, an associate of his and a friend of the Bastidon family, to ask Catherine's hand on his behalf. Their marriage lasted sixteen years, until Catherine's death, and was apparently an extremely happy one.

Derzhavin left a touching cycle of love poetry devoted to his first wife, whom he affectionately addressed as "Plenira" (a name suggesting the Latin for "fullness" or "plenty"). Derzhavin's poems to Plenira constitute the first cycle of love lyrics from a husband to a wife ever written in Russia. Composed over several years, the cycle begins with a poem composed to celebrate their wedding, "Neveste" (To the Bride), later renamed "K Plenire" (To Plenira) by the author. The next poem in the cycle, "Prepiatstvie k svidaniiu s suprugoiu" (Obstacle to Meeting with My Spouse) – published as "Pesenka otsutsvuishchago muzha" (Song of an Absent Husband) – was written after the Kama River, which was blocked with accumulated ice, temporarily prevented Derzhavin from rejoining his wife. This incident, described in the poem, seems to have inspired Derzhavin with a vision of the river as an elemental force and perhaps served as a point of departure for the poet's rich reworkings of traditional images of water in such mature poems as "Kliuch" (Spring) and "Vodopad" (The Waterfall), as well as in his last poem, composed shortly before his death, "Reka vremen v svoem stremlenii . . . " (The River of Time in Its Ceaseless Course). The image of a river also takes on special importance in the last poem Derzhavin devoted to his wife, "Prizyvanie i iavlenie Pleniry" (Summons and Appearance of Plenira), supposedly written a day after her death in 1794. The poem describes how Plenira's spirit appeared to Derzhavin in the form of a white fog, flowing like a river from the open doors of a cupboard.

In the late 1770s Derzhavin continued polishing his poetic voice in such pioneering works as "Stikhi na rozhdenie v Severe porfirorodnago otroka . . . " (Verses on the Birth in the North of a Porphyrogennete Child [Alexander I], 1779), one of the first powerful depictions of the Russian winter, and "Oda. Prelozhenie 81-go psalma" (Ode. Trans-

position of Psalm 82), subsequently known as "Vlastiteliam i sudiiam" (To Rulers and Judges), which was suppressed and deleted from its proposed publication in the *Sanktpeterburgskii vestnik* (Saint Petersburg Herald) for November 1780 because of its allegedly antimonarchist sentiments; it was finally published seventeen years later.

At the end of the 1770s Derzhavin's poetry suddenly revealed a maturity and skill that greatly surpassed the quality of his previous work. Among his works of this period was "Kliuch," written shortly after the incident at the Kama River. "Kliuch" celebrates the publication of Mikhail Kheraskov's *Rossiiada* (1778), the first complete Russian epic poem, as a newfound source for inspiration. Derzhavin's poem is modeled on Horace's ode 13 from book 3. Instead of Horace's description of the sacrificial goat whose blood was to mix with the waters of the sacred spring of Bandusia, Derzhavin has the landscape around the spring at Kheraskov's estate express the sacrifice by manifesting various hues of red, images of which imbue the entire poem.

That Derzhavin was able to turn to Horace reflected new intellectual and literary influences in his life. Derzhavin's wife had introduced him into the house of the chief prosecutor of the Senate A. A. D'iakov, a superbly educated man and a patron of the arts. Connected with the house was a circle of Russian literati headed by Nikolai L'vov. The circle included some of the best talents in Russia, including Ivan Khemnitser, Vasilii Kapnist, and Mikhail Murav'ev; also closely associated with the circle were Iakov Kniazhnin and the actor Ivan Dmitrevsky. Kapnist and L'vov married two of D'iakov's daughters, who were close friends of Derzhavin's wife Catherine, and after her death Derzhavin took another of the five D'iakov daughters, Dar'ia, as his second wife.

In this circle of newly found friends Derzhavin's poetry began to mature. He found there not only admirers of his talent, but badly needed friendly critics, who, possessing a broad cultural framework that he lacked, were able to channel his poetic talent in directions he might not have discovered on his own. German was the only foreign language Derzhavin knew, and the group's members were able to introduce him to French, Latin, Greek, and English literatures. They did this by translating for Derzhavin both works of classical poetry unavailable in Russian (much of Horace, for example, was apparently translated for him personally by Kapnist) and works of more recent poets.

As a result of this productive interplay of ideas and persons, Derzhavin composed some of his best poetry. Thus, as an obvious response to Edward

Young's *Night Thoughts on Life, Death and Immortality* (1742–1745) – or rather to its translation by A. M. Kutuzov as *Plach, ili noshchnyia mysli o smerti i bezsmertii* (Weeping; or, Night Thoughts, 1777) – Derzhavin wrote his first universally recognized great ode "Na smert' kniazia Meshcherskogo" (On the Death of Prince Meshchersky), first published in 1779 in the paper *Sanktpeterburgskii vestnik*. As opposed to his early attempts at ode writing, this work was truly original, a marvelous transformation of some of the somber imagery found in Young's works. Its beginning is memorable for its powerful euphonic organization, the first so obviously rich since Lomonosov:

> Глагол времен! металла звон!
> Твой страшный глас меня смущает;
> Зовет меня, зовет твой стон,
> Зовет--и к гробу приближает.

> (Loud peal of time! cold metal's sound!
> Your dreadful chant is most disturbing;
> It calls, it calls me with its moan,
> It calls--and brings nearer the grave.)

As in the ode on Bibikov's death, Derzhavin depicted the death of a prince he hardly knew in personal terms. If the purpose of Young's image of death is to show the inescapable power of God, and, by means of rather simple syllogistic reasoning, to force mortals to accept God's domain after death, the power of Derzhavin's poem lies precisely in its depiction of the absurdity of any reasoning on this question. After a kaleidoscopic series of stark images of death, Derzhavin turns to Prince Meshchersky's corpse and comes to the most potent question of the poem:

> Здесь персть твоя, а духа нет.
> Где же он?--Он там.--Где там?--Не знаем.
> Мы только плачем и взываем:
> «О горе нам, рожденным в свет!»

> (Your dust is here, but not your spirit.
> Where then?--Out there.--Where's there?--Don't
>   know.
> We only weep and call in prayer:
> "Oh, woe to us in this world born!")

Derzhavin displays his thoughts "on life, death, and immortality," challenging those of Young by showing the uselessness of answering questions about the afterlife. This challenge becomes particularly incisive in the final stanza, in which the author invites the poem's addressee, Stepan Perfil'ev, a friend of Meshchersky, to accept the fact that "life is but a moment's gift of Heaven," and "not to torment yourself and grieve that your friend did not live forever," but rather to "say blessings on the blows of fate." Composed of eleven octaves, the ode to Prince Meshchersky recalls the octaves on the Book of Job transposed by Lomonosov almost three decades earlier. Derzhavin's ode "Bog" – composed a year later but not finished until 1784 – also recalls Lomonosov in its overall pathos.

Unlike all of the odes he had published since 1779, "Bog" was the first ode Derzhavin signed and published under his name. Contrary to popular opinion, he was not, properly speaking, original in the conception of this magnificent ode; rather, "Bog," like the ode on Prince Meshchersky's death, should be seen within the context of the genre which in Russia is most often known as the "sacred ode." In most of its manifestations this variant of the ode was similar, at least on the formal level, to panegyrical odes to earthly rulers, except for the fact that it was addressed to God and commonly employed biblical imagery, mostly from the Book of Psalms. The tradition of composing such odes had been inaugurated in Russia by the anonymous publication of Vasilii Trediakovsky, Aleksandr Sumarokov, and Lomonosov's *Tri Ody Parafrasticheskiia Psalma 143 sochinennyia chrez trekh Stikhotvortsov iz kotorykh kazhdoi odnu slozhil osoblivo* (Three Transposed Odes of Psalm 143 by Three Poets Each of Whom Composed a Separate One, 1743). Notably, Derzhavin's "Bog" alludes to Trediakovsky's psalm transposition, employing several of its rhymes and images. However, the greatest examples of sacred verse in eighteenth-century Russian poetry were by Lomonosov. His "Vechernee razmyshlenie o Bozhiem Velichestve pri sluchae velikago severnago siianiia" (Evening Meditation on the Majesty of God on the Occasion of the Great Northern Lights) inspired Sumarokov, Kheraskov, Ippolit Bogdanovich, Maikov, Murav'ev, Kapnist, and Kniazhnin to try their hands at this type of verse. Many of the images found in Lomonosov's "Vechernee razmyshlenie" and its companion "Utrenee razmyshlenie" (Morning Meditation) – such as "lampada" (icon lamp), "bezdna" (abyss), "mnozhestvo svetil" (multitude of luminaries), "luchi" (rays), and "peshchinka" (speck of sand) – became the basis for a shared pool of poetic figures in Russian sacred odes, and Derzhavin made productive use of them in "Bog."

But while he was not averse to borrowing images or even entire lines from other poets (most particularly from Kheraskov's ode of the same title), there is at least one thing that separates Derzhavin from all those who preceded him – his image of the poet. As opposed to Lomonosov, who underscored the distance between man (likened to a speck of dust) and the indescribable greatness of God, Derzhavin stressed the unity of the poet with the Creator:

Когда дерзну сравнить с Тобою,
Лишь будет точкою одною:
А я перед Тобой--ничто.

Ничто!--Но Ты во мне сияешь
Величеством Твоих доброт;
Во мне Себя изображаешь,
Как солнце в малой капле вод.

(When I dare compare [myriads of worlds] with You,
They comprise no more than a single dot:
And what then am I before You--nothing.

Nothing!--Yet You shine within me
By the majesty of your goodness;
In me You reflect Yourself,
Like the sun in a small drop of water.)

If Lomonosov's climb in his meditations from the familiar contours of an earthly landscape into the abyss of space betrays a linear perception of the universe in which man is alone and can only beg his silent Creator "to extend his rays of wisdom," Derzhavin offers a far more optimistic view. The poet's persona reflects not only his Creator's universe, but God himself. As opposed to Lomonosov, who sees man as a dwarf before God, obscured by darkness even in the face of a blazing sun, Derzhavin's analogy of man to a drop of water allows his persona not only to reflect the rays of a radiant sun, but to embrace God, thus overcoming Lomonosov's sense of emptiness.

By 1780 Derzhavin's poetry had come to be esteemed by connoisseurs of Russian poetry, and his name was recognized in the highest circles of Russian society. When Derzhavin's ode to Prince Meshchersky was published anonymously in 1779, the poet Ivan Dmitriev was so overwhelmed by it that he took it upon himself to search out its author; he subsequently became one of Derzhavin's most trusted friends. What finally assured Derzhavin's poetry a broad appreciation was Catherine the Great's recognition and patronage after the publication of Derzhavin's ode "Felitsa," which celebrated the virtues of the empress. Written in 1782 and published in the following year in the journal *Sobesednik liubitelei rossiiskogo slova* (Interlocutor of the Lovers of the Russian Word), "Felitsa" is one of Derzhavin's best-known and most anthologized poems. Its name was taken from an allegorical children's tale written

Title page for a collection of Derzhavin's poetry, with a portrait depicting him as the Russian Anacreon

by Catherine and published in 1781. The tale recounts how the young Prince Khlor, aided by an agent of Princess Felitsa (from the Latin, suggesting "felicity" or "good fortune"), ultimately succeeds in his quest for virtue, symbolized as a thornless rose, which he finds on a distant mountaintop. In Derzhavin's ode, virtue is unmistakably connected with Catherine. As opposed to the previous tradition of serious, lofty panegyrics, Derzhavin's ode was rendered in a delightfully light and humorous way whenever the focus of his attention shifted from the idealized, yet human, portrait of Catherine to her courtiers and to the poet himself, who is portrayed as replete with such forgivably human vices as excessive beer drinking, oversleeping, card playing, womanizing, and laziness. Although this portrait was in itself a profound departure from the previously abstract pose of the odic persona, lost in the heights of lyrical rapture, the great novelty of the ode also lay in the fact that it offered unambiguous satiric portraits of some of Catherine's main courtiers, depicted as embodiments of corruption, sloth, and ineptitude.

So well did Derzhavin hit the mark that many of the dignitaries lampooned in the ode spread rumors that the sole reason Derzhavin had written the poem was to improve his position in society. Derzhavin's ode was, in fact, quickly noted by Catherine II, who sent him a handsome gift of a diamond-encrusted box filled with gold, and his career subsequent to its writing was no less than meteoric, ending in senatorial and ministerial appointments. However, there is no need to contend, as have many scholars, that the author was disingenuous in writing the ode. Like the poems devoted to his wife, "Felitsa" belongs to a large group of texts, in this case devoted to the empress, beginning with his ode to Greatness (at Chitalagai mountain) and ending with a manuscript submitted as a gift to Catherine shortly before her death. Among the poems devoted to Catherine, many, such as "Blagodarnost' Felitse" (Gratitude to Felitsa) and "Videnie Murzy" (A Murza's Vision), were written precisely to deny the contention of the poet's ulterior motives in writing "Felitsa."

"Videnie Murzy," written shortly after "Felitsa" and published in *Moskovskii zhurnal* (Moscow Journal) in 1791, is perhaps Derzhavin's most inspired vision of Catherine. Imbued with elements of the fantastic, this ode offers one of the most eerie and memorable city nightscapes in Russian literature. Its first two verses, which depict a golden moon floating in a dark blue ether of the glittering Neva River and Baltic Sea, introduce the same liquid theme which unites the cycle of poems dedicated to Plenira. In this dreamlike setting, the poet describes his entire household, including his sleeping wife. He alone is awake, and he suddenly sees a vision of Catherine descending to him as a goddess from the heavens. Like the ghost of Plenira in Derzhavin's later "Prizyvanie i iavlenie Pleniry" (Summons and Appearance of Plenira), Catherine appears in a white fluid form, floating on a silvery wave, and speaks to the poet about his purpose in life. In the Plenira poem the ghost of his dead wife begs the poet not to grieve over her but to marry her best friend Dar'ia; Felitsa commands him to remain a true poet, since poetry is a gift of the gods. In these two works, Derzhavin's two Catherines, his wife and his empress, combine to present a single unified image of the feminine inspiration behind his poetry.

After "Felitsa" Derzhavin came into personal contact with the empress, although the more familiar he became with her and the more successful his career became, the less he wrote about her. Indeed, in the early 1790s, when Derzhavin was working as Catherine's private secretary, he produced no odes to her, despite her repeated requests. This might have been due not to his unwillingness to praise her, nor to a measure of disenchantment with her, as some scholars have suggested, but rather to the fact that Derzhavin took his official responsibilities seriously and did not let writing poetry interfere with them. Throughout his career as an administrator Derzhavin tried to introduce bureaucratic improvements whenever he could (and, it seems, whether or not reforms were necessary). His inordinate sense of justice, coupled with a hot temper — at times explosively manifested in matters in which he was clearly wrong — resulted in Derzhavin's inability to hold any government position for long. Thus each of the three major appointments he held between 1784 and 1789 — as state counselor in the Senate, governor of Olonets, and governor of Tambov — ended in his being relieved of his duties due to his inability to get along with others in authority. Catherine, who had taken it upon herself to protect the easily excitable poet whenever she could, recorded her meeting with him in 1789 after his most recent dispute: "I told him that a person of rank must respect the rank of another; since he was unable to get along already at his third post, he should seek the cause in himself. He became over-agitated even during my presence. Let him write poetry instead." Catherine then invited Derzhavin to become her personal secretary, although he did not last long in that position either.

Nevertheless, after the accession of Alexander I, Derzhavin's advancement continued — and with such rapidity that it seems as if the government was afraid that he would run into trouble if he held any one post for long. From 2 April to 25 November 1800 Derzhavin received no less than eight promotions to such different posts as member of the new Law Commission, president of the Commerce Department, minister of Finance, and member of the Supreme Council. However, he continued to be too much of a maverick to serve as a successful administrator, and, shortly after becoming minister of Justice (one of the highest posts in Russia), he was finally forced to retire in 1803. From that time on he devoted himself to family and to literature.

Despite his zealous and oft-rewarded efforts to succeed as a career civil servant, Derzhavin was not remembered as a particularly outstanding administrator, senator, or minister. Rather he made his mark in poetry, a realm in which even his manifest disadvantages, such as his poor education and unremarkable grammatical skills, often worked to his advantage. His strange spelling and substandard, colloquial Russian were often responsible for his creating fresh turns of phrase that gave power to clichéd expressions; his scant knowledge of foreign languages forced him to rely on translations, which, in turn, often resulted in interesting departures from the texts upon which his works were modeled. However, from the time of his association with the L'vov circle he came to understand that in literature a mere leap to the top did not suffice and that there was much more to the heritage of world poetry than he had imagined. He began to read Horace, Pindar, Ovid, Friedrich Klopstock, Young, and many others with serious interest.

Derzhavin understood that in order to transcend the ordinary he had to find a way to compete with the poetry of extraordinary authors. But ever since he began to model his poetry after that of Lomonosov, Derzhavin found himself unable to sustain Lomonosov's high-flown style or to hold to the linguistic rules governing the use of such style. Yet with time this inability resulted in a lucky find, as Derzhavin realized that the sense of Lomonosov's pathos could be just as compelling if set in contrast to bathetic, low-style elements. Derzhavin's ironic attitude with respect to the image of the poet's "I" was a major discovery and makes his poetry qualitatively different from that of Lomonosov. It did not prevent Derzhavin from describing lofty subjects, as the ode "Bog" demonstrates, and it allowed the organizing center of lyrical expression to attain a much more multifaceted and human dimension than did Lomonosov's more formal, rhetorical pose. Indeed it is through the "debased" image of the poet, who is not above using colloquial expressions and describing prosaic scenes of his domestic life (which in the ode to "Felitsa" include such mundane details as having his hair searched for lice by his wife), that Derzhavin chose to view the magnificence of the world.

This device of an earthy, yet often enchanted, observer of his surroundings allowed Derzhavin to introduce subjects heretofore unsung in Russian poetry, such as the feast in "Priglashenie k obedu" (Invitation to Dinner, 1795), which begins:

Шекснинска стрелядь золотая,
Каймак и борщ уже стоят;
В графинах вина, пунш, блистая
То льдом, то искрами манят . . .

(Gold sturgeon from Sheksna,
Kaimak and borshch already wait;
Wines and punch in carafes, shining

They allure with ice, and sparkle. . . .)

Whatever Derzhavin's aims might have been in a particular poem, he depicted the sound, the feel, the smell, and the color of everyday objects, presented through a prism uniquely his own and unmatched by any of his contemporaries. The objects of Derzhavin's mature poetic vision are as richly vibrant as the most accomplished still lifes by seventeenth-century Dutch painters: their specificity is attained not only by depictions of their visual, oral, and tactile texture, but their origin as well. Hence his fish was either from the river Sheksna or from Astrakhan, his beer Russian or English, his ham Westphalian, his seltzer water drunk from crystal glasses from Vienna, his coffee sipped from Chinese faience. Incidentally, in mentioning such items as "kaimak," "borshch," and "pirogi," Derzhavin introduced Russian cuisine into literature and implicitly gave it high cultural status.

Even when the subjects of Derzhavin's verse take on allegorical or emblematic weight – such as the bird in "Lastochka" (Swallow), which represents the soul of his departed wife, or the bird in "Solovei" (Nightingale), representing inspiration – they have concrete and developed lives of their own. These birds turn in flight, sing, and celebrate life. They teach the poet that despite the transitoriness of earthly things – a continual theme in Derzhavin's work – there is value in the specificity of the moment. Such is the case in Derzhavin's "Vodopad" (Waterfall, 1798):

Алмазна сыплется гора
С высот четырмя скалами,
Жемчугу бездна и сребра
Кипит внизу, бьет вверх бургами;
От брызгов синий холм стоит,
Далече рев в лесу гремит.

(A diamantine mountain rains
Down from the heights in four-tiered cliffs.
A chasm of pearls in an abyss of silver
Churns far below, fumes up in mounds.
The boiling forms a hill of blue,
The roar resounds in distant woods.)

Although later in the poem Derzhavin turns to such questions as "Does not this waterfall portray for us the course of man's existence?" and seeks the meaning of the lives of Grigorii Potemkin and Rumiantsev, the military heroes eulogized by the poem, the immediate sense of the grandeur of this particular waterfall resounds throughout the poem. Near the end of the poem, just before Derzhavin describes an even grander spectacle, the junction of the majestic Suna and Onega rivers, the poet turns again to the waterfall:

> Шуми, шуми, о водопад! . . .
> И в поздней памяти людей
> Живи лишь красотой твоей!

> (Roar on, roar on, O waterfall! . . .
> And in later memories of people
> Live on by your beauty alone!)

"Vodopad" illustrates Derzhavin's special way of joining the majesty of a momentary impression with the grandeur of timelessness it represents.

Similarly, Derzhavin's concept of his own immortality as a poet is not presented as some abstract idea but as something dependent on his ability to express the fabric of things he touched, the substance of people he knew, the nature of places he visited, and the feeling of time in which he lived. Nearly every poem he composed is stamped with his personality, and every object he describes is permeated with his keen sense of the physicality of being.

Communion with a poet's space-time can be achieved as long as his poetry is read — even whispered, as Derzhavin begs his close friend Metropolitan Evgenii Bolkhovitinov to do at the end of his Horatian epistle, "Evgeniiu. Zhizn' Zvanskaia" (To Evgenii. Life at Zvanka, 1807). This work is a unique celebration of life, depicting an ordinary day at Zvanka in all of its sensual fullness. The sounds of birds, horses, lambs, human songs, chatter, gossip, horns, harps, and other musical instruments, blend in with the aromas, smells, tastes, and resplendent patterns and colors of the poet's surroundings to re-create his experience of life, enjoyed amid cow barns, beehives, birdhouses, and ponds; amid the gold of butter, honeycombs, and leaves; amid the purple of berries and the velvet down of mushrooms. At midday meal he sees a flower garden of dishes, set out in patterns on the table and comprised of

> Багряна ветчина, зелены щи с желтком,
> Румяно-желт пирог, сыр белый, раки красны,
> Что смоль, янтарь--икра, и с голубым пером
>   Там щука пестрая: прекрасны!

> (Crimson ham, green sorrel soup with yolk of yellow,
> Rouge-golden pie, white cheese, red crayfish,
> Caviar, [black as] pitch or [golden like] amber--
>   and there is the blue fin

Derzhavin in later years; lithograph by I. Pozhalostin after an 1815 portrait by A. Vasil'evsky

Of a rainbow pike: beautiful!)

At the end of the poem Derzhavin, resting on a hill overlooking the Volkhov River, expresses doubts about the future of Zvanka. He prophetically predicts that it "will be torn down, its forest and garden will wither," so that only "fire-green eyes of owls will peer from the hollows" where it used to be. Yet he also understands that his and its immortality have already been achieved through his poetry.

Here, as in almost all of Derzhavin's verse, the image of the poet is at the center and clearly reflects the circumstances of Derzhavin's biography. Through the unifying, if polymorphous, nature of his lyric persona, with its autobiographical aspects, Derzhavin expanded traditional notions of genre and perhaps contributed to their destruction. Under the umbrella of Derzhavin's persona, for example, the ode could incorporate practically all other forms of lyric expression, including the elegy, songs, and even such "trifles" as album poetry. The use of such forms would have seemed inconceivable to Lomonosov the ode writer or to literary purists like Sumarokov, though it might have been understood to a degree by Trediakovsky, who once described the ode as a genre that subsumed all types of lyric poetry.

It is to Trediakovsky's wider understanding of the function of the ode that Derzhavin turned in his monumental treatise in its defense, "Razsuzhdenie o liricheskoi poezii ili ob ode" (A Discourse on Lyric Poetry, or On the Ode), written over the course of the last six years of his life with considerable help from his erudite friend Evgenii Bolkhovitinov and originally published in installments in the journal *Chtenie v Besede liubitelei russkago slova* (Readings in the Society of Lovers of the Russian Word). The discourse is mostly cited for Derzhavin's unambiguous stress on the faculty of "inspiration," which he sees as the source for all lyric poetry. This emphasis on inspiration has led several historians to view the poet as pre-Romantic or even Romantic. However, for Derzhavin the concept of inspiration was nearly equivalent to the concept of "celebration," either of God or of life in all its manifestations. It is primarily for this reason that Derzhavin equates the ode, which he saw as the highest form of celebration, with "lyricism" itself, the highest faculty of inspiration (hence their link in the title of the discourse). In this sense Derzhavin responded to specifically eighteenth-century Russian aspirations, rather than to those of Romanticism.

Derzhavin's need to imbue lyric poetry with a greater range of emotional tonality than offered by the traditional Russian ode led the poet, perhaps perplexed by the nature of his own innovations, to drop the designation of ode from much of the poetry he wrote during his later years. This, together with Derzhavin's general lack of interest in the Russian classicist system of genres, has led some scholars to see him as making a revolutionary break with the petrified norms of classicism, and alternately to cast him as an exponent of neobaroque or pre-Romantic trends. To be sure, Derzhavin's poetry provides rich material for such approaches, since it offers an inimitable arabesque of stylistically opposed levels. Whether he appeared in the guise of the Russian Pindar, Horace, or Anacreon, the three leading classical models for the ode, Derzhavin often ignored the formal and thematic limitations imposed on the genre by Russian tradition. At the same time, he seemed to fulfill the prescription for the ode advocated by Nicholas Boileau in his *L'art poétique* (1674), the principal text on which Russian classicism was built. Paraphrasing Boileau, it could be said that in Derzhavin's hands the ode at last became "vigorous, in its ambitious flight to heaven"; was finally able to hold "poetical converse with God"; frequently "hymned dusty conquerors at the end of their course"; and led Russian "bloodstained heroes to the banks of rivers." Just as Boileau had ordered, "the impetuous style" of Derzhavin's odes "moved at random" and "a fine disorder in them was an effect of [his] art." In this important sense, Derzhavin's career is the fulfillment of the ideals with which Russian classicism came into being.

On the other hand, Russian Romanticism learned important lessons from Derzhavin's literary practice, in particular his emphasis on the "image of the poet" and the attendant breakdown of the classical notion of genre. In this sense Derzhavin's poetry was a crucial precedent for such works as Pushkin's novel in verse *Evgenii Onegin* (Eugene Onegin, 1833), which is unified by a complex image of the poet-author. Certainly Derzhavin was alert to the literary ferment surrounding him. For example, he shared the young generation's enthusiasm for the poetry of Ossian — James Macpherson's famous literary hoax. Yet for all his eclecticism and breaking down of generic boundaries Derzhavin never embraced the kind of Romanticism that saw the world as disjointed, to be written about in fragments. Derzhavin's world was preeminently one of bright colors, rather than the dark gloom and melancholy characteristic of early Russian Romantics. Indeed, as Vladimir A. Zapadov has noted, Derzhavin's "Evgeniiu. Zhizn' zvanskaia" was clearly written as a rejection of the Romanticism espoused in V. A. Zhukovsky's "Vecher" (Evening, 1807). Moreover, the political leanings of the younger generation (often under the influence of ideas from revolutionary France) were quite different than those of the elder Derzhavin. Gone were the days when young Russians could be thrilled by the prospect of a career in state service. Far more significantly, when they spoke of inspiration, it rarely derived from their immediate or social surroundings, as it often did in Derzhavin's case. Rather they turned to nature, unspoiled by civilization, or to far-off places, such as Finland, the South Seas, the Caucasus, or the Orient, to seek inspiration and the thrill of the exotic — something Derzhavin found in ordinary Russian life.

For all his fame and admirers, Derzhavin did not establish a school of poetry, nor did he seek to do so. On the contrary, in 1807 he opened his residence on the Fontanka River in Saint Petersburg to Russian literati of various persuasions for literary gatherings and continued to do so on an ad hoc basis until his death. Derzhavin was eclectic in his approach to the literary factions of his day. While his house became the gathering place for Shishkov's Beseda group, an organization of conservative Russian writers who opposed Karamzin's linguistic and literary reforms, Derzhavin and his house remained just as open and receptive to Karamzin and some of his followers.

Derzhavin died, childless, on 9 July 1816. Contemplating Russia's advances in his anthology of Russian poetry of 1821, John Bowring wrote that in Russia "the foundation is now laid, on which the proud edifice of civilization will be raised," and continued, "but of all the poets of Russia, Derzhavin is in my opinion entitled to the very first place. His compositions breathe a high and sublime spirit; they are full of inspiration. His versification is sonorous, original, characteristic; his subjects generally such as allowed him to give full scope to his ardent imagination and lofty conceptions."

Biographies:

Evgenii Bolkhovitinov, "Novyi Opyt istoricheskago slovaria o Rossiiskikh pisateliakh," *Drug Prosveshcheniia,* 1 (March 1806): 274–288;

Vladimir A. Zapadov, *G. R. Derzhavin: Biografiia* (Moscow & Leningrad: Prosveshchenie, 1965);

Jesse V. Clardy, *G. R. Derzhavin: A Political Biography* (The Hague & Paris: Mouton, 1967);

Il'ia Z. Serman, *Derzhavin* (Leningrad: Prosveshchenie, 1967);

Pierre R. Hart, *G. R. Derzhavin: A Poet's Progress* (Columbus, Ohio: Slavica, 1978).

References:

Sergei T. Aksakov, "Znakomstvo s Derzhavinym," in his *Sobranie sochinenii,* volume 2 (Moscow: Khudozhestvennaia literatura, 1955), pp. 314–336;

Mark G. Al'tshuller (Altshuller), "Literaturnoteoreticheskie vzgliady Derzhavina i 'Beseda Liubitelei russkogo slova,'" *XVIII vek,* 8 (1969): 103–113;

Claude Backvis, "Dans quelle mesure Derzhavin est-il un Baroque?," *Studies in Russian and Polish Literature,* edited by Z. Folejewski and others (The Hague: Mouton, 1962), pp. 72–104;

Pavel N. Berkov, "Derzhavin i Karamzin v istorii russkoi literatury kontsa XVIII-nachala XIX veka," *XVIII vek,* 8 (1969): 5–18;

B. B. Blagoi, "Gavrila Romanovich Derzhavin," in G. R. Derzhavin's *Stikhotvoreniia,* edited by Blagoi, Biblioteka poeta, bol'shaia seriia (Leningrad: Sovetskii pisatel', 1957), pp. 5–74;

John Bowring, *Specimens of the Russian Poets. With Preliminary Remarks and Biographical Notices,* second

Derzhavin's grave, in Novgorod

enlarged edition (London: 1821), pp. xii–xiii, 3–44;

William E. Brown, "Gavriil Romanovich Derzhavin" in his *A History of 18th Century Russian Literature* (Ann Arbor, Mich.: Ardis, 1980), pp. 381–415;

I. I. Dmitriev, "Vzgliad na moiu zhizn'," in his *Sochineniia,* volume 2, edited by A. A. Floridov (Saint Petersburg, 1893);

Natalia I. Glinka, *Derzhavin v Peterburge* (Leningrad: Lenizdat, 1985);

Iakov K. Grot, "Primechaniia i prilozheniia k 'Zhizni Derzhavina,'" in Derzhavin's *Sochineniia,* volume 9, edited by Grot (Saint Petersburg: Akademia nauk, 1883);

Grot, "Zhizn' Derzhavina," in Derzhavin's *Sochineniia,* volume 8, edited by Grot (Saint Petersburg: Akademia nauk, 1880);

G. A. Gukovsky, "G. R. Derzhavin," in G. R. Derzhavin, *Stikhotvoreniia*, edited by Gukovsky, Biblioteka poeta, malaia seriia (Moscow, 1947);

Gukovsky, "Literaturnoe nasledstvo Derzhavina," in *Literaturnoe nasledstvo*, 9–10 (1933): 369–396;

Gukovsky, "Pervye gody poezii Derzhavina," in his *Russkaia poeziia XVIII veka* (Leningrad: Akademia, 1927), pp. 183–201;

Jane G. Harris, "The Creative Imagination in Evolution: A Stylistic Analysis of G. R. Derzhavin's Panegyric and Meditative Odes (1774–94)," Ph.D. dissertation, Columbia University, 1969;

Henry R. Hedrick, "The Poetry of Derzhavin," Ph.D. dissertation, Princeton University, 1966;

Vladimir F. Khodasevich, *Derzhavin* (Paris: Sovremennye Zapiski, 1931);

L. I. Kulakova, "O spornykh voprosakh v estetike Derzhavina," *XVIII vek*, 8 (1969): 25–40;

H. Kulle, *Farbe, Light und Klang in der Malenden Poesie Derzhavins* (Munich: Fink, 1966);

Alexander A. Levitsky, "The Sacred Ode in Eighteenth Century Russian Literary Culture," Ph.D. dissertation, University of Michigan, 1977;

Evgenii A. Maimin, "Derzhavinskie traditsii i filosofskaia poeziia 20–30kh godov XIX veka," *XVIII vek*, 8 (1969): 127–143;

Leslie O'Bell, "The Spirit of Derzhavin's Anacreontic Verse," *Die Welt Der Slaven: Halbjahres-schrift für Slavistik*, 29, no. 1 (1984): 62–87;

I. I. Podol'skaia, " 'Prekhodiashchee' i 'vechnoe' v poezii Derzhavina," *Izvestiia AN SSSR: Seriia literatury i iazyka*, 41 (July–August, 1982): 359–368;

N. B. Rusanova, "Epitety Derzhavina," *XVIII vek*, 8 (1969): 92–102;

E. A. Salias, *G. R. Derzhavin: Pravitel' Tambovskago Namestnichestva* (Tambov: Gubernskoe Namestnichestvo, 1871);

Harold B. Segel, "Gavrila R. Derzhavin" in his *The Literature of Eighteenth-Century Russia*, volume 2 (New York: Dutton, 1967), pp. 254–317;

Helena Smorczewska, H. "Motyw nocy w tworczosci Gawryly Dierzawina," *Slavia Orientalis*, 35, no. 3 (1988): 359–374;

Arnold R. Springer, "The Public Career and Political Views of G. R. Derzhavin," Ph.D. dissertation University of California, Los Angeles, 1971;

W. Waldenberg, *Derzhavin: Opyt kharakteristiki ego mirosozertsania* (Petrograd: Smirnov, 1916);

Thomas J. Watts, "G. R. Derzhavin's Path to the Pre-Romantic Lyric," Ph.D. dissertation, New York University, 1976;

Richard Wortman, "Gavrila Romanovich Derzhavin and his Zapiski," in Derzhavin's *Zapiski 1743–1812* (Cambridge: Oriental Research Partners, 1973), pp. 1–8;

Vladimir A. Zapadov, "Derzhavin i russkaia rifma XVIII v.," *XVIII vek*, 8 (1969): 54–91;

Zapadov, "Rabota G. R. Derzhavina nad 'Rassuzhdeniem o liricheskoi poezii,' " *XVIII vek*, 15 (1986): 229–283; 16 (1989): 289–319.

Papers:

Gavriil Romanovich Derzhavin's literary archive is divided between the State Public Library in Saint Petersburg (fond no. 247); the Institute of Russian Literature (Pushkin House) in Saint Petersburg (fond nos. 88 and 96); and the Central State Archive of Literature and Art in Moscow (fond no. 180).

Ivan Ivanovich Dmitriev

(10 September 1760 – 3 October 1837)

Natal'ia Dmitrievna Kochetkova
Institute of Russian Literature (Pushkin House), Saint Petersburg

BOOKS: *Na razbitie Kostiushki: Glas patriota* (Saint Petersburg, 1794);

I moi bezdelki (Moscow: Kh. Ridiger i Kh. Klaudi, 1795);

Stikhi e.i.v. Pavlu Pervomu pri vosshestvii na vserossiiskii prestol (Moscow: Kh. Ridiger i Kh. Klaudi, 1796);

Basni i skazki (Saint Petersburg: Gos. meditsinskaia kollegiia, 1798); revised as *Basni,* volume 1 (Saint Petersburg: Shnor, 1810);

Stikhi na sluchai sviashchennogo koronovaniia e.i.v. velichestva imperatora Aleksandra Pervogo (Moscow, 1801);

Sochineniia i perevody, 3 volumes (Moscow: Platon Beketov, 1803–1805; revised and enlarged edition, Moscow: Universitetskaia tipografiia, 1818); revised and abridged as *Stikhotvoreniia,* 2 volumes (Saint Petersburg: N. Grech, 1823);

Puteshestvie NN v Parizh i London, pisannoe za tri dnia do puteshestviia (Moscow: P. P. Beketova, 1808);

Apologi v chetverostishiakh (Moscow: Avgust Semen, 1826);

Jermak, czyli Zawojowana Syberya (Saint Petersburg: Karol Kray, 1830).

Editions: *Vzgliad na moiu zhizn': Zapiski Ivana Ivanovicha Dmitrieva,* 3 volumes (Moscow: V. Got'e, 1866);

Sochineniia, 2 volumes, edited by A. A. Floridov (Saint Petersburg: Ia. Sokolov, 1895);

Izbrannye stikhotvoreniia, by Dmitriev and N. M. Karamzin, edited by A. Ia. Kucherova, Biblioteka poeta, bol'shaia seriia (Leningrad: Sovetskii pisatel', 1953);

Polnoe sobranie stikhotvorenii, edited by Georgii P. Makogonenko, Biblioteka poeta, bol'shaia seriia (Leningrad: Sovetskii pisatel', 1967).

OTHER: Louis Sébastien Mercier (Mers'e), *Filosof zhivushchii u khlebnogo rynku,* translated by Dmitriev (Saint Petersburg: Vil'kovsky & Galchenkov, 1786);

Ivan Ivanovich Dmitriev

D. I. Fonvizin, *Zhizn' grafa Nikity Ivanovicha Panina,* translated by Dmitriev (Saint Petersburg: Vil'kovsky & Galchenkov, 1786);

Karmannyi pesennik ili Sobranie luchshikh svetskikh i prostonarodnikh pesen, 3 volumes, edited by Dmitriev (Moscow: Ponomarev, 1796).

Ivan Ivanovich Dmitriev was a literary ally and close friend of Nikolai Karamzin. According to his contemporaries, Dmitriev's contributions to Russian poetry mirrored Karamzin's in prose. Unlike Karamzin, however, Dmitriev never became a professional man of letters but instead devoted much of his life to a service career, eventually attaining high government positions. Dmitriev's work, like Karamzin's, primarily developed in a sentimentalist direction. Yet in many respects Dmitriev's position was contradictory: he adhered to many of the tenets of classicism while still brilliantly mocking the epigones of the movement. Dmitriev's innovation was primarily in the development of a revived system of poetic genres. Like Gavriil Derzhavin he transformed the Russian ode. He also helped to bring together different genres and cultivated poetic trifles — minor poetic forms such as madrigals and epigrams. His poetry enjoyed broad popularity toward the end of the eighteenth and beginning of the nineteenth centuries; it was committed to memory and, according to the fashion of the literary salons, recopied into albums. As Dmitriev recalls in his memoir *Vzgliad na moiu zhizn'* (A Look at My Life, 1866), "Hardly any of my contemporaries survived the writer's calling with less effort and greater success."

Dmitriev was born 10 September 1760 in the village of Bogorodskoe, not far from the city of Syzran in the province of Simbirsk. He was a descendant of an ancient line of Smolensk princes. His father, Ivan Gavrilovich Dmitriev, was a wealthy, educated landowner; he had a sizable library and a special interest in the theater. In the evenings the family members read aloud to each other, in particular from the works of Mikhail Lomonosov. Dmitriev's mother, Ekaterina Afanas'evna (née Beketova) was personally acquainted with Aleksandr Sumarokov and liked to recite his poetry. Dmitriev himself was an ardent reader from early childhood. From the ages of seven to ten he studied at private schools in Kazan and Simbirsk; thereafter he continued his education on his own. Having whetted his literary appetite on translated foreign novels, Dmitriev learned French in order to read them in the original. In 1774 Dmitriev moved to Saint Petersburg and entered into military service in the Semenovsk Regiment. As was the practice of the time, he had been enlisted while still a child. In the regimental school he studied mathematics, sketching, religion, and geography. During a trip to Moscow with his regiment in January 1775, Dmitriev witnessed the execution of Emel'ian Pugachev, the infamous leader of the peasant rebellion. He later described the event in great detail in his memoirs. Back in Saint Petersburg, and still in the service, Dmitriev went often to the theater, and he read voraciously; he also befriended Mikhail Murav'ev and several other young writers.

Starting in 1777, "between drills and guard duty" (in his words), Dmitriev began to write poetry, most of it satiric, the greater part of which he subsequently burned. He ran across a solicitation in Nikolai Novikov's weekly *Sankt-Peterburgskie uchenye vedomosti* (Saint Petersburg Scholarly News) for inscriptions for portraits of several famous Russians, and he composed the "Nadpis' k[niaziu] Antiokhu Dmitrievichu Kantemiru" (Inscription to P[rince] Antiokh Dmitrievich Kantemir). This modest piece, which appeared in Novikov's journal in 1777, was Dmitriev's first published work. In 1782 he submitted several poems anonymously to Petr Alekseevich Plavil'shchikov's journal, *Utra* (Mornings). Shortly thereafter, however, while at the theater, he overheard someone express an annihilatingly bad opinion of his poetry, and he subsequently took a more critical attitude toward his work and was in less of a hurry to publish. Dmitriev also decided to increase his knowledge of literary history and theory and studied the works of such Russian and French authors as Lomonosov, Charles Batteux, and Jean-François Marmontel.

In 1783 Dmitriev met Karamzin in Saint Petersburg; their families in Simbirsk knew each other and were even distantly related. The two writers became practically inseparable, sharing their ideas about literature and their various efforts at translation. After Karamzin left for Moscow they began a written correspondence. Their friendship, beneficial for both parties, lasted until Karamzin's death in 1826. Though he was Karamzin's senior in age (by six years) and in rank, Dmitriev unreservedly admitted his insignificance in comparison to his talented friend. He often revised his poetry according to Karamzin's suggestions. Derzhavin, whose works Dmitriev was already reading in the 1770s, also asserted a strong influence. Beginning in 1792 Dmitriev frequently visited Derzhavin's home, where he met several other writers, including Ippolit Bogdanovich, Vasilii Kapnist, and Nikolai Aleksandrovich L'vov. It was here as well that Dmitriev also met Denis Fonvizin on the eve of the playwright's death, a meeting which he described in detail in his memoirs.

In 1786 in the journal *Zerkalo sveta* (Mirror of the World) Dmitriev published two unsigned prose translations from French: Louis Sébastien Mercier's *Le Philosophe du Port Bled* — in Russian, *Filosof zhivushchii u khlebnogo rynku* (The Philosopher of the Bread Market) — and Fonvizin's *Zhizn' grafa Nikity Ivanovicha Panina* (Life of Count Nikita Ivanovich Panin), originally published anonymously in French as *Précis historique de la vie du comte Nikita Iwanowitsch de Panin* (Historical Summary of the Life of Count Nikita Ivanovich Panin, 1784). Both subsequently appeared in separate editions in 1786 and were republished in 1787 and 1792. Mercier's work includes a political exhortation to a young ruler and lays out a program for enlightened government. Fonvizin's essay was dedicated to the late Panin, an influential government figure who had headed a movement of loyal opposition to Catherine the Great. Dmitriev's choice of subject matter for translation demonstrated his interest in social and political issues. In 1789 he published several of his own poems in the journal *Utrennie chasy* (Morning Hours). Two of them, the fable "Lestnitsa" (The Staircase) and the idyll "Dve grobnitsy" (Two Tombs), were signed with his initials, "I. D."

Dmitriev's contributions to the *Moskovskii zhurnal* (Moscow Journal), published by Karamzin in 1791 and 1792, marked an important stage in his career as a writer. At the request of his friend, Dmitriev gave Karamzin a manuscript collection of his poetry, from which Karamzin selected works for publication. More than forty of his pieces were first printed in this periodical: songs, tales in verse, fables, and other works, all bearing the signature "I." Dmitriev became well known for his verse tale "Modnaia zhena" (A Fashionable Wife), a refined and witty account of an unfaithful woman, published in the *Moskovskii zhurnal* in 1791, and for his song "Sizyi golubochek" (The Blue-Gray Dove) of 1792 (later published untitled; the first line begins: "Stonet sizyi golubochek . . . " [A blue-grey dove moans . . .]), which was a reworking of a folk song in the sentimentalist style. Several composers wrote music to Dmitriev's words, most notably Fedor Dubiansky; for several decades the song remained in the repertory of Russian romances and inspired numerous imitations.

Dmitriev considered 1794 to be his "finest poetic year." At the time he was living with relatives in the city of Syzran, and from there he took a trip by sailboat up the Volga to Tsaritsyn. Sitting on deck he read and enjoyed the scenery, and during the evenings he wrote poetry in his cabin. His impressions were reflected in the poem "K Volge" (To the Volga), a description of Russia's natural beauty and a paean to the river. The poem was part of the tradition of high odic lyricism of the eighteenth century, best represented by Lomonosov, Sumarokov, and Mikhail Kheraskov. Yet in the same year Dmitriev also composed "Chuzhoi tolk" (Other Folks' Chatter), a verse satire which mocks epigonic ode writers. In it the poet ridicules the established clichés of Russian odes and their high-sounding phrases that contain little original feeling or inspiration. "Priroda delaet pevtsa, a ne

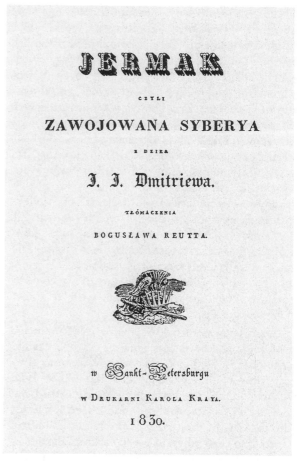

Title page for Dmitriev's poem about a sixteenth-century Cossack chieftain

uchen'e" (Nature, not study, makes the songster), he asserts. In his satire he also attacks the widespread servility of eighteenth-century Russian poetry and taunts those authors whose aim is "nagrada persten'kom, neredko sto rublei il' druzhestvo s kniaz'kom" (the reward of a ring, the occasional hundred rubles or friendship with a princeling). Dmitriev's most effective attempt to reform the ode was the poem "Ermak" (1794), about the sixteenth-century Cossack chieftain who helped conquer Siberia for Russia. The work is structured as a dramatic scene, a dialogue between two Siberian shamans who recollect their past greatness and discuss Ermak's victory over them. The mysterious and gloomy landscapes and the exotic costumes of the shamans set a lyrical mood and demonstrate pre-Romantic tendencies in Dmitriev's work. Also among the poems written in 1794 is the epistle "K G. R. Derzhavinu" (To G. R. Derzhavin), which Dmitriev wrote upon hearing of the death of his friend's wife. Thanking Dmitriev for the poem, Derzhavin responded that he could not read it "without sobbing." Another poem Dmitriev sent to Derzhavin at the same time was "Glas patriota na vziatie Varshavy" (Voice of a Patriot on the Taking of Warsaw), which he had written when rumor reached Syzran that the Russians had conquered the Polish capital. The rumor was premature, but just when the poem arrived in Saint Petersburg it was rendered true. Derzhavin presented the poem to Catherine the Great, and at her request it was published under the title *Na razbitie Kostiushki: Glas patriota* (On Kosciuszko's Destruction: The Voice of a Patriot, 1794).

Following the publication of Karamzin's collection *Moi bezdelki* (My Trifles, 1794), Dmitriev came out with his own under the title *I moi bezdelki* (My Trifles Too, 1795). These publications introduced a new type of poetry in Russia, with a markedly intimate quality; both were notable for their small format and for emphasizing their authors' individuality above all. In 1796 Dmitriev published the *Karmannyi pesennik, ili Sobranie luchshikh svetskikh i prostonarodnikh pesen* (The Pocket Songbook, or Collection of the Best Fashionable and Folk Songs), which included songs by contemporary authors — including Karamzin, Iurii Neledinsky-Meletsky, and Dmitriev — as well as some genuine folk songs.

In November 1796 Dmitriev retired with the rank of colonel. He greeted Russia's new ruler, Paul I, with *Stikhi e.i.v. Pavlu Pervomu pri vosshestvii na vserossiiskii prestol* (Verses to His Imperial Majesty Paul the First Upon His Ascension to the All-Russian Throne). However, early in 1797 Dmitriev was unexpectedly arrested and held for three days, accused of conspiring to assassinate the czar. When the falsity of the charges became apparent, Paul demonstrated his goodwill by naming Dmitriev the *ober-prokuror* of the senate. With this appointment began a second long and successful service career marked with new ranks and many honors, during which time Dmitriev's interest in literature began to diminish. He later confessed that he even tried to forget poetry in order to better assimilate the "barbarian style" of official documents.

Nevertheless, he continued to write poetry and to translate. One of the finest examples of his verse translations was his "Poslanie ot angliiskogo stikhotvortsa Popa k doktoru Arbutnotu" (1798), based on a French translation of Alexander Pope's popular satire "An Epistle to Dr. Arbuthnot" (1735). Several of Dmitriev's new poems appeared in Karamzin's almanac *Aonidy* (Aonides, 1796–

1799), and in 1798 Dmitriev published the collection *Basni i skazki* (Fables and Tales). Unlike Sumarokov and his successors, Dmitriev no longer considered the fable a low genre. Sharp wit and subtle irony, mixed at times with wistful contempt, characterize Dmitriev's fables. His work in the genre is sometimes elegiac, as in "Dva golubia" (Two Doves), and at other times idyllic, as in "Don Kishot" (Don Quixote); still other examples recall his verse tales.

Dmitriev contributed significantly to the development of the verse tale, which had become popular throughout Russia by the end of the eighteenth and beginning of the nineteenth centuries. His "Modnaia zhena," "Prichudnitsa" (The Crank), "Vozdushnye bashni" (Towers in the Sky), "Iskateli fortuny" (Fortune Seekers), and others became well known. There is a direct line from Dmitriev's tales to nineteenth-century Russian humorous poems such as Aleksandr Pushkin's "Graf Nulin" (Count Nulin, 1825). The larger part of Dmitriev's fables and tales were free translations or adaptations of the works of Voltaire, Jean-Pierre Florian, Jean de La Fontaine and other authors, most of them French. Dmitriev's works were nevertheless a major phenomenon in Russian poetry and not only enriched it with new subjects but, more important, significantly broadened the potential of its language. The poet Konstantin Batiushkov, commenting on Dmitriev's work, notes particularly his "witty, inimitable tales" and fables, "in which he rivaled La Fontaine and often surpassed him."

Dmitriev retired from civil service on 30 December 1799 at the rank of privy councillor and moved from Saint Petersburg to Moscow. There he remained in contact with Karamzin; visited Kheraskov, the "patriarch of contemporary poets"; and associated with young writers such as Vasilii Zhukovsky, Aleksandr Izmailov, and Pushkin. As if concluding his literary career, he began compiling a three-volume collected works, *Sochineniia i perevody* (Works and Translations, 1803–1805). The selection process for this publication was stringent, and he excluded many of his earlier published works. From 1800 to 1805 Dmitriev also contributed to several journals: *Vestnik Evropy* (European Herald), *Drug prosveshcheniia* (Friend of Enlightenment), *Severnyi vestnik* (Northern Herald), and *Moskovskii vestnik* (Moscow Herald).

In addition to new works of poetry, Dmitriev published literary criticism. His article "On Russian Comedies" appeared in the seventh number of the *Vestnik Evropy* (European Herald) for 1802. Noting the shortcomings of several contemporary plays,

Dmitriev outlined the main characteristics which, in his opinion, a good comedy must have: "consistent characters," "an intricate but natural plot," "humorous situations," "subtle jokes," "pure language," and a "moral goal." In journal publications of the time, as well as in letters and epigrams that circulated in literary circles, Dmitriev carried on a skillfully veiled but consistent polemic with his literary opponents, the "archaizers," including Pavel Golenyshchev-Kutuzov, Pavel L'vov, Dmitrii Khvostov, and Admiral Shishkov. He answered Mikhail Kachenovsky's critical review of *Sochineniia i perevody* – which had appeared in the *Vestnik Evropy* in 1806 – with a biting epigram: "Nakhal'stvo, Aristarkh, talantu ne zamena" (Impudence, Aristarchus, is no substitute for talent). Dmitriev's "Letter to the Publisher of the Journal," published in P. I. Shalikov's *Moskovskii nabliudatel'* (Moscow Spectator) in 1806, argued for the necessity and benefit of literary criticism, asserting that the review section is the most important part of a journal. On Dmitriev's recommendation Petr Shalikov's journal published the first fables of his future rival Ivan Krylov. Among these was "Dub i trost' " (The Oak and the Cane), a retelling of Dmitriev's fable of the same name. Krylov's friend Mikhail Lobanov recalled that Dmitriev told Krylov after reading his fables that "this is truly your genre, you have finally found it." In 1808 Dmitriev published a limited edition (about fifty copies) of his humorous poem *Puteshestvie NN v Parizh i London, pisannoe za tri dnia do puteshestviia* (The Travels of NN to Paris and London, Written Three Days Before the Trip). "NN" refers to Vasilii Pushkin, the great poet's uncle and a popular poet of his day, known for his good-heartedness and enthusiasm. The younger Pushkin called this work "a model of light-hearted playfulness and lively, harmless joking."

On 6 February 1806 Alexander I named Dmitriev a senator of the Moscow district, and Dmitriev was thus obliged to return to civil service. In the same year he was appointed to inspect the *zemskoe voisko* (national guard), in which regard he toured the Kostroma, Vologoda, Nizhegorodskaia, and Kazan provinces. In 1808 he traveled to Riazan to investigate a scandal involving the wine concession, and then to Kostroma to conduct an audit. At the beginning of 1810 the czar summoned Dmitriev to Saint Petersburg and appointed him a member of the state council and minister of justice. Dmitriev continued to receive medals and honors, but differences of opinion and clashes with other civil servants, including Derzhavin, drove him to request retirement again, which was granted on 30

ИВАНЪ ИВАНОВИЧЬ ДМИТРІЕВЪ

Dmitriev, circa 1818; engraving by E. Skotnikov after a sketch by Reichel

August 1814 with a yearly pension of ten thousand rubles.

Abandoning Saint Petersburg, Dmitriev again settled in Moscow, where he built a new house and occupied himself with his sizable library, stamp collection, and garden. He remained a bachelor to the end of his life. He loved to frequent society and was a permanent fixture at the English Club. He devoted considerable attention to his appearance and dressed like a dandy, wearing dress coats and wigs of assorted colors, some quite exuberant. He seemed cold and aloof to many, but his hospitality was exceptional, and he was a clever raconteur. Mikhail Dmitriev, the poet's nephew, describes his uncle's domestic routine: "Having been accustomed since childhood to the outdoors, a simple and active life, Ivan Ivanovich Dmitriev rose very early in the morning, prepared his own coffee, and dressed in a hurry. On very rare occasions I would catch him in his robe, but then only if he were ill. He took a long walk every day, persisting in this habit even as minister – he had enough time for everything. In Moscow, during his walks he would listen to the conversations of the simple folk, and often joined in. Sometimes he would return from his stroll with very accurate observations about the character of the Russian people, which he could imitate with peerless artistry. His jokes, always delivered with a straight face, were unusually sharp and funny. He read very much and consistently followed current affairs and the latest in literature."

After 1810 Dmitriev almost completely stopped writing poetry, but the circle of his literary contacts was as wide as always, and he took many young writers under his wing. Among those who enjoyed his support were Konstantin Batiushkov, Nikolai Grammatin, and Mikhail Milonov. The members of the famous literary circle Arzamas (1815–1818) chose Dmitriev as an honorary member. He carried on a wide-ranging correspondence (with Petr Viazemsky, Vasilii Zhukovsky, and many others), and his letters are of significant historical, literary, and cultural interest. In 1816 Alexander I appointed Dmitriev to lead a commission to help Moscow residents who had suffered losses during Napoleon's invasion of 1812. The commission's work was finished in 1819, and Dmitriev was generously rewarded; he received the rank of actual privy councillor and the Order of Saint Vladimir, First Degree. Elected a member of the Russian Academy in 1797, he was awarded its gold medal in 1823. Moscow and Kharkov universities and many other academic and literary societies counted him an honored member.

Several times during the 1810s and 1820s Dmitriev republished his collected works. The sixth and last publication of his works during his life, *Stikhotvoreniia* (Poems, 1823) was greatly abridged, again demonstrating Dmitriev's exacting standards toward his own work. The edition included a biographical essay by Viazemsky which describes the poet as a "model writer" and devotes special attention to Dmitriev's contribution to the development of the Russian literary language. In 1826 Dmitriev published a small volume titled *Apologi v chetverostishiakh* (Apologues in Quatrains), a selection of translations of French moralizing poetry. Several of these apologues (short fictitious or allegorical tales) had appeared in Dmitriev's earlier publications under the heading *basni* (fables).

By the 1820s Dmitriev's literary authority was extremely high in the eyes of his contemporaries. In a letter to the poet dated 11 February 1823, Zhukovsky wrote: "You are my teacher in poetry. I do not consider myself a worthy student, but I still reserve the right to thank you for acquainting me with the living joys of poetry, the highest aim and best reward for a poet." Aleksandr Voeikov, Viazemsky, Vladimir Izmailov, and many others spoke about the merits of Dmitriev's poetry. Viazemsky, in the article cited above, compares Dmitriev's fables with those by Krylov and declares his preference for the former. Aleksandr Pushkin, however, decisively rebutted Viazemsky in a letter dated 8 March 1824: "And who is Dmitriev? All of his fables together do not measure up to one by Krylov; all of his satires are not worth one of yours; and everything else is outweighed by even Zhukovsky's first poem." Relations between Dmitriev and Pushkin varied over the years. Dmitriev disliked Pushkin's "Ruslan and Liudmilla" (1820). Later, however, he recognized Pushkin's talent and spoke highly of such works as "Mozart and Salieri" and *Boris Godunov*. In the 1830s the poets frequently met and corresponded. Pushkin respected Dmitriev's literary accomplishments and took his epigraph for the seventh chapter of *Evgenii Onegin* (Eugene Onegin, 1833) from Dmitriev's poem "Osvobozhdenie Moskvy" (The Liberation of Moscow). Dmitriev outlived Pushkin; it was he who, in 1837, broke the news of Pushkin's death to his father. Dmitriev died not long afterward, on 3 October 1837.

It was not until 1866 that Dmitriev's memoir, *Vzgliad na moiu zhizn'* (A Look at My Life), was published. Written between 1823 and 1825, it presents an interesting and lively account of the works and career of the poet and civil servant, as well as portraits of many of his most outstanding contemporaries. It provides a clear profile of an epoch and its literary life and offers valuable information about Karamzin, Derzhavin, Bogdanovich, Vasilii Petrov, and many other writers.

Letters:

Pis'ma I. I. Dmitrieva k kniaziu P. A. Viazemskomu 1810–1836 godov: Iz Ostaf'evskogo arkhiva, edited by Nikolai Barsukov (Saint Petersburg: M. Stasiulevich, 1898).

References:

Konstantin N. Batiushkov, "Rech' o vliianii legkoi poezii na iazyk," in his *Opyty v stikhakh i proze,* edited by Irina M. Semenko (Moscow: Nauka, 1977), pp. 8–19;

V. M. Chulitsky, "I. I. Dmitriev," *Zhurnal Ministerstva narodnogo prosveshcheniia,* nos. 3–5 (1902);

Anthony G. Cross, "Dmitriev and Gessner," *Study Group on Eighteenth-Century Russia Newsletter,* 2 (1974): 32–39;

Cross, "The Reluctant Memoirist," in Dmitriev's *Vzgliad na moiu zhizn'* (Cambridge: Oriental Research Partners, 1974), pp. i–xii;

Mikhail A. Dmitriev, *Melochi iz zapasa moei pamiati* (Moscow: Grachev, 1869);

Ludmila I. Eremenko, "I. I. Dmitriev – satirik-polemist ('Chuzhoi tolk')," *Vestnik Leningradskogo gos. universiteta,* 20 (October 1982): 52–57;

Iakov Grot and Petr Pekarsky, eds., *Pis'ma N. M. Karamzina k I. I. Dmitrievu* (Saint Petersburg: Akademiia nauk, 1866);

I. A. Krylov v vospominaniiakh sovremennikov (Moscow: Khudozhestvennaia literatura, 1982);

Elizaveta N. Kupreianova, "Dmitriev i poety karamzinskoi shkoly," in *Istoriia russkoi literatury,* volume 5, part 1 (Moscow & Leningrad: Akademiia nauk, 1941), pp. 121–144;

Georgi P. Makogonenko, "Dmitriev, Ivan Ivanovich," in *Slovar' russkikh pisatelei XVIII veka,* volume 1 (Leningrad: Nauka, 1988), pp. 269–272;

Makogonenko, "Pushkin i Dmitriev," *Russkaia literatura,* no. 4 (1966): 19–36;

Galina G. Silinskaia, "'Karmannyi pesennik' I. I. Dmitrieva," *Russkaia literatura,* no. 3 (1982): 143–149;

Vladimir P. Stepanov, "Zametki o V. L. Pushkine," in *Pushkin: Issledovaniia i materialy,* 11 (Leningrad: Nauka, 1983), pp. 250–262;

Halina Swidzinska, "I. I. Dmitriev: A Classicist and a Sentimentalist in the Context of the World and Russian Fable," Ph.D. dissertation, University of Pittsburgh, 1972.

Papers:
A large portion of Ivan Ivanovich Dmitriev's archive is preserved in the Central State Archive of Literature and Art in Moscow, fond. 1060 (forty-two archival units from 1791 to 1907).

Fedor Aleksandrovich Emin

(circa 1735 – 18 April 1770)

Thomas Barran
Brooklyn College, City University of New York

BOOKS: *Nepostoiannaia fortuna, ili Pokhozhdenie Miramonda,* 3 volumes (Saint Petersburg: [Sukhoputnyi kadetskii korpus], 1763);

Prikliucheniia Femistokla i raznye politicheskiia, grazhdanskiia, filosoficheskiia, fizicheskiia i voennyia ego s synom svoim razgovory; postoiannaia zhizn' i zhestokost' fortuny ego goniashchei (Saint Petersburg: [Sukhoputnyi kadetskii korpus], 1763);

Nagrazhdennaia postoiannost', ili prikliucheniia Lizarka i Sarmandy (Saint Petersburg: [Akademiia nauk], 1764);

Nravouchitel'nyia basni (Saint Petersburg: Akademiia nauk, 1764);

Pis'ma Ernesta i Doravry, 4 volumes (Saint Petersburg: [Akademiia nauk], 1766);

Rossiiskaia istoriia zhizni vsekh drevnikh ot samago nachala Rossii gosudarei vse velikiia i vechnoi dostoinyia pamiati imp. Petra Velikago deistviia, ego naslednits i naslednikov emu posledovanie i opisanie v Severe zlatago veka vo vremia tsarstvovoniia Ekateriny Velikoi v sebe zakliuchaiushchaia, 3 volumes (Saint Petersburg: Akademiia nauk, 1767–1769);

Kratkoe opisanie drevneishago i noveishago sostoianiia Ottomanskoi Porty (Saint Petersburg: Morskoi Shliakhetnyi kadetskii korpus, 1769);

Put' k spaseniiu, ili Raznyia nabozhnyia razmyshleniia v kotorykh zakliuchaetsia nuzhneishaia k obshchemu zhaniiu chast' bogosloviia (Saint Petersburg: [Sukhoputnyi kadetskii korpus], 1780).

OTHER: Gabriele Martiano, *Beshchastnyi Floridor istoriia o printse rakalmutskom,* translated by Emin (Saint Petersburg: Sukhoputnyi kadetskii korpus, 1763);

Liubovnyi vertograd, ili Nepreoborimoe postoianstvo Kambera i Ariseny, translated by Emin (Saint Petersburg: Sukhoputnyi kadetskii korpus, 1763);

Gorestnaia liubov' markiza de Toledo, translated by Emin (Saint Petersburg: Sukhoputnyi kadetskii korpus, 1764);

Pierre Solignac (Solin'iak), *Istoriia pol'skaia,* 2 volumes, translated by Emin (Saint Petersburg: Akademiia nauk, 1766);

Smes', novoe ezhenedel'noe izdanie, nos. 1–40 (1 April 1769–December 1769), edited by Emin;

Adskaia pochta, ili Perepiski khromonogago besa s krivym (July 1769–December 1769), edited and written by Emin; republished, in one volume, as *Adskaia pochta ili Kurier iz ada s pis'mami* (Saint Petersburg: [P. I. Bogdanovich], 1788).

Fedor Aleksandrovich Emin earned his place in literary history as Russia's first novelist. The distinction holds true not only in the literal sense that Emin published the first original novel written in the Russian language; he also brought the genre to Russia in a social and economic sense. From the middle of the eighteenth century in western Europe, the novel existed as a literary genre that presented recognizable descriptions of everyday life and more or less believable characters; these elements appeared in the novel and journalism at roughly the same time. Emin brought Russian novelistic prose close to journalistic discourse, in that his novels included much factual information and what today would be called editorial opinion. The novel as an object to be purchased and read privately at home also introduced new patterns of literary consumption; in this sense Emin presided over the commodification of Russian prose fiction. At a time when such creatures were rare, Emin made his living as a professional writer.

Emin's early years were long shrouded in mystery, and scholars are still uncertain about his early biography. It is generally accepted that he led a wandering, adventurous life before he settled in Saint Petersburg, but Emin seems to have regarded his life story in much the same way as one of his adventure novels. He gave several versions of it to different people at different times, not even bothering to maintain consistency of details. As Nikolai Karamzin put it in his *Panteon rossiiskikh Avtorov* (Pantheon of Russian Authors, 1801–1802), the most fascinating of Emin's novels was his biography, as he related it to friends. Indeed Emin seems to be one of the first Russian writers to take advantage of the market value of a carefully manipulated biographical myth. Nonetheless, recent archival research has yielded evidence to support the validity of the most fantastic of all his versions of his early life.

The first version of Emin's early years appears in Nikolai Novikov's *Opyt istoricheskogo slovaria o rossiiskikh pisateliakh* (Attempt at a Historical Dictionary of Russian Writers, 1772), which reports that Emin was born either in Poland or in a Russian town near the Polish border. A Catholic, he received tutoring in Latin and other subjects from a Jesuit, who later took the young pupil with him on his travels. After wandering in Europe and Asia, they arrived in Turkey, where Emin was involved in some sort of incident (the details were never revealed) that threatened him with imprisonment. To avoid this outcome Emin converted to Islam and served for several years as a Janissary. He managed to leave Turkey on an English ship bound for London, where he presented himself before the Russian ambassador, A. M. Golitsyn, in order to reconvert to Christianity, this time to Russian Orthodoxy. In 1761 he arrived in Saint Petersburg.

Emin's publisher S. L. Kopnin wrote a second version of the writer's biography, which he included as an appendix to Emin's final book, *Put' k spaseniiu* (The Path to Salvation, 1780), published posthumously. According to Kopnin, Emin was born near the Turkish border in a Hungarian town named Lippe, to a Hungarian father and Polish mother. During hostilities in 1737 he and his mother were captured and held hostage by the Turks, but his mother managed to continue Emin's Catholic education during their captivity. They were returned to Hungary at the end of the war. Educated there in a Jesuit school, he accompanied one of the priests on a missionary trip to Asia. Kopnin's version of Emin's adventures in Turkey does not differ from Novikov's, but according to the former, Emin spent his time in London studying all the Christian sects before settling on Russian Orthodoxy as the most authentic.

Kopnin subsequently sold the rights to Emin's last work to a publisher named M. K. Ovchinnikov, who added to the 1784 edition of the work another account of Emin's life by a man who had supposedly studied for the priesthood with Emin at the Kiev Academy. According to this unnamed source,

Emin was born either in a Russian town or in a Polish settlement near Kiev.

The fourth and most fantastic version of Emin's early years came to light in the nineteenth century from an archival source, Emin's 1761 petition to the College of Foreign Affairs for permission to enter Russian service. In the biographical data he provides with this petition, Emin states that he was born in Constantinople to a family of Polish descent. His father was the governor of Lepanto, his mother a Christian captive. Raised in the Islamic faith, he studied Polish and Latin at home and then went to Venice to study Italian, a language necessary for anyone involved in Levantine trade. Upon returning to Constantinople, he learned that his father had been deposed and exiled. Father and son fled to Algiers, where they took part in the war between Algiers and Tunis. When his father died of wounds received in this war, Emin returned to Constantinople, promised his mother that he would convert to Christianity, and set out for Europe on a venture in the spice trade. On the way his ship was attacked by pirates, and he was captured but managed to escape to a Portuguese fortress. When he announced his desire to convert to Christianity, he was sent to Lisbon and, on the personal orders of the king, was given instructions in the faith by the cardinal himself. During his instructions, however, he came to the conclusion that he preferred Orthodoxy to Catholicism and put off his baptism. Emin then left for London, where he presented himself to the Russian ambassador for baptism in the Russian Orthodox faith.

As fantastic as this last version sounds, it seems to be the most probable, judging by recent archival research conducted by M. A. Arzumanova and Evgenii B. Beshenkovsky. The latter researched the Russian Foreign Policy Archives, where he found a passport issued to Emin in Lisbon on 18 November 1760, an attestation by one Baron Depius of the arrival of the "Mahomet Emin, a Turkish noble of Constantinople," and records of correspondence with the Russian ambassador to Turkey regarding Emin's relatives in Constantinople. Archival records show that several well-known people confirmed Emin's story that his father was indeed Gen. Hussein Bey. The archives also contain an attestation by Cardinal-Rector Cremento Ruiz de Carvallo confirming Emin's religious instruction and his wish to postpone baptism. Independent historical sources reveal that one Hussein Bey did command the Algerian forces during the Algiers-Tunis War and that he had blue eyes, which would add credence to Emin's claim that his parents were of Polish extraction.

If the final version of Emin's early life contains the most truth, why were less exotic versions created? For one thing, Emin treated his biography as something of a literary property, fictionally recasting parts of it in his first novel, *Nepostoiannaia fortuna, ili Pokhozhdenie Miramonda* (Inconstant Fortune, or The Adventures of Miramond, 1763), and regaling his Saint Petersburg acquaintances with autobiographical stories. As he gained more success in his writing, he realized that the public perception of an author's biography can help or hinder the reception of a book. When war broke out between the Russians and Turks in 1768, Emin simply decided to rewrite his biography, downplaying his Turkish origins, which explains the version Novikov claimed to have heard from the author. After all, he had converted to Orthodoxy and claimed to be of Slavic descent: why arouse the kind of suspicions inevitable during wartime against people who have had dealings with the enemy? Another explanation has to do with Emin's last book, *Put' k spaseniiu,* which remained a profitable best-seller until the end of the nineteenth century. The publishers who owned the rights to this work, Kopnin and Ovchinnikov, contributed versions of Emin's life story that stress his religiosity. Both claim that he was born and reared a Christian. Kopnin portrays him as settling on Orthodoxy after a long period of spiritual study, while Ovchinnikov has him attending the Kiev Academy, thus making Emin Orthodox from birth. They added authority to their book by representing the author as a lifelong Christian rather than a recent convert.

Emin chose Saint Petersburg as the place where he would make his fortune. Judging from evidence in petitions he sent during his first years in the northern capital, as well as from autobiographical passages in his first novel, Emin initially expected to be treated in a manner befitting the station he had occupied in the Ottoman Empire. Unfortunately, he incurred heavy debts while waiting for a profitable position in the Russian Foreign Service that never materialized. He worked in the College of Foreign Affairs but could not advance in that agency because of the suspicions raised by his background. A. M. Obreskov, the Russian envoy in Turkey, refrained from making inquiries about him but advised his colleagues in Saint Petersburg to keep Emin out of all Turkish affairs and away from the borders of the empire. He further counseled them to obstruct any correspondence Emin might attempt to carry on with people in foreign lands.

To supplement the meager income from his service position, Emin took additional jobs teaching Italian at the Noble Infantry Cadet Corps and the Academy of Arts. He finally resorted to literature when the combined income from all of his positions did not meet his needs. His situation improved somewhat in 1763, when he began working as a translator in the cabinet of the new empress, Catherine II; he could now avail himself of financial assistance from the state in writing and publishing his books. To pay off his debts Emin borrowed twenty-five hundred rubles from the empress against the anticipated profits from future writings. By the end of his life, Emin could command an advance of eight thousand rubles from the publisher Kopnin for his works.

Emin consistently admitted that he wrote for money and lived by the earnings of his pen. Having a lively sense of the developing book trade, he aimed his novels at a popular audience and knew they could not pass for great literature. As a struggling writer Emin felt great sympathy for the marginal economic conditions in which authors often found themselves. He presented himself as a noble adventurer, acquainted with numerous languages and cultures, who had fallen on hard times. He did not conceal his resentment toward the rich and powerful who offered no help to struggling intellectuals. His traffic in popular literature did not hinder his appreciation for serious contributions to the arts and sciences or his awareness that his own work did not fall into that category.

Once he had settled on writing as his source of income, Emin worked with astonishing productivity. In the seven years of his literary career, he produced nineteen volumes of original and translated works. His books enjoyed great popularity during his lifetime and in the decades following his death; however, the haste with which Emin wrote, his aim of appealing to the widest possible readership, and the fact that he composed in a language that was not his native tongue compromised the quality of his works. His syntax is tortuous, his characterizations two-dimensional, and his plots improbable. Today his works are largely forgotten. None of his books has appeared in a full English translation, and one can only get a taste of his work from excerpts in anthologies or from quotes in scholarly articles.

To the literary historian, however, Emin represents a key figure in the development of Russian prose fiction and in the shaping of a popular Russian reading audience. Since his goal in writing was above all financial, he did not remain partial to any one type of novel but essayed many styles, from that of the fantastic adventure novel and the philosophical novel in the manner of François Fenelon's *Télémaque* (1699) to the contemporary sentimental, epistolary format employed by Samuel Richardson and Jean-Jacques Rousseau. Emin provides a fascinating picture of a literary craftsman keeping an eye on the literary trends of western Europe, as he tests and educates the untapped Russian market for prose fiction.

Emin's first novel, *Nepostoiannaia fortuna, ili Pokhozhdenie Miramonda,* was dedicated to Grigorii Orlov, who in addition to being Catherine the Great's lover was one of the prime movers behind the coup that had put her on the throne; this dedication reveals Emin's sharp instinct in seeking patronage. Emin contracted the printing of the novel with the press of the Infantry Cadet Corps, ordering a printing of twelve hundred copies. The novel appeared in three volumes, each approximately three hundred pages.

Of all Emin's novels, *Miramond* holds the reader's interest most effectively. It enjoyed great popularity in eighteenth-century Russia: Novikov published a second edition at his Moscow University Press in 1781, while Sytin's press put out a third edition in Saint Petersburg in 1792, along with the biography of Emin that had appeared in *Put' k spaseniiu.* In *Miramond* Emin alternates his hero's relatively fast-moving adventures (kidnappings by pirates, wars, and love intrigues in Lisbon and Cairo) with detailed descriptions of the geography and mores of the Mediterranean and the Levant (in the section on Morocco the author provides a recipe for couscous, and in the Egyptian episode he describes the wedding customs of the inhabitants). The information Emin provides varies in accuracy and believability, making it difficult to determine how much he culled from his own experiences and how much he drew from his reading or simply made up. Nonetheless, Emin gave the adventures in his novel more verisimilitude by adding contemporary material; for example, he gives a description of the devastation caused by the Lisbon earthquake of 1755, as well as details of intrigues between the Jesuits and the court of Lisbon. In all, he manages to add to *Miramond* some of the immediacy of journalism, the discourse which probably contributed more than any other to the transformation of the novel into its modern form.

Whether the edition initially sold poorly or Emin, in his inexperience, had signed a disadvantageous contract, he owed the press money after the printing of *Miramond.* To liquidate the debt he sold them two manuscripts, which he claimed were translations, for the sum of three hundred rubles. One of these, *Beshchastnyi Floridor* (Unfortunate Floridor, 1763), was a loose rendering of Gabriele Martiano's *Il Floridoro, o vero historia del conte de Racalmuto* (Floridor, or True History of the Count of Racalmuto). Emin claimed that he had translated the other, *Liubovnyi vertograd* (Love's Bower, 1763), from a Portuguese manuscript, but the original of this work has not been found; several scholars, in fact, think that Emin himself wrote this novel. Its style and content bear remarkable similarities to *Miramond.* Emin may have denied its authorship for several reasons: if *Miramond* had not produced a profit, the press might have refused to accept any more of Emin's original manuscripts in payment for his debt; translations of western European literature had excellent chances of winning patronage for their authors in the early years of Catherine II's reign; or Emin may have employed the tactic of authorial disavowal, frequently used by writers of eighteenth-century prose fiction in order to increase a work's appeal and verisimilitude.

Emin shared many of the intellectual presuppositions of the Enlightenment and used his novels to propagandize them. Some of his psychological and religious views, however, bear more of a resemblance to those of the moralists of seventeenth-century France than to those of the philosophes. The Lisbon earthquake had prompted one of the major debates of the Enlightenment, sending Voltaire into a spiritual crisis that made him question God's benevolence. Rousseau in turn defended Providence on the grounds that God created the world with benevolent intentions, but that humanity brings about its own catastrophes. Emin claimed in *Miramond* that the earthquake occurred as divine retribution for the sins of the Portuguese. While Rousseau, Claude Helvétius, and Denis Diderot were examining and rehabilitating the human passions as possible motivations for great actions and deeds, Emin employed the vocabulary of the previous century, regarding passions as universally destructive. In *Miramond* and later works Emin uses images of disease and poison when referring to erotic passion.

His ability to adapt the latest western European trends in the novel emerges most noticeably in *Pis'ma Ernesta i Doravry* (Letters of Ernest and Doravra, 1766), an epistolary novel modeled on Rousseau's *Julie, ou la nouvelle Héloïse* (1761). Emin's novel has none of the literary quality of Rousseau's masterpiece, but his rapid recognition of the popular appeal of *Julie* and his attempt to exploit this market in Russia mark an important point in Russian literary history. Its artificiality and awkwardness notwithstanding, *Pis'ma Ernesta i Doravry* stands as the first novel written in Russian that explores psychology and the passions from a subjective point of view in a first-person narrative.

Emin wrote two separate prefaces for this novel, as Rousseau had done in *Julie*. In one, again following Rousseau, he plays the game of authorial disavowal with his readers, raising questions over the writer of the letters and then refusing to resolve them. In both prefaces Emin draws a distinction between high literary art and the kind of popular fiction he is writing. He also addresses the question, hotly debated at the time, of the moral influence of novels on their readers. Emin claims that he wants to find a median audience between the prudes and the libertines, those who wish to witness or to participate vicariously in the conflict between virtue and passion. He also wants his novel to seem authentic. Anticipating the objection that some of his letters are too long, Emin invokes Rousseau, whose letters are even longer, he reminds his reader.

Even if Emin retreats from his denial of authorship, he does so to defend the verisimilitude of the correspondence presented in his novel.

Emin drew much of the plot of *Pis'ma Ernesta i Doravry* from Rousseau. Ernest, an impoverished nobleman, falls in love with Doravra. Her father objects to their alliance because of the inequality of their fortunes. Ernest obtains a diplomatic post and travels to Paris and London. While he is away, his past catches up with him: his wife, whom he had married at his father's urging and whom he thought was long dead, arrives and conclusively ruins his chances with Doravra. Doravra marries another, Ernest's wife dies, and Ernest withdraws to a solitary retreat where he nurses his bitterness and writes philosophical prose. Similarities to Rousseau's *Julie* abound. In both novels the lovers have confidantes who add their own letters and provide a credible means for the exchange of information and letters between the protagonists. Both heroes travel to Paris and write their observations of that city. Moreover in both novels the father of the heroine poses a formidable obstacle to the young couple's union.

Emin, however, did not slavishly mimic Rousseau's original. While he did not alter Rousseau's model considerably with regard to plot and characters, he rewrote the social conflict. Whereas in *Julie* St. Preux is a commoner while Julie belongs to the nobility, Emin's Ernest and Doravra both belong to the nobility. The conflict in Emin's novel arises from a difference in wealth: Ernest is poor, while Doravra's family is well-to-do.

Emin's most extreme departure from Rousseau lies in the philosophical and psychological presuppositions of the novel. Emin followed an older attitude toward erotic passion, rejecting Rousseau's belief that this drive, when properly channeled, can prove to be a remarkable force for good. In *Julie* St. Preux lives with Julie and her husband, serving as a tutor for their children. St. Preux and Julie's sexual passion undergoes a metamorphosis in which it is purified and contributes its energy to the virtue that enables them to live chastely under one roof. Emin wanted nothing to do with Rousseau's attempt to rehabilitate the passions. While the ménage à trois serves as Rousseau's primary metaphor for the possibility of channeling passion for noble ends, Emin rejects this vision by having Ernest twice refuse invitations to live chastely in the same household with Doravra because his passion for Doravra has not yet died.

The moral theme of Emin's novel lies in its treatment of passion as consistently destructive. When Ernest and Doravra begin their correspondence, they agree that love causes more suffering than happiness. Human virtue consists in the control of passion by reason and adherence to duty, as Doravra asserts in letter 15 of part 1: "No matter how strongly virtue rules our hearts, passion is stronger than our human nature and can shake its foundations unless it is tamed by reason." Emin differs little in this respect from the great French tragedians of the seventeenth century, but while this moral scheme succeeds in the plays of Jean Racine, the psychological prose of a novel needs more complexity and ambivalence in order to sustain the reader's interest.

Ernest's letters, especially those in the third part of the novel when he is living in isolation, contain a great deal of philosophical and political discussion relating to the controversies of the Enlightenment in general as well as to particular political and social issues of Catherine II's Russia. Part 3 reflects many of the issues that would be discussed in Catherine's Legislative Commission of 1766–1768 and would concern Catherine for most of her reign: the problems of serfdom, education, and the lack of a thriving middle class in Russia. Emin defends serfdom as an institution but condemns individual cases in which landlords abuse their powers. Regarding the merchant class, twice in the novel Ernest praises their contribution to the state: once when he is in England and learns that even the nobility there engage in commerce and add much to the state as a result; and the second time in his ruminations on education, when he declares that the "merchant class is the soul of the state." Ernest's thoughts on education draw much from Rousseau's theories in *Emile:* both authors recommend that the child be given as much physical freedom as possible and that the body be strengthened along with the mind; both believe that reason, far from being an innate faculty, develops in a child at a relatively late stage.

At the end of *Pis'ma Ernesta i Doravry,* Ippolit warns Ernest that he risks public disapproval and personal danger if he continues to make moral judgments about specific people in his philosophical writings. Ippolit counsels him to moderate in his truth-telling if he wants to enjoy his solitary life. This novelistic development reflects an actual turn of events in Emin's life. In January 1769 Catherine II sponsored and contributed to a satiric journal, *Vsyakaia vsiachina* (All Sorts and Sundries), based on the English journals of Joseph Addison and Richard Steele. The journal openly encouraged Russian writers to start other such journals, with the goal of instituting a public satire that would ridicule and correct the human vices that hindered progress and moral improvement. The program called for gentle satire that would criticize universal human failings, but several of the journals that sprang up began satirizing identifiable Saint Petersburg events and personalities. Emin was not one to miss an opportunity to cash in on a new literary trend; his weekly *Smes'* (Miscellany) was the first to begin satire *na litso* (against specific individuals), although Catherine publicly debated the desirability of such personal satire with Novikov, whose journals stand as the masterpieces of this era.

In 1769 Emin began another satiric journal called *Adskaia pochta* (Hell's Post), which again defended the practice of satire targeting recognizable individuals, although he rarely employed it. Much of the material in *Adskaia pochta* made use of free translations from a series of French pamphlets by Eustache Le Noble, which in turn had appeared as sequels to Alain René Lesage's popular novel *Le Diable boiteux* (1707). Not many readers in Saint Petersburg would have known the contents of Le Noble's pamphlets, and Emin seems to have intended eventually to reveal his source as a joke on those who interpreted his borrowed material as personal attacks.

After writing *Pis'ma Ernesta i Doravry* Emin turned to nonfiction genres. His attempt at writing Russian history, *Rossiiskaia istoriia zhizni vsekh drevnikh ot samago nachala Rossii gosudarei* (Russian History of the Life of All Ancient Rulers from the Very Beginning of Russia, 1767–1769), proved an utter failure. He did not use the extant primary sources, the chronicles and other documents that he could readily have consulted. He did not even consult the histories of Russia already written by Vasilii Tatishchev and Mikhail Lomonosov. It is difficult to determine which is worse, his misuse of the sources he consulted or his utter fabrication of much of his material. This ill-conceived book earned him some justifiably caustic verses in Mikhail Chulkov's satiric journal *I to i sio* (Both This and That) of 1769, which refer to Emin as a fool. Emin underestimated the importance that accurate historical writing was assuming at the time. Karamzin, who himself would write a monumental history of Russia, reserved his severest criticism of Emin for this book. In this instance Emin's acute sense of the literary marketplace seems to have failed him.

Emin died at the age of thirty-five, leaving a wife, Ul'iana, and a son, Nikolai, who would earn a reputation as an author of sentimentalist fiction. Emin sustained an astonishing level of literary productivity for the last seven years of his life, working with great rapidity in his adopted language. The author is said to have completed *Pis'ma Ernesta i Doravry,* a novel of four volumes totaling over eight hundred printed pages, in less than two months. Emin's frantic literary activity reflected the intellectual promise of the first decade of Catherine's reign, the years of her correspondence with Voltaire and the philosophes, her *Nakaz* (Instruction) and Legislative Commission, and her encouragement of satiric journals. A man of considerable experience and erudition, Emin foresaw the potential of the growing Russian book trade and possessed a real sense of literature and journalism as salable commodities. He wrote to earn money, but he seems to have had a sense that his activity was fundamentally honorable. By writing for a middlebrow audience, Emin retained the sense of participating in the Enlightenment project of improving humanity through education and the spread of information.

References:

M. A. Arzumanova, "Novoe o F. Emine," *Russkaia literatura,* no. 1 (1961): 182–186;

Evgenii B. Beshenkovsky, "Zhizn' Fedora Emina," *XVIII vek,* 11 (1976): 186–203;

David E. Budgen, "Fedor Emin and the Beginnings of the Russian Novel," in *Russian Literature in the Age of Catherine the Great,* edited by Anthony G. Cross (Oxford: Meeuws, 1976), pp. 67–94;

Grigorii A. Gukovsky, "Emin," *Istoriia russkoi literatury,* volume 4, edited by Gukovsky and Vasilii A. Desnitsky (Moscow & Leningrad: Akademiia nauk, 1947), pp. 256–264;

Gukovsky, "Emin i Sumarokov," *XVIII vek,* 2 (1940): 77–94;

Gukovsky, "Ideologiia russkogo burzhuaznogo pisatelia XVIII v.," *Izvestiia Akademii Nauk: Otd. obshchestvennykh nauk,* 3 (1936): 429–458;

O. L. Kalashnikova, "Zhanrovye modifikatsii romana v tvorchestve F. Emina," *Voprosy russkoi literatury,* 1, no. 57 (1991): 43–51;

A. I. Liashchenko, *K istorii russkogo romana: Publitsisticheskii element v romanakh F. A. Emina* (Saint Petersburg, 1898);

V. V. Pukhov, "Kto zhe izdaval zhurnal *Smes'*?," *Russkaia literatura,* no. 2 (1981): 159–162;

V. D. Rak, "*Adskaia pochta* i ee frantsuzskii istochnik," *XVIII vek,* 15 (1986): 169–197;

L. I. Reznichenko, "O zhanrovom svoeobrazii romanov F. A. Emina," in *Problemy izucheniia russkoi literatury XVIII veka,* edited by Vladimir A. Zapadov (Leningrad: Gos. Ped. Inst. im Gertsena, 1974), pp. 33–44;

Il'ia Z. Serman, "Iz istorii literaturnoi bor'by 60-kh godov XVIII veka: Neizdannaia komediia Fedora Emina *Uchenaia shaika*," *XVIII vek,* 3 (1958): 207–225;

Vasilii V. Sipovsky, *Ocherki iz istorii russkogo romana,* volume 1 (Saint Petersburg, 1910), pp. 393–406, 497–508, 649–671.

Papers:

A manuscript of Fedor Aleksandrovich Emin's unpublished comedy "Uchenaia shaika" (circa 1767) is located in the Rukopisnoe otdelenie, Lenin Library, Moscow (f. 526, sobranie A. V. Fedorova, no. 2968).

Denis Ivanovich Fonvizin

(3 April 1744 or 1745 – 1 December 1792)

Natal'ia Dmitrievna Kochetkova
Institute of Russian Literature (Pushkin House), Saint Petersburg

BOOKS: *Slovo na vyzdorovlenie e. i. v. gosudaria tsesarevicha i velikogo kniazia Pavla Petrovicha* (Saint Petersburg: Morskoi kadetskii korpus, 1771);

Nedorosl', komediia v piati deistviiakh. Predstavlena v pervyi raz v Sanktpeterburge Sentiabria 24 dnia 1782 (Saint Petersburg: Shnor, 1783; revised edition, Saint Petersburg, 1800); translated by George R. Noyes and George R. Parick as "The Young Hopeful," in *Masterpieces of the Russian Drama,* volume 1, edited by Noyes (New York & London: Appleton, 1933), pp. 27–84; translated by Frank D. Reeve as "The Minor," in *An Anthology of Russian Plays,* volume 1, edited by Reeve (New York: Vintage, 1961), pp. 21–83; translated by Marvin Kantor as "The Minor," in *Dramatic Works of D. I. Fonvizin* (Bern: Herbert Lang / Frankfurt am Main: Peter Lang, 1974), pp. 87–134;

Précis historique de la vie du comte Nikita Iwanowitsch de Panin (London, 1784); published in Russian as *Zhizn' grafa Nikity Ivanovicha Panina,* translated by Ivan Dmitriev (Saint Petersburg: Vil'kovsky i Galchenkov, 1786);

Poslanie k slugam moim Shumilovu, Van'ke i Petrushke ([Saint Petersburg: Bogdanovich, 1788]);

Brigadir, komediia v piati deistviiakh (Saint Petersburg: Bogdanovich, 1792?); translated as "The Brigadier," in *The Literature of Eighteenth-Century Russia,* volume 2, edited by Harold B. Segel (New York: Dutton, 1967), pp. 321–373; translated by Kantor in *Dramatic Works of D. I. Fonvizin,* pp. 49–86.

Editions: *Sobranie sochinenii i perevodov* (Moscow: Universitetskaia Tipografiia, 1829);

Polnoe sobranie sochinenii, edited by Platon Beketov, 4 volumes (Moscow: I. G. Salaev, 1830) – includes "Chistoserdechnoe priznanie v delakh moikh i pomyshleniiakh";

Sobranie original'nykh dramaticheskikh sochinenii i perevodov, 3 volumes (Moscow: N. Stepanov, 1830);

Denis Ivanovich Fonvizin

Sochineniia (Saint Petersburg: A. Smirdin, 1846);

Izbrannye sochinenia (Saint Petersburg: Eduard Veimar, 1858);

Sochineniia, pis'ma i izbrannye perevody, edited by Piotr A. Efremov (Saint Petersburg: I. I. Glazunov, 1866);

Pervoe polnoe sobranie sochinenii, kak original'nykh, tak i perevodnykh 1761–1792 (Saint Petersburg & Moscow: K. K. Shamov, 1888);

Sochineniia. Polnoe sobranie original'nykh proizvedenii, edited by A. I. Vvedensky (Saint Petersburg: A. F. Marks, 1893);

Sobranie sochinenii (Saint Petersburg: Kopeika, 1914);

Izbrannye sochinenii i pis'ma, edited by Leonid Svetlov (Moscow: Iskusstvo, 1946);

Sobranie sochinenii, 2 volumes, edited by Georgii P. Makogonenko (Moscow & Leningrad: Khudozhestvennaia literatura, 1959).

Editions in English: *Dramatic Works of D. I. Fonvizin,* translated by Marvin Kantor (Bern: Herbert Lang / Frankfurt: Peter Lang, 1974);

The Political and Legal Writings of Denis Fonvizin, translated by Walter Gleason (Ann Arbor, Mich.: Ardis, 1985).

OTHER: "Rassduzhdenie o nepremennykh gosudarstvennykh zakonakh," in E. S. Shumigorsky, *Imperator Pavel I, Zhizn' i tsarstvovanie* (Saint Petersburg: V. D. Smirnov, 1907).

TRANSLATIONS: Ludvig Holberg (Gol'berg), *Basni nravouchitel'nye s iz"iasneniiami* (Moscow: Moskovskii universitet, 1761; enlarged, 1765);

Johann Gottfried Reichel, *Slovo, govorennoe po sovershenii vysochaishego koronovaniia . . . Ekateriny Vtoryia . . . v publichnom sobranii Imp. Moskovskago universiteta oktiabria 3 dnia, 1762 godu istorii professorom, universitetskim bibliotekarem i Leiptsigskago sobraniia svobodnykh nauk chlenom, Iogannom Gotfridom Reikhelem, o tom, chto nauki i khudozhestva protsvetaiut zashchishcheniem i pokrovitel'stvom vladeiushchikh osob i velikikh liudei v gosudarstve* (Moscow: Moskovskii universitet, 1762);

Jean Terrasson, *Geroiskaia dobrodetel', ili Zhizn' Sifa, tsaria egipetskogo, iz tainstvennykh svidetel'stv drevnego Egipta vziataia,* 4 volumes (Moscow: Moskovskii universitet, 1762–1768);

Jean-Jacques Barthélémy (Bartelemi), *Liubov' Karity i Polidora* (Saint Petersburg: Sukhoputnyi kadetskii korpus, 1763);

Gabriel François Coyer (Koie), *Torguiushchee dvorianstvo, protivupulozhennoe dvorianstvu voennomu, ili Dva rassuzhdeniia o tom, sluzhit li to k blagopoluchiiu gosudarstva, chtoby dvorianstvo vstupalo v kupechestvo? S pribavleniem osoblivogo o tom zhe rassuzhdeniia g. Iustiia* (Saint Petersburg: [Akademiia nauk], 1766);

François-Thomas-Marie de Baculard d'Arnaud, *Sidnei i Silli; ili, Blagodeianie i blagodarnost'* (Moscow: Moskovskii universitet, 1769);

Paul-Jérémie Bitaubé (Bitobe), *Iosif,* 2 volumes (Moscow: Moskovskii universitet, 1769);

Antoine-Léonard Thomas (Tomas), *Slovo pokhval'noe Marku Avreliiu* (Saint Petersburg: Veitbrekht i Shnor, 1777);

Johann G. Zimmermann (Tsimmerman), *Rassuzhdeniia o natsional'nom liubochestii* (Saint Petersburg: Shnor, 1785).

Denis Ivanovich Fonvizin was the most distinguished Russian playwright of the eighteenth century, whose fame rests mainly upon his comedy *Nedorosl'* (The Minor, 1783). According to tradition, after reading the work, Catherine the Great's favorite Grigorii Potemkin told the author, "Denis, either die or stop writing! This one play alone has immortalized your name." After more than two centuries the comedy continues to be staged. Fonvizin's talent, which was primarily in satire, also expressed itself in prose genres and journalism. His lively, expressive style paved the way in many respects for Aleksandr Pushkin, who always referred to Fonvizin with great respect and warmth. In *Evgenii Onegin* (Eugene Onegin, 1833) Pushkin praised Fonvizin as a master of satire.

Denis Ivanovich Fonvizin was born in Moscow on 3 April 1744 or 1745. The confusion in year results from the inscription on the writer's gravestone in the Nevsky Monastery in Saint Petersburg: "born 3 April 1745, died 1 December 1792, lived 48 years, seven months, 28 days." The apparent mistake in the inscription has been interpreted in various ways, but most likely 1745 is correct. Fonvizin descended from a German knight who was captured during the reign of Ivan the Terrible in the sixteenth century and whose offspring had become thoroughly Russified. The family name was preserved as "Von Vizin" or "Vizin" for some time, but Pushkin later protested against this spelling, which reflects German pronunciation, saying that Fonvizin was "iz pererusskikh russkii" (a pun meaning both "a Russian of the Russianized" and "more Russian than Russians"). "Fonvizin" became the accepted spelling in the later tradition.

Fonvizin's father, Ivan Andreevich, served under Peter I, first in the Russian fleet and then in the infantry. In 1762 he transferred to the civil service, specifically the inspection department. In his unfinished memoirs, "Chistoserdechnoe priznanie v delakh moikh i pomyshleniiakh" (An Open-Hearted Confession of My Deeds and Designs), first published in full in Platon Beketov's 1830 edition of Fonvizin's works, the writer recalled that his father "had a very hot temper" but was not rancorous and cared for his serfs "with kindness." The story of his first marriage, as related by Fonvizin, demonstrated his father's magnanimity. In order to assist his brother, who had fallen into severe debt, Ivan Andreevich Fonvizin agreed to marry an elderly woman who was extremely rich and had fallen in love with him. Over the course of the next twelve years, in Fonvizin's words, his father "tried to make her old age comfortable." His second wife (the writer's mother) was Ekaterina Vasil'evna Dmitrieva-Mamonova, from an ancient Russian aristocratic family.

Fonvizin's parents were landowners of middle standing, possessing around five hundred serfs, but because they had eight children (four sons and four daughters), they could not afford to hire foreign-language tutors. At the age of four Fonvizin began learning to read and write Russian, and his father later made him read Slavonic during religious services at home. When Moscow University opened in 1755, Denis and his younger brother Pavel, also subsequently a man of letters, were immediately enrolled in the university's gymnasium for children of noble families. However, the level of education it offered was not high. Nevertheless, while at the gymnasium Fonvizin mastered Latin and, even more important, German. The main thing he acquired during his years at the university gymnasium, in Fonvizin's words, was "a taste for the philological sciences." He became interested in the theater and took part in amateur theatrical productions staged at the university after 1756. Fonvizin's academic achievements were honored at the yearly public assemblies held at the university from 1756 to 1761.

In winter 1759–1760 a group of the best students, including Fonvizin and his brother, took part in a trip to Saint Petersburg organized by the university's director Ivan Melissino. In Saint Petersburg the students were brought before Ivan Shuvalov, the curator of the university, and greeted him with speeches and poetry. In Shuvalov's home Fonvizin met Mikhail Lomonosov, who was already highly acclaimed as a poet, scholar, and scientist. Fonvizin never forgot this meeting, but it was an invitation to the court theater that made the most significant impression on him. Fonvizin saw the greatest actors of the time: Fedor Volkov, Ivan Dmitrevsky, and Iakov Shumsky. Shortly afterward he made the acquaintance of Volkov and Dmitrevsky in his uncle's home. In Saint Petersburg another episode occurred which revealed an important aspect of the future writer's personality. In casual conversation at the theater, the son of a certain highly placed individual derided Fonvizin for his inability to speak French, which at the time had become the fashion among the Russian gentry. Upon his return to Moscow Fonvizin immediately undertook the serious study of that language and came to know it well. In 1760 he received the rank of sergeant; ac-

cording to eighteenth-century custom he had been assigned to the Semenovsky Regiment as a child (since 1754). However, he did not find military service to his taste; as he put it, he much preferred studying to "being on guard duty."

The writer recalled that he was drawn to satire early on and that his barbed words often "made the rounds throughout Moscow." At the same time, according to the testimony of one of Fonvizin's contemporaries, "despite the sharpest and quickest wit, he never deliberately offended anyone – unless it was someone who had challenged him to a war of words." While still a student, he began to publish translations. His first significant work, *Basni nravouchitel'nye s iz"iasneniiami* (Edifying Fables with Explanation), by the Danish writer Ludvig Holberg, was translated from the German (1761). Like the original, Fonvizin's translation is in prose and is on the whole quite accurate. Fonvizin also published several prose translations in the journals *Poleznoe uveselenie* (Useful Amusement) and *Sobranie luchshikh sochinenii* (A Collection of the Best Compositions). These translations were mostly moralistic pieces by French and German authors such as Johann Gottlieb Krueger, J. G. B. Pfeil, and Antoine Yart. Fonvizin's interest in political questions was attested by his decision to translate the philosophical novel *Séthos* (1731) by the French author Jean Terrasson. In the foreword to his translation, *Geroiskaia dobrodetel', ili Zhizn' Sifa, tsaria egipetskogo* (Heroic Virtue, or the Life of the Egyptian King Sif, 1762–1768), Fonvizin remarks that the work attracted him because of its "good intention to be useful to society." In 1762 Johann Gottfried Reichel, a professor at Moscow University, praised this translation in the highest terms, noting Fonvizin's excellent command of German. It was thus no surprise that in the same year Reichel entrusted Fonvizin with the translation from German to Russian of his address to a Moscow University public assembly. In the spring of the same year Fonvizin transferred from the university gymnasium to the university. However, in June he applied to serve in the Foreign Office; successfully passed tests in Latin, German, and French; and was taken on as a translator.

At the end of 1762 Fonvizin was sent on a diplomatic mission to Germany to bestow a decoration on Duchess Meklenburg-Shverinskaia. Although he still had not fully mastered etiquette, as he recalled in his memoirs, he was helped by his erudition, his powers of observation, and his "natural wit." In 1763 he moved to Saint Petersburg, where the College of Foreign Affairs was located. He wrote of his life in Saint Petersburg in great detail to his father and to his favorite sister, Fedos'ia Ivanovna Fonvizina (subsequently Argamakova), who was one year his elder. He was present at receptions for foreign ambassadors and attended events at the palace, including balls and masquerades. Fonvizin spoke ironically about the diversions of the gentry in the capital but was nevertheless a full-fledged man of society: he dressed in stylish, expensive clothing and loved to play cards and to show off his wit in conversation. He was known for his entertaining stories; his ability to impersonate masterfully the voice and manners of other people invariably provoked laughter. In particular he was well known for his comic impersonation of the poet Aleksandr Sumarokov.

Fonvizin's interest in the theater continued, and he tried to attend every interesting performance, also maintaining his acquaintance with actors. He became a close friend of Dmitrevsky. They spent a great deal of time together, despite the fact that Fonvizin's parents thought it unworthy of a nobleman to have friendly relations with "comedians" from the third estate. During this time (1762 to the beginning of 1764), perhaps reacting to his parents' attitude, the writer worked on a treatise titled "Kratkoe iz"iasnenie o vol'nosti frantsuzskogo dvorianstva i o pol'ze tret'ego china" (A Brief Explanation of the Freedom of the French Nobility and on the Utility of the Third Estate), which was partly original and partly a translation of an unknown source.

In 1763 Fonvizin's translation of Jean-Jacques Barthélémy's story *Les amours de Carite et Polydore* (1760) was published in Saint Petersburg as *Liubov' Karity i Polidora* (The Love of Carita and Polydore). The action takes place in ancient Greece, and the plot concerns the myth of the Minotaur and the plight of the young boys and girls sacrificed to it. Fonvizin hoped to make a profit on this venture and sent part of the edition to his sister in Moscow, asking her to help in the book's distribution and sale and to send him money as soon as possible. Because life in the capital required a sizable income, he felt constant financial pressure.

In fall 1763 Fonvizin completed a verse translation of Voltaire's *Alzire* (1736) as "Al'zira" and submitted manuscript copies of the work to Catherine II's favorite Count Grigorii Orlov and to his brother Fedor Orlov. The translation contained errors (for example, Fonvizin confused the French *sabre* [saber] and *sable* [sand]), which were soon the subject of a mocking epigram by the poet Aleksandr Khvostov. Fonvizin was critical of the work as well and did not attempt to have it published. Neverthe-

Nikita Panin, head of the College of Foreign Affairs under Catherine II. Fonvizin became Panin's secretary in December 1769.

less, the translation had its good points and according to Fonvizin attracted attention in literary circles, where it was circulated in manuscript form. As a result, the young writer came to the attention of Catherine's main personal secretary, Ivan Elagin, who was himself interested in writing and enjoyed patronizing beginning authors. Still listed as an employee of the College of Foreign Affairs, Fonvizin began to work for Elagin as a secretary and at the same time became a member of a literary circle that included Elagin's other secretary, Vladimir Lukin, as well as Bogdan El'chaninov, Fedor Kozlovsky, and Elagin. These were men of diverse social rank, from hereditary noblemen to the son of a house servant (Lukin), but they were all drawn to the theater and interested in writing plays. Wishing to augment the existing Russian comedic repertory, they "adapted" plays by foreign authors "to Russian mores"; that is, while utilizing the basic plot, they Russified the text, introducing Russian titles and names and occasionally even adding completely new episodes. Fonvizin thus reworked Jean-Baptiste Louis Gresset's drama *Sidney* (1745) as *Korion*. This comedy in verse was successfully staged at the court theater in 1764 and 1765. The play's hero, Korion, is a man disappointed in love and life. However, his lover's betrayal turns out to be only in Korion's imagination, and the hero's attempted suicide is prevented by a keen-witted servant who gives his master water instead of poison. Fonvizin introduced a new character into the play, Krest'ianin (Peasant), who complains of the hardship of quitrent and of oppression and illegal extortion. At the same time Krest'ianin's speech is peppered with slang, and he comes across as a comic figure. The character delighted the ten-year-old heir to the throne, Pavel Petrovich, who reportedly laughed throughout the play's performance. Despite this mark of "favor from above," the play was assailed by critics. Iakov Kniazhnin's satiric poem "Boi stikhotvortsev" (The Battle of the Versifiers, 1765), which circulated in literary circles, leveled sharp abuse at both the play and its author, as well as at the other members of the Elagin circle. Kniazhnin's mockery in turn provoked a sarcastic "Druzheskoe uveshchanie Kniazhninu" (Friendly Admonition to Kniazhnin), also in verse and ascribed to Fonvizin.

By the 1760s Fonvizin was well known as an author of satiric poems. The most noteworthy was the *Poslanie k slugam moim Shumilovu, Van'ke i Petrushke* (Epistle to My Servants Shumilov, Van'ka and Petrushka, 1788). The work is structured as a conversation between the poet and his servants, based on actual people; Fonvizin saw no reason to change their names for the poem. Arguing about "why the world was created," the participants speak out ironically not only about the powers that be but also about the clergy, whose only concern, they note, is to fill their pockets. "Because of this work many considered me an atheist," Fonvizin wrote in his "Chistoserdechnoe priznanie," and he explained that the work had been written during the years of his friendship with the young man of letters Prince F. A. Kozlovsky, at a time when their "favorite pastime consisted in blaspheming and mockery."

Fonvizin also continued to work on translations apart from his official duties, and in 1764–1765 he rendered Johann Justi's social-political work *Der Grundriss einer guten Regierung* (1759) as "O pravitel'stvakh" (On Governments) and a translation by Justi of a French treatise by Gabriel François Coyer as *Torguiushchee dvorianstvo, protivupolozhnoe dvorianstvu voennomu* (The Trading Nobility versus the Military Nobility, 1766). At the same time Fonvizin's service under Elagin became unpleasant, mostly because of an increasing enmity between him and Lukin. More and more he thought of leaving Elagin's service. In a letter dated 11 September 1768 Fonvizin declared that life with Elagin had become intolerable, and that he would eventually like to enter the service of someone else, and not [have to work with] such a pervert."

In fall 1768 Fonvizin took an extended leave of absence and visited his family in Moscow. During this time he fell in love with a certain woman "pleniaiushchego razuma" (of captivating intelligence), whom he recalled throughout his later life. His beloved was married, and only upon parting did she confess her mutual feelings for him. "I so respected this woman," the writer recalled, "that I didn't dare even to think of taking advantage of her confession, but, agreeing only to correspond with her, said goodbye, and left her crying most bitter tears."

During this Moscow leave Fonvizin continued his writing and translating. As always, he selected works to translate that were close to his own interests. He translated François-Thomas-Marie de Baculard d'Arnaud's *Sidnei et Silli, ou La Bienfaisance et la reconnaissance* (1766) as *Sidnei i Sillii; ili, Blagodeianie i blagodarnost'* (Sidney and Silli, or Charity and Gratitude, 1769), which praised the generosity and devotion of friendship. He also translated Paul Jérémie Bitaubé's poem in prose *Joseph* (1767) as *Iosif* (published four times between 1769 and 1790). In his memoirs Fonvizin notes that his father had introduced him to Bible stories, and that the story of Joseph sold into slavery by his brothers had inspired him with "uncontrollable weeping" as a child; the writer remarks that he knew of many who shed tears over his translation of Bitaubé. Its language is archaic, purposefully laden with slavonicisms; in the introduction Fonvizin argues for the need to combine the "seriousness" of Slavonic with the "clarity" of contemporary Russian when dealing with texts of this sort.

Fonvizin's main work during this period, which amply testifies to his creative independence, was the comedy *Brigadir* (The Brigadier, 1792?), completed in the first half of 1769. Upon returning from Moscow, he read his play to friends. He was a masterful reader and made his listeners laugh out loud. After hearing him read the play, Grigorii Orlov suggested that Fonvizin read it to the empress, and on 29 June 1769 the playwright read *Brigadir* to Catherine at the palace at Peterhof with great success. Three days later he was invited to see the heir to the throne, Pavel Petrovich, and after that, as Fonvizin recalled, he was "invited daily to dine and read" in the homes of the most powerful and influential figures in Saint Petersburg.

Drawing upon the works of European playwrights – most notably Denis Diderot and Pierre-Augustin de Beaumarchais – and upon Russian satiric tradition, Fonvizin presents in his play a spectrum of Russian social types, throwing a humorous light on the daily life of ignorant landowners. The main characters are the crude and narrow-minded Brigadier (an eighteenth-century Russian military rank between colonel and general); his wife, the Brigadirsha, stupid and miserly to the point of absurdity, but sympathetic because of the cruel manner in which her husband treats her; the bigoted and corrupt civil-service counselor; and the counselor's wife and the brigadier's son Ivanushka, two empty-headed fops who praise everything foreign.

Nikita Panin, tutor to Pavel Petrovich and head of the College of Foreign Affairs, told Fonvizin apropos his new comedy that "I see you know our morals and manners well, for your Brigadirsha is Russian through and through; no one can say they don't have their own Akulina Timofeevna, a grandmother, auntie, or some other relation [just like her] ... this is the first comedy on our [own Russian] mores." Panin offered Fonvizin a position working in his service, and in December 1769 the playwright became his secretary. Fonvizin fulfilled many important diplomatic duties and became not only a colleague of Panin's but also his trusted friend. According to one contemporary, "You could say that they were of one heart and soul." Fonvizin became part of the political faction Panin headed, which included Panin's brother, Petr Panin, an important military leader, and Princess Ekaterina Romanovna Dashkova, director of both the Academy of Sciences and the Russian Academy. The precise nature of the faction's political goals is the subject of debate among historians. Panin's position was quite complicated. He had supported Catherine and helped her seize the throne in 1762. However, Catherine rejected the constitutional projects that he had proposed to the empress soon after. Their relations became increasingly strained, and the Panin group placed its hopes for reform on Pavel Petrovich.

By the 1770s Fonvizin's literary reputation had solidified. When Nikolai Novikov published Fonvizin's "Poslanie k slugam moim" in his journal *Pustomel'ia* (The Tattler), he noted that "The pen that wrote this [work] is well known to Russian educated society and to all who love literature. Many of this author's written works are passed from hand to hand, read with the greatest enjoyment, and praised as much for their clarity and purity of style as for their sharp and lively wit, and their light and pleasant expression." Novikov and Fonvizin were bound together by both common Enlightenment convic-

tions and literary interests. The article on Fonvizin in Novikov's *Opyt istoricheskogo slovaria o rossiiskikh pisateliakh* (Attempt at a Historical Dictionary of Russian Writers, 1772) noted that Fonvizin "wrote many clever and extremely good poems" and that "his prose is as pure, pleasant, and fluid as his poetry." *Brigadir* is especially singled out: "It captures our customs and morals exactly; its characterizations are consistent, and the denouement is the most simple and natural." As if predicting the playwright's future fame, Novikov's article concluded that "Russia hopes to see in him a first-class writer." Also in 1772 Novikov republished Fonvizin's *Slovo na vyzdorovlenie e. i. v. gosudaria tsesarevicha i velikogo kniazia Pavla Petrovicha* (Speech on the Recovery of His Imperial Majesty the Tsarevich and Grand Prince Pavel Petrovich) – which had been published separately in 1771 – in his journal *Zhivopisets* (The Painter). In this polemical work Fonvizin outlines a program for enlightenment in Russia, countering many of the ideas of Panin's opponents. Many anonymous pieces appearing in *Zhivopisets* in 1772–1773 have been convincingly attributed to Fonvizin as well. In content and narrative method the satiric "Pis'ma k Falaleiu" (Letters to Falelei) – ostensibly written by provincial landowners to their son and nephew Falalei, who lives in Saint Petersburg – is particularly reminiscent of Fonvizin's other writings. The author masterfully imitates the speech of uncultured landowners who commit acts of violence against their serfs with impunity and who self-confidently assert, "Da na chto oni krest'iane – ego takoe i delo, chto rabotai bez otydykha!" (That's why they are peasants – it is their job to work without rest!).

In 1772–1773 the opposition to Catherine culminated with the coming of age of her son Pavel Petrovich and hopes for his accession to the throne. According to tradition, Fonvizin even took part in a conspiracy against the empress. In September 1773 Pavel Petrovich married, and Panin's tutorship was terminated; this helped Catherine consolidate her power. With Panin's loss of influence, Fonvizin's situation became precarious. He wrote to his sister: "[I am in] dreadful condition. I ask God only that he deliver me safely from this hell." Nonetheless, Fonvizin continued to work in the College of Foreign Affairs, which Panin still headed. Catherine, always the consummate politician, rewarded Panin generously for his previous services. Panin divided the empress's largesse up with his secretaries, and thus Fonvizin suddenly found himself the owner of lands in Belarus and possessor of more than a thousand serfs.

Fonvizin's marriage to Ekaterina Ivanovna Khlopova (née Rogovikova) in 1774 also improved his financial situation. After losing her parents she had been raised in the home of her uncle and had married her first husband against her guardian's wishes. As a result, her relatives refused to give her her rightful inheritance of around three hundred thousand rubles, and she filed suit against them. During the course of the long proceeding her husband died, and Ekaterina Ivanovna had to continue alone. Fonvizin, who took part in settling the suit, tried to help her, and then, in order to put an end to gossip about their relationship, he married her. Because she was the daughter of a merchant, many people, including Fonvizin's parents, did not approve of the union. However, judging from his letters, the writer held her in unwavering respect and affection. They moved into her house on Galernaia Street in Saint Petersburg. Guests were common in the Fonvizin house, where there were card tables, a clavichord, and a table that could seat twenty; the walls were decorated with prints in golden frames. In the 1770s Fonvizin was friends with many writers, including Mikhail Kheraskov, Mikhail Murav'ev, Vasilii Maikov, and even Kniazhnin; his earlier dispute with the latter apparently did not interfere with their subsequent relations, and their positions on many questions were close. Fonvizin also continued to write. In 1777 his translation of Antoine-Léonard Thomas's *Eloge de Marc-Aurèle* (Eulogy for Marcus Aureleus, 1775) was published. This book, which condemned despotism and presented an idealized picture of a king, must have had immediate relevance for contemporary Russian readers.

In 1777–1778 Fonvizin and his wife made a trip to France. They were accompanied by the Saint Petersburg book dealer Germann Johann Klostermann, with whom Fonvizin had developed excellent business contacts and the most cordial personal relations. The purpose of the trip was to treat Fonvizin's sick wife, and they traveled as private citizens. However, the writer was so well known in diplomatic circles that more than once the travelers were made guests of honor at official receptions. They arrived in France at the end of 1777 and spent around three months in Montpellier and spring and summer 1778 in Paris. They visited the theater and art galleries and made the acquaintance of many important figures, including Benjamin Franklin. They saw Voltaire during one of his triumphs before the theatrical public, which had ecstatically greeted the great author as he entered his box.

Fonvizin tutoring a student; engraving by Böm

During his trip Fonvizin wrote detailed letters to his sister and to Petr Panin. These letters, which Fonvizin was unable to publish during his life, draw a comprehensive picture of the political and cultural scene in prerevolutionary France and contain interesting sketches of day-to-day life and contemporary morals. Fonvizin's judgments are predominantly negative: he notes political and judicial corruption and the ostentatious luxury of the nobility. With irony he relates how he saw people singe the hair off a pig right in the middle of the street in Lyons and similar details of low European realia. He criticizes the writers and philosophers of the French Enlightenment rather sharply, deriding, for example, Jean Le Rond d'Alembert's physical appearance. Fonvizin's one-sided judgments may be explained to a large extent by his polemical opposition to Russian Gallophiles, whom the writer had already satirized in *Brigadir*. At the same time, Fonvizin, in criticizing the abuses and disorder in the cultured society of France, continually draws parallels to analogous phenomena in Russia. Written in a lively and engaging style, Fonvizin's letters are one of the best examples of eighteenth-century Russian epistolary and polemical writing.

Upon his return to Saint Petersburg in 1778, Fonvizin continued to work at the College of Foreign Affairs. In 1781 he was assigned to the postal department, and he worked to reform the Russian postal system. At the same time he was able to complete work on a new play, the comedy *Nedorosl'* (1783), which he had begun as early as 1779. In March 1782 Fonvizin read the play in several private circles, and his reading created a sensation. Postal Director B. V. Pestel' recalled: "A large number of literary people and connoisseurs gathered for dinner; the guests' curiosity [about the play] was so great that the host urgently entreated the author, who was a fine actor, if he wouldn't read at least one scene from it. He satisfied the general desire, but when he finished . . . those present were so captivated that they asked him to continue the reading. Food was brought to and from the table but no one sat down to dinner until Fonvizin had finished the entire comedy, and after dinner Dmitrevsky, ceding to the general demand, was obliged to read the entire play through a second time from the beginning."

The staging of the play was set for May. However, serious problems arose, apparently because the play was too outspoken. Contemporaries recalled that *Nedorosl'* was subject to a good deal of persecution and that the actors did not want to perform in it because of the threat of repercussions. On 28 May 1782 the tutor to Prince Aleksandr Kurakin, a Frenchman named Picard, complained from Saint Petersburg that "We will not see Mr. Fon-Vizin's new comedy called *Nedorosl'* here, as we had previously hoped. . . . This is truly a deprivation for the public, who have long justly appreciated Mr. Fon-Vizin's tremendous talent. Several enlightened figures, who heard the play read, assert that this is the greatest Russian theatrical piece in the comic genre." In contrast to *Brigadir,* which was met with approval at court, *Nedorosl'* could have offended many important people, first of all the empress herself. Catherine had long seen in Petr Panin a potential political danger, and she felt a similar distrust for his good friend Fonvizin. Panin had been excluded from politics in an increasingly visible way, and when Fonvizin retired from service in March 1782, it may have been to protest this situation.

Fonvizin's friend the actor Dmitrevsky took a spirited part in trying to have *Nedorosl'* staged, and at a benefit performance of 24 September 1782 the premiere of the play finally took place at Karl Knipper's "vol'nyi" (free) theater in Saint Petersburg, which unlike the court theater was open to the entire public. Fonvizin helped cast the play and did readings of each role for the actors, thus helping to direct the play as well. The best Russian actors of the day took part: Dmitrevsky, Petr Plavil'shchikov, and the celebrated comic actor Shumsky, who brilliantly played the role of Eremeevna, the wet nurse (men customarily played this role, inevitably increasing its comic effect). Karamzin, however, who was present at the premiere, recalled that although the comic scenes provoked passing laughter, the more serious scenes were what held the audience's attention.

Nedorosl' raises topical political and social questions and at the same time mocks vices common to people of all times and places. Ignorant, self-assured landowners who have become accustomed to ruling tyrannically over their serfs and servants are presented onstage, and Fonvizin's contemporaries apparently listened with rapt attention to the bold tirades of his positive heroes who denounce behavior at court. The eternal themes of education and the relationship between parents and children are organically fused with an attack upon the "bad morals" reigning in contemporary Russian society. The name of Mitrofan, the eponymous "minor" who has been spoiled by his mother, became a household word in Russia, as did the word *nedorosl'*, as young noblemen who had not yet entered service were called in the eighteenth century; the term took on new connotations suggesting a young person's laziness, effeminacy, and ignorance. One of Mitrofan's lines became a popular saying: "Ne khochu uchit'sia, khochu zhenit'sia" (I don't want to study; I want to get married). Masterfully structured comic scenes, lively and expressive dialogue evoking each character's individuality, and brilliant acting all contributed to the success of the play, and as a sign of their overwhelming approval the audience threw purses of money onto the stage. *Nedorosl'* was published in 1783 and in May of the same year was staged in Moscow; it has been a standard of the Russian theatrical repertory ever since.

The political ideas expressed in *Nedorosl'* closely correspond to the contents of a document written by Fonvizin on Panin's suggestion in 1782 and early 1783, the "Rassuzhdenie o nepremennykh gosudarstvennykh zakonakh" (Discourse on Necessary State Laws), known widely as "Zaveshchanie Panina" (Panin's Testament). The discourse sharply condemns despotic government and speaks of the need for social reform and restricting the monarchy's power by potent legal means.

Fonvizin's contemporaries could easily discern Catherine in the figure of the absolute monarch, dominated by vice and surrounded by "sycophantic incompetents." Panin died on 31 March 1783, and although Fonvizin was unable to publish the discourse, he preserved a copy of the text and gave it to trusted friends for safekeeping. Fonvizin's brother Pavel had one copy, which later turned up in the possession of his other brother, Aleksandr, father of the future Decembrist rebel Mikhail Fonvizin, and the work circulated among members of the secret political societies that appeared in Russia after 1812. This bold political tract was not published until 1907, in the appendix to E. S. Shumigorsky's book *Imperator Pavel I, Zhizn' i tsarstvovanie* (The Life and Reign of Emperor Paul I).

Fonvizin turned to other ways of expressing his criticism of the government. In 1783 he took part in a curious polemic with Catherine in the pages of the journal *Sobesednik liubitelei rossiiskogo slova* (Interlocutor of Lovers of the Russian Word), published by Dashkova, who had been named head of the Academy of Sciences in January of that year. Catherine had been taking a silent part in the journal's publication and attempting to convert it into an organ of the government. Dashkova, however, was able to assert the independence of *Sobesednik liubitelei rossiiskogo slova* and secured the participation of many of Russia's leading literary figures: Fonvizin, Gavriil Derzhavin, Petr Bogdanovich, Kniazhnin, Vasilii Kapnist, Ermil Kostrov, Murav'ev, and others. Anonymously, Fonvizin published a list of "Neskol'ko voprosov, mogushchikh vozbudit' v umnykh i chestnykh liudiakh osoblivoe vnimanie" (Several Questions Designed to Arouse the Special Interest of Intelligent and Honest People), and alongside the questions appeared Catherine's answers, also anonymously. The empress was clearly angered by "the loose tongue" of the author of the questions, which address such issues as the serious shortcomings of Russian law and the preponderance of favoritism in the government. Significantly, Fonvizin, who had himself recently left civil service, asked, "why do we see so many good people resigning from service?" To this Catherine rather cynically answered, "many people are leaving service apparently because they find retirement profitable." The questions and answers were printed in the third issue of the journal, and in the fifth a clever "letter from the questioner" appeared. Despite complimentary formulas praising the "most wise monarch" and the letter's ostensibly penitential tone, Fonvizin was able to continue his debate with the empress. In particular he returned

to the question of retirement, noting, "I have seen many such persons who serve, or rather, occupy places in the service, only so that they can ride around in pairs [that is, enjoy the right of state employees to ride in carriages drawn by a pair of horses]. I have seen many others who resigned the minute they attained the right to harness a team of four."

During this period Fonvizin evidently found writing the most acceptable form of social activity. In addition to the questions, he published several other works in the *Sobesednik liubitelei rossiiskogo slova*. Particularly topical was his "Chelobitnaia rossiiskoi Minerve ot rossiiskikh pisatelei" (A Petition to the Russian Minerva from Russian Writers), published in the fourth issue. The article spoke of "renowned ignoramuses" who dismiss "all those who practice in the literary sciences" from public service, referring to Derzhavin, who at the time was being subjected to administrative persecution by his superior Aleksandr Viazemsky, *ober-prokuror* of the senate and head of the secret police. Fonvizin satirized Saint Petersburg court life in his uncompleted "Povestvovanie mnimogo glukhogo i nemogo" (Tale of a Sham Deaf Mute), installments of which appeared in the fourth and seventh issues of *Sobesednik liubitelei rossiiskogo slova*. Speaking of the excesses of a certain provincial landowner, the author recalls his powerful patron — the palace janitor. The story also contains a lively description of Russian provincial life, to some degree anticipating Nikolai Gogol's *Mertvye dushi* (Dead Souls, 1842).

In 1783 Fonvizin, together with Derzhavin, Kheraskov, Bogdanovich, and many other writers, joined the Russian Academy, which had just opened with Dashkova at its head. The academy's first task was to compile the first scientific dictionary of the Russian language. Fonvizin took exceptional interest in this project. He became one of a "detachment" of four whose job it was to develop principles for compiling the dictionary and, in fact, took upon himself the writing of the "Nachertanie dlia sostavleniia tolkovogo slovaria slaviano-rossiiskogo iazyka" (Outline for Compiling an Explanatory Dictionary of the Slaveno-Russian Language). Fonvizin proposed that church dictionaries as well as the works of the best writers, past and present, be used as sources (these included the works of Lomonosov and Sumarokov and eighteenth-century Russian periodicals). On 11 November 1783 Fonvizin read the text of his "Nachertanie" at a session of the academy. A week later discussions were held, and the plan was approved. Fonvizin was assigned the task of compiling words beginning with the letters *K* and *L*. On 22 January 1784 he wrote to Dashkova to inform her that he had completed the job, and he appended to the material he had assembled a list of words derived from the verb *dat'* (to give), as well as a list of hunting terms, dictated by Petr Panin, an enthusiast of the sport. Because of a trip to Moscow, Fonvizin was unable to attend several subsequent meetings of the Russian Academy at which the well-known historian Ivan Boltin criticized the "Nachertanie." Fonvizin answered his objections in a detailed letter. Later work on the dictionary validated most of Fonvizin's proposals (such as excluding proper names from the dictionary). The *Slovar' Akademii Rossiiskoi* (Dictionary of the Russian Academy) appeared in six volumes from 1789 to 1794.

At the same time Fonvizin continued to write. In 1784 his French *Précis historique de la vie du comte Nikita Iwanowitsch de Panin* (Historical Summary of the Life of Count Nikita Ivanovich Panin) was published anonymously in London. Portraying Panin as an ideal state official and citizen, Fonvizin again risked Catherine's wrath. However, after only two years, a Russian translation by Dmitriev was published in a Saint Petersburg journal, and it was subsequently republished three more times, albeit still anonymously and with the sharpest passages deleted.

Not wishing to return to state service, Fonvizin occupied his leisure time with his favorite activities. He was seriously interested in art and had a fine appreciation of painting and graphics. He loved music and attended the Musical Club, where concerts were performed twice a week; he himself played the violin. In collaboration with his longtime friend the bookseller Klostermann, Fonvizin became involved in selling art objects. Klostermann traded in artworks as well as books, and he sold several paintings, bronze statues, and other valuable objects to the Hermitage. Fonvizin also continued to work as a translator, producing a Russian version of *Vom Nationalstolze* (1758), by the German Enlightener Johann G. Zimmermann, as *Rassuzhdeniia o natsional'nom liubochestii* (Discourse on National Pride, 1785). The ideas it propounded were close to Fonvizin's own: love for one's country, inextricably tied to the love of freedom, is presented as a fundamental civic virtue.

Fonvizin and his wife went on another trip abroad in 1784, this time Italy, where they saw the sights and attended the theater, concerts, and art galleries. One of the goals of this trip was to obtain works of art. From Italy the travelers headed to Belarus to visit Fonvizin's estate, after stops in Vi-

Fonvizin's grave, in the Aleksandr Nevsky Monastery in Saint Petersburg (photograph by Marcus Levitt)

enna and Kraków. During their journey a peasant uprising began at Fonvizin's estate, due to the oppressive management of his lessee, Baron F. A. Medem, who had also failed to pay Fonvizin the money owed him. A long legal dispute broke out between the two, which cost Fonvizin a great deal of money. In August 1785 Fonvizin left to visit his relatives in Moscow, where on 29 August he was overcome by a severe paralysis and for a while was completely unable to move or speak. Gradually, his condition improved.

A year later Fonvizin and his wife traveled abroad for the sake of his health. He spent winter 1787 in Vienna and spring in Karlovy Vary (Karlsbad), Czechoslovakia. The trip did not achieve the desired result, but despite his illness Fonvizin continued to participate in literary life. In 1786 the journal *Ezhemesiachnye sochineniia* (Monthly Works) published his "Kallisfen," a "Greek tale" which contained direct political allusions about the current situation in Russia. In 1787 students at the Noble Pension of

Moscow University prepared a collection called *Raspuskaiushchiisia tsvetok* (The Blossoming Flower), in which Fonvizin's verse satire "Lisitsa-Koznodei" (The Fox Intriguer) – a free translation of the German prose fable by Christian Friedrich Schubart, "In Lybien starb 'mal ein Löwe" (1774) – appeared. The fable, which mocks sycophantic courtiers, once again turned out to be topical for Russian readers. In publishing the translation, the editors expressed gratitude "to the great poet, famous throughout the world for his many great works" for his contribution.

Around the end of 1787 Fonvizin began to prepare his own journal, "Drug chestnykh liudei, ili Starodum" (Friend of Honest People, or Starodum), for publication – although it was not to appear in print until the 1830 Beketov edition of Fonvizin's works. The title recalled Starodum ("Wise Old Man"), the *raisoneur* and positive hero of *Nedorosl'*, into whose mouth the playwright had put many of his own ideas. Subscriptions to the journal were solicited in the newspaper *Sankt Peterburgskie vedomosti* (Saint Petersburg News) from February to March 1788; however, in a letter of 4 April 1788 Fonvizin informed a correspondent that "the police have refused to allow *Starodum*'s publication." Fonvizin's articles for the journal began to circulate in manuscript, and his "Vseobshchaia pridvornaia grammatika" (Universal Court Grammar) gained special notoriety. Aleksandr Radishchev referred to it in his *Puteshestvie iz Peterburga v Moskvu* (Journey from Petersburg to Moscow, 1790). Brilliantly parodying school textbooks, Fonvizin depicts the corrupt ways of those close to the throne, dividing them up into *glasnye* (vowels), *bezglasnye* (nonvowels), and *poluglasnye* (semivowels), with a pun on *glasnyi*, which may also mean "vocal" or "public."

Despite the failure of "Starodum," Fonvizin undertook the publication of his collected works and translations. In May and June 1788 subscriptions were advertised, but this project did not come to pass either. Meanwhile the writer's health deteriorated. In summer 1789 he and his wife once again went abroad for his health's sake, this time to Riga, Baldon, and Mitava, but there was no significant improvement. In 1791 Fonvizin suffered several apoplectic strokes, but to the end of his life he continued his literary pursuits. One of his final works was the memoir "Chistoserdechnoe priznanie v delakh moikh i pomyshleniiakh," which he did not manage to complete. In line with the tradition of Jean-Jacques Rousseau's *Confessions* and to some extent polemicizing with it, Fonvizin relates his childhood, youth, and first years of his literary career in a lively and captivating manner. The work is also of interest for its subtle psychological observations and acute satiric sketches.

Fonvizin never lost hopes of publishing his collected works and tried to undertake the project again in 1792 with the help of the Saint Petersburg publisher Bogdanovich, who had already published several of his works. When he republished the life of Panin in 1792, Bogdanovich included a list of forthcoming titles, and among them was a complete edition of Fonvizin's works in five volumes, but this edition never appeared.

Failures to publish and physical weakness did not crush Fonvizin's good-natured wit and interest in life. In November 1792, returning to Saint Petersburg from a recent trip to Belarus, he paid a visit to Derzhavin and spent the last evening of his life at the poet's home. Dmitriev, who met the famous playwright then for the first time, described the event: "He entered Derzhavin's study, supported by two young officers. . . . He could no longer use one of his arms, and one leg had also become deadened; both had been stricken by paralysis. He spoke with extreme effort, and pronounced each word in a hoarse and wild voice, but his eyes sparkled with animation. His first glance addressed to me was disconcerting. The conversation dropped off. He began to ask me questions about his works. . . . From the start it seemed as if he was trying to weigh my intelligence and character." Dmitriev noted that Fonvizin had brought Derzhavin a new comedy called "Gofmeister" (The Household Steward), which has not survived; one of the officers accompanying him began to read it. During the reading Fonvizin "tried to emphasize the expressions that pleased him with his eyes, head movements, and his good hand." He took active part in the ensuing conversation and told a few amusing anecdotes. The next morning, 1 December 1792, Fonvizin died. He was buried in the Aleksandr Nevsky Monastery in Saint Petersburg.

At the beginning of the nineteenth century Fonvizin's papers passed into the hands of Beketov, who prepared Fonvizin's collected works, published in 1830 by the bookseller I. G. Salaev. Several unpublished works by Fonvizin were subsequently discovered by scholars and have been published in later editions of his works.

Letters:

Sobranie sochinenii, volume 2, edited by Georgii P. Makogonenko (Moscow & Leningrad: Khudozhestvennaia literatura, 1959), pp. 317–562.

Biographies:

Kirill V. Pigarev, *Tvorchestvo Fonvizina* (Moscow: Akademiia nauk, 1954);

Georgii P. Makogonenko, *Denis Fonvizin: Tvorcheskii put'* (Moscow & Leningrad: Goslitizdat, 1961);

Lubov I. Kulakova, *Denis Ivanovich Fonvizin: Biografiia pisatelia* (Moscow: Prosveshchenie, 1966);

Alexis Strycek, *Denis Fonvizine* (Paris: Librarie des cinq continents, 1976);

Charles A. Moser, *Denis Fonvizin* (Boston: Twayne, 1979);

Natal'ia D. Kochetkova, *Fonvizin v Peterburge* (Leningrad: Leningradskoe izdatel'stvo, 1984);

Stanislav Rassadin, *Satiry smelyi vlastelin: Kniga o D. I. Fonvizine* (Moscow: Kniga, 1985).

References:

Pimen Arapov, *Letopis' russkogo teatra* (Saint Petersburg: N. Tiblen, 1861);

Thomas Barran, "Rousseau and Fonvizin: *Emile* as a Source for 'The Minor,'" *Ulbandus Review*, 2 (Fall 1982): 5–22;

Pavel N. Berkov, *Istoriia russkoi komedii XVIII v.* (Leningrad: Nauka, 1977);

Berkov, *Istoriia russkoi zhurnalistiki XVIII veka* (Moscow & Leningrad: Akademiia nauk, 1952);

Berkov, "Materialy dlia biografii D. I. Fonvizina (K voprosu ob ego ukhode v otstavku)," *Nauchnyi biulleten' Leningradskogo gos. universiteta*, 6 (1946): 24–25;

Berkov, "Teatr Fonvizina i russkaia kul'tura," in his *Russkie klassiki i teatr* (Leningrad & Moscow: Iskusstvo, 1947), pp. 7–108;

Anthony G. Cross, "Fonvizin's *Nedorosl'*: An Overlooked English Critique," *Study Group on Eighteenth Century Russia Newsletter*, 5 (1977): 27–33;

Ivan A. Dmitrievsky, "D. I. Fonvizin," *Drug prosveshcheniia*, 3, no. 9 (1805): 245–255;

Irina Isakovich, *"Brigadir" i "Nedorosl'" D. I. Fonvizina* (Leningrad: Khudozhestvennaia literatura, 1979);

Istoriia russkogo dramaticheskogo teatra, volume 1 (Moscow: Iskusstvo, 1977);

Istoriia russkoi dramaturgii: XVIII – pervaia polovina XIX veka (Leningrad: Nauka, 1982);

Marvin Kantor, "Fonvizin and Holberg: A Comparison of *The Brigadier* and *Jean de France*," *Canadian-American Slavic Studies*, 7 (Winter 1973): 475–484;

Kantor, "Life and Writings" in *Dramatic Works of D. I. Fonvizin*, translated by Kantor (Bern: Herbert Lang / Frankfurt: Peter Lang, 1974), pp. 11–45;

Germann I. Klosterman, "Fonvizin (Iz neizdannykh zapisok)," *Russkii arkhiv*, 3, no. 2 (1881): 291–299;

Charles A. Moser, *Fonvizin, Russia and Europe*, Kennan Institute for Advanced Russian Studies Occasional Paper 26 (Washington, D.C.: Kennan Institute for Advanced Russian Studies, 1978);

David Patterson, "Fonvizin's *Nedorosl'* as a Russian Representative of the *genre sérieux*," *Comparative Literature Studies*, 14 (1977): 196–204;

Il'ia Z. Serman, "Fonvizin and Fénélon," *Study Group on Eighteenth Century Russia Newsletter*, 5 (1977): 33–36;

Iurii V. Stennik, *Russkaia satira XVIII veka* (Leningrad: Nauka, 1985);

Mikhail I. Sukhomlinov, "D. I. Fonvizin," in his *Istoriia rossiiskoi akademii*, volume 7 (Saint Petersburg, 1885), pp. 10–22;

Nikolai S. Tikhonravov, "Biografiia D. I. Fonvizina," in his *Sochineniia*, volume 3 (Moscow, 1898), pp. 90–129;

Reuel K. Wilson, *The Literary Travelogue: A Comparative Study with Special Relevance to Russian Literature from Fonvizin to Pushkin* (The Hague: Nijhoff, 1973).

Papers:

The main portion of Fonvizin's archive is located in the Central State Archive of Literature and Art (fond 517) and in the State Russian Library (formerly the Lenin Library, fond 178), both in Moscow.

Gedeon (Georgii Andreevich Krinovsky)
(circa 1730 – 22 June 1763)

Victor M. Zhikov
Institute of the Russian Language, Moscow

BOOK: *Sobranie raznykh pouchitel'nykh slov, pri Vysochaishem Dvore e.i.v. skazyvannykh Pridvornym propovednikom Ieromonakhom Gedeonom,* 4 volumes (Saint Petersburg: Academy of Sciences, 1755–1759); republished in 2 volumes (Moscow: Synod, 1760); republished in 6 volumes (Moscow: Synod, 1828); republished in 4 volumes (Moscow: Synod, 1855).

A major religious figure and one of the central figures in the history of Russian homiletics, Gedeon Krinovsky was the first to preach in Russian rather than in Church Slavonic, and at the same time he modified the rhetorical structure of the sermon. In his homilies the central place was not given to theological debate with examples taken from divine history, as had been characteristic of the earlier homiletic tradition, but to entertaining stories – often from classical rather than biblical sources – interspersed with edifying teachings. As a rule, Gedeon's sermons were lacking in serious theological content, focusing instead on elementary ethical postulates. His sermons were written for the court and brought Gedeon exceptional fame in his position as court preacher.

Gedeon Krinovsky (born Georgii Andreevich) was born in Kazan into the family of a sacristan. The exact date of his birth is not known, but it is most likely around 1729–1730; in the records of the Kazan seminary for 1738 he is mentioned as a pupil and his age listed as nine, and Metropolitan Platon (Levshin) writes in his memoirs that at the time of Gedeon's death in 1763, he was no more than thirty-three years old. Less trustworthy sources list the year of his birth as 1726. There is also some disagreement as to whether he was of Ukrainian or Russian extraction; the latter seems more probable.

Gedeon entered the Kazan seminary in 1738, during a relatively flourishing period of its existence, when Luka Konashevich became bishop of Kazan. He graduated in 1746, having completed seven courses of study. He was tonsured as a monk, assumed the name Gedeon, and taught at the seminary for five years. In 1751 he fled to Moscow, hoping to be accepted into the Dukhovnaia akademiia (Spiritual Academy, a theological academy of higher education) to receive an education that would pave the way for his advancement in church service. Despite the objections of Bishop Luka, who demanded that Gedeon return to the Kazan seminary, he remained in Moscow, suggesting that he had already acquired influential protectors there. On 9 December 1751 the Holy Synod accepted Gedeon into the Moscow academy and permitted him to serve and preach at the Zaikonospassky Monastery, which was attached to it.

From this moment Gedeon's brilliant career began. At the end of 1752 Empress Elizabeth came to Moscow, and Gedeon had the opportunity to preach in her presence. The empress, moved by the young monk's eloquence, made him her court preacher. His duties included regular preaching in the court church, and the sermons that he gave there comprise his literary legacy. Gedeon's closeness to the empress insured his quick advancement in church service. On 21 January 1757 he was named archimandrite (abbot) of the Savvino-Storozhevsky Monastery, a position that gave title and salary but did not require his actual presence; he visited the monastery only once. In 1758 Gedeon became a member of the Holy Synod, the government body that ran church affairs, and shortly afterward became archimandrite of the richest and most noteworthy Russian monastery, the Trinity–Saint Sergius *Lavra* (principal monastery); yet he resided there for only three months. On 7 October 1761 Gedeon was made bishop of Pskov and Narva, which, because of its proximity to Saint Petersburg, was one of the most desirable pulpits. Gedeon also remained the court preacher up until the death of Empress Elizabeth. After that his influence declined, although he kept his position in the synod. In the summer of 1763 Gedeon set out to visit his diocese, but along the way he fell ill and died on 22

Gedeon (Georgii Andreevich Krinovsky)

June 1763, in the Panteleimonov Monastery, two miles from Pskov.

Gedeon's career was rather unusual but indicative of an epoch in which cleverness and the ability to understand and popularize the latest cultural trends could provide entry into Saint Petersburg high society. In Petr V. Znamensky's characterization, Gedeon was an emancipated monk who was connected to the court and had been rewarded and promoted by the secular powers. He was known for his luxurious attire; his assorted velvet and satin cassocks filled an entire dressing room. Rumor had it that he wore shoes decorated with diamond buckles worth more than 10,000 rubles. (After his death, however, he left behind only 5,855 rubles and 75 kopecks.) In the last years of Elizabeth's rule, Gedeon was, despite his youth, probably the most influential figure in the Russian church hierarchy. The two most prominent ecclesiastical figures of Catherine's reign, the Petersburg Metropolitan Gavriil (Petrov) and the Moscow Metropolitan Platon (Levshin), both owed their initial success to Gedeon's sponsorship.

Having become a grandee in his way, Gedeon also adopted the accepted cultural codes dictating how a magnate should act. One element of such be-

havior at mid century was apparently petty tyranny, and anecdotes about Gedeon ascribe such behavior to him. For example, it is said that while walking through the Trinity–Saint Serguis Monastery with his protégé Platon Leshvin (the future metropolitan of Moscow; at the time a simple priest), Gedeon noticed the valuable silk cassock Platon was wearing and pushed him into a pond. Afterwards he reportedly made an admonition that someone of a lower rank should not be upset when a superior jokes with him and thereupon presented Platon with two expensive cassocks to replace the one that had been ruined. This story should not be viewed as an accurate description of Gedeon's character; rather, it reveals the spirit of the age and the way in which Gedeon assimilated it, as well as how representatives of lower social groups adapted themselves to the elitist and Europeanized culture of the gentry.

Gedeon, according to Platon, was not particularly well educated and apparently attached little value to learning. As archimandrite of the Trinity–Saint Sergius Monastery, he administered the Trinity Seminary, one of the main educational institutions in the empire, but his concerns were mainly managerial and disciplinary (for example, he devised uniforms for the seminarists). He did introduce the study of French and German and made geography and arithmetic mandatory, changes which testify more to Gedeon's desire to bring seminary education in line with secular schools than to an aspiration to upgrade its quality. The contents of his personal library, a catalogue of which was compiled after his death, indicates his broad if not deep interests. A large part of the collection comprised theological works and works concerning church history; there were also classical authors (to whom he often referred in sermons), as well as guides to good manners.

In his sermons Gedeon strove to attract his listeners' attention not so much by moral pathos as by sensitivity to the tastes of his upper-class audience; that is, he followed the same orientation here as can be observed in his career as a whole. This applies to the basic moral postulates of his sermons as well. Gedeon often maintained that the salvation of the soul is not contingent upon rejecting worldly goods but only upon faithfully carrying out one's duties, as in his "Slovo o tom, chto nikakiia zvaniia ne prepiatstvuiut ko spaseniiu, tol'ko b po nadlezhashchemu upravliaemy byli" (Sermon on How No Calling [or Title] Is an Impediment to Salvation, If Only It Is Directed to the Proper End).

As far as the larger tradition of Russian homiletics is concerned, Gedeon's sermons do not give the impression of anything unusual or original, although his contemporaries considered his preaching as something fundamentally new and sharply different from the rhetorical practices of previous religious orators. Alexander Sumarokov praised Gedeon highly, calling him "Rossiiskii Flesher" (the Russian Fléchier) and asserting that he had more *tsvetnost'* (coloration) than Feofan Prokopovich. Sumarokov lauded Gedeon's oratorical skills, claiming that he had filled a void in this area left by the death of Prokopovich. Later writers have basically repeated this assessment.

These judgments to a large degree also concur with what Gedeon said of himself and were most likely formulated with Gedeon's words in mind. In the foreword to his sermons "K chitateliu" (To the Reader, 1755) Gedeon wrote:

Сочинитель за истинное почитая оное в некотором письме у Сенеки изображенное мнение: Что как тому, который говорит, так и тому, который слушает, иметь надлежит намерение одно; то есть, чтоб той пользовал, а сей пользовался; ни о чем больше не старался, только чтоб, как можно, внятнее представить народу, о чем когда намерен был говорить к нему. А понеже между

народом большая всегда бывает часть неученых и простых, которым высокостильных бесед разуметь трудно и не возможно; то уже он ради произведения в действо своего намерения за такия меры и непременно приняться был должен, которыя б и самым некнижным простолюдинам могли зделать слова его легко уразумительными.

The author considers the opinion described in one of Seneca's letters as the truth: That he who speaks and he who listens must have a single intention. One offers, and the other receives. He aimed for nothing so much as presenting the people what he meant to say as intelligibly as possible. And since among the people there is always a large part who are simple and unschooled, and for whom discussions in a high style would be difficult or impossible, therefore, in order to put his intention into action, it was very necessary to take measures so that his words would be easily understood by even the least literate of the simple folk.

This emphasis on simplicity and accessibility of presentation had a distinct antirhetorical aspect; Gedeon juxtaposed his sermons to traditional learned homiletics based upon complex rhetorical constructions. At the same time, he recommended his sermons as a new model. Thus in the "Nastavlenie iunoshestvu" (Admonition to Youth), which prefaced the last volume of his works, Gedeon wrote:

Известно всякому, столь мало таких, которые бы к Вашему примеру служить могли, особливо Российских печатных Авторов имеется в нашем отечестве; не упоминая о том, что некоторые из тех самих не только младому, как ваш, возрасту не подражательны, но и зрелым умам не удобь понятны: а здесь найдете вы, коим образом без дальных глубокостей и украшений слог ваш народу, котораго вы пользе себя посвятили, полезным учинить можете. Я никогда не старался, чтоб очень привязывать меня к Риторике, но где она слову Божию услужить сама хотела, употреблял ее ... Я только сожалею, что столь многие молчат, затем, что сладкоречиво говорить не могут, и тем теряется та польза, которую бы имел народ от их хотя и не витийственным образом сочиненной проповеди.

It is well known to all how few published Russian Authors in our fatherland there are who could serve as a model for you, not to mention that several of those who are [published] are not only unsuitable for you, the young, as worthy of emulation, but neither are they easily comprehended by more mature ears. But here you will find in what way, without remote profundities and stylistic embellishments, you can be of use to our people, to whose service you have dedicated yourselves. I have never tried to tether myself too much to Rhetoric, but where she herself desired to serve the word of God, I have made use of her . . . I am only sorry that so many remain silent when they cannot speak in a smooth style (sladkorechivo), and hence the value that people might have obtained from their sermons – even if not composed with great oratory – is lost.

Gedeon's "Slovo v nedeliu 21-iu po soshestvii sv. Dukha" (Sermon for the Twenty-First Week After Pentecost) includes a similar attack on those who value rhetoric in religious oratory. His description of the previous (Church Slavonic) homiletic tradition as being difficult to comprehend recalls Prokopovich's analogous assertions and is one of a whole tradition of similar statements about the need for simplicity; criticism of one's forerunners serves as a way to justify one's own innovations. At the same time, an analysis of Gedeon's sermons only reveals innovation and original design to a very limited degree. He never puts into practice his desire, described in the preface, to aim his sermon at "the least literate of the simple folk"; on the contrary, Gedeon's sermons demonstrate his own sort of erudition, aimed, if not at the most learned, then still at a self-consciously elite audience.

All of Gedeon's sermons strictly observe the traditional division of the sermon into the *exordium, narratio,* and *peroratio.* The introduction includes the traditional presentation of the main theme, and often the usual self-deprecating claim about the author's inadequacy and his appeal to the audience for their attention and compassion. Gedeon often includes direct addresses to the empress – he asserts that she has a natural understanding of the moral principle to be presented in the given homily, and this allows him to speak as if not merely in his own name but in hers. In his "Slovo v nedeliu mytaria i fariseia" (Sermon of the Week of the Beggar and the Pharisee), for example, Gedeon says that he performs his sermon "blagonadezhen sovershenno buduchi, chto VASHEMU Sviashchenneishemu IMPERATORSKOMU VELICHESTVU kak v krotosti i smirenii izvestnoi Khristopodrazhatel'nitse, sie moe predpriiatie ne ne priiatno, i vsem khotiashchim za krotchaishim, na Sionskoi gore bogoslovom vidennym, posledovat' agntsem, ne ne polezno byt' imeet" (being perfectly assured that YOUR most Holy IMPERIAL HIGHNESS, in meekness and humility a well-known Imitator of Christ, will find this my undertaking not unworthy; and to all of those who wish to follow that meekest lamb, seen on Mount Zion by [John the] Theologian, it will not be unuseful). In this passage Gedeon distinguishes the empress from all other lis-

teners and points to her as a model for emulation. In his "Pervoe slovo so sviatoi i velikii Piatok" (First Sermon on the Great and Holy Friday), Gedeon speaks of the souls who follow Christ and places the Empress at their head: "Osoblivo VASHEGO IMPERATORSKOGO VELICHESTVA sviashchenneishaia, iazvy Gospoda svoego dukhovne izobrazheny na sebe nosiashchaia dusha" (Especially YOUR most Holy IMPERIAL HIGHNESS, who spiritually bears the image of Our Lord's wounds upon your own soul). This strategy is often used by Gedeon and helped create a norm for court preaching; it was presumably one of the reasons for Gedeon's success as an orator and at least to some degree helps explain his sermons' official reception. According to Evgenii Bolkhovitnov, the Empress Elizabeth sometimes assigned subjects to Gedeon, and apparently she was always satisfied with the results. Gedeon's sermons thus served to emphasize the empress's particular concerns and her special virtues of the moment, insofar as her subjects had, according to Gedeon, "Monarkhinia, kotoraia sama v primer vsiakoi propoveduemoi . . . dobrodeteli byt' mozhet" (a Monarch who herself could serve as an example for any kind of virtue one might preach).

The other parts of Gedeon's sermons have no particularly outstanding traits. The exposition in most cases follows the logical development of the argument, which is, as a rule, quite obvious and free of intellectual play or complex constructions. Several sermons do not so much develop an argument as simply string ideas together. In the "Slovo v nedeliu chetvertuiu o rasslablennom" (Sermon on the Sixth Week on the Enfeebled), in which Gedeon polemicizes with the Calvinist doctrine of predestination, or in the "Slovo v nedeliu shestuiu po Soshestvii Sv. Dukha" (Sermon on the Sixth Week After Pentecost), where Gedeon examines the nature of blasphemy and polemicizes with freethinkers and atheists, elements of scholarly disputation appear – that is, they alternate arguments and their refutation (*confutatio*). However, this structure was not characteristic of Gedeon's sermons, which were neither publicistic or polemical (as had been the case of sermons of the Petrine era) but rather moralistic and admonitory.

Gedeon's homilies make frequent use of exempla (examples, models) and their explanation. Their organization, more or less free in their internal logic, forms the basis of the narrative structures Gedeon uses. This method of organization was what Sumarokov had in mind when he said that Gedeon filled his homilies with stories and fables probably aimed at an uncultured audience unable to appreciate more subtle constructions. Bible stories served as one source for Gedeon's exempla, tales from classical history as another. Often his historical anecdotes are tied to the theme of the sermon in a very superficial way, and in many instances it is obvious that their main function is not to illustrate the author's ideas but to entertain the audience. Thus, for example, in speaking of how the soul may be damned "za liubov' prelestnago mira" (through love for the world's charms), Gedeon adds: "Prikhodit mne teper' na pamiat' Kleopatra Egipetskaia. Ona liubia Antoniia Konsula Rimskago, kak skazuiut, dragotsennuiu Margaritu tsenoiu protivo vsego tsarstviia eia (ezhel' pravda) stóiavshuiu, v prakh melkii istershi vypit' emu v vine dala. Glupaia ta vo istinu zhena, byla glupaia, chto tak naprasno kamen' toi izgubila" (The Egyptian Cleopatra comes to mind here. It is said that for the love of Anthony, the Roman Consul, she gave him (if what they say is true) a precious Pearl worth the whole of her kingdom, ground up to drink in a cup of wine. This woman was foolish, truly foolish, to destroy such a stone for no reason).

Gedeon's writings are filled with similar vignettes. He probably took them partly from the Roman historians he had read at the seminary and partly from the collections of historical anecdotes that circulated widely in eighteenth-century Russia. He also used material from sources that were part of the common literary legacy of the medieval Slavic world, such as the *Aleksandriia* (a mythologized history of Alexander the Great); episodes from Alexander's life appear in nearly every fourth sermon. Stories from natural history also appear (such as the story of the lion who would not harm anything lying down, but who tore to pieces anything standing); these may also derive from Slavic sources. In general, Gedeon draws material for his exempla from traditional sources and is thus reminiscent of Ukrainian baroque homiletics (for example, those of Ioannikii Galiatovsky and Lazar Baranovich); in this respect Gedeon reveals a dependence upon existing tradition rather than an opposition to it. What distinguishes Gedeon is that in his works the exempla acquire independent importance and are not merely illustrative. Because they are not restricted by theme, the use of exempla is greatly emphasized and becomes a defining characteristic of Gedeon's sermons. It has been suggested that Gedeon was attempting to imitate the famous early eighteenth-century Greek preacher Elias Miniates, from whom he allegedly borrowed entire fragments; a comparison of texts, however, does not support this view. Gedeon was transforming the Kievan tradition, but it was a tradition he knew very well, and innovation does not exclude continuity. Gedeon's ties with the Kievan school are evident in his patristic references, in which Latin authors (Augustine, Jerome, Ambrose) occupy a prominent place.

If Gedeon's innovations in the realm of content were limited, in his means of expression he introduced significant new elements into Russian homiletics. He apparently introduced new methods of delivery, though the details of his innovations are unknown. Platon claimed that Gedeon could read his homilies so that his audience "byvali kak by vne sebia i boialis', chtoby on perestal govorit'" (would be beside itself and feared that he would stop speaking). This statement seems to refer not to Gedeon's individual method of speaking but to a new technique, and Platon asserts that Gedeon was his main guide in how to deliver sermons.

In language there can be no doubt that Gedeon was an innovator. He was the first to write his homilies in Russian and not Church Slavonic, as the church historian Filaret Gumilevsky points out, "okonchaniia slov, izmeneniia ikh i sintaksis i nego — russkie" (his word endings, inflexions, and syntax are all Russian). Earlier homiletic tradition was tied to a hybrid variant of Church Slavonic. Texts using this variant are notable for their occasional or systematic use of specific Church Slavonic grammatical elements (for example, its unique past-tense forms), which served as a kind of sign or semiotic marker of the work's linguistic register. Gedeon rejected such markers of Church Slavonic, preserving them only in citations from Holy Scripture and in a few specific phrases. Considering the great significance of the choice of language in the eighteenth-century Russian cultural context, these formal innovations demonstrated a clear break with tradition and a reformist orientation. There is reason to assume that Gedeon's linguistic notions were based on ideas developed by the secular writers of his day. His homilies characteristically include well-worn phrases from contemporary secular panegyric odes, especially those of Lomonosov, such as "pylaiushchaia zloboi Etna" (Etna aflame with malice) or "skrezheshchushchii zubami Tatar" (Tartarus gnashing his teeth).

In this way Gedeon distanced himself from the exclusively religious tradition and sought a rapprochement with Europeanized gentry culture. His reformist orientation in language was especially important in its influence on his two famous pupils, Gavriil Petrov and Platon Levshin. His legacy to them was precisely in the choice of language, as they did not follow his lead in the realms of stylistics or rhetoric. Petrov and Levshin's use of Russian had tremendous influence during the reign of Catherine II and was taken up by Russian homiletics as a whole; from that time Russian became the accepted language of sermons. In this respect Gedeon's literary activity ushered in a new era in the history of Russian homiletics.

Biography:

Fedor Titov, *K biografii Gedeona Krinovskogo, episkopa pskovskogo i narvskogo* (Kazan, 1907).

References:

Evgenii Bolkhovitinov, *Slovar' istoricheskii o byvshikh v Rossii pisateliakh dukhovnogo china greko-rossiiskoi tserkvi,* second edition, volume 1 (Saint Petersburg: I. Glazunova, 1827), pp. 85–88;

Filaret Gumilevsky, *Obzor russkoi dukhovnoi literatury, 862–1863,* third edition (Saint Petersburg, 1884), pp. 332–333;

Hans Albert Lennart Kjellberg, *La langue de Gedeon Krinovskij, prédicateur russe du XVIIIe siècle,* I. (Uppsala: Publications de l'Institut Slave d'Upsal, 1957);

[Platon (Levshin)], "Zapiski o zhizni Platona mitropolita moskovsogo, im samim pisannye, i okonchennye Samuilom kostromskim episkopom," *Zhizn' moskovskogo mitropolita Platona,* edited by I. M. Snegirev, volume 2, fourth edition (Moscow, 1891), pp. 201–263;

Aleksandr P. Sumarokov, "O rossiiskom dukhovnom krasnorechii," in his *Polnoe sobranie sochinenii,* second edition, volume 6 (Moscow: Novikov, 1781), pp. 277–284;

P. Zavedeev, *Istoriia russkogo propovednichestva ot XVII veka do nastoiashchego vremeni* (Tula: N. I. Sokolova, 1879);

V. M. Zhivov, *Kul'turnye konflikty v istorii russkogo literaturnogo iazyka XVIII – nachala XIX veka* (Moscow: Institut russkogo iazyka, 1990);

Petr V. Znamensky, "Chteniia iz istorii russkoi tserkvi za vremia tsarstvovaniia Ekateriny II," *Pravoslavnyi sobesednik,* no. 2 (1875): 99–143.

Stefan Iavorsky

(1658 – 24 November 1722)

Sergei Nikolaev
Institute of Russian Literature (Pushkin House), Saint Petersburg

BOOKS: *Hercules post Atlantem infracto virtutum robore honorarium pondus sustinens* (Chernigov: Tipografiia Troitskaia, [circa 1685]);

Echo glosu wolajacego na puszczy od serdecznej refleksji pochodzace (Kiev: Kievo-Pecherskaia lavra, 1689);

Arctos coeli Rossiaci in gentilibus syderibus resplendens (Kiev: Kievo-Pecherskaia lavra, 1690);

Pelnia nieubywajacej chwaly w herbowym ksiezycu . . . reprezentowana (Kiev: Kievo-Pecherskaia lavra, 1691);

Vinograd Khristov, v nem zhe letorasl' edina ot trekh si est' brak chesnyi edin ot trekh chinov devstvuiushchikh, vdovstvuiushchikh i supruzhnykh v chest' Bogu v Troitsi sviatoi pokloniaemomu, obretaiushchikhsia (N.p., 1698);

Znameniia prishestviia Antikhristova i konchiny veka ot pisanii bozhestvennykh iavlenna (Moscow: Pechatnyi dvor, 1703);

Kamen' very pravoslavnym tserkve sviatyia synom, na utverzhdenie i dukhovnoe sozidanie, pretykaiushchimsia zhe o kamen' pretykaniia i soblasna na vostanie i ispravlenie (Moscow: Synod, 1728); republished in 3 volumes (Moscow, 1843).

Editions: *Propovedi,* 3 volumes (Moscow: Synod, 1804–1805);

Neizdannye propovedi Stefana Iavorskogo, edited by I. Chistovich (Saint Petersburg: Departament udelov, 1867);

Ritoricheskaia ruka, translated from Latin by F. Polikarpov (Saint Petersburg: Obshchestvo liubitelei drevnei pis'mennosti, 1878).

SELECTED PERIODICAL PUBLICATIONS – UNCOLLECTED: "Neizdannye propovedi . . . Stefana Iavorskogo," edited by Arkhimandrit Nikodim, *Pribavleniia k izdaniiu tvorenii svuatykh otsev v russkom perevode,* 22 (1863): 249–270;

"Poslanie k preosviashchennym Aleksiiu Sarskomu i Podonskomu i Varlaamu Tverskomu i Kashinskomu [1718]," *Chteniia v Obshchestve*

Stefan Iavorsky

istorii i drevnostei rossiiskikh, 4, section 5 (1864): 5–8.

Stefan Iavorsky was one of the most educated and prominent figures in the Russian church during the Petrine period: he became, despite his wishes, the head of the Russian Orthodox church during the difficult period of its subordination to the state under Peter the Great's reforms. Throughout his life, he aspired to a quiet life of independent literary activity rather than a great career, and it was precisely his involvement in church politics and polemics that hindered him in fully developing his considerable literary talent. As he complained to his close friend Dimitrii Rostovsky in 1707: "Believe me, the man who has lived happily is the one who has been able to hide himself away. Pray, divine prelate, for the deliverance of the unfree – of whom the first am I!"

Stefan Iavorsky, whose lay name was Semen Ivanovich, was born in 1658 into a wealthy noble family on the right bank of Ukraine in the city of Iavor (the exact location of which is unknown). After this land became a part of Poland in 1667, the Iavorsky family, which was Orthodox, relocated to the left bank, to the village of Krasilovka near Nezhin. Around 1673 Iavorsky enrolled in the Kiev Mohyla Collegium, the leading Orthodox educational institution of its time, and he completed its course of study. The gifted student found a patron in rector Varlaam Iasinsky, on whose counsel he traveled to Poland in 1684 to continue his education. First, Iavorsky was compelled to become a member of the Uniate church – a common procedure for Kievan students who desired to continue their education in Jesuit colleges in the West – and to adopt the name Stanislav (Simon). Iavorsky spent five years abroad, studying philosophy in Lvov and Lublin and theology in Poznan and Vilnius. He finished his education in Vilnius with the degree of *artium liberalium et philosophiae magister, consummatus theologus*. The Vilnius Jesuits offered him the position of rector of the Congregation of the Holy Virgin, but in 1689 Iavorsky returned to his native country.

In Kiev the first thing Iavorsky did was break from the Uniate church and return to Eastern Orthodoxy; he then passed a series of examinations at the Mohyla Collegium, not only in philosophy and theology but also in poetics and rhetoric. Iavorsky displayed such a great talent for writing verse in Latin and Polish that the Mohyla faculty awarded him the honorary title of "poet laureate" – the only time it was ever conferred in the entire history of the institution.

By the time of his return to Kiev, Iavorsky had already published his panegyric *Hercules post Atlantem* (circa 1685), dedicated to Iasinsky, who succeeded Innokentii Gizel' as the archimandrite of the Kiev Caves Monastery. The panegyric was a complex rhetorical construction of Latin prose with poems in Latin and Polish; its theme was the life of Iasinsky, who, like Hercules, takes on the heavy labors of his predecessor. The author is inexhaustible in his display of images and tropes drawn from the arsenal of classical antiquity; he heaps up lush and extraordinary baroque comparisons, and the work sparkles with erudition. Immediately after his return Iavorsky published another panegyric, *Echo glosu wołajacego na puszczy* (Echo of a Voice Crying in the Wilderness, 1689), dedicated to the Ukrainian Hetman, Ivan Mazepa. It is just as rhetorically elaborate as the previous work and is also written in Polish and Latin.

In 1689 Iavorsky took his monastic vows under the name of Stefan and was accepted into the care of his alma mater. In the following year, he published two more panegyrics to Iasinsky, the *Arctos coeli* (Constellation of the Heavens, 1690) and *Pelnia nieubywajacej chwaly* (Abundance of Unlessening Glory, 1691), confirming once and for all his reputation as the collegium's premier poet. In his *Poetics* of 1705 Iavorsky's future nemesis Feofan Prokopovich cited Iavorsky's magnificent poem in Russian, "Ty, oblechenna v solntse, Devo Bogomati" (You, Divine Virgin Mother, Swathed in Sunlight), calling its author "a most famous and educated man, greatly merited among his colleagues." In the eighteenth century, Iavorsky's poems continued to be cited as model works in courses on poetics at the Mohyla Academy.

In 1690 Iavorsky became professor at the collegium (soon to be redesignated academy), first teaching rhetoric (1690–1691), then philosophy (1691–1693), and finally theology (1693–1697). His contemporaries in Kiev considered him the embodiment of European scholarship. However, both in philosophy and theology, Iavorsky was a traditionalist, following Aristotle and Thomas Aquinas, and he gave no significance to more recent humanistic developments in modern philosophy. He mocked the great Polish Renaissance scholar Copernicus in one of his sermons, and in his course on rhetoric (of which only a Russian translation of 1705 has been preserved) he denounced Descartes. Iavorsky's courses were not progressive and did not pretend to be; from a Western point of view they did not in any way reflect the latest in contemporary scholarship. Iavorsky did not consider himself a philosopher; his main interests were philological and historical – not the search for truth but its exposition and propagation.

In 1697 Iavorsky became hegumen of the Holy Nikol'sky Monastery, as well as prefect of its collegium. He also began to preach, which soon made his name known in Kiev. One of his sermons entitled *Vinograd Khristov* (The Vineyard of Christ, 1698) was published on the occasion of the wedding of his disciple Ivan Obidovsky. Iavorsky wrote that he did not envy Aristotle and Seneca, insofar as the former had educated the "bandit" Alexander of Macedon and the latter the "bloodthirsty" Nero; Iavorsky, on the other hand, trained a man adorned with all manner of Christian virtue.

The life Iavorsky led at the monastery was in all probability close to his ideal. Scholarly activity, preaching, and poetry – this circle of interests seemed to satisfy him fully. However, with the new century the course of his life changed radically. At the beginning of 1700 Iavorsky visited Moscow on business for the Kiev metropolitanate. In February of that year Field Marshall Aleksei Shein died, and Patriarch Adrian commissioned the orator from Kiev to present the eulogy. This pleased Peter the Great so much that he had Iavorsky remain in Moscow and ordered that a new position be found for him. In April, Iavorsky was made metropolitan of Riazan and Murom. Shortly thereafter, Adrian also died, and Peter, who had already decided to reform the Russian church, appointed Iavorsky the locum tenens of the patriarchal throne. Thus in the course of several months Iavorsky ascended from the humble position of father superior to the highest office in the entire church. Iavorsky had never desired such an appointment and even attempted to avoid it, but Peter was unyielding. Iavorsky's credentials suited the czar's purposes: the prelate was not a progressive or a reformer, but he was an authoritative figure with a European education, of which there were still few in Russia.

Iavorsky's life changed dramatically as he was faced with new and immense concerns. He lived in Moscow, Saint Petersburg, and Riazan in turn, and only rarely, with the permission of the czar, visited Ukraine. At Peter's command he worked to reform the Moscow Slavonic-Greek-Latin Academy on the model of the Kiev Academy. As the head of the church he was obligated to concern himself with the struggle between religious factions and heresies within the church. Almost immediately after his appointment he presided over the highly publicized case of Grigorii Talitsky, who had proclaimed that the Antichrist was already reigning over the world and that his name was Czar Peter. Talitsky was condemned, but the matter attracted a great deal of attention; and Iavorsky wrote a public refutation of Talitsky entitled *Znameniia prishestviia Antikhristova i konchiny veka* (Signs of the Arrival of the Antichrist and the End of the Age, 1703), which was reprinted many times during the eighteenth century.

However, Iavorsky published no further works up to the time of his death. He often gave sermons, primarily on the occasion of church holidays, about three hundred of which have been preserved. They hardly reflect the vividness of the epoch. If Iavorsky touched upon the victories of the Russian army in the Great Northern War, for example, he would always take the opportunity to delve into the essence of things hidden behind external events. With a masterly command of baroque rhetorical de-

vices, he created complex and fantastic constructions, startling his audience with allegories or etymological figures of speech. The power of his oratorical art was even admitted by his ill-wishers. The anonymous author of the pamphlet *Molotok na Kamen' very* (Hammer on the Rock of Faith, circa 1740) – a repudiation of Iavorsky's treatise *Kamen' very* (Rock of Faith, 1728; written 1713–1715) – admits that Iavorsky was able to bring his audience first to tears and then to laughter.

At first Iavorsky unconditionally supported all of Peter's efforts, but the reforms came to restrict the rights of the church to such an extent that even Iavorsky came to oppose them. He was limited in his power as mere placeholder of the patriarchal throne, however, and many functions previously under the control of the patriarch were transferred to secular jurisdiction. The relations between Iavorsky and the czar cooled considerably in 1712. On 12 March the priest read a homily on the occasion of Czarevitch Aleksei's name day in which he likened the czarevitch's visit abroad to the wanderings of the popular second-century saint known as Aleksei, Man of God. In his sermon Iavorsky called the czarevitch "Russia's only hope" and dropped several hints criticizing the czar's personal life. (Aleksei, who became standard-bearer of the conservative opposition to Peter's reforms, was later arrested for treason and died in the Peter Paul Fortress in 1718, probably as the result of torture.) The text of Iavorsky's sermon was seized and shown to the czar, and as a result, Peter forbade Iavorsky to preach in public. He did not renew the privilege for three years, and relations between the two were never set straight.

Iavorsky turned his attention to theological matters. He directed a commission on correcting the translation of the Bible and wrote *Kamen' very*, an enormous treatise on Orthodox dogma that was sharply anti-Protestant in spirit. Peter prevented its publication, finally permitted in 1728 under Peter II. Iavorsky's influence on the life of the church continuously diminished, and with the appointment of Prokopovich as bishop in 1718, it became nominal. Prokopovich, Peter's close collaborator and the brilliant propagandist of his reforms, had a background similar to Iavorsky's (both had studied at the Kiev Academy and in Europe), but the new bishop fully embraced the Enlightenment philosophical trends which Iavorsky rejected. When the Holy Synod was established in 1721 according to Prokopovich's plan – as a secular, governmental body in control of the church – Iavorsky became its president, but the real authority was concentrated in the hands of Prokopovich, its vice-president. Iavorsky found himself isolated both from Peter and from the conservative opposition, which associated him with the innovative European educational trends within the church.

During the Moscow period of his life, Iavorsky wrote a few poems in Russian: a long epitaph in 1707 to Iasinsky, his beloved mentor; an epitaph to his friend Rostovsky in 1709; and, in the same year, verses denouncing the disloyalty of Mazepa, whom Iavorsky had once lauded. At the end of his life, Iavorsky returned to writing poetry in Latin. When he compiled the catalog of his library, he added a touching Latin elegy that was translated into Russian several times during the eighteenth century. At the same time, he also composed a quatrain on the futility of title seeking.

Iavorsky had one last example of the futility of worldly fame when, shortly before his death, the already-sick priest was interrogated in his home by members of the synod and senate. He was suspected of being involved in a proclamation that declared Peter to be the Antichrist. It is possible that only his death saved Iavorsky from punishment. He died in Moscow, a city he called Babylon, on 24 November 1722, far from his native land, surrounded with outward marks of honor but in an atmosphere of cabal and mistrust.

References:

Ilarion A. Chistovich, *Feofan Prokopovich i ego vremia* (Saint Petersburg: Akademiia nauk, 1868);

Dmitry Izvekov, "Iz istorii bogoslovskoi polemicheskoi literatury XVIII stoletiia," *Pravoslavnoe obozrenie,* no. 8 (1871): 139–171; no. 9 (1871): 267–307;

Aleksandr Korolev, "Stefan Iavorsky," in *Russkii biograficheskii slovar'* (Saint Petersburg, 1909), pp. 413–422;

Łużny (Luzhnyi), "Izdaniia na pol'skom iazyke v literature epokhi Petra I," *XVIII vek,* 9 (1974): 304–312;

Łużny, "Stefan Jaworski – poeta nieznany," *Slavia Orientalis,* 4 (1967): 363–376;

Mikhail Maksimovich, "Knizhnaia starina iuzhnorusskaia," *Kievlianin,* 3 (1850): 133–136;

Sergei I. Maslov, *Biblioteka Stefana Iavorskogo* (Kiev: M. T. Meinandea, 1914);

Ioann Morev, *"Kamen' very" mitropolita Stefana Iavorskogo, ego mesto sredi otechestvennykh protivoprotestanskikh sochinenii* (Saint Petersburg, 1904);

Aleksandr A. Morozov, "Metafora i allegoriia u Stefana Iavorskogo," *Poetika i stilistika russkoi literatury: Pamiati akademika Viktora Vladimirovicha Vinogradova* (Leningrad: Nauka, 1971), pp. 35–44;

Valeriia M. Nichik, *Iz istorii otechestvennoi filosofii kontsa XVII-nachala XVIII v.* (Kiev: Naukova dumka, 1978);

Anton Nikol'sky, *Opisanie rukopisei, khraniashchikhsia v arkhive sviateishego pravitel'stvuiushchego Sinoda,* volume 2, part 1 (Saint Petersburg: Synod, 1906), pp. 381–426;

V. P[evnitsky], "Slova Stefana Iavorskogo, mitropolita Riazanskogo i Muromskogo," *Trudy Kievskoi dukhovnoi akademii,* 7 (1874): 72–121;

Iurii F. Samarin, *Stefan Iavorskii i Feofan Prokopovich* (Moskva: A. I. Mamontov, 1880);

Iurij Serech, "Stefan Yavorsky and the Conflict of the Ideologies in the Age of Peter I," *Slavonic and East European Review,* 30 (December 1951): 40–62;

Filipp A. Ternovskii, "Mitropolit Stefan Iavorsky (Biograficheskii ocherk)," *Trudy Kievskoi dukhovnoi akademii,* no. 1 (1864): 36–70; no. 3 (1864): 237–290; no. 6 (1864): 137–186;

Igor S. Zakhara, *Bor'ba idei v filosofskoi mysli na Ukraine na rybezhe XVII–XVIII vv. (Stefan Iavorsky)* (Kiev: Naukova dumka, 1982).

Antiokh Dmitrievich Kantemir

(8 September 1708 – 31 March 1744)

Galina Nikolaevna Moiseeva
Institute of Russian Literature (Pushkin House), Saint Petersburg

BOOKS: *Simfoniia na psaltyr'* (Saint Petersburg: Synod, 1727);

Satyres de M. le Prince Cantemir, avec l'histoire de sa vie, traduites en François (London: Nourse, 1749);

Heinrich Eberhards, Freyherr von Spilcker, versuchte freye Uebersetzung der Satyren des Prinzen Kantemir . . . (Berlin, 1752);

Satiry i drugie stikhotvorcheskie sochineniia s istoricheskimi primechaniiami i s kratkim opisaniem zhizni (Saint Petersburg: Akademiia nauk, 1762).

Editions: *Sochineniia kn. Antiokha Kantemira. Polnoe sobranie sochinenii russkikh avtorov*, volume 20 (Saint Petersburg: A. Smirdin, 1847);

Izbrannye sochineniia (Moscow: P. Perevlessky, 1849);

Sochineniia, pis'ma i izbrannye perevody, 2 volumes, edited by P. A. Efremov, with an introduction and notes by V. Ia. Stoiunin (Saint Petersburg: V. Ia. Glazunov, 1867–1868);

Sobraniie stikhotvorenii, second edition, edited by Z. I. Gershkovich, Biblioteka poeta, Bol'shaia seriia (Leningrad: Sovetskii pisatel', 1956).

TRANSLATIONS: Bernard le Bovier de Fontenelle, *Razgovory o mnozhestve mirov . . .* (Saint Petersburg: Akademiia nauk, 1740);

Horace, *Desiat' pisem pervoi knigi* (Saint Petersburg: Akademiia nauk, 1744).

SELECTED PERIODICAL PUBLICATION – UNCOLLECTED: "Petrida," edited by N. S. Tikhonravov, *Letopisi russkoi literatury i drevnostei*, 1, no. 3 (1859): 16–22.

Antiokh Dmitrievich Kantemir

Antiokh Kantemir's poetry represents a vivid expression of the Petrine reforms and of the Europeanization of eighteenth-century Russian culture. Secular in content yet nationalistic in language and style, Kantemir's writings helped bring Russian literature into the orbit of European culture and anticipated many of the peculiar features that would shape Russian literature in the eighteenth and early nineteenth centuries. A scathing satirist, diplomat, and arguably Russia's first indigenous Enlightenment man of letters, the European-educated Kantemir was, in the apt phrase of the nineteenth-century critic Vissarion Belinsky, "the first [writer] in Russia to unite literature with life."

Prince Antiokh Dmitrievich Kantemir was born on 8 September 1708 in the city of Iassy (in Moldova) to the family of Prince Dmitrii Kantemir (or Cantemir) and his wife Kassandra Kantakuzen, a descendant of the Byzantine imperial family. Dmitrii Kantemir spent his early years at the Turkish court as a hostage for the Moldavian lord, Prince Constantine, and was a highly educated man and an expert on Turkish history, culture, and music. In 1711, during Peter the Great's Prutsk campaign, Dmitrii Kantemir found asylum with the czar and accepted Russian citizenship. On one occasion he and his family found themselves in the czar's camp when it was surrounded by Turkish troops, and the sultan demanded his return. Peter's response is well known: he said that he would be willing to surrender a city in hopes of winning it back later but that he would never surrender people who had entrusted themselves to him. The five small children of the Moldavian prince, of whom Antiokh was the youngest, were reportedly hidden away in Peter's imperial carriage to ensure their safety.

Dmitrii Kantemir and his family were subsequently given estates near Moscow and in the Ukraine. The domestic situation in which Antiokh grew up was unusually conducive to his all-around intellectual development. Prince Dmitrii, who was, according to Peter the Great, "a very intelligent man and capable of [giving sound] advice," labored over several scholarly works, including a history of the Ottoman Empire and *Kniga sistima, ili Sostoianie mukhammedanskoi religii* (System or State of the Mohammedan Religion, 1722). He took the education of his children seriously. Antiokh was tutored by the Greek priest Anastasii Kondoidi and by Ivan Il'insky, subsequently a translator for the Petersburg Academy of Sciences. Kondoidi instructed the children in Greek and Latin, and thus Antiokh was introduced to classical literature (and to Italian, as well) at an early age, while Il'insky taught them the Russian language and guided Antiokh's first experiments in writing poetry.

For a short time Kantemir studied at the Slavonic-Greek-Latin Academy in Moscow, and in 1718, in the presence of Peter the Great, the ten-year-old recited a eulogy (in Greek) to Saint Dimitrius of Thessalonika. Several years later, after the death of Princess Kassandra, Prince Dmitrii was married again, to Princess Anastasiia Trubetskaia, and moved with his family to Saint Petersburg. The beautiful young princess, who had received a European-style education in Sweden, managed her household according to the fashion of the day, and a wave of receptions, visits, balls, and entertainments swept into the life of the Kantemirs. All of the aristocracy of Saint Petersburg — the Princes Golitsyn, Trubetskoi, Dolgoruky, F. D. Romodanovsky, and many others — frequented the home of the Moldavian lord; the czar's right-hand man, A. D. Men'shikov, was also an intimate, and the czar himself often dropped in without ceremony. This period lasted until May 1722, when Peter gave Dmitrii Kantemir administrative command over the Persian campaign.

Prince Kantemir set out with his entire family, with the exception of his young wife. From Moscow they traveled to Murom, Nizhnii, and then down the Volga to Astrakhan, from whence they set out to march on Derbent, with stops in large towns and in villages. The inquisitive, fourteen-year-old Antiokh had the opportunity to observe the way of life not only of aristocratic circles but of all of Russia. His acquaintance with the way of life along the Volga was later reflected in his satires.

During the return trip from the campaign, Dmitrii Kantemir fell ill. He died on 21 August 1723 at his Sevsk village of Dmitrievskoe. In his will he admonished his children to concern themselves with their education and named as his heir whichever son excelled the most in his studies by the time of his coming of age; he also noted that Antiokh, the youngest, was "the best of all in intelligence and learning." The indefiniteness of the will regarding the inheritance later resulted in lengthy family disputes.

On 25 May 1724 Kantemir petitioned the czar for permission to go abroad to study "new and ancient history, geography, law and all that belongs to the field of politics," as well as mathematics and painting. For unknown reasons, the request was rejected, and the prince was obliged to complete his education under the direction of the first members of the newly instituted Saint Petersburg Academy of Sciences: Daniel Bernulli, Georg-Bernhard Bulfinger, Gottlieb Siegfried Bayer, Christian Gross, and Friedrich Christian Mayer. In addition to his other studies he began to study French, one result of which was his 1726 translation of a short satiric work, to which he appended some "virshi" (syllabic rhymed verse) of his own. In the same year, Kantemir compiled a *Simfoniia na psaltyr'* (Concordance to the Psalter, 1727), dedicated to Empress Catherine I. These first creative endeavors, however, were still imitative and amateurish: his teacher Il'insky was at that time composing a *Simfoniia na Chetveroevangelie i Deianiia apostol'skie* (Concordance to the Gospels and the Acts of the Apostles, 1727). The real beginning of Kantemir's literary activity came in 1729, when he wrote several short poems and songs and transpositions of Psalms 36 and 72, all written in syllabic verse. His first verse satires — on which his literary fame primarily rests — also date to this period.

In spite of his youth, Kantemir was already a notable figure, remarkable for his cultural sophistication. But it was not only his education that attracted attention. During the period after Peter's death, a time of general malaise and political reaction had set in, especially under the short-lived rule (1727–1730) of Peter's grandson, Emperor Peter II, the son of Aleksei Petrovich, whom Peter had put to death for treason. During the rule of this teenage czar various factions jockeyed for power, and favoritism reigned supreme. Kantemir, now a young lieutenant in the Preobrazhensky regiment, clearly asserted his political loyalties by allying himself with Feofan Prokopovich, one of the main architects of the Petrine reforms, which then seemed in increasing jeopardy.

Kantemir's personal circumstances were also very difficult at that time; in 1729 his father's entire personal inheritance, consisting of more than ten thousand serfs, was awarded to his brother Constantine, thanks to Constantine's marriage to the daughter of Prince D. M. Golitsyn, a prominent member of the Supreme Secret Council. Kantemir felt that he had been cheated and expressed his disappointment in several elegies; however, convinced that his personal adversity reflected the arbitrary rule then plaguing Russia as a whole, he hoped that with the restoration of "true autocracy" – the ascension of Anna Ioannovna after Peter II's death in 1730 – "nastupit liubago polnyi den' pokoia" (a complete day of serenity will come for everyone). Kantemir took a conspicuous part in the struggle against the members of the Supreme Secret Council, who had prepared a list of "konditsii" (conditions) to which Anna Ioannovna had been forced to consent prior to her assuming the throne; these conditions would have established constitutional rule and made the empress subordinate to the council in all important matters of internal and external politics. Kantemir, in cooperation with Feofan Prokopovich, the historian V. N. Tatishchev, and other political figures who supported the Petrine program – including strong, autocratic rule – composed an address to the empress in the name of the Russian nobility urging her to rescind all of the conditions, a course which the new empress was pleased to follow.

In 1731 Kantemir was named "resident" (ambassador) to England, and he departed on 1 January 1732. This journey marked the end of his direct participation in Russian life, for he spent the rest of his life abroad. His main literary achievement was his nine verse satires, five of which were written before he left Russia. His early satires – bold exposés of Russian social and political ills – reflect the years of struggle during the tense last period of Peter II's reign. His first and probably most famous satire, "Na

khuliashchikh ucheniia" (On the Detractors of Learning, 1729), bears the subtitle "K umu svoevu" (To My Mind) and is directed against "those who despise the sciences," primarily against the reactionary clergy. In it Kantemir creates a satiric gallery of clergymen, as in the portrait of the sanctimonious hypocrite and ignoramus Kriton (a name invented by Kantemir apparently to suggest duplicity):

Расколы и ереси науки суть дети;
Больше врет, кому далось больше разумети;
Приходит в безбожие, кто над книгой тает,--
Критон с четками в руках ворчит и вздыхает,
И просит, свята душа, с горькими слезами
Смотреть, сколь семя наук вредно между нами.

(Schisms and heresies are learning's sons;
The more one knows, the more truth one shuns;
Book work into atheism tumbles,--
Thus, beads in hand, old Kriton sighs and grumbles,
And, pious soul, with bitter tears beseeks
To view what harm among us knowledge wreaks.)
– translation by Harold B. Segel (in his *The Literature of Eighteenth-Century Russia*, 1967)

Encouraged by the success of his first satire and the praise of Feofan Prokopovich, who wrote him a well-known verse epistle, Kantemir, in his own words, "applied himself further to the composition of satires," and four more quickly followed. In the third, dedicated to Prokopovich, Kantemir draws a vivid satiric sketch of Archimandrite Varlaam (Anna Ioannovna's confessor), who was one of the candidates for patriarch:

Варлам смирен, молчалив, как в палату войдет,--
Всем низко поклонится, к всякому подойдет.
В угол отвернувшись потом, глаза в землю втупит;
Чуть слыхать, что говорит; чуть, как ходит, ступит.
Когда в гостях, за столом-и мясо противно,
И вина не хочет пить; да то и не дивно;
Дома съел целый каплун, и на жир и сало
Бутылки венгерского с нуждой запить стало.
Жалки ему в похотях погибшие люди,
Но жадно пялит с под лба глаз на круглы груди . . .

(Varlam is humble and silent when he enters the hall,
He bows low to everybody and approaches all.
Then turning to face the corner, he lowers his eyes to the ground;
You can hardly hear what he is saying, hardly hear his footsteps when he walks.
When a guest at table, he disdains meat
And refuses wine; but that is not surprising;
At home he ate an entire capon, and [to wash down] the fat and suet
He needed to drink [many] bottles of Hungarian [wine].
He is sorry for those who have perished in their lusts,

But secretly stares greedily at those beautiful round breasts . . . [.])

The anticlericism of Kantemir's satires connects his work with that of many Renaissance writers who denounced the clergy from the perspective of a secular humanist worldview. Both in the novellas of Giovanni Boccaccio and in the "harsh" satires of the Polish Renaissance writer Krzysztof Opalinski, for example, as well as in the anonymous facetiae (Russian *fatsetsii,* short comical novellas that began to appear in Russia in the later seventeenth century via Poland), which reflected the sentiments of lower levels of society, the image of the clergy was almost always negative, marked by greediness, shamelessness, and stupidity.

Although Kantemir was a deeply religious man, his anticlericism marked his fundamental support for Peter the Great's reform program, which consistently juxtaposed the power of church and state, religious and secular cultures. According to the Petrine ideology, it was the clergy, taking active advantage of their power and influence, that was hindering Russia's progress and enlightenment. Without doubt, in the difficult circumstances of the late 1720s and 1730s, when ignorant favorites held positions of authority in Russia, they were often supported by members of the clergy, and it took great courage on Kantemir's part to expose their influence. The first satire ends with verses that satirize not abstract images of clerical abuse but concrete representatives of the Russian clergy who were hostile to the Petrine reforms, such as Archbishop Georgii Dashkov. Kantemir's satires mark one of the first instances of the anticlerical theme in Russian literature, a theme later to be taken up by Mikhail Lomonosov when he wrote several satires on the clergy, including the well-known "Gimn borode" (Hymn to a Beard, 1756–1757).

However, Kantemir's satires did not attack only the reactionary clergy. Kantemir was a committed proponent of Peter's measures, making merit and utility to the state the basic criteria for career advancement rather than "good breeding" or inherited wealth, and he was the first to introduce the theme of the "corrupt nobleman" into Russian literature. His second satire, which is constructed in the form of a dialogue between Evgenii (from the Greek, "of noble birth") and Filaret (from the Greek, "lover of virtue"), is devoted to this as well as other topical questions of Russian social life of the early 1730s. Evgenii complains that although he is of noteworthy ancestry, rank and honor have come not to him but rather to those "kto ne vse ster

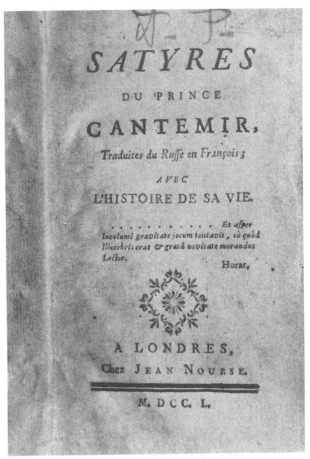

Title page for an early French edition of Kantemir's satires

s grubykh ruk mozoli" (from whose coarse hands the callouses have not yet rubbed off). With indignation he lists all those "newcomers" who have replaced the boyar aristocracy and taken over distinguished positions in the government. Filaret, who clearly expresses the author's point of view, explains that "virtue alone" makes people noble. Filaret defends those sensible and knowledgeable people "koi chrez svoi trudy is podlosti v znatnuiu stepen' proiskhodiat" (who by their labors rise above their baseness to an exulted station).

In this satire Kantemir also touches upon a related issue that was just becoming topical in the late 1720s, that of the young men returning from foreign shores. Sent abroad by Peter to study, they return to Russia not with a desire to serve but interested only in the latest fashions and bear an insuperable prejudice against anything Russian. These were the first portraits of those "novomanirnogo shlakhetstva" (new-mannered nobility), the *shchegol'* and *shchegolikha* (dandy and female dandy), who in the name of fashionable raiment were prepared to "derevniu vzdet' na sebia . . . tselu" (put their entire village on their backs – that is, to sell or mortgage their estates to pay the tailor). Denunciation of corrupt noblemen was to become a central theme of eighteenth-century Russian literature, reflected in the work of Denis Fonvizin, Nikolai Novikov, Aleksandr Radishchev, Ivan Krylov, and many others.

The literary form of Kantemir's satires was largely determined by his sources. Kantemir made use both of the classical tradition (Juvenal, Persius) and French classicism, the most vivid and popular exponent of which was Nicholas Boileau, literary theoretician and author of highly lauded satires. Yet it is also evident that Kantemir was familiar with Molière and especially de la Bruyère, who satirized French social evils in his *Les Caractères ou les Moeurs de ce siècle* (The Characters or Morals of this Century, 1688). Kantemir created his own satires with these illustrious examples of European literature in mind, consciously striving to assimilate the best achievements of European artistic thought into Russia.

In his satires Kantemir creates a spectrum of human shortcomings, with portraits of misers, prodigals, drunkards, hypocrites, and arrogant boasters. While the mark of foreign literary influence is unmistakably evident, Kantemir so thoroughly fills his descriptions with the details of Russian everyday life that his bold denunciations clearly characterize his own day and time. Kantemir also portrayed many concrete features of the social and historical reality of 1730s in other works during this period, such as his fables in imitation of Aesop, which touch on contemporary political problems. Furthermore, Kantemir introduced colloquial language of a wide range of social groups. He generously employs Russian proverbs and folk sayings and saturates his characters' speech with colloquialisms. A feeling of deep respect for the lower social orders and a desire to encapsulate popular wisdom characterize Kantemir the satirist.

Kantemir did not publish his satires during his lifetime, despite repeated attempts to do so. However, they became widely known via numerous handwritten copies. It was only five years after the poet's death, in 1749, that Abbot Guasco first published the satires in a French prose translation. This edition was republished in 1750, and a German translation from the French appeared two years later. Thus Kantemir became the first Russian writer to achieve literary celebrity in Europe. The first Russian edition of the satires appeared in 1762, eighteen years after Kantemir's death, thanks to the efforts of Lomonosov.

Kantemir was one of the first Russian philologists, and his notes to the satires include a wealth of information about the history of literature, classical culture, and contemporary natural sciences; Kantemir clearly wanted them to reflect the latest developments in Russian and European learning. The notes are included in a manuscript copy of the satires that Kantemir sent to Russia from Paris in 1743 and were prepared for publication in the 1762 edition by the poet Ivan Barkov, probably under Lomonosov's editorial direction.

At the end of the 1720s Kantemir also began work on an epic poem dedicated to Peter the Great, which he called the "Petrida, ili Opisanie stikhotvornoe smerti Petra Velikogo, imperatora vserossiiskogo" (The Petriad, or a Verse Description of the Death of Peter the Great, Emperor of All the Russias), first published in 1859. It begins with the story of Peter's impending death:

Печаль неутешную России рыдаю:
Смеху дав прежде вину, к слезам побуждаю;
Плачу гибель чрезмерну в роксолян народе
Юже введе смерть Петра перва в царском роде.

(I weep Russia's inconsolable woe:
Having earlier given cause for laughter, I now arouse tears;
I bemoan the horrible consequences for the Roksolanian people [a pseudo-historical name for Russians],
Which the death of Peter I has wrought in the czar's clan.)

The "Petrida" as conceived by Kantemir had a political as well as artistic agenda: to defend Peter's reforms and to present him as a model of a wise sovereign, a graphic example for the Empress Anna, his niece.

Kantemir's work in Peter's personal archive on the historical sources for the poem was interrupted in the fall of 1731, when the question of his appointment as envoy to England arose. An interest in Russian history characterized all of the members of Feofan Prokopovich's "uchenaia druzhina" (learned guard), to which Kantemir belonged. During the years of his friendship with Kantemir, Prokopovich not only studied ancient Russian history but also wrote *Kratkaia povest' o smerti Petra Velikogo* (A Short Tale on the Death of Peter the Great, 1725) and participated in editing the *Podennyi zhurnal Petra Velikogo* (Daily Journal of Peter the Great) and other historical works. Another member of the group, the historian V. N. Tatishchev, was collecting materials for his projected multivolume *Istoriia Rossiskaia* (History of Russia, 1768–1848), which he saw as the realization of Peter's own behest. Under the direction of his father's secretary, I. Fokerodt, and that of Prof. G. S. Bayer of the Saint Petersburg Academy of Sciences, Kantemir also studied early Russian history. A copy of Kantemir's unpublished "Gospodina filosofa Konstantina Maneisa Sinposis istoricheskii" (Historical Synopsis of the Philosopher Constantine Manasses, 1725), a translation and conspectus of the Byzantine historian's twelfth-century chronicle, has been preserved.

Kantemir made a significant contribution to Russia's familiarization with classical heritage. His translation of Horace's *Epistles* was published by the Academy of Sciences in 1744, after Kantemir's death and with no mention of the translator's name. Kantemir also translated what were known in the eighteenth century as the poems of Anacreon, but they unfortunately remained unpublished and unknown to his contemporaries; they were not published until the nineteenth century and had no influence on Russian eighteenth-century Anacreontic poetry. Kantemir also translated Fontenelle's *Entretiens sur la pluralité des mondes* (1686), the French enlightener's popular exposition of Copernicus's heliocentric system. The translation was completed in 1730 and published in 1740. While abroad at the end of the 1730s, Kantemir worked on a Russian translation of Justinus's *History* and a version of Francesco Algarotti's *Il newtonianismo per le dame* (1737).

On 30 March 1732 Kantemir arrived in London and immediately began his diplomatic activity. At the time tact and caution were needed to preserve harmony between the English and Russian governments, but Kantemir was equal to the task. He successfully negotiated the sending of an English ambassador to Saint Petersburg, as a result of which he was promoted to the position of *chrezvychainyi poslannik* (extraordinary envoy).

Despite the promotion, Kantemir's salary remained the same, and he was often compelled to write letters petitioning money from various influential persons because his income was insufficient to maintain a standard of living consistent with his position. He also enlisted the help of his sister Maria, who lived in Saint Petersburg, to procure onetime grants of money and raises in salary. His financial situation declined even further when the estates that the empress had granted him were confiscated because of a suit his stepmother filed over his father's inheritance. Although these estates were later returned to him, he expended much energy in legal battles. This episode, the need to take care of Russian visitors to London, the execution of all kinds of orders – from shipping books and instru-

ments to the Academy of Sciences to purchasing material for dresses – together with his immediate duties as ambassador occupied practically all of Kantemir's time during the early years of his life in England and left none for literary work. Later, after his position in the service had become more secure, he resumed writing. In 1735 he wrote the philosophical ode or song "Na zlobnogo cheloveka" (To a Malicious Person), in 1736 the ode "Na vziatie Azova" (On the Capture of Azov), and in 1737 the fables "Gorodskaia i polevaia mysh' " (The City Mouse and the Country Mouse) and "Chizh i snegir' " (The Siskin and the Bullfinch). He also reworked some of his earlier satires.

At the same time, Kantemir began to develop an intimate circle of friends, mostly Italians; they called themselves a club and spent their leisure time together. They were all members of the diplomatic corps, highly educated men who took an active interest in the sciences, literature, and art. Under their influence Kantemir became well acquainted with Italian literature (especially the works of Torquato Tasso, Ludovico Ariosto, Francesco Algarotti, Paolo Rotti, L. Riccoboni, and Pietro Bembo), renewed his interest in painting, and became fascinated by opera. The circle maintained contact with writers (Rolli, Algarotti), composers (Porpora), and well-known actors and actresses.

Kantemir placed high value on feminine intelligence and believed that "the sharpness of the feminine intellect is quicker and more penetrating than ours, and their imagination more vivid and clear." He had many women friends, including the Marquise de Monconseil, who lived in Paris and with whom Kantemir maintained an active correspondence on questions of art, literature, and politics. He met her in Paris, where he was being treated (from 6 August to 5 September 1736) for a persistent eye disease that had refused to yield to the efforts of London doctors. The goal of the trip was achieved: the well-known oculist Dr. C. D. V. Gendron was able to cure his illness over the course of several years and became his personal physician.

While he took up Italian, and later English literature (especially the works of John Locke, John Milton, Alexander Pope, and John Wilmot, Earl of Rochester), Kantemir continued to follow the development of Russian literature and subscribed to all of the publications of the Academy of Sciences. Thus in 1735 he became acquainted with Trediakovsky's *Novyi i kratkii sposob k slozheniiu stikhov Rossiiskikh* (New and Brief Method for Composing Russian Verse), which introduced a tonic system of Russian versification based on regularly stressed metric feet rather than on the number of syllables in a line, as in "syllabic" verse. Kantemir, however, never accepted the new system. His rejection of it may be explained in part by the fact that Trediakovsky's attempt was theoretically contradictory and inconsistent: he insisted, for example, that the only correct use of a tonic system was in "long verses" written in trochaic meter. Lomonosov also reacted critically to Trediakovsky's treatise. The literary environment of Paris, where syllabic poetry writing prevailed, also probably played a part in Kantemir's nonacceptance of the tonic system.

In his "Pis'mo Kharitona Makentina" (Letter of Khariton Makentin – the name being an anagram of Antiokh Kantemir), Kantemir criticizes Trediakovsky's *Novyi i kratkii sposob,* defends syllabic versification, and sets forth many theoretical ideas about perfecting that type of verse. It was appended to his translation of Horace, *Desiat' pisem* (Ten Epistles, 1744). Kantemir also began to rework his early satires, introducing compulsory stress on the seventh or fifth syllable of his thirteen-syllable syllabic line, in which – as in the French Alexandrine – stress always fell on the penultimate syllable in the line. This acknowledgment of the importance of rhythmic regularity of syllabic verse was a significant development in Kantemir's poetry.

Kantemir's London circle reflected his ideal of a life lived in conformity with the Horatian prototype, filled with lofty spiritual interests. In his sixth satire, "O istinnom blazhenstve" (On True Bliss, 1738), Kantemir paints a picture of the quiet prosperity of a moderate and normal cultured life, lived in seclusion "mezh mertvymi greki i latyni" (amidst dead Greeks and Romans) with a small circle of chosen friends. This life is opposed to the noisy and troubled life of official activities, connected with hypocrisy, cruelty, and the trampling of human dignity.

Affairs of the heart were not forgotten, either. Allusions to Kantemir's love interests are found in his correspondence with his sister Maria, who, for example, cautioned her brother that he not allow "anything serious to develop out of friendly kisses and conversations, and most important, that [they] not incur any unpleasantness and offend his fiancee." Princess Maria was referring to her active effort to arrange the marriage of her brother to Princess V. A. Cherkasskaia, a possibility that had been raised even prior to Kantemir's departure for England. Cherkasskaia's father was sympathetic to the proposed marriage, but her mother was not, and consequently the matter was delayed. At the start of his stay in London, Kantemir still hoped that the

Title page for the first Russian publication of Kantemir's satires

marriage might work out and even sent his fiancée presents; later, tired of waiting and distracted by new interests, he changed his mind and wrote categorically to his sister in 1740 that "as far as the tigress is concerned, I no longer think about her at all: I am so fed up with these never-ending, fruitless conversations about her that I have lost all patience with them." In 1742 Cherkasskaia's father died, bringing an end to the long courtship; in the following year the princess married P. B. Sheremetev. Kantemir remained a bachelor, albeit with some regrets.

In England, Kantemir successfully undertook the publication of his father's works. While still a student at the Saint Petersburg Academy of Sciences, Kantemir had befriended the young professor G. S. Bayer, who held the chair of Eastern and Ancient Languages. Bayer reportedly had proposed to publish a "Turkish History by Prince Kantemir in Latin with Notes and a Description of the Author's Life" but the plan was hindered by Kantemir's departure for England. Kantemir took the originals of his father's manuscripts abroad with him, and in 1734 the first edition of Dmitrii Kantemir's *The History of the Growth and Decay of the Ottoman Empire,* which the author had begun in Constantinople in 1714 and finished in Russia in 1716, was published in English in London. The translation from the original Latin, made "from the author's own manuscript" (as the title page states), was prepared by N. Tindal, with Kantemir's help.

On 18 April 1738 Kantemir was awarded the title of *kamerger* (chamberlain) and appointed plenipotentiary minister to France, where he arrived on 8 September. His position in the French court proved extremely difficult: it was his job to defend Russia's foreign policy, which was then hostile to several of France's allies – Sweden, Poland, and Turkey – and friendly to Austria, France's longtime enemy. In view of this, it was difficult to preserve peaceable relations between France and Russia; moreover, the French government was not particularly well disposed to Kantemir, whom they assumed was devoted to England and Austria. He was put under secret surveillance, and a plan was devised to force him out of the country. At first Kantemir was so burdened with his new assignment that he neglected to write to his friends in London. Gradually, his official duties became easier, but life in an atmosphere full of mistrust and intrigue affected his mood. Kantemir sadly recalled his London friends and the pleasure he found in their company.

He became acquainted with Voltaire, the Abbot Guasko (his future biographer), and the Duchess Eugen, but these new contacts were unable to help him become accustomed to the Paris environment. "I always wanted to visit Paris [again] sometime," Kantemir wrote to his sister. "Now I am here enjoying all manner of life's comforts, but nonetheless can hardly wait for the hour when I shall get out of here." The noisy and brilliant life of Paris, the various amusements and card games in which he was compelled to participate "against his own desire," and the diplomatic service "in spite of all its advantages and honors" seemed oppressive.

After the change of government in Russia in 1740–1741 vague rumors that Kantemir would be recalled from Paris held him in agonizing uncertainty. He wanted to return home to live with his brothers and sister, "even if poorly, but on the other hand in peace." He dreamed of exchanging his diplomatic career for a duty closer to his heart – to be president of the Academy of Sciences.

Living in Paris, Kantemir continued to concern himself with his father's literary legacy. He made great efforts to arrange for the publication of *The History of the Growth and Decay of the Ottoman Empire* in French. The work was known in France in manuscript even before its publication there; in letters of 13 March and 19 April 1739 Voltaire thanked Kantemir for the use of his father's work "in the original." Two editions of the work were published in Paris in 1743,

in two and four volumes. The translation was done by M. Joncquiers, and, in distinction from the 1734 English edition, both French editions included a biography of Dmitrii Kantemir written by his son. During these years Antiokh Kantemir also worked on translating the work into Italian with the help of Abbot Guasko, but he never finished this project.

The Parisian climate was unfavorable to Kantemir's health. He took the waters at Aix-en-Provence in 1741 and in 1743 at Plombières, and in 1744 he petitioned Empress Elizabeth "in tears" for permission and a subsidy to travel to Italy for medical treatment. Permission was granted, but without financial assistance. However, due to his acute condition Kantemir was unable to profit from this authorization, and he died on 31 March 1744. His remains, in accordance with his will, were transported back to Russia, and he was buried in Moscow in the church of the Greek Nikol'sky Monastery, alongside his father.

G. F. Miller preserved information about the unfortunate demise of Kantemir's library and the fate of his papers. The writer's brothers Sergei and Matvei ordered that Kantemir's books be sold in Paris and that "only original works and translations of their brother" be forwarded to Russia. In 1780, upon the death of Sergei, the last surviving brother, all remaining manuscripts of Dmitrii and Antiokh Kantemir were transferred to the archive of the College of Foreign Affairs in Moscow (currently the Central State Archive of Ancient Acts) by N. N. Bantysh-Kamensky, a relative of the family, who became director of the archive in 1783.

Bibliographies:

Grigorii N. Gennadi, "Dannye dlia polnogo sobraniia sochinenii Kantemira," *Bibliografischeskie zapiski*, no. 3 (1858);

Pavel N. Berkov and V. P. Stepanov, "Materialy dlia bibliografii izdanii A. D. i D. K. Kantemirov i literatury o nikh (1917–1959)," in *Problemy russkogo Prosveshcheniia v literature XVIII veka*, edited by Berkov (Moscow & Leningrad: Akademiia nauk, 1961), pp. 260–270.

Biographies:

Vladimir Ia. Stoiunin, "Kniaz' Antiokh Kantemir," in *Sochineniia, pis'ma i izbrannye perevody*, volume 2 (Saint Petersburg: Glazunov, 1867);

Leonid N. Maikov, *Materialy dlia biografii kn. A. D. Kantemira* (Saint Petersburg: Akademiia nauk, 1903);

Helmut Grasshoff, *Antioch Dmitrevič Kantemir und Westeuropa* (Berlin: Akademie-Verlag, 1966).

References:

Vasilii N. Aleksandrenko, *Russkie diplomaticheskie agenty v Londone v XVIII veka,* 2 volumes (Warsaw: Varshavskago Uchebnago Okruga, 1897);

Mikhail P. Alekseev, " 'Proroche rogatyi' Feofana Prokopovicha," in *Iz istorii russkikh literaturnikh otnoshenii XVIII–XX vekov* (Moscow: Akademiia nauk, 1959), pp. 17–43;

Charles L. Drage, "The Anacreontea and 18th-Century Russian Poetry," *Slavonic and East European Review,* 41, no. 96 (1962): 110–134;

R. J. M. Evans, "Antiokh Kantemir and His First Biographer and Translator," *Slavonic and East European Review,* 37 (1958): 184–195;

Evans, "Antiokh Kantemir and His German Translators," *Slavonic and East European Review,* 36 (December 1957): 150–158;

Zinovii I. Gershkovich, "K biografii A. D. Kantemira," *XVIII vek,* 3 (1958): 456–459;

T. M. Glagoleva, *K literaturnoi istorii satir kn. A. D. Kantemira (Vliianie Bualo i Labriuiera)* (Saint Petersburg, 1913);

Glagoleva, "Satiry kn. A. D. Kantemira i russkii byt pervoi poloviny XVIII veka," *Filologicheskie zapiski,* 3, no. 6 (1914): 398–432; 4, no. 3 (1914): 489–503;

Paulin Lewin, *Intermedia wschodniosłowiańskie XVI–XVIII wieku* (Warsaw & Kraków, 1967);

Galina N. Moiseeva, "Ivan Barkov i izdanie satir Antiokha Kantemira 1762 goda," *Russkaia literatura,* no. 2 (1967): 102–115;

Moiseeva, "K voprosu o russko-pol'skikh literaturnykh sviaziakh vtoroi poloviny XVII–XVIII vekov," in *Problemy slavianskogo literaturovedeniia, fol'klora i stilistiki* (Moscow, 1963);

Moiseeva, "Natsional'no-istorecheskaia tema v epicheskoi poeme XVIII veka," *Russkaia literatura,* no. 4 (1974): 33–53;

Moiseeva, "Stanovleniie novoi russkoi literatury i fol'klor," in *Russkaia literatura i fol'klor (XI–XVIII vv.),* edited by V. G. Bazanov and others (Leningrad: Nauka, 1970);

Moiseeva, "Sud'ba rukopisnogo naslediia Dmitriia Kantemira," in *Nasledie Dmitriia Kantemira i sovremennost'* (Kishinev: Kartia Moldoveniaske, 1976), pp. 127–143;

Petr P. Pekarsky, "Podrobnosti o pechatanii 'Simfonii na psaltyr' ' kniazia Antiokha Kantemira, posviashchenie i predislovie etoi knigi," *Bibliograficheskie zapiski,* no. 17 (1858): 531–535;

Fedor Ia. Priima, "Antiokh Kantemir i ego frantsuzskie literaturnye sviazi," in *Russkaia literatura: Trudy Otdela novoi russkoi literatury,* volume 1 (Leningrad: Akademiia nauk, 1957), pp. 7–45;

Lev V. Pumpiansky, "Kantemir i ital'ianskaia kul'tura," *XVIII vek,* [1] (1935): 83–132;

Moisei I. Radovsky, *Antiokh Kantemir i Petersburgskaia Akademiia nauk* (Leningrad: Akademiia nauk, 1959);

Ivan Shimko, *Novye dannye k biografii kn. A. D. Kantemira i ego blizhaishikh rodstvennikov (Po dokumentam, khraniashchimsia v Moskovskom Arkhive Ministerstva iustitsii)* (Saint Petersburg, 1891);

Rimvydas Silbajoris, "Rhythm and Meaning in Kantemir's 'Letter to Prince Nikita Jur'evich Trubeckoj,' " *Slavic and East European Journal,* 16 (Summer 1972): 163–172;

Silbajoris, *Russian Versification: The Theories of Trediakovskij, Lomonosov, and Kantemir* (New York: Columbia University Press, 1968);

Iurii V. Stennik, "K voprosu o poeticheskom sostiazanii 1743 goda," *Russkaia literatura,* no. 4 (1984): 100–104;

Stennik, *Russkaia satira XVIII veka* (Leningrad: Nauka, 1985);

Valentin P. Vompersky, "Stilisticheskaia teoriia A. D. Kantemira," *Filologicheskie nauki,* 1, no. 91 (1976): 55–66.

Vasilii Vasil'evich Kapnist
(12 February 1758? – 28 October 1823)

Charles L. Byrd
Indiana University

BOOKS: *Ode à l'occasion de la paix conclue entre la Russie et la Porte Ottomane à Kaynardgi le 10 juillet. Anno 1774* (Saint Petersburg, 1775);

Oda na vseradostnoe obruchenie ikh imp. vysochestv velikago kniazia Aleksandra Pavlovicha i velikoi kniazhny Elizavety Alekseevny sovershivsheesia 1793 goda, maiia v 10 den' (Saint Petersburg: Imperatorskaia tipografiia, [1793]);

Sochineniia (Saint Petersburg: Gos. Meditsinskaia kollegiia, 1796);

Iabeda komediia v piati deistviiakh (Saint Petersburg: Imperatorskaia tipografiia, 1798); translated into French by A. Legrelle as *La Chicane* (N. p.: Gang, 1886) – includes a previously unpublished preface attributed to Kapnist;

Klorida i Milon pastusheskaia opera v odnom deistvii (Saint Petersburg: Gubernskoe pravlenie, 1800);

Liricheskie sochineniia (Saint Petersburg, 1806);

Sochineniia (Saint Petersburg: A. Smirdin, 1849).

Editions: *Izbrannye sochineniia,* edited by B. I. Koplan, Biblioteka poeta, bol'shaia seriia (Leningrad: Sovetskii pisatel', 1941);

Sochineniia, edited by Iurii D. Ivanov (Moscow: Goslitizdat, 1959);

Sobranie sochinenii, 2 volumes, edited by Dmitrii S. Babkin (Moscow & Leningrad: Akademiia nauk, 1960);

Izbrannye proizvedeniia, edited by Babkin and G. V. Ermakovna-Bitner, Biblioteka poeta, bol'shaia seriia (Leningrad: Sovetskii pisatel', 1973).

Vasilii Vasil'evich Kapnist achieved fame with a single masterpiece, the satiric five-act verse comedy *Iabeda* (Chicanery, 1798). A work of adroit rhymes and ingenious stagecraft, *Iabeda* continuously attracted audiences into the 1850s, when other plays from the extensive eighteenth-century Russian tradition of full-length verse comedy had been largely forgotten. Rivaling for some spectators and readers Aleksandr Griboedev's more famous comedy, *Gore ot Uma* (Woe from Wit, 1833), Kapnist's masterwork was successfully revived in 1970. The

Vasilii Vasil'evich Kapnist; engraving by A. Osipov

author's enduring popularity as a satiric playwright has overshadowed the other achievements of a remarkably varied literary and administrative career. Indeed Kapnist was much more active as a poet throughout his life than as a playwright.

Although it is certain that Kapnist was born to the son of a Greek immigrant in the Ukrainian village of Obuhovka, it is difficult to determine the poet's precise date of birth. Kapnist claims in a letter to his wife dated 17 February 1788 that he was born on 12 February 1758. But family legend, reported by the poet's granddaughter, has the future author born out of wedlock in 1756 to a Turkish servant, then later deceived about his origins for the sake of propriety. Still other sources list 1757 as the year of birth. The competing testimonies and hint of deceit are indicative of the legal chaos and deceptions that characterized the era and which were to become Kapnist's most important literary themes.

In any case Kapnist never knew his father, Vasilii Petrovich Kapnist, a brigadier who died in battle in 1757. The future poet was brought up by his Ukrainian mother (or stepmother) and received an excellent education at home, especially in German and French. French was to become the language of Kapnist's first literary endeavor, a patriotic ode written in 1774 on the peace established between Russia and the Ottoman Empire. More important, French gave the future playwright access to Molière, whose *Sganarelle, ou le cocu imaginaire* (Sganarelle, or The Imaginary Cuckold, 1660) he translated into Russian verse as *Sganarev ili mnimaia nevernost'* in the 1780s.

At the age of thirteen Kapnist was sent to Saint Petersburg, where he attended the military school of the Izmailovsky Guards. Having performed well at the school, Kapnist was transferred within two years to the Preobrazhensky Regiment, where he met Gavriil Derzhavin, whose poetic career was just beginning. The two poets became friends for life and would frequently comment on one another's work and exchange letters.

In 1775 Kapnist withdrew from military service to concentrate on literary activities. He became active in the circle of writers, actors, musicians, and painters surrounding the charismatic poet and architect Nikolai L'vov, another friend of Derzhavin. The association with L'vov had important consequences for Kapnist's personal as well as his literary life. In 1781 Kapnist married Aleksandra Alekseevna D'iakova, whose sister, Maria Alekseevna, L'vov secretly married. Some fifteen years later, after his first wife's death, Derzhavin married the youngest of the three D'iakova sisters, further strengthening his bonds with Kapnist.

Through L'vov, Kapnist came into contact with fellow poets such as Mikhail Murav'ev and Ivan Khemnitser. All the poets of the L'vov circle were interested in alternatives to classicist, odic verse and turned for inspiration to foreign sentimentalist writers such as James Thomson, whose long nature poem, *The Seasons* (1726–1730), they particularly admired. Jean-Jacques Rousseau was also avidly read and discussed, and his influence is apparent in Kapnist's long poems on the condition of the peasantry written during the early 1780s.

Kapnist shared with Khemnitser alone a keenly satiric disposition and profound dissatisfaction with the social vices of the era. Khemnitser brought to the L'vov circle his formal verse satires on such subjects as bad judges and profit-hungry poetasters, character types who also figure prominently in Kapnist's writings. But while Khemnitser prudently made no effort to publish his satires, since Catherine II did not like to have the corruption of her regime denounced, Kapnist boldly published his "Satira I" in 1780 in *Sanktpeterburgskii vestnik* (The Saint Petersburg Herald). The work proved controversial enough to jeopardize Kapnist's marriage plans, for Aleksandra D'iakova's mother was among the poem's many critics and refused to receive Kapnist for several months.

Ostensibly a satire of human vices, especially stupidity, in the thematic tradition of Antiokh Kantemir and Aleksandr Sumarokov, the poem contains thinly veiled derogatory references to specific poets, such as the contemporary ode writer Vasilii Ruban, easily recognizable as "Rubov," in Kapnist's list of poets who write *gnusnye* (vile) verses for money. "Satira I" also catalogues various types of corrupt legal officials under Catherine: the well-meaning but thoroughly inept judge, nicknamed Bestolkov (Clueless); Zavistov (N. V. Nobles), a mistrustful judge of low rank; and the respected but thieving judge, Vredov (Harmer). In this poem and in the thematically related *Iabeda,* Kapnist invented some of Russian literature's greatest satiric names. Unfortunately, his onomastic wit is as resistant to translation as his genius for the rhymed couplet, so it is inevitable that his reputation abroad will never equal that in Russia.

Increasingly disgusted with the mores of Saint Petersburg, Kapnist withdrew in 1783 from a position he had obtained in the postal service and departed for his Ukrainian home. The sudden move may have been provoked by Catherine's 3 May decree indenturing the previously free peasants of three Ukrainian provinces to their local landowners. This new law prompted Kapnist's compassionate, ironically titled "Oda na rabstvo" (Ode to Slavery), written at Obuchovka in 1783.

Although Khemnitser had broken with the classicist tradition of the panegyric ode in such satiric poems as "Oda na pod'iachikh" (Ode to Petty Bureaucrats), Kapnist's "Oda na rabstvo" is notable for its introduction of lachrymose motifs, in the tradition of western European sentimentalism, to the genre. The poet's odic lyre has been washed by a "river of tears," his eye by "a flood" of them, all in response to the "enslavement" of the peasantry. Rousseauistic imagery of the people "in chains" recurs throughout the poem, interspersed with a series of addresses to the empress. The argument of these apostrophes is ironic to the point of sarcasm. The poet appeals to Catherine as a protectress of the people who, witnessing their plight, will liberate them, receiving the applause of their unchained hands and the glory of the poet's song. Such a virulently ironic treatment of the empress could hardly be published during her lifetime and was withheld until 1806 when the ode was collected in Kapnist's *Liricheskie sochineniia* (Lyrical Works).

Ironic praise for Catherine also characterizes Kapnist's later "Oda na istreblenie v Rossii zvaniia raba Ekaterinoiu Vtoroiu" (Ode on Catherine II's Abolition of the Title [or, Condition] of Slave in Russia, 1786). In 1786 Catherine decreed that petitions to the throne would no longer be signed "your Majesty's slave (*rab*)." Catherine's act, of course, did nothing to abolish serfdom, but Kapnist's poetic persona in the ode misinterprets the minor change in courtly protocol and glibly goes on to praise Catherine as the great emancipator of her "chained" people. In response to the poem, Catherine is reported to have remarked: "You want it [the destruction of slavery] in actual fact. How dare you! The words are enough." Catherine's alleged response contains a mocking Ukrainianism, "Zas' " (How dare you), which, if it did in fact reach the poet, could only have reinforced his antipathy for the empress and his allegiance to his Ukrainian homeland.

Kapnist responded critically not only to Catherine's political acts but also to the highly sympathetic image of her created by Derzhavin in his series of poems addressed to "Felitsa." Kapnist mocks Derzhavin's hyperbolic praise in "Otvet Rafela pevtsu Felitsy" (Raphael's Answer to the Singer of Felitsa). This playful work takes Derzhavin's *Izobrazhenie Felitsy* (Depiction of Felitsa), in which Derzhavin calls upon the Renaissance painter Raphael to paint Catherine's portrait, as its pretext. In Kapnist's work Raphael is reluctant to paint so great a subject as Catherine, whose portrait would require unobtainable materials: "Dlia ram obshirnoi tol' kartiny / Mal les vsei zdeshnei Palestiny" (For the frame of such a picture / The forests of all Palestine would not suffice). The humorous rhyme parodies the exaggerated, rococo style of Derzhavin's panegyrics. Derzhavin was hardly delighted with Kapnist's parody, but the two remained close friends. Kapnist had even named one of his sons for his fellow poet and would write one of his most moving funerary odes for Derzhavin's first wife.

During the last two decades of the eighteenth century Kapnist was deeply troubled by a series of personal misfortunes. In 1784 the death of the poet's one-year-old son Aleksei moved Kapnist to write the twenty-six stanzas of "Oda na smert' syna moego" (Ode on the Death of My Son). Suggesting a larger, political context for personal sufferings, the introduc-

tion alludes to the "enslavement" of the surrounding lands. Although written in the form of the Lomonosovian ten-line odic stanza (*aBaBccDeeD*), the poem's mood is typically sentimentalist, reminiscent of Thomas Gray's *Elegy Written in a Country Churchyard* (1751) and Edward Young's *Night Thoughts on Life, Death and Immortality* (1742–1746). The speaker takes consolation in natural images of loss: "the dark clouds which cut down the grain with hard rain," "the wind, carrying away the leaves," and "the plant-killing frost." The poem impressed contemporaries with its musicality. Its last two stanzas, beginning with the lines "Teper' uzh ia tvoiu grobnitsu / Ne vozmushchu moei toskoi" (No longer will I perturb your grave with my sorrow), were set to music by Kapnist's brother-in-law, Grigorii D'iakov.

The death of Kapnist's baby daughter in 1788 prompted another elegiac work, "Na smert' Iulii" (On the Death of Julia), which became a popular folk song. Many of the devices are the same as in "Oda na smert' syna moego": the poet speaks as if standing beside the grave; he takes comfort in his surroundings, including the moon, "friend of the sorrowful"; and in a typically sentimentalist conceit, the life of the child is compared to the life of a rose. Yet the two poems differ greatly in scope. A short work of only four simple *ababcdcd* stanzas, "Na smert' Iulii" is indicative of the many alternatives to the formal ode and elegy becoming widely accepted toward the end of the century.

In a later elegy written after the death of Derzhavin's first wife in 1794, "Oda na smert' Pleniry" (Ode on the Death of Plenira), Kapnist returned to the longer, more solemn form of the classicist funerary ode. The poem consists of fourteen Lomosovian stanzas. "Plenira" was a pet name for Ekaterina Derzhavina. In the context of the poem, the name suggests the plentitude of her love for humanity. Much of the poem is addressed to Derzhavin, but the work also includes the speaker's own meditative discourse:

Но что жизнь? В родах--мученье,
В детстве--раболепства гнет,
В юности--страстей волненье,
В мужестве-труды сует.

(But what is life? at birth--torture,
In childhood--the oppression of servility.
In youth--the disturbance of the passions.
In adult life--the labors of vanity.)

The poet's pessimistic resignation is reminiscent of his statement in "Oda na smert' syna moego": "Schast'e brennee stekla" (Happiness is more fragile than glass). Such meditations also characterize a second poem Kapnist wrote in memory of Derzhavin's wife and a series of more properly philosophical odes, including his "Oda na Unynie" (Ode to Dejection).

The melancholy tone of Kapnist's poems from the 1780s and 1790s contrasts with the affection and bustle of his letters of the period. Constantly traveling because of his new administrative duties, Kapnist occasionally complained of loneliness, but he more often playfully chastised his wife for not writing enough and inquired warmly after their remaining children. In 1785 Kapnist had been elected marshall of the nobility for the province of Kiev, a city to which he was expected to travel regularly. He also journeyed frequently to Saint Petersburg, the imperial capital he called a "uzhasnyi labirint" (terrible labyrinth). One of his longest trips there was in connection with his special project to form a Cossack volunteer regiment. In 1775 Catherine had dissolved the Zaporozhian Cossack government, but in 1788, under the combined threats of Turkish invasion from the south and Swedish naval attack on the Baltic Sea, Kapnist proposed to mobilize the half-million or so Cossacks who already possessed good military training. Kapnist had hoped that such services performed for the common social good would help him to "gain distinction" and "acquire friends," but he soon saw the error of such hopes. Kapnist's proposal was sent to Grigorii Potemkin for final approval but was soon lost among Potemkin's papers.

In his many travels to Saint Petersburg, Kapnist also attempted to resolve a burdensome family lawsuit against the wife of a certain Colonel Tarnovsky, who allegedly broke the law in seizing an estate in the Saratov province which belonged to Kapnist's brother. The case dragged on for more than fifteen years, and its impact is felt in Kapnist's masterful satire against legal corruption, the comedy *Iabeda,* begun in 1791. It is remarkable that such an enduring play was produced by an author with only minimal experience in playwriting. Kapnist's only prior work for the theater had been his version in rhymed Russian couplets of Molière's *Sganarelle, ou le cocu imaginaire.* The first draft of *Iabeda* was titled "Iabednik" (The Slanderer) in the tradition of Molière's dominating character types, for which his comedies are usually named. This tradition had been continued in Russia by Iakov Kniazhnin, without whose verse comedy, *Khvastun* (The Braggart, 1786), *Iabeda* would have been impossible, as Kapnist himself acknowledged.

Я Б Е Д А,

КОМЕДІЯ

ВЪ ПЯТИ ДѢЙСТВІЯХЪ.

Съ дозволенія Санктпетербургской Цензуры.

ВЪ Санктпетербургѣ, 1798.
Печатано въ Императорской Типографіи.
Иждивеніемъ г. Крупницкого.

Title page for Kapnist's finest work, a five-act verse satire

The final title of *Iabeda* and its plot reflect Kapnist's disdain for what may be variously translated into English as "chicanery" or "fraud" and its attendant vices: perjury, slander, flattery, and bribery. The plot revolves around the plans of one character, Pravolov (Lawtrapper), to cheat Major Priamikov (Straightguy) of his father's estate. In order to win his suit, Pravolov ingratiates himself to the president of the local legal court, Krivosudov (Crookjudge), with bribes and feigned interest in marrying his daughter, Sofia. Pravolov must also win the favors of five other local legal officials: Bul'bul'kin, a drunk whose name imitates the sound of liquor being poured out of a bottle; Atuev (from *Atu,* the Russian hunter's call), who takes leashes for hunting dogs as bribes; Radbyn, a stammerer; Parol'kin (from *parole,* a French card-player's term), a gambler; Kochtin (Claws), the court secretary; and Khvataiko (Grabbit), the court procurator. Only a deus ex machina in the form of a summons from afar for the arrest of Pravolov spoils his plan to seize Priamikov's estate.

The plot of *Iabeda* combines the best of classicism with vestiges of Aristophanic old comedy. In the tradition of Greek new comedy and classicism, there is a central love story, with Priamikov eventually marrying Sofia. But it is clearly of less overall interest than the satire against legal officials in the tradition of Aristophanic comedy. Kapnist adheres strictly to the unity of time and place. The play's action transpires within twenty-four hours, and all scenes — including legal hearings — occur at Krivosudov's house; the local law court is said to have burned down. The heavy drinking in act 3 at Krivosudov's name-day party is reminiscent of Aristophanic device; in *The Wasps* Aristophanes' lawyers are stumbling drunks. More generally, the name-day party at the center of Kapnist's comedy excites memories of the feast that traditionally accompanied the performance of Greek old comedy.

Much of the comedy's charm, however, comes not from the ironies of its theme but from the brilliance of its verbal wit. The character Radbyn's stammering is perfectly written into the iambic hexameter rhyme scheme: "Do-do-do-vodi-dit i-i-inonogda / Nas pra-pra-pravdoiu do-do-do sty-styda" (So-so-some-t-t-times the-th tr-truth is plain / And le-le-leads-u-us to gr-gr-gr-great shame). The stammering contrasts with the loquacious casuistry and flattery of the eloquent liars who surround Radbyn. Among the corrupt officials, he alone, in the tradition of stammering holy fools, is occasionally gifted with insight. His speech impediment offsets and exposes the lucid mendaciousness that typifies the other characters' discourse.

Khvataiko's rhetoric epitomizes the corruption of language among the smooth-talking lawyers. He teaches the others, including his sidekick Naumych, a song that includes some of the most memorable lines of the entire comedy:

Хватайко: Бери, большой тут нет науки,
             Бери, что только можно взять.
             На что же привешены нам руки,
             Как не на то, чтоб брать?

Все: Брать, брать, брать.

Наумыч: ... И драть.

(Khvataiko: Take [a bribe], there's no great science
    here,
          Take, whatever you may grab.
          What are hands hung on us for,
          If not to take?

All: To take, take, take.

Naumych: ... and to fight.)

It is reported that during one early-nineteenth-century performance in the provinces, these lines so delighted some audience members that they interrupted the action with spontaneous applause, pointed to a local official in attendance, and shouted: "That's you! That's you!" A subsequent stanza of Khvataiko's ditty includes a rhyming pseudoproverb: "Chto vziato, to sviato" (That which is taken [i.e., a bribe], is holy). Verging on blasphemy, such lines suggest the reversal of all moral values under Catherine and significantly darken the comedy, which the censors initially perceived as too threatening for print or performance.

After years of haggling, Kapnist was finally permitted to publish and produce the play under Emperor Paul I in 1798. But the printed copies were promptly seized and not released for sale until 1804. The 1798 Saint Petersburg stage production was closed by imperial decree after only four performances, and *Iabeda* was not performed again until 1805. Surprisingly, on 31 October 1799, while the comedy was still forbidden, Paul appointed Kapnist to a position in the Directorate of the Imperial Theater. Kapnist's duties included the review and "correction" of works submitted for production. The precise motivation for Paul's decision to make Kapnist a censor is unknown; perhaps he hoped to mollify the writer's satiric indignation. Perhaps, as one report suggests, a special private performance of *Iabeda* had so impressed Paul that he wished to reward the author. In any case Kapnist apparently enjoyed neither his duties nor the irony of the situation; he retired from the post on 14 August 1801.

None of the works written by Kapnist in the last two decades of his life achieved the recognition eventually gained by his earlier satiric verse and by *Iabeda*, often considered a major influence on the comedies of Nikolai Gogol. He published a one-act pastoral opera in 1800 and then abandoned comic genres and turned to tragedy, but he produced only two works, both strongly influenced by those of Vladislav Ozerov. His most successful nineteenth-century poems were responses to international political events and adaptations of Horace.

Kapnist saw in the Napoleonic invasion of Russia evidence for his life's conviction that the Russian government had been weakened by corruption. "Videnie plachushchego nad Moskvoiu rossianina" (Vision of a Russian Lamenting Over Moscow), dated 28 October 1812, is rich in historical allusion. One of the former Moscow patriarchs, Hermogen, appears to the poet in a dream. Hermogen was known for having denounced a pretender to the Russian throne and for having been tortured by Polish interventionists in 1612. A Jeremiadic figure embodying the uncompromising moral standards of old Moscow, Hermogen voices tirades against the corrupt Russian nobility – consonant with the author's own disdain for the widespread vice of his times.

In the last two decades of his life, Kapnist wrote over twenty-five adaptations of Horace. These can hardly be called translations in the ordinary sense, for Kapnist knew little Latin and worked from French and German versions in consultation with colleagues. Kapnist also wrote several original works which were Horatian in their spirit of praise for moderation and the simple pleasures of country life.

"Obuchovka," usually considered the best of Kapnist's later poems, catalogues the virtues of life on the poet's Ukrainian estate. He describes himself as happily living at peace with neighbors and in harmony with his own conscience, and his house as "umerennosti skromnyi khram" (a humble temple of moderation), a metaphor suggesting his faith in Horatian values. Like Derzhavin's similar country-house poem, "Evgeniiu. Zhizn' Zvanskaia" (To Eugene. Life at Zvanka, 1807), Kapnist's work conducts readers on a stroll around his estate. In a birch tree leaning out over the river Psel, Kapnist sees a figure of destruction: the tree will fall into the depths of the water during a storm. Kapnist so cherished this tree that he later wrote a lyric about it and requested that its wood be used for his coffin, a wish his children fulfilled. Kapnist died of pneumonia on 28 October 1823 and was buried on his estate. He had been, to use the words of the epitaph he envisaged for himself in "Obuchova," a "friend of the Muses" as well as "a friend of his homeland."

References:

Dmitrii S. Babkin, "V. V. Kapnist i A. N. Radishchev," *XVIII vek,* 4 (1959): 269–288;

Babkin, "V. V. Kapnist, kritiko-biograficheskii ocherk," in Kapnist's *Sobranie sochinenii,* volume 1, edited by Babkin (Moscow & Leningrad: Akademiia nauk, 1960), pp. 12–65;

Pavel N. Berkov, "V. V. Kapnist kak iavlenie russkoi kul'tury XVIII Veka," *XVIII vek,* 4 (1959): 257–268;

Berkov, *Vasilii Vasil'evich Kapnist (1750–1823)* (Moscow & Leningrad: Iskusstvo, 1950);

William B. Edgerton, "Laying a Legend to Rest: The Poet Kapnist and Ukraino-German Intrigue," *Slavic Review,* 30 (September 1971): 551–559;

Edgerton, "A Textological Puzzle in Kapnist's 'Ode on Slavery,'" in *Serta Selavica in memoriam Aloisii Schmaus,* edited by Wolfgang Geseman, Joannes Holthusen, Erwin Koschmieder, Ilse Kunert, Peter Rehder, and Erwin Wedel (Munich: R. Trofenik, 1971), pp. 435–444;

Galina A. Lapkina, "O teatral'nykh sviaziakh V. V. Kapnista," *XVIII vek,* 4 (1959): 304–312;

Aleksandr I. Matsai, *"Iabeda" V. V. Kapnista* (Kiev: Kievskii universitet, 1958);

Il'ia Z. Serman, "V. V. Kapnist i russkaia poeziia nachala XIX veka," *XVIII vek,* 4 (1959): 289–303.

Nikolai Mikhailovich Karamzin

(1 December 1766 – 22 May 1826)

Gitta Hammarberg
Macalester College

BOOKS: *Pesn' mira* (N.p., 1792);

Moi bezdelki, 2 volumes (Moscow: Ridiger i Klaudii, 1794);

Bednaia Liza (Moscow; Ridiger i Klaudii, 1796);

Iuliia (Moscow: Ridiger i Klaudii, 1796);

Oda na sluchai prisiagi moskovskikh zhitelei e. i. v. Pavlu Pervomu, samoderzhtsu vserossiiskomu (Moscow: Ridiger i Klaudii, 1796);

Razgovor o shchastii (Moscow: Ridiger i Klaudii, 1797);

Pis'ma russkogo puteshestvennika, 6 volumes (Moscow: Ridiger i Klaudii, 1797–1801); 5 volumes (Moscow: Ridiger i Klaudii, 1797–1801); republished, in 2 volumes (Saint Petersburg; A. S. Suvorin, 1887); edited by V. A. Grikhin (Moscow: Sovetskaia Rossiia, 1983); edited by Iurii M. Lotman, N. A. Marchenko, and Boris A. Uspensky. Literaturnye pamiatniki (Leningrad: Nauka, 1984);

E. i. v. Aleksandru I, Samoderzhtsu Vserossiiskomu, na vosshestvie ego na prestol (Moscow, 1801);

Na torzhestvennoe koronovanie e. i. v. Aleksandra I, Samoderzhtsa Vserossiiskogo (Moscow, 1801);

Panteon rossiiskikh avtorov, edited by Platon Beketov, volume 1 (Moscow: Selivanovsky, 1801–1802);

Istoricheskoe pokhval'noe slovo Ekaterine II (Moscow, 1802);

Sochineniia, 8 volumes (Moscow: S. Selivanovsky, 1803–1804); enlarged edition, 8 volumes (Moscow: S. Selivanovsky, 1814); revised and enlarged edition, 9 volumes (Moscow: S. Selivanovsky, 1820); enlarged edition, 3 volumes (Saint Petersburg: A. Smirdin, 1848);

Istoriia Gosudarstva Rossiiskogo, 8 volumes (Saint Petersburg: 1816–1818); revised edition, 12 volumes (Saint Petersburg: N. Grech, 1818–1829); fifth edition, in 3 volumes (Saint Petersburg: I. Einerling, 1842–1843); facsimile of fifth edition, with index by P. M. Stroev, and introductory essays by Iu. Lotman, V. P. Kozlov, and S. O. Shmidt (Moscow: Kniga,

Nikolai Mikhailovich Karamzin

1988); another edition, 12 volumes, edited by A. N. Sakharov (Leningrad: Nauka, 1988–); another edition, 4 volumes, edited by A. F. Smirnov (Rostov-on-Don: Knizhnoe Izdatel'stvo, 1988);

O drevnei i novoi Rossii v ee politicheskom i grazhdanskom otnosheniiakh (Berlin: F. Schneider, 1861); republished as *Zapiska o drevnei i novoi Rossii,* edited by Vasilii V. Sipovsky (Saint Petersburg: M. N. Tolstaia, 1914).

Editions: *Neizdannye sochineniia i perepiska,* volume 1 (Saint Petersburg: N. Tiblen i Ko., 1862);

N. Karamzin. I. Dmitriev. Izbrannye stikhotvoreniia, edited by A. Ia. Kucherov, Biblioteka poeta, bol'shaia seriia (Leningrad: Sovetskii pisatel', 1953);

N. M. Karamzin i I. I. Dmitriev. Stikhotvoreniia, edited by A. Ia. Kucherov, Biblioteka poeta, malaia seriia (Leningrad: Sovetskii pisatel', 1958);

Izbrannye sochineniia, edited by Pavel N. Berkov and Georgii P. Makogonenko, 2 volumes (Moscow & Leningrad: Khudozhestvennaia literatura, 1964);

Polnoe sobranie stikhotvorenii, edited by Iurii M. Lotman, Biblioteka poeta, bol'shaia seriia (Moscow & Leningrad: Sovetskii pisatel', 1966);

Pis'ma russkogo puteshestvennika. Povesti, edited by N. N. Akopova, Makogonenko, and M. V. Ivanov (Moscow: Pravda, 1980);

Izbrannye stat'i i pis'ma, edited by A. F. Smirnov (Moscow: Sovremennik, 1982);

Izbrannoe, edited by Berkov and Makogonenko (Moscow: Pravda, 1984);

Sochineniia, edited by G. P. Makogonenko, 2 volumes (Leningrad: Khudozhestvennaia literatura, 1984);

Zapiski starogo moskovskogo zhitelia: Izbrannaia proza, edited by Vl. Murav'ev (Moscow: Moskovskii rabochii, 1986);

Predaniia vekov: Skazaniia, legendy, rasskazy iz 'Istorii gosudarstva Rossiiskogo', edited by Makogonenko and M. V. Ivanov (Moscow: Pravda, 1987).

Editions in English: *Karamsin's Julia translated from the Russian to the French by Mr du Bouillier and from the French in to the English by Ann P[renser] H[awkins]* (Saint Petersburg, 1803);

Travels from Moscow through Prussia, Germany, Switzerland, France and England, translated by A. A. Feldborg, 3 volumes (London: Printed for J. Badcock by G. Sidney, 1803);

Russian Tales by Nicolai Karamsin, translated by John B. Elrington (London: Sidney, 1803);

Tales, from the Russian of Nicolai Karamsin, translated by A. A. Feldborg (London: G. Sidney, 1804);

Letters of a Russian Traveler, 1789–1790, translated and abridged by Florence Jonas (New York: Columbia University Press, 1957);

Karamzin's Memoir on Ancient and Modern Russia: A Translation and Analysis, translated by Richard Pipes (Cambridge, Mass.: Harvard University Press, 1959);

Selected Prose of N. M. Karamzin, translated by Henry M. Nebel (Evanston, Ill.: Northwestern University Press, 1969);

Selected Aesthetic Works of Sumarokov and Karamzin, translated by Henry M. Nebel, Jr. (Washington, D.C.: University Press of America, 1981).

OTHER: Salomon Gessner, *Dereviannaia noga: Shveitsarskaia idiliia,* translated by Karamzin (Saint Petersburg, 1783);

Albrecht von Haller, *O proiskhozhdenii zla, poema velikogo Gallera,* translated by Karamzin (Moscow: Tipograficheskaia kompaniia, 1786);

Detskoe chtenie dlia serdtsa i razuma, 9–20 (January 1787–December 1789), edited by Karamzin and A. A. Petrov;

William Shakespeare, *Iulii Tsezar',* translated by Karamzin (Moscow, 1787);

Gotthold E. Lessing, *Emiliia Galotti,* translated by Karamzin (Moscow, 1788);

Moskovskii zhurnal, 1–8 (January 1791–December 1792), edited by Karamzin;

Aglaia, almanakh, 1–2 (1794–1795), edited by Karamzin;

Jean-François Marmontel, *Novye Marmontelevy povesti,* translated by Karamzin, 2 volumes (Moscow, 1794–1798);

Madame de Staël, *Melina,* translated by Karamzin (Moscow, 1795);

Aonidi, ili Sobranie raznykh novykh stikhotvorenii, 1–3 (1796–1799), edited by Karamzin;

"Lettre au Spectateur sur la littérature russe," *Spectateur du Nord,* 4 (1797): 53–71;

Panteon inostrannoi slovesnosti, compiled and translated by Karamzin, 3 volumes (Moscow: Ridiger i Klaudii, 1798);

Vestnik Evropy, 1–12 (1802–1803), edited by Karamzin;

"[Avtobiografiia]," edited by Ia. K. Grot, *Zapiski Imperatorskoi Akademii Nauk,* 8, no. 2 (1866): 97–98.

The period from the 1790s to the 1820s in Russian literature is commonly referred to as the Karamzin era. Karamzin set the tone for Russian sentimentalism, the movement that dominated Russian literature at the turn of the century. His literary works, particularly his prose fiction, provided models for his fellow sentimentalists and initiated genres that were to blossom among his successors. His works finally bestowed legitimacy on Russian prose fiction. His contributions to Russian intellectual life reached far beyond literature: his ideas on literary language gained wide acceptance and gave rise to one of the most fruitful linguistic polemics in the history of Russian literature; his activities as a journalist enlightened the Russian public and popularized European culture in Russia. In fact, Karamzin is generally credited with creating the Russian reading public, particularly the woman reader. He was one of the first Russian professional men of letters who actually earned his livelihood by writing. The last decades of his life were spent as an official court historian, opening up for Russians their national past. On a more modest scale he also introduced Russian literature to European readers.

Karamzin's paternal ancestry can be traced to the Tatar prince Kara-Murza, while his earliest known maternal ancestor, Fedor Pasukh, served under Ivan III. His parents were Mikhail Egorovich Karamzin, a retired army captain, and Ekaterina Petrovna Karamzina (née Pasukhina). Nikolai, their second son, was born on 1 December 1766 on a small family estate on the Volga, not far from the provincial capital, Simbirsk. His mother died when he was two years old, and his father remarried about a year later – a marriage that made Karamzin a distant relative to Ivan Dmitriev, a lifelong friend and fellow poet.

Karamzin's education began at home, where he was taught by the family physician and educated neighbors. He read all he could, including Charles Rollin's ten-volume *Histoire ancienne* (Ancient History, 1730–1738) in Vasilii Trediakovsky's translation. In 1777–1778 he attended Monsieur Fauvel's boarding school in Simbirsk, followed by the Moscow boarding school of Johann Matthias Schaden, a Tübingen professor of moral philosophy at Moscow University, whose lectures Karamzin also attended. These experiences, together with continued independent study, gave Karamzin a solid background in the humanities, including a knowledge of German, French, and some English, and familiarity with European literatures and cultures.

After graduating in 1781 he moved to Saint Petersburg, where his father had enrolled him in the Preobrazhensky Guards regiment. Literary pursuits were more appealing to Karamzin than military service, and he befriended, among other authors, Ivan Dmitriev, who encouraged his literary interests, including translation. Karamzin's first published piece was the 1783 translation of Salomon Gessner's idyll "Das hölzerne Bein" (The Wooden Leg, 1772) – a choice of genre that influenced the direction of Karamzin's own writing.

After his father's death, Karamzin retired from the army in 1784 and returned to Simbirsk to put estate matters in order. While reading widely (Voltaire, Edward Young, William Shakespeare) and planning future translations, he also lived the typical high-society life in salons and at the card tables. In Simbirsk he met Ivan Turgenev and became a member of his Masonic lodge, Zlatoi venets (The Golden Crown). This association gave a more spiritual direction to Karamzin's energies, setting him on a lifelong path of self-improvement. He moved back to Moscow

and joined Nikolai Novikov's Druzheskoe uchenoe obshchestvo (Friendly Learned Society), aimed at spreading enlightenment to the people, and encouraged conscious self-improvement and practical philanthropy. Taking advantage of Catherine's 1783 edict legalizing private presses, they organized a typography in 1784 and acquired property to house their publishing ventures and serve as living quarters for some of the "brothers." Karamzin moved in with Semen Gamaleia, Aleksei Kutuzov, Aleksandr Petrov (his closest literary role model), and the German poet Jacob Lenz. Masonic teachings, German Sturm und Drang ideas, and the brotherly friendships nurtured by the group had a lasting impact on Karamzin's literary activities and tastes. During this period he published his translations of Albrecht von Haller's poem *Über den Urspung des Übels* (On the Source of Evil, 1734; translated as *O proiskhozhdenii zla,* 1786), Shakespeare's *Julius Caesar* (1599; translated as *Iulii Tsezar,* 1787) and Gotthold E. Lessing's *Emilia Galotti* (1772; translated as *Emiliia Galotti,* 1788).

Karamzin's career both as a writer and as a journalist was launched with his participation in Novikov's publishing ventures. He participated in serially issued translations of works by Christoph Christian Sturm. He also contributed translations and original pieces to Novikov's journal *Detskoe chtenie dlia serdtsa i razuma* (Children's Reading for Heart and Mind) – the first Russian children's journal – which he and Petrov edited from 1787 to 1789. The translations include versions of James Thomson's *The Seasons* (1726–1730); several *contes moraux,* mainly from the works of Mme. de Genlis; a pastoral drama from Christian Weisse's journal *Der Kinderfreund* (The Children's Friend); and selections from Alexander Pope.

Karamzin's most important original prose works published in the journal were "Evgenii i Iuliia" (Eugene and Julia) and "Progulka" (A Promenade). The former is Karamzin's first sentimental tale, and "Progulka" can be read as a fictional expression of his artistic credo. It illustrates major sentimentalist principles: a solipsistic focus on the individual and the importance of a highly sensitized heart and mind for artistic creation and reception; and the idea that aesthetics is inherently ethical. It traces the history of art from the original divine Creation as a series of subsequent re-creations (or more properly, cocreations) of that primary work by subsequent artists. The idyllic structure of this minor work reveals the essential features of all of Karamzin's subsequent prose fiction: an insignificant plot is enveloped by an emotional and expressive narrator's voice, which is directly addressed to the reader in the opening and conclusion of the work and colors all of the events related.

Karamzin's first original poems appeared in *Detskoe Chtenie* – unimportant except as indications of the forms (idylls, elegies, Anacreontic verse) and melancholic tone that became staples of sentimentalism. A more important, longer poem, "Poeziia" (Poetry), was written at the time, although it was not published until 1792 in *Moskovskii zhurnal* (Moscow Journal). It is a companion piece to "Progulka" in that it too outlines a history of poetry and enumerates the idyllic poets most favored by Russian sentimentalist writers. Idyllists set the tone for Karamzin's verse and prose, and the absence of French and Russian writers in this poem has been read as a deliberate rejection of Russian classicism, along with its French intermediary. "Poeziia" conveys a sense of innovation: it ends predicting a new era in Russian literature and a (not immodest) hint at Karamzin's own role in creating it.

The Pleshcheev family provided a nurturing environment for Karamzin at this time and contributed to defining the cult of friendship characteristic of sentimentalism. Aleksei Pleshcheev, whom Karamzin had known since boarding school, was to remain a close friend; Karamzin established a long sentimental friendship with his wife, Anastasiia Pleshcheeva; and her sister, Elizaveta Ivanovna Protasova, was later to become his wife. Pleshcheeva, under the sobriquet Aglaia, figured in many of Karamzin's works; others were addressed or dedicated to her; and one of his almanacs was named *Aglaia*.

In 1789 Karamzin set out on a grand tour of Europe. Few Russian travelers before or after could match this journey as an in-depth study of Western culture. Besides Karamzin's interest in literature, he engrossed himself in art, architecture, music, theater, political systems, philosophy, foreign customs, and geography. The journey was in a profound sense also a personal journey of the type made popular by Laurence Sterne in his *A Sentimental Journey* (1768). Karamzin traveled as a "reader" of texts in the widest sense and as an "author" generating a future literary work. He visited an impressive number of representatives of the intellectual elite, including Immanuel Kant, Christoph Friedrich Nicolai, Karl Moritz, Ernst Platner, Christian Weisse, Johann Gottfried Herder, Christoph Martin Wieland, Charles Bonnet, Johann Lavater (with whom he had corresponded already well before his journey), Jean-François Marmontel, and Jean-Jacques Barthélemy (Johann Wolfgang von Goethe was also on his agenda, but a meeting did not occur). To other favorite writers, such as Sterne, Jean-Jacques Rousseau, Voltaire, Salomon Gessner, and

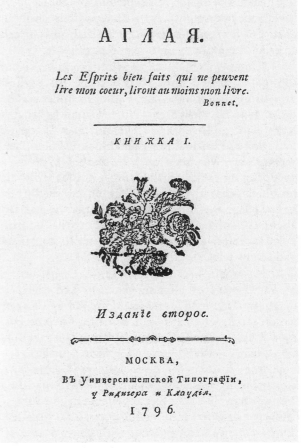

Title page for a one-volume republication of Karamzin's short-lived almanac, originally published in 1794–1795

Albrecht von Haller, he paid homage by visiting places connected with their lives and works.

Upon his return to Russia, Karamzin created one of his most important works, the *Pis'ma russkogo puteshestvennika* (Letters of a Russian Traveler, 1797–1801). This epistolary work, while a true encyclopedia of European culture, is a typical sentimentalist literary work in which the reader finds out as much about its narrator – his moods, opinions, and emotional reactions – as about the European topics he relates. The solipsistic focus on the narrator is most pointedly revealed in the last letter, where he describes the work as a "mirror of my soul," which he himself in twenty years will find a pleasant way to recall "what I was like, how I thought and dreamt." In the foreword to the new edition, written in 1793, Karamzin emphasizes spontaneous writing and justifies his attention to trifling details by the fact that novelists such as Samuel Richardson and Henry Fielding do the same thing. The simple and natural manners of a traveler are contrasted to the official and learned styles of government servants or professors who write for their colleagues, and readers interested only in statistical or geographical data are directed to other works. The emphasis on "trivia" and the narrator's intimate pose became hallmarks of sentimentalist fiction, and Karamzin's comparison of his work to the British novel clearly highlights its fictional rather than factual emphases (although the work is in fact filled with factual data).

About half of the *Pis'ma russkogo puteshestvennika* appeared serially in the new journal Karamzin published upon his return from Europe, *Moskovskii zhurnal* (Moscow Journal, 1791–1792). The literary and educational significance of *Moskovskii zhurnal* can hardly be exaggerated – it had more readers than most eighteenth-century journals, and it circulated both in the capital and the provinces. Anthony Cross has aptly called *Moskovskii zhurnal* the "broadsheet of Russian Sentimentalism" – it included Russian literary works in prose and verse, foreign literary works, reviews of Russian books (both original and translations), notices of plays performed in Moscow, and a section of noteworthy events and anecdotes about famous modern authors. Karamzin excluded "works which are theological, mystical, too academic, too pedantic or too dry," thereby breaking both with the Masons and their journals and with the one-sided emphasis of earlier satirical periodicals. *Moskovskii zhurnal* was modeled on the best contemporary European literary magazines and is justly regarded as the first truly balanced modern Russian literary journal. Although some of Karamzin's Masonic friends regarded the enterprise skeptically and as presumptuous for a budding author, its very audacity as well as Karamzin's growing popularity attracted many major writers to the journal – including authors as diverse as Mikhail Kheraskov, Gavriil Derzhavin, and Dmitriev.

Karamzin's original works made up an important part of the journal. Although *Pis'ma russkogo puteshestvennika* was not the first published Russian epistolary travelogue, it was tremendously influential, and the intimate pose of the traveling sentimental narrator was widely imitated (and abused) in travelogues. Karamzin's short prose fiction published in *Moskovskii zhurnal* was even more influential. The *malaia forma* (short form) and the close attention to style it promoted sharply distinguished sentimentalist fiction from earlier Russian novels (by authors such as Mikhail Chulkov, Fedor Emin, Matvei Komarov, and Kheraskov), which were usually several volumes long and stylistically cumbersome. Several of Karamzin's early prose works can be broadly characterized as "idylls," including

"Derevnia" (The Countryside), "Palemon i Dafnis," (Palemon and Daphnis) "Navodnenie" (The Flood), "Posviashchenie kushchi" (Dedication of a Grove), "Noch' " (Night), and "Nevinnost' " (Innocence). They share the characteristics of "Progulka": its structure, small-scale natural settings (with commonplaces of the idyll such as shepherds and shepherdesses, swirling brooks, flowering meadows, and light breezes), the focus on intimate experiences (often firsthand by the narrator), pleasant or melancholy moods, and a sensitive central narrator. The poetic style of these short works has been noted: passages are rhythmically structured in anaphoric and often alliterative repetitive cadences, often paratactically linked. Some, such as "Noch'," even approximate the stanza structure of verse. "Frol Silin" varies the pattern by describing the good deeds of a real, though idealized, Russian peasant and the village in which he lives. This modest work popularized the anecdote as a literary genre. Other works incorporate features of salon culture and address women readers. "Nevinnost' " is a virtually plotless allegory of innocence personified as one of the graces but with a typically Karamzinian twist: it is a compliment to his Aglaia/Pleshcheeva. In "Raiskaia ptichka" a monk goes out in the forest to gather figs, is sidetracked by the beautiful song of the nightingale, does not notice the passage of time, returns to his monastery only to find everything changed – a thousand years have passed – and dies. This elaborate plot is also converted into a compliment to Aglaia as a singer and to the narrator himself as an ideal listener. These two works anticipate Karamzin's next periodical, the yearly almanac *Aglaia*.

The pose of close friendship between narrator and reader is also characteristic of Karamzin's sentimentalist tales, two of the best-known of which were first published in *Moskovskii zhurnal:* "Bednaia Liza" (Poor Liza) and "Natal'ia, boiarskaia doch' " (Natal'ia, the Boyar's Daughter). "Bednaia Liza," the textbook example of sentimentalism, is an *idyll manqué* (lost idyll) – a typical pattern. While peddling flowers in Moscow, a young innocent peasant girl, Liza, meets a gentleman, Erast. A fervent reader of idylls and novels, Erast is enraptured by Liza's country graces, seduces her, abandons her to fight in the war, and returns to Moscow only to marry a rich widow. He dismisses Liza, who is devastated and drowns herself in a pond. The narrator relates the story as he heard it from Erast, reliving Liza's tragedy, with the appropriate sighs and tears, while also reveling in his own sensitivities. The reaction to "Bednaia Liza" echoed the tremendous

German response to Goethe's *Die Leiden des jungen Werthers* (The Sorrows of Young Werther, 1774), and there are many contemporary accounts of melancholy pilgrimages to "Liza's pond." In "Natal'ia" a potential love idyll between young Natal'ia and her beloved, Aleksei, is temporarily thwarted by his father's official disgrace. The young couple elopes to a forest hideout, then both of them (Natal'ia disguised as a boy-soldier) enter the war Muscovy is waging with Lithuania. They distinguish themselves and are rewarded by the czar. The treatment of Aleksei's father is recognized as unfair, and the young couple marries and lives happily ever after.

Both tales have a vaguely Russian setting, but in neither is geographical or historical description by any means realistic. Karamzin retains his fondness for idyllic parameters and the emotive narrator. In "Bednaia Liza" the narrator is a serious (although also somewhat ironic) cosufferer, eager to evoke sympathetic tears and melancholy moods in his reader; in "Natal'ia" a humorous, jesting narrator aims to move his reader to laughter; his personal digressions and whimsical humor recall the narrator of Sterne's *Tristram Shandy* (1759–1767). Russian sentimentalism definitely has a humorous strain – a fact often overlooked in the context of sighs, tears, and melancholy moods most often identified with the movement. Karamzin's fiction sets the pattern for this strain as well.

"Liodor," a peculiar, fragmented tale (a form typical for sentimentalism), is a sensitive hero's *idyll manqué*. The narrator presents the hero's story as a consolation to his Aglaia, who mourns the loss of mutual friends. "Liodor" is a good example of the sentimentalist enjoyment of virtue in distress: distress activates a sensitive heart, but discovering and dwelling on one's own feelings and artistic sensibilities also brings intense pleasure. Together with the compliments to Aglaia, this consolation illustrates how nonliterary genres were used to invigorate literature. In "Prekrasnaia tsarevna i shchastlivoi karla" (The Beautiful Princess and the Fortunate Dwarf) the traditional fairy-tale theme of the beauty and the beast is "sentimentalized" in a humorous way similar to "Natal'ia." Both works engage in the ironic banter and humorous jesting that was to culminate in Karamzin's last prose fiction.

The themes, the tonalities, and the style of Karamzin's prose were strikingly similar to those in his poetry. The Russian scholar Iurii Lotman has noted that Karamzin "poeticized" his prose and "prosaicized" his verse. Many of his prose works include verse sections, and he pioneered intermediate forms: the prose idyll "Noch'" has a discernible

stanzaic structure, and the modest "Pesniia tsiurikhskogo iunoshi" (Song of a Zurich Youngster) is a poem in prose, a genre Karamzin later perfected in the dedication to the second book of *Aglaia*. Karamzin was at his most experimental in his early verse, and his experimentation with unrhymed verse in *Moskovskii zhurnal* is part of the general "prosaization." He was particularly creative in experimenting with different combinations of dactyls and trochees, and his use of both rhymed and unrhymed trochaic tetrameter stands out against the prevailing dominance of iambic meters in Russian poetry. He drew attention to his metrical innovations by printing the metrical schemes above some of his poems.

Karamzin largely ignored the traditional notion of "genre," together with the entire prescriptive classicist genre-style system. He consistently set the personal and trivial against the magnificent and the official, reacting against the prestige attached to classicist odes and epics. He emphasized middle registers, rejecting both excessively high, lofty genres and styles and excessively low, coarse ones. He infused middle genres, such as the idyll and the elegy, with new life by incorporating the elegance and lighthearted wit characteristic of minor nonliterary genres (compliments, jokes, anecdotes, games) and the oral intonations of conversation. Karamzin used his linguistic ingenuity to create a new style – a simple language without the artifice of the cumbersome *Slaveno-rossiiskii* written literary language – and he made it artistically viable. As Lotman points out, the very refusal to use sanctioned artistic devices that readers had come to expect, the rejection of fancy metaphors and tropes, was an effective artistic "minus device."

Ordinariness was in fact carefully crafted "artifice," as was Karamzin's use of women as artistic resources. For example, the author presented the ballad "Alina" as a suggestion from a woman the traveler met on the road, and the poem's speech and thoughts are presumably taken from Alina's journal, meant for herself only, even though they are in ballad form. Conversations inspired poems in overt or hidden dialogue form. "Mishen'ke" (To Mishen'ka) is addressed to a child; the melodrama "Petr Velikii" (Peter the Great) alternates a child's questions and adult answers; and other poems are birthday greetings, get-well wishes, compliments, or witty repartees. "Kladbishche" (The Cemetery), an adaptation of a German original, incorporates in alternating stanzas a pleasant idyllic voice and a horror-filled Gothic voice, illustrating two major tonalities emerging in Russian sentimentalism. Karamzin helped popularize short forms such as inscriptions (on park benches, trees, snow monuments, and statues) and "simple" epitaphs. Another poem in *Moskovskii zhurnal,* "Strannye liudi" (Strange People), is structured as a riddle. Games, such as riddles, *bouts-rimés,* and charades, which were to become staples in ladies' albums and literary journals around the turn of the century, also gained literary status.

Several poems besides "Poeziia" address the topic of art. In an epistle to Dmitriev, Karamzin assesses the state of Russian poetry. He notes (with a tear) that there are few great bards left who can move the heart or bring ecstasy to the soul. The poet concludes on the same optimistic and self-congratulatory note as "Poeziia," in effect proclaiming himself the new Homer, Gessner, Heinrich von Kleist, and Anacreon of the Neva. Other poems from this period show a more modest self-image. "Anakreonticheskie stikhi A. A. P." (Anacreontic verses to A. A. P[etrov]) outlines the poet's attempts to become a second Isaac Newton, then perceived as simply a wise philosopher, and finally a James Thomson – but he laments his lack of talent. Still, poetic aspirations are affirmed, and the image of the sensitive melancholic, parted from his friend, seeking solace in nature and lacking any obvious talents, emerges as an image of the ideal poet.

Through the use of similar "minus devices" in other poems, Karamzin orchestrates a reversal of traditional "odic" values; less becomes more, weakness becomes strength, lack of elegance and beauty becomes a reason for loving a woman. Even for soldiers, bravery is less important than a tender heart. "Voennaia pesn' " (War Song) uses five stanzas for exhortation to bravery and killing but ends with an unexpected about-face:

> Губи!--Когда же враг погибнет,
> Сраженный храбростью твоей,
> Смой кровь с себя слезами сердца:
> Ты близних, братий поразил!

> (Kill!--and when the enemy perishes,
> Beaten by your courage,
> Wash off the blood with tears from your heart:
> You have struck your own, your brethren!)

Similarly, in praising czars Karamzin chooses not to extol their heroic qualities, their majestic powers, the might of their realms, battles won, or other typical objects of praise in odes and solemn oratory. In the poem that bears his name Peter the Great is praised for forgetting his rank and the luxuries of court, for leaving his throne and royal man-

Title page for the first book publication of Karamzin's travelogue, based on his grand tour of Europe in 1789–1790

tle, and for exchanging a ruler's orb for a traveler's staff. In "K Milosti" (To Mercy) Catherine II is presented as the personification of mercy, not unlike Karamzin's shepherdesses. Under her rule poets and citizen-children are happy as long as maternal kindness allows human rights and freedoms to thrive. This rhetoric did not obscure the poem's significance as a courageous plea on behalf of Novikov and the persecuted Masons, victims of a less maternal and less merciful Catherine.

Karamzin's views on literature were most directly expressed in his reviews. Literary criticism was not entirely new in Russian journals, but Karamzin made it a regular feature of his journal and developed it according to consistent principles. His reviews were moderately critical, guided by his sense of good taste. He usually gave a general assessment of the work and a descriptive synopsis of it, as well as specific commentary on selected passages. His drama criticism shows his likes (Sophocles, Shakespeare – whom he virtually introduced to Russia – Lessing, Friedrich von Schiller, August von Kotzebue) and dislikes (French classicist tragedy) and his expertise both in the literary and performative aspects of drama. Karamzin's only original drama, "Sophia" – a justly forgotten play that unsuccessfully mixes Kotzebue with Shakespeare – also appeared in *Moskovskii zhurnal.*

Karamzin's translations in the journal consist both of fiction and nonfiction. Among the most prominently featured authors are Marmontel, Jean-Pierre Florian, Louis-Sébastien Mercier, Barthélemy, Goethe, Schiller, Christoph Wieland, Kotzebue, Sterne, and James MacPherson's "Ossian" poems. Karamzin proved an astute critic of others' translations and his own skills as a translator had developed quite remarkably as compared to his earliest efforts.

The French Revolution had bitter consequences for the literary climate in Catherine's Russia. In 1790 Aleksandr Radishchev was exiled to Siberia as a "spreader of the French venom" for his *Puteshestvie iz Peterburga v Moskvu* (Journey from Petersburg to Moscow, 1790), seen by Catherine as part of a Masonic plot against her. The persecution of the Masons continued, and in 1792 Novikov's publications were impounded, he was imprisoned, and Karamzin's Masonic friends were exiled to their estates. Rumors circulated that Karamzin too had been exiled and was in disgrace. Many writers chose to abandon literature, at least for a time. Karamzin's apprehensions about events in Europe and about literary repression in Russia were compounded by personal misfortunes. Petrov died in 1793, and the Pleshcheevs suffered a financial crisis. With characteristic generosity, Karamzin sold his share in the family estate in order to help them. He spent much of his time from 1793 to 1795 at Znamenskoe, the Pleshcheev estate. He largely removed himself from the "official world" to the "small world" of domesticity and close friendships, which was a productive environment for him as a writer.

Due to the success of *Moskovskii zhurnal,* Karamzin was persuaded to publish a separate collection of his original works from the periodical (with some additional new works). This two-part collection was entitled *Moi bezdelki* (My Trifles, 1794), reflecting the new emphasis on the trivial and personal as literary values. It was tremendously popular, and a second edition appeared in 1797. Dmitriev followed Karamzin's example and called his collection *I moi bezdelki* (My Trifles Too), and soon this authorial pose became a fad, as well as an object of parody by the literary opposition.

Trivia were, however, taken quite seriously by Karamzin. Lotman and his disciples have recently discovered a French-language booklet published in 1794. Titled *Les amusemens de Znamenskoé: Lisez-le, ne lisez pas,* it contains a variety of literary games in which Karamzin participated and stories composed on set words, providing an interesting "missing link" between domestic amusements and "trifles" as bona fide literature. One of the stories included is the French original of Karamzin's tale "Dremuchii les" (The Deep Forest), published in Russian in his almanac, *Aglaia.* As Karamzin stated in his prepublication announcement, *Aglaia* was to publish only original Russian works in "the purest, most carefully polished style," and "Dremuchii les" may be seen as the literary expression of these family amusements, stylizing and poeticizing small world values. Many of Karamzin's works from this period contrast this kind of nurturing intimacy to the horrors of the world at large, and, more so than in his earlier work, the reader senses Karamzin's pessimism and skepticism about human progress.

The first issue of *Aglaia* was introduced with a poem, "Prinoshenie gratsiiam" (Offering to the Graces), about the "goddesses of friendship" who make life worth living for sensitive souls. The poet presents the almanac as the fruit of his solitude, dedicated to nature and the Muses. It is a wreath woven of flowers moistened with a tear, and the poet sees the Graces as his only consolation. The losses of Petrov and other friends are mourned in "K solov'iu" (To the Nightingale), where pleasant birdsong cannot console the poet. Without friends he cannot enjoy nature, and his thoughts turn to his own death. Even nature in its full might, personified as "mother Volga," will ultimately die, the poet reflects in "Volga." The dedication of the second volume of *Aglaia* to Pleshcheeva similarly voices disenchantment with "the sad world" but also points to love and friendship as consolation – although in the second book even consolation sounds tenuous. The works of this period are the gloomiest of Karamzin's entire oeuvre. In epitaphs (to Charles Bonnet, to Caliph Adulraman), obituaries (to Petrov – entitled "Tsvetok na grob moego Agatona" [A Blossom on the Grave of My Agathon]), in the poems within the tale "Afinskaia zhizn'" (Athenian Life), as well as in the dark tonalities of the story "Ostrov Borngol'm" (Bornholm Island) and the elegiac sensibilities of "Sierra-Morena," Karamzin expresses the aesthetics of grief and horror, characteristic of contemporary European pre-Romanticism.

Karamzin helped popularize the prominent Gothic themes of death and graveyards, often contrasted in his works to the sentimental idyll or to art. Gothic elements are evident in "Ostrov Borngol'm", which details the adventures of the narrator-traveler who follows hints about a mysterious unhappy love affair (overheard in an elegiac song in Gravesend) to the Danish island of Bornholm, complete with a Gothic castle and a dungeon housing a damsel in distress. The implied horrors are left untold, but the narrator's quest for a story is satisfied, and his emotions are appropriately heightened. "Ostrov Borngol'm" is a particularly good illustration of sentimentalist priorities: the tale is less important than its teller, and the fragment is exploited as an artistic form. Another tale, "Afinskaia zhizn' " (Athenian Life), contrasts a dream visit to ancient Athens with sad contemporary reality, and in "Sierra-Morena" the Spanish setting of "Liodor" is used for two intersecting failed love idylls. An oath, innocently broken, leads to Alonzo's death, to seclusion in a nunnery for Elvira, and to the narrator's silent alienation.

These tales stand out as among Karamzin's finest, and the plots are much more interesting than those of his earlier tales. The gloomy tonality in "Sierra-Morena" is the end point of one particular line of Karamzin's sentimentalism. From the joyous early idyll to the sentimental tale with its increasing tendency toward an *idyll manqué,* Karamzin has arrived at an anti-idyll and a narrator alienated from "the mad creatures called men." Such works anticipate the Romantic movement. They also reflect Karamzin's evolving views of art. In an article written during this period, "Nechto o naukakh, iskusstvakh i prosveshchenii" (On the Sciences, Arts and Enlightenment, 1794), the elegy replaces the joyous hymns to Creation as the first art form. Karamzin's work evolved from the aesthetics of the joyous to that of the grievous — both emotions, however, he held to be equally pleasurable. Other works, such as the epistolary exchange between Melodor and Filalet, show two philosophical views of enlightenment and the prospects for human happiness: one optimistic, the other pessimistic.

The essay "Chto nuzhno avtoru?" (What Does an Author Need?, 1794) is one of Karamzin's most explicit statements on sentimentalist art, stressing a sensitive heart and personal experience over technical skill and knowledge of literary rules. Again he stresses art as an ethical venture — "Durnoi chelovek ne mozhet byt' khoroshim avtorom" (a bad person cannot be a good author) — and points to aesthetics of horror. The form of this publicistic essay anticipates Karamzin's later journalism.

A third volume of *Aglaia* did not materialize, and items intended for it were published elsewhere: the prose tale *Iuliia* (Julia) was published separately in 1796, and other stories appeared in the Saint Petersburg journal *Muza* (The Muse). *Iuliia* initiated another Romantic genre, the society tale. It depicts a coquettish heroine, who, after succumbing to social temptations and the charms of a princely social lion, realizes her errors and finds satisfaction in motherhood and simple country life with a less glamorous husband.

Karamzin's work with trivia was channeled in two directions during this period: a section of miscellaneous contents, titled "Smes', " which ran in the newspaper *Moskovskie vedomosti* (Moscow News) in 1795, and verse for a new almanac, *Aonidy, ili sobranie raznykh novykh stikhotvenenii* (Aonides, or A Collection of Various New Poems), which began publication in 1796. The newspaper section is an eclectic mix of original and translated pieces, "*Moskovskii zhurnal* in microcosm," as Cross has put it. Karamzin kept up this activity for a year until *Aonidy* took shape. In a letter to Dmitriev he outlined his plan for a Russian "Almanach des Muses" to provide a forum for both established poets and talented novices and excluding all that is "base, impure, and caricature-like." Refined female tastes are reflected in Karamzin's specific exclusions and also in his attention to the publication's external elegance (engravings, Dutch paper), as well as in his desire to present a "small booklet of verse" that "our ladies will not be ashamed of carrying in their pockets." Three volumes of *Aonidy* appeared, and the idea of an almanac took root among the poets of the next generation. Karamzin's almanac published poetry by the foremost poets of the era, including Kheraskov, Derzhavin, Dmitriev, Murav'ev, Iurii Neledinsky-Meletsky, Nikolai L'vov, Vasilii Kapnist, Ermil Kostrov, and Vasilii Pushkin.

If the idea for the almanac and its design were inspired by women readers, Karamzin's poetry from this time also reflects his interpretation of female tastes. It is less experimental and written in the more conventional iambic meters — because, according to Dmitriev, women wanted rhymed and regular verse. At the same time (and possibly for similar reasons) Karamzin's poetry from this period shows his continued fondness for literary trifles, salon poetry, and literary games.

Karamzin's epics also reveal a tendency to miniaturize and feminize literature. The *bogatyrskaia skazka* (heroic epic tale) "Il'ia Muromets" is a good illustration of his experimentation with meter and genre and an example of the sentimentalist use of nonliterary folklore for literary innovation. Its irregular trochaic tetrameter with dactylic clausula is explained as "completely Russian" and the verse of "almost all of our old songs." This meter had previously been used to some extent, but Karamzin made it popular and (mistakenly) identified it with the Russian *bylina* (the oral heroic folk epic); as such it was subsequently used by Kheraskov, Radishchev, and Aleksandr Pushkin. It also helped initiate a long debate among Russian poets over the nature of genuine "Russkii stikh" (Russian verse). Although Karamzin's protagonist is introduced as a true *bogatyr* (hero of the *bylina*) the "deeds" related in the poem are limited to the kind of voyeuristic dreaming common in Karamzin's early idylls. "Il'ia Muromets" plays with the Russian epic tradition and with sentimentalist clichés and also points to the more pronounced role Karamzin ascribes to imagination in art: poetry is viewed as fantasy, a means for forgetting grim reality. The epic muse he invokes is the goddess "Lozh', Nepravda, prizrak istiny" (Falsehood, Untruth, mere semblance of truth). Variations on the theme occur in other poems as well. "Bednomu poetu" (To a Poor Poet), for example, concludes with a concise definition of the poet as a skillful liar.

During this period, women are one of the most pervasive topics of Karamzin's poetry. Female sensibilities and natural virtues are portrayed as the most desirable qualities in *all* authors. Women, he asserts, bring out the best qualities in men, and their domesticity and innocent elegance soften the roughness and base instincts that tempt men to power, riches, and fame. The poem "Darovaniia" (Gifts) once again traces the history of art, rehearsing many of Karamzin's earlier ideas, but gives a more prominent place to women as sources for poetic perfection. Women also figure in some of Karamzin's best love poetry, and their significance is eloquently stated in his "Poslanie k zhenshchinam" (Epistle to Women), which concludes with the epitaph for a poet: ". . . On liubil: / On nezhnoi zhenshchiny nezhneishim drugom bul!" (. . . He loved: / He was a tender woman's tend'rest friend!). The epistle is an extended compliment to women in all their varied roles, both in the poet's personal life and in his literary evolution. Although the poetic I cannot be directly equated with Karamzin, the poem abounds in autobiographical references (for example, to Karamzin's early loss of his mother and to his ten-year attachment to Pleshcheeva). Allusions to specific works form an important subtext for the poem. It is perhaps Karamzin's most eloquent statement

ИСТОРІЯ

ГОСУДАРСТВА РОССІЙСКАГО.

ТОМЪ I.

САНКТПЕТЕРБУРГЪ.

Печатано въ Военной Типографіи Главнаго Штаба
ЕГО ИМПЕРАТОРСКАГО ВЕЛИЧЕСТВА.

Title page for the first volume of Karamzin's monumental history of Russia

on the gendering of his literary works, and hence on the feminization of sentimentalism.

Light verse was the most obvious expression of this feminization, and although Karamzin was not Russia's first nor best practitioner of light verse (Dmitriev, Neledinsky-Meletsky, and Vasilii Pushkin were particularly skilled in this area), his almanacs were crucial in bestowing literary legitimacy on its "trifling" forms. Furthermore, Karamzin's attention to women as the arbiters of good taste and his promotion of reading and writing among women was to find wide resonance among his contemporaries and successors, who recognized Karamzin's role in this reevaluation of gender. After Karamzin, Russian authors at least began to include women as potential readers. The first important Russian women's journals began to appear, women started to contribute to literary journals, and editors started to solicit their works and to "serve the Graces" in their own writings. Some writers (such as Petr Makarov) even championed the right of women to pursue higher education.

Boris Uspensky traces Karamzin's program of the feminization of language and literature back to Trediakovsky and the French salon tradition. Light verse was popularized in seventeenth-century French women's salons, and French poets were particularly influential on Karamzin's light verse of this period. Many of these "insignificant" short pieces are addressed to women or describe women, and many are written for private occasions. Lengthy titles are supplied to explain the context to the general reader. The poems address topics found in virtually every woman's album through the 1820s (such as love and friendship, beauty, constancy and inconstancy, flower symbolism). Hackneyed topics, strictly prescribed forms, and the demand for elegant wit challenge the poet's originality, and the impression of effortless creation is deceptive.

That Karamzin intended his poems as models is clear from his careful explanations of the rules for poems such as the triolet. That he encouraged women writers is evident from the fact that women sent him their poems and Karamzin responded in kind. For instance, his "Otvet na stikhi odnoi devitsy, v kotorykh ona klaniaetsia Khloe, drugu svoemu, liubit' ee plamenno i vechno, ostavliaia dlia Kupidona tol'ko malen'kii ugolok v serdtse" (Response to Verses of a Certain Young Lady in Which She Vows to Khloia, Her Friend, To Love Her Ardently and Forever, Leaving for Cupid Only a Small Corner in Her Heart) is his response to a poem he received from Ekaterina Sushkova. Some of his titles indicate the nature of his poetic trifles: "Triolet Alete v tot den' kak ei ispolnilos' 14 let" (Triolet for Aleta on the Day She Turned Fourteen); "Nadpis' k portretu zhestokoi" (Inscription to the Portrait of a Cruel Woman); "Impromptu Grafine R**, kotoroi v odnoi sviatochnoi igre dostalos' byt' korolevoiu" (Impromptu for Countess R**, Who in a Yuletide Play Managed To Be Queen); "Impromptu dvum molodym damam, kotorye v maskakh podoshli k avtoru i khoteli uverit' ego, chto on ikh ne uznaet" (Impromptu for Two Young Ladies, Who Came up to the Author in Masks, and Wanted to Convince Him that He Would Not Recognize Them); and "Nadpisi na statuiu Kupidona" (Inscriptions on a Statue of Cupid), which consists of inscriptions for each part of Cupid's body and includes a footnote describing how the author saw a marble cupid and got the hostess's permission to inscribe it from head to foot.

The poem "Protei, ili nesoglasovaniia stikhotvortsa" (Proteus, or the Poet's Contradic-

tions) is another statement of Karamzin's poetic credo. It affirms earlier sentimentalist convictions about poetic license to write whatever the heart bids and to use any genre and any topic in accord with the poet's inclinations. The solipsistic primacy of the individual remained basic in sentimentalism and in Karamzin's poetry. In addition to light verse, he continued to address philosophical questions, as in his adaptations of Voltaire and Jacques Delille. In his 1793 poem "Otvet k drugu" (Answer to a Friend) he refused to write a panegyric ode to Catherine because the lofty topic was unsuitable to his "quiet lyre." In "K Milosti" (To Mercy) he had praised what was lacking in Catherine's reign — human freedoms and mercy. The climate changed with the ascension of Paul I, and the ode Karamzin wrote for the occasion predicts a new Age of Astrea, ruled by a wise czar and a loving father to his children, seen in characteristic sentimental terms as a descendant of the Muses, "dear to our hearts." It is an interesting sequel to "K Milosti" in that Paul is also praised for what Catherine failed to do: "I dver' v temnitsakh otvorilas'; / Svoboda s milost'iu iavilas' " (And the prison doors opened; / Freedom appeared together with mercy). Karamzin praises Paul in feminine terms, using Empress Maria Fedorovna's philanthrophy as a worthy role model for the emperor. The ode is traditional in formal terms, but "the quiet lyre" of a sentimentalist is heard.

Paul's reign turned out to be even more repressive than the last years of Catherine's reign, and Karamzin had his share of trouble with censors. He continued to write minor verse while frequenting Moscow salons and suffering through an unhappy love affair and domestic upheavals in the Pleshcheev family. His *Razgovor o shchastii* (Dialogue on Happiness, 1797) continued the philosophical exchange between Melodor and Filalet. His personal correspondence and a few surviving notebook pages reveal a mood of resigned stoicism and yet a steadfast faith in enlightenment.

In 1798 he compiled and translated the *Panteon inostrannoi slovesnosti* (Pantheon of Foreign Literature), selections from classical and modern authors. His aim was to familiarize Russian readers with the ideas of foreign authors and to provide examples of good style. This in effect meant ideas sympathetic to him and his own "new style," which gave a surprising unity to the great variety in selection. At the request of the editor of *Spectateur du Nord*, a journal published in French in Hamburg, Karamzin supplied an essay, "Lettre sur la littérature russe," in 1797. The journal had earlier published a translation of his *Iuliia* to prove that Russian literature was not as "barbaric" as European readers tended to believe. "Lettre sur la littérature russe" makes generalizations and offers an apologia for the lack of Russian literary achievement. Extracts from *Pis'ma russkogo puteshestvennika* (provided at the editor's request) included the first publication of sections on the French Revolution. In his article Karamzin also briefly discusses the twelfth-century *Slovo o polku Igoreve* (The Tale of Igor's Campaign), the major manuscript discovery of the era, and comments favorably on Russian folk songs, in keeping with the European vogue for folklore and national epics. All mention of modern Russian authors, with the exception of Karamzin, is lacking. In disregarding Russian classicism and in indicating a promising future for Russian letters, Karamzin's "Lettre sur la littérature russe" echoed his "Poeziia."

In another project started around the same time (with Platon Beketov), Karamzin embarked on a history of Russian literature. *Panteon Rossiiskikh avtorov* (Pantheon of Russian Authors, 1801) contains brief entries on major Russian authors together with their portraits, chronologically arranged from "Boian," the bard of *Slovo o polku Igoreve,* to Lomonosov. It omits authors of Karamzin's generation, although what he refers to as "our era" is characterized by "its attractiveness of style," once more highlighting his own achievements and using his "new style" as a period label.

Karamzin's optimism at the beginning of the new century reflected personal and political events. In 1801 he married Elizaveta Ivanovna Protasova, the "Emiliia" of his subsequent verse. In two odes of the same year he greeted Alexander's ascension to the throne optimistically as a "sweet spring" appearing after "winter's black horrors." His "Istoricheskoe pokhval'noe slovo Ekaterine II" (Historical Panegyric Oration to Catherine II) draws on Alexander's avowals to rule in the spirit of Catherine. He defends autocracy as the only possible form for a vast empire such as Russia at its particular stage of development. On the other hand, he also voices his preference for a republican form of government based on civic virtue and repeats his concern for public enlightenment in his praise for Catherine's educational reforms.

Karamzin gradually became more preoccupied with politics and history, and his new interests are reflected in his last journal, *Vestnik Evropy* (Herald of Europe, 1802–1803). The journal had two sections: "Politics" and "Literature and Miscellany." The political section was the more substantial and innovative and made *Vestnik Evropy* Russia's first unofficial,

privately published political journal, the forerunner of later Russian "thick journals." It served as Karamzin's personal political platform and was his major attempt at shaping public opinion. He emerges as a pacifist, a promoter of general education, and a supporter of a strong, enlightened autocrat who is actively involved in the well-being of his subjects and capable of appointing advisers based on merit rather than political affiliations; for much of the duration of the journal Napoleon is held up as the ideal ruler. Karamzin speaks out against weak rulers and particularly against an oligarchy of aristocrats interested only in furthering their own power, rank, and fame. A strong central power is, in his opinion, a guarantee against anarchy, while good advisers prevent tyranny and despotism. Yet Karamzin remains "a republican at heart," and Lotman characterizes his preferences as representing a Rousseauian "republican monarchy," or a Jeffersonian democracy.

Karamzin also rejects emancipation of the serfs before enlightenment has spread to all classes and remained an apologist for the nobility and defender of the existing Russian social and political system. In fact, the tone of the journal became increasingly nationalistic and patriotic. Russian history and language are portrayed as sources for national pride, and Karamzin often emphasizes that Russia has the same potential for enlightenment as other nations. He notes the increased prestige Russia enjoys in Europe. He advocates the enlightenment of all classes and welcomes the spread of bookstores to the provinces and the emergence of private libraries. He encourages the reading "even of novels," however mediocre they might be. Education is seen as the primary obligation of parents, and the custom of using foreign tutors is strongly censured. The essay "Strannost'" (An Aberration) describes education by foreign tutors at its most ridiculous: a Frenchman offering to teach Russian to Russian children. An essay published in *Vestnik Evropy* titled "Otchego v Rossii malo avtorskikh talantov?" (Why Are There Few Authors of Talent in Russia?, 1804) answers the question posed by the title: not because of the cold climate, not for lack of talent, but because of the specific civic circumstances in Russia. Talent, he asserts, must be complemented by constant reading and conversation with women (who unfortunately still speak French), and he recommends that Russian authors invent new expressions and pay attention to the potential of the spoken language. In general, the essays in *Vestnik Evropy* increasingly view literature as a national priority rather than an exclusively private pleasure. Literary criticism is featured less than it had been in *Moskovskii zhurnal,* although announcements and brief reviews of foreign and Russian literature appeared. Karamzin's long review article in *Vestnik Evropy,* "O Bogdanoviche i ego sochineniiakh" (On Bogdanovich and His Works, 1803), remains one of the most perceptive analyses of *Dushen'ka* (1783) and a model of sentimentalist literary criticism.

Karamzin continued to include his own works in the journal. Some poems continue the line of light verse, others address his "Emiliia" and one poem is written on the death of the writer Petr Pel'sky. "Gimn gluptsam" (Hymn to Fools) is another creative use of the "minus device," praising fools for their lack of truly important qualities, and "K Emiliiu" (To Emilia), a poem about married bliss, concludes by stating the impossibility of verse devoted to that topic. Some prose works, such as "Chuvstvitel'nyi i kholodnyi" (The Sensitive and the Cold), fall squarely within the typical sentimental paradigm. Others, such as "Moia Ispoved'" (My Confession) and "Rytsar' nashego vremeni" (A Knight of Our Time) fully develop the potentials of literature as humorous play.

"Moia ispoved'" takes typical sentimentalist themes, structures, and genres and exposes their abuses by parodic exaggeration. The most treasured sensitivities are turned into Sadean amoral sensuality, the familiar virtues are flaunted by their absence, women are mercilessly exploited, and love and friendship are travestied. Specific autobiographical references abound, although the attitudes expressed on education, language, and literature are diametrically opposite to those in Karamzin's other works. It is simultaneously a satire on contemporary Russian gentry mores and a parody both of contemporary didactic novels and Karamzin's own literary practice. "Rytsar' nashego vremeni," frequently used to reconstruct Karamzin's early biography, is no more a serious autobiography than "Moia ispoved'." It traces the hero's childhood and concludes with an adolescent Peeping Tom incident reminiscent of "Liodor." Karamzin utilizes all the literary devices made famous in Sterne's *Tristram Shandy,* from nonsensical chapter headings to playful digressions and narratorial games with the reader. It is Karamzin's only novel, (or so it is labeled, although it is only sixty pages long in its published form – twenty-two in modern print) but is also a lighthearted parody of the eighteenth-century Russian novel in all its variety: Emin-type adventure novels, Eastern tales and romances, Kheraskovian historical-philosophical novels, and earlier sentimentalist idylls and tales. With this work sentimen-

talist prose fiction had come full circle, and its self-parodic stance signaled the impending demise of sentimentalism.

Elsewhere in *Vestnik Evropy* Karamzin recommended the use of folklore and history as literary sources, and one of his tales, "Marfa Posadnitsa, ili Pokorenie Novagoroda" (Martha the Mayoress, or the Subjugation of Novgorod), is labeled a historical tale. This story, based on an episode from Russia's sixteenth century, uses the "found manuscript" device and invokes a lofty, oratorical civic pathos – a different stylistic register than most of Karamzin's earlier fiction – but it is no less sentimentalist than his other works. Here the narrator's style fits his patriotic fervor, which echoes that of his historical personages. The feminization of literature surfaces in Martha's emphasis on domestic values, even when she speaks as a Demosthenes – as Karamzin's contemporary adversaries were quick to point out. Novgorod fights for ancient freedoms, while Czar Ivan's Muscovites victoriously proclaim the virtues of a strong central state with a good and merciful ruler. The tale voices Karamzin's conservative political position and his support for a strong autocracy, although Novgorodian democracy is also viewed with some sympathy. Novgorodian values captured the imagination of the younger generation, and Novgorod became particularly important as a symbol in Romantic historical tales, a genre Karamzin virtually initiated with "Marfa Posadnitsa."

While *Vestnik Evropy* was being published successfully, Karamzin's personal life was less fortunate. His wife died shortly after their first daughter, Sofia, was born in 1802. Constant troubles with the censors did not improve his mood. His reputation as a writer was perhaps at its height when he decided to quit literature and devote himself to history. In 1803 he was appointed court historiographer with a pension of two thousand rubles per year. He had earlier been offered a position as university professor but declined it, considering his talent unsuitable to the responsibilities it entailed.

Around this time Karamzin frequented the house of Prince Andrei Viazemsky, which had become a kind of salon for poets, particularly those who would later be called "Karamzinists" (as opposed to the so-called Shishkovites, after Admiral Aleksandr Shishkov, who opposed Karamzin's linguistic reforms). Early in 1803 he married Ekaterina Andreevna Kolyvanova, Viazemsky's illegitimate daughter. Their marriage was a happy one, and the Viazemsky-Karamzin household at the Ostaf'evo estate near Moscow provided the ideal environment for Karamzin's work on his magnum opus, the

Istoriia Gosudarstva Rossiiskogo (History of the Russian State, 1816–1829). In the twelve volumes of this work that Karamzin produced over the last twenty-three years of his life, he presented the history of the Russian state from its modest beginnings through its rise to power, and, ironically perhaps, to its disintegration during the Time of Troubles. As official historian, Karamzin was given access to libraries, archives, and documents (both from Russia and abroad), which he used with characteristic energy and professionalism. He discovered important historical documents, such as the Hypatian Chronicle, and his scholarly excitement about such discoveries is evident from his letters.

Karamzin's time was now devoted to history and to his growing family, with occasional interruptions for illnesses or visits from friends. Through his family connection Karamzin also became the main tutor to Petr Viazemsky, the future poet. By the time of the Napoleonic Wars Karamzin was working on the fifth and sixth volumes. In 1811 he befriended Grand Duchess Ekaterina Pavlovna, the czar's sister, and became a welcome guest at her Tver' estate. Here they discussed the Russian past, and at her suggestion Karamzin wrote his *Zapiska o drevnei i novoi Rossii* (Note on Ancient and Modern Russia; first published as *O drevnei i novoi Rossii v ee politicheskom i grazhdanskom otnosheniiakh,* 1861), which was presented to Alexander I. Karamzin's conservative ideas (similar to those in "Marfa Posadnitsa") ran contrary to many of Alexander's beliefs, and the *Zapiska o drevnei i novoi Rossii* could be construed as particularly critical of Alexander's liberal advisers. For a long time it remained unpublished. Karamzin fell out of favor and was subjected to various forms of degrading treatment both by Alexander and his notorious minister Aleksei Arakcheev during the early stages of the publication of the *Istoriia Gosudarstva Rossiiskogo.*

Napoleon's entry into Moscow in 1812 forced the family to evacuate their home, which together with Karamzin's valuable library was lost in the subsequent fire. In the years immediately following, Karamzin continued to work in Moscow and at Ostaf'evo and managed to complete eight volumes of the *Istoriia Gosudarstva Rossiiskogo* by 1816. To facilitate the publication of the work, the family moved to Saint Petersburg, and in 1818 the first eight volumes, dedicated to Alexander, appeared in a large print run of three thousand copies. It turned out to be the literary event of the era. All copies sold out within less than a month – a new record. Soon Alexander became more favorably disposed toward Karamzin, and he was awarded various dec-

Monument to Karamzin in Simbirsk

orations, appointed member of the Russian Academy, and invited to give speeches there and elsewhere. Even his old adversary Admiral Shishkov changed his opinion of Karamzin's "new style" when he read the *Istoriia Gosudarstva Rossiiskogo.*

Karamzin's last decade was spent in Saint Petersburg or nearby Tsarskoe Selo, in close proximity to the court. He would converse with the czar as a friend and was not afraid to state his opinions, however unpopular he knew they would be. He managed to retain both his political and literary independence despite being so close to the throne. He continued his research and writing and was personally involved in all aspects of publishing his work. Younger poets were frequent guests in his home, particularly the poets of the Tsarskoe Selo Lyceum, including young Aleksandr Pushkin. Although many of them disagreed strongly with Karamzin's political views and found his literary practice old-fashioned, he gained almost universal respect for his decency and honesty in all matters.

In 1825, while working on the twelfth volume of his *Istoriia Gosudarstva Rossiiskogo* Karamzin was already seriously ill, and Alexander's death and the subsequent Decembrist revolt, to which he was an eyewitness, placed him in a sensitive position at court. His health deteriorated further, and in 1826 he decided to abandon work on his history and travel to Italy. Nicholas I agreed to a generous pension for Karamzin and provided travel accommodations. Lotman suggests that Karamzin had negotiated a post for himself as Russian consul in Florence, but he died before this journey could take place.

Karamzin had a long-standing interest in history, and many of his essays in *Vestnik Evropy* are devoted to Russian history as a subject for artists. They describe how to select and embellish chronicle accounts to "affect the imagination strongly," "to move the heart," "to evoke pity," and how "sensitivity ought to be the artist's inspiration." As late as 1824, during a dinner conversation recorded by a German traveler, Karamzin once more affirmed that the national past was of primary interest to every Russian and that a historian should neither distort nor exaggerate facts but depict both what is glorious in the past and what is shameful. Karamzin describes national history as the most interesting of all literary works. His *Istoriia Gosudarstva Rossiiskogo* is also a literary work, and the literary method he uses is in a profound sense sentimentalist: the voice of the narrator-historian is heard, rejoicing and grieving with his heroes, his own emotions penetrating the events he relates; hence the structure of this work is as bivocal as is that of "Bednaia Liza." The author-historian is presented as a reader and cocreator with his chroniclers-predecessors. His expressive voice provides unity to the whole, in the same way as the epistolary pose provided unity to the traveler's disparate European experiences. The great length of the *Istoriia Gosudarstva Rossiiskogo* does not contradict its sentimentalist structure, and the fact that old Russian styles and folkloric genres are more prominent in it than in Karamzin's earlier works should not obscure the fact that they are still subordinated to the narrator's "new style" framework. This profound bivocality explains why most readers could find something appealing in the work, and even readers such as Nikolai Turgenev, who profoundly disliked the ideology expressed, could admire Karamzin's style. In uniting the most disparate genres and styles within one whole, Karamzin's sentimentalist "polyphonic epic" (as Evgenii I. Osetrov calls the *Istoriia*

Gosudarstva Rossiiskogo) anticipates the nineteenth-century Russian novel.

Karamzin's monumental history served the same prestigious function within sentimentalism as the epic had served within classicism. Its success among readers far surpassed the reception given to the various epic "Rossiadas" and "Petriadas." It was the ultimate sentimentalist accomplishment, its crowning glory. Karamzin's history demonstrated the flexibility of the sentimentalist movement and also exhausted its potentials. Although it was published in the nineteenth century, it serves as a powerful coda to eighteenth-century Russian literature while also providing a rich resource for a new generation of poets who would create the Golden Age of Russian literature that Karamzin had predicted.

Letters:

Pis'ma N. M. Karamzina k A. F. Malinovskomu i pis'ma A. S. Griboedova k S. N. Begichevu, edited by Mikhail N. Longinov (Moscow: Obshchestvo liubitelei rossiiskoi slovesnosti, 1860);

Pis'ma N. M. Karamzina k I. I. Dmitrievu, edited by Iakov Grot and Petr Pekarsky (Saint Petersburg: Akademiia Nauk, 1866);

"Perepiska Karamzina s Lafaterom," edited by I. Waldman and Grot, *Zapiski Imperatorskoi Akademii Nauk,* 1, no. 73 (1893): 1–67;

Pis'ma N. M. Karamzina k kniaziu P. A. Viazemskomu 1810–1826 (iz Ostaf'evskogo arkhiva), edited by Nikolai Barsukov (Saint Petersburg, 1897).

Bibliographies:

V. I. Mezhov, *Iubilei Lomonosova, Karamzina i Krylova: Bibliograficheskii ukazatel' knig i statei, vyshedshikh po povodu etikh iubileev,* enlarged edition (Saint Petersburg, 1887);

Anthony G. Cross, "Karamzin Studies: For the Bicentenary of the Birth of N. M. Karamzin (1766–1826)," *Slavonic and East European Review,* 45 (January 1967): 1–11;

N. I. Nikitina and V. A. Sukailo, comps., *N. M. Karamzin: Biobibliograficheskii ukazatel',* edited by I. E. Baranovskaia (Ul'ianovsk: Ul'ianovskaia oblastnaia nauchnaia biblioteka, 1990).

Biographies:

Adal'bert V. Starchevsky, *Nikolai Mikhailovich Karamzin* (Saint Petersburg: Karl Krai, 1849);

Nikolai N. Bulich, *Biograficheskii ocherk N. M. Karamzina i razvitie ego literaturnoi deiatel'nosti* (Kazan': Universitetskaia tipografiia, 1866);

Mikhail N. Pogodin, *Nikolai Mikhailovich Karamzin po ego sochinenüam, pis'mam i otzyvam sovremennikov,* 2 volumes (Moscow: A. I. Mamontov, 1866);

E. Solov'ev, *N. M. Karamzin: Ego zhizn' i nauchno-literaturnaia deiatel'nost'* (Saint Petersburg: E. Evdokimov, 1894);

Henry M. Nebel, *N. M. Karamzin: A Russian Sentimentalist* (The Hague: Mouton, 1967);

Anthony G. Cross, *N. M. Karamzin: A Study of His Literary Career 1783–1803* (Carbondale: Southern Illinois University Press, 1971);

Iurii M. Lotman, *Sotvorenie Karamzina* (Moscow: Kniga, 1987);

Evgenii I. Osetrov, *Tri zhizni Karamzina: Roman-issledovanie,* revised edition (Moscow: Moskovskii rabochii, 1989).

References:

Roger B. Anderson, *N. M. Karamzin's Prose: The Teller in the Tale. A Study in Narrative Technique* (Houston: Cordovan, 1974);

Joseph L. Black, ed., *Essays on Karamzin: Russian Man-of-Letters, Political Thinker, Historian, 1766–1826* (The Hague: Mouton, 1975);

Natan Eidel'man, *Poslednii letopisets* (Moscow: Kniga, 1983);

Boris M. Eikhenbaum, "Karamzin," in his *Skvoz literaturu: Sbornik statei* (Leningrad: Academia, 1924), pp. 5–36;

John G. Garrard, "Karamzin in Recent Soviet Criticism: A Review Article," *Slavic and East European Journal,* 11 (Winter 1967): 464–472;

Gitta Hammarberg, *From the Idyll to the Novel: Karamzin's Sentimentalist Prose* (Cambridge: Cambridge University Press, 1991);

Faina Z. Kanunova, *Iz istorii russkoi povesti (Istoriko-literaturnoe znachenie N. M. Karamzina)* (Tomsk: Tomskii universitet, 1967);

Nataliia D. Kochetkova, *Nikolay Karamzin* (Boston: G. K. Hall/Twayne, 1975);

L. V. Krestova, "A. I. Pleshcheeva v zhizni i tvorchestve Karamzina," *XVIII vek,* 10 (1975): 265–270;

Viktor D. Levin, *Ocherk stilistiki russkogo literaturnogo iazyka kontsa XVIII–nachala XIX v. (Leksika)* (Moscow: Nauka, 1964), pp. 115–294;

Nikolai I. Mordovchenko, *Russkaia kritika pervoi chetverti XIX veka* (Moscow: Akademiia nauk, 1959), pp. 17–77;

Rudolf Neuheuser, *Towards the Romantic Age: Essays on Sentimental and Preromantic Literature in Russia* (The Hague: Martinus Nijhoff, 1974);

Pavel A. Orlov, *Russkii sentimentalizm* (Moscow: Moskovskii universitet, 1977), pp. 197–269;

Hans Rothe, *N. M. Karamzins europäische Reise: Der Beginn des russischen Romans. Philosophische Untersuchungen* (Bad Homburg v.d.H.: Verlag Gehlen, 1968);

Vasilii V. Sipovsky, *N. M. Karamzin, avtor 'Pisem russkogo puteshestvennika'* (Saint Petersburg: Demakov, 1899);

Boris A. Uspensky, *Iz istorii russkogo literaturnogo iazyka XVIII–nachala XIX veka: Iazykovaia programma Karamzina i ee istoricheskie korni* (Moscow: Moskovskii universitet, 1985);

Vadim E. Vatsuro, "Podvig chestnogo cheloveka," in Vatsuro and Maksim I. Gillel'son, eds., *Skvoz' 'umstvennye plotiny': Ocherki o knigakh i presse pushkinskoi pory* (Moscow, 1986), pp. 29–113;

Viktor V. Vinogradov, "O stile Karamzina i ego razvitii (Ispravlenie teksta povestei)," in *Protsessy formirovaniia leksiki russkogo literaturnogo iazyka (ot Kantemira do Karamzina),* edited by Iurii S. Sorokin (Moscow: Nauka, 1966), pp. 237–258;

Vinogradov, *Problema avtorstva i teoriia stilei* (Moscow: Khudozhestvennaia literatura, 1961), pp. 221–365.

Ivan Ivanovich Khemnitser

(5 January 1745 – 20 March 1784)

Thomas Barran
Brooklyn College, City University of New York

BOOKS: *Oda na slavnuiu pobedu, oderzhannuiu pobedonosnuiu armieiu ee imperatorskogo velichestva nad nepriiatelem pri gorode Zhurzhe i na zavladenie onago goroda fevralia 4 dnia 1770 goda* ([Saint Petersburg: Akademiia nauk, 1770]);

Oda na slavnuiu pobedu oderzhannuiu pobedonosnym oruzhiem eia imp. velichestva nad turkami i tatarami pri ust'e reki Kaguly pod predvoditel'stvom ego siiatel'stva vysokopovelitel'nago gospodina generalfel'dmarshala grafa Petra Aleksandrovicha Rumiantsova, iiulia 21, 1770 goda ([Saint Petersburg: Akademiia nauk], 1770);

Siiatel'neishemu grafu Alekseiiu Grigor'evichu Orlovu general anshefu, eia imp. velichestva general ad'iutantu, kavalergardskago korpusa porutchiku, leib gvardii Preobrazhenskago polku podpolkovniku i vsekh rossiiskikh ordenov kavaleru, na vtorichnoe iz Arkhipelaga v Sankt-Peterburg pribytie (Saint Petersburg: [Akademiia nauk], 1773);

Basni i skazki N. . . N. . . (Saint Petersburg: [Gornoe uchilishche, 1779]); enlarged edition, 2 volumes (Saint Petersburg: I. K. Shnor, 1782).

Editions: *Basni i skazki,* 3 volumes, edited by Nikolai L'vov and Vasilii Kapnist (Saint Petersburg: Imperatorskaia tipografiia, 1799);

Sochineniia (Saint Petersburg: A. Smirdin, 1847);

Sochineniia i pis'ma, edited by Iakov K. Grot (Saint Petersburg, 1873);

Polnoe sobranie stikhotvorenii, edited by L. E. Bobrova and V. E. Vatsuro, Biblioteka poeta, bol'shaia seriia (Moscow & Leningrad, 1963).

TRANSLATION: Claude-Joseph Dorat, *Pis'mo Barnvelia k Trumanu iz temnitsy. Geroida* (Saint Petersburg, 1774).

Ivan Ivanovich Khemnitser

Ivan Ivanovich Khemnitser earned a lasting place in the history of Russian literature with less than a hundred verse fables. He gave final form to the genre that Ivan Krylov would later use so successfully, and until the middle of the nineteenth century his fables rivaled those of Krylov in popularity.

Khemnitser enjoys a distinction shared by few Russian writers: passages from his fables entered the Russian language as proverbial expressions.

Ironically Khemnitser grew up in a household where only German was spoken. His father, Johann Chemnizer, was born in Saxony and went to Saint Petersburg to serve as an army medic. His service took him to Astrakhan Province, where his son Ivan was born on 5 January 1745. To judge by the awkward German in the memoir he left after his son's death, Johann Chemnizer did not receive much of an education. He nonetheless took every opportunity to provide his son with an education in spite of the remoteness of the location in which the family was stationed. He hired tutors to teach the boy German, Latin, Russian, mathematics, and geometry.

In 1755 Johann took his family back to Saint Petersburg, where he had been appointed inspector of the Infantry Hospital. Once they settled in the capital, Ivan enrolled in a medical school associated with the Infantry Hospital, where he studied history, geography, and osteology; he continued his study of Latin at home with the aid of tutors. Young Khemnitser seemed destined to follow his father's career when, suddenly and inexplicably, he enrolled at the age of twelve in the Noteborg Infantry Regiment. He probably soon regretted his impulsiveness, as he had to work his way up from the bottom and held only the rank of lieutenant when he left the service twelve years later. Both father and son saw service in the Seven Years' War (1756–1763). Khemnitser's career prospects improved considerably once he left military service; in 1770 he began working in the Department of Mines, which was later upgraded to the College of Mines.

Khemnitser developed a close personal relationship with the director of the Department of Mines, the ober-prokuror of the senate Mikhail Soimonov while working under his supervision and for most of his career enjoyed his protection and patronage. Khemnitser also became friends with one of Soimonov's relatives, the poet and architect Nikolai L'vov, who would exert a decisive influence on Khemnitser's literary career. In 1773 Soimonov founded the School of Mines in Saint Petersburg. Khemnitser held a position on the scholarly committee of this institution from 1774 to 1779.

In 1770 Akademiia nauk (the Academy of Sciences) published two of Khemnitser's odes celebrating Russian victories in the Turkish Wars, followed by a 1773 publication of his poem celebrating Count Aleksey Grigor'evich Orlov's return to Saint Petersburg from his naval command in the Mediterranean. The following year the poet's translation of a heroic epistle by Claude-Joseph Dorat was published. These early works represent exercises in established genres in high style and have little to distinguish them.

Khemnitser's travels in Europe proved to be pivotal in his intellectual development and literary career. The opportunity to travel arose when Soimonov decided to spend some time at European spas to improve his health and asked L'vov and Khemnitser to accompany him. The travels provided Khemnitser and L'vov with the time and opportunity to immerse themselves in the cultural life of Germany, Holland, and especially Paris. L'vov, who was six years younger than Khemnitser, later recorded several anecdotes from this trip concerning Khemnitser's impulsiveness and absentmindedness, apparently with the intention of showing in hindsight that his friend had some of the character traits of the French fabulist Jean de La Fontaine.

When he returned to Saint Petersburg Khemnitser enjoyed nearly five years of fruitful literary activity. A loose association of brilliant young Saint Petersburg poets, which in addition to Khemnitser included Gavriil Derzhavin and Vasilii Kapnist, formed under the nominal leadership of L'vov. During his association with these talents, Khemnitser developed the fable as a genre with a deceptively simple surface, in which he combined ordinary language and homeliness of detail reflecting the mundane realities of Russian life.

Under this surface, however, lay sophisticated commentaries on several of the philosophical works that Khemnitser read and discussed with his literary colleagues. In one of his fables, "Mukha i pauk" (The Spider and the Fly), two insects discuss the origin of the magnificent building in which they happen to be sitting. The spider claims that the orderliness of the construction manifests the art and intention of a builder. The fly responds with his theory that the structure came together by itself from little pebbles. The fable concludes:

> Такое мухи рассужденье,
>   Как мухе, можно извинить;
> Но что о тех умах великих заключить,
> Которые весь свет случайным быть считают,
> И лучше в нем судьбе слепой подвластны быть,
>   Чем Бога признавать, решились?
> Тех, кажется, никак не можно извинить,
> А только сожалеть об них, что повредились.

> (Such are a fly's reasonings,
>   For which a fly might be excused;
> But what can one conclude of those great minds,
> Who take the whole world for a chance occurrence,
> And find it better to submit to blind fate,
>   Than to recognize God?
> One can find no excuse for these,
> But can only pity them and their insanity.)

This conclusion – one of the few in which Khemnitser felt it necessary to articulate the moral lesson – obviously condemns the materialist philosophers of the Enlightenment.

Khemnitser published his first collection of thirty-three fables under the title *Basni i skazki N... N...* (Fables and Tales of N. N., 1779). His name did not appear on the work because he feared that

БАСНИ и СКАЗКИ

И. И. Хемницера,

Въ трехъ частяхъ.

Въ природѣ, въ простотѣ онъ истинну искалъ:
Какъ видѣлъ, такъ ее списалъ.

Печатано въ Императорской Типографіи.
Въ Санктпетербургѣ, 1799.
Съ дозволенія Цензуры.

Title page for the first complete collection of Khemnitser's fables

the satire in the fables would cause him difficulties in the service if he were acknowledged as the author. An enlarged edition appeared in 1782, also anonymously, adding thirty-six new fables. Khemnitser's friends had by this time associated themselves with the journal *Sankt-Peterburgskii vestnik* (Saint Petersburg Messenger), where they gave Khemnitser's collection a favorable review; privately they tried, but without success, to persuade him to acknowledge himself as the author.

In all, Khemnitser composed ninety-one fables. For approximately one-third of these, he adapted the work of Western fabulists. His favorite was Christian Furchtegott Gellert (1715–1769), eighteen of whose fables he reworked into Russian. He only took five from La Fontaine and one each from Voltaire, Dorat, and Nozhan. Khemnitser developed a mastery over the compression and conciseness needed for the genre. From extant drafts, scholars have reconstructed his method of composition: he began by jotting down prose outlines of the

plots or topics he wanted to treat and gradually worked them into verse, using iambic lines of varying length with fairly simple rhyme schemes, usually couplets. While Russian authors such as Aleksandr Sumarokov had already written fables, Khemnitser raised the genre from one of crude satire, vulgarity, and imitated peasant speech to a middle conversational style. His language, though simple, admits discussion of higher philosophical and moral themes.

Khemnitser included a dedicatory poem to an unnamed woman in his first edition of fables. According to L'vov, the addressee was Maria D'iakova, the daughter of A. A. D'iakov, the ober-prokuror of the senate, and in subsequent editions the initials N. N. were replaced by her initials. Her well-known portrait by D. G. Levitsky presently hangs in the Tretiakov Gallery in Moscow. The three D'iakov sisters married members of L'vov's poetry circle: L'vov married Maria, while Derzhavin and Kapnist married her sisters. Maria D'iakova guessed the identity of the author of the book that was proving to be so popular in the northern capital and published a poem in the *Sankt-Petersburgskii vestnik* announcing that she had discovered the secret. Khemnitser's name was, of course, left blank in the published version.

Khemnitser's relationship to D'iakova has given rise to considerable speculation. According to one version, he fell in love with her and proposed marriage but was rejected because she had already secretly wed L'vov. Because of objections on the part of her family, the couple could not reveal their status until years later. Another tradition ascribes Khemnitser's failure with D'iakova to his physical unattractiveness. According to this story, one of the L'vov sisters had a bureau decorated with Khemnitser's image and two cupids; one cupid was turning away from him in fright, while another had already fled. This speculation also remains unsubstantiated and may reflect an attempt to liken the Russian fabulist to Aesop.

In 1782 Khemnitser accepted a diplomatic position as the Russian consul to the Turkish city of Smyrna. Some literary historians have speculated that he accepted such a distant post because of his heartbreak at Maria Diakova's refusal. A. V. Desnitsky suggests that L'vov resented Khemnitser's attentions to his wife and secretly intrigued to have him posted far away. The truth is probably far simpler: the School of Mines was about to undergo administrative changes, in advance of which Soimonov tendered his resignation. With his protector gone, Khemnitser had to look for new work. He had never accumulated much money in the service or with his writings and had no estate or family fortune on which to fall back, as did many of his richer literary friends. Clearly, he had to remain in the service in order to earn a living. Furthermore, the diplomatic post in Smyrna, far from being a type of exile, represented a career advancement.

Khemnitser left Saint Petersburg in June 1782. Once he reached the Black Sea, he had to wait for two weeks at the port of Kherson for the yacht designated to take him to Constantinople. He arrived in the Ottoman capital in August, during the observance of Ramadan, so he was forced to wait for another month until the Porte could issue a directive sending him to Smyrna. While in the Turkish capital, he got an early indication of the type of diplomatic tensions he would have to handle. When a fire broke out, rumors circulated that Russians had set it in order to divert Turkish attention from Crimea, which the Russians had recently conquered during the Russo-Turkish War. Khemnitser's ap-

pointment to such a sensitive diplomatic post, in an empire that his nation had just defeated in war, shows the extent to which he was trusted in high places.

Once in Smyrna, Khemnitser handled his duties well. He defended Russian interests energetically, especially in demanding toleration of Russian Orthodox religious practices in the Moslem Ottoman Empire. While in Smyrna Khemnitser fell into a state of alienation and depression. For one thing, his expenditures far outstripped his meager resources, and he was unable to learn whether or not he should draw his salary from the consular funds. Most people in Russian diplomatic posts had private means on which to fall back; others did not scruple to embezzle. While it was common practice to steal from the till in Russian diplomatic positions, Khemnitser was unusually punctilious about such matters.

Khemnitser's most serious distress, however, came from his sense of personal isolation. His letters speak plaintively of the necessity to stifle his impulses and curb any spontaneous utterances, lest he offend the inhabitants of the city. He rejoiced at the advantageous Treaty of Kuchuk-Kainardji but could not express his joy because he lived in the midst of the vanquished. The stress of isolation and occupational anxieties, combined with the unaccustomed climate and unfamiliar diet, may have undermined his health. He fell ill and died on 20 March 1784, a month after he had been named to the Russian Academy.

L'vov and Kapnist published an edition of Khemnitser's works in 1799. It included several fables found among the author's papers. To avoid provoking the authorities, L'vov and Kapnist edited many of these fables to dull their satiric content. The intellectual climate of the Russian Empire had grown harsher during the final years of Catherine II's reign, and Paul I's unpredictability and pathological suspiciousness called for a great deal of caution on the part of those who had earlier identified themselves with the literature and ideas of the West.

In addition to the editorial alterations, Khemnitser's friends added a biographical essay about the poet to the 1799 edition. They describe an impractical, absentminded poet, a creature not of this world. While the poet may have had his moments of abstraction, the personality created for him posthumously does not agree with the facts of his biography. One who worked his way up from the lower ranks of the army to pursue an academic career in applied science, who dabbled successfully in literature, and who finally ended his career as a diplomat — such a career is far too demanding of a variety of abilities and skills to be achieved by someone as forgetful and silly as his friends portray. Kapnist and L'vov created an identity for Khemnitser that corresponded to the fables, no doubt drawing on some of the characteristics of the author but exaggerating his foibles, perhaps wishing to associate him with the French fabulist La Fontaine, reputed to have been absentminded.

References:

G. V. Bitner, "Khemnitser," *Istoriia russkoi literatury,* volume 4, part 2, edited by G. A. Gukovsky and V. A. Desnitsky (Moscow & Leningrad: Akademiia nauk, 1947), pp. 473–484;

L. E. Bobrova, " 'Epigrammy i prochie nadpisi' Khemnitsera," *Uchenye zapiski Leningradskogo gos. ped. inst. im A. I. Gertsena,* 168 (1958): 3–30;

Bobrova, "O sotsial'nykh motivakh basen I. I. Khemnitsera," *Uchenye zapiski Leningradskogo gos. ped. inst. im A. I. Gertsena,* 170 (1958): 29–39;

A. V. Desnitsky, "Krylov i Khemnitser," *Uchenye zapiski Leningradskogo gos. ped. inst. im A. I. Gertsena,* 168 (1958): 31–57;

Iakov Grot, "Biograficheskiia izvestiia ob Ivane Ivanoviche Khemnitsere po novym rukopisnym istochnikam," in *Russkaia poeziia: Sobranie proizvedenii russkikh poetov chast'iu v polnom sostave, chast'iu v izvlecheniiakh, s vazhneishimi kritiko-biograficheskimi stat'iami, biograficheskimi primechaniiami i portretami,* volume 1, edited by Semen Vengerov (Saint Petersburg, 1897), pp. 453–462;

Aleksandr E. Izmailov, "Razbor Khemnitserovoi basni 'Volia i nevolia,' " in *Polnoe sobranie sochinenii,* volume 2 (Moscow, 1890), pp. 398–406;

Vadim E. Vatsuro, "K voprosu o filosofskikh vzgliadakh Khemnitsera," *XVIII vek,* 6 (1964): 129–145.

Mikhail Matveevich Kheraskov

(25 October 1733 – 27 September 1807)

Alexander Levitsky
Brown University

SELECTED BOOKS: *Oda . . . Elizavete Petrovne . . . sochinennaia na torzhestvennoe vospominanie pobedy Petra Velikogo nad shvedami pod Poltavoiu . . .* (Saint Petersburg: Akademiia nauk, 1751);

Venetsianskaia Monakhinia tragediia (Moscow: Moskovskii universitet, 1758; revised and enlarged edition, Moscow: I. Zelennikov & B. Sokolov, 1793);

Bezbozhnik: geroicheskaia komediia (Moscow: Moskovskii universitet, 1761);

Plody nauk poema (Moscow: Moskovskii universitet, 1761);

Novye Ody (Moscow: [Universitetskaia tipografiia], 1762);

Oda . . . Petru Feodorovichu . . . na vseradostneishee vosshestvie na prestol (Moscow: Moskovskii universitet, [1762]);

Oda . . . Ekaterine Alekseevne . . . na vseradostnoe vosshestvie na prestol (Moscow: Moskovskii universitet, [1762]);

Epistola ko vsepresvetleishei, derzhavneishei, velikoi gosudarnye imperatritse Ekaterine Alekseevne . . . v den' vysokotorzhestvennago koronovaniia eia imp. velichestva (Moscow: Moskovskii universitet, [1763]);

Nravouchitel'nyia basni, 2 volumes ([Moscow: Universitetskaia tipografiia, 1764]);

Plamena tragediia (Moscow: Moskovskii universitet, 1765);

Pocherpnutyia mysli iz Ekklesiasta (Moscow: Moskovskii universitet, 1765; revised edition, Moscow: Novikov, 1779);

Marteziia i Falestra tragediia (Moscow: Moskovskii universitet, 1767);

Oda . . . Ekaterine Alekseevne . . . na ustanovliaemye vnov' premudrye zakony i na preslavnyia dela eia imperatorskogo velichestva (Moscow: Moskovskii universitet, [1767]);

Torzhestvennaia pesn' imperatriste Ekaterine Alekseevne . . . na vseradostnoe pribytie iz Kazani v Moskvu 1767 goda, iiunia 14 dnia (Moscow: Moskovskii universitet, [1767]);

Mikhail Matveevich Kheraskov

Numa Pompilii, ili Protsvetaiushchii Rim (Moscow: Moskovskii universitet, 1768; revised and enlarged edition, Moscow: I. Zelennikov & B. Sokolov, 1793);

Filosoficheskiia ody ili pesni (Moscow: Novikov, 1769);

Oda . . . Ekaterine Alekseevne . . . na torzhestvennuiu pobedu pri gorode Chesme nad turetskim flotom (Saint Petersburg: [Senatskaia tipografia], 1770);

Chesmesskii boi (Saint Petersburg: Akademiia nauk, 1771);

Selim i Selima poema (Saint Petersburg: Morskoi kadetskii korpus, 1773);

Borislav (Saint Petersburg: [Akademiia nauk], 1774);

Drug neshchastnykh: Sleznaia dramma (Saint Petersburg: [Sukhuputnyi kadetskii korpus], 1774);

Gonimyia sleznaia drama (Moscow: Moskovskii universitet, 1775);

Khram rossiiskago blagodenstviia, posviashchennyi sooruzhitel'nitse onago e. i. v. vsemilostiveishei gosudarnye Ekaterine Alekseevne Vtoroi (Moscow: Moskovskii universitet, [1775]);

Rossiiada iroicheskaia poema (Moscow: Moskovskii universitet, 1779; revised and enlarged edition, Moscow: Novikov, 1786); republished as *Rossiada* (Saint Petersburg: I. Glazunov, 1895);

Nenavistnik (Moscow: Universitetskaia tipografiia [Novikov], 1779);

Dobrye soldaty (Saint Petersburg: Veitbrekht i Shnor, 1779);

Zolotoi prut: Vostochnaia povest'. Perevedena s arabskogo iazyka ([Moscow: Novikov], 1782);

Idolopoklonniki ili Gorislava (Moscow: Novikov, 1782);

Uteshenie greshnykh (Moscow: Novikov, 1783);

Vladimir vozrozhedennyi (Moscow: Novikov, 1785);

Epicheskiia tvorennia, 2 volumes (Moscow: Novikov, 1786–1787);

Shchastlivaia Rossiia ili 25 letnii iubilei: Prolog ([Moscow]: Kh. Klaudii, 1787);

Kadm i Garmoniia drevnee povestvovanie, 2 volumes (Moscow: Novikov, 1789);

Polidor, syn Kadma i Garmonii, 3 volumes (Moscow: I. Zelennikov, 1794);

Piligrimy, ili Iskateli Shchastiia (Moscow: K. Ridiger i K. Klaudii, 1795);

Oda . . . Pavlu Pervomu . . . podnesennaia pri ego vseradostnom vstuplenii na praroditel'skii prestol ot Moskovskago universiteta 1796 goda, noiabria 12 dnia (Moscow: Ridiger i Klaudii, [1796]);

Stikhi na konchinu ego siiatel'stva grafa Fedora Grigor'evicha Orlova, posledovavshuiu 1796 goda maiia 17 dnia ([Moscow: Ridiger i Klaudii, 1796]);

Tsar', ili Spasennyi Novgorod: stikhotvornaia povest' (Moscow: Ridiger i Klaudii, 1796–1800);

Tvoreniia, 12 volumes (Moscow: Ridiger i Klaudii, 1796–1803);

Pesn' e. i. v., vsemilostiveishemu gosudariu Pavlu Petrovichu . . . vo iz"iavlenie vsepoddannicheskoi blagodarnosti za poluchennuiu vysochaishuiu milost' posviashchaet ([Moscow: Universitetskaia tipografiia, 1797]);

Osvobozhdennaia Moskva (Moscow: Ridiger i Klaudii, 1798);

Bakhariana, ili Neizvestnyi: Volshebnaia povest', pocherpnutaia iz russkikh skazok (Moscow: Universitetskaia tipografiia, 1803);

Zareida i Rostislav (Moscow: Rossiiskaia Akademiia, 1809);

Izbrannye proizvedeniia, edited by A. V. Zapadov, Biblioteka poeta, bol'shaia seria (Leningrad: Sovetskii pisatel', 1961);

Veseliashiaisia Rossiia: Prolog ([Moscow: Universitetskaia tipografiia], n.d.).

OTHER: *Poleznoe uveselenie* (January 1760–June 1762), edited by Kheraskov;

Svobodnye chasy, 1 (January 1763–December 1763), edited by Kheraskov.

TRANSLATION: Alexander Pope, *Khram slavy: Poema* ([Moscow: Universitetskaia tipografiia, 1761]).

The slim volume of poetry with which Mikhail Matveevich Kheraskov's oeuvre is represented in this century does not even begin to outline the influence this poet had on the development of Russian literature, nor does it give any idea of his actual importance for Russian cultural history. Cliché formulas about Kheraskov, mostly generated during the period following his death and generally hostile to his legacy, abound even among scholars of eighteenth-century literature. Much of this unjust posthumous assessment stems from the fact that Kheraskov simply is not read. If his complete works were ever published, they would fill the space on bookshelves occupied only by the most prolific of poets. His only published collected works (1796–1803) comprise twelve volumes but account for only about half of his writings. Besides being scarce, Kheraskov's works are but a pale reflection of a man who left his imprint on practically every genre practiced during his long life and who helped shaped the aesthetic norms of his age.

Kheraskov was one of the century's most important men of letters, who contributed in a major way to the growth of Russian literature and the institutions of Russian literary life. The volume of Kheraskov's accomplishments probably speaks better than his works of his actual place in Russian literary history. A most versatile writer of poetry, drama, and prose; founder of the first Russian literary salon, in which his wife, E. V. Kheraskova, the first Russian female poet to be published, actively participated; publisher of the first Russian weekly devoted to literature and publisher and participant in a number of other journals; one of the first to introduce sentimentalism to Russian literature; a novelist and the creator of the first historical epic poem in Russia, the *Rossiiada* (The Rossiad, 1779); the overseer of Moscow University; an important Mason; and, finally, a colleague and patron to many Russian writers. The young Nikolai Karamzin declared Kheraskov to be Russia's greatest poet, and his works were generally considered classics during his lifetime.

Misperceptions about Kheraskov's role in literature have a variegated history with at least two phases. The first began in the midst of the Romantic movement, which in Russia was even more violently opposed to classicist literary norms than in Europe. The second phase began in the twentieth century and did not involve any hostility but was due rather to a conceptual fallacy by a pioneer in eighteenth-century literary studies, Grigorii A. Gukovsky, who took it upon himself to resurrect the stature of another important but nearly forgotten poet, Aleksandr Sumarokov. In doing so he tended to subordinate nearly every poet associated at some point of his life with Sumarokov to the status of his pupil, and Kheraskov was no exception.

The usual arguments for Kheraskov's inclusion in the "Sumarokov school" relate to his early biography. Mikhail (or Mikhailo) Matveevich Kheraskov, born on 25 October 1733, was sixteen years younger than Sumarokov and, hence, naturally suited to the role of pupil, particularly in view of the fact that he received his education at the same Sukhoputnyi shliakhetnyi kadetskii korpus (Noble Infantry Cadet Corps) from which Sumarokov had graduated. Kheraskov also belonged to the same social class as Sumarokov, the aristocracy, while the two other major poets of the older generation, Vasilii Trediakovsky and Mikhail Lomonosov, were of lowly origin.

However, their aristocratic heritage had quite different origins: Sumarokov came from an established Russian noble family, while Kheraskov was the child of an important Wallachian émigré who had entered Russia during the reign of Peter the Great. In this regard Kheraskov had more in common with such Russified foreigners as Antiokh Kantemir than with the rooted Russian gentry to whom Sumarokov addressed much of his writing. While Sumarokov was probably first introduced to literature during his time at the corps, Kheraskov had the advantage of having a stepfather (his own father died when Kheraskov was a year old), Nikita Iurievich Trubetskoi, a well-educated man and minor poet in his own right. Furthermore, Khe-

raskov entered the corps four years after Sumarokov had graduated, and Kheraskov's first two odes, of 1751 and 1753, bear the unmistakable influence of Lomonosov rather than Sumarokov. Possibly to underscore the connection, Kheraskov signed them with the same version of his first name as that which Lomonosov used – Mikhailo, rather than Mikhail.

The first important sampling of Kheraskov's work appeared in the journal *Ezhemesiachnyia sochineniia* (Monthly Compositions) in 1755. This periodical, put out by the Academy of Sciences, was at the time the only journal to print poetry in addition to writings in the sciences, arts, and humanities. Among these early poems were many that substantially differed from Sumarokov's, such as Kheraskov's programmatic "Sonet i Epitafiia" (Sonnet with an Epitaph), published in the August issue, two months after Sumarokov's sonnet "Kogda vstupil ja v svet, vstupiv v nego, vopil" (As I Entered the World, I Wailed). While Kheraskov's sonnet bears an obvious thematic likeness to Sumarokov's work, it also displayed important differences. First, its rhyme scheme was a departure from both Sumarokov's and Trediakovsky's earlier sonnets, and, even more markedly, it was composed from the vantage point of someone speaking from beyond the grave (hence the title). If Kheraskov's first sonnet was meant as a challenge to Sumarokov's earlier text, it also demonstrated his alertness to contemporary European interest in graveyard topics and the cultivation of sentiment in poetry. Thomas Gray's famous *Elegy Written in a Country Churchyard* (1751), which also ended with an epitaph and which helped gain recognition in English literature for such topics, was published only four years earlier.

At the same time Kheraskov's sonnet signaled what would become his intense interest in the Masonic movement; one of the initiation rituals in Freemasonry was spending some time in a grave or a coffin. Grave imagery even entered Kheraskov's amorous verse at the time, as in a madrigal that G. F. Miller (Müller), the editor of *Ezhemesiachnyia sochineniia,* refused to publish. In the poem Kheraskov's persona expresses a longing to transform himself into a flower on the breast of his beloved Phyllis and to "wilt in the grave" formed by her breasts. Kheraskov's sonnet also pointed the way to the closely related theme of the vanity of this world, which Kheraskov explored in an ode published three months later (in November 1755). This topic became dominant in his journals of the early 1760s.

Kheraskov showed his independence from Sumarokov most prominently in his first tragedy,

Venetsianskaia Monakhinia (The Venetian Nun, 1758), which violated nearly every canon of classicist tragedy that Sumarokov had tried to establish. It was a three-act play (instead of the normative five), presumably set in contemporary Venice (instead of the noble past), and it concerned itself with the tragic love of commoners (rather than of royalty or nobility). Of the three unities Kheraskov immediately violated that of place in his first act, dividing the setting between a monastery and an ambassador's residence. As in his sonnet the play demonstrates Kheraskov's awareness of up-to-date developments in European literary tastes. In its final act the heroine, Zaneta, enters the stage with blood gushing from self-inflicted wounds – she has blinded herself, following to the letter the biblical commandment, "If thine eye offend thee, pluck it out." This was much more akin to the devices of contemporary *Trauerspiel* (tragedies), popular in Germany and England, than to the principles of the French classicist drama, which avoided such ghastly spectacle.

At the time of writing *Venetsianskaia Monakhinia* Kheraskov was also separated from Sumarokov by geographic distance. Having resigned his commission in the army, in which he had served after his graduation from the cadet corps, he moved to Moscow in 1755 in order to assist in the opening of the first Russian university. Assuming the rank of collegiate assessor, he oversaw the students' study program, the library, and the printing office. This was the first of Kheraskov's many appointments at Moscow University, in the service of which he spent over forty years of his life. Most of his early efforts at the university were to convert its curriculum from Latin to Russian, as advocated by Lomonosov, the university's founder, and by Lomonosov's pupil N. N. Popovsky, one of its first professors.

Kheraskov's activities at the university were important for the further development of Russian letters. Probably his greatest service in this regard was the creation of the first Russian literary weekly in Moscow, *Poleznoe uveselenie* (Useful Amusement), which devoted its pages exclusively to literature and primarily to poetry. The two and a half years during which this journal was published, may be considered a pivotal episode for Russian literary culture. For the first time readers had the luxury of weekly contributions to various genres of poetry from many aspiring young poets, rather than having to follow the development of Russian literature from sporadic separate publications. In sharp contrast to the uncertainty reigning in the social and political sphere at the time due to the problems of dy-

Title page for an edition of Kheraskov's epic poem on the Christianization of Russia

nastic succession, with three rulers exchanging their hold on the throne and several private careers dashed in the process, Russian literature seems to have become endowed with an unmistakable sense of certainty about its own future.

Much of this certainty was no doubt due to Kheraskov's personal traits. In contrast to Sumarokov, whose irascibility and short temper were notorious, Kheraskov gained a reputation for gentleness and gentility. As early as 1760, soon after his marriage to the poet Elizaveta Neronova, his house became the principal attraction of Moscow's younger generation of aspiring poets, in fact the first Russian literary salon. But Kheraskov was no lawgiver for Russian literature in the sense that Trediakovsky, Lomonosov, and Sumarokov had individually aspired to be. The tone of Kheraskov's poetry, as well as of his personal life, was of suggestive persuasion rather than command; he united people by the charm of his character as much as by his poetry, leaving room for individual development of the poets who surrounded him. This aspect of Kheraskov's personality was also reflected in *Poleznoe uveselenie*. Indeed there is probably more justification in speaking of a "school of Kheraskov" or of a "Kheraskov Pleiade," as witnessed by this journal and several others that followed, rather than of the more generally accepted notion of a "Sumarokov school." Kheraskov helped to give several Russian writers their start, including Ipollit Bogdanovich, to whom Kheraskov provided free room and board in his own home when he came to Moscow as a fifteen-year-old student. Many others – Vasilii Maikov and Denis Fonvizin, to name the best known – began their careers working on Kheraskov's journals of the early 1760s.

In contrast to the constant squabbling of his predecessors, Kheraskov did not believe in coercion via attack; he abhorred satire, especially personal satire, and shunned emotional argument. All this found expression in the selection of topics in *Poleznoe uveselenie,* as well as in the style of his poetry, stripped of both bathetic constructions and high-style Church Slavonic elements. Notably, in his later poetry of the 1770s he revived some of Lomonosov's practices, but at this stage he closely held to the standard of Russian as spoken by the gentry class. *Poleznoe uveselenie* also reflected the aspirations of the Russian aristocracy of the time, which coincided in many ways with the ethical program advocated by Masonry, a movement to which most of the journal's contributors apparently belonged. Kheraskov believed, as did many Masons, in moving Russian society toward a more equitable social system by means of morally edifying its populace rather than by explicit social or political changes. The principal instrument in effecting such a movement was a literature that would establish a moral code of behavior for Russia's aristocracy, which would by its example affect the rest of the Russian people. This emphasis on spiritual rather than material values brought Kheraskov (in the midst of the supposed blossoming of Russian classicism, as some literary historians would like to characterize this period) to the embrace of such "baroque" themes as *vanitas vanitatum,* to which he devoted a number of odes, stanzas, madrigals, elegies, sonnets, and lyrics. Even by using the same theme in various genres Kheraskov violated classicist notions about the necessary distinctions of genres. The theme of the vanity of this world, introduced by Kheraskov's first published *stans* (stanza) in *Poleznoe uveselenie,* "Vse na svete sem prekhodit" (Everything in This World is Transient), had a number of subtopics concerned either with evils to be corrected, such as *zlato* (material wealth) or *zloba* (moral deficiency), or with alternatives to *vanitas,* such as good deeds and *dobrodetel'* (virtue) or *uedinenie, pokoi* (solitude). Each of these subtopics received competitive treatments, often

printed alongside one another, by various poets associated with the journal, including Bogdanovich, A. G. Karin, N. Krushchev, Maikov, the brothers A. V. and S. V. Naryshkin, Aleksei Rzhevsky, V. D. Sankovsky, and P. Zhukov, as well as Kheraskov's wife, Ekaterina, and other anonymous contributors.

Kheraskov's first published stanza characterizes the general thrust of his poetry (which included odes, madrigals, sonnets, prayers, rondos, and elegies) published in *Poleznoe uveselenie.* Typically, "Vse na svete sem prekhodit" was not an original work but a free translation of J. B. Rousseau's "Ode sur un commencement d'anné." However, Kheraskov not only changed the formal and thematic nature of his model – reducing the number of stanzas from fifteen to nine, shortening the verse line to trochaic tetrameter, avoiding Rousseau's "erotic Epicureanism" in stanza nine, and intensifying the use of antithetical constructions and oxymora – he also transformed the genre of Rousseau's poem, transforming it from an Aeonic ode (a variant of the solemn ode) into a meditative *stans* (a "middle ode" by Trediakovsky's definition). This fundamental change not only explains Kheraskov's failure to mention his source (after all, he created a different text than Rousseau's model) but also indicates Kheraskov's general modus operandi in his works of this period. Thematic and didactic considerations overruled the sanctity of model texts, as well as their generic allegiance. Kheraskov's purportedly Anacreontic *Novyie Ody* (New Odes, 1762) had little in common with Anacreon's celebrations of wine, women, and song, and his collected *Nravouchitel'nyia basni* (Didactic Fables, 1764) emphasized their didacticism, which neither Aesop nor Jean de La Fontaine found necessary to underscore explicitly, at the same time deemphasizing humorous elements typical of their fables. Kheraskov seemed to have been unable to find in the poetic models he used adequately stated ingredients of his program, which centered on the moral edification of his compatriots. For this reason he changed them to suit his own needs.

Thus one is faced with a curious phenomenon when discussing Kheraskov's poetry of the early 1760s. On the one hand, Kheraskov continued to cultivate the same kinds of poetry as Sumarokov had in the late 1750s, as far as their generic designations are concerned. On the other hand, he transformed many of these genres by subjugating them to his didactic goals and early sentimentalist sensibility. In so doing he often destroyed what had been conceived by Sumarokov as their generic essence.

All this did not prevent Kheraskov from displaying in his verse of the period a keen interest in metric and stanzaic variability. Indeed it seems that he considered the difference between genres as residing primarily in the varied rhythmic realizations of the poems, while the message conveyed to his readers could remain more or less the same – an attitude suggested by the dozens of generically different poems written by Kheraskov in the 1760s that explore the same basic themes in a great variety of metric realizations. Further, Kheraskov's collection *Novyia Ody* offered for the first time odes rendered in unrhymed iambic tetrameters and trochaic tetrameters and not divided into stanzas; they were "new odes" precisely because of their rhythmic actualizations.

Kheraskov's *Pocherpnutyia mysli iz Ekklesiasta* (Thoughts Gathered from Ecclesiastes, 1765) combined meditative poetry with a display of technical virtuosity. Published as a separate booklet, it was a free variation of both the Book of Ecclesiastes and Voltaire's "Précis de l'Ecclesiaste." *Pocherpnutyia mysli iz Ekklesiasta* consists of forty stanzas of varied lengths (four and six lines) and feet (from iambic trimeter to hexameter) and should be considered as a synthesis of previous contributions both to the topic of *sueta* (vanity) and the genre of stanzas; it is the longest work of its kind in Russian literature. The last lines of the first five stanzas repeat the word *sueta* in a rondeaulike manner, and this rhythmic device is further enhanced by a large degree of variability in the work's rhyming patterns, which exhaust virtually all of the possible permutations for four- and six-line stanzas. Just as his *Novyie Ody* had little to do with Anacreon, so did his *Pocherpnutyia mysli iz Ekklesiasta* derive little from Voltaire, even though Kheraskov claimed to have been inspired by the French writer's work.

While of obvious didactic content, *Pocherpnutyia mysli iz Ekklesiasta* may also be seen as one of the earliest harbingers of Romantic diction. The images in such lines as "V kipiashchei mladosti moei" (In my burning youth), "Iskal begushchego dushi moei pokoiu" (I sought fleeting peace for my soul), "Kipiashcha krov' vo mne prostynet i zamerznet, / Pomerknet vzor, i mysl' pritupitsia moia" (My boiling blood will cool and freeze, / My sight shall blur and my mind be blunted), and in the entire seventh stanza on the theme of *toska* (ennui) became commonplaces of Russian Romantic poetry. Kheraskov's stylistic principles not only differed from the goal posited in Lomonosov's *Ritorika* (Rhetoric, 1748) – "to speak colorfully about any given subject and thereby sway others to one's own opinion about

it" – but also rejected Sumarokov's insistence in his 1747 epistle concerning Russian poetry on good style, clarity, and reason. In Kheraskov's first epistle, published in *Poleznoe uveselenie,* he described one of the primary purposes of literature as its ability "chtob tronut' chem nibud' chitatelei serdtsa!" (by some means to touch readers' hearts) rather than their minds. In one of his first elegies published in *Poleznoe uveselenie,* Kheraskov purposefully added the oxymoron "icy fires" which Boileau had expressly banned from this genre eighty-five years before as impermissibly irrational.

Kheraskov's interest in finding appropriate vocabulary for expressing emotional states was undoubtedly one of his pioneering accomplishments in Russian literature, yet he is consistently remembered only in connection with his didactic efforts. These culminated in his collection *Filosoficheskiia ody ili pesni* (Philosophical Odes or Songs, 1769), later titled *Nravouchitel'nyia Ody* (Didactic Odes, in volume seven of his *Tvoreniia* [Works, 1796–1803]). Whichever literary format Kheraskov chose, his need to instruct overcame his need to entertain. Kheraskov's early didacticism was informed by his naive belief that literature could improve the morals of his compatriots. In fact, he was rumored to have been disappointed when, after the first year of his attempts in *Poleznoe uveselenie* to affect improvement in social behavior, he saw little change.

Still the aesthetic impact of his works on Russian literary sensibility was significant. Specifically, Kheraskov provided a language that allowed the rise of Russian esoteric thought and metaphysical poetry. His experiments in religious verse, begun in the early 1760s in *Poleznoe uveselenie* and its continuation *Svobodnye chasy* (Idle Hours), continued in such journals of the 1770s as *Vechera* (Evenings) and *Utrennii svet* (Morning Light). Later works worthy of note are his versified chapters of Proverbs and several magnificent sacred odes composed in the manner of Lomonosov's solemn odes, including "Oda o Velichestve Bozhii" (Ode on the Majesty of God, first published in volume three of *Opyt Trudov Vol'nago rossiiskago sobraniia* [Works of the Free Russian Assembly, 1776]); "Bog" (God, published in *Utrennii svet,* October 1777), which played a vital role in shaping Derzhavin's famous ode of the same title; and "Mir" (The World, in the January 1778 issue of *Utrennii svet*). In addition, Kheraskov wrote numerous Masonic hymns, verse transpositions of Psalms, the poem "Uteshenie greshnykh" (Consolation for Sinners), and the over thirteen-hundred-line culmination of his religious poetry, the Christian epic "Vselennaia" (The Universe), completed in 1790.

Most of these works reflect Kheraskov's interest in Masonry, which may have also helped account for the divergent path he took from Sumarokov. While Sumarokov was also a Mason, he belonged to the lower orders, which were traditionally assigned to concentrate on the rational aspect of human life, while middle-level Masons, such as Kheraskov, were to explore the emotional realm. Only Masons of the highest rank were initiated into the revelatory aspects of spiritual life. That Kheraskov achieved such rank is suggested in part by "Vselennaia." Sumarokov, on the other hand, never wrote anything of this kind. From this perspective the poetic practice of Sumarokov and Kheraskov in the 1750s and 1760s may be complementary rather than antagonistic; Sumarokov stressed reason, Kheraskov emotion, yet both were part of a larger philosophical system.

Kheraskov also wrote in genres that Sumarokov explicitly banned. Among these was the novel. Sumarokov had warned against the pernicious effects of novels in a famous article, "O chtenii romanov" (On Reading Novels, 1759) and held firmly to this view for the rest of his life. Kheraskov's first novel, *Numa Pompilii, ili Protsvetaiushchii Rim* (Numa Pompilius, or Rome in its Bloom), was published in 1768, followed by two more: *Kadm i Garmoniia* (Cadmus and Harmonia, 1789) and its three-part sequel, *Polidor, syn Kadma i Garmonii* (Polydore, Son of Cadmus and Harmonia, 1794). Moved by didactic concerns more than literary ones, in *Numa Pompilii* Kheraskov gave unambiguous advice to the monarch on how to create a utopian society. The other two, as Stephen L. Baehr has shown, were meant as sophisticated Masonic allegories.

After his first novel was published, Catherine II apparently became alarmed by Kheraskov's views and activities and had him transferred from Moscow to the capital in 1770 to assume the post of a vice-president of the *bergkollegiia* (Department of Mines). The move, while technically a promotion, did not, of course, reflect Catherine's wish to be instructed by the author of *Numa Pompilius* or to turn herself into the ideal philosopher-king as advocated in Kheraskov's novel. Rather it seems to have been her way of bringing under close supervision a writer who was gaining in influence.

Thus ended the first fifteen years of Kheraskov's engagement with Moscow University. Kheraskov's literary and social activity in the 1760s had been nothing less than remarkable: he was al-

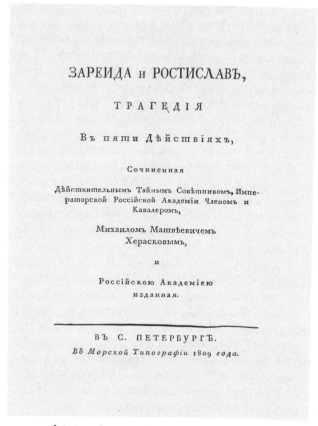

Title page for a posthumous publication of one of Kheraskov's tragedies

ready a seasoned author of hundreds of poems and several books and an important journal editor-publisher. He also translated important articles on poetry, philology, magic, and other subjects for a three-volume Russian translation (1767) of Diderot's *Encyclopédie, ou Dictionnaire raisonneé des sciences, des arts et des métiers* (1751–1780).

Kheraskov's less-acknowledged role in the 1760s was that of dramatist. During the years after 1761, when Sumarokov's tenure as director of the Saint Petersburg Russian Theater ended, the elder writer had stopped writing for the stage, and during this time Kheraskov helped fill the vacuum. Kheraskov supplied Russian audiences with the first samples of bourgeois drama, sentimental and Christian tragedy, and traditional classicist comedy, of which he wrote the first in verse, entitled *Bezbozhnik* (The Atheist, 1761). Kheraskov's engagement with dramaturgy resulted in twenty works for the theater, including a prologue and an opera. Kheraskov's unique and independent role in the development of Russian drama has been largely ignored, with the notable exception of the pioneering studies by Michael A. Green.

Almost immediately after his transfer to Saint Petersburg, Kheraskov organized new weekly gatherings at his residence in the capital. They were attended by some of the leading poets of the day, including many of those who had taken part in Kheraskov's journals: his wife, Maikov, Rzhevsky, Bogdanovich, A. V. Khrapovitsky, and other poets. The gatherings resulted in the publication of a literary weekly, *Vechera* (Evenings), published during 1772–1773. *Vechera* dealt with many of the themes that had occupied *Poleznoe uveselenie* but with a new inclination toward the nocturnal, mystical, and transcendental, in marked contrast to the tone of the so-called satiric journals of the period. The periodical's interest in mystical aspects of experience heralded a fascination with such topics characteristic of Russian journalism in the second half of the 1770s and the early 1780s. By that time many journals were under the direct influence of Masonic lodges.

About this time Kheraskov became close to Nikolai Novikov, a former student at Moscow University, and this friendship had immediate negative consequences. Catherine had begun to harbor personal resentment against Novikov, ever since his satiric journal, *Truten'* (The Drone, 1769–1770), had successfully outperformed *Vsiakaia vsiachina* (All Sorts and Sundries), the journal she had sponsored. Catherine's displeasure with Novikov eventually led to his imprisonment 1792, but long before that Catherine began to view all Masons with great suspicion, most particularly those who were associated with Novikov. Apparently as a result of his Masonic activities, Kheraskov was forced into early retirement in 1775.

Kheraskov's period of political disfavor came to an end, however, with his completion of the *Rossiiada,* a work on which he labored for eight years. The first Russian heroic epic on a historical subject, the *Rossiiada* brought Kheraskov his greatest fame as a writer. Replete with patriotic themes, the work also won Catherine's approval and certainly contributed to Kheraskov's reinstatement at Moscow University as its rector in the late 1770s.

The *Rossiiada* was not Kheraskov's first effort in long narrative verse, nor was it his last. In 1761 he had composed a long didactic poem, titled *Plody nauk* (The Fruits of Learning), modeled on Lomonosov's epistle "O pol'ze stekla" (On the Usefulness of Glass, 1755). Kheraskov's work on the usefulness of the sciences was directed in part against Rousseau's *Discours sur les sciences et les arts* (1750). *Plody nauk* was subtitled *poema* (long poem) and represented a sort of a hybrid between the didactic content of traditional epistles and the longer, epic form.

It set a precedent for future Russian poets, who, somewhat ambiguously, came to call any work in verse of substantial length a *poema,* whether it had anything to do with epic content or not.

Far closer to the traditional forms of the epic was Kheraskov's second attempt at a long narrative poem, composed ten years later and titled *Chesmesskii boi* (The Battle of Chesme, 1771). Written in response to one of Russia's most extraordinary naval victories, which had resulted in complete annihilation of the Turkish fleet, the poem expressed Kheraskov's inspired patriotism. No doubt emboldened by the success of *Chesmesski boi,* Kheraskov decided to undertake the *Rossiiada,* which he hoped would be a full-fledged national epic, based not on a contemporary event (like the work on Chesme) but on a decisive moment in history which had set Russia on the path of national self-determination. His choice fell on the taking of Kazan in 1551 by Ivan IV ("the Terrible"). This choice was fortunate, since it not only involved an event of true historical significance but also accorded well with Catherine's foreign-policy objectives of the period. The *Rossiiada* depicted in historically accurate detail that particular stage in history when the Russian state, after centuries of foreign domination following Russia's invasion by the Golden Horde in 1237, regained control of its destiny. It began a sequence of events that resulted not only in Russia's capture of Kazan, a capital of the Golden Horde, but of all the territories still under Tartar control. The final stage of this policy was reached in Catherine's annexation of the Crimea shortly after *Rossiiada* was completed. Kheraskov's epic, composed of twelve cantos, was replete with all the embellishments thought appropriate for an epic, including celestial apparitions, prophetic dreams, and magic agents, as the long siege of Kazan was invested with cosmic significance. Kheraskov was dubbed the "Russian Homer," a reputation he enjoyed for many decades.

The poet quickly capitalized on his return to favor. As rector of Moscow University, he invited Novikov to lease the university's press for ten years, in hopes of improving its dismal publishing record. The verve with which Novikov took up this challenge was nothing short of spectacular and represents a celebrated chapter in Russian publishing history. Novikov's views on the educational role of literature had germinated during those years when he studied at Moscow University under the spell of Kheraskov's ideas, and his intellectual program for Russia was nearly a duplicate of Kheraskov's. Among other things, Kheraskov served as a liaison for Novikov, putting him in touch with many important figures, including a young German-educated teacher of the occult and an important Mason, Johann Georg Schwarz, whom Kheraskov appointed professor of German at Moscow University in 1779. Schwarz's emphasis on the revelatory and mystical aspects of attaining true wisdom – as described in his *O trekh poznaniiakh* (On Three Types of Knowledge, 1782) – were based on the teachings of the seventeenth-century philosopher and mystic Jacob Boehme. Boehme's ideas fell on fertile ground with people like Novikov and Kheraskov, who were disenchanted with the form of Masonry introduced into Russia by the Prussian baron von Reichel in the early 1770s, as well as with the casual fraternal activities practiced in the Great Provincial Lodge (whose organizer was Ivan Elagin and its grand secretary, the poet Maikov). This variant of Masonry was of English origin and introduced into Russia in the mid 1770s. Schwarz was a charismatic lecturer, who in 1780 attracted such illustrious listeners as Joseph II of Austria and Prince Frederick of Prussia. He drew around him a host of young student admirers who were to contribute to the intellectual ferment in Russia lasting far into the next century. Schwarz's and Novikov's common Masonic interests soon grew into a close friendship and inspired the already-prolific Novikov to an outpouring of new publications. With the financial and moral help of the Druzheskoe uchenoe obshchestvo (Fraternal Learned Society), organized by Schwarz, the press disseminated original and translated works of literature in accord with Masonic ideals.

Thus in the early 1780s Kheraskov was at the center of a dynamic movement with the institutional ability to advance its notions about the moral perfectibility of humanity and the inner spiritual aspects of human existence. Kheraskov presided over Moscow University, a cultural mecca for Russia at the time. With the help of Schwarz, Kheraskov was able to integrate Masonic notions into Russian higher education. Together they organized a "sobranie universitetskikh pitomtsev" (gathering of university alumni), the first secret student society in Russian history. Kheraskov also appointed Schwarz inspector of a new pedagogical seminary, so that he could assert his influence over primary education.

Together with Novikov, Kheraskov was able to assume nearly absolute control over what was published in Moscow. If the amount of printed matter that suddenly flooded the Russian market in the early 1780s was attributable to Novikov's organizational skills, the funding and thematic range of the material he published was to a large extent influenced by the Bratiia Rozovago kresta (Rosicrucian

Order of Masons), which Kheraskov helped to organize. Along with manuals on mathematics and foreign languages, Russian readers could purchase books of neo-Christian and Evangelical content. The brotherhood controlled not only the presses of Moscow University but also two major free typographies, one of which was owned by Novikov and the other by Ivan Lopukhin, Novikov's and Kheraskov's fellow Rosicrucian. These presses published mystical and didactic tracts in large editions, ranging from Boehme's *Path to Christ* to such compilations as *The Errors of Reason* and *The Secrets of the Cross* and Lopukhin's monumental five-volume edition of Johann Arndt's *On True Christianity* (1784). Nocturnal topics, didacticism, and mysticism – themes earlier advanced by Kheraskov in *Poleznoe uveselenie* and revived in *Vechera* – were again an integral part of Russian literary life. Kheraskov may have felt that the proof of his contention that literature vitally affected social matters was finally at hand. Perhaps he felt that he was on the threshold of realizing the foundations for the social utopia he had advanced in 1768; this is suggested by the elaborate sequel to his first novel *Numa Pompilii* titled *Kadm i Garmoniia,* which he completed in 1786.

The year 1784 marked a watershed in Kheraskov's career, not only because of the period of reaction following the French Revolution but for a variety of personal and literary reasons. Kheraskov grew to feel increasingly isolated. Despite the fame of the *Rossiiada,* several new poets on the scene began to threaten his literary preeminence. His former protégé Bogdanovich published his immensely successful, mock-erotic, long narrative poem *Dushen'ka* (The Little Soul, 1783), while in lyric poetry Derzhavin's name began to loom ever larger – his ode "Bog" (God, 1784) outshone Kheraskov's ode of the same title. Furthermore, Kheraskov suffered the unexpected loss of Schwarz, who, exhausted by the excesses he imposed upon himself in his ascetic quest for inner perfection, died in February. Novikov's phenomenal success as a publisher brought about intense scrutiny from Catherine, who became increasingly mistrustful of the Masons. Beginning with an edict in 1785, she ordered a series of interrogations of Novikov as well as the close supervision of all Masonic presses, a process that eventually led to the publisher's imprisonment in 1792.

Kheraskov was forced to disassociate the university gradually from overtly Masonic ties. Within a few years Kheraskov was horrified at the activities of some branches of the Masonic movement during the French Revolution, and he voiced his criticism in

РОССІЯДА
ИРОИЧЕСКАЯ ПОЕМА.

печатана
при
Императорскомъ Московскомъ
Университетѣ
1779 года.

Title page for Kheraskov's narrative poem about Ivan IV (Ivan the Terrible). Kheraskov's popular poem was the first Russian heroic epic on a historical subject.

"Vselennaia." This fact may have helped Kheraskov escape Catherine's campaign against the Masons (or "Martinists" as she called them), when in 1791 Derzhavin interceded with her on his behalf (via her current favorite, Platon Zubov).

Kheraskov's gradual isolation did not, however, result in any lessening of his literary productivity. In 1785 Kheraskov finished another epic poem in eighteen cantos entitled *Vladimir vozrozhedennyi* (Vladimir Reborn), which was devoted to the Christianization of Russia. In his last years Kheraskov composed at least three more tragedies and other works of drama. In the 1790s he wrote one of his longest novels, *Polidor, syn Kadma i Garmonii*. Despite his advanced age Kheraskov managed to revitalize his verse in the early years of the nineteenth century, after his retirement from Moscow University in 1802. He shocked the reading public with his unique narrative poem/fantasy tale, *Bakhariana, ili Neizvestnyi* (1803), by far his longest poetic creation, composed of fourteen cantos of unrhymed dactyls and trochees, a meter that was thought at the time to be truly Russian.

But time finally took its toll. After four decades of service to Moscow University and fifty years as a published writer, Kheraskov died at his home in Moscow in 1807. His wife's death followed in 1809. During Napoleon's occupation of Moscow in 1812, his house burned to the ground, thus robbing historians of what must have been a colossal archive consisting not only of Kheraskov's works and his library but of letters and papers from the many individuals whose lives he affected.

At the end of his life Kheraskov found in Karamzin probably his most talented student and heir. The continuities between these two figures, whose names became associated with two epochs of Russian literary culture, have yet to be examined in detail. The political and aeshetic profile of Karamzin, who attended Moscow University and who became an associate of Novikov, is unusually close to that of Kheraskov. In the 1780s Karamzin proclaimed that Kheraskov was Russia's greatest poet and in the 1790s helped to establish the "cult of feeling," which had been anticipated by Kheraskov thirty years before. Karamzin applied some of Kheraskov's stylistic discoveries and political ideas to the writing of his twelve-volume *Istoriia Gosudarstva Rossiiskogo* (History of the Russian State, 1816–1829). The image of the ideal ruler in Kheraskov's novels and epics (mostly directed at Catherine), is in many ways close to Karamzin's implicit understanding of such an ideal in the *Istoriia,* as well as in his explicit statements to Alexander I in the second decade of the nineteenth century. Finally, both Kheraskov and Karamzin were inclined to didacticism and moralizing, although Kheraskov had the misfortune of having his name associated almost solely with its excesses. Greater familiarity with Kheraskov's oeuvre would go a long way to rectify the image of a poet whose words, chosen for the Russian national hymn, "Kol' slaven" (How Glorious), taken from one of his Psalm transpositions, were sung to represent his country.

References:

Stephen L. Baehr, "The Masonic Component in Eighteenth Century Russian Literature," in *Russian Literature in the Age of Catherine the Great,* edited by A. G. Cross (Oxford: W. A. Meeuws, 1976), pp. 121–139;

Ia. L. Barskov, *Perepiska moskovskikh masonov XVIII veka: 1780–1792 gg.* (Petrograd, 1915);

William E. Brown, "Mikhail Kheraskov and the National Epic," in his *A History of 18th Century Russian Literature* (Ann Arbor, Mich.: Ardis, 1980), pp. 246–267;

Michael A. Green, "Diderot and Kheraskov: Sentimentalism in its Classicist Stage," in *Russia and the West in the Eighteenth Century,* edited by Cross (Newtonville, Mass.: Oriental Research Partners, 1983), pp. 206–213;

Green, "Kheraskov and the Christian Tragedy," *California Slavic Studies,* 9 (1976): 1–26;

Green, "Kheraskov's *Gonimye:* Shakespeare's Second Appearance in Russia," *Slavic Review,* 35, no. 2 (1976): 249–257;

Green, "Kotzebue and Kheraskov: Sentimentalism in Its Pre-Romantic Stage," *Study Group on Eighteenth-Century Russia Newsletter,* 10 (1982): 20–29;

Grigorii A. Gukovsky, *Russkaia poeziia XVIII veka* (Leningrad, 1927), pp. 48–102;

L. I. Kulakova, "M. M. Kheraskov," in *Istoriia russkoi literatury,* volume 4 (Moscow & Leningrad: Institut russkoi literatury, 1947), pp. 320–341;

Alexander A. Levitsky, "Masonic Elements in Russian Eighteenth-Century Religious Poetry: Preliminary Questions and Observations to the Theoretical Stance and Practices of Sumarokov and Kheraskov," in *Russia and the World of the Eighteenth Century,* edited by R. P. Bartlett, Cross, and Karen Rasmussen (Columbus, Ohio: Slavica, 1988), pp. 419–436;

I. N. Rozanov, "Mikhail Matveevich Kheraskov," in *Masonstvo v ego proshlom i nastoiashchem,* volume 2, edited by S. P. Mel'gunov and N. P. Sidorov (Moscow: Zagruga & Nekrasov, 1915), pp. 38–51;

A. P. Vlasto, "A Noble Failure – Kheraskov's *Vladimir Vozrozhdyonny,*" in *Gorski vijenac: A Garland of Essays Offered to Professor Elizabeth Mary Hill,* edited by R. Auty, L. R. Lewitter, and Vlasto (Cambridge: Modern Humanities Research Association, 1970), pp. 276–289;

A. P. Zapadov, "Tvorchestvo Kheraskova," in Kheraskov's *Izbrannye proizvedeniia,* edited by Zapadov (Moscow & Leningrad: Sovetskii pisatel', 1961), pp. 5–56.

Dmitrii Ivanovich Khvostov

(19 July 1757 – 22 October 1835)

Mark G. Altshuller
University of Pittsburgh

BOOKS: *Pis'mo ego siiatel'stvu grafu Aleksandru Vasil'evichu Suvorovu-Rymnikskomu. Na sluchai porazheniia viziria so glavnymi silami pri reke Rymnike 1789 goda, sentiabria 11 dnia* (Moscow: Okorokov, 1789);

Izbrannye pritchi iz luchshikh sochinitelei rossiiskimi stikhami (Saint Petersburg, 1802);

Liricheskie tvoreniia (Saint Petersburg, 1810);

Oda na osviashchenie Kazanskiia tserkvi 1811 goda, sentiabria 15 dnia (Saint Petersburg, 1811);

Poslaniia v stikhax (Saint Petersburg, 1814);

Polnoe sobranie stikhotvorenii, 4 volumes (Saint Petersburg, 1817–1818); 5 volumes (Saint Petersburg, 1821–1827); expanded edition, 7 volumes (Saint Petersburg, 1828–1834).

OTHER: Jean Racine, *Andromakha tragediia,* translated by Khvostov (Saint Petersburg: Akademiia nauk, 1794);

Nicolas Boileau-Despréaux, *Nauka o stikhotvorstve,* translated by Khvostov (Saint Petersburg, 1808);

"Poslanie k NN o navodvnii Petropolia byvshem 1824 goda 7 noiabr'a," in *Nevskii al'manakh,* edited by Egor Aladin (Saint Petersburg: Naradnogo prosveshcheniia, 1825).

Dmitrii Ivanovich Khvostov

Count Dmitrii Ivanovich Khvostov occupies a unique place in the history of Russian literature – as an object of scorn. Generations of Russian literati sharpened their wit at the expense of Khvostov's writings. Even after he was no longer read, Russians continued to make fun of his name, regardless of what he had actually written. Later generations came to forget Khvostov's writings completely but always remembered his reputation as a literary buffoon, which had been indelibly etched into Russian literary consciousness. This image of Khvostov's literary biography presents a striking contrast to his actual life and career. Active, energetic, well respected as a government official, he did not in the least resemble a clown. Neither did the kind, intelligent, humble, and compassionate man resemble the graphomaniac convinced of his own genius who became the butt of countless jokes and epigrams.

Dmitrii Ivanovich Khvostov was born in Saint Petersburg on 19 July 1757 to a noble family whose lineage could be traced back to the thirteenth century. His father, Ivan Mikhailovich, was a second lieutenant in the guards; his mother, Vera Grigor'evna Karina, was the sister of three writers, one of whom, Fedor, later became friends with her son. Many men of letters frequented the Khvostovs' home, including the renowned poet and dramatist Aleksandr Sumarokov, the famous satiric poet Vasilii Maikov, and the future poet's uncle, Aleksei Karin. Literature was so significant in the Khvostov family that Khvostov's older brother Aleksei, who died at the age of sixteen in 1772, published a translation of a French comedy by Marc Legrand in 1770.

Khvostov studied at home until the age of eighteen, then in the boarding school of the well-known educator Professor Litke. By this time his family had moved to Moscow, and he was able to attend lectures at Moscow University, where he studied French, Italian, and Latin. His uncle Aleksei Karin died in 1769 and left his nephew a splendid library (three thousand volumes) of French and Italian books. In 1772 Khvostov was enlisted as a private in the *leibgvardiia* of the Preobrazhensky Regiment in Saint Petersburg (Russian nobles often began their service as privates in such privileged regiments). Here he befriended Prince Dimitry Gorchakov, a renowned satiric poet. At the beginning of 1779 Khvostov resigned from the guards with the rank of lieutenant, and on 10 March he entered into civil service. From 1783 to 1787 he served in the senate under the supervision of Prince Andrei Viazemsky, under whom he fulfilled the duties of *stolonachal'nik* (desk chief) and *ekzekutor* (administrator), at a rank roughly equivalent to that of a major in the military. Khvostov did not advance far in his career and apparently did not value the service, as he was relieved of his duties in 1787 for failure to report to work. He left for Moscow, where in 1798 he married Princess Agrafena Ivanovna Gorchakova, the niece of the well-known general Aleksandr Suvorov. In verses Khvostov invariably called his wife Temira.

Becoming a relative of Suvorov helped further Khvostov's career. The famous military leader got along well with his nephew and highly valued his practical qualities, although according to tradition he made fun of Khvostov's "metromania" (that is, his passion for meter, or verse). There is a story that on Suvorov's deathbed (he died 6 May 1800, in Khvostov's Saint Petersburg home) he said to Khvostov: "Liubeznyi Mitia, ty dobryi i chestnyi chelovek! Zaklinaiu tebia vsem, chto dlia tebia est' sviotogo, bros' tvoe virsheslagatel'stvo" (Dear Mitia, you are a good and honorable man! I adjure you by everything that you hold sacred, give up your versifying). Khvostov allegedly took this advice to be the ravings of a dying man.

With Suvorov's intercession, Khvostov was promoted to lieutenant colonel in 1790 and assigned to serve under him. He accompanied Suvorov on his campaigns, acted as his secretary, and collected and preserved many of the general's papers. In 1795, again due to Suvorov's interces-

sion, Khvostov was granted the court rank of *kameriunker* (gentleman of the monarch's bedchamber). This title was usually conferred on young aristocrats and served as an indication of an outstanding future career. However, Khvostov was already close to forty years old and had never distinguished himself by his manners. Someone remarked to Empress Catherine that, judging by Khvostov's appearance, he should not have been given such a title. Catherine answered: "Chto mne delat', ia ni v chem ne mogu otkazat' Suvorovu; ia by etogo cheloveka cdelala freilinoi, esli by on etogo potreboval!" (What can I do? I cannot refuse Suvorov anything: I would make this man a maid of honor if he so demanded!) The simple-hearted Khvostov recorded this story in his notes in praise of Suvorov.

When Suvorov fell out of favor with Emperor Paul I, Khvostov remained loyal to the disgraced general. His devotion even raised the ire of the emperor, whose favor was regained by a testimonial ode celebrating Paul's election as the grand master of the order of Malta. On 30 May 1797 Khvostov was promoted to a full state counselor (a general's rank) and appointed *ober procurator* to the senate. He attained the same position in the Most Holy Synod in 1799. When Suvorov returned from exile and was sent to command the armies in Italy, Khvostov wrote to him on behalf of Paul. In 1799 Suvorov became a Sardinian prince and requested of King Karl-Emmanuel IV the title of Sardinian count for Khvostov, which was granted on 4 October 1799; he received the right to carry this title in Russia on 28 January 1802. After this episode, those who mocked Khvostov invariably hailed him as "the count," or the "Sardinian count," lending a special zest to jokes about the ill-starred poet, which became popular in the first decade of the nineteenth century.

Having begun his literary activity in the 1770s under the influence of Sumarokov and his immediate circle, Khvostov became a true disciple of classicism, the dominant literary trend of the time, and in his odes he followed the carefully worked out tradition of Mikhail Lomonosov. Khvostov's literary views never changed. By the end of the eighteenth century the reading public had become fully accustomed to classicist poetry, and Khvostov's literary exercises were sympathetically greeted in literary circles. On 4 July 1791 he was accepted as a member of the Russian Academy on the suggestion of its president, Princess Dashkova; and Ermil Kostrov, a popular poet at the time, referred to Khvostov in published verses as "liubimstem chistykh muz, drugom vernym

Apollona" (favorite of the pure Muses, true friend of Apollo).

However, the literary scene changed significantly at the beginning of the nineteenth century. In 1803 Aleksandr Shishkov's famous polemical treatise *Rassuzhdenie o starom i novom sloge rossiiskogo iazyka* (Discourse of the Old and New Style in the Russian Language) was published. In this book Shishkov argued against Nikolai Karamzin, the originator of Russian sentimentalism, and his many followers. A literary war began. Because of his classicist sympathies, Khvostov was hostile to sentimentalism and found himself on Shishkov's side, though literary relationships in this controversy were more complicated than any readymade patterns may suggest.

Karamzin's young, talented, and sharp-witted friends took up arms in his defense; these included Petr Viazemsky, Vasilii Zhukovsky, Konstantin Batiushkov, and Dmitrii Dashkov, later to be joined by the young Aleksandr Pushkin. They ridiculed Shishkov's ideas but chose Khvostov's poetry as their primary literary target.

In 1802 Khvostov's *Izbrannye pritchi iz luchshikh sochinitelei rossiiskimi stikhami* (Selected Parables from the Best Authors in Russian Verse) was published. The fable had always been considered one of the canonical genres of Russian classicism. Khvostov wrote a tract in verse about the theory of fable writing and addressed the subject in many of his unpublished letters. In full accordance with classicist ideas, Khvostov considered didacticism the most important element in a fable. He insisted on maintaining the fable's "unity of action," that is, that the author create a certain closed space within which the plot's brief action will develop and from which some sort of moral must arise. Khvostov followed a classicist conception of "verisimilitude" – understood not as the depiction of the world as it is but as reflecting the higher reality of an ideal abstract world especially arranged and purified so that the reader may best assimilate the author's ideas.

Starting from these propositions, Khvostov depicts his characters in whatever way he sees fit under the given circumstances of the fable. Thus a dove, having fallen into a snare, "razgryz zubami uzelki" (chewed the net with its teeth); a donkey, which needs to climb up a rowan tree, "krepko lapami za derevo khvataet, polzet" (firmly grabs the tree with its paws and crawls); a crow holds cheese in its lips; an elephant grows a hoof; a pike that is caught on a hook howls; and so on. Khvostov also changes the laws of perspective in the fables: from

far away, objects seem large; upon closer inspection, they get smaller. Objects in the fables may also transform from one thing into another: a little stone that has been tossed, having hit its target, becomes an arrow. A dog may be called a good person in order to show her responsiveness and kindheartedness, and a rabbit a *komolaia ptitsa* (hornless bird). However, all these absurdities form a system. Khvostov deliberately creates an unreal world in his fables, a world that answers his own artistic intentions and which bears some resemblance to the surrealist compositions of Salvador Dalí.

These timid protosurrealistic experiments were not appreciated by contemporaries, who perceived the fables as a manifestation of feeblemindedness and lack of writing skill. Thus the well-known critic and poet Aleksandr Izmailov wrote in one of his reviews: "Chego ne delaet vsemogushchaia poeziia? Prikosnetsia li magicheskim zhezlom svoim k Golubku, zaputavshemusia v seti – mgnovenno vyrastaiut u nego *zuby,* i on *razgryzaet imi uzelki* " (What can almighty poetry not accomplish? All it has to do is lightly touch its magic wand to a Pigeon that has blundered into a net and in an instant it grows *teeth* and can *chew its way through the net with them*). Only one of Khvostov's contemporaries – Nikolai Gnedich, the poet and translator of Homer's *Iliad* – although he derided Khvostov's verses along with everyone else, understood there was a certain system at work in the parables. He asserted that Khvostov had created a new world and populated it with his own creatures.

In 1802 Khvostov retired, moved to Moscow, and began to publish a journal, *Drug prosveshcheniia* (The Friend of Enlightenment, 1804–1806), together with Grigory Saltykov and Pavel Golenishchev-Kutuzov, two other supporters of Shishkov. The journal took an active part in literary debates. Khvostov contributed parodies, epigrams, and critical articles against the sentimentalists. Among his literary antagonists were Prince Petr Shalikov and the well-known poet and fabulist Ivan Dmitriev. In the heat of literary battle Khvostov's reputation as an ungifted graphomaniac was solidified, and afterward almost everything he wrote called forth a torrent of ridicule. People came to expect only stupidities and absurdities from him. After the journal ceased publishing, Khvostov returned to the civil service in Saint Petersburg and in 1807 became a senator.

In 1808 Khvostov published a translation of Nicolas Boileau-Despréaux's *L'art poétique* (1674). In spite of the similarity of their literary positions, the famous fabulist Ivan Krylov immediately penned an epigram about it:

> --Ты ль это Буало? . . . Какой смешной наряд!
> Тебя узнать нельзя: совсем переменился.
> --Молчи! Нарочно Я Графовым нарядился;
>   Сбираюсь в маскарад.

> ("Is that you Boileau? . . . What a funny getup!
> It is impossible to recognize you: you have changed
>   completely."
> "Shut up! I purposely dressed up like a count [that is,
>   like Khvostov];
>   I am going off to a masquerade.")

Khvostov's 1794 translation of Jean Racine's tragedy *Andromaque* (1667) was staged in 1810. The production was successful and continued for ten performances, but Khvostov's deriders did not spare him. Among the many epigrams was this one:

> Не все породисты собаки,
> Не всяк в отца боярский сын
> И переводчик «Андромахи»
> Еще далеко не Расин.

> (Not all dogs are purebred,
> Not every boyar's son is equal to his father,
> And the translator of "Andromaque"
> Is far from being Racine.)

Izmailov mocked Khvostov in his fable "Stikhotvorets i chert" (The Poet and the Devil, 1811), which enjoyed huge success. The poet of the title, lamenting the public's inattention, is forced to publish and purchase his books himself. He complains that he would be ready to sell his soul to the devil if only he would be willing to listen to his poems. The devil appears but can not bear the torture of the reading and cowardly takes flight.

In the same year the triumphant opening of the Kazan Cathedral took place in Saint Petersburg, and Khvostov wrote *Oda na osviashchenie Kazanskiia tserkvi 1811 goda, sentiabria 15 dnia* (Ode on the Consecration of the Kazan Church, 15 September 1811). Written in the best tradition of the Lomonosovian ode, the work compares favorably with some of the best poetry of the day, both in its aesthetic conception and poetic technique. Amid all the examples of Khvostoviana there appeared the seemingly lone instance of a more or less charitable epigram:

> Се храма нового неизреченно чудо!
> Хвостов стихи скропал--и, говорят, не худо.

> (The unspeakable wonder of this new cathedral!
> Khvostov scribbled some verses--and they say they are
> not bad).

In 1811 Shishkov and Gavriil Derzhavin founded an influential literary society, the Beseda liubitelei russkogo slova (Colloquy of Lovers of the Russian Word). Khvostov had been taking part in the informal gatherings of the literary archaists since his return to Saint Petersburg, and he became a full member of the new society. He joined its second division, where Derzhavin presided, and took an active part in Beseda's activities. He attended every meeting, participated in planning sessions, recited from his works, and regularly published in the society's journal. All of this activity made him an even more attractive target for his literary opponents.

In 1812 an event took place that was long remembered in the annals of Russian literary life. At a meeting of the well-known Vol'noe obshchestvo liubitelei slovesnosti, nauk i khudozhestv (Free Society of Lovers of Literature, Science, and Art), there was a proposal to elect Count Khvostov an honorary member. One member of the society, the young, brilliantly educated, and talented literary figure (later the minister of justice) Dashkov, declared himself against the nomination. When the majority voted for acceptance, Dashkov offered to read the welcoming speech, and his testimonial to Khvostov was an exercise in subtle mockery. Dashkov placed Khvostov higher than Pindar, Horace, Molière, Jean La Fontaine, and Racine and referred to him as "krasoi i chest'iu rossiiskogo Parnasa" (the beauty and honor of the Russian Parnassus) and "liubimstem Aonid i Feba" (the favorite of the Aonides and of Apollo). In conclusion, he proposed that at each subsequent meeting several exemplary pages from the count's works should be studied.

Khvostov reportedly did not show any offense. The next day he invited Dashkov to dinner, and though he felt awkward, Dashkov was obliged to accept. For the whole evening he was forced to sit and listen as Khvostov extolled his virtues. In parting, Khvostov told him, "Neuzheli vy dumaete, chto ia ne ponial vashei ironii? Konechno, vasha rech' byla ochen' zabavna, no nekhorosho, chto vy poshutili tak nad starikom, kororyi vam nichego durnogo ne sdelal. Vprochem, ia na vas ne serzhus', ostanemtes' znakomy po-prezhnemu" (Do you really think that I did not understand your irony? Of course, your speech was very amusing, but it is not proper to make fun of an old man who never did any harm to you. However, I am not angry with you; let us remain friends).

Despite the reconciliation, Dashkov was excluded from the society for his speech, but ironic praise became an increasingly common theme in the anti-Khvostov literature, and in literary polemics in general. At meetings of Arzamas, the pro-Karamzin literary society formed to do battle with Beseda, for example, its members (including Dashkov, Zhukovsky, Batiushkov, Viazemsky, and Pushkin) pronounced funereal eulogies over Beseda's "zhivye mertvetsy" (living dead) and recited parodies of the works of its members. Khvostov was a favorite target. Zhukovsky performed one eulogy in which the strange creatures of Khvostov's parables mourn their deceased author. Viazemsky wrote ten parodic fables in imitation of Khvostov, emphasizing the absurdity of Khvostov's works and their violation of everyday reality.

Meanwhile Khvostov's governmental career was progressing successfully. He continued to work in the senate, and as a man of unimpeachable integrity, he was chosen *sovestnyi sud'ia* (arbitration judge) for Saint Petersburg; his job was to try to resolve civil suits before they could reach regular governmental courts. In 1831 he was made a *deistvitel'nyi tainyi sovetnik* (full secret counselor), equal to the rank of lieutenant general, and took part in general sessions of the senate.

Khvostov was rich and was generous in helping others, especially writers. Many who received money from Khvostov were free with praise for his works, probably because they knew that the usually clearheaded and practical Khvostov was unable to resist such flattery. He became more convinced of his exceptional talent as a poet. As an epigraph to his works he naively chose one of his own lines: "Liubliu pisat' stikhi i otdvat' v pechat' " (I love to write poetry and have it published).

At his own expense Khvostov published three separate editions (comprising four, five, and seven volumes) of his "full works," *Polnoe sobranie stikhotvorenii,* between 1817 and 1834. When they did not sell, he had his agents buy and send them to acquaintances and state institutions – often at the same time as he was preparing further editions. Through such curious financial operations he managed to squander his large fortune. Pushkin joked, "[Za granitsei] pishut dlia deneg ... tam stikhami zhivut, a u nas Graf Khvostov prozhilsia na nikh" ([Abroad] they make a living from poetry, but among us Count Khvostov went broke because of it).

The aging Khvostov continued to write. Among his poems are many lines in which he speaks of his passion for writing with his former insistence, but also with effortless elegance:

Меня винят за поздний к Музе жар,

Все говорят писать стихи я стар;
Творец для дам сонетов, мадригалов,
Дитя сует и посетитель балов,
На ложе роз готовлюся заснуть
И парки нить, играя, протянуть.

(They accuse me of a belated passion for the Muse,
They say I am too old to write poetry;
Creator of sonnets and madrigals for ladies,
Child of vanity and frequenter of balls,
I am ready to fall asleep on a bed of roses
And playfully extend the thread of the Parcae [that is,
    of fate].)

No one, however, wanted to read Khvostov's poetry, whether good or bad. Khvostov's reputation had separated itself from the poet's actual person and works and become a sort of literary mask, even during his lifetime. Each of his published works was met with derision.

On 7 November 1824 a terrible flood occurred in Saint Petersburg. The event inspired Khvostov to write "Poslanie k NN o navodvnii Petropolia byvshem 1824 goda 7 noiabr'a" (Epistle to NN on the Flood of Petersburg on 7 November 1824), which was published in 1825. Almost immediately, Izmailov, who seems to have had a special file of material on Khvostov, composed a derisive epigram titled "Khvostoviad":

Господь послал на Питер воду,
А граф тотчас скропал и оду.
Пословица недаром говорит:
«Беда беду родит.»

(The Lord sent water onto Petersburg,
And the count immediately scribbled an ode.
Not for nothing runs the proverb:
"Sorrow begets sorrow.")

When Pushkin wrote his masterpiece *Mednyi vsadnik* (The Bronze Horseman, 1833), in which he described the flood, he made fun of Khvostov's "Poslanie," and of Khvostov himself, by praising him, just as Dashkov had done:

Граф Хвостов,
Поэт любимый небесами,
Уж пел бессмертными стихами
Несчастье Невских берегов.

(Count Khvostov
Poet beloved of the heavens,
Has already sung in immortal verses
The misfortune of the Neva's shores.)

In love with poetry, Khvostov collected and carefully preserved materials on the history of Russian literature in his vast archive. He even began to compile a dictionary of Russian writers, but the work unfortunately was never finished and remains unpublished.

Karamzin, writing in 1824, was one of the few to appreciate Khvostov's altruistic devotion to art and the uniqueness of this strange and idiosyncratic figure. He wrote, "Ia smotriu s umileniem na grafa Khvostova ... za ego postoiannuiu liubov' k stikhotvorstvu ... Eto redko i potomu dragotsenno v moikh glazukh ... on deistvuet chem-to razitel'nym na moiu dushu, chem-to teplym i zhivym. Uvizhu, uslyshu, chto graf eshche pishet stikhi, i govoriu sebe s priiatnym chuestvom: 'Vot liubov' dostoinaia talanta! On zasluzhivmet imet' ego, esli ne imeet' " (I look with tender admiration on Count Khvostov, for his steadfast love for poetry.... This is a rare thing, and hence precious in my eyes.... He touches my soul with something striking, something warm and alive. When I see or hear that the count is still writing poetry, I say to myself with an agreeable feeling. 'There is a love worthy of talent! He deserves to have it, if he does not).

Khvostov died in Saint Petersburg on 22 October 1835 at the age of seventy-eight. He had one son.

References:

Mark G. Altshuller, "D. I. Khvostov," in *Khvostov, Poety 1790–1810 godov,* edited by Altshuller, Biblioteka poeta, bol'shaia seriia (Leningrad: Sovetskii pisatel', 1960), pp. 424–426;

Altshuller, "Neizvestnyi epizod zhurnal'noi polemiki nachala XIX veka (*Drug prosveshcheniia i Moskovskii zritel'*)," *XVIII vek,* 10 (1975): 98–106;

Altshuller, *Predtechi slavianofil'stva v russkoi literature: Obshchestvo "Beseda liubitelei russkogo slova"* (Ann Arbor, Mich.: Ardis, 1984), pp. 177–209;

E. Kurganov and N. Okhotina, eds., *Russkii literaturnyi anekdot kontsa XVIII–nachala XIX veka* (Moscow: Khudozhestvennaia literatura, 1990), pp. 142–157;

P. O. Morozov, "Graf D. I. Khvostov," *Russkaia starina,* 6–8 (1892);

N. S. Tikhonravov, "D. V. Dashkov i graf D. I. Khvostov v Obshchestve liubitelei slovesnosti, nauk i khudozhestv v 18182 god," *Russkaia starina,* 43 (1884): 105–113;

Vadim E. Vatsuro, "I. I. Dmitriev v literaturnykh polemikakh nachala XIX veka," *XVIII vek,* 16 (1989): 139–179;

Aleksandr V. Zapadov, "D. I. Khvostov i ego *Zapiski,*" in *Literaturnyi arkhiv,* volume 1 (Moscow & Leningrad: Akademiia nauk, 1938), pp. 359–364.

Papers:

Dmitrii Ivanovich Khvostov's archive has been preserved in the Institute of Russian Literature (Pushkin House) in Saint Petersburg (Manuscript Division, fond 3222).

Iakov Borisovich Kniazhnin
(3 October 1740 – 14 January 1791)

Elena Dmitrievna Kukushkina
Institute of Russian Literature (Pushkin House), Saint Petersburg

BOOKS: *Oda eia imperatorskomu velichestvu vsemilostiveishei gosudaryne imperatritse Ekaterine Alekseevne i samodershitse vserossiiskoi* (Saint Petersburg: Kadetskii korpus, 1764);

Oda na torzhestvennoe brakosochetanie ikh imperatorskikh vysochestv velikogo kniazia Pavla Petrovicha i gosudaryni velikiia kniagini Natalii Alekseevny 1773 goda, sentiabria 29 dnia (Saint Petersburg: Artilleriiskii inzhenernyi shliakhetnyi kadetskii korpus, [1773]);

Neschastie ot karety, komicheskaia opera v dvukh deistviiakh (Saint Petersburg: Akademiia nauk, 1779); translated by J. Eyre as "The Ill-Fated Coach," *Slavonic Review*, 22, no. 58 (1944): 125–137; translated by Harold B. Segel as "Misfortune From a Coach," in his *The Literature of Eighteenth-Century Russia*, volume 2 (New York: Dutton, 1967), pp. 374–393;

Rosslav, tragediia v stikhakh, v piati deistviiakh (Saint Petersburg: Akademiia nauk, 1784);

Khvastun, komediia v stikhakh (Saint Petersburg: B. L. Gek, 1786);

Rech'govorennaia gospodam kadetam Imp. Sukhoputnogo shliakhetnogo kadetskogo korpusa v prisutstvii gospodina glavnogo nachal'nika, ego siiatel'stva grafa Angal'ta, shtab- i ober-ofitserov ([Saint Petersburg, 1787]);

Sobranie sochinenii, 4 volumes ([Saint Petersburg]: Gornoe uchilishche, 1787);

Komicheskaia opera Zbiten'shchik. V trekh deistviiakh (Moscow: F. Gippius, 1788); republished as *Sbiten'shchik komicheskaia opera v trekh destviiakh* (Saint Petersburg: Shnor, 1790);

Troe lenivykh, opera v odnom deistvii, sochinennaia na rossiiskom iazyke (Moscow: A. Svetushkin, 1789);

Vladisan, tragediia v piati deistviiakh, s khorami (Moscow: Senate, 1789);

Chudaki komediia v stikhakh, v piati deistviiakh (Saint Petersburg: Akademiia nauk, 1793);

Vadim Novgorodskii tragediia v stikhakh, v piati deistviiakh (Saint Petersburg: Akademiia nauk, 1793); translated by Richard Fortune as

Iakov Borisovich Kniazhnin

"Vadim of Novgorod," *Russian Literature Triquarterly*, 20 (1987): 59–106;

Traur, ili Uteshennaia vdova, v stikhakh. Komediia v dvukh deistviiakh (Saint Petersburg, 1794);

Skupoi, opera komicheskaia v odnom deistvii ([Moscow, 1801]);

Mysli nekotoroi gospozhi, dannyia avtoru k izobrazheniiu togo, kakim obrazom chelovek v prostom poniatii razumeet boga ([Saint Petersburg,] n.d.);

Neudachnyi primiritel', ili Bez obedu domoi poedu (N.p., n.d.).

Editions: *Sobranie sochinenii*, 5 volumes (Moscow: A. Reshetnikov, 1802);

Sochineniia, 5 volumes (Saint Petersburg: I. Glazunov, 1817–1818);

Sochineniia, 2 volumes (Saint Petersburg: A. Smirdin, 1847–1848);

Izbrannye proizvedeniia, edited by L. I. Kulakova, Biblioteka poeta, bol'shaia seria (Leningrad: Sovetskii pisatel', 1961);

Izbrannoe (Moscow: Pravda, 1991).

TRANSLATIONS: Vincenzo Maria Coronelli, *Zapiski istoriogeograficheskie o Morei, pokorennoi oruzhiem venetsianskim, o tsarstve negropontskom i o prochikh bliz lezhashchikh mestakh . . .* (Saint Petersburg: Akademiia nauk, 1769);

Charles Augustin de Ferriol d'Argental, *Nechastnye liubovniki, ili Istinnye prikliucheniia grafa Kominzha napolnennyia sobytii ves'ma zhalostnykh, i nezhnyia serdtsa chrezvychaino trogaiushchikh* (Saint Petersburg: Sukhpoutnyi kadestskii korpus, 1771);

Carlo Goldoni, *Domashnie nesoglasiia. Zabavnoe zrelishche v piati deistviiakh. Perevod iz Goldonieva featra s nebol'shimi po nashim obychaem otmenami* (Saint Petersburg: [Akademiia nauk], 1773);

Goldoni, *Lzhets, zabavnoe zrelishche. Vol'nyi perevod iz Goldoniia* (Saint Petersburg: Akademiia nauk, 1774);

Pierre Corneille, *Sid tragediia* (Saint Petersburg: Akademiia nauk, 1775);

Corneille, *Smert' Pompeeva, tragediia* (Saint Petersburg: Akademiia nauk, 1775);

Corneille, *Tsinna, ili Avgustovo miloserdie, tragediia* (Saint Petersburg: Akademiia nauk, 1775);

Voltaire, *Genriiada, geroicheskaia poema v desiati pesnaikh . . . perelozhennoe rossiiskimi belymi stikhami* (Saint Petersburg: Akademiia nauk, 1777);

Giambattista Marino, *Izbienie mladentsev, poema v chetyrekh pesniakh* (Moscow: Universitetskaia tipografiia, 1779);

Corneille, *Rodoguna tragediia* (Moscow: Kompaniia tipograficheskaia, 1788).

OTHER: *Izvestii Imperatorskogo Vospitatel'nogo doma, k udovol'stviiu obshchestva sluzhashchiia,* 1 (1779), 2–6 (1780, 1781, 1784–1787), edited by Kniazhnin.

Iakov Borisovich Kniazhnin was a leading representative of Russian classicism and one of the most significant Russian dramatists of the second half of the eighteenth century. His tragedies, comedies, and comic operas were highly regarded by his contemporaries and noticeably influenced both Russian literature and the social opinions of his time.

Kniazhnin's comedies and comic operas addressed burning issues of the day and furthered the development of these genres as well as Russian literature as a whole. While his works were successful with the public, they earned Kniazhnin the reputation of being derivative. During his life Kniazhnin tasted both glory and grievous hardship, and the circumstances surrounding his death remain a mystery.

Iakov Borisovich Kniazhnin was born in the ancient Russian city of Pskov on 3 October 1740 to a family of the old Russian nobility. He lived at home until the age of ten and received his initial education under the tutelage of his father. He was later sent to the gymnasium of the Saint Petersburg Academy of Sciences, where his studies were guided by Karl Friedrich Moderach, an adjunct at the academy. The young Kniazhnin received good preparation in mathematics, geography, and history and displayed great aptitude in the study of Italian, French, and German. He became enamored of the poetry of Albrecht von Haller and Salomon Gessner, did several translations, and even tried his hand at some original verses, which have not survived.

In 1755 Kniazhnin began civil service as a clerk in the department responsible for administering Russia's Baltic lands, and two years later he was accepted as a translator in the chancellery in charge of building houses and parks. He did not find this work satisfying, however, and in 1762 he transferred to military service. He began as a secretary to Fieldmarshal Count Kirill Razumovsky, who was also president of the Academy of Sciences, and in 1764, through the count's influence, was appointed secretary to the empress's general-adjutants on duty. The job was not much of a burden, and Kniazhnin was able to devote himself seriously to literary activities.

Kniazhnin made his debut as a dramatist in 1763, when his melodrama (a tragedy with music) *Orfei* (Orpheus) was produced, with music by G. Torelli (after 1791 replaced with music by Evstignei Fomin). The well-known actor Ivan Dmitrevsky played the role of Orpheus with great success, and the leading Russian tragic actress of the time, Tat'iana Troepol'skaia, performed the role of Euridice. Kniazhnin published an ode to Catherine in 1764, but the work is largely amateurish and unoriginal. However, his satirical poem "Boi stikhotvortsev" (The Battle of the Versifiers), written in 1765, shows that his literary views were already fully formed. Kniazhnin regarded the works of Mikhail Lomonosov and Aleksandr Sumarokov highly and in this satire sharply criticizes Ivan Elagin for his attacks on Sumarokov.

Kniazhnin's tragedy *Didona* (Dido, circa 1767) made him famous. The well-known episode from Virgil's *Aeneid* had long been a favorite among European dramatists, and, in fact, the plot of Kniazhnin's play resembled that of Jean-Jacques Lefranc, Marquis de Pompignan's *Didon* (1734). It was written in strict classical style, using the Russian equivalent of Alexandrine verse that Sumarokov had introduced. The play's action is based on the traditional struggle between feeling and duty, though Kniazhnin's work is set apart from other tragedies of its time by the greater depth of conflicting emotions experienced by its protagonists. *Didona* concludes with a striking scene: the hero Iarb, spurned by Dido, avenges himself by setting fire to Carthage, and Dido throws herself into the flames onstage. Such special effects were beginning to make their appearance in opera and ballet but were novelties in tragedy at that time.

Kniazhnin read *Didona* to his circle of friends, and eventually word of the play reached the empress, to whom it was dedicated. After reading the tragedy, she praised it and gave permission for it to be produced. Reports disagree as to whether the first staging of *Didona* occurred in 1767 or 1769. Soon after the tragedy's premiere it was staged in the court theater in Catherine's presence and was a success. According to legend, someone from the court, wishing to compliment Kniazhnin, called him the Russian Racine, to which the young dramatist answered: "Radi Boga, molchite, ne to kto-nibud' uslyshit vashi slova i vpred' ni v chem ne stanet vam verit'!" (Be silent, for the love of God, or someone might hear you and never trust you again!).

According to another anecdote, after the play's success, Kniazhnin traveled to Moscow to present the greatest dramatic authority of the day, Sumarokov, with the manuscript of *Didona*. Sumarokov's approval confirmed Kniazhnin's intention to devote himself to literature. It was reportedly on this occasion that Kniazhnin made the acquaintance of Sumarokov's daughter Ekaterina, who subsequently became his wife. Further legends accrue to Ekaterina Aleksandrovna Kniazhnina (née Sumarokova, 1746–1797), for example, that she was one of Russia's first female poets — on the basis of some verses printed in 1759 in Sumarokov's journal *Trudoliubivaiu pchela* (The Industrious Bee) that were probably by her father. Be that as it may, the union of Kniazhnin and Sumarokova seemed entirely appropriate in literary circles. A brilliant future seemed to open up before the young dramatist.

However, life in high society held dangerous temptations. Kniazhnin played cards and gambled away more than five thousand rubles of public money. Although he was ready to pay back more than two thousand rubles, and a lieutenant of the cavalry guard regiment, G. F. Shilovsky, was prepared to put up the remaining sum on his behalf, in 1773 a court ordered Kniazhnin stripped of his noble title and his rank of captain and sentenced him to death by hanging and at the same time ordered that his estate be confiscated. Kniazhnin, in irons, awaited execution.

Thanks to the intercession of Count Razumovsky, who appealed to Catherine for a pardon, Kniazhnin was released from prison. He was made a private in the Saint Petersburg garrison and then deprived of his rank in the civil service as well. Some modern scholars suggest that the unusually harsh sentence given to Kniazhnin was a result of the role he may have played in the struggle for power between Catherine and the sympathizers of her son, or that it was a reaction to Kniazhnin's new tragedy *Ol'ga* (1772), a free adaptation of Voltaire's *Mérope* (1743). The heroine Ol'ga's speech about her renunciation of the throne on behalf of her son might have been taken as a reference to Catherine's refusal to relinquish the throne to her son and heir, the Grand Duke Pavel Petrovich, who had recently come of age.

For four years Kniazhnin earned a living and supported his wife and two sons by translations and home tutoring. He became a teacher in the home of Prince Aleksandr Khovansky, whose son, Grigorii Aleksandrovich, later a sentimentalist poet, retained a deep respect for Kniazhnin his entire life. During these years of disgrace Kniazhnin translated Corneille's tragedies *Rodogune* (1644), *Le Cid* (1637), *La mort de Pompée* (1642), and *Cinna* (1640); did a loose translation of Carlo Goldoni's comedies *Il Bugiardo* (The Liar, 1753) and *I Puntigli Domestici* (Domestic Squabbles, circa 1755); translated Voltaire's epic poem *La Henriade* (1723) in free verse; and completed a prose translation of Giambattista Marino's poem *La strage degli Innocenti* (The Massacre of the Innocents, 1632). Kniazhnin's translations of *Le Cid, La mort de Pompée,* and *Cinna* were to have comprised the first part of an unrealized publication of Corneille's complete tragedic works. Six hundred copies of these translations were printed in October 1775, although they were not bound as a volume as was originally intended and went on sale separately in 1779.

In 1777 Kniazhnin regained his captain's rank and at his own request started his civil service career over again, beginning as a translator in the chancellery in charge of building houses and parks where he once worked. In 1778 he accepted the chancellery head Ivan Betsky's invitation to become his secretary, and he served in this capacity to the end of his life. A prominent and high-ranking official, Betsky was not only the head of the chancellery but also directed various institutions of higher learning: the Academy of Arts, the Vospitatel'nyi Dom (Foundling Home) for orphans and abandoned children, the Smol'ny Monastery School for Noblewomen, and the Cadet Corps, where children of the nobility prepared for military service and children of lower orders studied to become teachers. Kniazhnin became Betsky's indispensable assistant. Beginning in 1779 Kniazhnin edited the journal *Izvestii Imperatorskogo Vospitatel'nogo doma* (News of the Imperial Foundling Home), and he was assigned to deliver reports concerning the problems of child development at celebratory gatherings at the Academy of Arts in 1779 and the Cadet Corps in 1789. He also taught Russian literature at the Cadet Corps. In his memoirs one of Kniazhnin's pupils, the writer Sergei Glinka, recalled his teacher as a good and broadly educated professor who was very perceptive to new trends in literature. Kniazhnin read Karamzin's *Pis'ma russkogo puteshestvennika* (Letters of a Russian Traveler, 1797–1801) aloud to his students while it was still in manuscript and passionately praised its author, who, he claimed, was in the process of creating "novyi, zhivoi, odushevlennyi slog" (a new, living, animated language). According to Glinka, Kniazhnin no longer placed any importance on luxury, did not boast of any of his literary successes, and was extremely attentive to those around him. On his way to work Kniazhnin was reported to have given away the money intended for his cab fare to a beggar or servant and had then been obliged to make his way on foot, despite inclement weather.

Kniazhnin's literary activity blossomed at the end of the 1770s and 1780s. Throughout this period his new dramatic works appeared onstage and in print; several had evidently been written during his period of disgrace. Kniazhnin's poetry also appeared in popular literary journals along with that of well-known authors such as Gavriil Derzhavin, Vasilii Kapnist, Ippolit Bogdanovich, and Apollon Maikov. In his lyric works Kniazhnin wrote about the superiority of a "blagorodnoe serdtse" (noble heart) that lives an everyday existence over those people who, succumbing to worldly vanity, revel in

Title page for Kniazhnin's final tragedy, which was declared subversive by Catherine II. She ordered all published copies to be confiscated and publicly burned, but a few copies survived.

flattery and riches. Motifs characteristic of "light poetry" appear in Kniazhnin's "Utro" (Morning), "Vecher" (Evening), and a few other poems, all of which Kniazhnin called "odes." Kniazhnin's satiric poetry and his fables are marked by the use of lively colloquial and vulgar language. Kniazhnin's skill in conveying conversation in verse unites his poetry with his dramatic works.

Kniazhnin was successful with his comic operas *Neschastie ot karety* (Misfortune from a Coach, 1779), *Skupoi* (The Miser, performed 1782; published 1801), and *Sbiten'shchik* (The Seller of Sbiten', performed 1783; published 1788). Popular in contemporary Europe, comic opera was new to Russia in the 1770s, and its success indicated the democratization of literature and the theater in Russia, as well as a greater interest in Russian folklore. Comic opera appealed to Russian audiences with its combination of comedy and music, its catchy lyrics, and its use of popular folk songs.

Neschastie ot karety was first produced with the music of Vasilii Pashkevich at the Hermitage Theater in the presence of Catherine II. In a letter to

Dmitrii Khvostov on 19 November 1779, Mikhail Murav'ev reported the play's great success: "We are all being amused here [in Saint Petersburg] by a Russian comic opera. . . . You cannot imagine with what universal pleasure the birth of this new type of production has been received."

The opera ridicules the ignorance of the Russian landed gentry, and in particular the manner in which they despise all things Russian and bow and scrape before the French. In the play a landowner wants to sell a peasant and use the profits to buy a new coach. However, after he discovers that the peasant knows a few words in French, he orders that his chains be removed and permits him to marry the girl he loves. The opera's action develops in a lively manner, without extraneous dialogue, and it never loses the audience's attention (something which characterizes all of Kniazhnin's plays).

In *Skupoi,* with music by Vasilii Pashkevich, Kniazhnin developed a scenic situation from Molière's *L'avare* (1668), in which a shrewd servant woman undertakes to outsmart the master with the help of a woman who passes herself off as an aristocrat. In Kniazhnin's version of the story, in order to get the hand of his beloved, who lives with her uncle Skriagin (whose name comes from the word for "miser" or "skinflint"), the young hero sends a servant woman to Skriagin in the guise of a countess who supposedly owns several villages "near China." The clever and seductive "countess" lures the heroine's money away from her uncle and gives it to the hero as the girl's dowry. The opera was regularly performed until the middle of the 1810s and was revived by the Moscow Chamber Music Theater in the late 1970s.

Kniazhnin's most popular comic opera, *Sbiten'shchik,* with music by Jean Bulant, a French composer living in Russia, was performed until the 1820s. The plot was adapted from Molière's *L'école des femmes* (School for Wives, 1662). However, Kniazhnin introduced new characters and scenes into the well-known comic script. *Sbiten'shchik* depicts the philosophy of life of the urban bourgeoisie and profiles the middle social strata. Stepan the sbiten'-seller (*sbiten'* is a hot, mulled honey drink) is reminiscent of the irrepressible Figaro from Beaumarchais's *Le Barbier de Séville* (The Barber of Seville, 1775), as well as the hero of the anonymous, seventeenth-century Russian picaresque novel *Povest' o Frole Skobeeve* (Tale of Frol Skobeev). The opera's Russian coloration is demonstrated in its first aria, which evokes the sounds of vendors at a market. In his memoirs the literary man Dmitrii Runich recalls

that everyone at the time knew "those marvellous couplets" from *Sbiten'shchik:*

Счастье строит все на свете,
Без него куда с умом?
Ездит счастие в карете,
А с умом идет пешком!

(Happiness [or: Good Fortune] arranges everything in life,
Where can you get with brainy talk?
Happiness rides in a carriage,
With brains alone you'll have to walk!)

Kniazhnin's comedy *Khvastun* (The Braggart, 1786) concerns the rapid rise to power of political opportunists. Although somewhat similar in plot to David Augustin de Brueys's *L'Important* (1693), the play's allusions to contemporary politics were apparent to Kniazhnin's contemporaries, who considered the play both funny and courageous. Verkholet, the protagonist of the comedy, is a nobody but poses as a grandee, bragging about his alleged intimacy with court circles. Everyone around immediately begins to flatter him and try to take advantage of his acquaintance, but at the end both the boaster and his luckless devotees are ruined. Notably, Nikolai Gogol was to use the same dramatic situation in his comedy *Revizor* (The Inspector General, 1836).

In his comedies and comedic operas, Kniazhnin abandoned the didacticism characteristic of drama of his time and placed greater importance on the dynamic development of plot. His characters' language was set apart by its expressiveness and lack of constraint, enriched by the playwright's use of clever and apt folk sayings, elements which helped guarantee the success of his plays. At the same time, because Kniazhnin culled the plots of many of his works from foreign sources, he acquired the reputation of a derivative writer, or in Pushkin's phrase, "pereimchivyi" (imitational). This reputation was solidified by Ivan Krylov's comedy *Prokazniki* (The Pranksters, 1788), in which Kniazhnin – in the guise of the egotistical writer Rifmokrad (Rhyme-Stealer) – and his family are mercilessly ridiculed. Scholars speculate about the cause of the conflict between the two writers, who had enjoyed a friendly relationship: when Krylov first came to Saint Petersburg he lived at Kniazhnin's home for a time. Vladimir V. Kallash suggests that Kniazhnin's comedy *Chudaki* (The Eccentrics, 1793) may have been an appropriation of one of Krylov's ideas. According to several witnesses, however, the enmity arose out of an insulting conversation between the sharp-tongued

Ekaterina Kniazhnina and the young Krylov. She allegedly made fun of the beginning writer, who in exchange for his translations of French and Italian operas had only been given free entrance to the orchestra of the theater, by calling him "cheap" and a "pisatel' za piat' rublei" (five-ruble writer). Supposedly, *Prokazniki* was Krylov's response. Sorely insulted by the play, Kniazhnin wrote an outraged letter to Dmitrevsky, who passed it on to Krylov; Krylov in turn answered Kniazhnin's letter with a note full of venomous wit. Ostensibly denying the resemblance of his comedy's heroes to Kniazhnin's friends and family, Krylov further underscored the similarities between them. It is not known if this letter reached its addressee, but it circulated in copies.

Such accusations aside, Kniazhnin composed at a time when borrowing the plots of European dramatic works and adapting them to Russian mores was an accepted procedure. Early examples of this practice date to the early 1760s in adaptations by Vladimir Lukin and Ivan Elagin. Other writers who transposed western European dramaturgy included Mikhail Popov, Ivan Dmitrevsky, and Sumarokov. In answer to continued criticism of his father's adaptations of foreign plots, Kniazhnin's son responded with an article about his father in Metropolitan Evgenii's *Slovar' svetskikh pisatelei, sootvechestvennikov i chuzhestrantsev, pisavshikh v Rossii* (Dictionary of Secular Writers, Native and Foreign, who wrote in Russia, 1845). He argues that his father wrote for the public rather than for critics, and hence was more concerned with producing good theater than with the status of the original works. The relationship of Kniazhnin's comedies to their European models has been analyzed in detail by Boris Neiman.

Kniazhnin's comedies may have occasionally provoked conflicting responses, but his authority as a tragedian was unquestionable. At the time of Kniazhnin's disgrace his tragedy *Didona* was not produced in public theaters. However, in 1778 the poet Mikhail Murav'ev wrote to his sister about its production in the D'iakov home theater and expressed his belief that Kniazhnin showed evidence of becoming a greater tragedian than Sumarokov.

Kniazhnin lived up to his friend's expectations and in 1784 presented his new tragedy *Rosslav*. In the letter of dedication to the president of the Russian Academy, Princess Dashkova, he pointed out what he considered the main feature of his new work: instead of depicting the passion of love, "which is the only thing represented in Russian theaters," he exhibited "the passion of great souls, and love for the fatherland." As the basis for *Rosslav*,

Kniazhnin chose an episode relating to the early sixteenth century, and Sweden's war for independence – indicative of contemporary curiosity in Russia about Scandinavia. Kniazhnin did not strive for historical accuracy but instead focused his attention on the leading character; he wanted Rosslav to be the embodiment of the ideal Russian, a person in whom all aspects of behavior are governed by love of the fatherland. Thus Rosslav is taken prisoner by the Swedish king yet does not betray his allies, and when a Russian prince wants to free him by releasing Swedish prisoners of war captured in Russia, Rosslav refuses to go along with the plan, since he values the interests of the fatherland over his own.

Rosslav premiered on 8 February 1784 and enjoyed outstanding success. The delighted audience refused to stop applauding and demanded the author take the stage. According to Glinka, the modest Kniazhnin hastily ran out of the theater. As the tumult continued, Dmitrevsky, who had performed the role of Rosslav, turned to the public and said that though the author was not in the theater, he would relay the audience's flattering respects to him. After the triumph of *Rosslav*, and despite Kniazhnin's reaction, it became standard practice in Russian theater to call the author to the stage after the performance as a mark of the production's success.

In 1785 Kniazhnin began to work on a commission for Catherine. She wished to see a dramatic portrayal of the Roman emperor Titus, traditionally considered to be an ideal monarch who cared exclusively about the good of his people. Kniazhnin took as the basis for his play Pietro Metastasio's opera *La Clemenza de Tito* (1734), and in three weeks the first Russian musical tragedy, *Titovo miloserdie* (The Clemency of Titus), was ready. The play differs appreciably from typical tragedies, as it includes music, a chorus, crowd scenes, and ballet. One of the characters formulates the idea of the tragedy in the words "Ne Tit zdes' tsarstvuet, zdes' tsarstvuet zakon" (It is not Titus who rules here, here rules the law). Although some scholars perceived veiled criticism of Catherine in the play, the empress was evidently pleased with it and rewarded Kniazhnin with a diamond-covered snuffbox.

One further result of the playwright's new favor was that Catherine agreed to the publication of Kniazhnin's collected works. Moreover, she ordered that they be published at her cost but that Kniazhnin keep the profits from the edition. His *Sobranie sochinenii* in four volumes appeared in print in 1787.

Kniazhnin's tragedies *Vladisan* (1789) and *Sofonisba* (both written around 1785) combined traits of classical tragedy with features new to Russian drama. The action of the musical tragedy *Vladisan* (with music by Jean Bulant) takes place in old Russia, but all of its characters are fictitious. The play opposes a good czar with a tyrant whose tyranny is perpetuated by flattering and self-interested courtiers. In *Sofonisba* Kniazhnin turned to a subject from Roman history already familiar in plays by Jean Mairet, Pierre Corneille, and Voltaire. For the first time a Russian drama did not indict a particular czar-tyrant but the monarchy as a whole.

Neither of these tragedies enjoyed much success. By the early 1790s significant changes had occurred in the Russian theater; the genre of tragedy was in crisis and being supplanted by other types of drama. For the most part, the language of the theater was drawing closer to natural conversational speech, and the long pompous monologues of traditional classical tragedy began to seem outdated. The well-known actor Aleksei Iakovlev, who made his debut in 1794, confessed that the role of Rosslav was not to his taste, consisting, in his view, mostly of bragging.

During this time Kniazhnin's last comedy, *Chudaki* (The Eccentrics, 1793), written between 1787 and 1791, was performed with great success. In it Kniazhnin utilized various situations and characters from Philippe Destouches's *L'homme singulier* (circa 1764) and from Carlo Goldoni's comedy *La Cameriera brilliante* (1757). The play's action takes place in the home of a wealthy nobleman who has arrived in Saint Petersburg in search of a bridegroom for his daughter, and its plot is built on the rivalry of prospective bridegrooms, who include a ruined aristocrat, a bribe-taking judge, a retired major, and a fashionable poet. Evidently some of these characters were meant as criticism of Krylov and his close circle of friends. The comedy satirizes courtly arrogance, voluntary toadying before the nobility, and "fashionable" (bad) upbringing. *Chudaki* was produced in the Tsarskosel'sky Lycee during the period when Pushkin studied there. The play remained in the Saint Petersburg and Moscow repertoires through the 1830s.

Despite the success of Kniazhnin's dramatic works, his finances remained strained. At the end of the 1780s Betsky began to lose his sight and became increasingly despotic. Service under him weighed heavily on Kniazhnin, and in a letter dated July 1789 Kniazhnin complained that he felt like Betsky's slave. A month earlier Kniazhnin had approached the Moscow Trustee Council with a request that he be compensated for his work for the

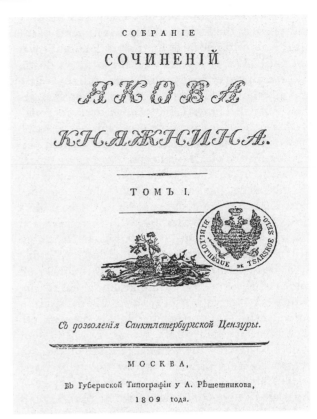

Title page for the first volume of Kniazhnin's collected works

Foundling Home, and the council agreed to award him 300 rubles. However, he was only given the pitiful sum of 150 rubles for his previous six years' work. Oppressed by need, he signed a promissory note for 175 rubles, and in September the possessor of the note demanded payment of the debt or a lien on Kniazhnin's salary. Persecuted by creditors, Kniazhnin had to pawn his household items and then buy them back with credit extended to him by the Saint Petersburg Trustee Council.

On 21 January 1790 Kniazhnin's friends staged a benefit for the writer at the Petrovsky Theater. Two of Kniazhnin's works were presented, his early tragedy *Vladimir i Iaropolk* (1772) and the comic opera *Neschastie ot karety*. The proceeds did not remedy his financial difficulties, however, and even after his death a year later creditors came to the Trustee Council demanding payment for Kniazhnin's loans.

In 1789 Kniazhnin brought his last tragedy, *Vadim Novgorodskii* (Vadim of Novgorod, 1793), to the theater. This play, fated to be the acme of Russian classicist dramaturgy, itself had a dramatic fate. While it was being prepared for performance and its leading roles were being rehearsed by the renowned actors Iakov Shusherin and Petr Plavil'shchikov, the French Revolution began. Anticipating unpleasantness over the antimonarchical sentiments of the play, Kniazhnin decided to halt production. It was not until 1793, two years after the author's death, that the play was finally published, both separately and in volume thirty-nine of the collection *Rossiiskii featr* (Russian Theater). The event caused a scandal. Catherine reprimanded the president of the Academy of Sciences, Dashkova, who had granted permission for the play's publication, and many others for assisting in the publication, including Kniazhnin's niece, his son Aleksandr, the bookseller Ivan Glazunov, and the guardian of Kniazhnin's children, P. Ia. Chikhachev, who had preserved Kniazhnin's unpublished manuscripts. In December 1793 the senate pronounced its decision, confirmed by a decree from Catherine, to burn publicly all copies of the tragedy, on the grounds that it contained "nekotorye slova, ne tol'ko soblazn podaiushchie k narusheniiu blagosostoianiia obshchestva" (certain words, which not only tempt people to destroy the welfare of Russian society) but which were directed "protiv zakonnoi vlasti tsarei" (against the lawful rule of czars). Copies of the tragedy were confiscated from bookstores, and texts of the play were torn from *Rossiiskii featr,* and all were burned on Aleksandr Square in Saint Petersburg, facing the Aleksandr Nevsky Monastery. A secret order was also issued by the senate and sent to all districts demanding that all copies of the tragedy be collected and returned to Saint Petersburg for incineration; this order was repeated in 1794 and 1798.

What was it in Kniazhnin's tragedy that seemed so dangerous to the throne? The plot was based on an actual uprising which took place at the end of the ninth century, led by the mayor (*posadnik*) of Novgorod, Vadim, against Prince Riurik. Catherine herself had already used this episode, based on Russian chronicles, in her play *Istoricheskoe predstavlenie iz zhizni Riurika* (Historical Scene from the Life of Riurik, 1786), in which Riurik was presented as an ideal monarch and Vadim as someone envious and ambitious. In Kniazhnin's play the conflict did not center on psychological issues or on abstract passions, as was traditional in Russian tragedy, but shifted to social and historical ones, which were embodied in the clash between an ideal monarch and an ideal republican. However, the play suggests that monarchies are always false and hypocritical and that they deceive the people because they fear them. Kniazhnin's tragedy also hinted at specific aspects of Catherine's rule, which to many observers had come to represent a tyranny that liked to pass itself off as enlightened and democratic. Printed soon after the execution of Louis XVI, Kniazhnin's tragedy seemed to be in sympathy with revolutionary events.

The extreme nature of actions taken against Kniazhnin's play gave rise to several accounts of the sudden death of its author on 14 January 1791. In the ambiguous words of Kniazhnin's son, his father had died following "zleishaia goriachka" (a most evil fever), resulting from "zhestochaishaia prostuda" (the cruelest of chills). Glinka felt that a crucial role in Kniazhnin's fate had been played by a manuscript of his entitled "Gore moemu otechestvu" (Woe to My Fatherland), which fell into unauthorized hands and was misinterpreted, perhaps intentionally. Glinka, whose version of events is unclear and contradictory, acknowledged that he had only read a few rough pages of this manuscript (which has not been preserved), but he stressed that Kniazhnin's main idea was that the French Revolution had given new direction to the century, and that in order to prevent a similar catastrophe in Russia it was necessary to make reforms. Glinka concluded that "Kniazhnin's patriotic thoughts seemed untimely," and that "he did not survive the experience." Notably, neither Kniazhnin's son nor Glinka even mention the tragedy *Vadim Novgorodskii.*

According to another version, because of the play Kniazhnin was imprisoned in the Peter-Paul Fortress and then flogged to death in the Secret Chancellery by the Saint Petersburg police chief Sheshkovsky. According to V. Selivanov's memoirs, based on the testimony of his father, who had studied under Kniazhnin at the Cadet Corps, the cadets firmly believed this account. The Decembrists, who took part in the uprising of December 1825 on Senate Square in Saint Petersburg, also accepted it as true. Mikhail Lunin, enumerating the victims of autocracy, included Kniazhnin, who "for the brave truths [voiced] in his tragedy was subjected to torture in the secret chancellery." The story was also included by the Decembrist Aleksandr Brigen in his historical works, and it was known to the young Pushkin, who noted that Kniazhnin "umer pod rozgami" (died under the rod).

In the 1810s and 1820s *Vadim Novgorodskii* circulated widely among educated Russian youth. A few volumes that had escaped incineration were copied by hand and circulated. The dramatization of ancient freedoms in Russia in *Vadim Novgorodskii* inspired the Decembrist poets, who dedicated many verses to ancient Russian liberty and the fate of ancient Novgorod.

Kniazhnin was buried in the Smolensk Orthodox Cemetery in Saint Petersburg. A simple stone, which subsequently disappeared, was reportedly erected on his grave and bore the following inscription:

Творенья Княжнина Россия не забудет.
Он был и нет его. Он есть и вечно будет.

(Russia will never forget Kniazhnin's works.
He was, and is no more. He is, and forever will be.)

The precise location of the grave is not known.

Letters:

"Dvenadtsat' let iz zhizni Ia. B. Kniazhnina (Po neizdannym pis'mam G. Gogeliu 1779–1790). Publikatsiia iz arkhiva pisatelia," in *Zapiski Otdela rukopisei (Gosudarstvennaia biblioteka im. Lenina),* volume 24 (Moscow, 1961), pp. 259–351.

Biography:

Liubov' I. Kulakova, *Ia. B. Kniazhnin* (Moscow & Leningrad: Iskusstvo, 1951).

References:

Pavel N. Berkov, *Istoriia russkoi komedii XVIII v.* (Leningrad: Nauka, 1977);

Viktor A. Bochkarev, *Russkaia istoricheskaia dramaturgiia poslednei treti XVIII veka* (Kuibyshev: Kuibishevskii gos. pedagogicheskii institut, 1985);

Aleksandr Brigen, *Pis'ma. Istoricheskie sochineniia* (Irkutsk: Vostochno-Sibirskoe knizhnoe izdatel'stvo, 1986), p. 450;

Vasilii Desnitsky, "Krylov i Kniazhnin (nachalo vzaimootnoshenii)," *Uchenye zapiski Leningradskogo gos. pedagogicheskogo instituta im. A. I. Gertsena,* 321 (1967): 40–57;

William Edgerton, "Ambivalence as the Key to Kniazhnin's Tragedy 'Vadim Novgorodskii,'" in *Russia and the World of the Eighteenth Century* (Columbus, Ohio: Slavica, 1988), pp. 306–315;

Sergei N. Glinka, *Zapiski* (Saint Petersburg, 1895);

Vladimir V. Kallash, "Primechaniia k komedii 'Prokazniki,'" in Ivan A. Krylov's *Sochineniia,* volume 1 (Saint Petersburg, 1901), p. 17;

Simon Karlinsky, *Russian Drama from Its Beginnings to the Age of Pushkin* (Berkeley: University of California Press, 1985), pp. 132–149;

A. Ia. Kniazhnin, "Kniazhnin, Iakov Borisovich," in Evgenii Bolkhovitnov's *Slovar' russkikh svetskikh pisatelei, sootechestvennikov i chuzhestrantsev, pisavshikh v Rossii* (Moscow: M. P. Pogodin, 1845);

Kniazhnin, "Kratkoe nachertanie zhizni Ia. B. Kniazhnina," in Ia. B. Kniazhnin's *Sobranie sochinenii,* volume 1 (Moscow, 1802);

Liubov I. Kulakova, "Boi stikhtvortsev. Neizdannaia poema Ia. B. Kniazhnina (Epizod iz istorii literatunoi polemiki 1765 goda s prilozheniem teksta poemy 'Boi stikhotvortsev,'" *Russkaia literatura i obshchestvenno-politicheskaia bor'ba XVII–XIX vekov, Uchenye zapiski Leningradskogo gos. pedagogicheskogo instituta im. A. I. Gertsena,* 414 (1971): 73–93;

Kulakova, "Zhizn' i tvorchestvo Ia. B. Kniazhnina," in Ia. B. Kniazhnin's *Izbrannye proizvedeniia,* Biblioteka Poeta, bol'shaia seria (Leningrad: Sovetskii pisatel', 1961), pp. 5–58;

Mikhail S. Lunin, *Sochineniia. Pis'ma. Dokumenty* (Irkutsk: Vostochno-Sibirskoe knizhnoe izdatel'stvo, 1988), p. 147;

Boris V. Neiman, "Komedii Ia. B. Kniazhnina," in *Problemy realizma v russkoi literature XVIII veka* (Moscow & Leningrad, 1940), pp. 121–182;

D. P. Runich, "Sto let tomu nazad. Iz zapisok D. P. Runina," *Russkaia starina,* 88, no. 11 (1896): 304;

Iurii V. Stennik, *Zhanr tragedii v russkoi literature* (Leningrad: Nauka, 1981);

Aleksandr P. Valagin, "Kto smeet umeret'," in Ia. B. Kniazhnin's *Izbrannoe* (Moscow: Pravda, 1991), pp. 5–26;

Iurii A. Veselovsky, "Ideinyi dramatyrg ekaterininskoi epokhi Kniazhnin i ego tragedii," in his *Literaturnye ocherki* (Moscow, 1900), pp. 349–379;

Stepan P. Zhikharev, *Zapiski sovremennina,* volume 2 (Leningrad: Iskusstvo, 1989).

Matvei Komarov

(circa 1730 – 1812)

David Gasperetti
University of Notre Dame

BOOKS: *Pis'mo ego siiatel'stvu kniaziu Alekseiu Vasil'evichu Khovanskomu. Pisannoe v Ruzskoi ego votchine v sele Bogorodskom, v kotorom neskol'ko familei imeli ubezhishcha ot byvshei v Moskve morovoi iazvy* (Moscow: Senate, 1771);

Obstoiatel'noe i vernoe opisanie dobrykh i zlykh del rossiiskogo moshennika, vora, razboinika i byvshego moskovskogo syshchika Van'ki Kaina, vsei ego zhizni i strannykh pokhozhdenii (Saint Petersburg: Senate, 1779); revised as *Obstoiatel'nye i vernye istorii dvukh moshennikov: pervogo rossiiskogo slavnogo vora, razboinika i byvshego moskovskogo syshchika Van'ki Kaina so vsemi ego syskami, rozyskami, sumozbrodnoiu svad'boiu, zabavnymi raznymi ego pesniami, i portretom ego. Vtorogo frantsuzskogo moshennika Kartusha i ego sotovarishchei* (Saint Petersburg: Senate, 1779); published as *Obstoiatel'naia i vernaia istoriia rossiiskogo moshennika slavnogo vora, razboinika i byvshego moskovskogo syshchika Van'ki Kaina so vsemi ego syskami, rozyskami, sumozbrodnoiu svad'boiu i raznymi zabavnymi ego pesniami; i ego sotovarishchei* (Saint Petersburg: Sytin, 1793);

Povest' o prikliuchenii aglinskogo milorda Georga i o brandeburgskoi markgrafine Friderike Luize (Saint Petersburg: Shnor, 1782); revised as *Povest' o prikliuchenii aglinskogo milorda Georga i o brandeburgskoi markgrafine Friderike Luize s prisovokupleniem k onoi istorii byvshego turetskogo viziria Martsimirisa i sardinskoi korolevny Terezii*, 3 volumes (Moscow: Ponomarev, 1785); revised as *Povest' o prikliuchenii aglinskogo milorda Georga i o brandeburgskoi markgrafine Friderike Luize; s prisovokupleniem k onoi istorii byvshego turetskogo viziria Martsimirisa i sardonskoi korolevny Terezii*, 3 volumes (Moscow: Reshetnikov, 1791);

Nevidimka. Istoriia o fetsskom koroleviche Aridese i o brate ego Polumedese s raznymi liubopytnymi povestiami (Moscow: Reshetnikov, 1789).

OTHER: *Opisanie trinattsati starinnykh svadeb, velikikh rossiiskikh kniazei i gosudarei, kakie vo vremia onykh po togdashnemu obyknoveniiu proiskhodili obriady. V tom zhe chisle nakhoditsia svad'ba kazanskogo plennogo tsaria Simeona, i samozvantsa Grishki Rostrigi*, edited by Komarov (Moscow: Ponomarev, 1785);

Starinnye pis'ma kitaiskogo imperatora k rossiiskomu gosudariu, pisannye ot nyneshnego vremeni s lishkom za 150 let, naideny mezhdu ostavshimi pis'mami posle pokoinogo grafa Nikity Moiseevicha Zotova, kotoryi, po izvestiiu vernykh rossiiskikh pisatelei, byl u gosudaria imp. Petra Velikogo uchitelem; a nyne izdany v pechat' byvshim u ego naslednikov sluzhitelem M. K., edited by Komarov (Moscow: Ponomarev, 1787);

Raznye pis'mennye materii, sobrannye dlia udovol'stviia liubopytnykh chitatelei, compiled by Komarov (Moscow: Reshetnikov, 1791).

With his three novels, two historical publications, and wide-ranging miscellany, Matvei Komarov became Russia's first best-selling literary figure. From the late 1770s through the October Revolution of 1917 his works were issued in more than thirty editions, a remarkable achievement for eighteenth-century Russian letters. Komarov did not consider himself an author, and it would be stretching facts to say that he "wrote" any of the works that were published under his name. Komarov can best be described as an editor, compiler, and adapter, whose real strength lay in transforming popular legends, adventure stories, and folktales into publishable works of literature. Taking advantage of the open form of the novel, he combined the disparate sources at his disposal to forge one of the first working idioms for Russian prose fiction. In the process he acquired a readership that probably has never been surpassed by any other Russian writer and helped to lay the foundation for the modern Russian literary aesthetic.

Komarov succeeded so well with the rapidly expanding reading public of Catherine the Great's reign because his work melded the two major artistic trends of eighteenth-century Russian society. On the one hand Komarov worked under the stigma of having the arbiters of literary taste dismiss the novel as a pernicious waste of time. As was the case with many other writers of prose fiction at the time, Komarov responded to the challenge by attempting to ground his work on the concepts of authority and logic. To this end he interpolated episodes based on classical themes into his adventure stories, helped readers make sense of references to distant cultures with the judicious use of footnotes, and, in his first novel, *Obstoiatel'noe i vernoe opisanie dobrykh i zlykh del rossiiskogo moshennika, vora, razboinika i byvshego moskovskogo syshchika Van'ki Kaina* (A True and Detailed Account of the Good and Evil Deeds of the Russian Scoundrel, Thief, Robber, and Former Moscow Police Spy, Van'ka Kain, 1779), employed a moralizing, supervising narrator to keep readers on track. On the other hand, as his humble origins and literary output suggest, Komarov was a man of the carnivalesque subculture: the real building blocks of his work are folklore, the satiric humor of the broadsides and popular fiction known in Russia as *lubok,* and a mocking sense of folk humor. With these inherently antiauthoritarian elements at the center of his pioneering work in the novel, Komarov seems to be undermining the conventions of official culture as often as he tries to appease them.

Virtually nothing is known of Komarov's life, especially the time that precedes and follows his literary activity. A biography has never been written, and whatever can be said about his life must be gleaned from the prefatory material in his publications. Tracing the genealogy of all the families mentioned in the dedications of Komarov's works, Viktor Shklovsky concludes that he was a *dvorovyi chelovek* (house serf) who gained his freedom only toward the end of his literary career. Whatever his social status, Komarov admitted that his educational background was modest. In the introduction to *Nevidimka* (1789) he confesses: "ia sam nakhodias' v chisle nizskogo sostoianiia liudei, i ne buduchi obuchen nikakim naukam krome odnoi russkoi gramote" (I myself am among those of low condition and am not learned in anything other than Russian letters). Komarov sheds little more light than this on his personal history, adding only that his education began with the reading of religious books and proceeded to secular works. Just which titles constitute the self-taught Komarov's educational canon remain a mystery. The erudition and cultural awareness found in his first publication, *Pis'mo ego siiatel'stvu kniaziu Alekseiu Vasil'evichu Khovanskomu* (A Letter to His Excellency Prince Aleksei Vasilevich Khovansky, 1771), suggest a work-

manlike literary competence, yet this does little to bring the sketchy outline of his educational background and personal life into sharper focus.

The letter is a short and simple treatise in verse on the value of reason. In 1771 Anna Loginovna Eikhler, Komarov's probable owner, visited the Volga estate of her son-in-law Aleksei Khovansky to escape the effects of a plague ravaging Moscow. Traveling with Eikhler, Komarov was impressed by Khovansky's enlightened attitude toward the containment of the plague and in homage to these efforts wrote his letter. It begins with a general assessment of human character: there are as many different types of people as there are individuals on earth, from geniuses who know all about life to denser folk who do not even understand themselves. Some people are such ignoramuses, Komarov continues, that they are no better than unthinking animals. When confronted by a calamity they do not understand, they simply dismiss it as the workings of fate or the hand of God. Komarov argues that such people are truly blind to one aspect of the real power of God, his gift of reason, with which humans may overcome difficulties. Owing to the blindness and carelessness of some, the plague has sent thousands to their graves. Khovansky, on the other hand, with his diligent and rational approach to the problem, has saved many people. Komarov ends by proudly proclaiming that he has written his letter in the hope that Khovansky's deeds will be remembered and praised long after his death.

The simplicity and unevenness of Komarov's letter shed a great deal of light on what would become the trademark of his career. On the one hand, Komarov reveals a knowledge and appreciation of the basic components of Enlightenment culture; on the other, he lacks the sophistication and skill to create a truly convincing work out of them. His discussion of human nature and reason fits in well with Enlightenment teachings on these subjects, but even with references to Copernicus and Aristotle it remains rather pedestrian. As would prove the case throughout his career, however, Komarov makes his most memorable statements with the aid of humor. For example, when attacking those who see the hand of fate in every calamity, he asks rhetorically whether, if he became dead drunk and then set off on the ocean in a small boat and drowned, fate would be the guilty party. In matters of style Komarov approximates yet never masters the norms of belles lettres. A high percentage of the lines constituting the letter are written in iambs, but, without any apparent reason or pattern, trochaic and even nonmetrical lines are scattered throughout the work. Lines of uneven length and repetitive rhymes give the impression of a mind that understands the rules of the game but either is not interested in it or not adept at playing it.

In his first novel, *Van'ka Kain,* Komarov adapted a popular, allegedly autobiographical account of his subject's life. Born Ivan Osipov in 1718, Kain was a serf who escaped from his master and joined a group of bandits. Eventually becoming their leader, Kain terrorized the countryside and turned into something of a folk hero. Later in his career he became a police informer and was given virtual carte blanche to pursue a life of crime. Using this protected position, he worked to put his criminal competition out of business and became the de facto police chief of Moscow. Order was restored only when troops were sent in to bring Kain to justice. He was eventually sentenced to life imprisonment, during which time he supposedly wrote the autobiography that served as the source of Komarov's novel.

Often called a documentary novel, Komarov's adaptation of the autobiography underscores his attempt to legitimize prose fiction. To make this tale more attractive to arbiters of literary taste, Komarov effaced the nonliterary, mostly oral features of the story and interjected a moralistic narrator into the work. Various reflections of dialectal speech and special jargon — including thieves' cant, the comic patter of the carnival known as *balagurstvo* (the language of the marketplace), and even chancellery language — were either eliminated from the narrative or translated into standard literary language, although these features were often retained in the dialogue, probably with the intention of distinguishing it from the narrator's more literary discourse. Moreover, the whole tale was turned into a third-person narration in which a moral consciousness or evaluative center was inscribed. With the addition of a moralizing narrator Komarov could deploy and interpret Kain's outlaw adventures for maximum effect. In fulfilling the intention announced in the first pages of the novel — to expose the wicked outcome of an improper upbringing among disreputable people — Komarov sought to establish the sense of authority and morality required of a work of legitimate literature.

Despite Komarov's attempts to sanitize the often bawdy legend of Van'ka Kain, his version of the tale retains a degree of the original's anti-authoritarian or carnivalesque orientation to literature. Both the dialogue and the narration include the satiric, jinglelike rhymes known as *pribautki* that often

took officialdom as their target. When describing Kain's riotous adventures, the narrator always concludes with a moral denunciation of his subject's behavior. Before he gets to this perfunctory condemnation, however, he seems to relish taking an inordinate amount of time describing the crafty, bizarre, and comic aspects of the given event. Moreover, Komarov selected a subject that could not help but become a vehicle for subversion of the status quo. Rising from the lowest ranks of society to become the unchallenged and officially sanctioned leader of the Moscow underworld, Kain is the perfect example of the temporary king of the carnival. Through his joking, thieving, and subterfuge he subverts the normal order of things until the lowly are made high and the high are turned into fools. The popular, carnivalesque elements of the novel are most likely the prime reason for the unprecedented success it enjoyed.

First published in 1779, *Van'ka Kain* succeeded to the point of meriting the rare feat of a second printing in the same year, this time with a translation of the story of the French brigand Cartouche appended. Republished an astounding five more times by the end of the century, Komarov's version of the notorious brigand's life can truly be called Russia's first best-selling novel. Shklovsky notes that since there was no such thing as copyright in late-eighteenth-century Russia, Komarov's tale was basically fair game for anyone who wanted to publish it, and the number of times his novel was reprinted was probably much greater than is generally recognized. *Van'ka Kain* continued to find a large reading public well into the nineteenth century. Aleksandr Pushkin owned a copy, and it drew the attention of such prominent critics as Vissarion Belinsky and Nikolai Dobroliubov. In general, critics have dismissed *Van'ka Kain* as a second-rate piece of popular fiction suitable only for the lowest type of literary taste. There is no doubt, however, that the work reached more readers than almost any other Russian novel, with a publication history spanning close to one hundred years.

Encouraged by the success of *Van'ka Kain,* Komarov soon issued a second novel, *Povest' o prikliuchenii aglinskogo milorda Georga i o brandeburgskoi markgrafine Friderike Luize* (The Story of the Adventures of the English Milord George and the Brandenburg Margravine Friderika Luiza, 1782). Like *Van'ka Kain, Milord George* was an adaptation of an already popular tale. Prior to Komarov's treatment of the subject, at least seven manuscript versions existed that could have served as the basis of the novel. Acting as an editor, or as Shklovsky calls him, a "historian-commentator," Komarov shaped the manuscript by expunging some of its blatant eroticism and adding an appendix to clarify the many references to classical antiquity in the work. As with *Van'ka Kain,* Komarov selected a source that was steeped in the folkloric tradition. This time, instead of focusing on a popular hero, he chose to adapt a work replete with reflections of *lubok,* Russian folktales, and incidents from *1001 Arabian Nights.*

The plot of *Milord George* revolves around the motif of continence as exemplified by two sets of would-be lovers, George and Luiza and Martsimiris and Theresa. The story opens as George loses his way in a fairy-tale forest only to find an enchanted castle, where he falls in love with the sorceress Friderika Luiza. Through the intercession of an evil spell George and Luiza are to be separated for six years before they may consummate their love. The story follows George as he remains loyal to Luiza despite the most exacting challenges. He is captured by pirates, thrown into a pit full of worms, and subjected to the constant advances of a Moorish queen who loves to parade naked before her English captive, but George remains faithful. His constancy is rewarded as he is finally reunited six years later with Luiza on board her ship. Just as they are about to retire to their quarters, however, Luiza decides that they must listen to the lengthy life story of the ship's captain, Martsimiris. As in the story that frames it, dense forests, magic spells, and an unconsummated love affair lie at the heart of Martsimiris's tale. An abduction by pirates, service in the army, and appointment to the rank of Turkish grand vizier serve as the prelude to Martsimiris's great disappointment in his courtship of Theresa. At first separated from each other, when the lovers are reunited, they labor under a strange curse which has Theresa always falling asleep in Martsimiris's presence and awakening when he departs.

The third and final part of the novel begins after the conclusion of Martsimiris's sad tale. George and Luiza are about to overcome six years of frustrated desire when they are shipwrecked and separated yet again, with George ending up in Cartagena, Spain. After various erotic encounters, including those in an interpolated tale that derives most likely from Giovanni Boccaccio's *Decameron* (1353), George makes his way to Venice during carnival time. Caught up in the intrigues of the event, he finally realizes that a French dauphine who shows a strong interest in him is actually Luiza in disguise. After Luiza recounts how Martsimiris and Theresa finally broke the power of the enchantment

that had separated them, George and Luiza retire to Brandenburg and a life of eternal bliss.

As with his first novel, Komarov shaped the story of *Milord George* to emphasize didactic aims. Thus he lingers on descriptions of classical statuary with the single-mindedness of an instructor giving a lesson and includes a brief dictionary of classical gods and goddesses for his less sophisticated readers. Moreover, from the beginning of the novel Komarov stresses the favorite Enlightenment theme of education. The almost superhuman fortitude George displays in resisting various attempts at seduction is no doubt the result of his upbringing, which had at its core the reading of didactic stories. George's education had been supervised with care and industry by his uncle, who had not even allowed him to receive a visitor unattended lest he be polluted by empty or improper thoughts. George's upbringing is also responsible for his insistence that his wife be possessed of a "velikii razum" (healthy mind). To drive home the cardinal importance of education in one's life, George is compared to his friend Meralii. Schooled only in the science of amour and overindulged by his parents, Meralii is cursed to move from one meaningless dalliance to the next without ever finding true happiness. Even when he is able to identify his own vices, they are so ingrained that he is powerless to do anything about them.

Despite the Enlightenment elements in *Milord George,* the entire work is ultimately dominated by the tone and substance that made the novel such an outlaw genre for classicists such as Mikhailo Lomonosov and Aleksandr Sumarokov. Adventure, exotic tales, and eroticism attracted readers rather than moral digressions. The plot of *Milord George* may be based on the title character's iron will and fierce loyalty to Luiza, but from beginning to end its raison d'être is to bring about the sexual union of its hero and heroine, and George's rejection of the women who would replace Luiza is even more provocative than his expected reunion with the Brandenburg margravine. Such is the incident in which the Moorish queen shamelessly surrenders herself to George and exposes her entire body, calling his attention to her marvelously shaped breasts: "posmotri, milord, ty konechno v Londone takikh priiatnykh i nezhnykh chlenov ne vidyval" (Look, Milord, you surely never saw such beautiful and tender shapes as these in London). Such episodes not only counterbalance the didacticism of the novel but to some degree actually satirize attempts to legitimize the genre.

First published in the early 1780s, *Milord George* was even more successful than *Van'ka Kain.*

By 1799 it had come out in a fifth edition, and even though no edition issued after Komarov's death in 1812 carried his name on the title page, they all stayed close in tone and substance to the original version of 1782. In reviewing what was at least the ninth edition of *Milord George* in 1839, Belinsky went so far as to call the novel immortal, and indeed it was virtually impossible to counter its popular appeal. By the late nineteenth century, *Milord George* had already gone through dozens of editions, and Leo Tolstoy observed that the people were far more interested in *Milord George* than in the belles lettres and philosophy that the leading lights of Russian culture would have them read. Komarov's tale of the English lord remained a best-seller in Russia until the newly established Bolshevik state did what the cajoling of previous generations of critics never could: it confiscated an edition of the work that was at press in 1918, thus ending its remarkable 136-year publication history.

A comparison of two historical works that Komarov edited in the mid 1780s, *Opisanie trinattsati starinnykh svadeb, velikikh rossiiskikh kniazei i gosudarei* . . . (A Description of Thirteen Ancient Weddings of Great Russian Princes and Sovereigns . . . , 1785) and *Starinnye pis'ma kitaiskogo imperatora k rossiiskomu gosudariu* . . . (Ancient Letters of the Chinese Emperor to the Russian Sovereign . . . , 1787), offers a rare clue about his personal life. In the former work Komarov refers to himself as a *rab* (slave), whereas in the dedication of the latter he uses the term *sluga* (servant). Shklovsky concludes from this that Komarov gained his freedom sometime in between the publication of these two historical pieces, probably as the result of the death of his owner. This supposition is confirmed by an announcement in the *Moskovskie vedomosti* (Moscow News) of 12 June 1787 offering both works for sale. In addition to the advertisement of the books, Komarov uses the announcement to make an appeal for employment. Presumably fending for himself, he seeks the position of personal secretary to a nobleman or important merchant. Komarov's life must not have been comfortable at this time, for he also offers a small dog for sale, suggesting his precarious financial situation.

Komarov's self-proclaimed purpose in publishing *Opisanie trinattsati starinnykh svadeb* and *Starinnye pis'ma kitaiskogo imperatora* was to be of service to the public. In the former work he portrays the wedding ceremonies of Russian rulers from Basil III (1479–1533) to Aleksei Mikhailovich (1629–1676). True to his penchant for adapting or simply publishing already available material, Komarov claims that he

has exactly reproduced the historical sources at his disposal, his only contribution being the addition of footnotes. In *Starinnye pis'ma kitaiskogo imperatora* Komarov publishes the texts of five letters and the description of a sixth written by a Chinese emperor to the Russian court. Although no addressee is named, Komarov believes the letters were sent either to Mikhail Fedorovich Romanov (1596–1645), the czar who established the first Russian consulate in China, or his successor, Aleksei Mikhailovich. Translated from Latin and Mongolian into an antiquated, bookish mix of Russian and Slavonic, the letters consist of a series of complaints against the activities of the Russian enclave in the settlement of Iach'ch' on the Chinese border.

Although neither historical work received a second printing, evidence suggests that they found receptive audiences. In his introductory address to readers in the second work Komarov thanks the public for their favorable acceptance of his book describing ancient royal weddings. Even though the subject matter of these two works might seem strange to the modern consciousness, in late-eighteenth-century Russia they satisfied a widespread demand for historical writing.

In comparison with Komarov's next book, *Nevidimka. Istoriia o fetsskom koroleviche Aridese i o brate ego Polumedese s raznymi liubopytnymi povestiami* (The Invisibility Cap: The History of the Fetsian Prince Arides and His Brother Polumedes with Various Curious Stories, 1789), works like *Van'ka Kain* and *Milord George* seem well organized and tightly plotted. The heroes of *Nevidimka* are the two aristocratic brothers, Arides and Polumedes. Separated when Polumedes is captured by pirates, they find fortune and happiness and are reunited by the end of the novel. In the intervening pages, however, as the title page announces, readers witness a wide array of "curious stories" told in the manner of such popular genres of the day as the folktale, Eastern tale, and picaresque novel.

Set in ancient times in the mythical Kingdom of Fets, *Nevidimka* begins with a folktalelike episode in which the imprisoned knight Arides meets a magical snake who transforms into a beautiful sorceress and gives Arides the *shapka-nevidimka,* a cap that has the power to make its wearer invisible. With this device Arides eludes his captors and is soon on his way to a series of adventures. Using his wits and awesome physical strength (recalling the exploits of the knights of Russia's oral epics, the *bogatyri*), and with a significant amount of magic thrown in for good measure, Arides restores usurped thrones and wins the hearts of the women he meets. When they are not fighting for their own lives and loves, the brothers often spend their time listening to the tales of other unfortunate vagabonds. In fact, the novel reaches a level of narrative imbedding four or five layers deep as characters frequently recite interpolated tales, which always depend on the stock formulas of wit and magic to reunite separated lovers or overthrow oppressive monarchs.

As with Komarov's previous novels, *Nevidimka* combines the incompatible elements of Enlightenment moralizing and the subculture's fondness for fantasy and adventure. Characters frequently speak of the need to have reason govern one's life, and the protagonists Arides and Polumedes are known for their advanced minds and spiritual virtues. In fact, Arides is such a learned man that he is appointed tutor to the son of the Fetsian king. Moreover, the entire novel is intertwined with the names of distant and exotic places. Adventures are set in Morocco, Constantinople, India, Persia, and Venice. While anchoring the story with identifiable landmarks and thus increasing the verisimilitude of the work, this device also fulfills the Enlightenment goal of being instructive. Nevertheless, the basic spirit of *Nevidimka* runs completely counter to an Enlightenment aesthetic. The emphasis of what Komarov called his string of "simple folktales" is clearly on entertaining readers with a quick-moving, ever-changing story line. It would be hard to believe that the proponents of Enlightenment had much use for three-headed monsters or magic tablecloths.

Although *Nevidimka* did not enjoy the phenomenal reception accorded *Van'ka Kain* and *Milord George,* it was nevertheless successful. It received only two printings, but few works of belles lettres in eighteenth-century Russia could make such a claim. Komarov's success with *Nevidimka,* as with his earlier works, came as the result of targeting a wide audience. With its unusually large print and heavy reliance on folklore (the magical cap of the title being the most outstanding example), *Nevidimka* was directed at the least sophisticated of readers. Komarov acknowledges this fact in the introduction when he claims that "pisal ia prostym russkim slogom, ne upotrebliaia nikakogo retoricheskogo krasnorechiia, chtob chteniem onoi vsiakogo zvaniia mogli liudi pol'zovat'sia" (I wrote [this work] in a simple Russian style, without any sort of rhetorical eloquence, so that people of any walk of life could read it).

In his last published work, *Raznye pis'mennye materii* (Various Written Things, 1791), Komarov limited himself to the role of compiler. Without trying to edit or adapt, he simply offered readers a collection of dozens of relatively well-known works, both verse and prose, literary and nonliterary. In this miscellany readers could find, among other genres: lyrics, sonnets, and odes; riddles, fables, and folktales; and epistles, epitaphs, and instructions. While Komarov admits in the dedication that he does not deserve the title of author, his choices for the compilation indicate a well-developed literary consciousness. Komarov culled the selections in this miscellany from over a dozen sources, including such essential journals of the early stages of modern Russian culture as *Ezhemesiachnye sochineniia* (Monthly Writings, 1755–1764), *Poleznoe uveselenie* (Useful Diversions, 1760–1762), *Truten'* (The Drone, 1769–1770), *Pustomelia* (The Twaddler, 1770), and *Ekonomicheskii magazin* (The Economic Magazine, 1780–1789). Komarov may not have created original works of literature, but *Raznye pis'mennye materii* reveals his active, sensitive, and appreciative intellect.

Komarov's avowed purpose in the dedication of *Raznye pis'mennye materii* was, again, to be of service to society. Quoting Sumarokov's quintessentially Enlightenment credo that to live without being useful is to live in vain, he offers this work "dlia udovol'stviia liubopytnykh chitatelei, a osoblivo dlia takikh, kotorye ne imeiut sposobu chitat' mnogie knigi" (for the pleasure of curious readers, especially those who do not have the ability to read many books). In keeping with this civic-minded intent, Komarov includes the triumphant ode "Na vziatie Ochakova" (On the Taking of [the Fortress at] Ochakov); eulogies to great Enlightenment figures such as Peter the Great, Catherine the Great, and Lomonosov; a short dictionary of commonly used words of foreign derivation; and various instructions encouraging honest living and service to the state. In this vein he even reprints his own *Pis'mo . . . kniaziu Alekseiu Vasil'evichu Khovanskomu.* Nor is the favorite Enlightenment tool of satire overlooked in the collection: the section of epitaphs includes humorous sketches of the doctor who did not know how to heal, yet who became a rich man; the clerk who could make the straight crooked, the crooked straight; and the miser who even in his grave charged a fee for reading his epitaph. Komarov also offers Denis Fonvizin's "Poslanie k slugam Shumilovu, Van'ke i Petrushke" (Epistle to My Servants Shumilov, Van'ka, and Petrushka, 1788), in which the author decries the falseness of society and the suffering it produces for so many.

Counterbalancing the serious and didactic elements of *Raznye pis'mennye materii* is a healthy dose of whimsy and humor. It is interesting to note how Komarov frequently juxtaposes a mocking work with a serious one, as when a traditional madrigal and elegy on the subject of unrequited love are preceded by a series of lighthearted epigrams. Typical of the latter is the epigram in which a wife, responding to her husband's question of how many times she has been unfaithful, replies that she is not schooled in mathematics. Later in the miscellany Komarov follows a weighty dictionary of foreign words with a section of home remedies for such problems as bedbugs and cockroaches and tips on how to preserve fruit. In the most direct confrontation of humor and high-mindedness he compares Nikolai Nikolev's ode "Na vziatie Ochakova" (On the Taking [of the Fortress at] Ochakov) to Nikolev's parodic "Russkie soldaty: gudoshnaia pesnia na sluchai vziatiia Ochakova" (Russian Soldiers: A Jester's Song on the Occasion of the Taking of Ochakov, 1789). Komarov's intention in grouping works this way or what impact the volume's arrangement had on readers can probably never be known. At the very least, he presented his audience with an eclectic collection of reading material that did not privilege didacticism and philosophy over humor, parody, or the mundane. The ironic juxtaposition of texts in his final work may well have been an attempt to poke fun at the inflated self-image of Enlightenment culture.

After the completion of the miscellany, which apparently found a rather large readership, Komarov disappeared from the literary scene. His motivations are unknown. Perhaps, as Shklovsky speculates, the ever-growing reading public that made Komarov so popular also provided him at last with financial security. If this was in fact the case, it would make him one of the first commercially successful writers in the annals of Russian literature.

Komarov described himself as an editor, compiler, and publisher. In assessing his importance in the development of Russian literature, the term *literary weather vane* could also be added to the list. Although Komarov's literary achievements were modest at best, his work acquires great historical significance for revealing many of the forces that combined to form the first Russian novels. *Van'ka Kain, Milord George,* and *Nevidimka* incorporate many of the devices and attitudes of official literature. Moralizing narrators, satire, a pedagogical approach to the dissemination of knowledge, and certain stock Enlightenment themes show an unmistakable at-

tempt to legitimize the genre. On the other hand, Komarov's novels are saturated with the anti-authoritarian spirit and devices of the subculture. Folklore, *lubok* buffoonery, and a carnivalesque resistance to the status quo are the real building blocks of these works and most likely the true reasons for their great popularity. In his fusion of "high" and "low" culture Komarov presages Pushkin's *Ruslan i Liudmila* (1820), Nikolai Gogol's reliance on the Ukrainian puppet theater, and Fyodor Dostoyevsky's relationship to the hack journalism of the 1840s. Komarov might be second-rate as an author and original thinker, but his works are valuable as they provide some of the first examples of the role of the subculture in the Russian tradition of novel writing.

References:

Nikolai Dobroliubov, "Zhizn' Van'ki Kaina, im samim rasskazannaia. (Novoe izdanie Grigoriia Knizhnika. SPb., 1859)," in his *Sobranie sochinenii v desiati tomakh,* volume 4 (Moscow: Khudozhestvennaia literatura, 1962), pp. 271–274;

David Gasperetti, "The Carnivalesque Spirit of the Eighteenth-Century Russian Novel," *Russian Review,* 52 (April 1993): 166–183;

Nikolai V. Guberti, *Materialy dlia russkoi bibliografii: Khronologicheskoe obozrenie redkikh i zamechatel'nykh knig XVIII stoletiia napechatannykh v Rossii grazhdanskim shriftom 1725–1800,* 3 volumes (Leipzig: Zentralantiquariat der Deutschen Demokratischen Republik, 1980);

E. Mechnikova, "Na zare russkogo romana," *Golos minuvshego,* no. 6 (1914): 5–40;

Gunter Schaarschmidt, "The Lubok Novels: Russia's Immortal Best Sellers," *Canadian Review of Comparative Literature,* 9 (September 1982): 424–436;

Viktor Shklovsky, *Matvei Komarov: zhitel' goroda Moskvy* (Leningrad: Priboi, 1929);

Jurij Striedter, *Der Schelmenroman in Russland* (Berlin: Harrassowitz, 1961), pp. 121–156;

Irwin R. Titunik, "Matvei Komarov's *Van'ka Kain* and 18th-Century Russian Prose Fiction," *Slavic and East European Review,* 18 (Winter 1974): 341–356.

Ermil Ivanovich Kostrov
(6 January 1755 - 9 December 1796)

Mark G. Altshuller
University of Pittsburgh

BOOKS: *Stikhi Sviateishemu pravitel'stvuiushchago sinoda kontory chlenu, Novospasskago stavropigal'nago monastyria vysokoprepodomneishemu gospodinu ottsu arkhimandritu Ioannu, kotorye v chaianii milostivago blagoprizreniia i otecheskago miloserdiia k neshchastnym liubiteliam nauk derzaet prinest' Viatskoi seminarii uchenik, voblovitskoi ekonomicheskoi krest'ianin Ermil Kostrov* ([Moscow]: Moskovskii universitet, 1773);

Ego siiatel'stvu grafu Grigoriiu Aleksandrovichu Potemkinu . . . svoe vseuserdneishee vozblagodarenie nizhaishe prinosit Moskovskaia slavenogrekolatinskaia akademiia, za okazanie k nei osoblivago blagovoleniia laskovym priniatiem i ugoshcheniem eia popechitelei ([Moscow]: Moskovskii universitet, 1775);

Epistola Sviateishego pravitel'stvuiushchago sinoda chlenu, ikh imp. vysochestv v zakone uchiteliu velikomu gospodinu preosviashenneishemu arkhiepiskopu Moskovskomu i Kaluzhskomu i Sviatotroitskiia Sergievy Iavry sviashchennoarkhimandritu Platonu, kotoruiu vo vremia polucheniia ego preosviashchenstvom dragotsenneishiia mitry i panagii, predstavitel'stvom e. s. grafe Grigoriia Aleksandrovicha Potemkina . . . ([Moscow]: Moskovskii universitet, 1775);

Stikhi Sviateishego pravitel'stvuiushchago sinoda chlenu preosviashchenneishemu Platonu, arkhiepiskopu Moskovskomu i Kaluzhskomu i Sviatotroitskiia Sergievy Iavry sviashchennoarkhimandritu, protektoru i polnomu direktoru Moskovskoi slaveno-greko-latinskoi akademii, v znak . . . vysokopochitaniia i glubochaishego userdiia . . . v novyi 1776 god ([Moscow]: Moskovskii universitet, 1776);

Oda na vozhdelennoe rozhdenie e. i. v. gosudaria velikago kniazia Aleksandra Pavlovicha . . . (Moscow, 1778);

Oda na vseradostnyi den' koronatsii e. i. v. Ekaterine II . . . 1778 goda ([Moscow]: Moskovskii universitet, [1778]);

Oda ego vysokoprevoskhoditel'stvo deistvitel'nomu tainomu sovetniku, eia imp. velichestva ober-kamergeru,

Ermil Ivanovich Kostrov

raznykh ordenov kavaleru, Imp. Moskovskago universiteta kuratoru Ivanu Ivanovichu Shuvalovu. Na pribytie ego vysokoprevoskhoditel'stva iz S. Peterburga v Moskvu ([Moscow: Novikov], 1779);

Oda na den' rozhdeniia ego prevoskhoditel'stva, deistvitel'nago statskago sovetnika, Imp. Moskovskago universiteta kuratora, Mikhaila Matveevicha Kheraskova . . . Oktiabria 25 dnia, 1779 goda (Moscow: [Novikov, 1779]);

Oda na den' rozhdeniia ego vysokoprevoskhoditel'stva deistvitel'nago tainago sovetnika, dvora eia imp.

189

velichestva ober-kamergera ober-kamergera, Imp. Moskovskago universiteta kuratora ... Ivana Ivanovicha Shuvalova ... Noiabria 1 dnia, 1779 goda (Moscow: [Novikov, 1779]);

Oda na vseradostnyi den' rozhdeniia ... imp. i samoderzhitsy vserossiiskiia Ekaterine II. Aprelia 21 dnia 1779 goda ([Moscow]: Moskovskii universitet, [1779]);

Oda na vseradostnyi den' vosshestvie na vserossiiskii prestol e. i. v. ... Ekaterine II ... 1779 goda, iiunia 28 dnia ([Moscow]: Novikov, 1779]);

Oda ego svetlosti, kniaziu Grigoriu Aleksandrovichu Potemkinu; podnesennaia iiunia 9 dnia, 1780 goda (Moscow: Novikov, [1780]);

Oda na vseradostnyi den' rozhdeniia ... imp. i samoderzhitsy vserossiiskiia Ekaterine II i na prazdnestvo sovershivsheisia pervoi cherverti stoletiia ot uchrezhdeniia Imp. Moskovskago universiteta ... Aprelia 21 dnia, 1780 goda (Moscow: Novikov, 1780);

Oda na vseradostnyi den' vosshestvie na vserossiiskii prestol e. i. v. ... Ekaterine II ... iiunia 28 dnia 1780 goda (Moscow: Novikov, 1780);

Stikhi ego siiatel'stvu, grafu fon Falkensteinu, vo vremia ego poseshcheniia Imp. Moskovskago universiteta ([Moscow]: Novikov, 1780);

Oda na vseradostnyi den' rozhdeniia ... imp. i samoderzhitsy vserossiiskiia Ekaterine II ... aprelia 21 dnia 1781 goda (Moscow: Novikov, [1781]);

Oda na vyzdorovlenie ego vysokoprevoskhoditel'stva dvora eia imp. velichestva ober-kamergera, deistvitel'nogo tainago sovetnika, Imp. Moskovskago universiteta kuratora i raznykh ordenov kavalera Ivanu Ivanovichu Shuvalovu (Moscow: Novikov, 1781);

Oda e. i. v. ... Ekaterine II na otkrytie gubernii v stolichnom grade Moskve ... Oktiabria 5 dnia, 1782 goda (Moscow: Novikov, [1782]);

Oda na vysokotorzhestvennyi den' vosshestvie na prestol e. i. v. ... Ekaterine II ... iiunia 28 dnia, 1782 goda (Moscow: Novikov, 1782);

Oda na vseradostnoe pribytie eia imp. velichestva v Moskvu 1785 goda, iiunia 3 dnia, ot Imp. Moskovskago universiteta eia velichestvu podnesennaia (Moscow: Novikov, 1785);

Pesn' blagodarstvennaia e. i. v. Ekaterine II ... za okazannyia Moskve otlichnyia shchedroty v bytnost' eia velichestva v sei stolitse, chitannaia v publichnom sobranii Imp. Moskovskago universiteta v vysokotorzhestvennyi den' vozshestviia na prestol eia imp. velichestva, iiunia 28 dnia, 1785 goda (Moscow: Novikov, 1785);

Epistola na vseradostnyi den' vozshestviia na prestol e. i. v. Ekateriny II. Iiunia 28, 1786 goda (Saint Petersburg: Shnor, 1786);

Oda na den' torzhestvennago otkrytiia Obshchestva liubitelei uchenosti pri Imp. Moskovskogo universiteta, iiulia 2 dnia, 1789 goda (Moscow: A. Svetushkin, 1789);

Epistola ego siiatel'stvu grafu Aleksandru Vasil'evichu Suvorovu Rymnikskomu (Saint Petersburg: [Bogdanovich], 1791);

Epistola ego siiatel'stvu grafu Aleksandru Vasil'evichu Suvorovu-Rymnikskomu na vziatie Izmaila (Moscow: V. Okorokov, 1791);

Stikhi na osviashchenie khrama v Imp. Moskovskago universiteta, podnesennye Sviateishego pravitel'stvuiushchago sinoda chlenu, velikomu gospodinu vysokopreosviashchenneishemu Platonu, mitropolitu Moskovskomu i Kaluzhskomu i Sviato-Troitskiia Sergievy Iavry sviashchenno-arkhimandritu, 1791 goda, aprelia 5 dnia (Moscow: V. Okorokov, 1791);

Stikhi na konchinu ego prevoskhoditel'stva, tainago sovetnika senatora Petra Vasil'evicha Khitrova, posledovavshuiu aprelia 17 dnia, 1793 goda (Moscow: V. Okorokov, 1793);

Epistola ego siiatel'stvu general-fel'dmarshalu, grafu Aleksandru Vasil'evichu Suvorovu-Rymnikskomu, na vziatie Varshavy (Moscow: Ridiger & Klaudii, 1795);

Stikhi na konchinu e. s. Fedora Grigor'evica Orlova, dvora eia imp. velichestva deistvitel'nago i raznykh ordenov kavalera. 1796 goda, maia 17 dnia (Moscow: Ridiger & Klaudii, [1796]);

Stikhi na vysokotorzhestvennyi den' vozshestviia na prestol e. i. v. Ekaterine II ... 1796 goda, iiunia 28. (Moscow: Ridiger & Klaudii, [1796]).

Editions: Polnoe sobranie sochinenii i perevodov v stikhakh, 2 volumes (Saint Petersburg, 1802);

Sochineniia (Saint Petersburg: A. Smirdin, 1849).

TRANSLATIONS: François Thomas Marie de Baculard d'Arnaud, Poema El'vir' ... i Zenotemis, prikliuchenie marsel'skoe sochinenie (Moscow: N. Novikov, 1779);

Lucius Apuleius, Prevrashchenie, ili Zolotoi osel, 2 volumes (Moscow: N. Novikov, 1780–1781);

Homer, Iliada (Saint Petersburg: Shnor, 1787); continued in "Gomerovoi Iliady pesn' 7 i 8," Vestnik Evropy, 58, no. 14 (1811): 81–126; no. 15 (1811): 172–192;

Ossian (James Macpherson), Gal'skie stikhotvoreniia, 2 volumes (Moscow: V. Okorokov, 1792).

Ermil Ivanovich Kostrov entered the history of Russian literature principally as the translator of Homer's *Iliad* and the poems of Ossian. The personality of the poet played no less of a role in his posthumous fame. A simple-hearted man, gentle, talented, and completely indifferent to money, Kostrov was received by his contemporaries and immediate descendants as the embodiment of the romantic, unsettled, solitary poet. Stories of his poverty, early death, and even his frequent drunkenness lent a romantic aura to his name.

Ermil Ivanovich Kostrov was born on 6 January 1755 in the village of Sineglinskoe in the Slobodsky district of Viatka province. His father, Ivan Vukolovich Kostrov, a sexton in the local church, was twenty-six years old when Ermil was born; his mother, Ekaterina Artem'evna, was twenty-four. The future poet was their third child. He had a six-year-old sister, Ul'iana, and a three-year-old brother, Ivan. Nothing is known of their fate. Sineglinskoe was a small village, consisting of six or seven farmsteads lost among the swamps and forests of the immense but sparsely inhabited Viatka province. The village was part of the Voblovitsky section of the Uspensky monastery and was virtually the poorest place in Russia.

Although he was a peasant, Ivan Vukolovich was literate. He was responsible for church records, in which his signature has been preserved. It is possible that he instilled a taste for reading and writing in his youngest son at an early age. In this manner, it is not impossible that the early childhood of the poet passed in more favorable circumstances than one might expect.

The children of the clergy had the right to study free at ecclesiastical schools, and in 1766 Ermil Kostrov was enrolled in the Viatka seminary. He studied there for seven years, and his certificate of completion states that he "enjoyed impressive success, the kind one can demand only from a diligent pupil." At about this time Kostrov's father died, resulting in a serious blow to his son's education. Ivan Kostrov had been "posted to the sextonage," that is, not born into the clergy. Possibly, the decree on his appointment had not been formulated according to proper bureaucratic channels, or perhaps after his death the family automatically reverted to its previous status. Whatever the case, in 1773 Kostrov was excluded from the seminary as the son of a peasant. For a gifted youth of eighteen, this was a cruel blow.

Kostrov, however, did not lose heart. He addressed a request, in verse, to his kinsman Archimandrite Ioann (Cherepanov), a member of the synod who also studied, and later taught, at the Viatka seminary. These are Kostrov's first known verses, printed by the press of Moscow University in 1773. In his address to the archimandrite, calling himself "an unfortunate lover of science," the author was forced to acknowledge his official social position: a Voblovitskian economic peasant (one of those peasants who came under state supervision when church lands were secularized). In not very accomplished verses, the concrete facts of the young man's expulsion from the educational institution are glimpsed behind conventional poetic formulas. He speaks of his passion for science and laments the sudden interruption of his studies. At the end the author asks his high-placed addressee to help him enter the highest ecclesiastical school – the Moscow Slavonic-Greek-Latin Academy, where Vasilii Trediakovsky and Mikhail Lomonosov had once studied. The request produced favorable results. Having received a passport and a certificate from the Viatka seminary, Kostrov traveled to Moscow and began "unofficially" to attend lectures at the academy in philosophy and theology.

Two years later, in September 1775, Kostrov submitted a petition to the synod requesting that he be excluded from the peasantry and permitted to complete his education at the Moscow Academy. The application was supported by Platon, the director of the academy and the archbishop of Moscow; he asserted that Kostrov was honest, had an aptitude for theology, and had exhibited "impressive successes" in his studies. Kostrov's request was approved by the synod on 1 March 1776. The gifted youth was allowed to continue his studies and was elevated to the clergy.

His studies in the academy, however, did not continue for long. Like many other capable students from the clergy (such as Trediakovsky, Semen Bobrov, the statesman Mikhail Speransky, and many others), Kostrov preferred a secular education. In or around 1777 he transferred to Moscow University, and in January 1778, at the university celebrations, he read an ode on the birth of the future emperor Alexander I, which was published under the signature "university student Ermil Kostrov."

At the university Kostrov studied Greek and Latin philology with the famous Hellenic scholar Prof. Christian F. Mattei. Kostrov's successes are apparent in *Zolotoi osel* (1780–1781), his translation of Apuleius's *The Golden Ass*. The number of notes and references to various ancient authors Kostrov provides reflects the uncommon erudition of the translator. His work was so successful that when his

Zolotoi osel was reprinted in 1870, a reviewer praised the publisher for issuing the book "without any alterations or amendments," in spite of the almost century-old translation, and he made note of the clarity, accuracy, and elegance of Kostrov's language. This translation was republished in 1911.

Kostrov quickly completed his studies and was awarded a bachelor's degree, and by 1779 he was signing his verses "Baccalaureate of Moscow University." He remained at the university in the capacity of poet in residence. In 1782 he received the rather insignificant rank (eleventh class) of provincial secretary, which he retained until the end of his life. This was, however, decidedly not the role Kostrov had imagined for himself. Kostrov told an acquaintance, an eleven-year-old boy, that "universitetskoe schast'e mne ne na ruku i stikhotvorets rozhden pet', a ne uchit' . . . ia ne sovetoval by nikomu khodit' po moei tropinke" (university fortunes have not been kind to me: a poet is born to sing, and not to teach . . . I would not advise anyone to follow my path).

Kostrov's unfulfilled ambition strengthened his taste for alcohol. Many anecdotes testify to this weakness. Aleksandr Pushkin reported in his *Table-Talk* (1835–1836) that Kostrov, when needed to compose verse for some celebration, was often located drunk in a tavern or at the home of a drinking companion. If Kostrov were invited to an official celebration or to some dignitary's house for dinner, his friends would try to dress him ahead of time a bit more respectably and followed his strange, staggering progress to his appointed destination. Another contemporary, Mikhail A. Dmitriev, has left a picturesque description of Kostrov: "not very tall, a tiny little head, somewhat snub-nosed, his hair smoothed back, bent at the knees, not too steady on his feet." Andrei Bolotov wrote that "Kostrov . . . surprised me by his ugly and repulsive figure and appearance, and I wondered at his nature, which, having befouled him on the one hand, had endowed him in exchange with wondrous gifts, and I even regretted that I had happened to know him personally, because without knowing him I would have imagined him in an incomparably better condition."

Kostrov was always poor, in spite of receiving a salary as official university poet (Pushkin names a very respectable sum — fifteen hundred rubles annually). However, he had no care for money and could not hold onto it, drinking up and squandering everything he had. There is a well-known anecdote about how Kostrov, sitting in a tavern with a large sum of money in his pocket, overheard the desperate tale of an officer who had been threatened with prosecution for the loss of state funds. Deeply moved, the poet gave the poor man all that he had. Kostrov, at least in the last years of his life, did not even have a permanent lodging, and he lived first with one of his patrons, then with another. Once, the poet Ivan Dmitriev came to call on Kostrov, then living in Shuvalov's magnificent home. Dmitriev found Kostrov in the maids' rooms, where the humble poet was kindheartedly helping the servant women sew together some rags. An opened edition of Homer in Greek was lying alongside the scraps of cloth.

In the 1770s and 1780s Kostrov wrote approximately twenty celebratory odes dedicated to the empress, the courtiers Grigorii Potemkin and Shuvalov, distinguished visitors to the university, and others. These odes regularly appeared in celebration of official holidays, a birth in the royal family, and so on. The majority of these works were written in accordance with the strictly formed literary canon of Russian classicism: they praise highly placed personages and their deeds; have a clear-cut, prescribed compositional form; and are written in ten-line stanzas of iambic tetrameter and a high-flown, archaic language. Occasional echoes of Homer, Ossian, and biblical poetry testify to Kostrov's attention to early romantic trends.

Without a doubt such routine verse writing was burdensome to the talented poet. When Gavriil Derzhavin's ode "Felitsa" appeared in 1783, Kostrov was one of the first to understand the significance of Derzhavin's artistic discoveries. In the same year and in the same journal, *Sobesednik liubitelei rossiiskogo slova* (Interlocutor of Lovers of the Russian Word), Kostrov published the verse "Pis'mo k tvortsu ody, sochinennoi v pokhvalu Felitse" (Letter to the Author of the Ode, Written in Praise of Felitsa), in which with irony and skepticism he speaks of the ode as a genre:

Наш слух почти оглох от громких лирных тонов,
И полно, кажется, за облаки летать,
Чтоб равновесия не соблюдя законов,
Летя с высот, и рук и ног не изломать . . .

(Our ear has almost gone deaf from the loud tones of
    the lyre,
And it seems enough of flying beyond the clouds,
So that, having disdained the laws of balance,
Flying from the heights, one will not break one's arms
    and legs . . .)

He also concedes the ode's fast-approaching demise:

Признаться, видно, что из моды
Уж вывелись парящи оды
Ты простотой умел себя средь нас вознесть.

(One must admit, that the soaring ode
Has obviously already fallen out of fashion
By simplicity you were able to exalt yourself.)

Despite these acknowledgments, Derzhavin's artistic achievements did not have any significant effect on Kostrov's poetry. He continued to write commissioned verse, mostly keeping within the boundaries prescribed by the poetics of classicism, although he occasionally abandoned the traditional metric and strophic patterns by composing in trochees, stanzas of varying length, and so on. In his last years he wrote several refined poems, such as "K babochke" (To a Butterfly) and "Kliatva" (The Oath). The latter was very widely known and was considered a model of the gallant-sentimental style.

However, Kostrov's artistic originality, his true talent, and his deep understanding of the essence of literary processes are demonstrated in his translations, the most important of which was his unfinished translation of Homer's *Iliad,* upon which he worked from 1780 to 1786. During this period friends and patrons invited Kostrov to live in Saint Petersburg, but he hesitated, fearful of leaving his university position without the permission of Shuvalov. This permission must have been granted, because in the beginning of 1786 Kostrov moved to Saint Petersburg and apparently settled in Shuvalov's own home. In the following year, 1787, the first six cantos of the *Iliad* were published by Shnor's press. Despite several attempts, at the end of the eighteenth century Russian literature still did not have a verse translation of Homer. Kostrov's forerunner in the effort to translate classical epic into Russian verse was the poet and favorite of Catherine II, Vasilii Petrov, whose translation of the first six cantos of Virgil's *Aeneid* was published in 1770. Petrov's work was meant to be a model of the epic poem in accordance with the rules of classicism.

Kostrov did not like Petrov's verses, however, and the translation of the *Aeneid* did not satisfy him aesthetically. Kostrov tried to renounce the classicist scheme for his translation of the *Iliad,* although not very successfully. First of all, his choice of meter was decisive. Like Petrov, Kostrov translated using Alexandrines (lines of six iambs, rhyming in couplets). This meter was in keeping with the norms for the heroic poem as fixed by French classicism. (Voltaire's *La Henriade* [1728] – translated

into Russian as *Genriada* [1778] – and Mikhail Kheraskov's *Rossiada* [1779] were both written in this meter.) Although the Russian hexameter – in Russian poetry the equivalent of the ancient hexameter – had already been created by Trediakovsky, Kostrov was not ready for such a bold experiment as its use for the translation of the *Iliad,* nor would his readers have been prepared for such a thing. Kostrov's use of Alexandrine verse doomed Homer's epic to serious distortion, imbuing it with the spirit not of antiquity but of classicism.

Nevertheless, Kostrov, having a command of ancient languages and superlatively educated in philology, well appreciated the originality and distinctiveness of the ancient author. In the famous argument between the "ancients" and the "moderns" he, without a doubt, was on the side of the ancients. He strived to convey the immediacy and almost wild simplicity of the original, not inhibiting himself with classicist demands of "good taste." In this sense the ancients anticipated the ideas of early romanticism, and Kostrov clearly perceived this connection.

Thus, reproducing in translation scenes of the daily life of the ancient Greeks, Kostrov dares to describe Achilles and Patroclus cooking meat in a pan and on a spit, even though from the point of view of the moderns such trivial details were impermissible in a heroic poem. Petrov had avoided the details of feasting in the *Aeneid* (for example, the spit, carcasses of meat, bones, cauldrons, and campfires in canto 1, lines 210–215). Kostrov, on the other hand, does not shy away from calling the kings in Homer *psami* (dogs), and Odysseus in his version threatens Thersites with *rozgi* (birch rods).

The use of Slavonicisms plays a special role not only as a sign of high style but also as an intentional archaicizing – outdated words in the translation become signs of antiquity. In all these innovations Kostrov approached romantic notions of art as the expression of national spirit. For him Homer was not so much the author of the model epic as he was the brilliant poet of ancient Greece. Kostrov strove, therefore, to convey in Russian the most important characteristics of Homer's poetics, including such compound epithets as *gromonosiashchii* (thunder-carrying), *beloramennaia* (white-shouldered), *lepookaia* (having beautiful eyes), and many others.

Kostrov's translation of the *Iliad* was praised by contemporaries, who conferred on Kostrov the title of "the Russian Homer." Kostrov worked on his translation from approximately 1780 to 1786, and the time of its publication could not have been more felicitous. Hellenism was in fashion, and interest in everything concerning Greece was great. At

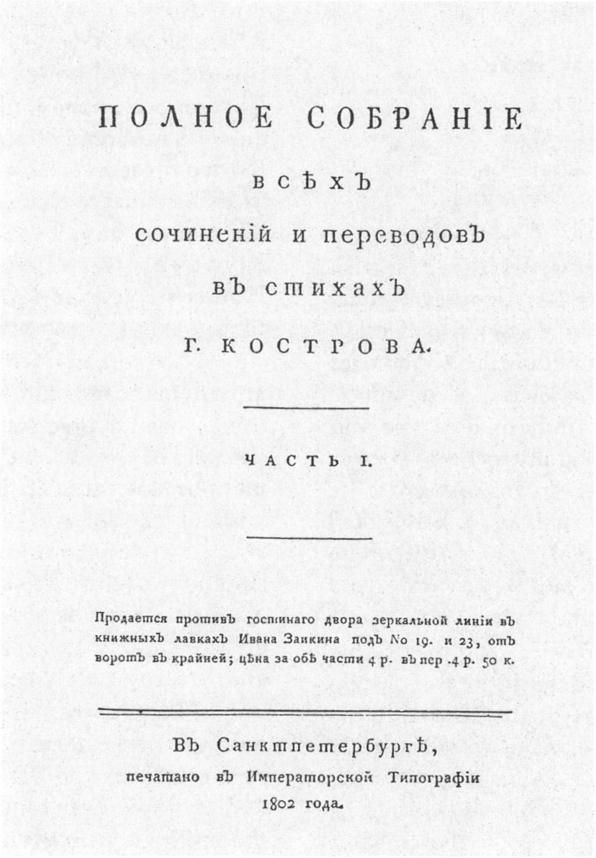

ПОЛНОЕ СОБРАНІЕ

в с ѣ х ъ

сочиненій и переводовъ

в ъ   с т и х а х ъ

Г. К О С Т Р О В А.

Ч А С Т Ь I.

Продается противъ гостинаго двора зеркальной линіи въ
книжныхъ лавкахъ Ивана Заикина подъ No 19. и 23, отъ
воротъ въ крайней; цѣна за обѣ части 4 р. въ пер .4 р. 50 к.

Въ Санктпетербургѣ,
печатано въ Императорской Типографіи
1802 года.

Title page for Kostrov's collected works

the time, preparations were being made for war with Turkey, and Catherine was entertaining the idea of creating an autonomous Greek state with its capital in Constantinople, headed by her grandson, Grand Prince Konstantin.

Kostrov's translation bore a verse dedication to Catherine the Great, in which the author compares Catherine to Homer's Minerva and predicts that the victory of Russian forces will bring freedom to the Greeks, Homer's descendants. Both the translation and the dedication earned the full approval of the empress. By her personal order, on 12 November 1787 Kostrov was awarded four hundred rubles for his translation. It may have been at this time that Catherine wanted to meet Kostrov, but the meeting never took place, because, according to legend, the poet gave all his money to a down-on-his-luck officer and "traded the palace for a tavern."

Having published the first six cantos, Kostrov prepared to publish six more. An announcement to readers at the end of the first printing suggests that Kostrov planned to issue four books (twenty-four cantos) in all. However, the second volume never

appeared, even though Kostrov continued to work on the *Iliad* for some time. In 1811, after Kostrov's death, the translations of the seventh, eighth, and part of the ninth cantos were discovered in the possession of a university employee, A. A. Artem'ev, and they were published in the journal *Vestnik Evropy* (European Herald). At the time Nikolai Gnedich was working on a continuation of Kostrov's translation and had already translated these cantos. Disheartened by the unexpected discovery, he quit the project, later beginning a new translation in hexameters. It was not until 1826 that Gnedich's work was finished and Russian literature finally received a standard translation of Homer.

The question arises as to why Kostrov gave up such a successful work. It is possible that he was dissatisfied with it, despite the translation's obvious and sensational success. The form chosen for the translation (Alexandrines) unavoidably doomed the translator to the creation of a heroic epic poem of the classicist type. Thus, Kostrov's attempt to present Homer as a Greek national poet, that is, to approach him from the position of the poetics of romanticism, was doomed to failure. Kostrov gave up translating the *Iliad* and turned to an author who had become the standard-bearer of the new romantic movement in the middle of the eighteenth century: the bard from Scotland, Ossian.

In December 1761 in London an exceptional work was published in quarto: *Fingal, an Ancient Epic Poem, in Six Books: together with Several Other Poems, composed by Ossian the Son of Fingal. Transl. from the Galic* (sic) *Language by James Macpherson.* The author, ostensibly the legendary third-century Gaelic warrior Ossian, was actually James Macpherson, who called himself the translator. "Ossian" 's poetry enjoyed enormous success. It would be difficult to overestimate the influence of this work — one of the most renowned forgeries in literary history — on the development of romantic ideas. Ossian and Homer, as expressive of spontaneous national creative spirits, were contrasted to Virgil, an author whose work was founded on cold rationality and on "rules." In this connection, Ossian was often preferred over Homer, and in light of these ideas, Kostrov's movement from Homer, whom he was unable to translate in a romantic key, to the unquestionably romantic Ossian seems quite natural. Johann Wolfgang von Goethe loved Ossian, and in his *Die Leiden des jungen Werthers* (The Sorrows of Young Werther, 1774), the hero, on the night before his suicide, reads to his beloved Charlotta his translations of the melancholy Scottish bard. Goethe's novel became Kostrov's favorite reading; it was reported that the drunken poet would force people to read to him from this novel, during which he wept copiously.

In 1792 two volumes of Kostrov's translation of Ossian were published as *Gal'skie stikhotvoreniia* (Gaelic Poems). Kostrov did not know English, and his translation was based on a popular 1777 French translation by Pierre Le Tourneur. Kostrov's version abounds in Slavonicisms and archaicisms, which give it a poetic loftiness that also distinguishes the French text from the wilder and syntactically more abrupt original. This stylistic elevation creates a darkly romantic mood. The translation was dedicated to Suvorov and accompanied by a poem addressed to the general, written in the spirit of Ossian and stressing the exotic warlike nature of the Scottish heroes:

Живописуемы в нем грозны виды браней,
Мечи, сверкающи лучом из бурных дланей,
Представят в мысль твою, как ты врагов сражал . . .

(The threatening images of battle depicted in it,

The swords flashing with light from stormy fists,
Will remind you how you battled your enemies . . .)

The translation became Suvorov's daily reading, and he carried it with him during military campaigns. "Ossian, moi sputnik menia vosplameniaet" (Ossian, my companion, inflames me), said Suvorov. "Chest' i slava pevtsam! Oni muzhaiut nas i delaiut tvortsami obshchikh blag" (Honor and glory to poets! They give us courage and contribute to the general good). The deeply moved general ordered that Kostrov be given one thousand rubles. The general's secretary, however, thought that one hundred rubles would be enough. It is not known if this award was ever made.

Kostrov's work was enthusiastically greeted by his contemporaries, and many readers considered the translation to be better than the original. Kostrov's was the first and only full Russian translation of Ossian until 1890. All the verse translations, revisions, and imitations of Ossian, of which there were many in Russian literature at the end of the eighteenth and beginning of the nineteenth centuries (by Vladislav Ozerov, Pushkin, Vasilii Zhukovsky, and others), to one degree or another all relied on Kostrov's translation.

The translation of Ossian was Kostrov's last major work. His health was deteriorating, as his alcoholism brought on the so-called "white fever," or delirium tremens. He began to have visions of devils dragging him to hell and recounting all his sins and of angels defending him and forcing him to pray and to renounce Voltaire and his followers. One moment he would be crying, the next begging for forgiveness, and then he would turn to those around him and recite poetry. Kostrov describes his visions vividly in a story published after his death in the anonymous book *Nekotorye liubopytnye prikliucheniia i sny iz drevnikh i novykh vremen* (A Few Curious Adventures and Dreams from Ancient and Modern Times, 1829); one of the storytellers, "Mister K," is a persona for the author and relates his visions. Doctors were able to get Kostrov on his feet, but he continued to suffer from intermittent bouts of fever and constant chills. "Strannoe delo" (It is a curious business), he said to Karamzin. "Vsiu zhizn' ia pil goriachee, a umiraiu ot kholodnogo" (my whole life I've drunk the hot stuff, and now I'm dying from cold).

Kostrov died 9 December 1796, arousing a fervent and sympathetic response. He was called *bessmertnym* (the immortal) transcriber of Homer, and in one epitaph it was said that Apollo had "prisek zhizn' bessmertnogo Kostrovo" (cut short the life of the immortal Kostrov) in order to remove Homer's most dangerous rival. A romantic aura of an inspired, destitute genius not of this world soon began to form around the name of the poet. In 1814 the fifteen-year-old Pushkin, in a programmatic poem on the fates of poets, placed Kostrov alongside the Portuguese poet Camoëns. Much later, the Romantic poet and dramatist Nestor Kukol'nik wrote *Ermil Ivanovich Kostrov* (1853), "a verse drama in five acts." Though unremarkable, the play enjoyed some success, undoubtedly because viewers continued to be attracted by the sympathetic figure of the good but wayward poet.

Biography:

Petr O. Morozov, *E. I. Kostrov, ego zhizn' i literaturnaia deiatel'nost'* (Voronezh, 1876).

References:

Mark Altshuller and Ivan Martynov, "Materialy dlia Biografii Ermily Ivanovicha Kostrova," *Study Group on Eighteenth-Century Russia Newsletter,* 10 (September 1982): 30–36;

V. A. Berdinsky, "Ermil Kostrov (nachalo biografii)," *Russkaia literatura,* 2 (Spring 1984): 160–161;

William Edward Brown, *A History of 18th Century Russian Literature* (Ann Arbor, Mich.: Ardis, 1980), pp. 475–483;

Andrei N. Egunov, *Gomer v russkikh perevodakh XVIII–XIX vekov* (Moscow & Leningrad: Akademiia nauk, 1964);

Grigorii A. Gukovsky, "Kostrov," in *Istoriia russkoi literatury,* volume 4 (Moscow & Leningrad: Akademiia nauk, 1947), pp. 462–472;

E. Kurganov, ed., *Russkii literaturnyi anekdot kontsa XVIII – nachala XIX veka* (Moscow: Khudozhestvennaia Literatura, 1990), pp. 65–68;

Iurii D. Levin, *Ossian v russkoi literature: Konets XVIII–pervaia tret' XIX veka* (Leningrad: Nauka, 1980), pp. 23–35;

N. M. Levina, "Dva neopublikovannykh pis'ma E. I. Kostrova," *XVIII vek,* 3 (1958): 505–510;

Petr O. Morozov, "Ermil Ivanovich Kostrov," in *Russkaia poeziia,* edited by Semen A. Vengerov (Saint Petersburg, 1897), pp. 296–313.

Ivan Andreevich Krylov
(2 February 1769 – 9 November 1844)

Iurii Vladimirovich Stennik
Institute of Russian Literature (Pushkin House), Saint Petersburg

BOOKS: *Oda . . . Imperatritse Ekaterine . . . na zakliuchenie mira Rossii so Shvetsieu* (Saint Petersburg: Shnor, 1790);

Amerikantsy, opera komicheskaia v dvukh deistviiakh (Saint Petersburg: Gubernskoe pravlenie, 1800);

Il'ia Bogatyr. Vol'shebnaia opera v chetyrekh deistviiakh (Saint Petersburg: Teatral'naia tipografiia, 1807);

Modnaia lavka. Komediia v trekh deistviiakh (Saint Petersburg: Teatral'naia tipografiia, 1807);

Urok dochkam. Komediia v odnom deistvii (Saint Petersburg: Teatral'naia tipografiia, 1807);

Basni (Saint Petersburg: Gubernskoe pravlenie, 1809; revised, 1811);

Novye basni (Saint Petersburg: Gubernskoe pravlenie, 1811);

Basni, 3 volumes (Saint Petersburg: Senate, 1815);

Novye basni, 2 volumes (Saint Petersburg: Imperatorskii teatr, 1816);

Basni, 6 volumes (Saint Petersburg: Imperatorskii teatr, 1819); revised and enlarged edition, 7 volumes (Saint Petersburg: Departament narodnogo prosveshcheniia, 1825); revised and enlarged again, 8 volumes (Saint Petersburg: A. Smirdin, 1830); published in 9 volumes (Saint Petersburg: Voenno-uchebnye zavedeniia, 1843);

Polnoe sobranie sochinenii, 3 volumes (Saint Petersburg: Iu. Iungmeister & E. Veimar, 1847).

Editions: *Polnoe sobranie sochinenii,* 4 volumes, edited by V. V. Kallash (Saint Petersburg: Prosveshchenie, 1904–1905);

Polnoe sobranie stikhotvorenii, 2 volumes, edited by B. I. Koplan and G. A. Gukovsky, Biblioteka poeta, bol'shaia seriia (Leningrad: Sovetskii pisatel', 1935–1937);

Polnoe sobranie sochinenii, 3 volumes, edited by D. Bednyi (Moscow: Goslitizdat, 1944–1946);

Ivan Andreevich Krylov; lithograph after a portrait by Volkov, 1812

Stikhotvoreniia, edited by A. P. Mogiliansky, Biblioteka poeta, bol'shaia seriia (Leningrad: Sovetskii pisatel', 1954);

Basni, edited by Mogiliansky (Moscow & Leningrad: Akademiia nauk, 1956);

Sochineniia, 2 volumes, edited by N. L. Stepanov (Moscow: Pravda, 1956);

Sochineniia, 2 volumes, edited by S. A. Fomichev (Moscow: Khudozhestvennaia literatura, 1984).

Editions in English: *Krilof and His Fables,* translated by W. R. S. Ralston (London: Strahan, 1869);

Krilof's Fables, Illustrating Russian Social Life, translated by J. Long (Calcutta: Englishman Press, 1869);

Kriloff's Original Fables, translated by I. Henry Harrison (London: Remington, 1883);

Kriloff's Fables, translated by C. Fillingham Coxwell (London: Kegan Paul, Trench & Trübner / New York: Dutton, [1920]);

Krylov's Fables, translated by Bernard Pares (London: Cape, [1926]);

Russian Fables of Ivan Krylov With Verse Translation by Bernard Pares (Harmondsworth, U.K.: Penguin, 1942);

15 Fables of Krylov, translated by Guy Daniels (New York: Macmillan, [1965]).

OTHER: *Pochta dukhov,* 1–2 (January 1789–August 1790), edited by Krylov;

Zritel', 1–3 (February 1792–December 1792), edited by Krylov, A. I. Kushin, P. A. Plavil'shchikov, and I. A. Dmitrevsky;

Filomela, in *Rossïiskïi featr,* volume 39 (Saint Petersburg: Akademiia nauk, 1793);

Kofeinitsa, edited by Iakov K. Grot, *Sbornik statei, chitannykh v Otdelenii russkogo iazyka i slovesnosti Akademiia Nauk,* 6 (1869): 219–292;

Trumf [*Podshchipa*], *Russkaia starina,* 3 (1871): 163–200, 536, 643–646.

Krylov occupies a special place in Russian literature. His popularity is comparable to Aleksandr Pushkin's, for even during his own lifetime he achieved nationwide fame. Krylov's works simultaneously belong to two historical and cultural epochs. Entering literature early in life, Krylov established himself as a brilliant dramatist and a talented satiric journalist at the end of the 1780s and the beginning of the 1790s. However, Krylov attained even greater fame in the nineteenth century as a fabulist. His fables were immensely popular, and contemporary readers considered them to be a genuine embodiment of the Russian national spirit.

Ivan Andreevich Krylov was born in Moscow on 2 February 1769 to the family of Staff Captain Andrei Prokhorovich Krylov, who had begun as a simple soldier and risen to officer's rank by dint of long service in the army. During the Pugachev peasant uprising of 1773–1775, Krylov's father commanded a garrison in the town of Iaik, and thanks to his courage and determination, the fort there held off the rebel forces. During this time his wife, Maria Alekseevna, and their five-year-old son, Ivan, lived in Orenburg, which was under siege. After the uprising was suppressed Andrei Krylov left military service, and the family settled in Tver, where he served as chairman of the provincial town council. In 1778 Ivan's father died, leaving nine-year-old

Ivan and his year-old brother, Lev, in the care of their mother. She educated Krylov in the basics of reading and writing and acquainted him with the fundamentals of arithmetic.

Krylov's family lived in straitened circumstances. In order to make ends meet, Maria Alekseevna often worked as a servant in rich households. Krylov himself began to work at an early age. Even while his father was still alive he had been assigned to serve in the *uyezd* court in the town of Koliazin, and later he became a *pisets* (scribe) for the Tver town council. While serving at these posts Krylov developed a passion for reading, for which he was occasionally punished. Circumstances helped the youth improve his education. At his mother's request Krylov was allowed to attend lessons with the children of the rich landowner N. P. L'vov and his brother, lessons which were given by the family tutor in their home. The gifted young boy quickly demonstrated his abilities, although from time to time when there were many guests in the house he was asked to help out as a servant. Thus in his childhood Krylov knew both need and humiliation. Spiritual vulnerability and a constant desire for independence formed a complex combination in Krylov, reflected in his lack of interest in a civil-service career or material wealth, in his egalitarian behavior, in his delight in deliberately shocking people, and in his compassion for the needy.

In the winter of 1782 Krylov's family moved to the capital, and by the next year he had found a position as a clerk in the Saint Petersburg Kazennaia palata (Revenue Department). Krylov began to take an interest in literature and the theater. In fact he had probably already written his first comic opera *Kofeinitsa* (The Reader of Coffee Grounds, 1869) in Tver. For all its immaturity, the selection of the subject, as well as the quality of its verse, testify to the erudition and undeniable talent of the young author. The didactic nature of the plot smoothly meshed with the opera's egalitarian pathos. A crafty shopkeeper wants to send a poor peasant into the army, falsely accusing him of stealing silver spoons from his mistress. He is aided in this by a fortune-teller's alleged reading of coffee grounds. The superstitious mistress, Novomodova (Fashion Plate), orders the innocent serf to be punished, but at the last minute the shopkeeper and his fraudulent conspirator are exposed.

The opera was never performed and remained unpublished during Krylov's lifetime. The young writer went to the publisher and book dealer Fedor Breitkopf and asked him to have the play set to music and to help him produce the work in the theater. Although he did not agree to the project,

Breitkopf encouraged the writer by offering him sixty rubles for the work. Krylov accepted but asked to be paid not in money, but in books, and he selected several volumes from Breitkopf's shop — works by Nicolas Boileau-Despréaux, Jean Racine, and Moliére. Nearly thirty years later, when Krylov was working in the Public Library, Breitkopf returned the manuscript of the play to him; it was published in 1869 in the journal *Sbornik statei, chitannykh v Otdelenii russkogo iazyka i slovesnosti Akademiia Nauk,* edited by Iakov Grot.

After *Kofeintitsa,* Krylov tried his hand at tragedy. Krylov presented his first attempt, called "Kleopatra" (Cleopatra), to the famous actor and translator Ivan Dmitrevsky, with whom Krylov had become friends, and asked for his impartial judgment. Dmitrevsky pointed out the play's shortcomings, and Krylov apparently destroyed it. His second attempt, entitled *Filomela* (Philomela), was more successful. It treated the classical story of Philomela's sufferings in the spirit of classicist tragedies about evil tyrants. It was published in volume thirty-nine of the collection *Rossiiskii featr* (Russian Theater) in 1793; the same volume included Iakov Kniazhnin's *Vadim Novgorodskii* (Vadim of Novgorod), for which reason it was subsequently burned, so most of the copies of Krylov's play were also lost. Later in life Krylov suggested that this was no great misfortune, since the play was largely derivative.

Krylov's attempts at comic genres were much more fruitful. From 1786 to 1788 he wrote two comic operas and two comedies. The first was the comic opera *Beshenaia sem'ia* (The Crazy Family). Written in 1786, the play reworks several typical farcical motifs from Italian comic opera. In the family of the rich miser Sumbur (Confusion) jealous passions are directed toward a young man, Postan (Constant). Several women are after him — Sumbur's grandmother, his mother, and his young niece — but Postan's heart is pledged to Sumbur's sister Priiata (Pleasant). The play's climax comes when the solicitations of the luckless love seekers reach an apogee in a farcical nocturnal scene of mass confessions of love.

Krylov's second opera of this period, *Amerikantsy* (The Americans), written in 1788, was of a different type — Krylov referred to it as a "geroicheskaia" (heroic) opera. Its plot, typical of eighteenth-century Enlightenment thought, juxtaposes the natural life of native Americans to the condition of Europeans, spoiled by wealth and overflowing with passions and aggression. The main characters of the opera are the proud

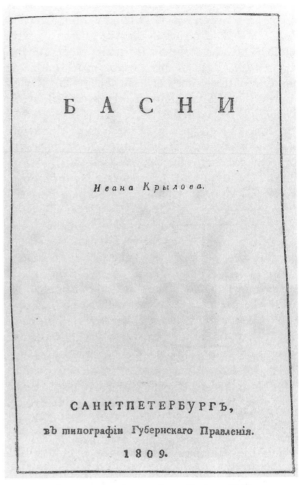

Title page for Krylov's first collection of fables

Spaniard don Guzman, who has fallen in love with the Indian girl Tsimara, and his sister Elvira, who has fallen in love with the tribal chief Atsem, Tsimara's brother. Romantic meetings alternate with military skirmishes. Taken captive, don Guzman and a friend are about to be burned at the stake but at the last minute are rescued by a Spanish detachment, who take Atsem and his warriors prisoner. Heeding his feelings toward Tsimara and the pleas of his sister, don Guzman refuses to take revenge upon Atsem and grants him freedom. The play ends with an idyllic scene of mutual reconciliation and brotherhood à la Jean-Jacques Rousseau.

Krylov's attempts to stage the opera in 1789 were unsuccessful. He had serious disagreements with P. A. Soimonov, director of the Russian Theater in Saint Petersburg, and he had become an enemy of Kniazhnin, the most important playwright of the day. Their opposition largely explains why most of Krylov's plays of the late 1780s failed to reach the stage. Echoes of Krylov's literary conflicts appear in his two comedies of that period, *Sochinitel' v prikhozhei* (The Writer in the Antechamber), written in 1786, and *Prokazniki* (Mischief Makers), written in 1788. Both of these works touch upon the question of the writer's place in society, but Krylov approaches the problem mainly as a satirist. In *Sochinitel' v prikhozhei* the satiric plan is suggested by the title. The play features versions of characters that had become traditional for eighteenth-century Russian comedy – the *petimetr* (self-satisfied fop) Count Dubovoi and the coquette Novodomova, who constantly flirt with one another. Between them scurries the poet Rifmokhvat (Rhyme Snatch), ready to compose verse for anybody and about anything for money. Along the way he is not averse to running after a comely servant girl, but his philandering costs Novodomova dearly. Rifmokhvat mixes up his notebooks, and instead of a book of his poetry he presents the count with Novodomova's notebook containing a list of her lovers. This caustic satire unambiguously reveals Krylov's attitude toward the demeaning practice of writing poetry to order.

No less sharp was Krylov's five-act comedy-lampoon, *Prokazniki* (Mischief Makers). It depicts the family of a certain poet Rifmokrad (Rhyme Stealer), who, in Krylov's words, "vykradyvaia loskutki iz frantzuzskikh i italianskikh avtorov, vydaet za svoi sochineniia i kotoryi svoimi kolkimi i dvoesmyslennymi uchtivostiami voskhishchaet durakov i obizhaet chestnykh liudei" (steals scraps from French and Italian authors and presents them as his own work, and who delights fools and affronts honest people with his caustic and ambiguous pleasantries). Rifmokrad's wife Taratora (Chatterbox) is wild about poetry and sets up a salon in their house in order to attract lovers. All of this was a merciless caricature – easily recognizable to contemporaries – of Kniazhnin, his wife Ekaterina Aleksandrovna (daughter of the poet Aleksandr Sumarokov), as well as some of their circle. Krylov did not merely attack Kniazhnin as an imitative writer but also as a family man, touching upon intimate aspects of his personal life. *Prokazniki* is full of farcical scenes in which the conceited Rifmokrad becomes a victim of the deceptions of his wife, friends, and servants.

The lampoon bordered on libel and evoked cries of protest from Kniazhnin. In response, Krylov wrote a letter of self-justification that circulated among literary people; full of sarcasm, his explanations of the play's content served as further mockery of the beleaguered Kniazhnin. The play was not

staged until 1793, after Kniazhnin's death, and although it was a popular success, its topical interest had been lost.

Krylov left his job in the Revenue Department in 1786 and entered service in the Gornaia ekspeditsiia (Department of Mines), where he served about a year. In 1788 his mother died, and the twenty-year-old writer, who had already made a name for himself in Saint Petersburg literary circles, left the Department of Mines to devote himself fully to literature. This new stage of his career was marked by his turn to journalism.

In 1788 Krylov made the acquaintance of Ivan Rakhmaninov, a captain in the guards known as a freethinker; he had translated Voltaire and owned his own printing press in Saint Petersburg. Krylov had published some poetry, including his first experiments in fables, in Rakhmaninov's journal *Utrennie chasy* (Morning Hours) during 1787 and 1788, and it was apparently then that Krylov got the idea to start his own journal. In January 1789, with Rakhmaninov's financial assistance, he began to publish *Pochta dukhov. Ezhemesiachnoe izdanie, ili uchenaia, nravstvennaia i kriticheskaia perepiska arabskogo filosofa Malikul'mul'ka s vodianymi, vozdushnymi i podzemnymi dukhami* (Spirits' Post; A Monthly Publication, or the Scholarly, Moralistic and Critical Correspondence of the Arab Philosopher Malikul'mul'k with Water Spirits, Spirits of the Heavens and from the Underworld).

Although published as a monthly periodical, *Pochta dukhov* was not a journal in the strict sense of the word. It was a unique, thematically heterogeneous satiric publication, framed by a single fantastic storyline, centered around the figure of the sorcerer-philosopher Malikul'mul'k. The work's unifying narrative conceit is established in the preface: seeking shelter from the rain in an abandoned house, the author falls under the sorcerer's power and is invited to become his personal secretary. Among his duties is editing the sorcerer's correspondence with various spirits, and the forty-eight letters he finds make up the contents of the journal. Malikul'mul'k's many correspondents have different, mostly satiric, functions. In letters sent from underground spirits – the gnomes Zor, Buriston, Vestodav, and Astarot – tales of the underground kingdom alternate with pictures of corruption and lechery that the spirits witness on earth, where they have been sent by Pluto on various commissions. Thus Buriston is sent up to find honest and unbiased judges for the underworld but despairs of fulfilling Pluto's assignment. In another letter, the gnome Zor describes his picturesque meetings

200

Parad na Tsaritsynom lugu *(The Review at the Tsaritsyn Meadow, 1832) by G. Chernetsov. Portrayed are Krylov, Aleksandr Pushkin, Vasilii Zhukovsky, and Nikolai Gnedich (from Nikolai Stepanov,* Krylov, *1963)*

on earth with the *petimetr* Pripryzhkin, who is courting a superannuated coquette, and with a Frenchwoman who runs a stylish shop that has become shelter to her brother, an escapee from the Bastille who plans to become a teacher in his new country – an episode reminiscent of the plot of one of Krylov's later comedies, *Modnaia Lavka* (The Stylish Shop, 1807).

Of an entirely different character are the letters sent to the sorcerer by heavenly spirits – the sylphs Dalnovid, Svetovid, and Vysprepar – as well as his correspondences with Astarot and Empedokol. For the most part these are philosophical and moral discussions, touching upon such important questions as the responsibilities of monarchs, the position of the nobility in society, and moral responsibility, which defines the "honest man." Mar-

garita Razumovskaia has established that these letters are largely Krylov's reworking of the *Lettres cabalistiques* (1737–1741) and *Lettres juives* (1736–1737) by the French writer and philosophe Jean-Baptiste de Boyer. The combination of entertaining qualities and serious, publicistic elements gives *Pochta dukhov* diversity. A significant place was allotted for literary polemics, and the young Krylov again mocked Kniazhnin and his patron Soimonov with invective. The journal ceased publication in August 1789.

Krylov returned to prose satire in 1792, about the time when he became close to the young litterateur Aleksei Klushin and to the actor and playwright Petr Plavil'shchikov. Together with Dmitrevsky they became partners in a new *tipografiia* (press) they called I. Krylov and Friends. In February 1792 they began to publish a new journal, *Zritel'* (Spectator). It published works by many authors and included prose, poetry, and review articles, but the most important contributions were by the publishers. The journal's editorial position was set out in several programmatic patriotic articles written by Plavil'shchikov and by Krylov's satiric writings. His moralistic "Nochi" (Nights) appeared in *Zritel'*, as did the satiric allegory "Kaib" and a cycle of parodic, pointedly satiric speeches.

"Nochi" is a fictionalized satire. Its fantastic denouement blurs the boundary between the nocturnal world of dreams where reason slumbers and that of people who are awake and active in the night. In the darkness the Queen of the Night appears to the author and asks him to record the night's events that he witnesses in order to find out when people commit more follies. The narrator describes all that happens over the course of two nights: the seduction of a young housemaid by a rich man, the misadventures of the deluded fop Vertushkin, and a nocturnal masquerade. It is hard to judge the underlying concept and genre of the work since it was never completed. But the general style and composition of the published part suggest that it was meant in the tradition of the picaresque novel.

"Kaib" is subtitled "Vostochnaia povest" (An Eastern Tale) and is a satiric allegory in the tradition of Voltaire's philosophical tales. The story relates how a powerful eastern potentate named Kaib, bored to death in his sumptuous palace and surrounded by greedy, servile courtiers, yearns to escape. Help comes unexpectedly from a mouse that is magically changed into a fairy after Kaib saves it from a cat. It tells Kaib that if he is to learn the secret of simple human happiness he must find a man who loves him and hates him simultaneously. Kaib sets out on a journey, having taken steps to conceal his departure. He learns how his subjects live and becomes convinced of the falsity of the idyllic pastoral depicted by sentimentalist poets; he discovers the true cost of those praises that hired versifiers heap upon monarchs in their sycophantic odes. Kaib's meeting with the family of an old man – his former minister who had been falsely denounced – and his love for the man's daughter, Roksana, fulfill the fairy's demand. Having returned to the palace, Kaib names the honest old man his vizier, punishes the thieves and slanderers, and, having married Roksana, attains happiness. Two structural aspects of the story clearly stand out: grotesque satire and sentimental utopianism. The idyllic finale of

"Kaib" and the miraculous role of the fairy wizard lend the narrative an ironic touch.

No less significant for denunciatory pathos are the satiric speeches Krylov published in *Zritel'*: "Rech', govorennaia povesoiu v sobranii durakov" (Speech, Delivered by a Rake in a Company of Fools), "Mysli filosofa po mode, ili Sposob kazat'sia razumnym, ne imeia ni kapli razuma" (Thoughts of a Philosopher Concerning Fashion, or a Method of Appearing Intelligent Without Having a Drop of Intelligence), and "Pokhval'naia rech' v pamiat' moemu dedushke govorennaia ego drugom v prisutstvii ego priiatelei za chasheiu punshu" (Panegyric in Memory of My Grandfather, Delivered by His Friend in the Company of His Comrades Over a Glass of Punch). The titles testify to the parodic character of these works, which lampoon panegyric speeches, one of the widespread types of rhetorical prose in the eighteenth century. The last of these works, for example, glorifies an elderly serf owner who died while on a hunt, a man who in his life provided a shining example of "kak dolzhno prozhivat' v nedeliu blagorodnomu cheloveku to, chto dve tysiachi podvlastnykh emu prostoliudinov vyrabatyvaiat v god; . . . il kak eti dve tysiachi chelovek mozhno peresech' v god raza dva-tri s pol'zoiu" (how a nobleman may run through in a week that which two thousand of his peasants earn in a year; . . . and how these two thousand may be flogged two or three times a year to good purpose).

Krylov's parodies of panegyrics also indicate the crisis Enlightenment ideas were undergoing in Russia after the French Revolution. Changes in the overall political situation in Russia also had an effect on the fate of *Zritel'*. In May 1792 the police searched Krylov's publishing house, looking for works that the government might perceive as dangerous. The police had heard about Krylov's publication of a story that mocked important government officials and about some politically questionable poetry by Klushin. In *Zhizn' i tvorchestvo Ivana Andreevicha Krylova* (Life and Works of Ivan Andreevich Krylov, 1847) Mikhail Lobanov recalls the writer's later account of the incident. Catherine II demanded to see the text of "Moi goriachki" (My Fevers), a story that had already been set in type. The story was confiscated, and the manuscript was lost. The police's attention toward the publishing house evidently did not stop and was apparently the reason Dmitrievsky and Plavil'shchikov withdrew from the venture. Thus, after eleven months of publication, *Zritel'* folded.

In 1793 Krylov and Klushin began to publish another journal, the *Sanktpeterburgskii Merkurii* (Saint Petersburg Mercury). Krylov only played a small part in

The house in Saint Petersburg where Krylov spent the last years of his life

it. His review of Klushin's comedy *Smekh i gore* (Laughter and Grief, 1793) was published here, as well as two more parodic speeches: "Pokhval'naia rech' nauke ubivat' vremia, govorennaia v novyi god" (Panegyric on the Science of Killing Time, Delivered at New Year's) and "Pokhval'naia rech' Ermalafidu, govorennaia v sobranii molodykh pisatelei" (Panegyric on Ermalafid, Delivered to a Company of Young Writers). In the first Krylov continues the tradition of attacking the parasitic morals of aristocratic fops. Most scholars consider the "Panegyric on Ermalafid" a lampoon of Karamzin and his followers. Attacks on sentimentalist excesses are combined with caustic mockeries of other literary tendencies.

The *Sanktpeterburgskii Merkurii* ceased publication in 1794. In one of its last numbers Krylov published the poem "K schast'iu" (To Happiness), in which he grieves over the ill fortune that has befallen him. Apparently the government forbade Krylov from continuing his publishing activities.

From the middle of the 1790s Krylov spent most of his time in the provinces, abandoning Saint Petersburg and literature for a time. In 1797 he became secretary to Prince S. F. Golitsyn and served in Moscow. When in 1797 the Golitsyn family moved to its estate, Kazatskoe, in Ukraine, Krylov accompanied them there and became the family tutor. He lived there until 1801.

While living at the Golitsyn estate, Krylov wrote one of his most original plays for the Golitsyn's family theater – the well-known *Podshchipa* or *Trumf* (1799, published 1871). Krylov's designation of the work as *shutotragediia* (comitragedy) indicates its parodic nature. But while parodying canonical motifs and structural traits of high classicist tragedy, Krylov also gave his play a sharply critical political subtext, making it into something of a political satire. The plot follows a traditional tragic structure. The troops of the German Prince Trumf conquer the capital of Czar Vakula's kingdom, and the prince demands the hand of the czar's daughter, Podshchipa. The princess, however, remains loyal to her betrothed, Prince Sliuniai. As the plot develops, traditional motifs of tragedy are travestied. For example, when Podshchipa suggests to Sliuniai that they accept death together in order to demonstrate their contempt for Trumf, the prince prefers to hide behind his decisive sweetheart. Krylov expertly caricatures the speech of the main characters, having

Trumf speak with a ponderous German accent and Sliuniai (whose name means "Slobberer") speak in a guttural babble. The monarch, Czar Vakula, is shown surrounded by his boyar counselors, of whom one is deaf, one mute, and the third ready to die of old age. The czar's favorite pastime is to play peg top, and the meeting of his ministers recalls a Russian children's game. The play is crowned by a farcical denouement, in which a gypsy girl puts laxative into the German soldiers' food, and they freely surrender to Vakula's troops.

Thus, in the tradition of popular farce, Krylov creates a clever satire in which he alludes to specific contemporary phenomena, including Emperor Paul I's accepting Prussian soldiers into the army and the mediocrity of his advisers. At the same time he mocks the outdated canon of classicist tragedy. Because of censorship, the play remained unpublished until 1871, when it appeared in the journal *Russkaia starina*.

While living at Kazatskoe, Krylov also wrote the one-act comedy *Pirog* (The Pie) in 1799. The comic situation concerns two servants, Van'ka and Dasha, who eat all of the filling from a pie that was sent to their master as a gift. The servants' misdeed inadvertently causes the union of two lovers, Milon and Prelesta, that their parents had opposed. As in Krylov's early work, the author's democratic sympathies are clearly defined in his depiction of the happy and resourceful servants and his ironic mockery of their luckless masters. Furthermore, as in *Podshchipa*, Krylov turns to parody, only this time the target is sentimentalism. In the depiction of Prelesta's mother, Uzhima (Simperer), Krylov deftly mocks the exalted sensibility and dreaminess of the heroes of sentimentalist novels and stories, which had become popular in the 1790s. The parody is often directed at the stylistic clichés that were trademarks of these works: Uzhima exclaims, "Akh, bozhe moi! Vy znaete moiu chuvstvitel'nost'; ia terzaius', gliadia na prepriatstviia, kotorye sud'ba polaguet vzaimnoi vashei nezhnosti .. . u nas 'budet santimental'nyi zavtrak, pod leskom u rucheika. Akh, esli b nezhnyi solovei ukrasil ego svoeiu garmonieiu!" (Oh, my God! You know how sensitive I am; I am in torment, seeing the obstacles to your mutual tenderness that fate has erected . . . we will have a sentimental breakfast beneath the trees by the streamlet. Oh, if only the tender nightingale would adorn it with its harmony!). Both *Podshchipa* and *Pirog* were staged at Golitsyn's home in Kazatskoe, with Krylov in the role of Trumf in *Podshchipa*.

At the end of 1805 Krylov returned to Saint Petersburg and began writing fables. He continued to write for the theater, however, and his later works include two comedies, a comic opera, and plans for an unfinished comedy titled "Lentiai" (The Sluggard). Krylov wrote these works during a period when Russia became increasingly anti-French, sparked by Napoleon's victory at Austerlitz in 1805 and the demeaning Tilsit peace treaty. In this atmosphere Krylov wrote the comedies *Modnaia Lavka* (The Fashionable Shop, 1807) and *Urok dochkam* (A Lesson for Daughters, 1807). In the first Krylov sarcastically mocks the perverting influence on Russians of French traders in fashionable wares. Madame Carré (Kare), the owner of a fashionable shop, and her relative Monsieur Trichet (Trishe), a speculator with a questionable past, are almost able to dupe Mrs. Sumburova, a provincial lady enamored of French styles. But thanks to the resourcefulness of a young Russian officer named Lestov, who is in love with Sumburova's daughter, Liza, all ends well. Trishe's plots are exposed, Mrs. Sumburova narrowly escapes disgrace, and the young lovers are united. The play enjoyed great success.

The second comedy, *Urok dochkam,* also involves the struggle against Gallomania. The peculiarity of the play is that Krylov borrowed the basic plot conflict from Molière's *Les Précieuse ridicules* (1659). The play takes place in the home of the landowner Velkarov. The place of Molière's Madelon and Cathos are taken by Velkarov's daughters, Fekla and Lukeria, who are both enamored of things French. The role of the pretend aristocrat is played by the servant Semen. He needs money in order to marry the maid, Dasha, and, learning of the daughters' caprices, he tricks them into thinking that he is a French marquis who had been robbed on the road and thus bilks them of money. Semen's exposure in the finale reveals the moral of the play, summarized in Velkarov's closing words: "Vot, gospozhi dochki, sledstvie vashego oslepleniia ko vsemu, chto tol'ko inostrannoe! Kto menia uverit, chtob i v gorode, v vashikh prelestnykh obshchestvakh, ne bylo markizov takogo zhe pokroiu, ot kotorykh vy nabiraetes' uma i pravil?" (Here, miss daughters, is the result of your being blinded by anything foreign! Who can assure me that even in the city, in your charming society circles, that there are no marquises of just such a stripe, who dictate your ideas and behavior?).

Krylov's comic opera, *Il'ia Bogatyr* (Ilya the Warrior, 1807), was written at the request of the director of the Imperial Theater, Aleksandr Naryshkin, and belongs to a group of plays on magical and fairy-tale subjects enjoying special popularity at the time. The plot concerns the marriage of Vladisil, prince of Chernigov, to the Bulgarian Princess

Vsemila and how the evil sorceress Zlomeka tries to stop it with the help of the powers of hell, led by Asmodei. With the help of the good sorceress Dobrada the evil intrigues are defeated. The main participant in the struggle is the fabled *bogatyr* (warrior) Il'ia, along with the prince's smart jester, Tarop. Il'ia defeats the Nightingale Bandit, obtains a magic sword, and frees Chernigov from the Pechenegs who are besieging it. Music for *Il'ia Bogatyr* was written by Catterino Cavos. The opera was a tremendous success and played in Saint Petersburg theaters for many seasons.

However, Krylov's interest in the stage soon passed, and he devoted all of his attention to fable writing. In 1805 he had shown the poet Ivan Dmitriev three of his fables, based on the fables of Jean de La Fontaine – "Dub i trost'" (The Oak and the Reed), "Razborchivaia nevesta" (The Fastidious Fiancée), and "Starik i troe molodykh" (The Old Man and the Three Youths). Dmitriev liked them and recommended that they be published. The first two appeared in *Moskovskii zritel'* (Moscow Spectator) in 1806. Encouraged, Krylov continued to write fables, and his first collection of twenty-three fables came out in 1809. More collections followed in 1811, 1815–1816, 1819, and 1825. Individual fables frequently appeared in journals. Shortly after Krylov's death a complete edition in nine volumes appeared. The edition includes more than two hundred fables, most of which have become classics of Russian literature.

In his fables Krylov's talent as a poet had the opportunity to develop fully. As the critic Vissarion Belinsky notes, Krylov not only created the Russian fable, having divined its aesthetic precepts, but also succeeded in expressing "zdravyi prakticheskii smysl russkogo narodnogo dukha, ego opytnuiu zhiteiskuiu mudrost', ego prostodushnuiu i zluiu ironiiu" (the healthy practical thought of the Russian popular spirit, its wisdom born of life experience, its guileless, and at times lethal, irony). Krylov's fables always tell a story, but their plots are allegorical. Their characters are usually animals, but beneath the guises of wolves, foxes, eagles, turtles, lions, and sheep are human beings, and the fables expose the egocentrism ruling human society. The motley world of animal passions that evokes the reader's laughter reveals the essential workings of social relationships, uncovering the true motivations of human behavior and the hidden mechanisms of power.

Krylov freed the fable from abstract didacticism. His best fables are sharp social satires. His animal characters always represent concrete human social psychologies; the main vices attacked in his fables are the predatoriness, deceit, and falsehood practiced by the powerful, as in "Volk i iagnenok" (The Wolf and the Lamb), "Lev i bars" (The Lion and the Snow Leopard), "Lisa i Volk" (The Fox and the Wolf), "Lisa-stroitel' " (The Fox Builder), "Shuka" (The Pike), "Lev na lovle" (The Lion on the Hunt), and "Ryb'i pliaski" (Fishy Dancing). The powerful rule the world, and the privileged are protected by corrupt courts, where the "guilty" parties always turn out to be sheep or other defenseless creatures, as in "Slon na voevodstve" (The Elephant in Charge), "Mirskaia skhodka" (The Peaceful Gathering), "Volki i ovtsy" (Wolves and Sheep), "Voronenok" (The Baby Crow), "Volk pastukh" (The Shepherd Wolf), and "Pestrye ovtsy" (Motley Sheep).

Such fables as "Krestian'e i reka" (The Peasants and the River) or "Lev i volk" (The Lion and the Wolf) attack not only the predatory practices of the upper classes but also the rationalizations they employ to maintain social inequity. Other fables, such as "Orel i Pchela" (The Eagle and the Bee), "Mukha i pchela" (The Fly and the Bee), "Listy i korni" (Leaves and Roots), and "Kamen' i cherviak" (The Stone and the Worm), present Krylov's positive ideal, presented in the image of a nameless laborer opposed to those who arrogantly lay claim to things they have not earned. Krylov's fables also, perhaps for the first time in Russian literature, explore the psychology of the Russian peasant – his common sense, subtle craftiness, and his openheartedness – as in "Krest'ianin i rabotnik" (The Peasant and the Worker), "Tri muzhika" (Three Muzhiks), "Mel'nik" (The Miller), "Krest'ianin i zmeia" (The Peasant and the Snake), and many others. The national and folk quality of Krylov's fables is demonstrated by the fact that many phrases from them became proverbs, such as "Usluzhlivyi durak opasnee vraga" (A helpful fool is more dangerous than an enemy) and "Na svete kto silen, tot delat' vse volen" (In this world the strong may do as they like).

A special place in Krylov's fables is occupied by those dedicated to the War of 1812 against Napoleon, including "Razdel" (The Allotment), "Vorona i kuritsa" (The Crow and the Chicken), "Volk na psarne" (The Wolf in the Kennel), "Oboz" (The Transport), and "Shuka i kot" (The Pike and the Cat). All of the fables in this cycle have original plots. In them Krylov was the first to express the Russian perspective on the war: in some of the best, for example, the wisdom of General Kutuzov is celebrated, long before Leo Tolstoy's *Voina i mir* (War and Peace, 1864–1869).

Krylov's popularity rose swiftly after his first collection of fables was published, and he became a prominent figure at various literary salons in Saint Petersburg. By 1805–1806 he had become friends with the family of Aleksei Olenin, a historian, archeologist, and subtle connoisseur of art who was also close to the court. Olenin was named director of the new Imperial Public Library in 1811, and in 1812 he invited Krylov to work there. Krylov's friend the writer and translator Nikolai Gnedich also worked there, as did the poet Anton Del'vig, the poet and linguist Aleksandr Vostokov, and the translator Mikhail Lobanov. Krylov also became a member of the literary group Beseda liubitelei rossiiskogo slova (Colloquium of Lovers of the Russian Word) and was soon elected to the Russian Academy. He enjoyed universal recognition. Thanks to Olenin, he was invited to court for dinners and other events. Once, after supper with the emperor's wife, Maria Fedorovna, she requested that Krylov recite his favorite fable, and he obliged with "Listy i korni" (Leaves and Roots). In 1838, on the occasion of his seventieth birthday, a commemorative medal was minted and a scholarship instituted in his name.

Krylov never married. His only close relative was his brother Lev, an officer stationed in Ukraine. They corresponded until Lev's death of fever in 1824. Although well known, Krylov led a solitary and measured existence. After work he would go to the English Club, where he dined and spent his evenings. During the summer he would visit the Olenin's *dacha* (villa) in Priiutino near Saint Petersburg. Krylov drew well and was an excellent violin player, and his passion for music lasted his whole life. He also gained a reputation as a subtle critic of painting. An active participant in the literary life of the 1810s and 1820s, he never took part in the polemics of the period. Many anecdotes and memoirs survive about his various activities, his inimitable wit, his habits, his likes, and his dislikes. In some he appears as a lazy provincial, an unprincipled man with a cold heart, and in some almost a glutton. Krylov did, in fact, have a passion for eating well, evidently as a way of recompensing himself for the deprivations of his childhood and hardships of youth. As far as his laziness and cold heart, a sober skepticism always characterized his attitude toward exalted feelings and displays of vanity, which in his opinion more often than not kept people from engaging in useful activity.

Toward the end of his life Krylov wrote nothing. In 1835 he composed his last fable, "Vel'mozha" (The Grandee), which is also one of his best; he recited it in 1836 at an imperial masquerade given at the Anichkov Palace. He retired in 1841 and moved to

Krylov in 1841 (portrait by K. Briullov; Tret'iakov Gallery, Moscow)

Vasil'evsky Island, an outlying section of Saint Petersburg, and rarely went anywhere. Krylov died on 9 November 1844. His final words were reported as: "Gospodi! Prosti mne pregresheniia moi!" (Lord, forgive my sins!). The church in which his funeral took place could not hold all the mourners. He was buried in the Aleksandr Nevsky Monastery, next to Nikolai Gnedich.

Bibliographies:

Vladislav Kenevich, *Bibliograficheskie i istoricheskie primechaniia k basniam Krylova* (Saint Petersburg: Otdelenie russkogo iazyka i slovesnosti Imp. Akademii nauk, 1868);

Afanasii Bychkov, "O basniakh Krylova v perevodakh na inostrannye iazyki," in *Sbornik statei, chitannykh v Otdelenii russkogo iazyka i slovesnosti Imperatorskoi Akademii Nauk,* volume 6 (Saint Petersburg, 1869), pp. 81–108;

Serafim Babintsev, *I. A. Krylov: Ukazatel' ego proizvedenii i literatury o nem,* edited by Boris M. Eikhenbaum and Iurii Mezhenko (Leningrad & Moscow: Iskusstvo, 1945).

Biographies:

Mikhail Lobanov, *Zhizn' i tvorchestvo Ivana Andreevicha Krylova* (Saint Petersburg: K. Zhernakov, 1847);

Petr Pletnev, *Zhizn' i sochineniia Ivana Andreevicha Krylova* (Saint Petersburg, 1859);

Sergei Durilyn, *I. A. Krylov: Kratkii ocherk zhizni i tvorchestva* (Moscow: Goslitizdat, 1944);

Aleksandr Zapadov, *Ivan Andreevich Krylov (1769–1844)* (Moscow & Leningrad: Iskusstvo, 1951);

Serafim Babintsev, *I. A. Krylov: Ocherk ego izdatel'skoi i bibliotechnoi deiatel'nosti* (Moscow: Akademiia nauk, 1955);

Nikolai Stepanov, *Krylov* (Moscow: Molodaia gvardiia, 1963);

Arkadii Gordin, *Krylov v Peterburge* (Leningrad: Lenizdat, 1969);

I. A. Krylov v vospominaniiakh sovremennikov, edited by Arkadii Gordin and Mikhail Gordin (Moscow: Khudozhestvennaia literatura, 1982).

References:

Vsevolod Arkhipov, *I. A. Krylov: Poeziia narodnoi mudrosti* (Moscow: Moskovskii rabochii, 1974);

Vissarion Belinsky, "Ivan Andreevich Krylov," in his *Polnoe sobranie sochinenii,* volume 8 (Moscow: Akademiia nauk, 1955), pp. 565–591;

Pavel Berkov, *Istoriia russkoi zhurnalistiki XVIII veka* (Moscow & Leningrad: Akademiia nauk, 1952), pp. 430–495;

Dmitri Blagoi and N. L. Brodsky, eds., *I. A. Krylov: Issledovaniia i materialy* (Moscow: Goslitizdat, 1947);

Anthony Cross, "The English and Krylov," *Oxford Slavonic Papers,* 16 (1983): 91–140;

Aleksandr Desnitsky, *Ivan Andreevich Krylov: Posobie dlia uchashchikhsia* (Moscow: Prosveshchenie, 1983);

Mikhail Gordin and Iakov Gordin, *Teatr Ivana Krylova* (Leningrad: Iskusstvo, 1983);

Pierre Hunt, "Ivan Krylov and the Aesopian Style of the Narrative Bestia," *Yearbook of the Beast Fable Society,* 2 (May 1990): 81–86;

Izrail' Iampol'sky, *Krylov i muzyka (1769–1969)* (Moscow: Muzyka, 1970);

Vladimir Perets, *Ivan Andreevich Krylov kak Dramaturg* (Saint Petersburg, 1895);

Margarita Razumovskaia, " 'Pochta dukhov' I. A. Krylova i romany markiza d'Arzhana," *Russkaia literatura,* 1 (1978): 103–115;

Il'ia Serman, ed., *Ivan Andreevich Krylov: Problemy tvorchestva* (Leningrad: Nauka, 1975);

Nikolai Stepanov, *Masterstvo Krylova basnopistsa* (Moscow: Sovetskii pisatel', 1956);

Stepanov, *Ivan Krylov* (New York: Twayne, 1973).

Mikhail Vasil'evich Lomonosov

(8 November 1711 – 4 April 1765)

Irina Reyfman
Columbia University

BOOKS: *Pervye trofei e. i. Ioanna III imp. i samoderzhtsa vserossiiskago chrez preslavnuiu nad shvedami pobedu avgusta 23 dnia 1741 goda v Finliandii postavlennye, i v vysokii den' tezoimenichestva ego velichestva avgusta 29 dnia 1741 goda v torzhestvennoi ode izobrazhennye ot vsepoddanneishago raba Mikhaila Lomonosova* (Saint Petersburg: Akademiia nauk, 1741);

Tri ody parafrasticheskie psalma 143, sochinennye chrez trekh stikhotvortsev, iz kotorykh kazhdyi odnu slozhil osoblivo, by Lomonosov, V. K. Trediakovsky, and A. P. Sumarokov (Saint Petersburg: Akademiia nauk, 1744);

Oda e. i. v. . . . velikoi gosudaryne Elizavete Petrovne . . . i ikh imp. vysochestvam . . . velikomu kniaziu Petru Feodorovichu i . . . velikoi kniagine Ekaterine Alekseevne na torzhestvennyi den' brachnago sochetaniia ikh vysochestv prinositsia v znak iskrenniago userdiia, blagogoveniia i radosti ot vsepoddaneishago raba Mikhaila Lomonsova khimii professora ([Saint Petersburg]: Akademiia nauk, 1745);

Oda e. i. v. . . . velikoi gosudaryne Elizavete Petrovne . . . kotoroiu v torzhestvennyi prazdnik rozhdenniia eia velichestva dekabria 18 dnia 1746 iskrennyia i vseuserdneishiia svoi zhelaniia prinosit vsepoddaneishaia Akademiia nauk ([Saint Petersburg]: Akademiia nauk, [1746]);

Oda na presvetlyi prazdnik vosshestviia na vserossiiskii prestol . . . velikiia gosudaryni Elizavety Petrovny . . . kotoroiu eia velichestvu vseuserdneishee pozdravlenie prinosit vsepoddanneishii rab Mikhailo Lomonosov 1746 noiabria 25 dnia ([Saint Petersburg]: Akademiia nauk, [1746]);

Radostnyia i blagodarstvennyia vosklitsaniia muz rossiiskikh, prozorlivostiiu Petra Velikago osnovannykh, tshchaniem shchedryia Ekateriny utverzhdennykh i neskazannym velikodushiem . . . velikiia gosudaryni imp. Elizavety Petrovny . . . obogashchennykh, ozhivlennykh i vosstavlennykh, kotoryia na presvetlyi i vseradostnyi prazdnik vosshestviia na vserossiiskii prestol eia velichestva noiabria 25 dnia 1747 goda prinosit vse-

Mikhail Vasil'evich Lomonosov; engraving by M. Shreiter

poddanneishaia Akademiia nauk (Saint Petersburg: Akademiia nauk, [1747]);

Oda e. i. v. . . . velikoi gosudaryne imp. Elizavete Petrovne . . . na presvetlyi prazdnik vosshestviia na vserossiiskii prestol eia velichestva prinositsia ot vsepoddaneishei Akademii nauk noiabria 25 dnia 1748 goda (Saint Petersburg: Akademiia nauk, [1748]);

Kratkoe rukovodstvo k krasnorechiiu, kniga pervaia, v kotoroi soderzhitsia ritorika pokazuiushchaia obshchie pravila oboego krasnorechiia, to est' oratorii i poezii (Saint Petersburg: Akademiia nauk, 1748);

Oda e. i. v. . . . velikoi gosudaryne imp. Elizavete Petrovne . . . kotoroiu za vysochaishuiu monarsheskuiu milost' okazannuiu v Sarskom sele vseuserdneishee blagodarenie prinosit vsepoddaneishii rab Mikhailo Lomonosov (Saint Petersburg: Akademiia nauk, 1750);

Tamira i Selim, tragediia (Saint Petersburg: Akademiia nauk, 1750);

Sobranie raznykh sochinenii v stikhakh i v proze ([Saint Petersburg]: Akademiia nauk, 1751);

Demofont tragediia (Saint Petersburg: Akademiia nauk, 1752);

Pis'mo o pol'ze stekla k deistvitel'nomu eia imp. velichestvu kamergeru Ivanu Ivanovichu Shuvalovu (Saint Petersburg: Akademiia nauk, 1752);

Vsepresvetleishei derzhavneishei velikoi gosudaryne imp. Elizavete Petrovne . . . na presvetlyi i vseradostnyi prazdnik vosshestviia na vserossiiskii prestol eia velichestva, noiabria 25 dnia 1752 goda, vo iz"iavlenie istinnago userdiia i radosti vsepoddaneishee pozdravlenie liricheskim stikhom izobrazhennoe vsenizhaishe prinosit vsepoddanneishii rab Mikhailo Lomonosov (Saint Petersburg: Akademiia nauk, 1752);

Opisanie illuminatsii i feierverka dlia iz"iavleniia obshchei radosti i userdiia vsepresvetleishei, derzhavneishei, velikoi gosudaryne imp. Elizavete Petrovne samoderzhitse vserossiiskoi predstavlennykh na novyi 1754 god v Moskve pred eia velichestva novosozdannym domom (Saint Petersburg: Akademiia nauk, [1753]);

Oda vsepresvetleishei derzhavneishei velikoi gosudaryne imp. Elizavete Petrovne . . . i nasledniku eia velichestva vnuku Petra Velikago . . . velikomu kniaziu Petru Feodorovichu i supruge ego . . . velikoi kniagine Ekaterine Alekseevne na vsevozhdelennoe rozhdenie . . . velikago kniazia Pavla Petrovicha sentiabria 20 dnia 1754 goda s iskrennim userdiem i revnost'iu prinesennaia ot vsepoddanneishago raba Mikhaila Lomonosova (Saint Petersburg: Akademiia nauk, [1754]);

Opisanie illuminatsii, kotoraia pri vysochaishem i vsemilostiveishem prisutstvii eia imp. velichestva k okazaniiu vseobshchei radosti o vozhdelenneishem rozhdenii ego imp. vysochestv gosudaria velikago kniazia Pavla Petrovicha byla predstavlena pred domom ego siiatel'stva gospodina generala anshefa, senatora, eia imp. velichestva deistvitel'nago kammergera, generala ad"iutanta, leibkompanii podporutchika i raznykh ordenov kavalera grafa Petra Ivanovicha Shuvalova v Sanktpeterburge oktiabria 26 dnia 1754 goda ([Saint Petersburg: Akademiia nauk, 1754]);

Opisanie feierverka kotoroi v prodolzhenie vsenarodnoi radosti o vozhdelenneishem rozhdenii ego imp. vysochestva velikago kniazia Pavla Petrovicha pri publichnom maskarade dannom eia imp. velichestva ot deistvitel'nago kammergera i raznykh ordenov kavalera Ivana Ivanovicha Shuvalova vnutr' dvora ego prevoskhoditel'st[v]a zazhzhen v Sanktpeterburge oktiabria 24 dnia 1754 goda ([Saint Petersburg: Akademiia nauk, 1754]);

Rossiiskaia grammatika (Saint Petersburg: Akademiia nauk, 1755 [1757]);

Slovo pokhval'noe blazhennyia i vechnodostoinyia pamiati gosudariu imp. Petru Velikomu v torzhestvennoe prazdnestvo koronovaniia . . . velikiia gosudaryni imp. Elizavety Petrovny . . . v publichnom sobranii Imp. Akademii nauk . . . aprelia 26 dnia 1755 goda ([Saint Petersburg]: Akademiia nauk, [1755]);

Slovo o proiskhozhdenii sveta novuiu teoriiu o tsvetakh predstavliaiushchee v publichnom sobranii Akademii nauk iiulia 1 dnia 1756 goda (Saint Petersburg: Akademiia nauk, [1756]);

Oda e. i. v. . . . velikoi gosudaryne imp. Elizvete Petrovne . . . na presvetlyi i torzhestvennyi prazdnik rozhdeniia eia velichestva i dlia vseradostnago rozhdeniia gosudaryni velikoi kniazny Anny Petrovny podnesennaia ot imp. Akademii nauk dekabria 18 dnia 1757 goda (Saint Petersburg: Akademiia nauk, [1757]);

Slovo o rozhdenii metallov ot triaseniia zemli, na torzhestvennyi prazdnik tezoimenitstva e. i. v. velikiia gosudaryni imp. Elizavety Petrovny . . . v publichnom sobranii Imp. Akademii nauk sentiabria 6 dnia 1757 goda (Saint Petersburg: Akademiia nauk, [1757]);

Sobranie raznykh sochinenii v stikhakh i v prose, 2 volumes (Moscow: Moskovskii universitet, 1758, 1765);

Oda e. i. v. . . . velikoi gosudaryne imp. Elizavete Petrovne . . . na torzhestvennyi prazdnik tezoimenichestva eia velichestva sentiabria 5 dnia 1759 goda, i na preslavnyia eia pobedy oderzhannyia nad korolem prusskim nyneshniago 1759 goda, kotoroiu prinositsia vsenizhaishee i vseuserdneishee pozdravlenie ot vsepoddanneishago raba Mikhaila Lomonosova (Saint Petersburg: Akademiia nauk, [1759]);

Rassuzhdenie o bol'shei tochnosti morskago puti, chitannoe v publichnom sobranii Imp. Akademii nauk maiia 8 dnia 1759 goda ([Saint Petersburg: Akademiia nauk, 1759]);

Kratkoi Rossiiskoi letopisets s rodosloviem (Saint Petersburg: Akademiia nauk, 1760);

Petr Velikii, geroicheskaia poema. Pesn' 1–2 ([Saint Petersburg: Akademiia nauk, 1760–1761]);

Rassuzhdenie o tverdosti i zhidkosti tel radi torzhestvennago prazdnika tezoimenitstva . . . velikiia gosudaryni imp. Elizavety Petrovny . . . v publichnom sobranii Imp. Akademii nauk sentiabria 6 dnia 1760 goda (Saint Petersburg: Akademiia nauk, [1760]);

Iavlenie Venery na Solntse nabliudennoe v Sanktpeterburgskoi Imp. Akademii nauk maiia 26 dnia 1761 goda ([Saint Petersburg: Akademiia nauk, 1761]);

Oda vsepresvetleishei derzhavneishei velikoi gosudaryne imp. Elizavete Petrovne . . . na presvetlyi torzhestvennyi prazdnik eia velichestva vosshestviia na vserossiiskii prestol noiabria 25 dnia 1761 goda v okazanie istinnoi radosti i revnostnago userdiia vsenizhaishe podnesennaia ot vsepoddaneishago raba Mikhaila Lomonosova (Saint Petersburg: Akademiia nauk, [1761]);

Oda torzhestvennaia e. i. v. . . . velikoi gosudaryne imp. Ekaterine Alekseevne... na preslavnoe eia vosshestviia na vserossiiskii imperatorskii prestol iiunia 28 dnia 1762 goda. V iz"iavlenie istinnyia radosti i vernopoddannago userdiia iskrenniago pozdravleniia prinositsia ot vsepoddaneishago raba Mikhaila Lomonosov (Saint Petersburg: Akademiia nauk, [1762]);

Oda vsepresvetleishemu derzhavneishemu velikomu gosudariu imp. Petru Feodorovichu . . . kotoruiu ego imp. velichestvu na vseradostnoe vosshestvie na vserossiiskii naslednyi imperatorskii prestol i kupno na novyi 1762 god v iz"iavlenie istinnyia radosti userdiia i blagogoveniia vsenizhaishe prinosit vsepoddaneishii rab Mikhailo Lomonosov (Saint Petersburg: Akademiia nauk, [1762]);

Oda vsepresvetleishei derzhavneishei velikoi gosudaryne imp. Ekaterine Alekseevne . . . kotoroiu eia velichestva v novyi 1764 god vsenizhaishe pozdravliaet vsepoddanneishii rab Mikhailo Lomonosov (Saint Petersburg: Akademiia nauk, [1763]);

Pervyia osnovaniia metalurgii, ili rudnykh del (Saint Petersburg: Akademiia nauk, 1763);

Ego siiatel'stvu milostivomu gosudariu grafu Grigor'iu Grigor'evichu Orlovu . . . na blagopoluchnoe vozvrashchenie eia velichestva iz Lifliandii pozdravitel'noe pis'mo ot statskogo sovetnika i professora Mikhaila Lomonosova, s Ruditskikh zavodov, iulia 19 dnia 1764 goda ([Saint Petersburg]: Akademiia nauk, [1764]);

Drevniaia Rossiiskaia istoriia ot nachala rossiiskogo naroda do konchiny velikogo kniazia Iaroslava pervogo, ili do 1054 goda (Saint Petersburg: Akademiia nauk, 1766);

Sobraniie raznykh sochinenii v stikhakh i v proze, 2 volumes ([Saint Petersburg]: Akademiia nauk, 1768).

Editions: *Sobraniie raznykh sochinenii v stikhakh i v proze,* edited by Damaskin (D. E. Semenov-Rudnev), 3 volumes (Moscow: Moskovskii universitet, 1778);

Polnoe sobranie sochinenii, 6 volumes (Saint Petersburg: Akademiia nauk, 1784–1787);

Sobranie sochinenii, 3 volumes (Saint Petersburg: Rossiiskaia Akademiia, 1840);

Sochineniia, 3 volumes (Saint Petersburg: A. Smirdin, 1847);

Sochineniia, 8 volumes (Saint Petersburg & Moscow: Akademiia nauk, 1891–1948);

Stikhotvoreniia, edited by A. S. Orlov, Biblioteka poeta, Bol'shaia seriia (Leningrad: Sovetskii pisatel', 1935);

Izbrannye filosofskie sochineniia, edited by G. S. Vasetsky (Moscow: Gos. sotsial'no-ekonomicheskoe izdatel'stvo, 1940);

Stikhotvoreniia, edited by Pavel Berkov, Biblioteka poeta, Malaia seriia (Leningrad: Sovetskii pisatel', 1948);

Polnoe sobranie sochinenii, 10 volumes (Moscow & Leningrad: Akademiia nauk, 1950–1959);

Izbrannye proizvedeniia, edited by A. A. Morozov, Biblioteka poeta, Bol'shaia seriia (Moscow & Leningrad: Sovetskii pisatel', 1965);

Izbrannaia proza, edited by V. A. Dmitriev (Moscow: Sovetskaia Rossia, 1980);

Izbrannye proizvedeniia, 2 volumes, edited by E. P. Karpeev and others (Moscow: Nauka, 1986).

OTHER: Marcus Tullius Cicero [Tsitseron], *Mneniia Tsitseronovy iz raznykh ego sochinenii sobrannye abbatom Olivetom, prezhde s frantsuzskogo iazyka na rossiiskii perevedeny kapitanom Ivanom Shishkinym; a nyne . . . ispravleny protiv podlinnykh latinskikh [M. V. Lomonosovym],* translated by Ivan Shishkin, edited by Lomonosov (Saint Petersburg: Akademiia nauk, 1752);

Jean Baptiste Rousseau, *Oda na shchastie sochineniia gospodina Russo, perevedennaia g. Sumarokovym i g. Lomonosovym,* translations by Lomonosov and Sumarokov ([Saint Petersburg]: n.d.);

"Stikhotvoreniia," in Lomonosov, Vasilii Trediakovsky, and Aleksandr Sumarokov, *Stikhotvoreniia,* edited by Berkov, Biblioteka poeta, Malaia seriia, 4 (Leningrad: Sovetskii pisatel', 1935), pp. 113–180.

Mikhail Vasil'evich Lomonosov was a figure of great prominence among mid-eighteenth-century

Russian writers and holds the reputation as one of the greatest Russian poets of his century. Coming from a geographic and cultural periphery of Russia and from a social station that traditionally was all but banned from education, he emerged as a leading figure of Russian science, scholarship, and literature. A man of encyclopedic knowledge, inexhaustible energy, and passionate temper, he was the first Russian chemist and physicist, a gifted linguist and a competent historian, but most of all an extraordinary poet. Lomonosov did not consider poetry his main occupation, viewing himself primarily as a scientist. However, his scientific accomplishments — often overrated by Russian students of his legacy — were not on a level with the achievements of his European contemporaries. Lomonosov contributed to the development of Russian science first of all as an indefatigable organizer and an enthusiastic educator. His interests were varied. He organized the first chemistry laboratory in Russia and began training students there. He encouraged the development of astronomy in Russia and was instrumental in organizing several important experiments. He promoted geologic and geographic research. He revived mosaic art in Russia and opened a colored-glass factory. Through his efforts the first Russian university, Moscow University (now named after Lomonosov), was established. But ultimately Lomonosov left his most significant mark on Russian culture through his poetry. He is remembered in Russia as a figure standing at the beginning of the modern literary tradition, the creator of modern Russian poetry and the reformer of the Russian literary language and versification.

The birthdate of Mikhail (or "Mikhailo" in the traditional form) Vasil'evich Lomonosov is not precisely known, but in the beginning of this century the Russian Academy of Sciences decreed to consider it 8 November 1711. He was born in Mishanovka, a small northern village on the island of Kurostrov in the delta of the Dvina River near Archangel. This part of Russia was populated by former citizens of the Novgorod region, which had known neither the Tatar yoke nor serfdom. Officially known as "state peasants" (having economic obligations not to an individual landowner but to the state), they could not depend for their living on agriculture, which was unprofitable in the far north, but had to earn their livelihood by such trades as shipbuilding, fishing, and sailing. Few formal schools existed in the region, but literacy was widespread and books were held in high regard.

Lomonosov's father, Vasilii Dorofeevich, was a prosperous shipowner who sailed the White and

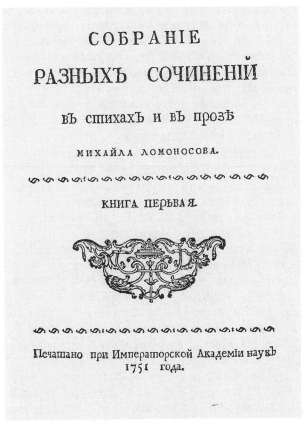

Title page for the earliest collection of Lomonosov's works

Barents seas fishing and delivering goods. His mother, Elena Ivanovna Sivkova, died when Mikhail was eight or nine. His father soon married again, and after his second wife also died he married a third time. His third wife, according to Lomonosov's later account, was a stern stepmother who did not approve of her stepson's passion for knowledge. Lomonosov also had a younger sister, Maria. Lomonosov's father drowned at sea in early 1741. According to a legend, Lomonosov had a prophetic dream about his father's death that enabled him to point out the island in the White Sea where the body of his father was subsequently found.

As a young boy of eight, Lomonosov went with his father on sea expeditions. He never forgot the experience and often referred to the natural beauty of the North in later years. When he was eleven or twelve, he learned how to read and write Church Slavonic from a neighbor and from a deacon of a local church. Soon Lomonosov became known locally for his expressive recitations of the Holy Scriptures. Around 1725 three books became available to him: Meletii Smotritsky's *Grammatika slavenskaia* (Slavic Grammar, probably the 1648 edition), Leontii Magnitsky's *Arifmetika* (Arithmetic, 1703), and Simeon Polotsky's *Psaltir' rifmotvornaia* (Rhymed Psalter, 1680). Smotritsky's fundamental grammar of Church Slavonic also contained the basics of rhetoric and versification; Magnitsky's textbook acquainted Lomonosov with the foundations of mathematics, astronomy, and physics; and the *Psaltir' rifmotvornaia* introduced him to poetry.

In his late teens Lomonosov decided to go to Moscow to continue his education. He left home in December 1730 and arrived in Moscow in mid January. Contrary to popular legend, Lomonosov's departure was rather prosaic. He did not flee in the middle of the night upon hearing a voice say "Quench not the spirit"; he left his village officially, with a valid passport. Nor did he go on foot, as the legend suggests – which would have been impossible at the height of winter – but traveled with a party of his fellow countrymen carrying frozen fish to Moscow markets. In Moscow he entered the Slavonic-Greek-Latin Academy, a religious school that provided higher education to many prominent Russians, mostly to children of the clergy and lower gentry. The school did not admit peasant children, and Lomonosov lied in declaring that he came from provincial gentry. He was accepted into the academy in January 1731 and placed with younger students since he did not know Latin, the language of instruction at the school. Having suffered some mockery from younger classmates for being a twenty-year-old "blockhead" in an elementary-level class, Lomonosov completed three grades in two years and was transferred to the intermediate class. At the academy Lomonosov learned Greek and Latin, studied poetics and rhetoric, and read classical authors. The academy library provided him with books in philosophy, physics, and mathematics that he read on his own. His teachers soon realized that he was an extraordinary student, which probably saved him from expulsion in 1734 when his peasant origin was discovered. He spent that year at the Kiev Academy, the older sister of the Moscow school, and soon after his return he was selected, with eleven other students, to continue his education at the newly organized gymnasium at the Academy of Sciences in Saint Petersburg.

Lomonosov arrived in the capital on 1 January 1736 and began his studies, but the academy superiors had other plans for him: in September he and two other students were on their way to Germany to become specialists in mining. The students arrived in Marburg in November and stayed for almost three years, studying mathematics, physics,

and mechanics under the supervision of Christian Wolff, a renowned philosopher and mathematician. The Russian students also took lessons in chemistry, French, fencing, and dancing. In July 1739 they proceeded to Freiberg to study chemistry and metallurgy with Johann Friedrich Henckel. Lomonosov remained there until May 1740, learning experimental chemistry and visiting local mines.

The circumstances of Lomonosov's departure from Freiburg anticipate his future clashes with colleagues and superiors. The Russian students' financial situation was poor, both because of their irregular lifestyle and because they did not receive their stipends on time. They had left debts and unpleasant memories of their rowdy behavior in Marburg. The academy officials instructed Henckel to supervise the students more closely and to take upon himself the management of their finances. Their new teacher was pedantic, harsh, and ill-tempered. Lomonosov soon began quarreling with him over money and teaching methods. One day in May 1740, after an especially heated quarrel, the young man left Freiburg without his supervisor's consent or knowledge. (It should be noted, however, that personal animosities did not prevent Henckel from praising Lomonosov's academic progress in a letter to the academy written in 1741.) Lomonosov attempted to return to Russia but failed to obtain either the money or the official permission that he needed. Not wishing to return to Freiburg, he went to Marburg instead. There he discovered that he had become a father: he had a daughter, Catherine Elizabeth, by Elizabeth Christina Zilch. He married the mother of his child on 6 June 1740 and soon left Marburg in another attempt to reach Russia. While traveling around Germany, Lomonosov was conscripted into the Prussian army but managed to escape. He eventually returned to Marburg, where he stayed until he received money from the Academy of Sciences for the trip home in May 1741. Having left behind his wife and child (whose existence he carefully concealed from his superiors at the academy), he arrived in Saint Petersburg on 8 June 1741. His family (including his brother-in-law, Johann Zilch, Lomonosov's future assistant in his work on mosaics) did not join him until October 1743. The Lomonosovs had another child, Ivan, who was born after his father's departure from Marburg and who died shortly after his birth. Lomonosov's daughter Catherine Elizabeth died soon after her arrival in Russia in 1743. His only child to survive to adulthood was Elena, born in 1749.

In January 1736, while still in Saint Petersburg, Lomonosov had bought a copy of Vasilii

Trediakovsky's book, *Novyi i kratkii sposob k slozheniiu rossiiskikh stikhov* (New and Brief Method for Composing Russian Verse, 1735). In it Trediakovsky proposed a reform of the syllabic system of versification that had dominated Russian poetry since the 1660s. He introduced the idea of the foot, borrowed from Greek and Latin poetry, as the basic unit of measurement in eleven- and thirteen-syllable verses, thus making the regular alternation of stressed and unstressed syllables the main rhythmic principle of Russian verse; he also suggested keeping the same foot (preferably trochaic) throughout the line. This innovation produced verse that Trediakovsky called "tonic." It was a precursor of the syllabo-tonic verse that is still predominant in Russian poetry. Lomonosov took Trediakovsky's book to Marburg and studied it carefully. It made a great impression on him, but he did not agree with some of Trediakovsky's ideas and expressed his disagreement with characteristic passion. The marginalia in Lomonosov's copy of *Novyi i kratkii sposob* (preserved in the Archives of the Academy of Sciences in Saint Petersburg, fond 20, op. 2, no. 3) are so abusive that an eighteenth-century reader wrote on the cover: "He is as fierce as the hound of Hell." Lomonosov disagreed with two major points: Trediakovsky's preference for trochees and his prohibition against alternating masculine and feminine rhymes. He also disapproved of Trediakovsky's style: the marginalia repeatedly ridicule what Lomonosov considered the author's mistakes — inversions, archaisms, and colloquialisms.

Trediakovsky's book inspired Lomonosov to experiment with syllabo-tonics. He was also influenced by German writers, especially by the poetry of Johann Christian Gunther, and by Johann Christoph Gottsched's works on the theory of literature. Lomonosov's first experiments were a translation of an Anacreontic ode that he found in one of Gottsched's essays and of an ode by François Fénelon, "Montagnes de qui l'audace" (1681). Against Trediakovsky's prohibition of syllabo-tonics in short verses, Lomonosov employed iambic trimeter in the former and trochaic tetrameter in the latter. In the fall of 1739 he summarized his ideas on syllabo-tonics in the essay "Pis'mo o pravilakh rossiiskogo stikhotvorstva" (Letter on the Rules of Russian Versification) and sent it to the Academy of Sciences together with his first solemn ode, "Na vziatie Khotina" (On the Taking of Khotin), commemorating the Russian victory in the Russo-Turkish war (1735–1739).

In the "Pis'mo" Lomonosov suggests using syllabo-tonic meters in verses of any length; advo-

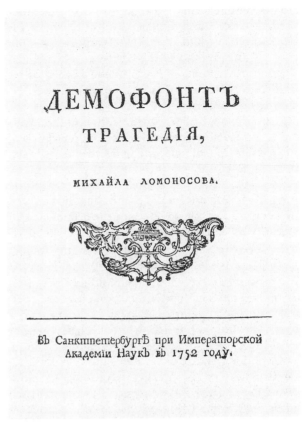

ДЕМОФОНТЪ

ТРАГЕДІЯ,

МИХАЙЛА ЛОМОНОСОВА.

Въ Санктпетербургѣ при Императорской
Академіи Наукъ въ 1752 году.

Title page for one of Lomonosov's tragedies written at the behest of Empress Elizabeth in 1750

cates the acceptance of all meters, including trisyllabics; and allows the combination of all types of rhymes. He includes original verse fragments to illustrate his new principles. Lomonosov's essay and ode were examined by the academy, and Trediakovsky was asked to write an answer. Aleksandr Sumarokov, at that time a supporter of Trediakovsky's innovations, wrote an epigram against Lomonosov, but neither the epigram nor Trediakovsky's letter has survived. The letter did not even reach Lomonosov at the time, for the academy decided to refrain from sending it in order to economize on postage. Lomonosov never forgot that Trediakovsky's and Sumarokov's first responses to his suggestions were not entirely enthusiastic.

According to legend, however, everyone at the academy and at court was so impressed by Lomonosov's literary debut that the ode was hailed as an exemplary literary work and immediately published. In fact, the ode was not published until 1751 in *Sobranie raznykh sochinenii,* and the essay in 1778, in another *Sobranie raznykh sochinenii.* Lomonosov significantly revised the ode for its

1751 publication, taking into account Trediakovsky's and Sumarokov's criticism of his ideas about versification. Contemporaries only knew the first version of the ode from excerpts that Lomonosov included in his 1743 and 1748 treatises on rhetoric. The first ode's later reputation as an extraordinary mature work was thus based on the 1751 version. It is true, however, that in the 1740s and 1750s Lomonosov established the standards of the Russian solemn ode: the obligatory use of iambic tetrameter, the ten-line stanza, the lofty and intense style, and the use of bold metaphors. Despite energetic objections on the part of Sumarokov and his disciples, Lomonosov became the acknowledged authority on solemn odes.

Upon his return to Saint Petersburg, Lomonosov maintained his affiliation with the academy. At first his duties were not defined, and he worked on several projects simultaneously: taking lessons in natural history, compiling a catalogue of the academy's mineral collection, translating his colleagues' articles for academy publications, and conducting some research on his own. He became an adjunct at the academy on 8 January 1742 and began teaching, first physics and later poetics and eloquence. Lomonosov's scientific work in the 1740s included several articles on physics and chemistry and a translation of a chapter from Ludwig Philipp Thümming's edition of Christian Wolff's textbook on physics, which he published under the title *Volfianskaia eksperimental'naia fizika* (Wolffian Experimental Physics, 1746). In July 1745 he was appointed professor of chemistry, becoming (together with Trediakovsky, who received the rank of professor of Latin and Russian eloquence) one of the two first Russian professors at the academy.

The early 1740s were the years of Lomonosov's fiercest clashes with his colleagues at the academy. His main quarrel was with Johann Daniel Schumacher, secretary of the academy's chancellery, who for thirty years had been, for all practical purposes, the head of the academy. Lomonosov accused him of corruption and of anti-Russian policies. The two high points of this battle were the fight that Lomonosov had in September 1742 with the family and guests of his neighbor, the academy gardener Johann Sturm, and a drunken brawl he caused at the academy conference in April 1743 for which he was put under arrest – first in the guardhouse and later at home – for more than six months. Throughout his life Lomonosov would claim injustices on the part of his German colleagues, but never again did he resort to violence.

In the 1740s Lomonosov continued to work as a poet and a literary scholar. He celebrated the brief reign of Ivan VI, the infant nephew of the late Empress Anna, with two solemn odes, but his real heroine became Elizabeth, the daughter of Peter I, who dethroned Ivan on 7 November 1741. Lomonosov devoted more than ten solemn odes to her, as well as many orations and laudatory inscriptions. In his odes to Elizabeth, Lomonosov pictured her as a monarch who restored the heroic and generous spirit of Peter the Great's reign which had been extinguished by his successors, especially Empress Anna. Lomonosov's solemn odes gained him the reputation of a "czars' flatterer," but the idealization of Elizabeth and contemporary Russian life in his odes can largely be accounted for by the requirements of the genre, as well as the poet's desire to inspire Elizabeth to return to the grandeur of her father's domestic and foreign policies.

While under arrest in 1743 Lomonosov composed his first work on rhetoric, "Kratkoe rukovodstvo k ritorike, na pol'zu liubitelei sladkorechiia sochinennoe" (Brief Handbook of Eloquence Composed for the Benefit of Lovers of Sweet-Tongued Speech), a relatively small essay that became known simply as the 1743 *Rhetoric*. In this essay, which was not published in Lomonosov's lifetime (it was first collected in *Sochineniia*, 1891–1948), the author quoted many of his early poems that have not survived in any other sources. The 1743 *Rhetoric* served as a starting point for Lomonosov's much more complete and detailed *Kratkoe rukovodstvo k krasnorechiiu, kniga pervaia, v kotoroi soderzhitsia ritorika pokazuiushchaia obshchie pravila oboego krasnorechiia, to est' oratorii i poezii* (Brief Handbook of Eloquence, Book One, Which Includes Rhetoric that Demonstrates General Rules of Both Eloquences, That Is, Oratory and Poetry, 1748), commonly referred to as the 1748 *Rhetoric*. The work was conceived as a three-volume enterprise, of which only the first volume, a general discussion of rhetoric, was published. The second volume, in which Lomonosov planned to examine oratorical works in prose, and the third, in which he was to consider the problems of poetics, were apparently never written. In the 1748 *Rhetoric* Lomonosov set forth his understanding of the rhetorical nature of socially important poetic genres such as solemn odes. The rhetorical principle was crucial to his idea of poetic discourse, especially his notion of the poetic word as polysemous. The treatise became a popular textbook and underwent several reprintings during Lomonosov's lifetime.

Lomonosov illustrated his ideas in the 1748 *Rhetoric* with original poetry and translations. One such work was the first Russian rendition of Horace's ode "Exegi monumentum aere perennius" (*Carmina* III, 30). Unlike Gavriil Derzhavin, Aleksandr Pushkin, and Valerii Briusov, later translators of this poem who introduced details from their own lives to emphasize the value of their contributions, Lomonosov, in his "Ia znak bessmertiia sebe vozdvignul" (I Have Erected a Monument of My Immortality), remained very close to the original. Nevertheless, he counted on his readers to notice an important similarity between Horace and himself: a rise to poetic greatness from humble origins. Lomonosov's "Vechernee razmyshlenie o Bozhiem velichestve pri sluchae velikogo sevenogo siianiia" (Evening Meditation Upon the Greatness of God, on the Occasion of the Great Northern Lights), written in 1743, was also included in the 1748 *Rhetoric*. The poem expresses the poet's admiration for God's power, displayed in natural phenomena and the beautifully designed universe. For Lomonosov the fact that the universe is infinite and contains countless worlds demonstrates God's greatness. The wisdom of God manifests itself through consistent and cognizable laws of nature. Unknown causes of phenomena such as the northern lights, he asserts, will eventually be explained scientifically. Lomonosov also admires the works of God, especially the sun, in "Utrenee razhmyshlenie o Bozhiem velichestve" (Morning Meditation upon the Greatness of God), written in 1743 or the late 1740s. He wonders what a scientist might see if it were possible to approach the sun. But not everything is open to the inquisitiveness of the human eye and mind, and this also proves God's might and grandeur. The combination of religious and scientific motifs is characteristic of Lomonosov's view of nature.

In the 1740s Lomonosov's relations with Trediakovsky and Sumarokov were friendly and cooperative. The three poets critiqued each other's poetry and discussed the principles of the new system of versification. One product of such discussions was a booklet, *Tri ody parafrasticheskie psalma 143, sochinennye chrez trekh stikhotvortsev, iz kotorykh kazhdoi odnu slozhil osoblivo* (Three Paraphrases of the 143rd Psalm, Composed by Three Poets, Each One Composing One Independently, 1744), in which the poets anonymously translated the same psalm and appealed to readers to resolve the theoretical question about whether or not meter must correspond to subject matter and theme. Lomonosov and Sumarokov maintained that the iamb was more suitable for the solemn diction of ode, whereas the trochee was better for "tender" genres, such as love

songs. Trediakovsky asserted that the meters are neutral with respect to subject matter. In their translations Lomonosov and Sumarokov used iambic tetrameter, while Trediakovsky employed trochaic tetrameter. Although Trediakovsky was right in theory, Lomonosov's preference for the iamb in odes prevailed.

In other cases Lomonosov was more responsive to suggestions. Thus he accepted criticism of one of the rules he had proposed in his version of syllabo-tonic reform. In "Pis'mo o pravilakh rossiiskogo stikhotvorstva" he insisted that an ideal iambic line should not allow pyrrhics; that is, every foot had to be stressed. This rule works for trisyllabics, since the average length of a word in Russian is three syllables, but in bisyllabics it unduly restricts the choice of words and produces an awkward, "stumbling" verse. In his 1743 *Rhetoric* Lomonosov was still insisting on the rule of "pure iambs," but around 1744 or 1745 he abandoned it. On the whole, the collaboration of the three poets during the 1740s was fruitful and allowed them to complete the reform of Russian versification and to formulate the general principles of syllabo-tonics as presented in Trediakovsky's 1752 *Sposob k slozheniiu Rossiiskikh stikhov* (Method for Composing Russian Verse).

The harmony, however, started to disintegrate in the late 1740s. The first conflicts were between Sumarokov and Trediakovsky. Then a bitter disagreement arose between Trediakovsky and Lomonosov over which of them deserved credit for the syllabo-tonic reform. Trediakovsky felt that priority was his, but Lomonosov vigorously contested his claim. Using his influence at the academy and its press, he tried to censure Trediakovsky's works dealing with this question and partially succeeded. The question was not entirely ceremonial: because of a normative aesthetic mentality in Russian letters that ascribed crucial importance to models, each of them strived to present his own works as the only correct examples for the newly emerging Russian literature.

In the beginning of the 1750s quarrels between Lomonosov and Sumarokov erupted. The most important point of their disagreement, sometimes presented as a clash between baroque and classicist aesthetics, was Lomonosov's concept of the poetic word. Sumarokov understood the word in poetry as having only one unchanging meaning, basically that of common usage, and a poet was supposed to respect this commonly accepted meaning. For Lomonosov the context helped determine the meaning of the word. Thus its sense could change, espe-

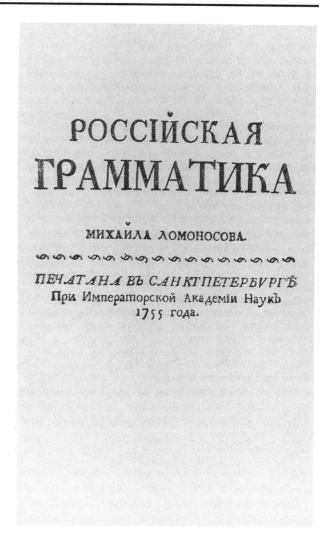

Frontispiece and title page for Lomonosov's Rossiiskaia grammatika, *the first Russian grammar to be published in Russian*

cially in tropes, revealing shades of meaning beyond those recorded in dictionaries. For Lomonosov this was the greatest source of power that poetry had over its audience. The unexpected, *deavtomatizirovannyi* ("disautomatized," in the terminology of Russian formalists) word, the unusual simile, and the metaphor that brings together disparate ideas were his means of creating artistic effects. Sumarokov considered this approach as not only idiosyncratic but wrong. He criticized Lomonosov's poetic usage as mistaken, ignorant, and sloppy. In his critical essays Sumarokov tried to prove that Lomonosov's practice was incorrect from the point of view of linguistics, and in brilliant parodies he demonstrated the alleged absurdity of Lomonosov's approach to the poetic word by taking it to extremes.

The disagreement between the two poets was aggravated by Lomonosov's intrusion into the genre of drama, which Sumarokov considered his own domain. In 1750 Elizabeth ordered Lomonosov and Trediakovsky to write a tragedy apiece. Lomonosov wrote *Tamira i Selim* (Tamira and Selim, 1750) and *Demofont* (Demophon, 1752). The first tragedy combines an oriental love story of a Baghdad prince and a Tatar princess whose romance is threatened by Mamai, the leader of the Golden Horde, with the historical story of Mamai's defeat in the battle of Kulikovo Field in 1380. The two narratives are not well integrated, since Lomonosov is obviously more interested in describing the glory of the Russian victory over the Mongols than in the romance between the fictional Selim and Tamira. Lomonosov employs unusual verse in his tragedy: instead of iambic hexameter couplets, advocated by Sumarokov as an imitation of French alexandrines, he uses cross-rhymes. Russian playwrights, however, ignored Lomonosov's experiment and followed Sumarokov's example.

In *Demofont* Lomonosov presented the story of Theseus's son, Demophon, and Phyllis, the daughter of a Thracian king, but he freely adapted the ancient plot. Creating a love triangle that ended in multiple violent deaths, he attempted to reconstruct the ancient, barbaric Greece of Homer's time. His characters, in contrast to those of Sumarokov's tragedies, are moved by passions and seem to be ignorant of the notion of duty; many students of *Demofont* have pointed out its similarity to Jean Racine's *Andromaque* (1667). *Demofont* and Trediakovsky's *Deidamiia* (1750) represent rare attempts to introduce classical plots into Russian tragedy. Their innovations were of little consequence for Russian theater: Sumarokov's preference for plots from Russian national history prevailed.

In 1751 Lomonosov published his *Sobranie raznykh sochinenii v stikhakh i v proze* (Collection of Various Works in Verse and in Prose). Of two planned volumes, only the first was printed. The collection opened with "Spiritual Odes," paraphrases of psalms and other biblical texts, the best-known of which is "Oda vybrannaia iz Iova, glavy 38, 39, 40 i 41" (Ode Selected from Job, Chapters 38, 39, 40, and 41). Lomonosov's rendition of the biblical text focuses on the glory of God as creator: the wisdom of God's creation and the beauty of a universe full of natural wonders once again inspires religious feelings in the poet.

A new vision of the "Oda na vziatie Khotina" opens the collection's next section, "Solemn Odes." A misprint – "Castilian spring" instead of "Castalian" – inspired a common joke that Lomonosov was drunk with "Castilian waters" when he composed the poem. The majority of other odes were written in the 1740s on the occasions of Elizabeth's birthdays, namedays, and anniversaries of her ascension. Collected under one cover for the first time, they reinforced the emerging canon of the Russian solemn ode. They also presented the image of Elizabeth as the mother of Russia and, occasionally, as Mother Russia. This image significantly influenced the formation of Russian patriotic discourse.

"Laudatory Inscriptions" is the title of the next section, which collects commissioned poetry, except for the "Nadpisi k statue Petra Velikogo" (Inscriptions for the Statue of Peter the Great). These five short poems, written between 1743 and 1747, describe the two statues of Peter designed by Carlo Rastrelli (one of them was eventually erected in 1799). The inscriptions develop the image of Peter the Great as the creator of new Russia, an image that had first appeared in Lomonosov's "Oda na vziatie Khotina":

Небесная отверзлась дверь,
Над войском облак вдруг развился,
Блеснул горящим вдруг лицем,
Умытым кровию мечем
Гоня врагов, Герой открылся.

(The celestial door opened,
A cloud suddenly unfolded over the troops,
And, his fiery face suddenly shining,
And with bloodied sword
The Hero appeared, pursuing his enemies.)

Lomonosov gives Peter the attributes of the thunder god:

Кругом его из облаков
Гремящие перуны блещут,
И чувствуя приход Петров,
Дубравы и поля трепещут.

(Around him from out of the clouds
The roaring thunderbolts flash,
And, sensing Peter's advance,
Woods and fields tremble.)

In the "Nadpisi" Lomonosov again stresses the divine nature of Peter, the creator of Russia:

И словом, се есть Петр, отечества Отец;
Земное божество Россия почитает . . .

(In a word, this is Peter, Father of the fatherland;
Russia worships the earthly divinity . . .)

However, Lomonosov adds a new trait to his portrait of the divine Peter and pictures him as a czar capable of temporarily shedding his divine and regal persona and assuming the humble role of one who labors for the benefit of his subjects:

Рожденны царствовать, простер в работу руки.
Монаршу власть скрывал, чтоб нам открыть науки.
Когда он строил град, сносил труды в войнах,
В землях далеких был и странствовал в морях,
Художников сбирал и обучал солдатов,
Домашних побеждал и внешних супостатов.

(Hands born to hold the scepter he extended to work.
He hid his kingly power in order to open up the sciences to us.
[He did that] when he built the city [Saint Petersburg], bore the labors of war,
Was in far-off lands and traveled upon the seas,
Gathered artists and trained soldiers,
And defeated his enemies both domestic and external.)

Both aspects of Peter's image, divine and human, were absorbed by Russian tradition and became integral elements of his reputation as the creator of modern Russia.

Lomonosov's tragedies and the publication of *Sobranie raznykh sochinenii* intensified the polemics between him and Sumarokov. Around this time Sumarokov produced his first "Ody vzdornye" (Nonsense Odes), as his parodies of Lomonosov later became known. Ivan Elagin composed a "Satira na petimetra i koketok" (Satire on a Fop and Coquettes, 1753), which asserted Sumarokov's superiority as a playwright. The satire incited a debate to which virtually all writers of the period contributed. Lomonosov's reaction included an epigram on Elagin and mockery of his satire in a letter to Ivan Shuvalov, Lomonosov's patron.

In 1755 Lomonosov finished his *Rossiiskaia grammatika* (Russian Grammar), published in 1757, although the title page bears the date of 1755. This was the first published grammar of the Russian language written in Russian, although several foreign grammars of Russian had appeared. The treatise managed to codify vernacular Russian, which had been in disarray since the cultural turmoil of Peter's reign. It addressed questions of orthography and alphabet and gave the first consistent overviews of Russian morphology and syntax. Lomonosov's stylistic comments in the book influenced contemporary usage. Despite vigorous criticism of *Rossiiskaia grammatika,* especially by Sumarokov, it remained the most widely used Russian grammar until the end of the eighteenth century.

In 1756 Lomonosov initiated another debate, this time more ideological than literary. His disciple, Nikolai Popovsky, had translated Alexander Pope's *Essay on Man* (1733–1734), but this translation was banned by the Holy Synod. Lomonosov reacted with "Gimn borode" (Hymn to the Beard), in which he mockingly lauded beards, a customary feature of masculine appearance in Russia before Peter's reforms and associated with the Russian Orthodox clergy, hence a symbol of obscurantism. The incident aggravated Lomonosov and Trediakovsky's conflict, as it related to the former's mistaken belief that the latter was the author of a letter, signed Kristofor Zubnitsky, accusing Lomonosov of atheism. It circulated together with an insulting poem, "Pereodetaia boroda, ili gimn p'ianoi golove" (The Disguised Beard, or Hymn to a Drunken Head), in which Lomonosov's low origin was ridiculed. Lomonosov's animosity was a strong contributing factor in Trediakovsky's decision to leave the academy in the late 1750s.

In 1758 the first volume of Lomonosov's two-volume collection *Sobranie raznykh sochinenii v stikhakh i proze* (Collection of Various Works in Verse and in Prose) was published, with a promise that the second volume would appear the following year; it was not published, however, until 1765. As the preface to the first volume, he printed one of his most influential works, "Predislovie o pol'ze knig tserkovnykh v Rossiiskom iazyke" (Preface on the Usefulness of Church Books in the Russian Tongue, 1758), an attempt to define the relationship between vernacular Russian and Church Slavonic, which before the eighteenth century had been the primary literary language. Lomonosov asserted the value of Church Slavonic for Russian culture as an intermediary between modern Russian and ancient Greek, which Lomonosov believed provided the structure of Slavonic, but at the same time he set limits on its usage in literary works. He tied the use of Slavonicisms to the hierarchy of genres accepted in eighteenth-century Russia, allowing commonly understood Slavonicisms in the so-called "high" genres (odes and epics), restricting them in "middle" genres (tragedies, epistles, elegies), and forbidding them in "low" genres (comedies, epigrams, songs). Lomonosov's adaptation of the theory of three styles to the Russian situation was so successful that it still constitutes the framework of Russian stylistic theory, although not literary practice.

Between 1756 and 1761 Lomonosov composed a work considered to be his credo. "Razgovor s Anakreonom" (A Conversation with Anacreon) consists of eight poems: translations of four odes ascribed to Anacreon and four replies by Lomonosov. In this dialogue the poet asserts the value of socially significant genres over love poetry and stresses the poet's responsibilities. The first and the last pairs are especially demonstrative. The first ode by Anacreon (a new translation of a poem Lomonosov translated while in Germany) describes a poet who wants to sing about heroes, but his instrument (*gusli,* in Lomonosov's translation) can sing only about love. In the answering poem Lomonosov claims that he would like to sing about love but is able only to laud heroes. The last pair of poems juxtaposes a portrait of Anacreon's beloved – a young, attractive girl – with a portrait of Lomonosov's "beloved mother," Russia, pictured as a mature woman with a robust body and breasts full of milk.

Lomonosov's reputation as a scientist and administrator grew in the 1750s. He studied atmospheric electricity (in one of the experiments in 1753, his colleague, Georg Richmann, was killed by lightning), continued research in physics and chemistry, and maintained his interest in mining and metallurgy. In 1754 he proposed a plan for a university in Moscow in a letter to Shuvalov, who helped to bring the project to fruition in 1755. Lomonosov's influence in the Academy of Sciences grew (although not at the rate Lomonosov would have preferred): in 1757 he became a member of the academy chancellery; in 1758, the head of the Department of Geography; and in 1760, the head of the academy gymnasium and university. At the same time he suffered some defeats in his war with fellow academicians. Thus in 1755 he did not succeed in a plan to reorganize the academy that would have given him the position of vice-president, and in 1757 he lost his chemistry laboratory to Ulrich Christoph Salchow, a chemist from Germany. His pet project in the 1750s was the introduction of the art of mosaics to Russia. In 1752 he completed his first mosaic work, a copy of Francesco Solimena's "Madonna," after which he received permission to build a colored-glass factory. A monument of his enthusiasm for glass in general and for mosaic in particular was his poem "Poslanie o pol'ze stekla" (Epistle on the Usefulness of Glass, 1752), in which he hailed the material as an invention of human genius and listed its various uses. Lomonosov's most famous mosaic works are his portrait of Peter the Great (1754) and his "The Battle of Poltava" (1764). For his achievements in this art form Lomonosov was made an honorary member of the Academy of Arts in 1763.

Lomonosov's poetic production in the 1760s was small. In 1760 he published the first canto of his heroic poem, *Petr Velikii* (Peter the Great), and the second canto in 1761. In these cantos (no more were ever written) Lomonosov further developed the image of Peter as divine creator of the Russian state. The work was one of many unsuccessful attempts to create a Russian national epic in the eighteenth century. In 1761 Lomonosov included two brief poems in his academy presentation concerning the planet Venus. One of them was a humorous piece, "Sluchilis' vmeste dva Astronoma v piru" (Two Astronomers Happened to Be Together at a Feast), in which the correctness of Copernicus's theory was inferred by a comparison of the sun to a hearth and the planets to a roast: nobody rotates the hearth around the roast. Lomonosov's odes to the new monarchs, first Peter III and then Catherine the Great, were not as significant as his odes to Elizabeth, nor were they as well received, and Lomonosov lost his position as Russia's de facto official panegyrist.

Lomonosov had become interested in the problems of Russian history in 1749, when he was

Lomonosov's grave in the Aleksandr Nevsky Monastery in Saint Petersburg (photograph by Marcus Levitt)

asked to evaluate the dissertation of a colleague, Gerhard Friedrich Müller, "De origine gentis et nominis Russorum" (On the Origin and Name of Russian People). Müller espoused the so-called Norman theory of the origins of Russian state, according to which the first Russian princes were Scandinavians. Lomonosov took a patriotic stance and accused Müller of denigrating the honor of the Russian nation. He had written two historical works in the 1750s, which appeared in print in the 1760s: the *Kratkoi Rossiiskoi letopisets s rodosloviem* (Brief Russian Chronicle with a Genealogy, 1760) and *Drevniaia Rossiiskaia istoriia ot nachala rossiiskogo naroda do konchiny velikogo kniazia Iaroslava pervogo, ili do 1054 goda* (Ancient Russian History from the Beginning of the Russian Nation to the Death of the Great Prince Iaroslav I, or to 1054, 1766). These works assert a patriotic version of Russian history, sometimes bending facts to fit his ideas. Both books, despite their bias, were popular in Russia and translated into foreign languages. Lomonosov also planned to write a history of Peter the Great, and as a specialist on this topic, he evaluated the manuscript of Voltaire's *Histoire de l'empire de Russie sous Pierre le Grand* (1761, 1763) and supplied the French author with materials.

Lomonosov's scientific projects in the 1760s included an article about a passage to India via the Arctic Ocean, a work on economics and population growth in Russia, and a book on mining and metallurgy. He was elected an honorary member of the Swedish Academy in 1760 and the Bologna Academy in 1764. Overall, however, Lomonosov was bitter in his last years. After Catherine the Great ascended the throne, he lost the protection of Shuvalov, and the new empress promoted his enemies at the academy. In July 1762 Lomonosov wrote a letter of resignation, which was accepted in May 1763, and he retired with the rank of state councillor. The retirement was soon reversed, however, and Lomonosov was even honored by Catherine's visit to his house, but he still felt that he had suffered a profound defeat in all of his enterprises. A chronic, unspecified illness, from which he had suffered since 1748, turned worse, and Lomonosov died on the second day of Easter, 4 April 1765. He was buried in the Aleksandr Nevsky Monastery in Saint Petersburg.

Soon after the writer's death, his image as the father of Russian literature began to form. He was portrayed as an extraordinary child, a youth overcoming insurmountable obstacles on his way to knowledge, a heroic fighter for the honor of Russian science and scholarship, and an inspired poet creating Russian literature out of nothing. By the end of the century he was portrayed as an authority in all fields of Russian literature, regardless of his actual achievements. The Romantic epoch, lukewarm to Lomonosov's poetry, admired his biography, picturing him as a genius, misunderstood and mistreated by his contemporaries. Soviet scholarship – especially during Josef Stalin's period, when a ten-volume collection of Lomonosov's complete works was produced – reinforced Lomonosov's heroic image as the creator of Russian literature and science and the defender of national culture. Lomonosov's heroic reputation ensured the popularity of the poetic principles he had advocated. Thus Lomonosov was largely responsible for the predominance of iambic tetrameter and rhymed verse in Russian poetry, as well as its reliance on tropes as the chief element of poetic diction and its relative indifference to stylistic experimentation. But most of all, it is as a personality, an embodiment of poetic genius, that Lomonosov has affected Russian cultural consciousness. Indeed, the perception of the poet as hero, characteristic of Russian culture, can be traced to Lomonosov's reputation as the father of Russian literature.

Letters:
M. V. Lomonosov, *Polnoe sobranie sochinenii,* volume 10 (Moscow & Leningrad: Akademiia nauk, 1957), pp. 415–599.

Bibliographies:
Boris Bukhshtab, *Lomonosov: Ukazatel' osnovnoi literatury* (Leningrad: [Publichnaia Biblioteka im. Saltykova-Shchedrina], 1940);

German M. Korovin, *M. V. Lomonosov: Ukazatel' osnovnoi nauchnoi literatury* (Moscow & Leningrad: Akademiia nauk, 1950);

E. B. Ryss, "Bibliografiia osnovnoi literatury o M. V. Lomonosove za 1911–1916 gg., " *Lomonosov: Sbornik statei i materialov,* 3 (1951): 587–607;

Ryss and Korovin, "Bibliografiia sochinenii M. V. Lomonosova i literatury o nem za 1917–1950 gg., " *Lomonosov: Sbornik statei i materialov,* 3 (1951): 501–586;

Ryss and Korovin, "Bibliografiia sochinenii M. V. Lomonosova i literatury o nem za 1951–1955 gg.," *Lomonosov: Sbornik statei i materialov,* 4 (1960): 401–438;

Ryss, "Bibliografiia sochinenii Lomonosova i literatury o nem za 1956–1960 gg., " *Lomonosov: Sbornik statei i materialov,* 6 (1961): 355–381.

Biographies:
P. P. Pekarsky, "Zhizneopisanie M. V. Lomonosova," in his *Istoriia Imperatorskoi Akademii Nauk v Peterburge,* volume 2 (Saint Petersburg: Akademiia nauk, 1873), pp. 259–963;

Boris N. Menshutkin, *M. V. Lomonosov: Zhizhneopisanie* (Saint Petersburg: Akademiia nauk, 1911); translated by Jeanette Eyre Thal and Edward J. Webster as *Russia's Lomonosov: Chemist, Courtier, Physicist, Poet* (Princeton: Princeton University Press, 1952);

Aleksandr A. Morozov, *M. V. Lomonosov: 1711–1765* (Moscow: Gazetno-zhurnal'noe i knizhnoe izdatel'stvo, 1952);

Morozov, *M. V. Lomonosov: Put' k zrelosti, 1711–1741* (Moscow & Leningrad: Akademiia nauk, 1962);

Galina E. Pavlova and Aleksandr S. Fedorov, *Mikhail Vasil'evich Lomonosov: His Life and Work,* translated by Artur Aksenov, edited by Richard Hainsworth (Moscow: Mir, 1984);

Evgenii N. Lebedev, *Lomonosov* (Moscow: Molodaia gvardiia, 1990).

References:

Pavel N. Berkov, *Lomonosov i literaturnaia polemika ego vremeni* (Moscow & Leningrad: Akademiia nauk, 1936);

Evgenii B. Beshenkovsky and E. S. Kuliabko, *Sud'ba biblioteki i arkhiva M. V. Lomonosova* (Leningrad: Nauka, 1975);

S. Chernov, "Literaturnoe nasledstvo M. V. Lomonosova," *Literaturnoe nasledstvo,* 9–10 (1933): 327–339;

Aleksandr S. Kurilov, ed. *Lomonosov i russkaia literatura* (Moscow: Nauka, 1987);

Lomonosov: Sbornik statei i materialov, 8 volumes, edited by A. I. Andreeva and L. B. Modzalevskogo (Moscow & Leningrad, 1940–1983);

L. B. Modzalevsky, *Rukopisi Lomonosova v Akademii nauk SSSR: Nauchnoe opisanie* (Leningrad: Akademiia nauk, 1937);

Aleksandr A. Morozov, "Lomonosov i barokko," *Russkaia literatura,* 2 (1965): 70–96;

Ilya Serman and Berkov, eds., *Literaturnoe tvorchestvo M. V. Lomonosova: Issledovaniia i materialy* (Moscow & Leningrad: Akademiia nauk, 1962);

Serman, *Mikhail Lomonosov: Life and Poetry,* translated by Stephany Hoffman (Jerusalem: Lexicon, 1988);

Serman, *Poeticheskii stil' Lomonosova* (Moscow & Leningrad: Nauka, 1966);

Rimvydas Silbajoris, *Russian Versification: The Theories of Trediakovskij, Lomonosov, and Kantemir* (New York: Columbia University Press, 1968);

Valentin P. Vompersky, *Stilisticheskoe uchenie M. V. Lomonosova i teoriia trekh stilei* (Moscow: Moskovskii universitet, 1970).

Nikolai Aleksandrovich L'vov

(1751 – 21 December 1803)

Konstantin Iur'evich Lappo-Danilevsky
Institute of Russian Literature (Pushkin House), Saint Petersburg

BOOKS: *Iamshchiki na podstave. Igrishche nevznachai* (Tambov: Vol'naia tipografiia, 1788);

Ruskoi 1791 god (Saint Petersburg: Gornoe uchilishche, [1791]);

Ruskaia pirostatika, ili Upotreblenie ispytannykh uzhe vozdushnykh pechei i kaminov . . ., 2 volumes (Saint Petersburg: Korpus chuzhestrannykh edinovertsev, 1795–1799);

O pol'ze i upotreblenii ruskogo zemlianogo uglia Sochinena v Galiche 1799 avgusta v 27 den' (Saint Petersburg: Shnor, 1799).

Edition: *Izbrannye sochineniia*, edited by Konstantin Iu. Lappo-Danilevsky (Saint Petersburg: Acropolis, 1994).

OTHER: Eunemond Alexandre Petitot, *Rassuzhdenie o perspektive, oblegchaiushchee upotreblenie onoi, v pol'zu narodnykh uchilishch*, translated by L'vov (Saint Petersburg: Gornoe uchilishche, 1789);

Sobranie narodnykh ruskikh pesen s ikh golosami. Na muzyku polozhil Ivan Prach, edited by L'vov (Saint Petersburg: Gornoe uchilishche, 1790);

Letopisets russkoi ot prishestviia Rurika do konchiny Ioanna Vasil'evicha, 5 volumes, edited by L'vov (Saint Petersburg: Gornoe uchilishche, 1792);

Paul Henri Mallet, *Pesn' norvezhskogo vitiazia Garal'da Khrabrogo, iz drevnei islandskoi letopisi Knitlinga saga g. Malletom vypisannaia, i v Datskoi istorii pomeshchennaia, perelozhena na rossiiskii iazyk obrazom drevniago stikhotvoreniia s primeru Ne zvezda blestit daleche vo chistom pole,* translated by L'vov ([Saint Petersburg], 1793);

Anacreon, *Stikhotvorenie Anakreona Tiiskogo,* 3 volumes, translated by L'vov (Saint Petersburg, 1794);

Andrea Palladio, *Chetyre knigi Palladievoi arkhitektury . . . ,* translated by L'vov (Saint Petersburg: Shnor, 1798);

Podrobnaia letopis' ot nachala Rossii do Poltavskoi batalii, 4 volumes, edited by L'vov (Saint Petersburg: Shnor, 1798–1799).

Nikolai Aleksandrovich L'vov

SELECTED PERIODICAL PUBLICATIONS – UNCOLLECTED: "Pesenka," *Sankt-Peterburgskii vestnik,* 6 (August 1780): 127;

"Idillia. Vecher 1780 goda noiabria 8," anonymous, *Sobesednik liubitelei rossiskogo slova,* 1 (May 1783): 28–32;

"Otryvok iz pis'ma A. M. B.," *Muza,* 2 (1796).

The L'vov-Derzhavin circle, inspired by Nikolai Aleksandrovich L'vov and lasting for more than thirty years, occupies an important position in the history of Russian letters. Starting in the 1770s, some of the most prominent Russian poets became associated with L'vov, including Gavriil Derzhavin, Vasilii Kapnist, Ivan Khemnitser, and Mikhail Murav'ev. The writers of this group were among the first to depart from classicist notions of art as the imitation of external models, classical or foreign, or as didactic propaganda designed to support an absolutist government. To them, literature (and art in general) was neither a craft open to everyone nor a hobby to which one devoted time after retirement – it was a fate and a calling.

L'vov helped acquaint his friends in Russia with Western culture, not only as a result of his wide travels in Europe, but also through his contacts in the aristocratic circles of Saint Petersburg and the friendships he cultivated with foreign artists and actors, primarily Italians. L'vov strove to emulate the Renaissance ideal of developing all sides of the human being. His interests went far beyond literature, and from the 1780s on he dedicated his time to architectural projects and to other activities such as collecting folklore, publishing early Russian chronicles, and leading geological surveys. Yet at no point did he abandon his literary pursuits, and perhaps it was as a result of his diverse interests that almost every one of his literary works was experimental, provoking new ideas and attacking literary stereotypes.

Nikolai Aleksandrovich L'vov was born in 1751 in the village of Cherenchitsy (in the Torzhok district of Tver province) to a noble family of modest means but with close ties to aristocratic relatives in Saint Petersburg. Little is known about his early years save that he had a boisterous and mischievous character. The loss of his father was the first hardship the young L'vov endured. As was common among the gentry of the time, L'vov was enlisted as a child in the Preobrazhensky Regiment, in which he began to serve in person at the end of 1769. From 1770 to 1771 he attended a school attached to the Izmailovsky Regiment and studied drawing, French, German, and other subjects. From March to July 1771 he took part in creating a manuscript journal entitled *Trudy chetyrekh razumnykh obshchnikov* (Works by Four Clever Companions). The undertaking was on a student level, and it is not surprising that it mostly consisted of translations – from Nicholas Boileau, Jean de La Fontaine, Voltaire, François Fénelon, Christian Gellert, and Gotthold Lessing. Already apparent, however, was the young poet's individual and lively manner. In one original poem he describes pranks that ended in his arrest; in another he heaps abuse on a colleague.

Active service in the Preobrazhensky Regiment (1771–1775) was hardly a burden for L'vov. Influen-

tial relatives helped him acquire a wide circle of contacts and even arranged trips for him to Denmark and Germany as a courier for the College of Foreign Affairs. With the sponsorship of P. V. Bakunin-Men'shoi, a relative highly positioned in Catherine II's court, L'vov received a post in the College of Foreign Affairs on 5 June 1776 as a translator, and he was awarded the rank of captain in consideration of his knowledge of Italian, French, and German. Notable among his assignments was a trip to London, Madrid, and Paris as a courier in 1776–1777. On the return trip he spent several months in Paris, where he met his uncle M. F. Soimonov, a member of Catherine's most intimate circle of friends, and the poet Ivan Khemnitser. The brilliant culture of the French capital during the epoch of the Encyclopedists fascinated the Russian visitors. They became regulars at the Comédie Française, the Comédie Italienne, and the Grand Opéra and occasionally attended the popular theaters "on the Boulevard." They enjoyed performances by the great actors of the day – Lekein, Larive, Brizard, Legras, and Clairval.

Upon returning to Saint Petersburg, L'vov started an amateur theater in the home of Bakunin-Men'shoi. It opened on 18 December 1777 with Jean-François Regnard's *Le Joeur* (The Gambler, 1696), in which L'vov played Géront, and Nicholas Framéry's comic opera *La Colonie* (1776), with music by Antonio Sacchini. The two shows were performed several times during the winter of 1777–1778. L'vov evidently also performed in Iakov Kniazhnin's tragedy *Didona* (Dido, first staged 1767 or 1769), staged at Bakunin-Men'shoi's theater in the author's presence.

The amateur theater played a significant role in L'vov's private life as well. The female roles in Regnard's, Framéry's, and Kniazhnin's plays were performed by the D'iakov sisters, and one of them, Maria, became L'vov's wife in 1780. The story of their romance has been passed down in the memoirs of Sofia Kapnist-Sealon. As the story goes, because of his poverty, L'vov's proposal of marriage was rejected by Maria's parents, even though she shared his affection. The poet Vasilii Kapnist, who was married to another sister, Aleksandra, had free access to the D'iakov house. While escorting the D'iakov sisters to a ball in the winter of 1780, he took them on a detour to the Church of the Life-Giving Trinity on Vasil'evsky Island, and L'vov and Maria D'iakova were secretly married. Several years later Maria's parents, still ignorant of the truth, finally agreed to their marriage, seeing that it was hopeless to stand in the way of young love. A date was fixed, and on the eve of their wedding the bride and groom revealed their secret. In 1794 Gavriil Derzhavin married the youngest of the D'iakov sisters, Dar'ia. Thus three outstanding eighteenth-century poets were linked not only by common aesthetic interests, but by marital ties as well.

A notebook preserved in the Institute of Russian Literature (Pushkin House) reveals a great deal about the development of L'vov's literary tastes during the 1770s. During these years he made a thorough study of French literature (Pierre Corneille, Jean Racine, François Fénelon, Jean-Jacques Rousseau, Jean-François Marmontel, and others). His attention was focused on works concerned with the individual's inner world – from Petrarch's sonnets to the epistolary novels of the Marquis d'Argens and Charles-Louis Montesquieu – an interest directly linked with the emergence of Russian sentimentalism. Among L'vov's original works from this period were a large number of unpublished songs (influenced strongly by Sumarokov) as well as madrigals, epigrams, epitaphs, and riddles. During the second half of the 1770s L'vov became close with Iakov Kniazhnin and B. F. Arndt, the publishers of the *Sankt-Peterburgskii vestnik* (Saint Petersburg Herald), and it is possible that he was responsible for several short notes on architecture in the journal. Without question L'vov was author of "Pesenka" (A Little Song), published in August 1780, with music written by D. S. Bortniansky.

L'vov's real literary debut, however, came with the publication of his poem "Idillia. Vecher 1780 goda noiabria 8" (Idyll. The Evening of 8 November 1780) in the journal *Sobesednik liubitelei rossiskogo slova* (Interlocutor of Lovers of the Russian Word) in the first number for 1783. Although the work was unsigned, its authorship was no secret to anyone in the literary world. The poem reflected L'vov's passion for French erotic poetry and anticipated early-nineteenth-century trends. Despite its favorable reception, this sort of poetry did not satisfy L'vov, and he soon came to value an absence of artifice and the use of artistic forms with more clearly national coloration.

L'vov's travels in Italy in 1781, evidently while delivering diplomatic documents to the Neapolitan court, asserted a tremendous influence on his aesthetic views. This influence is especially evident in his architectural projects, which were strongly influenced by the work of Andrea Palladio, whose *I quattro Libri dell' Architettura* (Four Books on Architecture, 1570) he later translated. On the return trip he spent some time in Rome and traveled through Livorno, Pisa, Florence, Bologna, Venice, and Vienna. The impressions from this trip were so strong that in Livorno, L'vov began to make notes and sketches. His notebook from the trip is unique among travelogues of eighteenth-century Russians in Italy because it virtually ignores daily life and ethnographic color; instead, it is devoted entirely to L'vov's impressions of art. L'vov's classicist tastes are clear: he is in raptures over the works of Raphael and Andrea del Sarto, while Michelangelo's technique leaves him cold.

Back in Russia, L'vov was appointed a *sovetnik* (councillor) in the Postal Ministry on 10 March 1782 and served in this position until 1797, fulfilling a broad range of tasks. This period in L'vov's life was a period of creative maturity and diverse undertakings. His first major architectural project was the Cathedral of Saint Joseph in Mogilev, erected to commemorate the meeting in that city between Catherine II and the Austrian emperor Joseph II in May 1780. He subsequently designed the Saint Petersburg Post Office (1782); the Cathedral of Boris and Gleb in Torzhok (1785); various estate structures near Torzhok; a church in Murino, near Saint Petersburg (1780s); the Grand Kremlin Palace in Moscow (1798); a priory in Gatchina (1798); the house of A. K. Razumovsky on his estate in Gorokhovoe pole, Moscow (1800–1802); and other architectural projects. L'vov also executed numerous drawings and engravings, including a study for the order of Saint Vladimir (1782), illustrations to Ovid's *Metamorphoses* (1790s), and vignettes for a deluxe edition of Catherine the Great's play *Nachal'noe upravlenie Olega* (The First Reign of Oleg, 1791).

Throughout his varied career L'vov continued to write. In the mid 1790s he published several poems in Russian periodicals: "K Doralize" (To Doraliza), "Muzyka, ili Semitoniia" (Music, or the Seven-tone Scale), "Otpusknaia dvum chizhikam" (The Emancipation of Two Siskins), "Stikhi na rosu" (Verses on a Rose), and "Pesnia na vziatie Varshavy" (Song on the Taking of Warsaw). Publishing in almanacs and journals reflected L'vov's connections with sentimentalist writers of Moscow and Saint Petersburg. By this time L'vov's position in the L'vov-Derzhavin circle had been clearly defined; his friends considered him a "genii vkusa" (genius of taste) whose opinions on questions of literary theory were authoritative.

L'vov's works from the 1790s fall into two distinct groups: those directed at a broad readership; and those addressed to his narrow circle of friends and relatives. The latter were primarily intended as experiments, attempts at creating new artistic forms and asserting freedom of expression, or as parodies of diverse literary traditions; they remained in manuscript. Some of these works represent an attempt to reform the genre of the ode and to create a Russian national variant – as with his "Novyi XIX vek v Rossii" (The New Nineteenth Century in Russia) and "Narodnoe voskliknovenie na vstuplenie novogo veka" (Popular Rejoicing at the Beginning of the New Century) of the 1800s. In other works L'vov tried to renew the song, as in his "Soldatskaia pesnia na golanskii maner" (A Soldier's Song in the Dutch Manner), "Pesnia dlia tsyganskoi pliaski" (Song for a Gypsy Dance), "Snegir'" (Bullfinch), and "Zima" (Winter, 1791), all from the 1790s. He also composed a cycle of autobiographical epigrams, unified by the image of a single author.

Of greater interest from a literary and historical point of view, however, are L'vov's "druzheskie poslaniia" (friendly epistles) written during the 1790s and 1800s, such as "Gavrile Romanovichu otvet" (Answer to Gavrilla Romanovich), "K Lizen'ke bol'noi, i k zdorovomu Oleniu" (To Ailing Lizen'ka and Healthy Olen'), "Ivanu Matveevichu Murav'evu, edushchemu v Etin" (To Ivan Matveievich Murav'ev, Who is Leaving for Etin), and "Tri net" (Three No's). At least one such epistle was published during the poet's lifetime – the "Otryvok iz pis'ma A. M. B[aku-ninu]" (Fragment of a Letter to A. M. B[akunin]). L'vov attempted in the epistle form to realize his theoretical demand for full poetic self-revelation, to establish an almost personal acquaintanceship between the author and his reader. Magical strings of closely packed images, flights of wondrous fancy, sudden changes of focus from the authorial point of view to narrative exposition, metrical innovations, and the combination of high, low, and nonstandard lexicon – all contribute to the unique poetics of L'vov's epistles, in which the creative personality takes center stage.

To a certain extent L'vov's three longer poems of the 1790s are comparable to his epistles; all employ educated Russian conversational language and freely varying lexicon. The first, "Zima," was published in an edition of so few copies that five years later I. I. Martynov published it in his journal *Muza* (Muse) as a new work. The originality of the poem lay in its composition; the first part is built on an elaborate comparison of the onset of winter to the arrival of a wealthy noblewoman who reshapes her surroundings according to whim. Defining the genre of "Zima" is difficult – there is little in it that may be called fantastic or magical, nor is there a real plot, so that the conventional label of *skazka* (tale) is inappropriate. Common themes, personification of natural phenomena, and elements of rhythm and rhyme all link the work to Derzhavin's "Stikhi na rozhdenie v Severe porfirorodnogo otroka" (Verses on the Birth in the North of a Child Born to the Purple, 1799). "Zima" is one of the most interesting and artistically perfect poems of the eighteenth century.

L'vov's second long poem, "Botanicheskoe puteshestvie na Dudorovu goru 1792, maia 8" (Botanic Expedition to Dudorov Mountain, 8 May 1792), falls into the category of humorous travelogues and was modeled on the well-known *Voyage de Chapelle et Bachaumont* (1656). The pretext for the poem was apparently provided by an excursion L'vov made with A. A. Musin-Pushkin and I. V. Beber to the Duderhof heights near Saint Petersburg, which were known for their wealth of endemic species. L'vov's poem is linked to its French predecessor by its humorous expository manner, the alternation of prose and poetry, the introduction of fantastic elements, and the fact that it is addressed to an actual living person (Musin-Pushkin). The "Botanicheskoe puteshestvie na Dudorovu goru 1792, maia 8," unpublished until soon after L'vov's death, was well received among the poet's circle of friends, who dubbed him "the Russian Chapelle."

L'vov's third long poem, "Dobrynia" (1804), is linked with the debates of the 1790s over the literary merits of the Russian epic meter (of the *bylina*) and serves as a response to Karamzin's chivalric tale *Il'ia Muromets* (1795). L'vov saw "Dobrynia" as a theoretical manifesto in which he hoped to demonstrate the full validity of the Russian style of *bylina* versification and challenged what he saw as Karamzin's superficial understanding of that tradition. The introductory parts of "Dobrynia" use various tonic folk meters, and L'vov clearly believed that he had accomplished his objective, although other matters distracted him, and he never completed the poem.

L'vov holds a place in the history of Russian dramaturgy as the author of four comic operas, the first of which, *Sil'f, ili Mechta molodoi zhenshchiny* (Sylph, or the Dream of a Young Woman, 1777), was an adaption of Marmontel's "Le Mari Sylphe" (from *Contes moraux*, 1761). L'vov introduced new characters, Russified the old ones, and compressed the action into twenty-four hours. The stimulus to write the play was apparently provided by L'vov's participation in the amateur productions at Bakunin-Men'shoi's house. One of the compositional elements of the opera is the contrast between the worlds of master and servant. A particularly successful characterization is that of the house serf Andrei, who completely misunderstands the reasons behind his master's whims. An absorbing plot (in which a nobleman, Nelest, wins the heart of his wife Mira by visiting her at night in the form of a sylph) and masterfully delineated characters mark the work's originality in relation to both Russian and western European comic opera.

In the middle of the 1780s L'vov's house in Saint Petersburg became a recital hall for frequent choral performances of folk songs, many of which were published in his *Sobranie narodnykh ruskikh pesen s ikh golosami* (A Collection of Russian Folk Songs With Musical Notes, 1790), which L'vov prepared for press in collaboration with the composer Jan Prác (Ivan Prach). The idea for L'vov's second comic opera, *Iamshchiki na podstave* (Coachmen on the Buckboard, 1791), the only one published during the author's lifetime, was closely connected to L'vov's enthusiasm for Russian folklore. The opera premiered in Saint Petersburg on 8 November 1787, set to music by E. I. Fomin. The innovative nature of the play, described by its author as an "igrishche nevznachai" (spontaneous farce), was the likely cause of its failure: in this comic opera, in which arias and recitatives are stylizations of folk songs, there is no romantic intrigue, the speech is full of dialect and colloquialisms, and, according to many scholars, the action is incomplete. The play, which sympathetically depicts the lives of Russian coachmen, reflects L'vov's political program, which held that harmony between the monarchy's interests (in the person of its service class, the nobility) and those of the peasantry is possible if existing laws are carried out and if the Russian people's traditional way of life is preserved inviolate.

L'vov's comic opera *Milet i Mileta* (Milet and Mileta) was written in 1794 in Cherenchitsy. As a leitmotiv for this *pastush'ia shutka* (pastoral joke) the author chose Derzhavin's poem "Mechta" (The Dream, 1797), connected with Derzhavin's marriage to Dar'ia D'iakova. A gentle irony permeates this pastorale, lending it unusual sophistication and making for one of the finest works of the L'vov-Derzhavin circle. L'vov's last comic opera, *Parisov sud* (The Judgment of Paris, 1796), carries the subtitle *geroicheskoe igrishche* (a heroic farce), which together with the dedication signed "Van'ka Iamshchik" (Vanka the Coachman) underscores its connection with the spontaneous farce *Iamshchiki na podstave*. In fact both plays are marked by their free use of Russian dialect, ignored or avoided by authors of other eighteenth-century musical plays. Mythological characters are significantly Russified and parodied. At the decisive moment, when the dull-witted Paris hesitates in his choice of goddess, Mercury hurries him along, asking: "Nu! Komu zhe dar vruchitsia, / Chuvstvam, serdtsu il' umu?" (Well! Who'll get the gift, / Feelings, heart or mind?). This couplet suggests that the goddesses in *Parisov sud* are meant not merely as mythological personalities but also as allegorical representations of the senses (Juno), the

heart (Venus), and the mind (Minerva). The play's conclusion thus acquires an additional meaning: no matter how hard a person strives to follow his rational judgment, at the last moment the emotions (Venus) will gain the upper hand.

If L'vov's verse translations of the 1770s show a tendency toward literalism, in the 1790s the poet developed his own original theory of artistic translation, in which the translator must not only accurately convey the idea of the lines but also render them accessible to the new audience. His first attempt along these lines was "Pesn' norvezhskogo vitiazia Garal'da Khrabrogo" (Song of the Norse Knight Harold the Brave, 1793), adapted from P. A. Mallet's *Histoire de Dannemarc* (1763). L'vov's views on translation are most clearly expressed in the introduction to his *Stikhotvorenie Anakreona Tiiskogo* (The Poetry of Anacreon of Teos, 1794). He claims that the uniqueness of the book lay in the fact that the translation and commentary comprise a single, original artistic unit. During his work on the translation, the poet was assisted by the Greek scholar Evgenii Bulgaris, who edited the Greek text (the 1794 edition was bilingual) and helped L'vov interpret it. The Russian poet also consulted translations of Anacreon in other European languages (those of Ann Lefèvre-Dacier, Hippolite Longepierre, Antoine Lafosse, François Gacon, Paolo Rolli, Jean-Jacques Moutonnet de Clairfons, and Johann Heinrich Friedrich Meineke), as well as the edition by I. B. Bodounius (1791). In his introduction L'vov touches upon such important issues as the tasks of literature, the place of the writer in society, and the debate between ancients and moderns. *Stikhotvorenie Anakreona Tiiskogo* was the first example in Russia of an annotated edition of poetry that tried to take European scholarship into account.

During the last years of his life L'vov became involved in coal mining. In the middle of the 1780s he had made several proposals to mine for coal and peat and in early July 1786 was sent on the personal order of Catherine to Borovichi, where he conducted a successful geological survey. But not until 1797, during the reign of Paul I, was he finally granted a concession for processing and marketing coal, and he was obliged to act at his own risk. In fall 1799 a large shipment of coal arrived in Saint Petersburg, but L'vov could find no buyers for it. The coal was refused a place for storage and was eventually dumped at L'vov's summer home near the Aleksandr Nevsky Monastery, where it caught fire, causing the poet huge financial losses. The incident inspired a poem, one of L'vov's most interesting on a nature-philosophy theme, "Na ugol'nyi pozhar" (On a Coal Fire, 1958). L'vov also wrote *O pol'ze i upotreblenii ruskogo zemlianogo uglia* (On the Exploitation and Use of Russian Coal, 1799), in which he summarized his thoughts about the necessity and benefits of mining this fuel.

L'vov worked processing coal in Borovichi until his death, and he devoted much time during the last years of his life to campaigning for the establishment of a specialized school for building homes by the method of *zemlebitnoe stroenie* (using unfired bricks). However, his strength was sapped by protracted illness, and in June 1803 L'vov departed for medical treatment in the Caucasus. Along the way he stopped to study mineral deposits around Mount Beshtau. After acquainting himself with the area, the poet drew up plans for a health resort with steam baths and showers to be built in a hillside where there were hot springs. During his stay in Taman, L'vov initiated plans to erect a pedestal for the well-known Rock of Tmutarakan, and he staved off its destruction. After returning to Moscow, the poet died there on 21 December 1803.

Letters:

Arkhiv kniazia Vorontsova, volume 32, edited by Petr I. Bartenev (Moscow, 1886).

Biographies:

Maria Budylina, O. I. Braitseva, and Anna Kharlamova, *Arkhitektor N. A. L'vov* (Moscow: Iskusstvo, 1961);

Natal'ia Nikulina, *Nikolai L'vov* (Leningrad: Lenizdat, 1971);

Aleksei Glumov, *N. A. L'vov* (Moscow: Iskusstvo, 1980);

K. Iu. Lappo-Danilevsky, *Literaturnaia deiatel'nost' N. A. L'vova. Avtoreferat* (Leningrad: Pushkinskii Dom, 1988).

References:

Zinaida Artamonova, "Neizdannye stikhi N. A. L'vova," *Literaturnoe nasledstvo*, 9–10 (1933): 264–286;

Lindsay Hughes, "N. A. L'vov and the Russian Country House," in *Russian and the World of the Eighteenth Century* (Columbus, Ohio: Slavica, 1988), pp. 289–300;

Aleksandr Kokorev, " 'Trudy razumnykh obshchnikov' (Rukopisnyi zhurnal N. A. L'vova i dr.)," *Uchenye zapiski Moskovskogo pedagogicheskogo instituta im. N. K. Krupskoi*, 86, no. 7 (1960): 3–46;

Boris I. Koplan, "K istorii zhizni i tvorchestva N. A. L'vova," *Izvestiia Akademii Nauk SSSR*, 7–8, series 6 (1927): 688–726;

Elena Kukushkina, "Komicheskaia opera N. A. L'vova 'Sil'f, ili Mechta molodoi zhenshchiny': K voprosu o metode L'vova-dramaturga," *Problemy izucheniia russkoi literatury XVIII veka*, 4 (1980): 48–53;

K. Iu. Lappo-Danilevsky, "K voprosu o tvorcheskom stanovlenii N. A. L'vova (po materialam chernovoi tetradi)," *XVIII vek*, 16 (1988): 256–270;

Lappo-Danilevsky, "Novye dannye k biografii N. A. L'vova (1770-e gody)," *Russkaia literatura*, 2 (1988): 48–53;

Lappo-Danilevsky and S. R. Dolgova, "Rabota N. A. L'vova po podgotovke vtorogo izdaniia perevoda iz Anakreona," *XVIII vek*, 17 (1990): 190–202;

Rimma Lazarchuk, "Poslanie N. A. L'vova i ego rol' v literaturnoi bor'be 1790-kh – 1800-kh gg.," *Uchenye zapiski Leningradskogo gos. pedagogicheskogo instituta, Filologicheskie nauki*, no. 480 (1970): 29–45;

Fedor P. L'vov, "L'vov," *Syn otechestva*, 77, no. 17 (1822): 108–121;

Alexander Rozanov, "Kompozitor N. P. Iakhontov," *Muzykal'noe nasledstvo*, 1 (1962): 11–64;

Viktor Vereshchagin, "Putevye zametki N. A. L'vova po Italii v 1781 g.," *Starye gody*, 5 (1909): 276–282;

Vladimir A. Zapadov, " 'L'vovskii kruzhok' i G. R. Derzhavin," in *XXI gertsenovskie chteniia: Filologicheskiie nauki* (Leningrad: Leningradskii gos. pedagogocheskii institut, 1969), pp. 90–93.

Papers:

The papers of Nikolai Aleksandrovich L'vov are preserved in Pushkin House and the State Public Library in Saint Petersburg.

Vasilii Ivanovich Maikov

(1728 – 17 June 1778)

Alexander Levitsky
Brown University

SELECTED BOOKS: *Igrok lombera* ([Moscow: Universitetskaia tipografiia], 1763; revised edition, Moscow: Moskovskii universitet, 1765);

Nravouchitel'nye basni, 2 volumes (Moscow: Moskovskii universitet, 1766–1767);

Sonet ko dniu prazdnovaniia, o blagopoluchnom vyzdorovlenii, ot privivnyia ospy, eia imp. velichestva i ego imp. vysochestva, pridvornago rossiiskago teatra akterami i aktrisami (Saint Petersburg: [Akademiia nauk], 1768);

Torzhestvuiushchii Parnass, prolog po vyzdorovlenii ot privivnyia ospy eia imp. velichestva i ego imp. vysochestva (Saint Petersburg: Akademiia nauk, 1768);

Nadpis' ko mramoram rossiiskim ([Saint Petersburg: Akademiia nauk, 1769]);

Stikhi k prazdnestvu Imperatorskoi Akademii khudozhestv ([Saint Petersburg: Akademiia nauk, 1770]);

Elisei, ili Razdrazhennyi Vakkh poema (Saint Petersburg: [Morskoi kadetskii korpus, 1771]); translated by Harold B. Segel as "Elisei, or Bacchus Enraged," in his *The Literature of Eighteenth-Century Russia,* volume 2 (New York: Dutton, 1967), pp. 123–179;

Raznye stikhotvoreniia, 2 volumes (Saint Petersburg: [Voennaia kollegiia, 1773]);

Agriopa tragediia (Moscow: [Voennaia kollegiia], 1775);

Femist i Ieronima tragediia (Moscow: [Voennaia kollegiia], 1775);

Opisanie raznykh uveselitel'nykh zrelishch, predstavlennykh vo vremia mirnogo torzhestva, zakliuchennago mezhdu Rossiiskoiu imperieiu i Ottomanskoiu Portoiu. V vysochaishem prisutstvii e.i.v. . . Ekateriny II i ikh imp. vysochestv, pri mnogochislennom sobranii naroda, bliz Moskvy na Khodynke, 1775 goda iiulia 16 dnia (Moscow: Voennaia kollegiia, [1775]);

Sonet ego siiatel'stvu grafu Grigor'iu Aleksandrovichu Potemkinu. 1775 goda sentiabria 30 dnia (Moscow: Voennaia kollegiia, 1775);

Khory na den' brachgnogo sochetaniia ego imp. vysochestva, gosudaria tsesarevicha i velikogo kniazia Pavla

Vasilii Ivanovich Maikov; engraving by I. Rozanov

Petrovicha, prazdnuemoi zdes' v Moskve, na pridvornom teatre, 1776 goda, oktiabria dnia ([Moscow]: Moskovskii universitet, 1776);

Oda o vkuse Aleksandru Petrovichu Sumarokovu ([Moscow: Universitetskaia tipografiia, 1776]);

Epistola e. v. gosudaryne Ekaterine Alekseevne . . . na torzhestvennyi den' koronovaniia eia (Moscow: Universitetskaia tipografiia, 1777);

Derevenskii prazdnik, ili Uvenchannaia dobrodetel', pastusheskaia dramma s muzykoiu. V dvukh deistviiakh ([Moscow]: Moskovskii universitet, [1777]);

Pigmalion, ili Sila liubvi. Dramma s muzykoiu v odnom deistvii (Moscow: Moskovskii universitet, 1779);

Sochineniia (Saint Petersburg, 1809).

Editions: *Sochineniia i perevody,* edited by P. A.
Efremov (Saint Petersburg: I. I. Glazunov,
1867);

Izbrannye proizvedeniia, edited by Aleksandr Zapadov
(Moscow & Leningrad: Sovetskii pisatel',
1966).

TRANSLATIONS: Frederick II, *Voennaia nauka: Iz
knigi Bezpechnyi filosof sochineniia e.v. korolia
prusskago* (Moscow: Moskovskii universitet,
1767);

Voltaire, *Meropa* (Moscow: Voennaia kollegiia,
1775);

Ovid, *Prevrashcheniia,* 4 volumes (Saint Petersburg:
Senatskaia tipografiia, 1775).

Vasilii Ivanovich Maikov was one of the most
gifted poets of his age. He successfully tried his
hand in several literary genres and made pioneering
contributions to the mock epic, the fable, and the
ode. Maikov's almost complete lack of knowledge
of foreign languages, which made him the object of
occasional ridicule, also prevented him from being
taken seriously as a poet on a par with Gavriil
Derzhavin, fifteen years his junior. Maikov shared a
whole series of personal traits and biographical details with the younger poet, including a provincial
background, simple beginnings as a soldier, and
brash behavior coupled with utter honesty. The two
writers ran in the same literary and official circles,
so that comparison between them is useful in gaug-
ing the development of Maikov's career and art. Despite Maikov's present relative obscurity, there is
no question that in the years prior to 1779, in which
Derzhavin began to be recognized as a major voice
in Russian literature, Maikov was regarded as one
of the two greatest living Russian poets (the other
being Mikhail Kheraskov).

Born into a family of a relatively wealthy
gentleman-landowner near Yaroslavl, Maikov was
brought up in an atmosphere conducive to the development of his literary talent. His father, Ivan
Stepanovich Maikov, was a typical product of the
Petrine reforms who spent more time in the army
than at home; even as a middle-aged man he participated in the first war between Russia and Turkey
(1735–1739) and in the campaign against Sweden
(1741–1742). Yet he still found time to be actively
involved in the creation of the local theater founded
by the talented actor Fedor Volkov, with whom the
younger Maikov became friends. Volkov's troupe
became the nucleus of the new national theater, and
after attending its opening in Saint Petersburg in

1756, Maikov had Volkov introduce him to the
theater's first director and (at the time) Russia's
leading playwright, Aleksandr Sumarokov. Sumarokov, in turn, was most probably the person responsible for introducing Maikov into the Russian literary scene; Sumarokov also first drew public attention to Maikov's talent in the 1760s.

Like Derzhavin, Maikov journeyed to Saint
Petersburg at the age of nineteen to begin military
service as a simple soldier. Like Derzhavin, he had
no high-powered patrons, which resulted in excruci-
atingly slow advancement in the ranks and the necessity of sharing his living quarters with soldiers of
low social status. He probably shared other aspects
of military life with them as well, including drinking, singing, and playing cards. He probably also
began to take note of their language, sayings, and
tales, which he later brilliantly reproduced in his
burlesque poems. Again like Derzhavin, drunken
brawls and card playing were to be incorporated
into his literary works in unique ways.

Opposed to Derzhavin, however, as well as to
his own father, Maikov never seemed interested in
making a career in the military. He seems to have
had a profound distaste for warfare and never participated in any military engagements. The closest
he came was in 1759, when he was assigned to take
a group of recruits to the front, but after having finished with this duty as expeditiously as possible, he
returned to his regiment in Saint Petersburg. On 25
December 1761 he resigned his commission with
the rank of captain and moved to Moscow. Apparently at this time he made the acquaintance of
Mikhail Kheraskov and joined the circle of writers
connected to the new journal *Poleznoe uveselenie* (Useful Amusement); he also joined their Masonic
order. Maikov's first literary efforts appeared the
following month, when the journal published an eclogue and an epigram by him. Both works display
considerable control of prosody, reflecting an established hand. They could hardly have been Maikov's
first attempts in verse, yet almost nothing is known
about any of his previous poetic efforts.

Within a short time Maikov established a distinct presence on the Moscow literary scene. He
wrote in various genres popular at the time and addressed new and unique topics. In two odes of 1762
(one to Catherine II and the other hailing the arrival of 1763) he emulated Mikhail Lomonosov.
Maikov's subsequent attempts at sacred odes, most
particularly his transpositions of psalms, are not
only among his greatest accomplishments but also, together with some of his philosophical odes, among
the most successful applications of Lomonosov's theory

of styles, as presented in the "Predislovie o pol'ze knig tserkovnykh v Rossiiskom iazyke" (Preface on the Usefulness of Church Books in the Russian Tongue, 1757). Maikov's early pro-Masonic leanings are reflected in a powerful ode published in the March 1763 issue of *Svobodnyia chasy* (Idle Hours, the successor to *Poleznoe uveselenie*), "Oda na strashnyi sud" (Ode on the Last Judgment), the first ode on the topic in Russian. The next month he tried his hand at a verse translation of Ovid's *Metamorphoses,* selections from which appeared in succeeding issues of the journal; twelve years later they were collected and revised in a separate book. These *basni* (fables), as the author called them, were rendered in iambic hexameter couplets (instead of Ovid's dactylic hexameters) and have not attracted much scholarly attention despite the fact that Maikov was the first Russian to translate Ovid's *Metamorphoses* into Russian verse. This is partly due to the fact that Maikov relied on a Russian prose translation of Ovid (most likely by Denis Fonvizin).

Maikov's first important success with the reading public occurred with the separate publication of *Igrok lombera* (The Player of Ombre, 1763), his first mock epic poem. The mock epic as a genre had been approved by Sumarokov in 1748 in his *Epistola o stikhotvorstve* (Epistle on Poetry), but it had never been successfully realized in Russian literature before Maikov. While the poem loses much of its effect without a detailed knowledge of ombre, a Spanish card game, it still retains much of its humor because of its clever stylistic mixing of opposed lexical levels. Maikov gives the cards such lofty names as David (the king of spades), Caesar (the king of diamonds), Judith (the queen of hearts), or Charlemagne (the king of hearts) and shows them engaged in "heroic" deeds. In his comedy *Iabeda* (Chicane, 1798) Vasilii Kapnist exploited the satiric potential of this card game, whose name derives from the Spanish word *hombre*. For Maikov, however, *Igrok lombera* was mainly a work of fun.

During the same year Maikov considerably expanded his circle of friends in Moscow. Among his new acquaintances were Fedor Kozlovsky, a talented poet who died before he could develop his gifts, and the brothers Aleksandr and Vasilii Bibikov, both well versed in literature and the arts. Kozlovsky was an officer in the Preobrazhensky Regiment in which Derzhavin served, and Derzhavin was once sent to deliver a package to him. He arrived while Kozlovsky was reading Maikov an excerpt from a tragedy he had written. After fulfilling his commission Derzhavin remained in the front hall listening to the reading, but Kozlovsky asked

him to leave, not wishing to be overheard by what he thought were "uneducated ears." The incident marks one of Derzhavin's first contacts with Russian writers.

Maikov's poetry later became an important model for Derzhavin, in part through his contact with Maikov's other friend, Aleksandr Bibikov. Maikov rendered Bibikov's *Voennaia nauka* (Military Science), a prose translation of a work by Frederick II, into verse, and it was published in book form in 1767. In 1773 Bibikov was appointed supreme commander of Catherine's forces to deal with the Pugachev rebellion, and it may have been under his influence that Derzhavin, under Bibikov's direct command, turned to the poetry of Frederick II (also available to him in Maikov's version) as a model for his Chitalagai odes.

While expanding the range of poetic experience through his Moscow contacts, Maikov also continued to follow Sumarokov's works with interest, especially his collection of fables published in 1762. In his own fables, collected as *Nravouchitel'nye basni* (Didactic Fables, 1766–1767), he followed Sumarokov's approach, particularly in his use of iambic lines of mixed length. If Maikov's legacy in the fable is usually understood as an intermediary between Sumarokov and Ivan Krylov, the most popular and accomplished Russian fabulist, such a position, however correct in technical terms, underrates Maikov's accomplishments in the genre. Endowed with a keen sense of humor, the author interweaves various stylistic levels of the Russian language, including its Slavonic and colloquial components. In his retellings of Aesop, Phaedrus, Ludvig Holberg, and other writers, Maikov creates a distinctly Russian brand of humor, often recalling Russian proverbs and folk expressions. Far from being overtly moralizing, despite the *didactic* in its title, the collection succeeds by the immediacy of the fables' chatter, what Russians call *boltovnia,* demonstrating Maikov's ability to converse with his readers rather than instruct them. Maikov also emulated Sumarokov in the genre of tragedy, as is clear from the first of his two published tragedies, *Agriopa* (staged in 1769; published, 1775), although the author was less successful than with his fables and the work did not remain on the stage for long.

In 1766 Maikov was appointed as an adviser to the governor of Moscow, I. I. Iushkov, a relative of Sumarokov's, and in the next year he was invited (apparently by Bibikov) to assume a central post in the work of Catherine II's Kommisiia o sochinenii novogo Ulozheniia (Legislative Commission for Composing a New Law Code). He became secretary of the Directorate Committee, which supervised the work done by the commission's deputies, and when the commission moved to Moscow in 1768, he moved there as well. With the dissolution of the commission by Catherine later that year, Maikov became temporarily unemployed until his old friend Count Z. G. Chernyshev invited him to become the procurator of the War College in March 1770. This appointment gave Maikov firsthand knowledge of the deficiencies in the Russian army and navy supply system and prompted him to open a plant specializing in the manufacture of canvas for sails. While Maikov did not begin this private enterprise strictly out of patriotic zeal (he had debts to repay in connection with a lien against his deceased mother's estate), he was one of the first Russian landowner-writers to go into manufacturing. Unfortunately for Maikov, however, the business, after showing initial profit, burned to the ground and incurred significant losses. By 1775, however, Maikov's financial affairs had improved following promotions and appointments within the service. His work alternated between Saint Petersburg and Moscow.

As opposed to the case of his friend, the poet Aleksei Rzhevsky, Maikov's service career did not deplete his interest in literature. In fact, in probably the busiest of all of his years, 1770–1771, when he simultaneously served as procurator of the War College, was an active member of the Free Economic Society, and started his own private enterprise, he was also able to complete work on what ultimately became his most cherished creation, the mock epic poem *Elisei, ili Razdrazhennyi Vakkh* (Elisei, or Bacchus Enraged, 1771). Written in response to the steep rise in the price of vodka declared by the government in order to generate income for its war efforts, the poem traces the adventures of Elisei, a peasant-turned-coachman, who is able to consume huge quantities of alcohol and hence is chosen by Bacchus to punish the *otkupshchiki* (excise-tax men), popularly deemed responsible for the price increase. At the same time, the poem parodies Vasilii Petrov's 1770 translation of the first book of Virgil's *Aeneid;* even the title *Elisei* is an unmistakable punning reference to Petrov's *Enei* (Aeneid). Maikov approached his poem in the spirit of Paul Scarron's *Virgile travestie* (Virgil Travestied, 1648–1658), employing the two types of mock epic described by Sumarokov in his epistle on Russian versification (involving combinations of low style with lofty subjects and vice versa). The result was a hilarious, rollicking tale, replete with folksy sayings and burlesque elements as well as episodes involv-

Title page for Maikov's popular mock epic

ing violence, drunkenness, scenes of transvestite transmogrification, and sex. The latter qualities were no doubt inspired by the master of obscene verse, Ivan Barkov, whom Maikov addresses in the beginning of *Elisei* as his "beloved Scarron," and the entire epic should probably be considered Maikov's postmortem apostrophe to Barkov, who died at the time Maikov was beginning *Elisei.*

Maikov's mock epic secured an exclusive niche for him in eighteenth-century Russian literature: he was at once the first to have satisfied the norms of the classicist genre of mock epic, while simultaneously achieving the more elusive ideal of "Russianness." It was primarily for the latter, as expressed in *Elisei* and in his fables, that Maikov was valued by contemporaries. When Denis Diderot visited Saint Petersburg in 1773–1774, he asked to be introduced to Maikov because of what he had heard about the distinctly national character of his writing. There was probably no other Russian writer at the time who felt the fabric of his native language to the same degree. If Maikov did not know foreign languages, he knew Russian and Church Slavonic as a connoisseur.

This knowledge was also evident in his sacred poetry, most of which had been published just prior to Diderot's visit to Russia. Maikov's turn to religious and philosophical themes had probably been precipitated by his intensified engagement with Masonry in the early 1770s and stimulated by Kheraskov's transfer to Saint Petersburg in 1770. The latter had organized a new literary circle at his residence, the result of which was the publication in 1772–1773 of the weekly journal *Vechera* (Evenings), in which some of Maikov's psalm translations were published. Most poets of the time tended to create versions of the psalms subject to current literary sensibility and notions of high style, often departing from the canonical models; some, like Ivan Bogdanovich, even created hybrids of several psalms strung together into new configurations. Maikov, however, based his versions on Lomonosov's theory of styles and often reintroduced Church Slavonic where other poets had used more-contemporary vernacular phrases. Comparing, for example, his version of Psalm 1 in *Vechera* to the two other anonymous versions of the same psalm published there reveals that his rendering was not only the most accomplished but also the closest to the canonical, Church Slavonic version, closer in some places in its use of Church Slavonic than even Lomonosov's version, completed a quarter of a century earlier. At the same time, psalms like this one (with its theme of moral perfectibility of man) and such odes as "Oda ishchushchim mudrosti" (Ode to Those Seeking Wisdom, 1778) and "Oda preosviashchennomu Platonu . . . o besmertii dushi" (Ode to the Right Reverend Platon . . . on the Immortality of the Soul, 1778) reflected Maikov's growing Masonic beliefs. He had risen in the Masonic ranks from a simple initiate in the Urania Lodge in 1770 to the post of grand secretary of the Great Provincial Lodge (headed by Ivan Perfil'evich Elagin) in 1775.

Just before he was to move to Saint Petersburg to assume the position of master of heraldry in 1778, Maikov died on 17 June while arranging his personal affairs for the move. He was buried in Moscow at the Donskoi Monastery.

Despite his varied accomplishments, including such works as the magnificent ode "Voina" (War, written in 1768–1769), the first in Russian literature to express pacifist sentiments, Maikov's name has been mostly remembered for the mock epic *Elisei*. Probably owing to his temperament rather than his abilities, Maikov was unable to sustain the lofty pitch required of the epic poem proper, and his only attempt in this regard, "Osvobozhdennaia Moskva" (Moscow Liberated), remained unfinished, as does the work of all his predecessors in this genre. This lacuna was finally filled by his lifelong friend Kheraskov, whose *Rossiiada* (The Rossiad, 1779) was published one year after Maikov's death. Kheraskov, on the other hand, despite his successes in other spheres of literary creativity, was never able to write humorous verse. Both poets were important predecessors to Derzhavin, the century's greatest poet. Derzhavin's famous ode "Bog" (God, 1784) could not have been written without Kheraskov's ode of the same title, and his development of the "zabavnyi russkii slog" (amusing Russian style) was directly indebted to Maikov's *Elisei*, which legitimized such a style for literary purposes. Herein lies Maikov's own greatness, since it was only after *Elisei* that the upper strata of Russian society began to understand what the lower strata had known all along in their *lubki* (chapbooks) and picaresque novels (to which genres *Elisei* also owes allegiance), namely that writing literature consists not only of *dulce et utile* (sweet utility), advanced by the dominant strain of Russian classicism, but also, simply, fun.

References:

William Edward Brown, "Vassily Ivanovich Maikov," in his *A History of 18th Century Russian Literature* (Ann Arbor, Mich.: Ardis, 1980), pp. 276–292;

James M. Curtis, "Vasily Maikov, an Eighteenth-Century Russian Poet," Ph.D. dissertation, Columbia University, 1968;

Grigorii A. Gukovky, "Maikov," in *Istoriia russkoi literatury,* volume 4, part 2 (Moscow & Leningrad: Akademiia nauk, 1947), pp. 201–226;

Leonid N. Maikov, "O zhizni i sochineniiakh V. I. Maikova," in his *Ocherki iz istorii russkoi literatury XVII i XVIII stoletiiakh* (Saint Petersburg: A. S. Suvorina, 1889), pp. 252–309;

Aleksandr V. Zapadov, "Tvorchestvo V. I. Maikova," in Maikov's *Izbrannye proizvedeniia,* edited by Zapadov (Moscow & Leningrad: Sovetskii pisatel', 1966), pp. 5–52.

Mikhail Nikitich Murav'ev
(25 October 1757 – 29 July 1807)

Vadim Dmitrievich Rak
Institute of Russian Literature (Pushkin House), Saint Petersburg

BOOKS: *Basni* (Saint Petersburg: [Sukhoputnyi kadetskii korpus], 1773);

Voennaia pesn' (Saint Petersburg: [Gosudarstvennaia voennaia kollegiia], 1774);

Oda e.i.v. gosudaryne Ekaterine II Imperatritse Vserossiiskoi, na zamirenie Rossii s Portoiu Otomanskoiu (Saint Petersburg: [Gosudarstvennaia voennaia kollegiia, 1774]);

Pokhval'noe slovo Mikhaile Vasil'evichu Lomonosovu (Saint Petersburg: [Akademiia nauk], 1774);

Ody ([Saint Petersburg: Akademiia nauk, 1775]);

Dobroe ditia. Drammaticheskaia skazochka (Saint Petersburg: Imperatorskaia tipografiia, 1789);

Emilievy pis'ma ([Saint Petersburg: Imperatorskaia tipografiia, 1789 or 1790]);

Obitatel' predmestiia, periodicheskie listy, 10 parts ([Saint Petersburg: Imperatorskaia tipografiia, 1790]); translated by C. L. Drage as "Mikhail Muravyov: An Inhabitant of a Suburb," in *Russian Literature Triquarterly,* 20 (1987): 111–132;

Poslanie k A. M. Br. 1783 g. ([Saint Petersburg: Imperatorskaia tipografiia], circa 1790);

Razgovory mertvykh (Saint Petersburg: [Imperatorskaia tipografiia], 1790);

Stikhi na konchinu Iakova Borisovicha Kniazhnina, prikliuchivshuiusia sego genvaria 14 dnia (N.p., [1791]);

Opyty istorii, pis'men i nravoucheniia ([Saint Petersburg]: Imperatorskaia tipografiia, 1796); published as *Opyty istorii, slovesnosti i nravoucheniia,* edited by N. M. Karamzin, 2 volumes (Moscow: Universitetskaia tipografiia, 1810);

Epokhi Rossiiskoi istorii ([Saint Petersburg: Imperatorskaia tipografiia], n.d.);

Feona ([Saint Petersburg: Imperatorskaia tipografiia], n.d.);

Istoricheskoe izobrazhenie Rossii v sed'mom-nadesiat' veke ([Saint Petersburg: Imperatorskaia tipografiia], n.d.);

Mikhail Nikitich Murav'ev; engraving by E. O. Skotnikov after a portrait by I. L. Mon'e, 1810

Nravstvennye izobrazheniia ([Saint Petersburg: Imperatorskaia tipografiia], n.d.);

Sobranie pisem razlichnykh tvortsov, drevnikh i novykh ([Saint Petersburg: Imperatorskaia tipografiia], n.d.);

Utrenniaia progulka ([Saint Petersburg: Imperatorskaia tipografiia], n.d.);

Utro ([Saint Petersburg: Imperatorskaia tipografiia], n.d.).

Editions: *Obitatel' predmestiia i Emilievy pis'ma,* edited by K. N. Batiushkov (Saint Petersburg: Akademiia nauk, 1815);

Polnoe sobranie sochinenii, edited by Batiushkov and V. A. Zhukovsky, 3 volumes (Saint Petersburg: Rossiiskaia akademiia, 1819–1820); published as *Sochineniia,* 2 volumes (Saint Petersburg: A. Smirdin, 1847);

Stikhotvoreniia, edited by L. I. Kulakova, Biblioteka poeta, bol'shaia seriia (Leningrad: Sovetskii pisatel', 1967).

OTHER: *Perevodnye stikhotvoreniia,* translated by Murav'ev (Saint Petersburg: Akademiia nauk, 1773);

Petronius, *Grazhdanskaia bran', poema,* translated by Murav'ev ([Saint Petersburg: Akademiia nauk, 1774]).

SELECTED PERIODICAL PUBLICATIONS – UNCOLLECTED: "Dshchitsy dlia zapisyvaniia," *Utrennii svet,* 4 (December 1778): 368–377; "Rassuzhdenie o razlichii slogov vysokogo, velikolepnogo, velichestvennogo, gromkogo i nadutogo," *Opyt trudov Vol'nogo Rossiiskogo sobraniia pri Imperatorskom Moskovskom universitete,* 6 (1783): 1–24.

Mikhail Nikitich Murav'ev's position in eighteenth-century Russian literature only came to be appreciated more than a hundred years after his death. His contemporaries did not realize the innovative nature of his writing because the majority of his work remained unknown to most of them, and that which was known was overshadowed by other aspects of his creative and civic biography. It was only in the 1930s that Grigorii Gukovsky and his pupil Liubov' Kulakova began to reveal the new directions that Murav'ev charted in Russian poetry of the 1770s and 1780s. One of the earliest representatives of Russian sentimentalism and pre-Romanticism, he was an important connecting link between the schools of Aleksandr Sumarokov and Nikolai Karamzin. Having paid tribute to Mikhail Lomonosov's "high-soaring" style and having assimilated the poetic lessons of Sumarokov and Mikhail Kheraskov, Murav'ev turned enthusiastically to European sentimentalist poetry (James Thomson, Edward Young, Ewald Christian von Kleist, Salomon Gessner, Albrecht von Haller, and Nicolas-Germain Leonard). At the same time, he remained an admirer of classical authors (especially Homer, Virgil, and Horace) and European

classicists of the seventeenth and eighteenth centuries. In his early works he presented a renewed version of classicist poetics, but from the mid 1770s he moved away from rationalism, contemplation, philosophizing, and moralizing in poetry and introduced subjective and emotional notes into his depiction of the world. His poetry became "tuman volshebnyi / Maniashchikh, sladostnykh i legkikh obrazóv" (a magical fog / Of beckoning, sweet and light images). In his hands Russian poetry became for the first time a chronicle of the human soul. Each poem seemed to be a page from a lyrical diary, with the language of feeling ousting the language of logical reasoning. Murav'ev constantly experimented in his works and moved away from traditional genres of classicism (the ode, didactic poetry, eclogues, and fables) to light verse, or, as he called it, "ubegaiushchaia" (fugitive) poetry – the friendly epistle, elegy, and ballad, which gained great popularity in Russia at the end of the eighteenth and beginning of the nineteenth centuries.

Mikhail Nikitich Murav'ev was born on 25 October 1757 in Smolensk, where his father, Nikita Artamonovich Murav'ev, who eventually became a privy councilor and senator, was then working in the civil service. Murav'ev left no written statements about his mother, Sofia Petrovna Murav'ev (née Izhorina), but throughout his life he maintained a close relationship with his father and with his sister Feodosiia. In 1760 Murav'ev's father was appointed vice-governor of Orenburg, where the future poet received his initial education at home. His father taught Mikhail the mathematical sciences, while tutors instructed him in French and German. However, a proper, comprehensive education was impossible in Orenburg, and in 1768 the family moved to Moscow, where on 15 January Mikhail entered the university gymnasium, directed at that time by the poet Kheraskov, whose patronage Murav'ev enjoyed for many years.

The boy was a good learner, repeatedly earning awards in various subjects, and at a gymnasium assembly on 17 December 1769 he gave two speeches, one in French and the other in German. In 1770 he transferred to the university, where he began to attend lectures on rhetoric by Anton Barsov, as well as lectures on philosophy by Johann Matthias Schaden. However, after only a short time at the university, Murav'ev had to withdraw when on 5 February 1770 he left for Archangel with his father, who had been ordered there by the senate. Cut off from the university, Murav'ev took up his own education seriously. He recalled how he "prossizhival dni za Korneliem" (sat for days over [Pierre]

Corneille), Jean Racine, and Nicholas Boileau while in Archangel, and in Vologda he read Virgil nonstop (completing the *Aeneid* in ten days in September 1772), although he only "razumel polovinu" (understood half of him).

At the gymnasium Murav'ev had already demonstrated an inclination for literary creation. In 1768, when he was eleven, he translated *La Vie d'Ernest le Pieux, duc de Saxe-Gotha* (1707), Antoine Teissier's French version of Elias Martin Eyring's *Vita Ernesti Pii ducis Saxoniae* (Life of Ernest the Pious, Duke of Saxony, 1704), and in his notebooks of 1768–1771 he began to translate Racine's *Phèdra* (1677) as well as Voltaire's *Zaïre* (1732) and Molière's *Le misanthrope* (The Misanthrope, 1666). Among his experiments of 1769–1772 were translations of Horace's satires, transpositions of several psalms, and his first original poems, which include "Stikhi na pobedu, oderzhannuiu 1770 goda, avgusta 21 dnia" (Verses on the Victory of 21 August 1770) and an "Ekloga" (Eclogue) in imitation of Virgil. Around 1771 he began to try his strength in dramatic genres and set to work on a comic opera called "Dobroi barin" (The Good Landlord); a heroic comedy, "Dobrodetel'naia lozh' " (The Virtuous Lie); and others. Moved by a "iunosheskim bredom tragedii" (youthful tragic delirium), he also began a tragedy, "Didona" (Dido), in which he attempted the ambitious task — obviously beyond his youthful skill — of liberating Virgil's plot from all of the extraneous elements which European writers (in particular, Jean-Jacques Lefranc in his *Didon* [1734]) had introduced into it. Murav'ev worked on this play for several years, but as with the other dramatic works, he never finished it.

In September 1772 N. A. Murav'ev's assignment to Archangel ended, and on 25 October he returned with his son to Saint Petersburg. On 31 October Mikhail became a soldier in the Izmailovsky Regiment. Shortly afterward his father received an appointment to the revenue department in Tver. Mikhail was not overzealous in military service and took many leaves of absence in order to travel to Tver and Moscow. His ascent through the ranks was slow for someone his age (on 24 November 1772 he became a corporal, on 22 September 1774 a sergeant, and on 1 January 1782 an ensign), but he was indifferent to promotion. Murav'ev directed his energy primarily toward writing and his education. Already fluent in French, German, and Latin, he now took up the study of Greek, Italian, and, at the end of the 1780s, English. He attended lectures by professors of the Academy of Sciences and studied mechanics, physics, mathematics, history, painting,

and music. He was drawn to classical philology and began to translate the *Iliad* in its original meter. He not only translated a Latin poem by Petronius but also worked on a translation of Lomonosov's *Petr Velikii* (Peter the Great, 1760) into Latin verse. At this time Murav'ev was also making many literary acquaintances – Vasilii Petrov, Mikhail Popov, Nikolai Novikov, Iakov Kniazhnin, Denis Fonvizin, and Vasilii Maikov (whom he considered his mentor in poetry). In the mid 1770s he became close to Nilokai L'vov, around whom had formed a literary circle which included the future luminaries of Russian poetry Ivan Khemnitser, Vasilii Kapnist, and Gavriil Derzhavin.

The 1770s and early 1780s were the years of Murav'ev's poetical flowering. From 1773 to 1775 several collections of his original and translated works appeared, as did individually published odes written to mark various occasions. The collection *Ody* (Odes, 1775) summed up Murav'ev's literary activities of the first half of the decade. Several poems on military themes continued the tradition of the official, solemn ode, while in others the influence of Kheraskov's philosophical odes was apparent. The last odes in the collection, including "Vesna" (Spring), exhibit a striving toward creative independence and indicate new interests whose logic would lead Murav'ev to sentimentalism.

On 3 December 1776, while in Moscow, Murav'ev was chosen as a member of the Vol'noe Rossiiskoe sobranie (Free Russian Society) at Moscow University, where at a meeting on 10 December he read his "Rassuzhdenie o razlichii slogov" (Discourse on the Distinctions of Styles), which he repeated "so vsemi dopolneniiami" (with lots of additions) on 6 May 1777. In this work clear signs of the decay of classicist aesthetics are evident. Murav'ev undermined the theory of three styles and formulated a new theory of individual styles.

After 1775 Murav'ev's works appeared sporadically in journals, and many remained unpublished, even though he put together the collections "Novye liricheskie opyty Mikhaila Murav'eva, 1776" (New Lyrical Experiments by Mikhail Murav'ev, 1776) and "Pièces fugitives," poems written from 1778 to 1784. Around 1790 he planned to publish a book of his poems from the 1780s, but only the first sheet was printed, which included the "Poslanie k A. M. Br[ianchaninovu]" (Epistle to A. M. Br[ianchaninov]) and two other poems. The reason these collections were never published is unclear; the poet's doubts about his own gifts — a leitmotiv

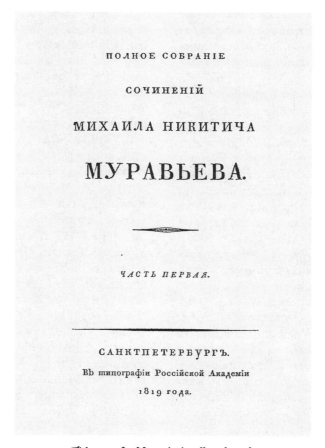

ПОЛНОЕ СОБРАНІЕ

СОЧИНЕНІЙ

МИХАИЛА НИКИТИЧА

МУРАВЬЕВА.

ЧАСТЬ ПЕРВАЯ.

САНКТПЕТЕРБУРГЪ.

Въ типографіи Россійской Академіи

1819 года.

Title page for Murav'ev's collected works

in his lyrics and the source of many melancholy reflections – may have played a role.

"Novye liricheskie opyty" included the first examples in Russian literature of exclusively personal, autobiographical, subjective lyrics, and the rudiments of those genres that were to have a rich future in pre-Romantic poetry. "Legkaia poeziia" (light poetry), adopted by Murav'ev under the influence of L'vov, from French writers (Voltaire, François-Joachim de Pierres de Bernis, Catherine-Stanislas Marquis de Bouflers, and Claude-Joseph Dorat), was an expression of incidental, momentary emotions and broke classical canons, freeing poetry from didacticism. At the same time, irony held sentimentality in check.

For all the subjectivity and autobiography of Murav'ev's lyrics, however, love motifs were the least developed. Various women's names, beginning with "Nina," are mentioned in his poetry, but the feelings expressed in works of this type carried a strong imprint of poetic convention and most likely had little or no connection to the actual facts of the poet's biography. In

1773 Murav'ev began writing the tragedy "Boleslav," based on twelfth-century Polish history and influenced by Voltaire's tragedy *Adélaïde du Guesclin* (1734). Murav'ev abandoned the work then returned to the play in 1776, and although he attached special importance to it, it remained unfinished, like his other experiments in dramatic genres. He used the plot of the tragedy in the ballad "Boleslav, korol' pol'skii" (Boleslav, King of Poland), written in the 1790s and first published in *Vestnik Evropy* in 1810. In 1781 he had written his first ballad, "Nevernost'" (Infidelity, 1967), the first Russian ballad of the new, English type.

For all his enthusiasm for literature, a young man with good connections in society could not help but abandon himself to the diversions of life in Saint Petersburg. When he had moved to the capital in 1772, he had formulated the motto "Soedinit' prelesti svetskogo cheloveka s uprazhneniiami literatora est' dukhovnoe dostoinstvo' " (To unite the charm of a man of society with the activities of a man of letters is of spiritual value). Later he changed his opinion, and, struck by pangs of conscience, in his notes he tried to justify his inactivity and expressed regret over the "rastochennykh minutakh suetnoi i nesvobodnoi zhizni" (squandered minutes of [his] vain and restricted life) in Saint Petersburg. "Bespredel'naia prazdnost' " (a boundless idleness) also overcame him during a nine-month stay in Tver in 1780.

In November 1785 Murav'ev's life took an abrupt turn. He was appointed *kavaler* (companion) to the Grand Prince Konstantin Pavlovich and then tutor to Alexander and Konstantin Pavlovich in moral philosophy, Russian philology, and Russian history. In 1792, when Alexander's fiancée arrived in Russia, Murav'ev was assigned to teach her Russian. In preparing his lessons, Murav'ev would draw up brief notes for his charges to indicate the most important points on various themes and aspects of their studies. He published these notes at the Imperial Press in limited editions intended for himself and the students to whom they were addressed. In his pedagogical practice, Murav'ev used varied instructional and literary genres. Thus were written the moralistic "dramatic tale" "Dobroe ditia" (The Good Child) and the series "Razgovory mertvykh" (Dialogues of the Dead), which were collected in 1790. Two works conceived earlier but completed in this period also took on pedagogical purposes: *Emilievy pis'ma* (Letters from Emile, 1789 or 1790) and *Obitatel' predmestiia* (Inhabitant of a Suburb, 1790).

The title *Emilievy pis'ma* obviously alludes to the hero of the well-known didactic novel *Emile* (1762) by Jean-Jacques Rousseau – a writer from whom, along with Ewald Christian von Kleist and Christoph Wieland, Murav'ev claimed to have "sdelal bylo sebe shchit . . . protivu razvrashcheniia serdsa" (fashioned myself a shield . . . against the corruption of the heart) and "prisvoival sebe ili, luchshe skazat', voobrazhal, chto prisvoival ikh iazykh, ikh chustvovaniia" (assumed, or better, imagined, that I had appropriated their language, their feelings). *Emilievy pis'ma* includes a concise historical sketch of western European literature from Homer to the 1770s. The sketch was meant as a guide for the sensitive person seeking virtue in harmony both with people and nature and as a handbook on which authors to read and how, and what kind of beauty may be found in their works. In preparing his charges to rule Russia, Murav'ev's other goal was to make them understand the proper relationship between landowners and peasants and to have them view the farmer's labor as "istochnik bogatstva, kotoroe obrashchaetsia po zhilam

gosudarstva" (the source of wealth which circulates in the state's veins), the foundation on which "poluchili rozhdenie obshchestvo, zakony, iskusstva" (society, laws, and the arts are conceived). Murav'ev was a supporter of serfdom, which he believed could be reformed according to humane and enlightened principles.

Obitatel' predmestiia, periodicheskie listy was published in the form of ten periodical papers dating from 2 August until 1 November 1790. They explore the advantages of rural life in a sentimentalist manner, and as in *Emilievy pis'ma* the figure of an ideal landowner is presented, in this case Graf Blagotvorov (Count Charitable), a wise master, philanthropist, and father figure to his serfs. Both *Emilievy pis'ma* and *Obitatel' predmestiia, periodicheskie listy* show the influence of Joseph Addison and Richard Steele's *The Spectator* and *The Tatler,* but there are traces of other sources as well. The friend of the late Emile who is supposed to have published the letters strolls about in the society of Will Honeycomb (of *The Spectator*) and Dick Ironside (invoking Nestor Ironside of *The Guardian*), while the "obitatel' predmestiia" (suburban inhabitant) and his neighbors establish a small friendly circle, similar to that of the eponymous Spectator.

Murav'ev's educational notes and synopses reveal his erudition, his interest in contemporary European Enlightenment thinkers, including Abbé Guillaume-Thomas-François Raynal, Charles-Louis Montesquieu, Claude-Adrien Helvetius, Gottfried Wilhelm von Leibnitz, John Locke, David Hume, the earl of Shaftesbury, Francis Hutcheson, Adam Ferguson, William Robertson, and Adam Smith. Murav'ev's goal was to raise his charges as enlightened sovereigns who would concern themselves with the development of agriculture, commerce, and industry, respect each subject as a human being, and encourage science and the arts. He placed sensitivity and enlightenment at the center of his ethical teaching, sensitivity being the main source of life's pleasure and enlightenment acquiring value as it leads a person to moral perfection and virtue, conceived primarily as the urge to do good for others. According to Murav'ev, art is only able to give aesthetic satisfaction when inspired by virtue.

Among the prose genres not related to the fulfillment of his pedagogical duties, Murav'ev put a great deal of energy into traveler's notes. Even when young, on a trip to Archangel with his father in 1770, he had sent one of his university friends (apparently Rozheshnikov) letters in which he shared impressions of the road. Murav'ev's correspondence of the later 1770s with relatives and friends played an important role in his creative evolution. For the writer, letter writing was a kind of school in sentimentalist attitudes toward the world and a place to develop a corresponding style. From 1785 to 1793 Murav'ev made several trips around the country, and diaries and fragments of correspondence from this period are preserved among his papers. He even conceived a title in English and Russian for the description of his last trip: "The Idle Traveller. Puteshestvie prazdnogo cheloveka, Novgorod, Tver', Moskva, Kolomna, Riazan'." None of these projects was realized, although on their basis Murav'ev wrote the poems "Puteshestvie" (The Journey, 1819) and "K Feone" (To Theona, 1810).

During his time as tutor Murav'ev married Ekaterina Fedorovna Kolokol'tseva. In September 1795 his son Nikita was born and named in honor of his grandfather; a second son, Aleksandr, was born in March 1802. Like his nephew Mikhail Lunin, both of Murav'ev's sons later participated in the Decembrist movement.

In February 1796, when Grand Prince Konstantin had completed his studies, Murav'ev was dismissed with the rank of brigadier. For reasons unknown, in June 1798 Emperor Paul refused to promote him to the rank of major general. Petitions and efforts by various friends produced no results, and, deeply disillusioned, Murav'ev transferred from military to civil service. In 1800 he was made a senator, and in 1801, upon the accession to the throne of his former student Alexander I, Murav'ev was appointed state secretary in the Department of Petitions. In 1801–1802 he prepared collections of his work under the titles "Sobranie stikhotvorenii" (Collected Poems) and "Izvlechenie iz stikhotvorenii" (Selected Poems), which, as with many earlier such projects, never came to fruition. In October 1803 he petitioned the emperor on behalf of Karamzin, who as a result was appointed historiographer and given sufficient means to work full-time on his *Istoriia Gosudarstva Rossiiskogo* (History of the Russian State, 1816–1829). Murav'ev also secured for Karamzin the right to use the archives and furnished him with books essential to his work.

On 21 November 1803 Murav'ev was appointed deputy minister of education and made the trustee of Moscow University. As trustee he energetically took part in the transformation of Russia's oldest institution of higher education and tried to create better conditions for the development of national studies. During his trusteeship, instructors at the university began to read lectures in public regularly, taking advantage of great interest on the part of the Muscovite public. Several scholarly societies were established with Murav'ev's cooperation: the Obshchestvo istorii i drevnostei rossiiskikh (Society for Russian History and Antiquities) in May 1804, the Obshchestvo ispytatelei prirody (Society of Natural Scientists) on 26 September 1804, and the Obshchestvo sorevnovaniia meditsinskikh i fizicheskikh nauk (Society for Advancing Medical and Physical Science) on 2 January 1805. Leasing of the university press to outside entrepeneurs was discontinued, and the press began to publish a large number of periodicals, including Karamzin's *Vestnik Evropy* (European Herald). Murav'ev took part in editing the *Moskovskie uchenye vedomosti* (Moscow Scholarly News, 1805–1807) and the *Zhurnal iziashchnykh iskusstv* (Journal of Fine Arts, 1807), and he drafted the editorial program of the journal *Drug iunoshestva* (Friend of Youth, 1807–1809). He was also involved in other reforms, including regulations that would permit the university more autonomy.

Murav'ev's reforming activity was not confined to Moscow University. He undertook the practical organization of the Ministry of Education and of several new academic institutions (the Demidov Lyceum in Iaroslavl, Kazan University, and a series of provincial gymnasiums), invited foreign professors to newly opened departments, and began to draft new regulations for the Academy of Sciences. Selected as a member of the academy on 28 May 1804, he presented several reviews of works and took part in work on the academy's dictionary of the Russian language.

Murav'ev died on 29 July 1807. His death elicited many sympathetic responses, all of which spoke of his high moral fiber and, in Karamzin's words, his "liubov' k obshchemu blagu" (love for the common good). As Vasilii Zhukovsky later noted, as a poet Murav'ev had little influence on his contemporaries because he hardly published anything. Even his close friends valued him primarily as a writer of prose rather than as a poet. When Karamzin, Zhukovsky, and the poet Konstantin Batiushkov (Murav'ev's nephew, who was raised in his home) edited his works posthumously, producing two books and the three-volume collected works (wrongly labeled as "full" on the title page), not only did they consider it unnecessary to print a huge portion of Murav'ev's poetic output, but they also made emendations in the poems they did select. For them, publishing Murav'ev's collected works was not so much a way of including him in the living literary process as a tribute to a man who had exerted a great moral influence on them and who had helped each of them in some way.

Letters:
"M. N. Murav'ev," edited by Liubov' I. Kulakova and Vladimir A. Zapadova, in *Pis'ma russkikh pisatelei XVIII veka,* edited by Georgii P. Makogonenko (Leningrad: Nauka, 1980), pp. 259–377.

References:
Aleksandr. N. Brukhansky, "M. N. Murav'ev i 'legkoe stikhotvorstvo,' " *XVIII vek,* 4 (1959): 157–171;

Irina Iu. Fomenko, "M. N. Murav'ev i problema individual'nogo stilia," in *Na putiakh k romantizmu: Sbornik nauchnykh trudov,* edited by Fedor Ia. Priima (Leningrad: Nauka, 1984), pp. 52–70;

Grigorii A. Gukovsky, *Ocherki po istorii russkoi literatury i obshchestvennoi mysli XVIII veka* (Leningrad: Khudozhestvennaia literatura, 1938);

Liubov' I. Kulakova, "M. N. Murav'ev," *Uchenye zapiski Leningradskogo gos. universiteta,* 47 (1939): 4–42;

Viktor D. Levin, "Karamzin, Batiushkov, Zhukovsky – redaktory sochinenii M. N. Murav'eva," in *Problemy sovremennoi filologii: Sbornik statei k semidesiatiletiiu akademika V. V. Vinogradova* (Moscow: Nauka, 1965), pp. 182–191;

Ian K. Lilly, "On the Rich Rhymes of M. N. Murav'ev," *International Journal of Slavic Linguistics and Poetics,* 23 (1981): 147–162;

Zinaida M. Petrova, "Epitety M. N. Murav'eva," in *Iazyk russkikh pisatelei XVIII veka,* edited by Iurii S. Sorokin (Leningrad: Nauka, 1981), pp. 151–166;

Laura Rossi, "Mikhail Murav'ev and English Culture," *Study Groups on Eighteenth Century Russia Newsletter,* 20 (September 1992): 18–19;

Hans Rothe, "Nabokov, Pushkin and Murav'ev," *Study Group on Eighteenth-Century Russia Newsletter,* 14 (September 1986): 38–39;

Vladimir A. Zapadov, "Derzhavin i Murav'ev," *XVIII vek,* 7 (1966): 245–253;

N. Zhinkin, "M. N. Murav'ev (Po povodu istekshego stoletiia so vremeni ego smerti)," *Izvestiia Otdeleniia russkogo iazyka i slovesnosti Imp. Akademii Nauk,* 18, no. 1 (1913): 273–352.

Papers:
The main portion of Murav'ev's archive, consisting of forty-one volumes of manuscripts – literary works, diaries, notes, correspondence, official papers, and preparatory notes for his lectures – are preserved in the Russian National Library (formerly the Saltykov-Shchedrin State Library) in Saint Petersburg. Parts of his correspondence are located in the State Historical Museum in Moscow and in the Institute of Russian Literature (Pushkin House) in Saint Petersburg.

Iurii Aleksandrovich Neledinsky-Meletsky

(6 October 1752 – 14 February 1828)

Konstantin Iur'evich Lappo-Danilevsky
Institute of Russian Literature (Pushkin House), Saint Petersburg

BOOKS: *Stikhi na konchinu ego siiatel'stva, kniazia Vasil'ia Mikhailovicha Dolgorukogo-Krymskogo posledovavshuiu v Moskve 30 genvaria 1782 goda* (Saint Petersburg: [Artilleriiskii i inzhenernyi kadetskii korpus], 1782);

Oda ego siiatel'stvu kniaziu Nikolaiu Vasil'evichu Repninu, na pobedu, oderzhannuiu im nad turetskimi silami za Dunaem v 28 den' iiunia, 1791 goda (N.p., [1791?]);

Gospodam konnym artilleristam (N.p., [1796]);

Khor. Torzhestvui! tvoia to dolia (N.p., [1796]);

Pesnia. Vydu ia na rechenku ([Moscow: N. Novikov], n.d.).

Editions: *Sochineniia* (Saint Petersburg: A. Smirdin, 1850);

Stikhotvoreniia (Saint Petersburg, 1876).

OTHER: Antoine Léonard Thomas, "Na vremia," and "Na dolzhnosti obshchestva . . . ," translated by Neledinsky-Meletsky in *Sokrovishche Parnassa, ili Perevody luchshikh stikhotvorenii g. Tomasa . . .* (Saint Petersburg: [Artilleriiskii i inzhenernyi kadetskii korpus], 1778), pp. 3–13;

Claude Joseph Dorat, *Pervoe pis'mo kanonissy lissabonskoi,* translated by Neledinsky-Meletsky (N.p., 1792);

"Polnoe sobranie stikhotvorenii," in *Russkaia poeziia,* edited by S. A. Vengerov, volume 1, part 7 (Saint Petersburg, 1901), pp. 1–54.

Iurii Aleksandrovich Neledinsky-Meletsky

Iurii Aleksandrovich Neledinsky-Meletsky left for literary posterity only a few dozen exquisite lyrics that reflect deep feeling and display genuine poetic talent. His importance in Russian literary history is all the more significant because his oeuvre belongs to a period when the literary language was taking shape and becoming a more sophisticated poetic medium. The unified style of his narratives, felicitous choice of vocabulary, and formal perfection of his works – for which his contemporaries valued him so highly – had a particular importance for his fellow writers.

Iurii Aleksandrovich Neledinsky-Meletsky was born in Moscow on 6 October 1752 into a family of the highest Russian aristocracy. His mother, born Princess Kurakina, was the niece of Counts Nikolai and Petr Panin, important government figures under Catherine II. She died when Neledinsky was not yet three years old, and his paternal grandmother, Anna Ivanovna Neledinskaia-Meletskaia, took over his care and upbringing. She belonged to the ancient Talyzin family, with connections to the old Muscovite nobility, and her nephew was Empress Elizabeth's all-powerful chancellor Aleksei Bestuzhev-Riumin. She owned extensive property in the province of Tver but rarely visited there and instead kept a house in Moscow near the Sukharev Tower, renowned for its luxury and opulence, its many servants, and its traditionally Russian style of life. The future poet's father, Aleksandr Neledinsky-Meletsky, took virtually no part in his son's education: soon after his wife's death he left for Paris, where he lived a life of ease, maintaining a broad range of acquaintances in intellectual circles. He became an admirer of Voltaire, who called him "un amiable Russe" (an amiable Russian) in one of his letters. In 1767 the retired colonel returned to Russia and entered court service. Thereupon he soon became one of the people closest to Catherine II and a devoted participant in her various amusements and card games.

While his father lived in Paris, the son was entrusted to the care of serfs in his grandmother's house, and when Neledinsky was nine a Frenchman named De Pexonne was hired to tutor him in mathematics, history, geography, French, Latin, and Italian. His studies were interrupted in 1764 when his grandmother died, and the twelve-year-old boy was entrusted to the care of his maternal grandmother, Aleksandra Kurakina (née Panina), who lived in Saint Petersburg. Neledinsky's cousins, Princes Kurakin and Lobanov-Rostovsky, also orphaned at an early age, were already living at his grandmother's house. The young Pavel Petrovich, future emperor Paul I, often visited the Kurakin home, which had become a unique boarding school for young nobles, and subsequently he always looked on his adolescent playmates — all destined for brilliant careers — with favor.

In the beginning of 1769 Neledinsky and his cousins were sent to study at the University of Strasbourg, but they were called home within a year due to complaints on the part of their tutor, who was angered by their mischief. Early in 1770 Neledinsky entered active service in the regiment in which he had been enrolled as a child, as was the custom of the time. Russia was then at war with Turkey, and the young man, despite his family's objections, was eager to take part in military activity. In May he was sent to the Second Army, which was laying siege to the city of Bendera, and he served as an orderly to his great-uncle, Petr Panin, the general in charge. In 1771, under the command of Vasilii Dolgoruky, he took part in the subjugation of the Crimea, in storming enemy trenches, and in occupying Kafa, for which he was promoted to captain. His regiment was then transferred to the Swedish border, and in 1774, having been assigned to Gen. M. F. Kamensky's vanguard corps, Neledinsky commanded an advance battalion at the battle at Koludzha. For bringing news of the victory to the capital, Neledinsky was promoted to the rank of second major. After Kamensky's march to Shumla, which forced the Turks into signing the Treaty of Kuchuk-Kainardji, Neledinsky took no further part in military campaigns. He returned to the capital for the peace celebrations and was further promoted to the rank of first major.

Later in 1774, Neledinsky accompanied Repnin to Constantinople, where his uncle was the new ambassador to Turkey, and then returned to join the Pskov infantry regiment, in which he served until 1779, when he was transferred as lieutenant colonel to the Kiev regiment. From this period date some of Neledinsky's first poetic endeavors, inspired by his love for a woman whose name he hid from even his closest friends. He also began work on a translation of Voltaire's tragedy Zaïre (1732) but never finished. In 1785 Neledinsky retired from the army with the rank of colonel as a sign of protest against Catherine's powerful favorite, Prince Grigorii Potemkin, who had insulted the battalion Neledinsky commanded. The poet moved back to Moscow, where he began to give greater attention to his literary interests. In 1786 he married Princess Ekaterina Khovanskaia, who had just graduated from the Smol'nyi Institute for Noblewomen in Saint Petersburg. In September of that year Neledinsky was appointed director of Moscow's Glavnoe narodnoe uchilishche (Principal National Institute), to which all of the lower state schools and private boarding schools in the city and province of Moscow were subordinated.

The first well-known poem by Neledinsky, "Strofy na mir s Turkami 1774 goda" (Stanzas on the Peace Treaty with the Turks in 1774), follows all the generic rules for the eighteenth-century panegyric ode and was intended for the festivities in Moscow on the occasion of the Kuchuk-Kainardji peace. A series of extant poetic fragments indicates that Neledinsky had been dedicating his leisure time to poetry even earlier. In 1782 the newspaper Moskovskie vedomosti (Moscow News) published his poem "Stikhi na konchinu kniazia V. M. Dolgorukogo-Krymskogo 1782 goda 30 ianvaria" (Verses on the Death of Prince V. M. Dolgoruky-Krymsky on 30 January 1782), written in the form of a panegyric inscription, and in 1783 his "Strofy na druzhbu" (Stanzas on Friendship) appeared in the journal Sobesednik liubitelei rossiiskogo slova (Interlocutor of

Lovers of the Russian Word). In the latter he praises friendship as the highest good in the traditional odic form.

Neledinsky's friendship with Dar'ia Ivanovna Golovina, to whom he dedicated several comic poems – including "Pis'mo D. I. Golovinoi iz Vitebska" (Letter to D. I. Golovina from Vitebsk) and "Epitalama D. I. Golovinoi" (Epithalamium to D. I. Golovina) both first published in his *Sochineniia* (1850) – dates from the beginning of the 1780s. She, like her younger sister, was known for her beautiful voice, and the sisters were the first to perform Neledinsky's songs. In his letters to Golovina, Neledinsky shared the secrets of his unrequited love. The object of his platonic worship is unknown; Neledinsky referred to her as "Temira." The poems dedicated to her are among the more vivid examples of the poetry of Russian sentimentalism. The alexandrine verse and the imagery in the first lyrical work of the cycle "Temira" (1782) reveal the strong influence of French poetry and may explain the somewhat constrained style in the lyric hero's expression of feelings. Another cycle, "Temire" (To Temira), written in iambic lines of varied length, is organized around the opposition between the harmony of nature and the experiences of the lyric hero. The world's perfection leaves him indifferent, and his disillusionment is total: "Na chto by ne vzglianul, vse dlia menia postylo" (Whatever I looked at, everything was hateful to me). Even his own work seems offensive to the poet.

"Temire," first published in June 1787 in *Novye ezhemesiachnye sochineniia* (New Monthly Compositions) together with some minor works, brought Neledinsky well-deserved recognition. The admiration of the poet's friends elicited Neledinsky's poem "Molitva" (A Prayer, 1787). It is permeated with deep religious feeling. At the same time, the poet confesses his inability to withstand temptation and, in the final reckoning, puts his trust in God's mercy. Original in form and different from traditional odes in its authorial confession of weakness, its publication was forbidden by the censor. Neledinsky's close association with the poets Mikhail Kheraskov and Ivan Dmitriev, and then with Nikolai Karamzin, all of whom shared his aesthetic tastes, dates to the end of the 1780s.

Neledinsky's songs, published in a variety of periodicals – *Moskovskii zhurnal* (Moscow Journal), *Magazin obshchepoleznykh znanii i izobretenii* (The Storehouse of Generally Useful Knowledge), *Aonidy* (Aonides) – had brought the poet broad recognition by the early 1790s. Many of these songs were re-published in Dmitriev's *Karmannyi pesennik* (Pocket Song-Book, 1796). The songs were soon set to music and performed in drawing rooms of the nobility. They subsequently spread throughout Russian society, aided by the fact that some of the texts had been written to the music of folk melodies. Almost all of Neledinsky's songs were written in trochaic meter, linking them to folk poetry. It is not surprising, therefore, that some of his songs were assimilated into folk culture and later perceived as of popular origin. The songs "Vydu ia na rechen'ku" (I'll Go to the Brook), "U kogo dushevny sily nachinaiut izmeniat'" (Whoever is Losing His Strength of Spirit), and "Ty velish' mne ravnodushnym" (You Order Me to Be Indifferent) enjoyed particular popularity. At the center of attention in these songs is the unrequited passion and suffering of unhappy love. In a manner stylistically close to these songs, Neledinsky translated Pietro Metastasio's well-known poem "K Nine" (To Nina), a translation which is one of the heights of his oeuvre.

Neledinsky's calm life was interrupted by Paul I's ascension after Catherine's death in November 1796. Paul immediately summoned his childhood friend to Saint Petersburg, gave him the rank of *deistvitel'nyi statskii sovetnik* (active councillor of state), and appointed him state secretary for accepting petitions. At Paul's coronation Neledinsky was awarded the Order of Saint Anna of the Second Degree and given eight hundred serfs. He soon developed a friendship with Empress Maria Fedorovna and with Paul's favorite, Ekaterina Nelidova. In 1798 Neledinsky used his influence to obtain permission for the performance and publication of Vasilii Kapnist's comedy *Iabeda* (Chicane). On 8 April 1798 Neledinsky was rewarded with the Order of Saint Anna of the First Degree, but two months later the poet was dismissed from his position and exiled from Saint Petersburg due to the intrigues of I. P. Kutaisov. In November 1800, however, Neledinsky was appointed *tainyi sovetnik* (privy councillor) and assigned to Moscow as a senator. After the death of Paul I in 1801, Neledinsky remained in Moscow and spent his summers at Pavlovsk, Maria Fedorovna's summer residence. During one of these visits he wrote "Strofy na Pavlovsk" (Stanzas on Pavlovsk, 1805), extolling the widowed empress's place of seclusion. Thanks to her, in 1807 Neledinsky was entrusted with supervising the educational programs at the schools of the Order of Saint Catherine in Moscow and at the schools for *meshchanskiie devitsy* (girls from families of the merchant class).

At the beginning of the nineteenth century Neledinsky turned much of his attention to occasional verse, choruses and marches, and impromptus and *bouts rimés,* some of which were written in French. The poet also translated many works, mainly from French: poems by Frédéric-César de La Harpe, Jean-Pierre Florian, Joseph Nicolas Delisle, Claude Joseph Dorat, and Antoine Léonard Thomas, and fables by Jean de La Fontaine. Most of the works he chose to translate are love lyrics, thematically similar to his original work. In his translations Neledinsky did not strive for literalness. While preserving the source's general train of thought, Neledinsky considered it more important to create perfect and original works in Russian.

Neledinsky moved with his family to Tver in 1808 and then back to Saint Petersburg in February 1813, where he served on the board of the Obshchestva blagorodnykh devits (Society of Young Noblewomen) and in the Senate. In 1813–1814 Neledinsky took part in composing choral verse for a choir to celebrate the Russian army's triumphant return from Paris. He continued in state service until 1823, when he retired and settled in Kaluga. He spent the last five years of his life in the close circle of his family. The poet died in Kaluga on 14 February 1828.

Neledinsky-Meletsky played a conspicuous role in the development of Russian literature despite the comparatively small number of his works published during his lifetime. His lyrical masterpieces (his songs most of all) lent greater psychological depth to Russian lyrics and refined the literary language, aiding in its rapprochement with the spoken language of educated society that was taking place at the end of the eighteenth century. In his "Rech' o vliianii legkoi poezii na iazyk" (Speech on the Influence of Light Poetry on Language, 1816), Konstantin Batiushkov considered Neledinsky one of the most outstanding representatives of light poetry, which he considered one of the main accomplishments of contemporary Russian literature, and in 1823 Aleksandr Pushkin ranked him higher than Dmitriev.

References:

Khronika nedavnei stariny (Iz arkhiva kn. Obolenskogo-Neledinskogo-Meletskogo i Karamzina) (Saint Petersburg, 1876);

Mikhail N. Mazaev, "Kul't liubvi (Stikhotvoreniia Neledinskogo-Meletskogo i Karamzina)," *Vestnik vsemirnoi istorii,* 10 (1901): 61–84;

Nikolai F. Samarin, "Iu. A. Neledinsky-Meletsky (Ocherki ego zhizni, bumagi i perepiska ego)," *Russkii arkhiv,* 1 (1867): 101–120.

Nikolai Petrovich Nikolev

(10 November 1758 – 24 January 1815)

Irwin R. Titunik

University of Michigan

SELECTED BOOKS: *Oda ee imperatorskomu velichestvu gosudaryne Ekaterine Alekseevne . . . na zakliuchenie slavoiu uvenchannogo mira* (Moscow: Moskovskii universitet, 1774);

Popytka ne shutka, ili Udachnyi opyt komediia, v trekh deistviiakh (Moscow: Moskovskii universitet, 1774);

Ispytannoe postoianstvo komediia, v odno deistvie ([Moscow: Universitetskaia tipografiia, 1776]);

Pis'mo k Fedoru Grigor'evichu Karinu na predstavlenie Aleksandra Petrovicha Sumarokova iz podmoskovnoi 5-go oktiabria ([Moscow: Universitetskaia tipografiia, 1777]);

Satira na obychai i nravy razvrashchennykh liudei nyneshnego veka ([Moscow: Universitetskaia tipografiia, 1777]);

Prikashchik, drammaticheskaia pustel'ga s golosami, v odnom deistvii (Moscow: N. Novikov, 1781);

Rozana i Liubim dramma s golosami v chetvertykh deistviiakh (Moscow: N. Novikov, 1781);

Dve ody na vziatie pobedonosnym Rossiiskim voinstvom goroda Ochakova 1788 goda dekabria 6 sochinennyia pervaia g. T . . . m v tsarstve mertvykh, vtoraia otstavnym soldatom Moiseem Sleptsovym ([Saint Petersburg: Rakhmaninov,] 1789);

Oda ee imperatorskomu velichestvu velikoi gosudaryne Ekaterine Alekseevne . . . na zakliuchenie mira s Ottomanskoiu Portoiu 1791 goda dekabria 29 dnia (Moscow: V. Okorokov, 1792);

Oda ee imperatorskomu velichestvu vsemilostiveishei gosudaryne Ekaterine Alekseevne . . . v svidetel'stvo dushevnogo blagodareniia kak voobshche za prolityia bozhestvennyia shchedroty na vsekh chad rossiiskikh obnarodovannym manifestom sentiabria vtorago dnia v leto tsarstvovanii eia; vserossiiskago, v tridesiat' vtoroe, tavricheskago v pervoe nadesiat', kak i sobno za okazannuiu vysochaishuiu milost' nagrazhdeniem maluiu zhertvu za velikiia blagotvoreniia prinesshago eia vernopodannago Nikolaia Nikoleva (Moscow: Kh. Klaudi, 1793);

Oda ee imperatorskomu velichestvu vsemilostliveishei gosudaryne Ekaterine Alekseevne na torzhestvo mira s

Ottomanskoiu Portoiu 1793 goda v sentiabre (Moscow: Kh. Klaudi, 1793; Saint Petersburg: Akademiia nauk, 1793);

Tvorenii, 5 volumes (Moscow: Kh. Ridiger & Kh. Klaudi, 1795–1798);

Oda ego imperatorskomu velichestvu vsepresvetleishemu gosudariu . . . Pavlu Pervomu, na den' vsevozhdelennogo ego pribytiia v Moskvu dlia sviashchennogo miropomazaniia 1797 goda, marta dnia (Moscow: Kh. Ridiger & Kh. Klaudi, [1797]);

Torzhestvennye venchanie i miropomazanie na tsarstvo ego imperatorskogo velichestva Pavla I . . . i blagovernoi gosudaryni Marii Fedorovny (Moscow, 1798);

Oda e. i. v. gosudariu Pavlu Petrovichu na sluchai vziatiia kreposti Brestsii i porazhenie vragov rossiiskim voinstvom pod predvoditel'stvom general-fel'dmarshala grafa Suvorova-Rymninskago (sic) (Saint Petersburg: Akademiia nauk, 1799);

Chustvovanie po sluchaiu konchiny svetleishego kniazia M. I. Golenishcheva-Kutuzova Smolenskogo (Moscow, 1813);

Tri liricheskie stikhotvoreniia, edited by Stepan Maslov (Moscow, 1814);

Stikhi na vyzdorovlenie grafa Petra Aleksandrovicha Rumiantsova ([Moscow: Universitetskaia tipografiia], n.d.).

OTHER: "Pal'mira," in *Rossiiskii featr,* volume 5 (Saint Petersburg: Akademiia nauk, 1787);

"Sorena i Zamir," in *Rossiiskii featr,* volume 5 (Saint Petersburg: Akademiia nauk, 1787);

"Samoliubivyi stikhotvorets," in *Rossiiskii featr,* volume 15 (Saint Petersburg: Akademiia nauk, 1787);

"Feniks," in *Rossiiskii featr,* volume 22 (Saint Petersburg: Akademiia nauk, 1788);

"Tochil'shchik," in *Rossiiskii featr,* volume 22 (Saint Petersburg: Akademiia nauk, 1788);

"Rech', govorennaia Vereiskoi Okrugi pomeshchikom N. P. Nikolevym sobstevennym i sosednim krest'ianam," in *Pamiatnik druzei N. P. Nikolevu* (Moscow, 1819).

Nikolai Petrovich Nikolev's literary career ran its course in the last quarter of the eighteenth century, when Russia witnessed the emergence of powerful new literary talents and interests that would shape the further evolution of Russian literature in the nineteenth century. This period of Russian literary history involved in part a summing up and innovative manipulation of the achievements of the Russian baroque and neoclassicist past, and in part a movement toward the new literary concerns and practices of the developing sentimentalist and pre-Romantic trends. A few Russian writers at the time, most notably Gavriil Derzhavin and Nikolai Karamzin, were proclaimed by their contemporaries to be the geniuses, leaders, and exemplars of their age and were granted niches in the pantheon of Russian literature by posterity. Nikolev, a prolific poet and playwright, although of lesser talent, similarly endeavored to embody his age and nation in his literary work, but, while attracting the enthusiastic following of a coterie and representing a force to be reckoned with by the literary community at large, he ultimately failed in realizing his ambitions and fell into almost complete oblivion in the nineteenth century. Despite and perhaps because of his failed ambitions, however, Nikolev merits recognition as a particularly vivid representative of the late-eighteenth-century period of transition in the history of Russian literature.

Nikolai Petrovich Nikolev was born on 10 November 1758 in Moscow or its environs to an aristocratic family. Princess Ekaterina Dashkova, a leading figure in Russian intellectual and political life and president of the Academy of Science from 1783 to 1793, was related to the Nikolevs, and she met Nikolai in Moscow in 1764. Impressed with the six-year-old boy, she decided to take him under her wing. It is probable that the young Nikolev accompanied her when she returned to Saint Petersburg in 1769. Dashkova arranged for his tutelage (Nikolev is said to have excelled in mathematics and in foreign languages). In the illustrious social and cultural environment that surrounded her, populated with such powerful and influential personalities as the "enlightened magnates," Counts Ivan Shuvalov and Nikita Panin, Nikolev's character, outlook, and ambitions took shape. Nikolev remained on cordial terms with Princess Dashkova and the members of her circle throughout his life.

As was common practice with sons of aristocratic families, Nikolev had as a child been pre-

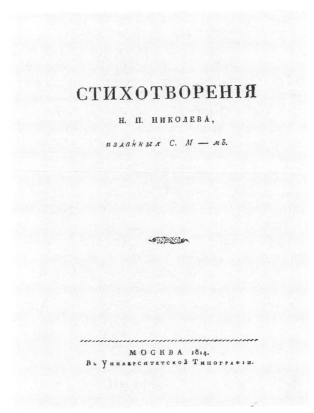

Title page for a book of poems by Nikolev, the last of his works to be published during his lifetime

enlisted in a guards' regiment. At sixteen years of age he reported for active duty and embarked upon a military career that lasted from four to fourteen years by various accounts, grievously cut short when Nikolev began to go blind, apparently as a consequence of an illness he contracted while on courier duty between the Crimea and Saint Petersburg. In 1784 (whether before or after that crisis is unknown) Nikolev married Princess Ekaterina Aleksandrovna Dolgorukaia.

After the onset of his blindness, Nikolev retired and proceeded to devote his time and energies to literary pursuits. The writing of poetry had been a favorite occupation since his thirteenth year, and he had written sizable compositions, (later collected into his published oeuvre) by the time he was sixteen or seventeen years of age. By 1795, when Nikolev began bringing out his *Tvorenii* (Works), the size and scope of his literary output had grown to such proportions that ten volumes were planned to accommodate it. Only five volumes were actually published, however, as public interest in Nikolev had apparently faded by the time the fifth volume came out in 1798. The contents of Nikolev's *Tvorenii* attest to the broad range of his poetic endeavors and to the thoroughly traditional nature of the kinds of poetry he chose to write: *dukhovnye ody* (spiritual odes), including psalm adaptations and versified prayers adapted from the New Testament and the Orthodox liturgy; panegyric odes, usually praising Empress Catherine II, even when the odes celebrated a victory of Russian arms; moralistic-didactic or philosophical odes; satires; fables; epistles; and songs, especially love songs and folk-style songs.

Of these verses a few items warrant special mention. In his "Liro-didakticheskoe poslanie k . . . Dashkovoi" (Lyro-Didactic Epistle to Dashkova, 1790), a poem of over one hundred panegyric-ode stanzas (*aBaBccDeeD*, in iambic tetrameter), Nikolev produced a full-blown *profession de foi,* apparently meant to represent the author's intellectual solidarity with Princess Dashkova (then president of the Academy of Sciences) and her circle. He attached such importance to this epistle that he devoted 270 pages of commentary to the version published in the third volume of his *Tvorenii.* The poem surveys the entire range of human intellectual endeavors, extolling the natural and physical sciences and the applied sciences (mechanics) but devoting approximately half its length to issues of language and literature. In those concerns Nikolev voiced the precepts of such classicist spokesmen as Nicholas Boileau and Aleksandr Sumarokov, espousing as the principles of his argument the same criteria of reason, decorum, and purity of literary genre. He also made ample use of the opportunity to rail at pedantry, censorius criticism, and authorial conceit, topics on which he had firsthand knowledge.

Among his moralistic-philosophical odes, two of 1796 – "Sovest'" (Conscience) and "Otets otechestva" (Father of the Fatherland), written in the same verse form as the "Liro-didakticheskoe poslanie k . . . Dashkovoi" – present Nikolev at his strongest and seem reminiscent (especially in their prosody, intonation, and vociferous stance against tyranny) of Aleksandr Radishchev's ode "Vol'nost'" (Liberty, circa 1783). But by far the most popular of Nikolev's poems were "Oda k premudroi Felitse ot starogo russkogo piity iz tsarstva mertvykh" (Ode to the Most Wise Felitsa by an Old Russian Poet from the Realm of the Dead, 1783–1787), "Oda rossiiskim soldatam na vziatie kreposti Ochakova . . . sochinennaia ot litsa nekoego drevnego rossiiskogo piity" (Ode to Russian Soldiers on the Taking of the Fortress of Ochakov Composed in the Person of a Certain Russian Poet of Yore), and "Russkie soldaty, gudoshnaia pesn' po sluchaiu vziatiia Ochakova" (Russian Soldiers, a Fiddling Song on the Occasion of the Taking of Ochakov), the latter two written in 1789 and revised in 1797. The first two were Nikolev's sui generis tributes to the success of Gavriil Derzhavin's first "Felitsa" ode. Nikolev came up with decidedly odd, parodic odes that use the trick of a mock speaker – in both cases, Vasilii Trediakovsky. Neither their verse form (dactylic tetrameter quatrains rhymed *aBaB*) nor their style is especially characteristic of Trediakovsky, but Nikolev doubtless knew that making fun of Trediakovsky, if only by invoking his image, would appeal to the prejudices and sense of humor of Catherine II, whose disdain for Trediakovsky was well known. The last of the three also uses a stand-in poet, this time of a folkish variety, named Moisei Sleptsov (Moses the Blind), an obvious alter ego of the poet. The verse form was the standard panegyric ode stanza but in trochaic meter, conventionally used in imitations of folk poetry. The folksy style of speech used by Nikolev's stand-in was not especially authentic or innovatory but an example of what Il'ia Serman has called in *Poety XVIII veka* (1972), "modnyi, zalikhvatskii psevdorusskii stil' " (the rollicking pseudo-Russian style then à la mode). One other poem of Nikolev's, a popular love song, gained a curious sort of notoriety by being quoted in Nikolai Gogol's story "Zapiski sumasshedshego" (Notes of a Madman, 1835), whose hero-narrator attributes it to Aleksandr Pushkin.

Nikolev's lyric poetry, despite his prolific production, did not form the basis of his reputation among contemporaries. That basis was supplied instead by his series of works for the stage, produced from early in his literary career to its end. Not all of his considerable dramaturgical output has survived, but nine works were performed, some several times, in Nikolev's lifetime. This set consists of two tragedies, four comic operas, and three comedies.

The uncontested masterpiece of the entire set of Nikolev's theatrical works was the tragedy *Sorena i Zamir* (Sorena and Zamir; collected in *Rossiiskii featr,* 1787), written in 1784 and performed on the Moscow stage from 1785 to 1795. The play is a highly original adaptation of motifs and ideas in Voltaire's *Alzire, ou les Américains* (1736), with Nikolev shifting the scene to Old Russia and making a Russian czar, Mstislav of Polotsk, the tyrant-villain, and his captives, the Polovetsian prince and princess Zamir and Sorena, two dignified and enlightened noble savages. (The play has no pretension to historical fact.) The governing motif of the play, as in many of Jean Racine's tragedies, is the disastrous effects of uncontrolled passion: Mstislav, madly in love with Sorena, schemes to possess her while she rebuffs him, remaining steadfastly faithful to her husband. Finally Sorena, driven to desperation by Mstislav's scheming (which includes Zamir's forced conversion to Christianity, thus annulling his marriage to the still-pagan Sorena), determines to assassinate him, but because of her anxiety and the darkness of night she accidentally kills Zamir instead, whereupon she takes her own life. Mstislav's remorse at the end of the play proves that he was not a thorough villain but a weak-willed victim of emotion. The tragedy has been much praised for its political daring (the tirades against tyranny and the pleas for human rights and tolerance put in the mouths of Zamir and Sorena). By some later accounts the play was banned after its initial performances by order of the Moscow authorities but Catherine II, who professed to see no reference to herself in the play's protests against tyranny, allowed it to resume. This account, however, may well be apocryphal, as it appeared in a partisan rebuttal of the negative reviews that *Sorena i Zamir* received upon its stage revival in 1810.

Curiously, the other most successful of Nikolev's works for the stage, the comic opera *Rozana i Liubim* (Rozana and Liubim) – written in 1776–1777, first performed in 1778, and published in 1781 – employs a similar plot, but of the "happy ending" variety. The tyrannical landowner Shchedrov abducts the serf girl Rozana, of whom he is enamored. Her serf fiancé Liubim's exemplary love for her and the dignified distress of her father finally touch the conscience of Shchedrov, and he returns her unharmed to marry Liubim. The play is an adaptation from a French original, *Annette et Lubin* (1766) by Charles Favart, and it has been praised for its daring in putting protests against gentry mistreatment of serfs into the mouths of its serf characters. The play bears the subtitle *dramma s golosami* (A Play with [singing] Voices), indicating a typical Russian comic-opera format: spoken dialogue with interpolated songs and choruses set to music. The music was composed by Joseph (or Michel) Kerzelli.

Nikolev's comedies seem to have achieved neither much esteem nor popularity. *Samoliubivyi stikhotvorets* (The Vainglorious Poet) – written in 1775 and first performed in 1781 – is typical of Nikolev's comedies. The play spins out a flimsy plot concerning an impediment to the marriage of two lovers, Milana and Chesnodum, and resorts for filler to buffoonery and to the satiric pronunciamentos of the servant girl Marina. The title character, Nadmen (Haughty), whose exalted notion of his poetic worth drives him to fury at the slightest hint of competition, supplies the plot's impediment: the protagonist, who wishes to marry Nadmen's niece, brings him a tragedy he has written, thinking thereby to ingratiate himself. The character of Nadmen is remarkable only as a lampoon on Aleksandr Sumarokov (whose vanity was legendary). It is reported (once again in a later memoir, by Aleksandr Shakhovskoi) that a performance of the play was hissed by the Kniazhnins (Iakov Kniazhnin was Sumarokov's son-in-law) and by other members of the audience offended on the great poet's behalf.

However, Nikolev's position with regard to the Sumarokov legacy, indeed with regard to the contemporary Russian literary scene, is a matter of confusion and dispute. He has been variously identified as a classicist, as a foremost representative of the latter-day Sumarokov school, as a fervent epigone of Mikhail Lomonosov's baroque-spirited odes, and as both a sharer in and a shunner of sentimentalism, then coming into fashion. He was probably in some degree all of these things – a contradictory and eclectic literary personality. A small coterie of well-bred and talented but minor literary figures including Fedor Karin, Dmitri Khvostov, and Dmitri Gorchakov looked up to Nikolev as the Russian literary genius of his age (they called him the "Russian Milton"), and the circle of his enthusiasts even included Ivan Krylov. But his most distinguished contemporaries, particularly Vasilii Kapnist, Derzhavin, Ivan Dmitriev, and Karamzin, could not abide his pretensions. Kapnist included a "Nikoshev" in his satiric gallery of bad poets; Karamzin described the effect of reading Nikolev's epistle to Dashkova as something like a blister on the brain, and he published a devastating review of one of Nikolev's comedies; Derzhavin and Dmitriev wrote stinging parodies of his odes, Derzhavin remarking that Nikolev was and would always be "sam na sebia satira" (a parody of himself).

Nikolev was, nevertheless, not deprived of official recognition. In 1792 he was elected to the Russian Academy; when Paul I ascended the throne, Nikolev enjoyed the emperor's special favor as his "aveugle clairvoyant" (blind seer); and even as late as 1811, the University of Moscow's Obshchestvo liubitelei Rossiiskoi slovesnosti (Society of Lovers of Russian Literature) made him an honorary member.

His last years were spent on his Moscow estate where, it is reported, with a vanity worthy of his own lampoon on Sumarokov, he received the homages of a few devoted but not altogether respectful admirers. He also continued his creative endeavors, working on a new tragedy, "Malek Adel'." In 1812 he had one last moment of glory when he rallied the neighboring peasants, panicked about the approach of Napoleon's forces, with an impassioned patriotic speech (published in *Pamiatnik druzei N. P. Nikolevu*, 1819). Nikolev died on 24 January 1815. Though he remains a frequent object of mention in the annals of Russian literary history and a few of his works are regularly reproduced in anthologies, Nikolev's name and legacy are mostly forgotten, and no major scholarly study has yet been devoted to him.

References:

Sergei T. Aksakov, *Sobranie sochinenii v piati tomakh*, volume 3 (Moscow: Pravda, 1966), pp. 8–16;

Mark G. Altshuller, "Liro-didakticheskoe poslanie' N. P. Nikoleva," *Russkaia literatura*, 72, no. 339 (1968): 208–214;

M. A. Arzumanova, "Iz istorii literaturno-obshchestvennoi bor'by 90-kh godov XVIII veka (N. P. Nikolev i N. M. Karamzin)," *Vestnik Leningradskogo universiteta*, 4, no. 20 (1965): 73–83;

A. A. Chebyshev, "N. P. Nikolev (istoriko-literaturnyi ocherk)," *Filologicheskie zapiski*, 3 (1890): 1–34; 4–5 (1890): 35–36;

Stepan A. Maslov, "Kratkaia biografiia N. P. Nikoleva," *Syn otechestva*, 36, no. 9 (1816): 197–212;

Iurii V. Stennik, "Lomonosov i Nikolev (Nekotorye tendentsii v razvitii zhanra pokhval'noi ody poslednei chetverti 18 veka)," in *Poetika i stilistika russkoi literatury (Pamiati akademika V. V. Vinogradova)*, edited by M. P. Alekseev and others (Leningrad: Nauka, 1971), pp. 59–68.

Nikolai Ivanovich Novikov

(27 April 1744 – 31 July 1818)

Gary Marker
State University of New York at Stony Brook

BOOKS: *Opyt istoricheskogo slovaria o rossiiskikh pisateliakh* (Saint Petersburg: [Akademiia nauk], 1772);

Drevniaia rossiiskaia idrografiia (Saint Petersburg: Akademiia nauk, 1773); published as *Kniga bol'shomu chertezhu ili drevniaia karta Rossiiskogo gosudarstva* (Saint Petersburg: Gornoe uchilishche, 1792).

Editions: *Izbrannye sochineniia,* edited by Georgii P. Makogonenko (Moscow: Khudozhestvennaia literatura, 1951);

Satirichskie zhurnaly N. I. Novikov, edited by P. N. Berkov (Moscow & Leningrad: Akademiia nauk, 1951);

Izbrannye pedagogicheskie sochineniia, edited by I. A. Trushin (Moscow: Khudozhestvennaia literatura, 1959);

N. I. Novikov i ego sovremenniki, edited by I. V. Malyshev (Moscow: Akademiia nauk, 1961), pp. 13–336, 481–515.

OTHER: *Truten',* 1, nos. 1–36 (May 1769–December 1769), 2, nos. 1–17 (5 January 1770–27 April 1770), edited by Novikov;

Pustomelia, 1 (June 1770–July 1770), edited by Novikov;

Zhivopisets, 1, nos. 1–26 (1772), edited by Novikov;

Drevniaia rossiiskaia vivliofika, ili Sobranie raznykh drevnikh sochinenii, 10 volumes, edited by Novikov (Saint Petersburg: [Akademiia nauk], 1773–1775); revised and enlarged edition, 20 volumes (Moscow: Tipograficheskaia kompaniia, 1788–1791);

Koshelek, 1, nos. 1–9 (1774), edited by Novikov;

Gorodskaia i derevenskaia biblioteka, 12 volumes, edited by Novikov (Moscow: N. Novikov, 1782–1786).

Nikolai Ivanovich Novikov

Although he wrote few original works and no novels, plays, or stories, Nikolai Ivanovich Novikov has been justly acclaimed as a towering figure of the Russian Enlightenment, equaled only by the Em-press Catherine the Great, Mikhail Lomonosov, Aleksandr Radishchev, and perhaps Nikolai Karamzin. As a philanthropist, as an editor, and above all as a publisher, Novikov had an enormous impact upon Russia's dawning secular intellectual life. Between 1765 and his arrest and incarceration in 1792, Novikov was responsible for bringing into print hundreds of new titles, and in his prime during the mid 1780s, his publishing empire in Moscow was producing nearly 40 percent of all titles generated by Russia's civil publishing houses. His undaunted energy on behalf of a fledgling intellectual world with few literary markets, along with the fact that his career was cut short by an act of political repression, secured for Novikov virtual lionization, at times almost beatification, among his peers and in subsequent scholarship. Historians have interpreted his career and ideas in sharply divergent ways, and none of them has made much headway in capturing his personality or private life. Still, high praise of Novikov has evoked almost no dissent within the academy.

Without denying his individual accomplishments, Novikov is best understood as part of the remarkable generation made up largely of aristocratic men who passed through secondary education together and went on to construct a framework within which Russian letters flourished. Born into a hereditary noble family on 27 April 1744 at the ancestral home in the village of Avdot'ino, not far from Moscow, Nikolai Ivanovich Novikov spent the first twelve years of his life at the family estate. Like most noble boys of the day, Novikov's initial education took place at home, where he lived with his parents and four siblings (he was the middle child, with two brothers and two sisters). His father had served in the navy and as a military governor but had retired to the estate in Avdot'ino by the time of Nikolai's birth.

In 1757 Novikov was sent to Moscow to attend the recently opened Moscow University gymnasium, where he lodged at the gymnasium's pension for young noblemen (there was a separate institution for the sons of commoners, the *raznochintsy*). During these years the gymnasium was noted less for the rigor of its pedagogy than for its atmosphere of high-minded conviviality. Language teachers particularly were ridiculed by the students, who attended classes for no more than several weeks a year. Still, most of the students learned enough French or German to be able to read widely in those languages and to translate a fair amount of what they read. They drew inspiration from the corps of scholars and writers who taught at the university, including Anton Barsov, Nikolai Popovsky, and Mikhail Kheraskov, and in the company of such teachers their devotion to reading and writing germinated.

Relatively little is known about Novikov's academic career. In 1758 the gymnasium awarded him a prize for scholastic achievement, but less than two years later his name was included on a list of students expelled for laziness and skipping classes. Secondary education had gained only a grudging acceptance among the Russian middle service nobility from which Novikov derived. Most, in fact, either studied at home or attended one of the cadet academies whose curricula devoted at least some atten-

tion to parade drills, marksmanship, and other skills of use to an officer, the career of choice for an aspiring eighteenth-century gentleman. Thus dismissal from the gymnasium brought Novikov no shame or loss of status.

After his expulsion Novikov spent about two additional years in Moscow before beginning his career in state service as an officer in the elite Izmailovsky Regiment in the capital of Saint Petersburg. He had had no prior military training or experience, but his father had followed the common practice of enlisting his son in the service lists years earlier, and, as a result, Novikov was immediately commissioned as a second lieutenant.

The year 1762 proved to be a good time to enter service. Prior to that year the nobility had been required to serve the state either in the military or in the civil administration, an obligation that was consistent with the principle of universal service that had guided the formal relationship between state and society in Russia for some time. But in 1762 Peter III issued a new edict that made noble service voluntary. His reasons for making such a change remain obscure, and its announcement seems to have evoked mostly bewilderment, but the timing proved to be fortunate for Novikov's generation.

In peacetime service in a regiment was no more burdensome than school had been. Moreover, it provided a salary, status, access to high places, and conviviality. Therefore, virtually everyone in Novikov's cohort continued to serve. They were free to devote time to the literary and journalistic endeavors that had grown up around their university associates, and, if they so chose, they now could leave service in order to become full-time intellectuals. By all accounts these literary activities were pleasurable, but much more was involved than pleasure. The young men imagined themselves as elite cosmopolitan servitors, newly minted gentlemen, and the natural leaders of a proud nation at once young (as a civilized European state) and rich in heritage (as a people with a centuries-old written tradition). They avidly imbibed the intoxicating optimism of the European Enlightenment and hastened to reproduce it in their own language. To be born into this generation meant engaging in a dawning secular literary culture, one that would provide a congenial setting for the humanistic turn the Russian Enlightenment was taking. These literati initiated the influential Russian literary journals. Their translations became the primary medium through which Russia's reading public experienced foreign literature.

To a large degree Russia's mid-century intellectuals, Novikov among them, set the terms of the Russian Enlightenment by raising issues that would define Russian letters for several generations. In their hands, national consciousness and modernity became abiding preoccupations, as the idealized Russia (typically cast as "new," "young," "untamed," and so on) came to be constructed primarily in relationship to an idealized Europe. Legitimized by social standing, education, history, and an Enlightenment-rooted vision of progress, they set about to remake Russia into a virtuous and civilized fatherland. The medium of choice in this endeavor was the printed word, and it was to the regenerative power of print that Novikov devoted most of his public life.

During the early 1760s Kheraskov, along with several present and former students, organized Moscow's first literary magazines. None lasted more than a few months or circulated far beyond the circles that produced them, but their appearance proclaimed the affinity between a commitment to moral influence and the pursuit of literary publishing that became an abiding creed of Russian intellectuals. Novikov appears to have played a small role in these short-lived ventures, but by 1765 he had taken his first steps toward a career in publishing by arranging for the publication of a contemporary's translation of François Fénelon's *Les Aventures d'Aristonous* (1699).

Much of Novikov's subsequent career parallels the reign of Catherine II, the Great (1762–1796). Catherine had come to power through a coup against Emperor Peter III, her mercurial and unpopular husband, carried out by leading members of the Izmailovsky Regiment at the end of June 1762. Novikov had just joined the regiment, but he was a part of the group that swore loyalty to Catherine, for which she rewarded him with a promotion in rank to *unter offitser*.

Over the next several years the "Izmailovtsy" occupied a visible position at Catherine's court, and they often accompanied the empress in Saint Petersburg and in the old capital of Moscow. When Catherine convened a commission in Moscow to deliberate over composing a new code of laws (the Legislative Commission of 1767–1769) Novikov was appointed as a recording secretary, a position of considerable prominence and visibility. When the commission ceased its activity, Novikov, along with the entire Izmailovsky Regiment, accompanied the empress back to Saint Petersburg.

Over the course of the next decade Catherine and Novikov developed a reciprocal – though not

Title page for the first issue of Novikov's influential weekly journal

intimate – literary relationship in which both participated as organizers and patrons of print culture. Catherine underwrote some of Novikov's projects (a relationship that continued into the 1780s), and more than once Novikov helped to organize support for the empress's own endeavors.

Between 1769 and 1774 Saint Petersburg witnessed the first true flowering of literary and moralistic journalism, in the form of several new, mostly weekly, magazines. Novikov was the primary editor of four of these satiric journals: *Truten'* (The Drone, 1769–1770); *Pustomelia* (The Tattler, 1770); *Zhivopisets* (The Painter, 1772–1773); and *Koshelek* (The Hair Net, 1774). Recent scholarship has pointed out that not all of these magazines were satiric, but the witty, ironic, and occasionally barbed exchanges between the various magazines united the participants in a common, modestly daring endeavor, transparently patterned after the English *The Spectator* (1711–1714) and *The Tatler* (1709–1711) of Richard Steele and Joseph Addison.

The literary world these weeklies helped to create reveals a great deal about Novikov's rise to prominence. On one hand none of the contributions bears its author's real name, even though several give broad hints to their identities. The printed texts offer an illusion of anonymity, a mask behind which one could engage in repartee with what might otherwise have been a dangerous opponent. On the other hand, nearly all of the participants in these activities, both writers and readers, came from the same small world of polite cosmopolitan society that all but precluded anonymity. The satiric discourse amounted to a journalistic masquerade, in which the names of the members of the group were not secret but the identities of individuals behind specific masks were. Novikov, everyone knew, was the major presence behind *Truten'* and *Zhivopisets,* but the identity cloaked in *Vsiakaia vsiachina* (All Sorts and Sundries, 1769–1770) – whether the empress's private secretary and the nominal editor, Grigorii Kozitsky, or the empress herself – was unknown. Therein lay the sport for contemporaries, and for subsequent literary historians as well.

The interchange between *Truten'* and *Vsiakaia vsiachina* caused a minor sensation in Russian educated society, which found itself invited to a spicy intellectual duel between Novikov, the young literator, and Catherine, the young empress. Current scholarship suggests that Kozitsky really did produce the journal and that Catherine provided mostly material support. But the mere possibility that Catherine was involved delighted cosmopolitan society, the intended audience for these magazines.

Until recently it was common, particularly among Soviet scholars, to characterize these exchanges as the beginnings of an ideological struggle between absolutist monarchy and a political opposition of liberal noblemen, the direct antecedents of the vaunted nineteenth-century intelligentsia. But this picture overstates the modest differences in political outlook that separated Novikov and his collaborators from Catherine. Moreover, it elevates the small volume of gentle social criticism that emanated from the weeklies to a prominence out of proportion to its standing in the journals. Rather, Catherine and Novikov were as cooperating in a common enterprise to enliven print and its attendant salon conversation among those who had moved back to the capital after the demise of the Legislative Commission. Central themes of these debates were moral improvement, individual virtue, and the welfare of the nation. Most of the barbs were directed against personal failings – posturing, dandyism, superficiality, and disrespect for the common folk rather than for political institutions or relations of authority.

Despite the bracing spirit of openness and respect for individual human potential they displayed, most of the satiric weeklies soon foundered in the market, as a result of the small audience they had found among Russian readers. Even with modest press runs (three hundred to six hundred) most ceased publication after a few months, and those that continued relied heavily on patronage. Novikov proved to be a partial exception to the rule, as he published a second printing of several issues of *Truten'* in 1769–1770 and a total of five reissues of most of *Zhivopisets* between 1772 and 1793. Despite their lack of success on the market, however, by the end of 1774 the satiric journals had shaped the capital's literary discourse, and Novikov proceeded to explore alternative venues for his publicism.

As the satiric magazines were winding down Novikov produced the only books that were to bear his name on the title page as author or primary editor, *Opyt istoricheskogo slovaria o rossiiskikh pisateliakh* (Attempt at a Historical Dictionary of Russian Writers, 1772) and *Drevniaia rossiiskaia idrografiia* (Ancient Russian Geography, 1773). Although the title page credited Novikov as the author, the *Drevniaia rossiiskaia idrografiia* was essentially a reissue of a seventeenth-century geography titled *Kniga bol'shogo chertezha* (Book of Large-Scale Mappings, 1627) consisting chiefly of extensive descriptions of the waterways, topography, and towns of the Muscovite state. *Opyt istoricheskogo slovaria o rossiiskikh pisateliakh,* however, was Novikov's own project. Culled from a variety of materials, both printed and archival, it included brief entries on 317 Russian writers. Most of the subjects were Novikov's contemporaries, and their status as "writers" was often based more on expectations than actual production. Novikov also included several noted figures from the seventeenth century, prefiguring, perhaps, the homages to old Russian culture that would become a distinctive feature of his program; however, a casual reader leafing through this volume would almost certainly have read it as a celebration of modernity. Page after page concentrated on contemporary writers. The message could not have been clearer: educated Russians were living amid a literary cornucopia, an unprecedented flowering of the pen and the press. Nevertheless, only 606 copies of the work were printed, of which Novikov received 450 (the remainder were held in escrow until 1784).

Novikov still held a position in state service — he had been made an official translator at the College of Foreign Affairs in 1770 — but most of his energy went to publishing, and much of that brought him ever closer to the empress. In 1773 a letter in *Zhivopisets* from "Liubomudrov iz Iaroslavlia" (The Lovers of Wisdom of Iaroslavl) made reference to a new Obshchestvo staraiushcheesia o napechatanii knig (Society Striving for Publishing Books), a publishing enterprise that Novikov had begun with the book dealer K. V. Muller and several of Novikov's literary contemporaries, including Aleksandr Radishchev and Mikhail Kheraskov. This society lasted about two years and brought several new and translated titles into print. Its renown, however, derived mostly from its relationship to the Obshchestvo staraiushcheesia o perevode inostrannykh knig (Society for the Translation of Foreign Books), which Catherine the Great had initiated in 1768 to publish Russian translations of Charles-Louis Montesquieu, Voltaire, Cicero, Henry Fielding, Jonathan Swift, and other classical and contemporary authors.

Catherine's ambitious vision quickly exhausted the five-thousand-ruble subsidy that she had granted the Academy of Sciences Press for production costs and salaries. Since the Translation Society's books sold poorly, and since the press could not very well send the empress rejection notices, the academy was obliged to solicit additional patronage. Novikov's society was founded largely to provide such assistance, and over the next few years the empress and Novikov, with Kozitsky as go-between, effectively constituted a publishing partnership. As a public sign of their union, Catherine bequeathed to the society the complete press run of the recently issued second edition of the Russian version (produced by a team of translators) of Jean-François Marmontel's *Bélisaire* (1766). Most scholars further believe that the "Lovers of Wisdom from Iaroslavl" was none other than the empress.

The publishing partnership was devoted to expanding and improving the limited range of texts that Russian readers were prepared to embrace. As Novikov wrote in *Zhivopisets:* "Kto by vo Frantsii poveril, ezheli by skazali, chto *Volshebnykh skazok* razoshlosia bol'she sochinenii *Rasinovykh?* A u nas eto sbyvaetsia: *Tysiacha odnoi nochi* prodano gorazdo bol'she sochinenii g. *Sumarokova*" (Who in France would believe it if we were to say that *Contes de fée* sold more widely than the works of Racine? But in Russia, *1001 Nights* has sold much better than the works of Sumarokov). Novikov was also hoping to encourage respect for Russia's traditions as a way of counterbalancing the mindless "gallomania" preva-

lent in some realms of cosmopolitan society. Defending Russia's honor and revering its past had become major themes in *Koshelek,* the last of the satiric weeklies, but these sentiments were elevated to high didacticism with the appearance of the ten-volume *Drevniaia rossiiskaia vivliofika* (Ancient Russian Library, 1773–1775) with press runs averaging around 1,150 copies per volume. Each issue reproduced from private and state archives texts that retraced old Russian customs, dress, faith, and law. Unlike the *Opyt istoricheskogo slovaria,* the *Drevniaia rossiiskaia vivliofika* included a great deal of material from past centuries, much of which had never been published. It devoted most of its space to the sixteenth and seventeenth centuries; special attention went to the reflections of Russian travelers abroad, such as Boris P. Sheremetev's journey to Poland and the Mediterranean in 1697.

Novikov hoped to stimulate his readers with curiosities from their own heritage and in the process to instill respect for what he believed was the worldliness and sophistication of Muscovy's not-so-distant past. Novikov's editions from these years seem to insist that Russian literature and writers were right to celebrate modernity, but that Russian civilization was old, rich, and virtuous. Those dandies who neglected Russia in order to embrace things French were fools and, far worse, risked losing touch with their own national identity.

Still, to reduce the entire publishing enterprise to the single agenda of Russia's worth vis-à-vis France would be too one-sided. Most of the titles that the publishing partnership produced came from French originals or from French translations of books in other languages. The reading audience would have had a difficult time discerning an anti-French or anti-Encyclopédiste message from Novikov's endeavors.

Whatever Novikov's expectations may have been, the end result proved to be a commercial fiasco, and patronage fell well short of compensating for weak sales. The *Drevniaia rossiiskaia vivliofika* fared best among these enterprises, thanks to an aggressive subscription campaign and a gift of one thousand rubles from the empress, but even it lost money. By the beginning of 1775 the publishing society had collapsed as a collective venture, and for the next several years Novikov devoted himself to individual publishing and philanthropic projects. The most important of these, the monthly *Utrennii svet* (Morning Light, 1777–1780) and the opening of the private academies of Saint Catherine's and Saint Aleksandr's, combined

Novikov's interests in publishing and lay-Christian education with his growing commitment to Freemasonry.

Little is known about the daily activities of Novikov's boarding schools. They operated in the capital as independently run private academies from 1777 to 1782, and as semi-independent for a few years more. It is widely believed that, under Novikov's watch, the pedagogy took on a distinctly religious and Masonic character, emphasizing personal piety, Christian charity, and good works. In any case, the Russian Orthodox church provided considerable support for the undertaking, first by housing the schools in two churches and then by helping to organize a subscription campaign to *Utrennii svet.*

Novikov had hoped that subscriptions to the journal would help subsidize the two schools, and the campaign did bring in several hundred subscribers, thanks in part to the activities of some provincial clerics. Whereas most literary journals, including those that cultivated a provincial audience, circulated almost exclusively among the nobility, *Utrennii svet* drew almost a third of its subscribers from the clergy.

This cooperation between prominent clerics and one of Russia's leading lay intellectuals was emblematic of the quality of Russia's Enlightenment up to this point. No one had ever accused the Orthodox church of reckless free thought, and yet numerous hierarchs were prepared to endorse and support a journal and two schools whose vision of spirituality drew some of its inspiration from Freemasonry. The corps of lay writers who directed the journal, conversely, saw no fundamental contradiction between their ideals and those of their faith. Instead they defended an engaged Christian humanism that parted company with the anti-Christian or anticlericalism of the French philosophes on one hand and critiqued obscurantist clerics who saw secular knowledge as being inimical to the church on the other.

Unfortunately, the accord between lay writers and clergy failed to stem the downward spiral of subscriptions, and by 1779 *Utrennii svet,* like most of its predecessors, was running deeply in the red. The list of subscribers — as high as 785 for the first year's run — had fallen well below 200, and by then Novikov was using revenue from the schools to prop up the journal. The last issue appeared in October 1780, and although Novikov tried to revive it under different names — *Vecherniaia zaria* (Evening Glow) and *Gorodskaia i derevenskaia biblioteka* (City and Country Library) — neither achieved a signifi-

Title page for a revised edition of Novikov's 1772–1774 satiric journal

cant circulation. The title pages of several of his publications from this period indicate that Novikov continued to try to subsidize the charity schools with his publishing ventures, but again he proved unsuccessful. By 1783 Saint Catherine's and Saint Aleksandr's had fallen out of his control. By then, however, Novikov had made a series of commitments that had made him the overseer of the largest publishing venture in Russia.

During a visit to Moscow in the summer of 1778 Novikov had proposed leasing Moscow University Press, the largest publishing house in the Russian Empire, for a ten-year period at a cost of forty-five hundred rubles per year. This lease was an immense and risky undertaking on Novikov's part, on behalf of which he resigned his commission in service, moved to Moscow, and became a full-time publisher.

At that time institutional presses still held a legal monopoly over publishing, and only a few individuals had successfully petitioned to operate private presses. The monopoly had not posed much of an impediment to Novikov and his contemporaries, since they had proven adept at gaining access to many scholastic presses over the preceding twenty years. Nevertheless, taking charge of such a large enterprise empowered Novikov with unprecedented access to Russian print for a private individual.

In the course of his tenure, Moscow University Press grew to the point where it was producing about seventy Russian-language titles annually, and it established itself as a magnet for able writers and translators. Novikov exploited the talents of his fellow Masons, as well as those of university instructors, students, and alumni. He took on all of the press's existing commitments, including textbooks and the biweekly newspaper *Moskovskie vedomosti* (The Moscow News), whose length he doubled to sixteen pages. He commissioned two new moralistic journals – *Moskovskoe ezhemesiachnoe izdanie* (The Moscow Monthly, 1781) and *Vecherniaia zaria* (Evening Glow, 1782) – several magazines, and dozens of new books.

Then, on 15 January 1783, a new law was passed permitting private individuals to purchase and operate their own presses without seeking special privilege. They were required to submit their publications to the local prefects of police, but the police had neither the means nor the interest to become actively engaged in censorship. For all practical purposes, therefore, Russia had acquired a relatively free press – a further indication of the continued amity between empress and literati.

Many private individuals took advantage of this opportunity, and Russian publishing underwent a dramatic shift toward privatization over the next decade. Novikov enlisted the financial support of his literary comrades, Masons, and wealthy patrons to help open two private enterprises: the Rosicrucian Press (1783), nominally owned by his friend Ivan Lopukhin; and the more eclectic but also Masonically inspired Typographical Company (1784). Until Novikov's arrest in 1792, these two publishing houses accounted for over 350 publications, and, along with the university press, they were responsible for nearly 40 percent of all Russian-language publications between 1785 and 1789.

Much earlier Novikov had made it clear that he was not in business to make a profit, and much of his activity in these years attests to the primacy of moral considerations over income. He was far from a commercial innocent, however, and many of the romances and adventure stories that he published during this time had an obvious commercial appeal. He negotiated contracts with several book dealers and expanded the provincial market for his publications to include as many as thirty regular outlets. He paid close attention to the technical and financial aspects of publishing and to the construction of a viable commercial network. His friend and collaborator Nikolai Karamzin commented in an 1802 article for *Vestnik Evropy* (European Herald) that Novikov had "torgovaval knigami, kak bogatyi gollandskii ili angliiskii kupets torguet proizvedeniiami vsekh zemel': to est', s umom, s dogadkoiu, s dal'novidnym soobrazheniem" (traded in books as a rich Dutch or English merchant trades in the products of all countries: that is, with sense, with integrity, and with foresighted imagination).

In the long run, however, the pursuit of moral improvement and philanthropy overwhelmed Novikov's finances. Records give only an approximate sense of his day-to-day business, press runs, and the like, but net proceeds probably ran between forty thousand and eighty thousand rubles in the 1780s, at a time when expenses almost certainly exceeded one hundred thousand rubles per year. Even with the generous support of patrons such as the wealthy Siberian merchant Grigorii Pokhodiashin, who provided him with tens of thousands of rubles in gifts and loans, Novikov's resources continued to dwindle.

The Typographical Company seems to have been perpetually so overextended that any interruption in the cash flow precipitated a crisis. Since Novikov, ever the philanthropist, regularly donated to charity and welfare, such interruptions proved endemic. Finances were further complicated by struggles for control of the company between Novikov's loyalists and the representatives of the Berlin Rosicrucians, most visibly Baron Friedrich Ludwig Schroder, who had come to Moscow specifically to oversee Novikov's activities after the death of the previous emissary, Novikov's friend and confidant Johann Schwartz.

Schwartz had been far more committed to Rosicrucianism than Novikov, but the two had collaborated closely for several years. Schwartz's death in February 1784, along with the atmosphere of press freedom, paradoxically increased Novikov's vulnerability to outside pressures. Nominally an independent impresario, Novikov soon found himself answerable to more masters than he could accommodate, let alone control: officials in Moscow were becoming uneasy over the relatively unrestricted private press, with unwelcome links to the highly secretive Rosicrucian order, which seemingly received its directions from abroad; the Berlin Rosicrucians demanded a major say in running the Typographical Company; and, finally, the market, as expressed through the book trade and subscription campaigns, was manifesting distressingly little enthusiasm for the inventory of Masonic and moralistic works, pulling private presses inexorably in a more lighthearted direction. Unable to survive professionally without the support of the state, the Rosicrucians, and the reading public, Novikov tried to satisfy all of them, but with diminishing success.

Beginning in 1784 both the state and the Rosicrucians conducted repeated inquiries, demanded explanations, and placed competing claims on Novikov's publishing activities. At various times Schroder attempted to take control of Novikov's lodge, his bookshop, and the directorate of the Typographical Company. Novikov parried many of these incursions, but he was obliged to make oral reports on his activities. He was helpless to intervene when Schroder purchased an expensive house to serve as a base for a variety of charities that he hoped to initiate, thereby committing the order to a mortgage of fifty thousand rubles that otherwise would have gone to sustaining the Typographical Company.

The state posed different but no less distracting problems for Novikov. His initial entanglements seemed innocent enough, arising from a simple case of copyright infringement that arose in 1784 when, at the urging of Moscow's governor-general, Novikov had issued editions of two books, *Sokrashchennyi katekhizis* (An Abbreviated Catechism) and *Rukovodstvo k chistopisaniiu* (A Guide to Proper Handwriting). The Public School Commission in Saint Petersburg held the copyrights, and when it protested, Novikov was obliged to surrender the entire runs of both editions. A year later Novikov's compilation of the *History of the Jesuit Order* ran afoul of the empress, who disliked its critical tone and ordered it banned. In the same year the Holy Synod of the Russian Orthodox church demanded unsuccessfully that Novikov's recent translation of Johann Arndt's pietistic treatise *Wahres Chrisenthum* (On True Christianity, 1605) be banned for its violations of faith.

None of these transgressions was particularly noteworthy, and several other individuals had drawn far more serious censure in the course of Catherine's reign. But the expressions of concern by Muscovite authorities (most notably the new governor-general, Count Iakov A. Bruce) over the potentially conspiratorial qualities of the seemingly German-controlled Rosicrucians and over the absence of meaningful controls over private printing convinced Catherine to sanction an inquiry.

On 7 October 1785 a five-member commission under the direction of Archbishop Platon of Moscow, an immensely erudite man with considerable regard for Novikov, looked first into Novikov's publishing activities and then into his fidelity to Orthodoxy. Concurrent with these reviews, Bruce conducted his own investigations into Novikov and the Rosicrucians.

Platon received copies of 461 titles attributed to Novikov's enterprises, of which 22 required further scrutiny. In the end 12 titles drew negative comments, some as being overly Masonic, others because they seemed too smitten by the French Encyclopédistes; six of the former were ordered withdrawn from circulation. For Novikov the investigation imposed a three-month pause in business, which under the circumstances constituted a severe blow to his shaky finances. Bruce, meanwhile, had convinced the empress of the danger of the Moscow lodges, and she assented to their closure.

In July 1787 Catherine ordered a nationwide raid on the empire's bookshops, nominally as a way of enforcing the Holy Synod's monopoly over printing works of faith. Over the next several months the Russian book trade was thrown into confusion, and in many towns it shut down. Once again Moscow and Novikov suffered the greatest assault as Bruce's agents seized a total of 142,000 volumes, constituting 313 separate titles, 166 of which had come out of Novikov's presses.

Eventually, only fourteen titles were banned, and the rest were returned to the shops, but Novikov found himself in an increasingly precarious financial and political position. Once again his trade had been suspended for several months, his ability to publish or trade in Masonic books and some potentially lucrative textbooks had essentially vanished, and his defenders at court were finding it almost impossible to intercede on his behalf. Finally, in October 1788 Novikov received word that Catherine would not allow a renewal of his lease on the Moscow University Press when it expired in May 1789.

Over the next three years Novikov had access only to the Typographical Company, and his publishing underwent a predictable and precipitous decline. His relationship with the empress had been poisoned by years of official mistrust, and the outbreak of revolution in France subjected him to further official suspicion; in the strained atmosphere of the 1790s even previously esteemed acts of charity, schools, hospitals, and famine relief were now construed as perfidious and potentially illegal. Under these circumstances Novikov could not sustain the career into which he had invested so much energy.

ДРЕВНЯЯ

РОССІЙСКАЯ

ВИВЛІОѲИКА,

Содержащая въ себѣ:

СОБРАНІЕ ДРЕВНОСТЕЙ РОССІЙСКИХЪ, ДО
ИСТОРІИ, ГЕОГРАФІИ и ГЕНЕАЛОГІИ
РОССІЙСКІЯ КАСАЮЩИХСЯ;

Изданная

Николаемъ Новиковымъ,

Членомъ Вольнаго Россійскаго Собра-
нія при ИМПЕРАТОРСКОМЪ
Московскомъ Университетѣ;

Изданіе Второе,

Вновь исправленное, умноженное и въ порядокъ Хроно-
логической по возможности приведенное.

ЧАСТЬ I.

М О С К В А,
Въ Типографіи Компаніи Типографической,
1 7 8 8.

Title page for an edition of Novikov's compilation of "drevnostei
rossiiskikh' " (Russian antiquities), texts
from state archives and private collections

Novikov's state of mind at this time is a matter of conjecture since he rarely allowed his personality or private affairs to filter into his public life. He had finally married in 1781, and the marriage produced two children, a daughter Varvara (born in 1782) and a son Ivan (born in 1783), but, beyond these facts, little is known of his family life. Much of this opacity reflected Enlightenment sensibilities, which privileged concreteness, materialism, and publicness over sentiment. Russia's philosophes valued inner morality and spiritual improvement, but they measured success by the yardstick of overt and demonstrable results.

Novikov went further than his contemporaries in submerging his identity in published works, which perhaps explains his failure to produce works of his own. Even when he published original works, as he presumably did in several of the literary and philosophical magazines, he left no clues through which his readership could identify him. Journalis-

tic conventions of the time preferred anonymous or imaginary authorship to real names, but many aspiring intellectuals published their own words through media other than journals and in genres that allowed their audiences to connect discrete texts with specific authors. Novikov, by contrast, was at once the omnipresent editor-publisher and a virtually untraceable author.

On those rare moments when Novikov permitted a glimpse into his repose, it took the form of a ritualized narrative in which a theatrical interchange among comrades is substituted for affect, personality, or domesticity. Thus an unpublished album entitled "Festive Days at Tikhvinskoe, 1788" purports to describe a late June celebration of the birthday of his friend Ivan Turgenev. In attendance were Novikov's family and several of his closest friends. The text speaks of "pleasant pictures of love . . . the sweet language of sincerity . . . the pure pleasure and innocent diversion of comradeship," in which the company of good fellows drinks and eats heartily, sings songs, and takes a pleasant walk through the gardens. The young Novikov children appear in this idyll not as members of a family but as symbols of youth and innocence, bearing garlands, adorned in flowers, and reciting short verses celebrating love and joy.

This text, though not intended for publication, narrates the well-rehearsed public face of Masonic fellowship and transposes it into a pastoral setting. It does seem to correspond to events in Novikov's life, as he spent most of his time tending to his wavering health and his estate at Avdot'ino (he owned 285 serfs, several hundred acres of land, and a considerable amount of livestock) and overseeing drought relief in his district.

Avdot'ino afforded no refuge from officialdom's suspicious glare, and on 21 April 1792 the new governor-general of Moscow, Prince A. A. Prozorovsky, sent a squadron of hussars to arrest Novikov and bring him to Moscow for interrogation and then to the Schlusselberg Fortress in Saint Petersburg. Charged again with producing and harboring illegal books and interrogated at great length about his business and Masonic activities, Novikov was convicted and sentenced to a term of fifteen years in Schlusselberg.

Those who were charged with him were also found guilty, but none received so severe a sentence, and most were amnestied over the next few years. Catherine took no pleasure in this outcome but displaced her remorse into hostility for Prozorovsky, whom she deemed the agency of Novikov's undoing. She gave orders to watch over Novikov's health but refused to have him released. Only after her death, in an amnesty decreed by the new emperor, Paul I, at the end of 1796, was Novikov finally released.

Novikov lived for another twenty-two years, during which time he retrieved his good name but eschewed his former cosmopolitan career. While maintaining contact with the reopened lodges and with many of his old literary confederates, Novikov spent most of the rest of his life in Avdot'ino tending to his property, opening a small cloth factory and later a distillery. Plagued by old debts, he devoted himself to modernizing his estate and receiving visitors. He died, following a stroke, on 31 July 1818.

Letters:

K biografii Novikova: Pis'ma ego k Labzinu, Chebotarevu, i dr. 1797–1815, edited by Boris Modzalevsky (Saint Petersburg, 1915);

"Iz neizdannykh pisem Nikolaia Ivanovicha Novikova," edited by Evgenii I. Katsprzhak and Artur P. Tolstiakov, *Kniga: issledovaniia i materialy,* 21 (1970): 163–192.

Biographies:

Mikhail N. Longinov, *Novikov i Shvarts: Materialy dlia istorii russkoi literatury v kontse XVIII veka* (Moscow: Katkova, 1857);

Longinov, *Novikov i moskovskie martinisty* (Moscow: Grachev, 1867);

Viacheslav Bogoliubov, *N. I. Novikov i ego vremia* (Moscow: M. Shabashnikov, 1916);

Vladimir P. Semennikov, *Knigoizdatel'skaia deiatel'nost' N. I. Novikova i Tipograficheskoi Kompanii* (Petrograd: Gos. izdatel'stvo, 1921);

Vladimir A. Rozenberg, *N. I. Novikov: podvizhnik russkoi knigi* (Berlin: YMCA Press, 1923);

Leonid B. Svetlov, *Izdatel'skaia deiatel'nost' N. I. Novikova* (Leningrad: Gizlegprom, 1946);

Georgii P. Makogonenko, *Nikolai Novikov i russkoe prosveshchenie XVIII veka* (Moscow: Nauka, 1952);

Aleksandr V. Zapadov, *Novikov* (Moscow: Molodaia gvardiia, 1968);

Ivan F. Martynov, *Knigoizdatel' Nikolai Novikov* (Moscow: Kniga, 1981);

Andre Monnier, *Un publiciste frondeur sous Catherine II: Nicholas Novikov* (Paris: Institute d'études slaves, 1981);

W. Gareth Jones, *Nikolay Novikov: Enlightener of Russia* (Cambridge: Cambridge University Press, 1984).

References:

Leonard A. Derbov, *Obshchestvenno-politicheskie i istoricheskie vzgliady N. I. Novikova* (Saratov: Saratovskii universitet, 1974);

W. Gareth Jones, "The Closure of Novikov's *Truten',*" *Slavonic and East European Review,* 50 (January 1972): 107–111;

Jones, "The Morning Light Charity Schools, 1777–80," *Slavonic and East European Review,* 56 (January 1978): 49–60;

Jones, "Novikov's Naturalized Spectator," in *The Eighteenth Century in Russia,* edited by John G. Garrard (Oxford: Clarendon Press, 1973), pp. 149–165;

Vasilii O. Kliuchevsky, "Vospominanie o N. I. Novikove i ego vremeni," in his *Ocherki i rechi* (Moscow: P. P. Riabushinsky, 1913);

Andrei I. Kondrat'ev, "Novikovskie izdaniia," in *Kniga v Rossii,* volume 1, edited by V. Ia. Adariukov and A. A. Sidorov (Moscow: Gos. izdatel'stvo, 1924), pp. 289–356;

Iurii D. Levin, "Angliiskaia prosvetitel'skaia zhurnalistika v russkoi literature XVIII veka," in *Epokkha Prosveshcheniia: Iz istorii mezhdunarodnykh sviazei russkoi literatury* (Leningrad: Nauka, 1967), pp. 3–109;

Gary J. Marker, "Novikov's Readers," *Modern Language Review,* 77 (October 1982): 194–205;

Marker, *Publishing, Printing, and the Origins of Intellectual Life in Russia, 1700–1800* (Princeton: Princeton University Press, 1985);

Gilbert McArthur, "Catherine II and the Masonic Circle of N. I. Novikov," *Canadian Slavic Studies,* 4 (1970): 529–546;

V. N. Mochul'sky, *Novikovskie zhurnaly XVIII veka* (Warsaw, 1909);

Aleksandr I. Nezelenov, *N. I. Novikov, izdatel' zhurnalov, 1769–1785 godov* (Saint Petersburg: V. S. Balashev, 1875);

N. I. Novikov i obshchestvenno-literaturnoe dvizhenie ego vremeni, XVIII vek, 11 (1976);

K. A. Papmehl, *Freedom of Expression in Eighteenth Century Russia* (The Hague: Mouton, 1971);

In-Ho Ryu, "Moscow Freemasons and the Rosicrucian Order: A Study in Organization and Control," in *The Eighteenth Century in Russia,* edited by John G. Garrard (Oxford: Clarendon Press, 1973), pp. 205–220;

Vladimir P. Semennikov, "Rannee izdatel'skoe obshchestvo N. I. Novikova," *Russkii bibliofil,* 5 (1912): 34–47;

Il'ia Z. Serman, "Novikov and *The Tattler,*" *Study Group on Eighteenth-Century Russia Newsletter,* 5 (1977): 37–38.

Nikolai Petrovich Osipov

(1751 - 19 May 1799)

Irwin R. Titunik
University of Michigan

SELECTED BOOKS: *Ne priamo v glaz, a v samuiu brov'* (Saint Petersburg: Imperatorskaia tipografiia, 1790);

Noveishei i sovershennoi rossiiskoi konskoi znatok, ezdok, okhotnik, zavodchik i konoval, ili Podrobnoe opisanie loshadinykh porod, statei, dobrot, nedostatkov, let i primet . . . , 2 volumes (Saint Petersburg: Imperatorskaia tipografiia, 1790);

Novoi i sovershennoi russkoi sadovnik, ili Podrobnoe nastavlenie rossiiskim sadovnikam, ogorodchikam, a naipache liubiteliam sadov . . . , 2 volumes (Saint Petersburg: Imperatorskaia tipografiia, 1790);

Starinnaia ruskaia khoziaika, kliuchnitsa i striapukha; ili Podrobnoe nastavlenie o prigotovlenii nastoiashchikh rossiiskikh kushan'ev, zaedok i napitkov . . . (Saint Petersburg: Imperatorskaia tipografiia, 1790);

Karmannaia kniga sel'skogo i domashnego khoziaistva (Saint Petersburg: Imperatorskaia tipografiia, 1791);

Podrobnoi slovar' dlia sel'skikh i gorodskikh okhotnikov i liubitelei botanicheskogo, uveselitel'nogo i khoziaistvennogo sadovstva . . . , 2 volumes (Saint Petersburg: I. K. Shnor, 1791-1792);

Virgilieva Eneida, vyvorochennaia na iznanku, 4 volumes (Saint Petersburg: I. K. Shnor, 1791-1796);

Krest'ianin skotovod ili Kratkoe nastavlenie derevenskim zhiteliam o vospityvanii i soderzhanii vsiakogo roda domashnei skotiny; o predokhranenii ikh ot boleznei, i o pol'zovanii ot onykh samymi prostymi, deshevymi i po bol'shei chasti domashnymi lekarstvami (Saint Petersburg: I. K. Shnor, 1792);

Liubopytnyi domovodets, ili Sobranie raznykh opytov i otkrytii otnosiashchikhsia k khoziaistvu gorodskomu i derevenskomu (Saint Petersburg: Krylov s tovarishchi, 1792);

Psovoi lekar', ili Opisanie sobach'ikh boleznei; s pokazaniem verneishikh i nadezhneishikh sredstv dlia lecheniia onykh (Saint Petersburg: I. K. Shnor, 1792);

Rossiiskoi khoziaistvennyi vinokur, pivovar, medovar, vodochnoi master, kvasnik, uksusnik, i pogrebshchik (Saint Petersburg: I. Glazunov, 1792); revised as *Novyi i polnyi Rossiiskoi khoziaistvennyi vinokur . . . ,* 2 volumes (Moscow: A. Reshetnikov, 1796);

Lakirovochnik ili Iasnoe i podrobnoe opisanie o zagotovlenii, sostavlenii i upotreblenii raznogo roda spirtovykh i maslenykh lakov i firnisov . . . (Saint Petersburg: Imperatorskaia tipographiia, 1798);

Nesbytochnye puteshestviia v nebyvalyia strany sveta (Saint Petersburg: F. Sveshnikov, 1799);

Ovidievy liubovnia tvoreniia, pererabotannia v Eneevskom vkuse . . . 1798 goda (Saint Petersburg: I. K. Shnor, 1803).

TRANSLATIONS: Frederick II, *Ostavshiesia tvoreniia Fridrikha Vtorogo korolia prusskogo,* 8 volumes (Saint Petersburg: I. K. Shnor, 1789-1791);

Rudolf Eric Raspe, *Ne liubo ne slushai, a lgat' ne meshai* (Saint Petersburg: I. K. Shnor, circa 1791); revised edition (Saint Petersburg: Imperatorskaia tipografiia, 1797);

Miguel de Cervantes, *Neslykhannyi chudodei, ili Neobychnye i udivitel'nye podvigi i prikliucheniia khrabrogo i znamenitogo stranstvuiushchego rytsaria Don Kishota,* 2 volumes (Saint Petersburg: Imperatorskaia tipografiia, 1791); republished as *Don Kishot La Mankhskii* (Moscow, 1812);

Novoi i sovershennoi raschetistyi kartezhnyi igrok, ili Podrobnoe opisanie vsekh upotrebliaemykh v obshchestve kartochnykh igr . . . , 2 volumes (Saint Petersburg: Imperatorskaia tipografiia, 1791);

Samuel Richardson, *Dostopamiatnaia zhizn' devitsy Klarissy Garlov, istinnaia povest',* 6 volumes, translated by Osipov and Petr Kil'dushevsky (Saint Petersburg: Sytin, 1791-1792);

Jean-Pierre Claris de Florian, *Gonzal'v Korduanskii, ili Obratno zavoevannaia Grenada,* 2 volumes (Saint Petersburg: I. K. Shnor, 1793);

August Gottlieb Meissner, *Alkiviad,* 4 volumes (Saint Petersburg: I. K. Shnor, 1794-1802);

Karmannyi konoval dlia dvorianina i konskogo okhotnika, ili Nastavlenie, kakim obrazom pomogat' v doroge loshadiam svoim v nuzhnykh sluchaiakh i kakie delat' zamechaniia pri pokupke onykh (Saint Petersburg: F. Meier, 1795);

Niccolo Forteguerri, *Rikhardet, poema,* 2 volumes (Saint Petersburg: Imperatorskaia tipografiia, 1800–1801).

OTHER: *Chto nibud' ot bezdel'ia na dosuge,* nos. 1–7 (1798), edited and written by Osipov; nos. 8–26 (1800), written by Osipov.

Nikolai Petrovich Osipov, along with such notables as Vasilii Ruban, Mikhail Chulkov, and Vasilii Levshin, was an outstanding member of eighteenth-century Russia's equivalent of Grubstreet. These writers wrote, compiled, translated, edited, and published massive amounts of factual and practical literature, such as almanacs, lexicons, guide books, and manuals; all were involved in the journalism of the day; all were translators of prose and/or verse; all combined the literary profession with another, "official" career. Osipov, unlike Ruban, did not publish reams of occasional verse or translate ancient classical writers; unlike Chulkov and Levshin, he did not deal in folkloristic materials or produce original fiction or write and translate plays. Osipov's literary activity consisted largely of compiling, editing, and publishing books of practical knowledge and in translating Western novels and stories. In one respect, however, he distinguished himself from his colleagues: in the course of his creative career he accomplished an enormous piece of work, a burlesque travesty of Virgil's *Aeneid,* which enjoyed high approbation, and although appreciation of it turned to neglect or even scorn after the 1830s, it stands as an undoubtable masterwork in the corpus of Russian eighteenth-century literature.

Nothing is known about the birth of Nikolai Petrovich Osipov except its year, 1751. The only other bits of information about his early life are that his father was an official of some sort and that the boy received his education first at home and then at pensions, from which it may be surmised that Osipov was of gentry origin. In 1769, as was typical for members of the gentry class, especially those of modest means, Osipov entered military service in the ranks. He was promoted to corporal in 1771 and to the most junior officer grade in 1773, when he was also transferred to a field regiment. During these years of military training Osipov also took his first steps in the literary profession. Joining forces with a regimental comrade, Nikolai L'vov, later to distinguish himself as a poet, musicologist, geologist

and architect, and with three other intellectually inclined fellow soldiers, Osipov collaborated in producing a manuscript periodical titled "Trudy chetyrekh razumnikh obshchnikov" (Works by Four Clever Companions), beginning on 17 March 1771. The periodical (never published) appeared at frequent but irregular intervals until 22 July and is reported to have consisted mostly of short original and translated verses. Osipov was the mainstay of this enterprise and continued to work at it singlehandedly when, toward the end, the others had ceased to participate.

In 1781 Osipov was forced to give up military service because of poor health. On retirement he was awarded the rank of first lieutenant. He settled in Saint Petersburg and attempted to earn a living at the literary trade, though with little success at the time, his only publications resulting from his work as part of a team of translators for collected works by and about Frederick the Great. In 1790 he managed to secure a position in the directorate of the Postal Service, but the year marked a turning point for Osipov in another respect. Earlier in the year he had purchased Aleksandr Radishchev's just-published *Puteshestvie iz Peterburga v Moskvu* (A Journey from Petersburg to Moscow) and had been questioned by the chief investigator of the "Radishchev affair," Catherine II's infamous henchman, Stepan Sheshkovsky. Osipov's sworn deposition, which survives, seems innocuous enough and did not in any way incriminate Radishchev, whom Osipov did not know; nevertheless, the episode appears to have besmirched Osipov's reputation in the eyes of future generations. Two things, however, suggest that Osipov's contact with Sheshkovsky was not entirely innocent. One is Osipov's subsequent acquaintance with Sheshkovsky's son, Ivan, to whom, moreover, he fulsomely dedicated his travesty of Virgil's *Aeneid* when it began to appear in 1791. The other is the fact that in 1796 Osipov was promoted to the rank of collegiate assessor and assigned to work as a translator, first in the secret branch of the Postal Service and later in the *Tainaia kantseliariia* (Secret Chancellery).

The early 1790s also marked the beginning of Osipov's success as a literary journeyman or hack. An impressive amount of his work was published that year: *Karmannaia kniga sel'skogo i domashnego khoziastva,* a manual on farm and household management, including a glossary of terms and a farmer's almanac; *Noveishei i sovershennoi rossiiskoi konskoi znatok . . . ili Podrobnoe opisanie loshadinykh porod, statei, dobrot, nedostatkov, let i primet . . . ,* a reference work on horses for horse farmers, hunters, and riders (republished the following year); *Novoi i sovershennoi russkoi sadovnik, ili Podrobnoe nastavlenie rossiiskim sadovnikam, ogorodchikam, a naipache liubiteliam sadov* ..., a reference book for town and country gardeners and for amateur botanists (a second edition in 1793 and a third without date appeared, followed by *Podrobnoi slovar' dlia sel'skikh i gorodskikh okhotnikov i liubitelei botanicheskogo, uveselitel'nogo i khoziaistvennogo sadovstva* ... [1791–1792], a botanical encyclopedia using the same material but reaching only the letter *K*); and *Starinnaia ruskaia khoziaika, kliuchnitsa i striapukha; ili Podrobnoe nastavlenie o prigotovlenii nastoiashchikh rossiiskikh kushan'ev zaedok i napitkov* ..., a guide for housewives, housekeepers, and cooks (republished in 1794). At the same time he produced a one-man compendium, resembling the popular satiric journals, titled *Ne priamo v glaz, a v samuiu brov'* (Not Straight In Your Eye But Right In Your Eyebrow, 1790). In the work Osipov emphasized the lighter, more comical, and even nonsensical aspects of satiric journalism, featuring such things as humorous glossaries, a grammar for fops, a monthly horoscope for "nebyvalyi god" (a year that never was or will be), a translation of the chapter "A Digression Concerning Critics" from Jonathan Swift's *A Tale of a Tub* (1704), and "Poslanie ot postel'noi sobachki k sochiniteliu" (Letter from a Lap Dog to the Author), which anticipates the letter-writing dog Medzhi in Nikolai Gogol's "Zapiski sumasshedshego" (Notes of a Madman, 1835).

Similar works occupied Osipov throughout his literary career, a new element added after 1790 being the translation of Western prose fiction. Among the largest and most important of these were a 1791 translation of a French version of Miguel de Cervantes's *Don Quixote* (1615; translated as *Neslykhannyi chudodei, ili Neobychnye i udivitel'nye podvigi i prikliucheniia khrabrogo i znamenitogo stranstvuiushchego rytsaria Don Kishota*); a 1791–1792 translation (together with Petr Kil'diushevsky) of Samuel Richardson's *Clarissa* (1747–1748; translated as *Dostopamiatnaia zhizn' devitsy Klarissy Garlov, istinnaia povest'*) from Abbé Prévost's French translation of that work; an abbreviated translation (probably published after 1790) of G. A. Bürger's German adaptation of Rudolf Eric Raspe's *Baron Munchhausen's Narrative of His Marvelous Travels and Campaigns in Russia* (1785; translated as *Ne liubo ne slushai, a lgat' ne meshai*); a 1793 translation of Jean-Pierre Claris de Florian's *Gonzalve de Cordoue, ou Grenade reconquise* (1791; translated as *Gonzal'v Korduanskii, ili Obratno zavoevannaia Grenada*); a trans-

lation of August Gottlieb Meissner's *Alcibiades* (1781–1788; translated as *Alkiviad,* 1794–1802); and an 1800–1801 translation of Niccolo Forteguerri's Italian epic *Ricciardetto* (1738; translated as *Rikhardet, poema*). Osipov's late effort at a weekly satiric journal, *Chto nibud' ot bezdel'ia na dosuge* (A Little Something from Nothing To Do at Leisure), appeared for seven weeks in 1798; the remaining numbers eight through twenty-six were published posthumously from Osipov's manuscripts in 1800.

It is something of a paradox that Osipov, for whom no other original poetry is extant and who translated verse originals into Russian prose, should have composed his one great achievement in verse. *Virgilieva Eneida, vyvorochennaia na iznanku* (Virgil's Aeneid Turned Inside Out), the first volume of which appeared in 1791, is a work of about fourteen hundred stanzas, each consisting of ten iambic tetrameter lines rhyming *aBaBccDeeD*. The stanza type is the standard eighteenth-century Russian panegyric ode stanza, and it worked wonderfully well for burlesque purposes, as Osipov may have learned from the unprintable but widely read and appreciated obscene parodic verses of Ivan Barkov, whose "Oda kulashnomu boitsu" (Ode to a Fistfighter), among others, had employed it. Osipov proved extraordinarily adept at the verse form, infusing it with special comic pungency and verve by his use of racy vernacular Russian laced with elements of various professional and social lingos, both urban and rural (the work is a veritable gold mine for investigators of eighteenth-century spoken Russian). The *Virgilieva Eneida, vyvorochennaia na iznanku* was immediately successful, provoking an enthusiastic review by Nikolai Karamzin in the *Moskovskii zhurnal* (Moscow Journal) in 1792 and a Ukrainian imitation by Ivan Kotliarevsky, whose *Eneida* (1798) has been credited with inaugurating modern Ukrainian literature. After the reputation of Osipov's *Virgilieva Eneida, vyvorochennaia na iznanku* experienced a severe decline in the nineteenth century, the work, somewhat ironically, drew scholarly attention only in connection with Kotliarevsky. This scholarship did, however, bring to light certain previously unknown aspects of the composition of Osipov's travesty.

Among the many burlesque travesties of Virgil's *Aeneid* in Western literature the one discovered to have had special influence on Osipov was *Die Abenteuer des frommen Helden Aeneas* (1782–1788) by the Austrian writer Aloys Blumauer. Such scholars as Nikolai Dashkevich and Ivan Steshenko claim that Osipov's travesty was in fact a close adaptation of Blumauer's text. Since Blumauer manipulated his travesty of Virgil so as to incorporate frequent, lengthy, and virulent satiric attacks on the Roman Catholic church, especially the Jesuit Order, and since Osipov had not followed Blumauer in that particular, scholars unanimously disparaged Osipov's version as the inferior work, one meant merely to cause laughter (laughter without some serious, preferably political, purpose has seemed to most Russian intellectuals since the 1830s an empty, even contemptible, frivolity). Recent, unbiased investigation, however, has discovered that, while Blumauer's travesty was undoubtedly a source, so was the masterpiece of Western travesties of the *Aeneid*, Paul Scarron's *Virgile travesti en vers burlesques* (1648–1652), which older scholars denied had any bearing on Osipov's version. Osipov seems to have followed a simple rule: wherever Blumauer launched into satires against the Roman Catholic church or omitted a key episode of the *Aeneid*, he made use of Scarron's text instead.

The question of the quality of Osipov's work is also open to reconsideration. When Osipov made use of Blumauer or Scarron, he did so, as unprejudiced reading discovers, in such a way as to transform creatively the models followed. His work, therefore, despite what it owes to Blumauer and Scarron, is legitimately to be regarded a thoroughly original one. Its skillful elaboration of the panegyric ode stanza is one example of Osipov's ingenuity, for instance, but by far its most transformational aspect is the Russification of its sources. The point of a burlesque travesty was to transpose a classic work of literature into an incongruous but equivalent set of linguistic, social, and ideological features wherein the high and serious values of the classic would be refracted in a comically inverted way ("carnivalesque" in Mikhail Bakhtin's terminology). This goal Osipov achieved by retelling the *Aeneid* in terms appropriate for Russian plebeian culture of the eighteenth century. The procedures involved are legion, but striking. Particulars include scenes of the Trojans swilling vodka and devouring typical Russian meals; the Cumaean Sybil expressing herself in Russian *tarabarshchina* (folk gibberish); King Latinus's use of Russian popular *lubki* (woodcuts) to decorate the quarters of his Trojan guests; and the employment of Russian Christmastide fortune-telling practices in relating Anchises' prophecies to Aeneas in the underworld. The result of these and many other comical incongruities was a hilarious *discordia concors* (harmonious discord), sustained for approxi-

mately fourteen thousand lines of verse – an achievement Osipov's contemporaries fully acknowledged and appreciated. The *Virgilieva Eneida, vyvorochennaia na iznanku* was published twice between 1791 and 1796 and went through two later editions in 1800 and 1801. Osipov, as had been true for Scarron and Blumauer, did not complete a travesty of the entire *Aeneid;* Osipov's travesty covered only the first seven books. Aleksandr Kotel'nitsky over the years 1802–1808 added to Osipov's opus his travesty of the five remaining books.

Late in life Osipov produced a second travesty, this time of Ovid, which was published posthumously in 1803. Entitled *Ovidievy liubovnia tvoreniia, pererabotannyia v Eneevskom vkuse . . . 1798 goda* (Ovid's Compositions on Love Reworked in the Aeneas Style), it comprises thirteen translations/adaptations of poems from Ovid's *Amores* (I: 1, 8, 9, 13; II: 4, 12, 15, 19; III: 4, 5, 8, 12, 15). Osipov took the opportunity to display a remarkable virtuosity in verse form, devising different line-foot-rhyme patterns for each poem (Ovid's Latin originals were in elegiac couplets throughout). Despite such virtuosity and recourse to many of the travesty techniques of *Virgilieva Eneida,* this work fell far short of its predecessor in quality and popularity. The choice of Ovid's *Amores,* poems already close to travesty and, moreover, unfamiliar to the Russian reading public of the time, may have contributed to the work's failure. One other burlesque, an unabashedly pornographic parody of Ippolit Bogdanovich's *Dushen'ka* (in a manuscript located in the Derzhavin archives at the Saltykov-Shchedrin Public Library in Saint Petersburg), has been attributed to Osipov, but its banal pornography and total lack of linguistic ingenuity, poetic flair, and vigorous humor suggest that it is almost certainly not his. The manuscript title page is signed. "N. Osipov," but the date, written in the same hand, is 1811, some twelve years after Nikolai Petrovich Osipov had died on 19 May 1799. His widow, Anna, had a gravestone erected with a verse epitaph whose final line boldly but erroneously asserts that "With his *Eneida* Osipov will live on in posterity."

References:

Nikolai Dashkevich, "Malorusskaia i drugie burlesknye (shutlivye) 'Eneidy,' " *Kievskaia starina,* 62, no. 9 (1898): 146–188;

Ivan Steshenko, "I. P. Kotliarevsky i Osipov v ikh vzaimootnosheniiakh," *Kievskaia starina,* nos. 7–8 (1898): 1–82;

Irwin R. Titunik, "A Note about Paul Scarron's *Virgile travesti* and N. P. Osipov's *Eneida,*" *Study Group on Eighteenth-Century Russia Newsletter,* 21 (1993): 51–56;

Boris Tomashevsky, "N. V. Osipov (biograficheskia spravka)," in *Iroi-komisheskaia poema,* edited by Tomashevsky, Biblioteka poeta, bol'shaia seriia (Leningrad: Izdatel'stvo pisatelei, 1933), pp. 263–266;

Boris O. Unbengaun, "Latinskoe voisko v travestirovannykh Eneidakh," in his *Russko-evropeiskie literaturnye sviazi: Sbornik statei k 70-letiiu so dnia rozhdeniia M. P. Alekseeva* (Moscow & Leningrad: Akademiia nauk, 1966), pp. 339–345;

S. A. Vengerov, *Russkaia poeziia. Sobranie proizvedenii russkikh poetov,* volume 1, part 2 (Saint Petersburg, 1897), pp. 806–810, and supplementary pp. 322–326.

Vladislav Aleksandrovich Ozerov

(30 September 1769 – 5 September 1816)

Mark G. Altshuller
University of Pittsburgh

BOOKS: *Sochineniia,* 2 volumes (Saint Petersburg: A. Pokhorsky, 1816–1817; revised edition, Saint Petersburg: I. Glazunov, 1828);

Sochineniia (Saint Petersburg: A. Smirdin, 1846);

Tragedii. Russkaia klassnaia biblioteka, 33 (Saint Petersburg: I. Glazunov, 1907);

Tragediia i stikhotvoreniia, edited by I. N. Medvedeva, Biblioteka poeta, bol'shaia seriia (Leningrad: Sovetskii pisatel', 1960).

OTHER: Alexander Pope, *Eloisa k Abelardu: Iroida,* translated by Ozerov (Saint Petersburg: Shliakhetnyi Sukhoputnyi kadetskii korpus, 1794).

The biography of Vladislav Aleksandrovich Ozerov is murky and full of riddles. He lived a short and strange life. He began to write late (at the age of thirty) and wrote only five tragedies, three of which enjoyed outstanding success. An official of the Ministry of Finance and a fairly powerful bureaucrat, he attained widespread fame suddenly and for several years was considered Russia's best dramatist. Just as suddenly he found himself in a remote village where he endured the failure of what may have been his best tragedy, went out of his mind, and soon died. He was quickly and undeservedly forgotten.

Vladislav Aleksandrovich Ozerov was born 30 September 1769 in the village of Kazanskoe (some accounts place his birth in Borka) in the Zubtsovsky district of Tver province. He belonged to an old but impoverished noble family. His father, Aleksandr Irinarkhovich, was a landowner of average means who lived very humbly, occupying himself with running his small estate.

The mother of the future dramatist died early, leaving behind several children. The father quickly remarried, to a widow with children of her own. The family was large (Ozerov's father had twenty-two children) and tightly budgeted. An expensive home education was well beyond the means of the parents. Family ties (among the relatives of the Ozerovs was an influential family, the Bludovs; the poet and government minister Gavriil Derzhavin; Field Marshal M. Kamensky; and others) helped to have Vladislav enrolled in the Sukhoputnyi shliakhetnyi kadetskii korpus (Noble Infantry Cadet Corps), where he was accepted 19 May 1776.

Many outstanding writers and government officials of the eighteenth century received their education at the corps, including Aleksandr Sumarokov, Mikhail Kheraskov, and Fieldmarshal Petr Rumiantsev. At the beginning of Catherine II's reign the academic program of the corps had been transformed on the basis of the pedagogical ideas of Jean-Jacques Rousseau and John Locke. The instructors strove for harmony between the natural sciences and the humanities and between physical and moral training. Special attention was paid to literature, especially French, an excellent knowledge of which Ozerov acquired at the corps. His contemporary, the writer and journalist Sergei Glinka, says in his *Zapiski* (Notes) that "Ozerov's memory contained the entire theater of [Pierre] Corneille, [Jean] Racine, Voltaire. He knew the French language excellently, played in French tragedies in the homes of courtiers and recited stunningly." In 1784 Iakov Kniazhnin, the renowned Russian dramatist who had just presented his famous tragedy *Rosslav* (1784), became Ozerov's literature instructor; his work would exhibit a strong influence on Ozerov. There was a long-standing tradition in the corps of students giving dramatic presentations, and in the same year Ozerov began performing on the corps's stage and soon became a good tragic actor, which undoubtedly served as preparation for his future dramatic writings.

But first Ozerov entered the service. On 16 November 1787 he finished the corps with a gold medal and the rank of lieutenant. He acted as adjutant to Count A. de Bol'men, who had been head of the corps and who apparently took on the graduate with great pleasure. A war with Turkey was then being fought, and Ozerov set off with his superior

Vladislav Aleksandrovich Ozerov

to join the active southern army, where in 1789 he took part in the taking of Fort Bendera.

In 1790 Ozerov returned to Petersburg. He had not severed his ties with his alma mater and in September 1792 he became adjutant to the director of the cadet corps, Fedor Angal'dt. In this capacity Ozerov dealt with all the pedagogical and financial problems of the institution. He often had business at court as well where he frequently came into contact with Catherine II's state secretary Aleksandr Khrapovitsky. A powerful grandee, Catherine's constant literary collaborator, and a member of her inner circle, Khrapovitsky is known as the author of *Pamiatnye zapiski* (Memoranda, 1782–1793), a diary in which he recorded the daily conversations and activities of the empress. He was also a graduate of the cadet corps, and he and Ozerov quickly found they had much in common. Khrapovitsky, twenty years older than Ozerov and much higher in rank, offered the young man his patronage. At the end of the 1790s Khrapovitsky and Ozerov exchanged verse epistles on the meaning of the words *chest'* (honor) and *chestnost'* (honesty). In his epistle Ozerov gives high marks to the integrity, fairness, and modesty of his older friend.

In 1794 Angal'dt died. Ozerov stayed with the corps for a little while, and then with the help of

Khrapovitsky he transferred to the Ekspeditsiia gosudarstvennogo khoziastva (Department of State Economy), where he dealt with problems concerning forestry. His service career developed successfully, and soon he held the rank of collegiate adviser (equal to a colonel in the army). He was an active and energetic official, frequently traveling on official business — inspecting and protecting the vast Russian forests. In 1798 a *Lesnoi departament* (Department of Forestry) was created under the admiralty, and in early 1800 Ozerov was transferred there, with the rank of major general.

Ozerov's literary experiments in these years were few and not very significant. His first published work, in 1794, was *Eloisa k Abelardu: Iroida,* a translation of the French poet Charles Pierre de Colardeau's *Lettre amoreuse d'Héloise à Abelard* (1758), which in turn was a "free translation" of Alexander Pope. In the introduction Ozerov tells the story of the unhappy lovers and Abelard's emasculation. This extensive poem takes the form of a passionate, fervent love letter from Heloise, who makes such statements as, "Ia plamemen goriu . . . zhar sil'nyi oshchushchaiu . . . / Obniav menia rukoi, prizhmi k grudi svoei" (I burn with flame . . . I feel an ardent fever . . . / Take me in your arms, press me to your breast). She demands from Abelard precisely that which he cannot give her: "Liubliu tebia, a ty ne mozhesh' uzh liubit'" " (I love you, but you are incapable of love).

This first published work of Ozerov's may be a key to several biographical riddles. Ozerov was never married. Nothing is known about his love relationships, with one exception. His cousin Dmitrii Bludov, in a letter dated 20 February 1817, told Ozerov's first biographer, Prince Petr Viazemsky, the story of the poet's youthful love for a woman: "with her he breathed deeply the raptures of platonic passion, he was often near happiness but was not happy, for the woman he loved was married and virtuous." This story can almost certainly be attributed to Ozerov, and it suggests that Ozerov's sexual life was not normal. Apparently he was never intimate with a woman. The American Slavist Simon Karlinsky notes that in the majority of Ozerov's plays the subject is not the love of a man for a woman – always pale and unexpressive – but the love of a bride for her dead lover, of a daughter for her father, or of a man for a friend.

In 1798 Ozerov wrote the tragedy *Iaropolk i Oleg* (Iaropolk and Oleg), based on the story from medieval Russian chronicles of the Kievan prince Iaropolk's murder of his brother, the Derevlian prince Oleg. Ozerov altered the tragedy, as often happened in the Russian tradition (in the works of Iakov Kniazhnin, Sumarokov, and Kheraskov), so that it ends happily – not with a murder, but only with an unsuccessful attempt on Oleg's life followed by the brothers' reconciliation. Iaropolk's confidant, the villain Svenel'd, who had paved the way for the fratricide, stabs himself and dies. The tragedy, again in keeping with Russian tradition, also operates as a political allegory. Paul I (Iaropolk), in spite of his instability, was distinguished by a chivalrous character, and it was natural for others to blame his cruelties on such villainous favorites as Kutaisov or Arakcheev (Svenel'd). In Ozerov's first tragedy the strong influence of Kniazhnin can be felt. Artistically, the play is quite weak; it was performed in Saint Petersburg on 16 May 1798 and then once more on 27 November 1805.

His literary pursuits drew Ozerov into several circles. He constantly visited the house of Aleksei Olenin, a powerful official, well-known patron of the arts, skilled graphic artist, brilliant connoisseur of ancient culture, and later the director of the public library and president of the Academy of Arts. Ozerov was a frequent guest at Olenin's suburban estate, characteristically named Priiutino (Place of Refuge), where many famous people of the epoch lived and worked,

often for months at a time. Among them were the fabulist Ivan Krylov, the poet Nikolai Gnedich (translator of the *Iliad*), Vasilii Kapnist, Vasilii Zhukovsky, and the dramatist Aleksandr Shakhovskoi. Ozerov may have conceived his tragedy about Oedipus under the influence of the Olenin circle's interest in classical literature.

Ozerov also frequented the home of a distant relative, the poet Derzhavin, who at this time, having quarreled with Paul I, was avoiding court service and living at his spacious home in Saint Petersburg on the banks of the Fontanka River. Derzhavin loved to gather young writers around him, praising their works (not always sincerely) and forcing them to recite their verses. Ozerov loved and respected Derzhavin, and in 1798 he wrote "Oda Gavriilu Romanovichu Derzhavinu," a testimonial ode (collected in his *Sochineniia*, 1817) in which he extolled the fairness, governmental wisdom, and poetic gift of the renowned poet. Later, however, relations soured between the two.

During the night of 11 March 1801 Emperor Paul I was murdered in the Mikhailovsky Fortress, and Alexander I became czar. Ozerov wrote an ode on his elevation to the throne. He did not have any selfish motive in this composition, since the ode was only published posthumously. Ozerov shared the hopes and aspirations of liberal circles of society, who expected a change for the better after the erratic, confused, and despotic reign of Paul I. In Alexander he saw a reformer and a sincere successor to Catherine II. However, for Ozerov, Alexander's reign began with serious difficulties: immediately after his coronation reforms were initiated in all areas of governmental administration. Ozerov was asked if it was not necessary to undertake reforms in his department. The painfully neurotic Ozerov decided that his superiors were dissatisfied with his work and resigned his post as senior counselor for the Forestry Department. On 10 July 1801 he was "relieved of duties because of sickness" (the usual excuse in such situations).

Soon Ozerov left for the country, where he lived with his father, who was always short of money. His father had forced his son into the service and was unhappy with his resignation. Life in the country was hard and did little to improve Ozerov's disposition. It was probably during this period that he had the idea for, and perhaps partly wrote, his next tragedy. Meanwhile, his cousin and devoted friend Bludov had transferred to the Ministry of Foreign Affairs in Saint Petersburg in October 1802. In his letters he exhorted Ozerov to return to service in the capital. Ozerov heeded this advice and on 21 November 1803 returned to his position at the Forestry Department.

Before long he presented his new tragedy, *Edip v Afinakh* (Oedipus in Athens) for the judgment of his friends, first of all Olenin and the head of the Imperial Theater's repertory department, Shakhovskoi. Its subject was taken from the ancient myth, treated by Sophocles in his famous Oedipus trilogy. Ozerov also made use of several French plays on the same theme.

Ozerov considerably altered both the plot and the characters of the story. Antigone and Oedipus do not perish but remain in Athens; Oedipus even forgives his repentant son Polynices. Ozerov's heroes are gentle and sensitive. They shed streams of tears, suffer, and feel pity, but they take no action. There is little action in the play – only the mounting tragic feelings of daughterly and fatherly love, the repentance of an unworthy son, and so on. In this manner Ozerov created a new genre in Russian literature: the sentimental-romantic tragedy. As in *Iaropolk i Oleg,* the play includes the kind of political allusions that had become usual for Russian classicist tragedy. In this practice he followed Sumarokov and especially his mentor, Kniazhnin. One of the most important heroes of the tragedy, the Athenian king Theseus, was meant to remind viewers of Alexander I. Theseus is good, just, peace loving, and even proclaims constitutional principles: "Gde na zakonakh vlast' tsarei ustanovlena, / Srazit' to obshchestvo ne mozhet i vselenna" (Where the power of kings is established by law, / Even the universe cannot strike down that society).

The tragedy delighted Olenin and Shakhovskoi. A connoisseur of antiquity, Olenin prepared sketches for the scenery and drawings of costumes, weapons, the interior of the temple, and so on, relying on his broad knowledge of classical archaeology. The sets were designed by the renowned Italian theatrical artist Pietro Gonzaga, who was a master of perspective. The spectator saw a panorama of Athens, the temple of the Eumenides, and a grove of cypress trees in the background; in the foreground was a field and the royal tent. Such staging was expensive, but there was no money in the theater's coffers, so Shakhovskoi, himself not rich, produced the tragedy at his own cost. The premiere was on 23 November 1804, and its success exceeded all expectations. Ozerov immediately became Russia's most acclaimed dramatist and its most popular poet. The tender, beautifully written monologues were perceived as elegiac poetry; people memorized them and recorded them in albums.

Inspired by this success, Ozerov began a new play, *Fingal.* This time, on the advice of Olenin, he turned from the clear skies of Greece to the clouds of Scotland, from the classical Sophocles to the romantic Ossian (James Macpherson). In fact, there was nothing surprising in this turn. Ozerov surveyed his Celtic heroes in the same sentimental-romantic key as he did the ancient Greeks. Dedicating the new tragedy to his friend and patron Olenin, he wrote: "I k pesniam bardov ia sklonil prel'shchennyi slukh, / Chtoby izvlech' cherty razitel'ny unyly" (I bent my fascinated ear to the songs of the bards, / In order to extract striking and despondent traits).

At the heart of the tragedy lies a story from the third canto of Ossian's epic *Fingal.* The Lochlin King Starno ("Starn" in Ozerov's version) has planned to ruin the hero Fingal (as revenge for the death of his son in Ozerov's version). He invites Fingal to marry his daughter, the black-haired beauty Agandeka (Ozerov changes her name to the more melodious Moina, taken from the same book). The enamored young woman forewarns Fingal, and her infuriated father stabs her to death before the eyes of her beloved. Fingal carries away the beautiful maiden's body and buries her on a high knoll above the sea.

Nothing remains of Ossian's stern northern warriors in Ozerov's heroes. They pine away and shed tears, thinking only about love. The lyrical theme dominates the tragedy, and the love scenes are written in memorable verses. Ozerov's heroes have little resemblance to those of classicist tragedy. The mighty Fingal readily renounces his religion and his longtime animosity with Starn in order to marry Moina. The heroine of a classicist tragedy was supposed to endure a deep inner conflict, a battle between duty and emotion. Moina does not waver for an instant, rising to the defense of her beloved against her own father.

While *Fingal* was playing on the Saint Petersburg stage with great success, Ozerov was finishing his next tragedy, *Dimitri Donskoi,* written during 1806; it premiered on 14 January 1807. This time Ozerov turned to his own country's history: the play depicts the triumphant battle of Kulikovo Field (1380), which led to the liberation of Russia from Tatar occupation. The work was a political tragedy with obvious contemporary allusions and was dedicated to Alexander I, who, Ozerov proclaimed, was destined to liberate Europe from the French, just as Dimitri had freed Russia from the Tatars. In this context the Tatar Khan Mamai represented Napoleon I, and the princes of the play various ministers and counselors to the czar. Ozerov invented the love story in the tragedy; Dimitri is in love with Princess Kseniia of Nizhnii Novgorod, who arrives at the Russian camp on the eve of battle, but Prince Tverskoi is a rival for her hand. Historically, by the time of the battle of Kulikovo, Dimitri had long been married. *Dimitri Donskoi* could hardly have appeared at a more propitious time, during the formation of the fourth anti-Napoleon coalition between Prussia, Russia, and Sweden and while Napoleon was winning brilliant victories in Prussia and swiftly advancing on Russia's borders. Russian society, patriotically inclined, was ready for war, thirsting to avenge the defeat at Austerlitz. Stepan Zhikharev includes in his memoirs a captivating account of the first performance of Ozerov's tragedy. He claims to have been violently affected by the play, becoming feverish, then crying, and finally applauding wildly and stamping his feet. The audience behaved as "madly" as Zhikarev, applauding so loudly at one point that the actors were forced to stop the performance for five minutes, waiting for the noise to subside.

Ozerov's fame had reached its apogee. However, besides friends among men of letters, he had fairly influential adversaries. One of these was Derzhavin, to whom Ozerov had dedicated *Edip v Afinakh*. The elder poet had aligned himself with Adm. Aleksandr Shishkov and his conservative political views and literary tastes. The liberalism and the sentimentality of the heroes in Ozerov's play were not to his liking. Additionally, he had intended to write a historical play and was jealous of the beginning dramatist's success. After having received Ozerov's deferential and enthusiastic dedication, Derzhavin did not react for a long time. Finally, in 1806, after almost half a year, he sent Ozerov a forced and ponderous poem, which could be read as praise only with difficulty. In a letter he promised "to review your work in the company of friends . . . to make note of its incomparable charms and few lapses." Derzhavin's analysis of Ozerov's play was never completed, but a draft preserved in his archives consists of a mean-spirited stylistic commentary, from which it is obvious that Ozerov's poetic system was not acceptable to Derzhavin and Shishkov. Neither did they approve of the "erroneus" liberal and constitutional ideas of Alexander I that Ozerov had put into the mouth of Theseus. Derzhavin criticized the play severely both in conversation with the emperor and at literary gatherings in his home.

Shishkov was even more outraged than Derzhavin by the "debasing" of the battle of Kulikovo's glorious hero, who, instead of praying to the saints' relics while in church, is transfixed by the face of a beautiful young maiden. Shishkov wrote extensive notes on the tragedy in which he also mocked Kseniia's trip to the military camp in order to hurriedly marry Dimitri there: "This is truly an original spectacle, not only for Russian warriors, but for everyone, to see a wedding, when they should see a battle! Well, and what if Tatars attacked at this moment? The devils would put out the marriage lights at once!"

From the same circle appeared a dramatic parody of Ozerov in 1810. Its author was a young officer and witty parodist named Petr Semenov, who had frequented Shishkov's house and taken part in domestic theatricals there. The play was called *Mitiukha Valdaisky* (Mitiukha of Valdai) — *Mitiukha* is a vulgar, colloquial variant of the name *Dimitri,* and Valdai is an area famous for its taverns, drunken coachmen, and ladies of easy virtue. Semenov preserved the story line of Ozerov's tragedy, turning it into a fight between the publicans of Valdai and coachmen from the neighboring settlement of Zimogor'e. The parody contains sharp criticism of the composition and plot of Ozerov's tragedy, which clearly took account of Derzhavin and Shishkov's remarks.

All this deeply hurt the hypersensitive Ozerov. He severed his relationship with Derzhavin and wanted to renounce writing completely. His friends encouraged him not to do so. Kapnist wrote a response to Marin's epigram in 1804 in which he praised Ozerov and tried to convince him to disdain the *zoily* ("Zoiluses," unjust and envious critics). Another well-known poet Konstantin Batiushkov, wrote a fable soon after the staging of *Dimitri Donskoi,* called "The Shepherd and the Nightingale." He called Ozerov's critics envious and untalented, croaking like frogs in the swamp. Batiushkov urged Ozerov to continue writing plays and not to give in to the attacks of his enemies: "Ty im molchan'em pet' okhotu pridaesh': / Kto budet slushat' ikh, kogda ty zapoesh'?" (By your silence you encourage them to drone, / Who will listen to them, when you begin to sing?).

Such friendly sympathy seems to have calmed Ozerov, who began work on his next tragedy, *Poliksena.* But he began to suffer difficulties connected with the service, which finally destroyed his vulnerable mental balance. In 1807 Fodor Golubtsov was appointed minister of finance, and the Forestry Department was put under his control. From the beginning of his service career Golubtsov had not gotten along with Ozerov. He summoned Ozerov to his office and in a sharp and unfriendly manner interrogated him on the condition of the Forestry Department, possibly in connection with a general inspection, in spite of Ozerov's irreproachable honesty and successful service. In a letter of 1810 Ozerov noted

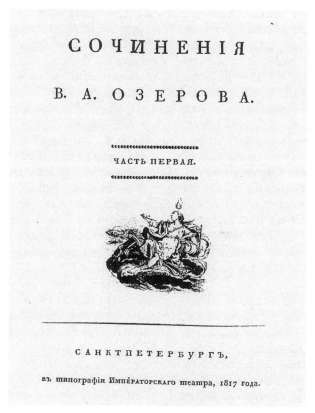

Title page for Ozerov's collected works

that in the course of seven years he had supplied the treasury more than one million rubles in profit. Considering Ozerov's sensitivity and morbid neuroses, it is not surprising that he felt deeply insulted. He submitted his resignation in July 1808, expecting to receive a pension and live in Saint Petersburg, occupying himself with dramaturgy. At the end of September 1808, having completed all his duties at the Forestry Department, he went to his little estate, Krasnyi Iar, in the province of Kazan. He took four acts from *Poliksena* with him and expected to finish writing the play quickly, as he usually did. However, his work came to a standstill. Ozerov missed the theater, contact with friends, and qualified literary advisers. His landowning neighbors exasperated him with their ignorance and pretensions. Nevertheless, on 29 October 1808 his last, and possibly best, tragedy was finished.

Its plot is taken from ancient mythology. It tells the story of the sacrifice of Poliksena, daughter of Hecuba and Priam, on the grave of Achilles after the fall of Troy. In contrast to Ozerov's other plays, *Poliksena* does not contain topical allusions, with the possible exception of Cassandra's prophecy that in the far-distant future the Russians will liberate the Greeks from a foreign yoke.

A dark mood prevails in Ozerov's tragedy. Everything recalls the downfall of Troy, streams of blood, cruel murders, and so on. Poliksena, destined to be sacrificed and in love with the dead Achilles, yearns for her own death as the only way to be united with her beloved. She stabs herself to death upon his grave. The play ends with Nestor's pessimistic philosophical meditations:

Среди тщеты сует, среди страстей борьбы
Мы бродим по земли игралищем судьбы.
Счастлив, кто в гроб скорей от жизни удалится,
Счастливее того, кто к жизни не родится.

(Among the vanity of vanities, among the passions
    of struggle
We wander the earth as playthings of fate.
Happy is he who quickly withdraws from life to
    the grave,
Happier is he, who was never born.)

Ozerov impatiently awaited the production of his play, but his friends were in no hurry. Shakhovskoi had more closely aligned himself with the "archaists" Derzhavin and Shishkov, and he had come to like Ozerov's plays with their tense emotion and sentimental characters less and less. The

270

friendly relationship between Olenin and Sha-khovskoi cooled, and minor disagreements and annoyances delayed the production. Finally, on 14 May 1809, the play premiered. The audience was small, box-office returns were minimal, and the play was performed only twice. The problem, however, was not that Shakhovskoi had cooled to Ozerov and was busy with other plays, nor was it that Olenin had had a falling out with Shakhovskoi. *Poliksena* lacked political topicality, and the sentimental, elegaic monologues of Ozerov's heroes were better grasped in reading than from the stage. The public was not able to appreciate the deep lyricism of *Poliksena* or its heightened tragic pathos.

Ozerov found the failure of his creation painful. At the same time, pressing service-related and financial difficulties befell him. At the beginning of April 1809 Ozerov received notice from Golubtsov that his resignation had been accepted, but that the czar had denied him a pension under the pretense that Ozerov had not served the final five years of the required thirty-five years necessary to get it. This rule was constantly broken, and Ozerov, having served long and productively, was completely disheartened. He wrote the minister a sharp and resentful letter.

There are various hypotheses regarding the czar's unexpected hard treatment of the celebrated dramatist, including Alexander's dissatisfaction with the historical allusions in a *Dimitri Donskoi*. The matter can probably be explained much more simply. As noted above, Ozerov had already resigned once, at the beginning of Alexander I's reign, when he had been dismissed with a pension and then, after two years, accepted back at his former position. Now he again suddenly submitted his resignation, possibly just before an inspection of his department. Alexander had a good memory, and these unpredictable actions must have disturbed him, especially as he was informed of them by a minister who was ill-disposed to Ozerov.

Although the dramatist had said in a letter to Olenin that "the glory of an author is more precious to me than the czar's favors and earthly treasures," he suffered from these blows, which seemed to rain down on him from all sides: the failure of his play; his service not being appreciated as it deserved to be; and not enough money to live on in the capital, let alone to finish building a country home. To crown his difficulties, the czar did not allow Ozerov to be paid the three thousand rubles promised him by the theater directorship upon the success of *Poliksena.*

Ozerov fell into an ever-deepening depression. He burned almost all his papers, including three acts of a tragedy – "Medea" – and plans for the tragedies "Osada Damaska" (The Siege of Damascus) and "Vel'gard Variag – Muchenik pri Vladimire" (Vel'gard the Varangian – Martyr in the Time of Vladimir). It is possible that outlines for a tragedy on Volynsky, a minister under Empress Anna, also perished in the fire. Ozerov began suffering nervous fits and was gradually going out of his mind. Heredity also may have played a part: his father had suffered for a long time in his youth from some sort of fits.

In winter 1810 Ozerov's father brought his son to his own estate, where Ozerov lived in a pitiful condition for six more years. He kept repeating the same senseless phrase, "Koroshi bol'shie, dev'at' priedut" (Good bigs, nine will come), and digging up the earth in the garden, trying to build a hill that had a little spiral path leading to its summit. He died 5 September 1816.

The writer's death inspired a literary battle. Young, talented poets, advocates of the "new style" (Zhukovsky, Batiushkov, Viazemsky, and the young Aleksandr Pushkin), accused the "archaists" of intrigues and envy that had led to Ozerov's death. Especially hard hit was Shakhovskoi, who (as has since become clear), although he did not show enthusiasm for the production of Ozerov's last play, also did not participate in any intrigues against him.

Ozerov's plays continued to be staged, but interest in them dwindled. In 1824, in the first chapter of *Evgenii Onegin,* Pushkin paid tribute to Ozerov as a glorious page in the history of the Russian theater, emphasizing the sentimentality of his dramaturgy. By 1826, however, Pushkin called Ozerov a "mediocre writer" and denied he possessed any dramatic artistry.

The Russian critic Vissarion Belinsky wrote in 1834 that Ozerov had already become wholly antiquated. By this time Ozerov's plays had disappeared from the stage, and his name was largely forgotten. But in 1914 the brilliant young poet Osip Mandelshtam wrote a short poem about Ozerov. These verses are surely among the best written about the dramatist and are the best evaluation of his significance for Russian culture. In the first stanza Mandelshtam condemns the generation of readers who consigned Ozerov to undeserved oblivion, and in the third and last stanza he contrasts the incorporeal and faceless heroes of symbolist theater to the majestic characters of classicist tragedy. He rightfully calls Ozerov's works the end and highest achievement of this movement in Russian literature:

> Что делать вам в театре полуслова
> И полумаск, герои и цари?
> И для меня явленье Озерова--
> Последний луч трагической зари.

> (What are you to do in [our] theater of indirect
>   suggestion
> And of half-masks, O heroes and kings?
> But for me the appearance of Ozerov
> Was the last ray of tragedy's sunset.)

— translation by Simon Karlinsky, (in his *Russian Drama from its Beginnings to the Age of Pushkin,* 1985)

Biographies:

P. O. Potapov, *Iz istorii russkogo teatra: Zhizn' i deiatel'nost' V. A. Ozerova* (Odessa, 1915);

Mikhail A. Gordin, *Vladislav Ozerov* (Leningrad: Iskusstvo, 1990).

References:

Viktor A. Bochkarev, *Russkaia istoricheskaia dramaturgiia nachala XIX-ogo veka (1800–1815)* (Kubishev, 1959), pp. 129–250;

Maksim I. Gillel'son, *Molodoi Pushkin i Arzamasskoe bratstvo* (Leningrad: Nauka, 1974);

Gillel'son, "V. A. Ozerov v perepiske P. A. Viazemskogo i D. N. Bludova," in his *P. A. Viazemsky: Zhizn' i tvorchestvo* (Leningrad: Nauka, 1969), pp. 365–378;

Simon Karlinsky, *Russian Drama from its Beginnings to the Age of Pushkin* (Berkeley: University of California Press, 1985), pp. 193–215;

Iurii D. Levin, *Ossian v russkoi literature* (Leningrad: Nauka, 1980), pp. 45–52;

Andrei Ia. Maksimovich, "Ozerov," in *Istoriia russkoj literatury,* volume 5 (Moscow & Leningrad: Akademiia nauk, 1941), pp. 156–180;

L. P. Sidorova, "Rukopisnye zamechaniia sovremennika na pervom izdanii tragedii V. A. Ozerova *Dimitri Donskoi,*" *Zapiski otdela rukopisei Vsesoiuznoi biblioteki imeni V. I. Lenina,* 18 (1956): 142–179.

Gavriil Petrov
(Petr Petrovich Shaposhnikov)
(18 May 1730 – 26 January 1801)

Viktor M. Zhivov
Institute of the Russian Language, Moscow

BOOKS: *Slovo v vysokotorzhestvennyi den' koronovaniia . . . imp. Ekateriny Alekseevny . . .* (Moscow: Moskovskii universitet, 1763);

Slovo v den' vosshestviia na prestol Ekateriny II (Moscow: Sinodal'naia, 1766);

Slovo v den' tezoimenitstva imp. Ekateriny II (Moscow: Sinodal'naia, 1766);

Slovo v torzhestvennyi den' vosshestviia na vserossiiskii prestol . . . imp. Ekateriny Alekseevny . . . (Saint Petersburg: Morskoi Kadetskii korpus, 1770);

O sluzhenii i chinopolozheniiakh Pravoslavnyia Grekorossiiskiia Tserkvi (Moscow, 1772; revised, Moscow: Sinodal'naia, 1797);

Slovo na vysokotorzhestvennyi den' koronovaniia . . . imp. Ekateriny Alekseevny . . . 1773 goda (Saint Petersburg: Akademiia Nauk, 1773);

Rech', kotoroiu privetstvoval Eia Imp. Velichestvo perverstvuiushchii Sviateishego pravitel'stvuiushchago sinoda chlen preosviashchennyi Gavriil . . . (Saint Petersburg: Akademiia Nauk, 1776);

Slovo v den' tezoimenitstva . . . imp. Ekateriny Alekseevny vseia Rossii propovedannoe v pridvornoi tserkve, pri vysochaishem Eia Velichestva i ikh Imp. Vysochestv prisutstvii (Saint Petersburg: Voennaia kollegiia, 1777);

Slovo pri nachatii otkryttia Sanktpeterburgskoi gubernii po vysochaishim uchrezhdeniiam . . . imp. Ekateriny Alekseevny . . . propovedannoe v sobornoi tserkvi Rozhdestva presviatyia Bogoroditsy, chto pri Nevskoi perspektive . . . (Saint Petersburg: Sukhoputnyi shliakhetnyi kadetskii korpus, 1780);

Slovo na otkrytie Vyborgskago namestnichestva . . . (Saint Petersburg: Shnor, 1784);

Tolkovaniia na sobornyia poslaniia Apostolov: Iakova, Petra, Ioanna i Iudy, by Petrov and Tikhon Malinin (Moscow: Sinodal'naia, 1794).

OTHER: *Sobranie raznykh pouchenii na vse voskresnye i prazdnichnye dni,* edited by Petrov, 3 volumes (Moscow: Sinodal'naia, 1775);

Kratkie poucheniia o glavneishikh spasitel'nykh dogmatov very, edited by Petrov (Moscow: Sinodal'naia, 1781);

Kniga kratkikh pouchenii o glavneishikh spasitel'nykh dogmatakh very, o zapovediakh Bozhiikh i o dolzhnostiakh iz raznykh sviatykh otets i uchitelei sobrannaia, edited by Petrov (Moscow: Sinodal'naia, 1795).

SELECTED PERIODICAL PUBLICATIONS – UNCOLLECTED: "Propoved' na den' rozhdeniia imperatora Petra III, skazannaia 10 fevralia 1762g. v Moskovskom Uspenskom sobore rektorom Gavriilom, 10 fevralia 1762 g.," *Moskovskie vedomosti,* no. 13 (2 December 1762);

"Slovo pri otkrytii komissii o sochinenii novogo ulozheniia," *Moskovskie vedomosti,* no. 62 (1767);

"Rech' imperatritse pri predstavlenii deputatsii ot komissii ulozheniia po sluchaiu dannogo Ekaterinoi pribavlenniia k Nakazu, skazannaia 9 aprelia 1768 g.," *Sanktpeterburgskie Vedomosti,* no. 40 (16 May 1768);

"Rech', skazannaia 22 noiabria 1768 g. pri pozdravlenii Ekateriny ot litsa komissii ulozheniia, s blagopoluchnym privitiem ospy," *Sanktpeterburgskie Vedomosti,* no. 103, 23 December 1768;

"Uveshchanie k narodu po sluchaiu morovogo povetriia 1771 g.," *Starina i Novizna,* 1 (1772): 78–79;

"Slovo pri osviashchenii khrama v uchrezhdennom v S.-Peterburge bogadel'nom dome, skazannoe 8 avgusta 1781 goda" *Sanktpeterburgskie Vedomosti,* no. 71 (3 September 1781);

"Tolkovaniia na zapovedi blazhenstva," *Khristianskoe chetenie,* 4 (1837): 50–83.

Metropolitan of Novgorod and Saint Petersburg, a major government figure, scholar, theologian, and philosopher, as well as famous homilist, Gavriil Petrov was one of the most prominent Russian church officials of the second half of the eighteenth century. Yet in the history of Russian literature and religion Gavriil remains to a large extent a paradoxical and equivocal personality. No other religious writer of the eighteenth century so consistently promoted the integration of Christian teachings with the ideology of the Enlightenment by asserting the unity of belief and rational thought, of Providence and natural law. The degree to which these views reflected the needs of the day, however, or how they fit into Gavriil's overall psychological makeup is unclear. One of the first and most important clergymen at the court of Catherine the Great, in his private life Gavriil was an ascetic who supported monasticism. His career took shape, as it were, against his will, while his spiritual goals found their expression in his support for monastic renewal and a return to patristic ascetic traditions. Gavriil's literary works reflect only his public self, that of a proponent of Enlightenment. His sermons and exegetical writings are remarkable for their rationalism and emphatic lack of rhetorical embellishments, rare for the day. Gavriil's activities as member of Catherine's Legislative Commission and as member of the Russian Academy testify to his scholarly industriousness while also obscuring the monastic and spiritual side of his life.

Gavriil Petrov (whose secular given name was Peter Petrovich Shaposhnikov) was born in Moscow on 18 May 1730 to the family of Petr Fedorovich Shaposhnikov, a subdeacon and later priest in the Russian Orthodox church; information concerning their last name is not entirely reliable. In 1740 Gavriil was sent to study at the Moscow Slavonic-Greek-Latin Academy, where he finished at the top of his class in 1753. Usually such success would have ensured a subsequent career, beginning with the position of junior instructor at the academy upon graduation. However, Gavriil was not offered such an appointment, and submitted a request to work as a baker of communion bread – a position usually occupied by old women – in order, as Boris Titlinov asserts in his 1916 biography, "imet' malen'kii kusok khleba i byt' vsegda pri tserkvi" (to have a small bit of bread and to always be at church). He became a *spravshchik* (editor) at the synodal printing house in Moscow, with a meager salary and negligible prospects for the future. Gavriil displayed his erudition and industriousness in his work on the second revised edition of Empress Elizabeth's Bible of 1756, which became the standard church text. Gavriil failed to advance because

he did not wish to become a monk, which at the time was a necessary condition for an ecclesiastical career. Gavriil was already developing a negative attitude toward the career of a scholar-monk, which he considered a profanation of monastic life, one which exchanged prayer and ascetic struggle for administrative and scholarly activity.

Nonetheless, in 1758 Gavriil became an instructor at the seminary attached to the *Lavra* (Laura, or principal monastery) of the Holy Trinity and Saint Sergius, and on 28 June of that year was almost forcibly tonsured as a monk by the monastery's archimandrite, Gedeon Krinovsky. Immediately upon his tonsure, Gavriil became a hieromonk (monastic priest) and rector of the seminary, and soon after, on 14 August 1758, *namestnik* (vicar) of the Lavra. On 8 August 1761 Gavriil was designated rector of the Slavonic-Greek-Latin Academy and archimandrite of the Zaikonospassky Monastery. This position brought him to the attention of Catherine II, who apparently valued both Gavriil's erudition (especially his knowledge of modern European languages – French and German – a rare trait for a clergyman) as well as the unique breadth of his views. The empress saw him as a man who was "ostryi i rezonabel'nyi i ne protivnika filosofii" (sharp and reasonable, no enemy of philosophy). Gavriil, in fact, humbly accepted the external dependence of the Russian church on the government and in particular its dependence on Catherine's "Voltairean" predilections and those of the *ober-prokurory* (chief procurators, or directors) of the synod appointed to administer church affairs. Gavriil primarily concerned himself with questions of spiritual and moral enlightenment and was interested in the inner reformation of church life. He imposed the rigor of monastic life not on others but on himself and his close entourage. To Catherine, the young archimandrite seemed a likely candidate for the role of enlightened hierarch, who with his erudition and tolerance would adorn the most liberal court in Europe, yet whose severe piety would satisfy the concerns of the Orthodox population.

The empress became involved in advancing Gavriil's career, and on 29 October 1763 he was designated bishop of Tver (the ordination took place in December, in the Peter-Paul Cathedral in Saint Petersburg). Catherine visited Gavriil in Tver in 1767 prior to her trip along the Volga. During these travels Catherine and her close associates translated Jean-François Marmontel's philosophical novel *Bélisaire* (1766), which had been banned by the Sorbonne as a freethinking manifesto of enlightened deism. Their translation was dedicated to

Gavriil, and the dedication clearly outlined those qualities that he – as a spiritual shepherd during the reign of an enlightened monarch – was supposed to embody: "krotost', smirenie, umerennost', prosveshchennoe nabozhestvo" (meekness, humility, moderation, and enlightened piety). The translators compared him to Belisarius, thus implicitly prescribing for Gavriil an ideological program.

In 1768 Gavriil was designated a member of the Legislative Commission for the Creation of a New Law Code, one of the most ambitious projects of the early years of Catherine's reign. He thus acceded to the role of representative of the entire clergy, replacing the recently deceased Saint Petersburg metropolitan, Dimitrii Sechenov. Gavriil took his responsibilities seriously, and he diligently worked to define new legislative principles. Although the commission never got as far as active legislation, Gavriil took an active part in its preliminary work. He wrote about Russia's need for comprehensible laws, about the regulation of education, and about laws governing the Old Believers and those of different faiths. He made a special effort to define the clergy as its own special estate, separate from the *srednii klass* (middle class) to which craftsmen and merchants were assigned, and to exempt ecclesiastics from corporal punishment.

Gavriil was appointed a member of the synod on 27 September 1769, and on 22 September 1770 he became the archbishop of Saint Petersburg and Revel, and prior of the Aleksandr Nevsky Monastery. Thus, before the age of forty Gavriil had come to occupy the most important ecclesiastical positions in Catherinian Russia. On 1 January 1775 Gavriil was also given control over the Novgorod See (which was often combined with that of Saint Petersburg), and on 22 September 1783 he was elevated to the rank of metropolitan. Gavriil enjoyed the favor of the empress until her death, and during her reign he was the de facto leader of the Russian church. He was especially concerned with strengthening the church's monastic communities, and he organized a seminary at the Aleksandr Nevsky Monastery.

At the beginning of his reign, Emperor Paul looked upon Gavriil with great favor. Gavriil was the first member of the clergy to whom he granted the Order of Saint Andrew and, subsequently, the Order of Aleksandr Nevsky. Later, however, as a result of the machinations of Amvrosii Podobedov, archbishop of Kazan, Paul changed his attitude toward Gavriil, and on 16 October 1799 he was deprived of his Saint Petersburg See (which was awarded to Amvrosii), although he was left in charge of the Novgorod See. Gavriil became extremely ill after moving to Novgorod and asked to be allowed to retire to the Simonov Monastery in Moscow. On 19 December 1800 he was relieved of his duties but ordered to remain in the bishop's residence in Novgorod. He died there on 26 January 1801 and was interred in the Cathedral of Saint Sofia in Novgorod. By some accounts, his remains did not decompose, and a local belief arose that prayers directed to Gavriil would relieve toothaches.

Gavriil's literary legacy is limited in volume but is not lacking in either cultural or historical and literary significance. During his lifetime Gavriil was famous as a homilist, although his fame in this area can be explained more by the author's high position rather than by purely literary considerations. Although Gavriil was hardly concerned with literary reforms, his sermons significantly differ from the usual homiletic production of the period; many are limited to topics of a purely moral nature and bring to mind moralistic argumentation rather than oratorical prose. This is true even of his panegyrical works, in which the demands of the genre, in particular the need for rhetorical embellishment, were most rigid.

For example, Gavriil dedicated his sermon on Catherine's name-day in 1777 to the theme of harmonizing the will of God and the human being. Gavriil writes that the desire for common welfare and harmony is directly related to the perfection of the human being, "ibo zdes' i chuvstva soglashaiutsia s razumom i pol'zy s pol'zami drugikh i namereniia s namereniiami Boga" (for in this feelings concur with reason, [our own] welfare with the welfare of others, and [human] intentions with the intentions of God). In his response to the question of theodicy Gavriil points out that "ne byl by Bog blag, est'lib ne soedinial s khudymi delami khudykh sledstvii" (God would not be good if He did not pair evil deeds with evil consequences), and he discusses the inability of human beings to know genuine righteousness. Given the general imperfect nature of society, the righteous person must inevitably "vkhodit' v techenie del liudei neblagonamerennykh" (enter into the flow of activities of those of ill will). This moralistic conclusion exhausts the sermon's theological message. The most important thing that harmonizes human will with that of God turns out to be enlightenment, which allows people to assimilate Christ's commands to love God and to love one's neighbor. Infringement of the divine order leads to the partial neglect of these commands, which are valid for eternity. Further on

Gavriil inserts a prayer, in which he hopes "chtob my onuiu zdes' nachali: chtob poznanie takovago sostoianiia bylo prakticheskoe" (that we begin it [eternity] here: so that our knowledge of such a state [that is, of God's order] be a matter of practice). Several concluding phrases dedicated to the empress are added to this argument. Gavriil explains that God "vveril khranenie Svoego zakona, a tem samym i nashego shchastiia Blagochestiveishei Monarkhine nashei" (has entrusted the preservation of His law – and hence our own happiness – to our Most Pious Monarch) and that her concerns and efforts are linked to the fulfillment of this task. Gavriil's panegyric is thus transformed into a work of moralistic edification.

This context explains Aleksandr Sumarokov's reaction to Gavriil's homiletic art; he asserted that Gavriil's sermons were directed more toward the presentation of a philosophical thesis than at exhibiting rhetorical figures, but he also praised Gavriil's graceful and forceful style, proclaiming that "Gavriil podoben reke bez shuma napolniaiushchei brega svoi i poriadochnym techeniem, nevykhodiashchei nikogda iz granits svoikh" (Gavriil is like a river which fills its banks noiselessly, with an even current, never overflowing its boundaries). M. I. Sukhomlinov's assessment that Gavriil's panegyrics never completely avoided the rhetorical routine of the period only actually applies to a few of Gavriil's laudatory speeches which occupy a marginal place in his literary legacy. The decision to lower the usual high homiletic style was clearly conscious on Gavriil's part.

However, Gavriil entered into the history of Russian homiletics not primarily as an author who departed from the generic canon of sermons, but rather as the editor of the Sobranie pouchenii na vse voskresenye i prazdnichnye dni (Collection of Homilies for All Sundays and Holidays, 1775). The publication of this collection was an important undertaking that reflected the religious policy of Catherine's reign, and it was approved and encouraged by the empress. Organized according to the liturgical calendar, these sermons were to be read "vo vsekh tserkvakh gradskikh i uezdnykh, i v monastyriakh bez vsiakiia peremeny, otlagatel'stva i izvineniia" (in all churches, urban and provincial, and in monasteries, without any changes, delays or apologies). Departure from this command would be punished, for example, by withholding the right to serve the mass, or suspension from duties. A clergyman could give his own sermon (after the appropriate censorship), in which case the stated duty was withdrawn; it is clear, however, that even if a clergyman de-

cided to substitute his own work for those approved by the Synod, he would still have to follow the norm they established. Thus the Sobranie pouchenii created a homiletic canon which continued to be in force through the first decades of the nineteenth century.

The Sobranie pouchenii rather explicitly contradicts Russian Orthodox tradition in its goals and spiritual precepts. Its introduction begins with the assertion that the church service does not only include prayers and the sacraments, but also and more important, the teaching of Divine law. This assertion of the primacy of nravouchenie (preaching, or "moral instruction") represented the rationalistic spirituality of the Age of Enlightenment rather than that of traditional Orthodoxy, which centered on the liturgy as the basis of the church's activity. The new order of things was consciously opposed to the traditional one. The introduction also argues that the usual church readings, from the fathers of the church or saint lives from the chet'i minei (menaea for reading), while offering examples for pious imitation, are not sufficient because they do not provide "obstoiatel'noe istolkovanie k nastavleniiu vsego zakona Bozhiia" (thorough commentary for instruction in all of Divine law). Furthermore, not only are the traditional sermons few and incomplete, their language is also declared to be temnyi (obscure) at times, made difficult by poor translations, which is increased by the slog (style) of Church Slavonic; "I potomu ne tokmo prostomu narodu, no inogda i uchenym nevrazumitel'ny, ili kogda neskol'ko i poniatny, no po slogu drevnemu i neiasnosti, takzhe inogda po dolgote, ne zelo usladitel'ny i pobuditel'ny" (And therefore they are incomprehensible not only to the simple folk but sometimes even to the learned, and when they are somewhat understandable, they are not very pleasing or stimulating due to their archaic style and ambiguity, and sometimes due to their length as well). The epithets usladitel'nyi (pleasing) and pobudutel'nyi (stimulating) are traditional requirements of oratorical art as established by rhetorical manuals, and the statement concerning the difficulty of understanding Church Slavonic reiterates Feofan Prokopovich's discussion from the Dukhovnyi Reglament (Ecclesiastical Regulation, 1721).

The stated goals of the Sobranie pouchenii were to provide new sermons containing instruction in the duties required of the true Christian and good citizen, and that this instruction be explained in a clear language that would be comprehensible to everyone. Hence the basic focus was not on the sacredness of church life but on rationalist enlightenment and edification. It was asserted that "neznanie zakona Bozhiia est' prichinoiu vsekh vo vsiakoi dolzhnosti neispravnistei i zloupotreblenii" (ignorance of Divine law is the reason for all of the abuses and faults in all occupations), and the source of *sueverstva* (superstitions) that "posramliaiut veru nashu" (bring shame on our faith). It is precisely ignorance – and not primal sin or evil human desires – which destroys the divine order, undermines the *obshchaia pol'za* (common good) and "narushaetsia obshchestvennyi pokoi i blagodenstve" (causes social stability and prosperity to be destroyed). It is obvious that in these formulations Enlightenment ideals of social harmony emerge from under the cover of Christian phraseology, and that "the law of God" is understood as an equivalent of the directives of Reason.

This ideology is reflected in Gavriil's selection and reworking of the sermons included in the collection. Of the 104 homilies chosen, nine were written by John Chrysostom, twelve by the eighteenth-century Greek homilist Elias Miniates, five by Bernard Joseph Saurin, five by Johann Lorenz von Mosheim, one by Louis Bourdaloue, thirty-seven by Platon Levshin, nineteen by Gedeon Krinovsky, eight by Gavriil, and five others compiled by Gavriil from various sources, including Bourdaloue and Salomon Gessner. All the homilies were abridged and edited and therefore form a literary unity. It is characteristic that, while reworking the homilies of Gedeon, Gavriil eliminated the entertaining anecdotes common in Gedeon's sermons, leaving primarily passages of moral edification. The emphasis on extraconfessional moralism is underscored by the inclusion in the *Sobranie pouchenii* of works by non-Slavic (primarily Protestant) authors, with Mosheim's *Heilige Reden* (1765) serving to a large degree as the model for its rhetoric.

Gavriil's commentaries on the Epistles, also intended to be read as sermons, manifest the same purely didactic character. They do not deal with topics relating either to church history or theology. The same may be said of his commentaries on the Beatitudes and of his "Rasmyshlenie o blagosti i miloserdii Bozhii k cheloveku" (Reflections on God's Beneficence and Mercy to Man), preserved in manuscript. Moralistic edification in a very concise form is also represented in the "Kratkoe khristianskoe nravouchenie" (A Short Christian Moral Admonition, 1770), published as a separate sheet.

Due to his scholarly reputation, Gavriil was often assigned the duty of editing church books (the prayer book for the first week of the Great Fast, the menologion, triodion, and others). As a liturgist, Gavriil was entrusted with the compilation of a popular explanation of the sacraments and rituals of the Orthodox church, which he set forth in *O sluzhenii i chinopolozheniiakh Pravoslavnyia Grekorossiiskiia Tserkvi* (On the Service and Liturgical Orders of the Orthodox Greco-Russian Church, 1772), which discusses the origins of the sacraments and basic rituals and presents a sequential commentary on the entire course of the service. Allegorical and mystical explanations, typical in the Orthodox tradition, are absent from this book: Gavriil refers the reader to other writings while restricting his own text to popular and, for the most part, rationalistic interpretations.

Gavriil's activities in the Russian Academy are also of some interest. He was elected into the academy at its founding in 1783 and was its foremost member, taking over the presidential duties when Dashkova was absent. The academy's principle undertaking was the compilation of the academic dictionary of the Russian language, and Gavriil took an active part in this work. He wrote a concordance to the homilies of John Chrysostom and edited parts of the dictionary, collecting both manuscript and old printed materials, composing a series of etymological remarks and explanations, and compiling lists of words.

From Gavriil's varied official and literary activities an image emerges of an enlightened, tolerant, and liberal religious figure who reconciled rationalism with faith, a man sparkling with erudition yet never avoiding scholarly work of a far-from-clerical nature, acquainted with the new philosophy and seeing an inner kinship between Christian charity and the theory of natural law. The evidence is diverse, yet the image remains illusory, and, like all of Russian Enlightenment culture created and controlled by Catherine, deceptive. All of the works by Gavriil discussed above were to a certain extent the tribute Gavriil rendered unto Caesar. As Georges Florovsky notes, "This magnificent and important Catherinean prelate . . . was a strict observer of fasts, man of prayer, and ascetic – not only in thought, but in life as well."

In this regard the notes of Feofan, Gavriil's cell attendant (who subsequently became archimandrite of the Kirillo-Novoezersiky Monastery), best depict Gavriil. Through Feofan, Gavriil was connected to the institution of elders (*starchestvo*), and in general with the nascent movement of monastic revival, which he fervently supported. Gavriil reestablished monasteries throughout his vast diocese and chose their abbots from among experienced monks who practiced asceticism. To this end Gavriil did not yield in his opposition to the synod, which advocated filling these positions only with those monks who had received an official academic education. Gavriil also partially restored the Valaamsky Monastery and saved the Simonov Monastery in Moscow from closure. He sanctioned monastic communalism and in 1796 composed rules for communal living, which he disseminated throughout the diocese. At the same time he also sent out to the monasteries the works of John Climacus (Ioann Lestvichnik) and Isaac the Syrian (Isaak Sirin), the main inspirers of Russian Orthodox asceticism. With Gavriil's direct support and supervision, in 1793 the *Dobrotoliubie* (the *Philokalia*, a compilation of Greek mystical writings) appeared in Moscow in the translation of Paisii Velichkovsky. Gavriil commissioned the Aleksandr Nevsky and the Trinity-Saint Sergius monasteries to review the book, which was to have supreme influence on Russian Orthodox spirituality in ensuing decades. This aspect of Gavriil's career leaves an imprint of elusiveness and complexity both on his portrait as a champion of Catherinian Enlightenment, as well as on the entire official church culture of Catherine's reign.

Bibliography:

Boris V. Titlinov, *Gavriil Petrov, mitropolit novgorodskii i sanktpeterburgskii* (Petrograd, 1916), pp. 1143–1152.

Biographies:

Makarii (Miroliubtsev), Arkhimandrit, *Skazanie o zhizni i trudakh Preosviashchenneishego Gavriila, mitropolita Novgorodskogo i Sanktpeterburgskogo* (Saint Petersburg, 1857);

Boris V. Titlinov, *Gavriil Petrov, mitropolit novgorodskii i sanktpeterburgskii* (Petrograd, 1916).

References:

Evgenii Bolkhovitinov, *Slovar' istoricheskii o byvshikh v Rossii pisateliakh dukhovnogo china greko-rossiiskoi tserkvi*, volume 1, 2nd edition (Saint Petersburg, 1827), pp. 81–85;

Arkhimandrit Feofan, "Zapiski O. Feofana, arkhimandrita Kirillo-Novoezerskogo monastyria, byvshego keleinika preosviashchennogo Gavriila, mitropolita Novgorodskogo i S. Peterburgskogo," *Strannik* (February 1862): 533–558;

Filaret (Gumilevsky), Episkop Chernigovskii, *Obzor russkoi dukhovnoi literatury 862–1863*, 3rd edition (Saint Petersburg, 1884), pp. 380–381;

A. Markos, "Gavriil Mitropolit Novgorodskii," *Syn otechestva*, 27 (1830): 26–42;

I. Pokrovsky, "Gavriil, mitropolit Novgorodskii i S-Peterburgskii, kak tserkovno-obshchestvennyi deiatel' (po povodu stoletiia s ego konchiny – 18 maia 1901 g.)," *Khristianskoe chtenie*, no. 10 (1901): 482–510; no. 11 (1901): 687–718;

V. Polenov, "Zhizneopisanie mitropolita Novgorodskogo i S. Peterburgskogo Gavriila," *Trudy Imp. Rossiiskoi Akademii*, volume 1 (Saint Petersburg, 1840), pp. 137–145;

Mikhail I. Sukhomlinov, *Istoriia Rossiikoi Akademii*, volume 1 (Saint Petersburg, 1874), pp. 58–139;

P. Zavedeev, *Istoriia russkogo propovednichestva ot XVII veka do nastoiashchego vremeni* (Tula, 1879);

P. V. Znamensky, "Chteniia iz istorii russkoi tserkvi za vremia tsarstvovaniia Ekateriny II," *Pravoslavnyi sobesednik*, no. 2 (1875): 99–143; no. 4 (1875): 392–418; no. 5 (1875): 3–44; no. 8 (1875): 327–347.

Vasilii Petrovich Petrov

(1736 – 4 December 1799)

Nadezhda Iurevna Alekseeva

Institute of Russian Literature (Pushkin House), Saint Petersburg

SELECTED BOOKS: *Oda na velikolepnyi karrusel' predstavlennyi v Sankt-Peterburge 1766 goda, v chetvertoe leto mirnogo vladeniia . . . gosudarnyi Ekateriny Vtoryia* (Moscow: Moskovskii universitet, 1766);

Epistola . . . imp. Ekaterine Alekseevne . . . po prichine dannykh eia velichestvom dostopamiatnykh otvetov, na podnosimuiu eia velichestvu, ot deputatov novago ulozheniia, imenem vsego gosudarstva, vysokuiu titlu, Velikiia Ekateriny, premudryia materi otechestva ([Moscow]: Moskovskii universitet, 1767);

Oda vsepresvetleishei, derzhavneishei, velikoi gosudaryne imperatritse Ekaterine Alekseevne, samoderzhitse vserossiiskoi, premudroi zakonadatel'nitse, istinnoi otectechestva materi, kotoruiu vo iz"iavlenie chuvstvitel'neishiia synov rossiiskikh radosti i iskrenneishego blagodareniia, vozbuzhdennogo v serdtsakh ikh vsevozhdelennym manifestom, v piatoe leto blagopoluchnogo eia velichestva gosudarstvovaniia izdannym, o izbranii deputatov k sochineniiu proekta novogo ulozheniia, prinosit vsenizhaishii i vse poddaneishii rab Vasilii Petrov ([Moscow:] Moskovskii universitet, 1767);

Nadpisi, kotorye vsenizhaishe podneseny ee imperatorskomu velichestvu samim sochinitelem ([Saint Petersburg]: Akademiia nauk, 1769);

Oda vsepresvetleishei . . . gosudaryne imp. Ekaterine Vtoroi . . . na pobedu nad turkami, v os'moe leto blagopoluchnogo eia velichestva gosudarstvovaniia rossiiskimi voiskami oderzhannuiu i na vziatie Khotina (Saint Petersburg: Akademiia nauk, 1769);

Oda vsepresvetleishei . . . gosudaryne imperatritse Ekaterine Vtoroi . . . na vziat'e Ias i pokorenie vsego Moldavskogo knaizhestva (Saint Petersburg: Akademiia nauk, 1769);

Pis'mo k ego siiatel'stvu . . . grafu Grigor'iu Grigor'evichu Orlovu ot tituliarnogo sovetnika Vasil'ia Petrova (Saint Petersburg: Akademiia nauk, 1769);

Oda na pobedy rossiiskogo flota, oderzhannyia nad turetskim, pod predvoditel'stvom grafa Alekseia Grigor'evicha Orlova, v Arkhipelage pri Khiose ([Saint Petersburg: Akademiia nauk], 1770);

Oda ego siiatel'stvu grafu Grigor'iu Grigor'evichu Orlovu 1771 genvaria 25 dnia ([Saint Petersburg: Akademiia nauk, 1771]);

Poema na pobedy Rossiiskago voinstva pod predvoditel'stvom generala fel'dmarshala grafa Rumiantsova, oderzhannyia nad tatarami i turkami, so vremeni ego voenachal'stva nad pervoiu armieiu, do vziat'ia goroda Zhurzhi ([Saint Petersburg: Akademiia nauk, 1772]);

Na pribytie ego siiatel'stva grafu Petra Aleksandrovicha Rumiantseva iz za Dunaia v Moskvu po zakliuchenii mira s turkami . . . (Moscow: Moskovskii universitet, 1775);

Sochineniia (Saint Petersburg: Shnor, 1782); enlarged, 3 volumes (Saint Petersburg: Meditsinskaia tipografiia, 1811);

Oda velikoi gosudaryne Ekaterine . . . na priobretenie Kryma (Saint Petersburg: Veitbrekht, 1784);

Pesn' imperatritse Ekaterine Vtoroi (Saint Petersburg, 1786);

Prikliucheniia Gustava III, korolia shvedskogo. 1788 iulia 6 dnia ([Saint Petersburg, 1788]);

Grecheskaia grammatika, v kotoroi sintaksis . . . i prosodiia . . . pravilami i primerami ob"iasneny (Saint Petersburg, 1788);

Plach' na konchinu ego svetlosti kniazia Grigor'ia Aleksandrovicha Potemkina Tavricheskago 1791 goda, oktiabria 5 dnia prestavl'shagosia v vere k bogu, v liubvi k otechestvu, v zhelanii blag rodu chelovecheskomu; muzha vsemi vysokimi titlami, no pache krotostiiu siiavshago; pokrovitelia nauk, pobedonostsa, mirotvortsa; vsem prosveshchennym, vsem blagorodnym dusham vozhdelennago, pochtennago, prisnopamiatnogo ([Moscow, 1791]);

Plach' i uteshenie Rossii k e.i.v. Pavlu Pervomu samoderzhtsu vserossiiskomu ([Moscow], 1796).

TRANSLATIONS: Virgil, *Enei. Geroicheskaia poema* (Saint Petersburg: Akademiia nauk, 1770; enlarged, 1781–1786);

John Milton, *Poteriannyi rai* (Saint Petersburg, 1777).

Vasilii Petrovich Petrov

Vasilii Petrovich Petrov was a leading writer during the reign of Catherine II and one of the most remarkable figures of the eighteenth-century Russian Parnassus. He was renowned for his odes, which, for the most part, glorify the main events of the period and its heroic military leaders, as well as Catherine, the "Russian Minerva." During his day Petrov's name was also closely associated with Virgil's *Aeneid,* which his contemporaries felt the poet had "mutilitated" in his translation. Petrov was one of the first to sense the decay of the triumphal ode by midcentury, and in his work the poet attempted to renovate the genre. Petrov's muse received the greatest recognition in the first quarter of the nineteenth century, when poets and critics noted the rare degree of erudition, the boldness, and the depth of intellect displayed in his verse.

Petrov is closely associated with Moscow. He was born there in 1736 into a poor clergyman's family and spent his childhood with his mother and sister after his father's early demise. The conditions in which he grew up were typical for many eighteenth-century Russian cultural figures: extreme poverty, a widowed mother who exhausted herself trying to make ends meet, an unsettled lifestyle, and a state of constant anxiety connected to the last unhappy years of Empress Anna's reign and palace revolu-

tions. Petrov retreated from these difficult circumstances into books, and from an early age he manifested an exceptional ability and passion for learning. In 1752 the future poet entered the Slavonic-Greek-Latin Academy, where he displayed the same zeal for learning and devoted all of his free time to the study of languages (besides those required, he also studied ancient Hebrew) and to reading the Greek and Latin classics.

However, the path into the temple of knowledge was not always smooth: in 1753 the seventeen-year-old Petrov was subjected to a flogging for an unknown offense. Though his studies enthralled him, Petrov's sense of personal insult and shamed honor were stronger, and he ran away from the academy to Saint Petersburg, where he found refuge with relatives and spent his time reading Virgil and Homer. However, Petrov soon heard of the retirement of Konstantin Brodovsky, the prefect who had dealt him the insult, and he returned to Moscow and was reinstated in the academy in 1754, despite the displeasure of several of his fellow students. In the upper grades Petrov distinguished himself by the sermons he delivered in the church of the Zaikonospassky Monastery (to which the academy was attached). These well-crafted sermons elicited the jealousy and displeasure of the Psalm instructor, but the academy's new rector valued and supported Petrov. On one occasion he reportedly asked Petrov for the text of one of his sermons, but Petrov revealed that he had improvised it. Much later, in a letter written not long before his death, Petrov assured his wife with his characteristic self-confidence that "Ia ne tol'ko vergilivshchinu, ia i tsitsironovshchinu mogu!" (I can do not only Virgil but Cicero too!). This was not empty boasting: both his contemporaries and literary descendants highly valued his oratorical skill. As the writer and critic P. A. Viazemsky later remarked, Petrov "magis oratoribus quam poetis enumerandus" (should be counted more as an orator than a poet), although even Viazemsky gave Petrov his due as a poet.

Upon finishing his studies in 1760, Petrov was given the position of instructor at the academy. First he taught stylistics, beginning in 1761; then poetry, in 1763; and, from 1767 on, rhetoric. The year 1766 was pivotal in Petrov's career. On the advice of his former schoolmate, N. N. Bantysh-Kamensky, Petrov composed his first ode, *Oda na velikolepnyi karrusel'* (Ode to a Magnificent Carousel), which immediately brought him to the attention of the literary world as well as the court. He was invited to the palace, where Catherine II awarded him a snuffbox containing two hundred gold pieces and granted him the privilege of carrying a sword (the prerogative of nobles). The sensational success of this ode was due to the vividness and freshness of Petrov's images and language. Petrov was a disciple of the "Russian Pindar," Mikhail Lomonosov, who had recently died, and in constructing his ode Petrov followed the principle of Lomonsov's *beau désordre* (beautiful disorder), producing traits characteristic of his subsequent verse: uneven and somewhat archaic language and rather tangled syntax. *Oda na velikolepnyi karrusel'* depicts a jousting tournament at a celebration organized in 1766 by the new empress. The fact that Petrov chose a mock battle as the subject of a triumphant ode was one of the main reasons he was frequently accused of a lack of concern for content. Nonetheless, the success of his first ode encouraged Petrov to continue writing poetry. In 1767 he wrote an ode celebrating Catherine's project for a new law code and his first epistle to the empress.

Petrov continued to teach, combining his work at the academy and giving lessons. His dream to go to Europe to complete his education was on the point of fruition, as several Moscow merchants, the fathers of Petrov's pupils, agreed to give the young teacher a thousand rubles for the trip. But

fate had its own plans for Petrov, and in 1768 he was invited to court in Saint Petersburg and appointed translator for the empress's personal affairs (attached to her *kabinet*) and her personal reader. It is not known to what benefactor the poet owed such an honored position; some have suggested that it was Grigorii Orlov, but it was more probably due to the influence of Catherine's new favorite, Grigorii Potemkin. According to the memorist Mikhail A. Dmitriev, Petrov and Potemkin had been friends since their student years. A mutual love for the classics and philosophy nurtured their friendship; as Petrov described it in his poem *Plach' na konchinu ego svetlosti kniazia Grigor'ia Aleksandrovicha Potemkina* (Lament on the Death of His Grace Grigorii Aleksandrovich Potemkin, 1791), they would argue about the meaning of life through long, cold Moscow nights: "Ty pren'ia vel so mnoi o promysle i roke, / O smerti, bytii i tselom mira toke" (You argued with me about Providence and fate / About death, being, and about the world's entire flow). The courtier and the poet preserved a mutual friendship and trust throughout their lives. When Potemkin left to fight the first Russo-Turkish War in 1769, Petrov served as the epistolary link between the empress and her young favorite.

The year 1769 was Petrov's first year of steady literary activity. He composed odes – *Oda presvetleishei . . . gosudaryne imperatritse Ekaterine Alekseevne . . . na vziat'e Ias i pokorenie vsego Moldavskogo kniazhestva* (Ode to the Most Radiant . . . Lord Empress Ekaterina Alekseevna . . . On the Taking of Iassy and the Subjugation of the Entire Moldavian Principate, 1769), *Oda presvetleishei . . . gosudaryne imp. Ekaterine Vtoroi . . . na pobedu nad turkami, v os'moe leto blagopoluchnogo eia velichestva gosudarstvovaniia rossiiskimi voiskami oderzhhannuiu i na vziatie Khotina* (Ode to the Most Radiant . . . Lord Empress Catherine II . . . on the Victory Over the Turks Gained by Russian Troops and the Taking of Khotin, In the Eighth Year of Her Highness's Successful Rule, 1769) – a *Pismo k ego siiatel'stvu . . . grafu Grigor'iu Grigor'evichu Orlovu ot tituliarnogo Sovetnika Vasil'ia Petrova* (Letter to His Highness . . . Count Grigorii Grigor'evich Orlov from Titular Counsellor Vasilii Petrov, 1769), inscriptions, and a translation of Antoine Thomas. In the same year he also worked on his translation of Virgil's *Aeneid,* the first six cantos of which were published in 1770. The archaic style of Petrov's odes and translation, which followed Trediakovsky's practice, as well as his court position as (in Catherine's words) her "karmannyi stikhotvorets" (pocket poet), elicited sharp criticism from many writers, and especially in the satiric journal *Smes'* (Miscellany). During this period Vasilii

Maikov wrote his epigram "Na perevod 'Eneidy'" (On the Translation of the *Aeneid,* 1770), and in 1771 he parodied the style of Petrov's translation in his mock-heroic poem *Elisei, ili Razdrazhennyi Vakkh* (Elisei, or Bacchus Enraged).

In the *Antidote,* published abroad and anonymously by Catherine in 1770, the empress defended her poet, praising his talent as greater than that of Lomonosov. Her overt protection, Petrov's privileged position, and perhaps his own idiosyncratic approach to poetry all contributed to the poet's isolation from literary society. The poet Mikhail Murav'ev remarked that it was impossible to get access to Petrov and that Petrov never spoke about poetry. Although united by close association with many noteworthy and cultured individuals of the period and possessed of considerable social skills and a wonderful sense of humor (judging from his letters), Petrov, it seems, had no social contact whatsoever with any of the literary figures of his time. The triumphant ode, which by this time had lost its popularity, continued to remain his primary genre. He continued to compose them, neither hearing praise from his fellow poets nor seeming to heed their abuse.

The year 1770 marked a new stage in Petrov's approach to ode writing. Whether due to the criticism of the journals or to his own sense that the ode form had exhausted itself, with the *Oda na pobedy rossiiskogo flota, oderzhannyia nad turetskim* (Ode on the Victory of the Russian Fleet over the Turks, 1770) Petrov began to experiment with the possibilities of the genre and to modify the odic practices associated with Lomonosov. His first experiments were concerned with replacing the classical strophic form with a variety of other verse forms. His innovations extended to content: he no longer constructed his odes as a series of individual pictures, and he replaced the usual descriptive or dramatic beginning with something more meditative; the triumphant ode became closer to the philosophical ode. Several years later, in 1779, Gavriil Derzhavin finally destroyed the canon of the triumphant ode and created a new ode of mixed form. Although, as he asserted, he had taken off "svoim sobstvennym putem" (on his own path), he had undoutedly taken stock of Petrov's work and its demonstration of the possibilities for the further development of the triumphant ode. Petrov's second ode to Count Orlov (1771) is remarkable in this respect. Imbued with a Horatian spirit, it contains strophes that could just as well have belonged to an elegy. In this ode Petrov anticipated Derzhavin, at least in part, by ten years, and the poem provides an interesting parallel to Derzhavin's "Pamiatniku Geroiu" (To a Monument to a Hero, 1781).

Petrov's long-standing dream was finally realized in 1772. With the permission of the empress, he set off for England, although it is unknown whether the poet chose this destination. If it was his choice, then it bespeaks his sensitivity to the cultural trends of the period, since Russian Gallomania was about to give way to Anglomania. Petrov traveled with G. I. Silov, a passionate young mathematician to whom the poet served, to some degree, as a mentor. The three-year period Petrov spent in England was a time of intensive work. Silov described Petrov to Catherine as a man who encouraged others to study by his own example. Petrov, besides being fluent in French and German, soon learned English and began to work on a translation of John Milton's *Paradise Lost* (1667).

However, the poet did not abandon his own work. While in London, Petrov composed a series of poetic epistles, as well as the epic poem *Na pobedy rossiiskogo voinstva* (On the Victories of Russian Troops, 1772). It is probable that Petrov had become acquainted with Nikolai Novikov's *Opyt istoricheskogo slovaria o rossiiskikh pisateliakh* (Attempt at a Historical Dictionary of Russian Writers, 1772) either in London or on the eve of his departure and had read the extremely unflattering description of his poetry. In response Petrov composed the satiric epistle "K . . . iz Londona" (To . . . from London; collected in his *Sochineniia,* 1811), addressed to Novikov, in which the poet provides a somewhat caustic analysis of the dictionary's principles of composition.

Literary projects did not stop Petrov from establishing close acquaintances with many noteworthy Russians who were in London at the time, including A. A. Samborsky, pastor of the Russian embassy's church; N. S. Mordvinov, enlightened patron of the arts and later admiral, with whom Petrov became friends for the rest of his life; and the Russian ambassador A. S. Musin-Pushkin. Petrov also made connections with such English notables as John Forster, John Paradise, and the Bentham family. His friendship with these people, especially with Paradise, allowed him to delve more seriously into English politics and culture. Besides Milton, Petrov became interested in the work of Alexander Pope, whose influence can be seen in Petrov's epistles from the period.

In fall 1773 Petrov left London to accompany the Duchess of Kingston to Rome and returned to London in July of the following year. Petrov rejoined Silov, and they soon received notice from

Catherine to return to Russia. Their request to prolong their stay was not granted, and in fall 1774 they set off for Russia by way of France and Germany. Petrov had probably arrived in Russia by early 1775, "ne ranen i ne branen" (neither wounded nor scolded), as he would jokingly say.

Upon his return Petrov was designated court librarian with a salary of twelve hundred rubles a year. Several times a year the poet "pozdravliaet" (would congratulate), as he put it, the empress and the military heroes Orlov, P. A. Rumiantsev, and Potemkin with odes, as he continued his experimentations in the genre. The language of his odes became even more archaic, their images more dense. Petrov completed his prose translation of Milton, which was published in 1777; according to Stepan Shevyrev, writing in 1862, even as late as the 1860s this translation remained "odnoi iz liubimykh knig nashego prostogo naroda" (one of the favorite books of our simple folk). Petrov continued to work on his translation of Virgil, which was published in its entirety between 1781 and 1786.

Petrov's health deteriorated during these years. His son related that on one occasion, when doctors predicted his demise, Petrov ordered that he be taken to Moscow. Once there, he made and took some sort of remedy, quickly recuperated, and then returned to Saint Petersburg. In 1780 he was nevertheless forced into retirement due to ill health. He left for his estate, Troitskoe, in the province of Orlov, having been granted the rank of collegiate councillor, with its corresponding salary as his pension. There Petrov lived out his life surrounded by his family. The poet occupied himself with educating his children and with agriculture (using English methods learned on his trip) and taught and instructed the peasant children, putting into practice the Horatian ideal of the country life in fashion at the time. In the winter he would travel with his family to Moscow to visit friends and to work at the library of the Slavonic-Greek-Latin Academy. Although he had withdrawn from society, Petrov kept up his connections with the court. He corresponded with Catherine, considering himself still in her service, and with his former diligence he continued to compose odes, epistles, and minor verse. In 1783 he was chosen a member of the Russian Academy, although he declined to participate in its activities because of his involvement with his own literary work.

In these later years Petrov composed odes that were more traditional and "correct"; he returned to the classical odic strophe, varying it only in rare instances, and these odes have greater clarity and simplicity than his earlier work. In the 1780s, however, Derzhavin became firmly and exclusively ensconced at the top of the Russian Parnassus, and by the end of the 1790s, Petrov had become a relic of the bygone epoch of classicism.

In the last years of his life Petrov suffered many losses. In 1791 Potemkin died, and Petrov responded with the *Plach' na konchinu ego svetlosti kniazia . . . Potemkina* (Lament on the Death of Prince . . . Potemkin, 1791), which both contemporaries and subsequent generations have considered to be his best work. In March 1795 Petrov suffered another loss with the death of one of his sons, Nikolai. His unpretentious "Na smert' moego syna" (On the Death of My Son, 1795) projects the simplicity of human grief and the poet's spiritual strength. Upon receiving news of Catherine's death in November 1796, Petrov suffered a stroke. Despite his illness, he composed his most morose and complex poem, *Plach' i uteshenie Rossii* (Russia's Lament and Consolation, 1796), which was addressed to the newly enthroned Paul I. In spring 1797 the sick, aged poet set off for Moscow with an ode of greeting for the coronation of the new emperor, in part to ensure the continuation of his pension.

In his last years Petrov often suffered from nervous attacks. He would pace his study for hours, composing poetry, laughing if the verses were happy and crying if they were sad. To the end he did not alter his accustomed way of life. According to his son, Petrov only slept for one hour a day and worked a great deal. His unquenchable desire for knowledge inspired the sixty-year-old poet to learn modern Greek. Petrov died on 4 December 1799. During the hours before he died he ordered that nothing be changed in the normal activities of the household, saying that his departure from this life was only part of the natural flow of events. He made his children promise to preserve their love for fatherland and virtue.

In his personal and creative life Petrov, more than any other figure in Russian classicism, embodied the ideal of the classical poet. His closeness to the court, friendship with Potemkin, and his free creativity all came easily to Petrov, without conflict, insult, or dissatisfaction. He conceived of poetry as following classical exemplars and fixed antique models. For Petrov, adhering to classical models primarily meant following the precedent of ancient Greece and Rome, and not that of western European classicism. Perhaps for this reason one of the favorite genres of the Russian eighteenth century — the spiritual ode — is almost completing lacking in Petrov's oeuvre. Petrov went his own independent way and had no imitators, no students, and no successors.

It was only later, with the generation of Konstantin Batiushkov and Aleksandr Pushkin, that Petrov's talent belatedly received due recognition. For Batiushkov, Petrov was without question a great lyric poet; for Pushkin, Viazemsky, and others, Petrov figured among the best poets of the previous century. Poets in Pushkin's era especially valued Petrov's language, from which they drew as from an inexhaustible well, and Petrov's odic style had a visible effect on Pushkin's late works. Petrov's contribution to Russian culture consists of not only his experiments in language and genre but also the vivid record he left of Catherine's brilliant age. Petrov was the kind of poet without which an epoch cannot be imagined but who passes away along with it.

References:

L. G. Barag, "O lomonosovskoi shkole v russkoi poezii XVIII veka (V. Petrov)," *Uchenye zapiski kafedry literatury i iazyka Minskogo pedagogicheskogo instituta,* 1 (1940): 68–92;

Anthony G. Cross, "Printing at Nicolaev, 1793–1803," *Transactions of the Cambridge Bibliographical Society,* 6, no. 3 (1974);

Cross, "Vasilii Petrov v Anglii 1772–1774," *XVIII vek,* 11 (1976): 229–246;

Ivan I. Dmitriev, *Vzgliad na moiu zhizn'* (Moscow: M. A. Dmitriev, 1866);

Mikhail A. Dmitriev, *Melochi iz zapasa moei pamiati* (Moscow: Grachev, 1869);

Grigorii A. Gukovsky, "Iz istorii russkoi ody XVIII v.," *Poetika,* 2 (1927): 129–147;

Ia. V. Petrov, "Zhizn' V. P. Petrova," *Sorevnovatel' prosveshcheniia i blagotvoreniia,* 1 (1818): 116–138;

Stepan P. Shevyrev, "Petrov. Perevody ego s inostrannykh iazykov, ody i poslaniia," in his *Lektsii o russkoi literature, chitannye v Parizhe v 1862 godu* (Saint Petersburg, 1884), pp. 180–184;

Il'ia Shliapkin, "V. P. Petrov, 'karmannyi' stikhotvorets Ekateriny II 1736–1799," *Istoricheskii vestnik,* 17 (1885): 381–405.

Platon
(Petr Egorovich Levshin)
(29 June 1737 – 11 November 1812)

K. A. Papmehl
University of Western Ontario

SELECTED BOOKS: *Pouchitel'nye slova pri vysochaishem dvore e. i. v. . . . gosudaryni Ekateriny Alekseevny* (Saint Petersburg: Academiia nauk, 1764);

Pozdravleniia ego imp. vysochestvu, ot uchitelia ego bogosloviia, ieromonahka Platona ([Saint Petersburg: Akademiia nauk, 1764]);

Prodolzhenie [pervoe] Pouchitel'nykh slov . . . (Saint Petersburg: Akademiia nauk, 1764);

Pravoslavnoe uchenie, ili Sokrashchennaia khristianskaia bogosloviia, dlia upotrebleniia . . . tsesarevicha i velikogo kniazia Pavla Petrovicha (Saint Petersburg: Akademiia nauk, [1765]); translated by R. Pinkerton as *The Present State of the Greek Church in Russia* (Edinburgh, 1814; reprinted, New York: AMS Press, 1973);

Prodolzhenie [vtoroe] Pouchitel'nykh slov . . . (Saint Petersburg: Akademiia nauk, 1765);

Prodolzhenie [tret'e] Pouchitel'nykh slov . . . (Saint Petersburg: Akademiia nauk, 1765);

Kratkii katikhizis dlia obucheniia malykh detei pravoslavnomu khristianskomu zakonu (Saint Petersburg: Akademiia nauk, 1766);

Prodolzhenie [chetvertoe] Pouchitel'nykh slov . . . (Saint Petersburg: Akademiia nauk, 1766);

Piatoe prodolzhenie Pouchitel'nykh slov . . . (Moscow: Moskovskii universitet, 1767);

Prodolzhenie shestoe Pouchitel'nykh slov . . . (Saint Petersburg: Akademiia nauk, 1769);

Slovo pri sluchae sovershaemykh molitv nad grobom Petra Velikogo, po prichine oderzhannoi flotom Rossiiskim nad Ottomanskim flotom vo Arkhipelage slavnoi pobedy, 1770 goda iiunia 24 dnia (Saint Petersburg: Akademiia nauk, 1770);

Prodolzhenie sed'moe Pouchitel'nykh slov . . . (Saint Petersburg: Akademiia nauk, circa 1770);

Prodolzhenie osmoe Pouchitel'nykh slov . . . (Saint Petersburg: Akademiia nauk, 1772);

Sokrashchennyi katikhizis ([Saint Petersburg: Akademiia nauk, 1773]);

Platon, metropolitan of Moscow

Pouchitel'nyia slova . . . s 1763 goda po 1778 god . . . , volumes 1–5 (Moscow: Senate Press, 1779–1780), volumes 6–10 (Moscow: F. Gippius, 1780–1782), volume 11 (Moscow: 1784), volume 12 (Moscow: Novikov, 1786), volumes 13–15 (Moscow: Synod, 1792), volumes 16–18 (Moscow: Kh. Ridiger & Kh. Klaudia, 1797–1798), and volumes 19–20 (Moscow: Synod, 1803, 1806);

Zhitie prepodobnogo i bogonosnogo ottsa nashego Sergiia, Radonezhskago chudotvortsa (Moscow: Novikov, 1784);

Kratkaia tserkovnaia rossiiskaia istoria, 2 volumes (Moscow: Synod, 1805);

Instruktsiiam blagochinnym iereiam, ili protoiereiam ([Moscow: Moskovskii Universitet], n.d.).

OTHER: "Zapiski o zhizni mitropolita Platona," in *Avtobiografia Platona, mitropolita Moskovskogo,* edited by Sergei K. Smirnov (Moscow, 1887);

"Putevye zapiski preosv. Mitropolita Platona . . . o puteshestvii v Iaroslavl', Kostromu i Vladimir 1792 goda," in *Zhizn' moskovskogo Mitropolita Platona,* edited by I. M. Snegirev (Moscow, 1890), pp. 151–168;

"Rech' po sovershenii Avgusteishego [E. I. V. Aleksandra I] koronovania, [15 September, 1801]," in *Zhizn' moskovskogo Mitropolita Platona,* edited by Snegirev (Moscow, 1890), pp. 177–181;

"Puteshestvie Mitropolita Platona v Kiev i po drugim russkim gorodam v 1804 g.," in *Zhizn' moskovskogo Mitropolita Platona,* edited by Snegirev (Moscow, 1890), pp. 107–148.

SELECTED PERIODICAL PUBLICATION – UNCOLLECTED: "Zapiski o zhizni Platona Mitropolita Moskovskogo im samim pisannye i okonchennye Samuilom Kostromskim Episkopom, 1810–1812," edited by Sergei K. Smirnov, *Dushepoleznoe chtenie,* 8–9 (1887).

Of humble social origin, but endowed with remarkable and varied intellectual and artistic talents, a brilliant orator, a leading educator and administrator, Platon began his ecclesiastical career in the mid eighteenth century, eventually rising to the top of the Russian church hierarchy. Concurrently, he made his mark on the broader cultural scene as an enlightened prelate, devoid of superstition or any trace of religious obscurantism, one capable of finding a common ground between the philosophical currents of his age and sincere religious belief. Appointed at age twenty-six as tutor in religion to Grand Duke Pavel Petrovich, the son and heir of Catherine the Great, he was closely associated for several years with the court at Saint Petersburg. This association exposed him to the most advanced current intellectual trends and provided opportunities for close contact with several prominent contemporaries, frequently resulting in lasting bonds of friendship. These ranged from his royal pupil, the future Emperor Paul I, to influential statesmen such as Nikita Panin and Grigorii Potemkin, to such leading literary figures as Aleksandr Sumarokov, Denis Fonvizin, Ekaterina Dashkova, Nikolai Novikov, and Gavriil Derzhavin. He met and de-

bated with Denis Diderot and was known to Voltaire. He acted as a guide to Prince Henry of Prussia (brother of Frederick II) and to Emperor Joseph II during their visits to Russia and was befriended by European royalty. These contacts represented a major factor in his intellectual development, although they did not lead to any significant involvement or influence in the political arena. His principal contribution to Russian literature of the period was through his sermons and speeches, written not in traditional Church Slavonic but in the new Russian literary language, *Slavenorossiiskii* (Slaveno-Russian), as contemporaries called it. Over six hundred of these were published in his lifetime, and some were translated into European and Asiatic languages.

The future Platon was born on 29 June 1737 as Petr Egorovich Levshinov (later abbreviated to Levshin). He was the second of four sons of a local sexton, who later became a priest serving in various village churches in the Moscow area, eventually retiring in Moscow. Although a simple man, born and bred in the peasant milieu, Platon's father appreciated the importance of a good education and spared no effort to give it to his sons, all of whom pursued ecclesiastical careers.

The future metropolitan received his basic formal education at the Slavonic-Greek-Latin Academy in Moscow, the highest institution of ecclesiastical learning in the country at the time. He studied there from 1746 to 1757, distinguishing himself as an able and hardworking scholar who augmented his studies with wide-ranging extracurricular reading. While still in his final year, he was appointed teacher at the academy, where he gave a successful series of lectures on the catechism to the general public in 1757–1758. The lectures were published in volume eight (1780) of his collected works, *Pouchitel'nye slova . . . s 1763 goda po 1778 god . . .* (1779–1806). In 1758 he was appointed teacher of rhetoric at the seminary attached to the Holy Trinity and Saint Sergius *Lavra* (laura, or principal monastery) at Sergiev Posad (known as Zagorsk from 1918 to 1991). There he took his monastic vows, assuming the name Platon, on 14 August 1758. Less than a year later he was ordained hieromonk (monastic priest) and appointed prefect (deputy rector) of the seminary. In 1761 he was promoted to rector and professor of theology.

Shortly after the accession of Catherine the Great, Platon's career took a new and unexpected turn. Following two encounters with the new empress at the *lavra,* he was appointed tutor in religion to the heir apparent, Grand Duke Pavel Petrovich, and moved to Saint Petersburg to take up his new duties in August 1763. These were not at all time-consuming, so that Platon was able to fill his ample leisure time with private study and preparation of sermons to be delivered at the imperial chapel and in a few other Saint Petersburg churches. These sermons soon established his reputation as an orator and enlightened priest. In 1764 the first volume of his sermons was published at the Akademia nauk (Academy of Sciences) press, to be followed by seven more published between 1764 and 1772. In 1765 the course of religious instruction he gave to Grand Duke Pavel Petrovich was published under the title *Pravoslavnoe uchenie, ili Sokrashchennaia khristianskaia bogosloviia* (The Orthodox Doctrine, or A Short Course in Christian Theology). This work, essentially an analysis and exposition of the Nicene Creed, soon became known beyond the borders of the Russian Empire. It was translated into German (1770), Latin (1774), Greek (1786), and English (1814).

Platon's thrice-weekly lessons with his royal pupil had lapsed by the summer of 1765, even though his appointment did not officially end until 1773. His association with the imperial court accorded him wide exposure and contacts with high-ranking Russian personalities as well as with many prominent foreigners, among them Diderot, whom he met in 1773 in Saint Petersburg. In 1766 he was invited, together with the bishops of Tver (Gavriil) and Pskov (Innokentii), to comment on the draft of Catherine's famous *Nakaz* (Instruction) to the Legislative Commission. In the same year he was appointed archimandrite of the Holy Trinity and Saint Sergius Monastery, a position he retained for life. With it came the membership in the Holy Synod, the ruling authority of the Russian church.

In 1770, Catherine elevated Platon to the episcopal rank, appointing him archbishop of Tver. In the same year he gave one of his best-known sermons at the tomb of Peter the Great to celebrate the naval victory over the Turkish fleet at Chesme. A French translation of this sermon was presented to Voltaire by Princess Dashkova in the spring of 1771.

During the five years of Platon's tenure as archbishop of Tver he was obliged to spend much of his time at Saint Petersburg, at meetings of the synod and at court. This period marks a definite cooling-off in the empress's attitude toward him, caused principally by Platon's closeness to the grand duke, who was coming of age and could be seen as the rightful heir to his father's throne. Early in 1775, without any prior warning, Platon was told to take over the Moscow eparchy, a move that he

interpreted as an overt sign of the monarch's displeasure. He applied himself to his new task with zeal, introducing reforms that brought generally positive results, most prominently in the realm of educating the clergy. One event of important literary and historical significance was Platon's role as religious examiner and censor in the investigation of Novikov and his Masonic circle in the mid 1780s. Platon exonerated Novikov from any suspicion of heresy and raised few objections to the content of the Masonic publications. Since the Moscow Freemasons were suspected by the empress of illicit links with the grand duke and a hostile foreign power (Prussia), Platon's lenient attitude toward them could not but deepen the estrangement between Catherine and her former protégé.

By 1780 a total of 180 of Platon's sermons had been published, an average of around 11 per year since 1764. His production in this field gradually increased to just over 16 per year, ending in 1806. In all, 603 of his sermons are included in the twenty volumes of his collected works. They range from homilies preached at church services to major orations with political overtones delivered on such major state occasions as coronations, funerals, and victory celebrations.

According to P. Zavedeev's history of Russian homiletics, Platon was the leading exponent of what he calls the moral-practical school, dominant in Russia in the second half of the eighteenth century. His sermons dealt primarily with moral and philosophical problems, as well as with combating current trends, whether secular or religious, that he found inimical to orthodoxy. A recurring theme in Platon's sermons is the harmony and connection between the duties of a Christian and those of a monarch's loyal subject. While approving of education in general, Platon held honesty and virtue to be the most precious fruits of all learning. One topical theme that Platon addresses on much the same lines as his contemporary and personal acquaintance, the playwright Fonvizin, is the fashion among the Russian nobility of employing foreign tutors for their children. In a sermon delivered in the late 1770s, Platon castigated this practice: "[Roditeli] poruchaiut liubeznyi zalog liudiam neizvestnym, prishel'tsam, nikakikh v sebe sledov chestnosti ne imeiushchim i chemu oni obuchaiut? Govorit' inostrannymi iazykami, pliasaniiu, kak obrashchat' mech', chtob v sluchae strastnogo zhara mog ego upotrebit' na pronzenie drugogo. A obuchenie zakonu gde? A iz"iasnenie sushchestvennykh poniatii dobra i zla gde? A vyrazumenie nastoiashchego chelovecheskogo blagopoluchiia i neshchastiia gde? Sii predostavliaiutsia sud'be" ([Parents] entrust their children to persons unknown, newcomers, devoid of even a trace of honesty. And what do these people teach? To speak foreign languages, to dance, to wield the sword so as to pierce an opponent with it. But where is the study of religion? Where is the explanation of the basic concepts of good and evil? Where is the understanding of man's true well-being and that of his misfortunes? All this is left to the vagaries of fate). A general feature found in Platon's sermons is a quaint blend of Christian images and concepts with those borrowed from classical mythology, mirroring the concurrent trend in secular Russian literature.

Platon's sermons generally received high praise from his contemporaries, beginning with Catherine, who more than once praised him for his "udivitel'nyi dar slova" (marvelous gift of eloquence). Sumarokov labeled Platon a disciple of Saint John Chrysostom and asserted that he consistently delighted his listeners and readers. Sumarokov also noted Platon's tendency to shine as an orator in his early sermons, while the later ones (Sumarokov died in 1777) show more of the "Christian simplicity and spiritual conviction with which he himself is imbued."

In the realm of language and style, Platon was a faithful adherent of Lomonosov's *Rossiiskaia grammatika* (Russian Grammar, 1755) and, perhaps to a less obvious extent, his theory of three styles. His writings show little evolution in this regard, so that his late works – notably the *Kratkaia tserkovnaia rossiiskaia istoria* (Short History of the Russian Church, 1805) – with their mid-eighteenth-century flavor, must have seemed out of date to contemporaries in this respect. Lexically, his sermons are reminiscent of the language of Fonvizin's "positive" characters, such as Starodum in *Nedorosl'* (The Minor, 1783). This similarity is an example of the cross-fertilization between the secular and spiritual branches of Russian literature at the time, also reflected in the desire to create a Slaveno-Russian literary language that would combine the lexical richness of Church Slavonic with the flexibility of modern vernacular.

In 1787, during one of her rare visits to Moscow, Catherine raised Platon to the rank of metropolitan. This promotion came without any prior warning in the middle of the service he was conducting at the Assumption Cathedral in the Kremlin. Any joy Platon may have felt on this occasion was marred by the fact that some of his junior colleagues had been accorded this honor a few years

Title page for Platon's ecclesiastical history

earlier, another sign of disfavor as far as he was concerned.

In 1792, responding to Platon's repeated requests, Catherine gave him permission to move his permanent residence to the *lavra,* beginning a period of semiretirement that was to last for nearly two decades, until 1811. Already in 1782 he had begun to build himself a retreat outside the main monastery, which he named Vifaniia (Bethany). It subsequently became a monastery in its own right and home to a seminary; it was also Platon's home in his declining years.

Paul I's accession in 1796 and his reversal of most of Catherine's policies did little, if anything, to improve Platon's relationship with the court at Saint Petersburg. Along with other friends and associates of the new emperor, he fell victim to the latter's erratic and unpredictable behavior and actually lost all personal contact with his former pupil after May 1798. He learned of Paul's death indirectly, through the official announcement of the accession of Alexander I in March 1801. In September

Platon officiated at the coronation of the new emperor and preached an eloquent, if not entirely original, sermon that received wide publicity and praise in western Europe as well as in Russia. Its English translation, by Dr. Matthew Guthrie, a longtime resident of Saint Petersburg, was published on the front page of the London *Chronicle* for 14–16 January 1802.

Platon's health progressively deteriorated, but he was able to complete in 1803 his *Kratkaia tserkovnaia rossiiskaia istoria* (Short History of the Russian Church). Published in two volumes, the work covers the period from approximately the mid tenth century to 1700 and ranks highly among contemporary historical works. It is based almost entirely on primary sources critically evaluated, and while concerned mostly with events within the church, it places them in a political and social perspective. At the same time the author carefully avoids any subjects that might be considered sensitive in the political context of his own time. Thus *Kratkaia tserkovnaia rossiikaia istoria* ends with the death of the last Moscow patriarch, leaving the task of describing the Petrine reforms to someone else. The *Kratkaia tserkovnaia rossiiskaia istoria* was conceived of and used as a textbook for religious schools. The student of the development of the Russian literary language might find in Platon's prose, alongside obsolescent grammatical and syntactic constructions, some lexical elements linking him to Admiral Shishkov and his Beseda liubitelei russkogo slova (Colloquium of Lovers of the Russian Word) of the early 1810s.

Another of Platon's works that might be classified as historical is his autobiography, begun circa 1792 and completed in 1810. The final two years of his life were written by one of his disciples, Samuil Zapol'sky-Platonov, later bishop of Kostroma. As a literary work it ranks alongside the *Kratkaia tserkovnaia rossiiskaia istoria* as an example of the Russian language of the period. Finally, in a closely related genre, Platon wrote two travelogues describing his journeys – he called them *palomnichestva* (pilgrimages) – to the religious centers of central Russia (Vladimir, Iaroslavl, Kostroma) in 1792 and to Kiev in 1804. Like the *Kratkaia tserkovnaia rossiiskaia istoria* they are addressed primarily to an ecclesiastical audience, with a strong didactic element.

In trying to assess Platon's position and significance within the general framework of Russian eighteenth-century culture, it is necessary to refer to his lasting contributions to the education of the Russian clergy. As archbishop of Tver, Platon had made the religious seminaries and the education of the clergy under his jurisdiction the prime object of his concern. But it was after taking over the Moscow eparchy that he made a deep and lasting impression. Probably as a result of his own personal exposure to learned foreigners, as well as his contacts with the Russian educated elite, he concentrated his efforts on changing the prevailing image of the Russian clergy as backward and ignorant of the realities of the contemporary world. To this end he revised the curricula of the Moscow Academy and the seminaries within his jurisdiction, introducing the teaching of foreign languages (Greek, French, and German) and of such secular subjects as history, geography, and classical mythology.

For the same reason Platon placed a high priority on proficiency in Latin – at the time a recognized international language – as a tool with which to defend orthodoxy in debates with representatives of other Christian faiths. He set the example by using Latin extensively in correspondence with his colleagues and ecclesiastical subordinates. In his insistence on Latin in the education of the clergy, an idea implanted by his early mentors, Platon found himself falling behind the times, especially toward the end of his career. For better or worse, his influence in a large measure accounts for the survival of the latinizing tendencies within the Russian church well into the nineteenth century.

In 1806 Platon suffered a stroke, which for a time left him partly paralyzed. His general health deteriorating further, he went into full retirement at the monastery of Vifaniia. The final months of his life coincided with the Napoleonic invasion of 1812. He lived long enough to learn of the French retreat from Moscow, and, after another stroke, he died at Vifaniia on 11 November 1812.

Assuming that one can legitimately speak of a spiritual or ecclesiastical branch of eighteenth-century Russian literature, Platon must be seen as its leading representative. As perceptively noted by the late Georgii Florovsky, Platon embodied all the cultural conflicts and contradictions of eighteenth-century Russia arising from its changing attitude toward the West. A champion and propagator of Latin in religious education, he was nevertheless openly hostile toward the "Latin" (Roman Catholic) church. Both as a preacher and as an educator he tried to bridge the gap between the ideas and fashions currently accepted by the educated segment of society, on the one hand, and strict adherence to the precepts of Russian Orthodox Christianity, on the other. Whatever the actual measure of his success in this regard, his contribution to the cultural reunification of Russian society, split by the effects of the reforms of Peter the Great, seems undeniable.

Letters:

Pis'ma Platona, mitropolita Moskovskogo, k preoviashchennym Amvrosiu i Avgustinu, edited by Sergei K. Smirnov (N.p., 1870?);

"Pis'ma Platona, mitropolita Moskovskogo, k preosviashchennomu Avgustinu," in *Pravoslavnoe obozrenie* (Moscow, 1870), pp. 89–136;

"Perepiska Moskovskogo mitropolita Platona s grafami I. P. Saltykovym i Iu. A. Golovkinym," *Russkii Arkhiv,* 2 (Spring 1897): 108–109.

Biographies:

Ivan M. Snegirev, *Zhizn' moskovskogo Mitropolita Platona* (Moscow, 1856);

K. A. Papmehl, *Metropolitan Platon of Moscow (Petr Levshin 1737–1812): The Enlightened Prelate, Scholar and Educator* (Newtonville, Mass.: Oriental Research Partners, 1983).

References:

A. A. Beliaev, *Mitropolit Platon kak stroitel' natsional'noi dukhovnoi shkoly* (Sergiev posad, 1913);

Georgii Florovsky, *Puti russkogo bogosloviia* (Paris: YMCA Press, 1937); translated by Robert L. Nichols as *Ways of Russian Theology, Collected Works,* volumes 5–6 (Vaduz: Buchervertreibsanstalt, n.d.);

Petr P. Pekarsky, "Razbor sochinenia g. Smirnova," in *Istoriia Troitskoi Lavrskoi seminarii* (Saint Petersburg, 1869);

V. P. Vinogradov, *Platon i Filaret, mitropolity Moskovskie* (Sergiev posad, 1913);

P. Zavedeev, *Istoriia russkogo propovednichestva ot XVII v. do nastoiashchego vremeni* (Tula: N. L. Sokolov, 1879).

Simeon Polotsky

(1629 – 25 August 1680)

Ronald Vroon
University of California, Los Angeles

BOOKS: *Zhezl pravleniia na pravitel'stvo myslennago stada pravoslavno-rossiiskiia tserkve* . . . (Moscow: Pechatnyi dvor, 1667);

Pouchenie o blagogoveinom stoianii vo khrame bozhii . . . and *Pouchenie ot iereov sushchym pod nimi v passtve ikh o ezhe prebyvati im vo vsiakom blagochestii i ne peti besovskikh pesnei* . . . ([Moscow: Pechatnyi dvor, 1674]);

Psaltir' tsaria i proroka Davida, khudozhestvom rifmotvornym ravnomerno slogi, i soglasnokonechno, po razlichnym stikhov rodom prelozhennaia and *Mesiatseslov* (Moscow: Tipografiia Verkhniaia, 1680);

Obed dushevnyi (Moscow: Tipografiia Verkhniaia, 1681);

Vecheria dushevnaia (Moscow: Tipografiia Verkhniaia, 1683);

Istoriia ili deistvie evangelskiia pritchi o bludnom syne (N.p., "1685" [mid eighteenth century]); republished as *Skolok s komedii iz pritchi o bludnom syne, prezh sego pechatannoi v 1685* (Moscow, 1795).

Editions: *Orel Rossiiskii. Tvorenie Simeona Polotskogo,* edited by N. A. Smirnov, Pamiatniki drevnei pis'mennosti, 133 (Petrograd: [Obshchestvo liubitelei drevnei pis'mennosti], 1915);

Izbrannye sochineniia, Literaturnye pamiatniki, edited by Igor P. Eremin (Moscow & Leningrad: Akademiia nauk, 1953);

Virshi, edited by V. K. Bylinin and L. U. Zvonareva (Minsk: Mastatskaia literatura, 1990).

OTHER: *Bukvar' iazyka slovenska,* edited by Polotsky (Moscow: Pechatnyi dvor, 1667);

Bukvar' iazyka slovenska, sirech' nachalo oucheniia detem, khotiashchym uchitisia chteniiu pisanii, edited by Polotsky (Moscow: Tipografiia Verkhniaia, 1679);

Testament, ili Zavet, Vasiliia, tsaria grecheskago, k synu ego Lvu Filosofu, edited by Polotsky (Moscow: Tipografiia Verkhniaia, 1680);

Simeon Polotsky

Istori[ia], ili povest' sviatago i prepodobnago ottsa nashego Ioanna, izhe ot damaska, o prepodobnom ottse Varlaame pustynnozhiteli: i o Ioasafe tsare Indiistem, edited by Polotsky (Moscow: Tipografiia Verkhniaia, 1680);

"Komidiia pritchi o bludnem syne," in *Drevniaia rossiiskaia vivliofika,* 10 volumes, edited by Nikolai I. Novikov (Moscow: Kompaniia tipograficheskaia, 1789), VIII: 34–60;

"O Navkhodonosore tsare, o tele zlate i o triekh otrotsekh, v peshchi ne sozhzhennykh," in *Drevniaia rossiiskaia vivliofika,* VIII: 158–169;

"Iz Sochinenii Simeona Polotskogo," in *Istoricheskaia khrestomatiia tserkovnoslavianskogo i drevnerusskogo iazykov,* compiled by Fedor Buslaev (Moscow: Universitetskaia tipografiia, 1861), pp. 1189–1214 – includes the abridged preface and Psalm 1 from *Psaltir' tsaria i proroka Davida*; "Glava mednaia glagolavshaia," "Obraz," "Slovo bozhie," and twelve other poems from "Vertograd mnogotsvenyi"; and "Stikhi na rozhdestvo Khristovo ko gosudaryni tsaritse ot gosudaria tsarevicha" and other abridged selections from "Rifmologion";

"Simeon Polotsky," in *Virshi. Sillabicheskaia poeziia XVII–XVIII vekov,* edited by Pavel Berkov, Biblioteka poeta, malaia seriia 3 (Leningrad: Sovetskii pisatel', 1935), pp. 97–119 – includes excerpts from six poems in "Rifmologion," among them the verse preface "Privetstvo B. M. Khitrovo ot ego vnuchka" and "Glas poslednii ko Gospodu Bogu tsaria Aleksiia Mikhailovicha," and twenty-nine poems from "Vertograd mnogotsvetnyi," including "Ikona Bogoroditsy," "Kupetsstvo," and "Iazyk";

"Simeon Polatski," in *Khrestamatyia pa starazhytnai belaruskai litaratury,* edited by Aleksandr Fomich Korshunaŭna Vuchebna-pedahahichnae vydavetstva Ministerstva asvety BSSR, 1959), pp. 337–356 – includes "Stikhi uteshnyi k litsu edinomu," "[Pryvital'nyia vershy tsaru Aliakseiu Mikhailavichu]," or "Metry", and "Stisi kraesoglasnii ko . . . velikomu gosudariu tsariu i velikomu kniaziu Aleksiiu Mikhailovichiu . . . otroki grada Polotska, pritekshimi vo tsarstvuiushchii grad Moskvu, glagolanii . . . v leto . . . 1660";

"Simeon Polotsky," in *Iz istorii filosofskoi i obshchestvenno-politicheskoi mysli Belorussii. Izbrannye proizvedeniia XVI – nachala XIX vv.,* edited by Vitalii Andreevich Serbenta and others (Minsk: Izd. AN BSSR, 1962), pp. 228–269 – includes "[Vo tsarstve edin imat' byti]," excerpts from "Glas poslednii ko Gospodu Bogu" and "Slovo k pravoslavnomu i khristoimenitomu zaporozhskomu voinstvu," and forty-five previously unpublished poems from "Vertograd mnogotsvetnyi," including "Srebro," "Bogatii ne udob' vkhodiat v nebo," and "Mir est' kniga";

"Simeon Polotsky," in *Russkaia sillabicheskaia poeziia XVII–XVIII vv.,* edited by Aleksandr Mikhailovich Panchenko, Biblioteka poeta, Bol'shaia seriia (Leningrad: Sovetskii pisatel', 1970), pp. 107–173 – includes 154 poems from "Vertograd mnogotsvetnyi," most of which are first publications, including the cycles "Avgust," "Pokhot'," "Smert'," and "Evangelisty."

SELECTED PERIODICAL PUBLICATIONS – UNCOLLECTED: Aleksandr Ivanovich Beletsky, "Stikhotvoreniia Simeona Polotskogo na temy iz vseobshchei istorii," *Sbornik statei v chest' Vladimira Petrovichha Buzeskula,* Sbornik Khar'kovskogo Istoriko-Filologicheskogo obshchestva, 21 (Kharkov: [pri Imperatorskom Khar'kovskom universitete], 1913–1914), pp. 587–668 – includes Polotsky's "Podpisanie obraza tsaria Konstantina," "Episkop," "Mest' ili otmshchenie," "Tsarie ili kesari Rima vetkhago," and "Tsarie Rima novago";

S. A. Shcheglova, "Deklamatsiia Simeona Polotskogo," *Sbornik statei v chest' akademika Alekseia Ivanovicha Sobolevskogo,* edited by Vladimir Nikolaevich Peretts, *Sbornik Otdeleniia russkogo iazyka i slovesnosti AN SSSR,* 101, no. 3 (1928): 5–9 – includes excerpts from Polotsky's "Stikhi kraesoglasnyi na Rozhdestvo Khristovo, glagolemyi v tserkvi vo slavu Khrista Boga";

Anthony Hippisley, "The Emblem in the Writings of Simeon Polockij," *Slavic and East European Journal,* 15 (Spring 1971): 167–183 – includes Polotsky's "Slovo neslushanie," "Kokosh," "Obrashchenie," "Roptanie," "Smirenomudrie," and "Vynu gorit."

Simeon Polotsky may rightly be regarded as Russia's first professional writer and the first major exponent of a tradition that would link belles lettres directly to the life of the state, its rulers, and its sociocultural development. A skilled orator, learned preacher, prolific versifier, devoted educator, and publisher, he brought his considerable talents to bear on the transformation of Russia from a state transfixed by its traditional ties to Byzantine culture to one that welcomed, however cautiously, the liberalizing influence of the Latin West. He was closely connected with the court of Czar Aleksei Mikhailovich and his successor, Czar Fedor Alekseevich, and contributed significantly to the creation of a cultural milieu that would facilitate the momentous reforms carried out by Peter the Great. At the same time, due to the vagaries of both literary and political history, his poetry did not immediately achieve a place in the canon commensurate with his status in society. While his homiletic works and verse renditions of the Psalms achieved widespread dissemination, the majority of his original poetic works circulated in manuscript form alone. Only in the last four decades have major efforts been made to publish them and to re-assess Simeon's legacy.

It is a mark of the general neglect Simeon has suffered that his birth name was confirmed only in 1988, on the basis of a thorough review of archival evidence by Lidiia Sazonova. He was born Samuil Gavriilovich Sitnianovich in 1629, probably in or around the city of Polotsk. After the death of his father, Hauryl Sitnianovich, his mother married Emial'ian Piatrouski, whose name the poet frequently appended to his own. He assumed the name Simeon many years later, when tonsured as a monk, and after moving to Moscow took on the surname Polotsky ("of Polotsk"), designating his place of origin. It is under the name Simeon Polotsky that he ultimately entered the world of Russian letters.

Of Simeon's early life virtually nothing is known. He was born into an Orthodox Belorussian family and had at least one sister and three half brothers, one of whom was also a monk. At the time of his birth the town of Polotsk, situated in what is now northern Belarus, was still under Polish rule. With a mixed Orthodox and Catholic population, it had historically been the site of political, cultural, and even physical conflict between the two religious constituencies but during peaceable interludes was also a favorable milieu for the transmission of cultural and religious values from the world of post-Tridentine Roman Catholicism to the deeply conservative world of Greco-Slavic Orthodoxy.

Sometime in the late 1630s or early 1640s Simeon left Polotsk and matriculated at the Mohyla Collegium (after 1689 the Mohyla Academy) in Kiev, the most important Orthodox educational institution of its time. His instructors and mentors at the academy included several representatives of what might be called the "Orthodox enlightenment": Lazar Baranovych, later appointed bishop of Chernigov; Innokentii Gizel', archimandrite of the Kiev Caves Monastery and author of one of the earliest Russian histories; and Ioannikii Haliatovs'ky, one of the foremost preachers of his day. The collegium, born of the merger of two monastery schools, had been established by Metropolitan Petro Mohyla in 1632 to counter the influence of the Jesuit colleges in Ukraine, which were enjoying considerable success in attracting Orthodox youth to Catholicism. Mohyla's collegium attempted to compete by adopting both the curriculum and the pedagogical practices of the Jesuit institutions. In doing so it instilled an appreciation for the learned disciplines cultivated in the Latin West but by the same token invited the very "adulteration" it wished to combat.

Simeon's subsequent career is ample evidence of such adulteration. Upon leaving the collegium in the late 1640s he proceeded to another institution, probably the Jesuit Academy in Vilnius, and continued his studies there until at least 1653. One of the more interesting pieces of evidence concerning his presence at the institution is a school mystery play written in the author's hand and signed "V chest' smerti Gospodnei: nekii bazilianin, v Vil'ne, na Pashku" (In Honor of the Lord's Death: a Certain Basilian, in Vilnius, for Easter). Of particular significance, in addition to the mention of Vilnius, is the poet's reference to himself as a "Basilian." Later in his life he identified himself in a handwritten ex libris as a member of the "Ordo Sancti Basilii Magni," a Catholic order of the Eastern Rite involved in propagandizing Catholicism in heterodox areas of Poland. It is not clear whether Simeon's association with the order was a matter of genuine conviction or a calculated move designed to gain entrance to or enhance his standing at the academy, but it does, in any case, testify to his profound personal contact with the intellectual and spiritual world of Roman Catholicism.

Simeon's training in Kiev and Vilnius was of critical significance in his subsequent development. His notebooks from these early years document his exposure to the seven liberal arts — grammar, rhetoric, dialectics, arithmetic, geometry, astronomy, and music. Particularly significant was his exposure to rhetoric and grammar. The former meant not only Aristotle, Cicero, and Quintilian but also some of the leading exponents of scholastic rhetoric and baroque poetics. There is strong evidence in Simeon's lecture notes and conspectuses that Jacobus Pontanus's *Institutiones poeticae* (1594) served as his introduction to poetics, and that a major representative of the Polish Baroque, Maciej Sarbiewski, served as one of his earliest poetic models. "Grammar" meant training in Latin, which served not only as the paradigm for the study of grammar in general but was also the principal language of instruction at both the Mohyla and Vilnius academies. Simeon's mastery of the language would be of momentous importance both for his worldview and his career: it opened the door to the classics of Western philosophy, science, and spirituality, as well as to leading representatives of neo-Latin literature, and it would later make him indispensable in Muscovite political and ecclesiastical circles. His failure to master Greek, on the other hand, would eventually make him suspect in the eyes of ecclesiastical rivals who favored Russia's traditional Byzantine orientation and were concerned about the inroads that the "Latin heresy" might make in Muscovy.

Sometime after 1653 Simeon returned to Polotsk, which had been overtaken by Russian forces at the outset of the Russo-Polish War (1654–1667). Here, in June 1656, he was shorn a monk in the Orthodox Theophany Monastery, taking Holy Orders shortly thereafter. At about the same time he began teaching in the monastery school, probably on the elementary level. His admission to the Orthodox monastic brotherhood, as his nineteenth-century biographer Ierofei Tatarsky has indicated, must have been motivated in part by his awareness that this was the most appropriate environment for pursuing the twin callings of poetry and pedagogy. As the poet was later to write in the introduction to the manuscript "Rifmologion, ili Stikhoslov" (Rhymebook), one of his major verse collections: "Trudniki slova Pavel pochitaet, / chest' im suguba dati uveshchaet. / Siiu mi polzu dadesia poznati, / po shchedroi Boga zhiva blagodati, / V iunosti verste, egda otrekokhsia / mira i v rizy cherny oblekokhsia. / Temzhe chto pisakh, tshchakhsia to khraniti, / znaia, iako vpred' mozhet v polzu byti." (Paul reveres workers of the word, / he advises us to accord them special honor. / It was given to me to recognize this benefit, / by the generous grace of the living God, / in my youth, when I renounced the world / and dressed myself in a black robe. / By the same token that which I wrote I strove to preserve, / knowing that it might be of use in the future).

The cloister and its school, while hardly rivaling the Kiev Caves Monastery and the Mohyla Collegium, nonetheless could boast several skilled writers, chief among them Ihnatsii Iiaulevich (Ignatii Ievlevich), the hegumen of the monastery and graduate of the Kievan fraternal school that gave birth to the collegium, and Filafei Utchytski (Filofei Utchitsky), who was to become hegumen in 1668. As supporters of the cause of Orthodox enlightenment, they undoubtedly found it expedient to overlook Simeon's temporary engagement with Catholicism, welcoming into their brotherhood a novice who was one of the most educated men of his day.

Within a few weeks of becoming a monk Simeon had the opportunity to display his talents in the most conspicuous way. Czar Aleksei Mikhailovich, now at war with Sweden, passed through Polotsk with his entourage during the first week of July, 1656. For the occasion the brotherhood of the Theophany Monastery prepared a declamation to be recited by twelve schoolboys in the czar's presence. Although the work was a collective effort, scholars generally attribute the final version to Simeon. In late October of the same year Aleksei returned to Polotsk from an unsuccessful siege of Riga and remained there for several days while awaiting the outcome of negotiations in Vilnius with the Polish crown. Once again the monastery brotherhood organized a reception for the czar at which panegyrics composed by Simeon were read. Simeon clearly impressed the czar as a learned and loyal subject, thereby preparing the way for his eventual move to Moscow.

A little over three years later, in the fall of 1659, Aleksei convened a church council to discuss the implications of Patriarch Nikon's unexpected withdrawal from the patriarchal see. Among those with whom he wished to consult was Simeon's father superior, Ihnatsii Iiaulevich. The latter formed a small traveling company – Simeon and a troupe of twelve youths from the Theophany school – to perform new declamations in Moscow. The first performance took place on 19 January 1660 with the recitation of a 162-line paean to the czar, his family, and advisers, composed for the occasion by Simeon. It was followed by declamations performed on February 12 in honor of the name-day of the czar's son, Aleksei Alekseevich, and on March 17 in honor of the czar on his patron saint's feast. Other declamations and dialogues in praise of the monarch and his family were written and perhaps performed during Simeon's nine-month sojourn in Moscow.

With the dismissal of the council in the fall of 1660 the Theophany Monastery delegation returned to Polotsk, and Simeon resumed his teaching activities. Within less than a year war broke out again between Muscovy and Poland, with Polotsk falling to Polish forces in 1661. The Theophany Monastery, the sole Orthodox cloister in the city, lost the privileges it had enjoyed since the czar's visit in 1656. It is fairly certain that, as a highly vocal supporter of Aleksei and his politics, Simeon's position at this point would not have been enviable. Several poems written between 1661 and 1663, in particular "Modlitwa w utropieniu" (Prayer in Time of Distress), "Prilog k prepodobnoi materi Efrosinii" (Petition to Holy Mother Efrosiniia), and "Molitva plachevnaia ko Presviatoi Bogoroditse, slozhennaia v leto 7171" (Plaintive Prayer to the Most Holy Theotokos, Composed in the Year 7171 [1663]) suggest that Simeon was subject to ridicule and threats and that he would have welcomed the opportunity to leave Polotsk and enter the czar's service in Moscow.

The period from the mid 1640s, when Simeon first began composing verse, to the early 1660s constitutes a distinct period in his evolution as a writer. During these years the poet wrote primarily in his native tongue, Belorussian, but also in Polish and

Latin, the principal languages of instruction at the Kiev and Vilnius academies. A few poems of the late 1650s are written in a relatively normative Church Slavonic, suggesting that around this time Simeon began to study the language seriously, recognizing it as the most appropriate medium for discourse in the world of Russian letters. No such texts, however, antedate the poet's first encounter with the czar in 1656. The verse, whether Polish, Belorussian or Church Slavonic, adheres to the Polish prosodic model of his time. The poems are isosyllabic in organization – in this respect they are structurally more rigorous than anything written by Simeon's predecessors – and are almost always arranged in rhymed couplets with feminine endings and obligatory caesura. Judging by the sampling of works that have been published, eleven- and thirteen-syllable lines constitute the overwhelming majority, with Sapphic verse occurring only on occasion.

Simeon's earliest known poem, dated 1648, is a Polish translation of the Akathistos to the Most Holy Theotokos, an ancient liturgical hymn of the Orthodox Church. This and other early poems may have been written as classroom exercises. Like many of those that followed during this period of poetic apprenticeship, they lack originality and are easily confused with the works of other, lesser-known writers. Indeed two major poems traditionally attributed to him – "Slova, iazhe Khristos raspiatyi na kreste movil do Boga ottsa" (The Words which Christ, Crucified on the Cross, Prayed to God the Father) and "Stisi kraeglasnii, slozhenii vo sretenie chudotvornoi ikony Presviatyia Bogoroditsy . . . " (Rhymed Verses Composed Upon Meeting the Wonderworking Icon of the Most Holy Theotokos . . .) – have been proven to be the works of his monastic brother, Filafei Utchytski, and some of the early declamations addressed to Czar Aleksei, including the frequently anthologized "Metry na prishestvie vo grad . . . Polotsk . . . Tsaria Aleksiia Mikhailovicha . . ." (Verses on the Arrival of . . . Czar Aleksei Mikhailovich in the . . . City of Polotsk) and the "Vitebskie virshi" (Vitebsk Verses), are known to be collective compositions.

His early verse reveals a wide variety of genres associated with the Polish, Ukrainian, and Belorussian Baroque: dialogues, a mystery play, odes, satires, epigrams, epitaphs, elegies, didactic and "scientific" verse, as well as various kinds of poetic curios (the *carmen echicum,* palindrome, zodiacum, and genethliacon). Many are declamations, a designation of performance rather than

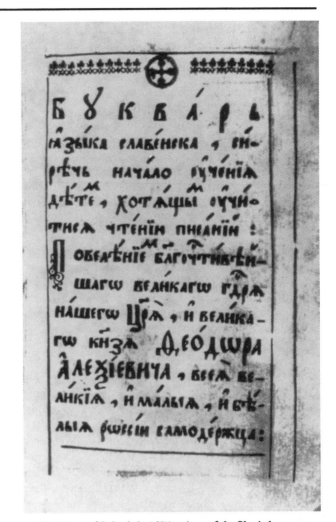

First page of Polotsky's 1679 primer of the Slavic language

genre. Those of a panegyric nature, honoring the czar and his family on some special occasion, occupy a position of particular prominence, as Simeon's biography graphically demonstrates. They are structured, for the most part, around a particular conceit in which the czar is likened to the sun and his family to heavenly bodies; the conceit in turn receives a multitude of thematic elaborations in the speeches of the declaimers.

Equally impressive, and certainly more complex in their imagerial structure, are the religious declamations written to be recited on particular feast days. The simpler examples, such as "Stikhi na Rozhdestvo Khristovo" (Verses on the Nativity of Christ) or "Stikhi na Voskresenie Khristovo" (Verses on Christ's Resurrection), consist of anonymous recitations with no marked beginning or ending. Somewhat more complex is "Stikhi kraesoglasnyia na Rozhdestvo Khristovo, glagolemyi v tserkvi vo slavu Khrista Boga" (Rhymed Verses on the Nativity of Christ, Recited in Church to the Glory of Christ [our] God), which follows the structure of and in many cases paraphrases the Nativity canon. The most complex of the pieces is "Wierszy w Wielky Piątek przy braniu płaszczenicy" (Verses on Good Friday at the Removal of the Shroud), a mystery play written in 1653 and probably recited at the service for Christ's burial on Good Friday. Framed by a prologue and epilogue, it consists of exchanges between the Pious Soul, an angel, and a chorus as they relive the major scenes of the Passion. All of these religious declamations, including the mystery play, adhere closely to the norms set forth in a late-seventeenth-century poetics conspectus of Jesuit provenance, "Regula poeseos et eloquentiae," and reveal Simeon's mastery of the received tradition of the scholastic baroque. Generically independent, but functionally similar, is Simeon's "Besedy pastuskiia ezhe est o voploshchenii Gospoda Boga i Spasa nashego I[isusa] Kh[rista] vidennago imi vo vertepe, ot prechistyia devy Marii pelenami povita i vo iaslekh polozhenna" (Pastoral Dialogue on the Incarnation of Our Lord, God and Saviour J[esus] Ch[rist], Wrapped in Swaddling Clothes and Laid in a Manger by the Immaculate Virgin Mary). While it observes in most respects the generic norms of the baroque pastoral, in particular the Polish "pastorałka," the dialogue is far more abstract and "learned." Virtually the entire work is written in Sapphic verse, and the language is a relatively pure Church Slavonic, indicating that already in Polotsk Simeon had mastered the language that was to serve as his exclusive medium of discourse in Moscow.

Recent scholarship has shown that even at this early stage Simeon was thoroughly familiar with the poetics of emblematic verse. The most obvious example is "Fron istinny, ezhe est' o blizhaishem sudii besedovanie" (The Throne of Truth, Concerning Imminent Judgement), a sequence of twelve poems that illustrate engravings on the theme of justice – Solomon judging the two women who claim to be mothers of the same child; Daniel bringing to justice the elders who slandered Susanna; Christ before Pilate; the Roman jurist Papinian's defiance of the emperor Caracalla and his subsequent murder; and others. Several didactic pieces reveal the author's familiarity with the leading emblem books of the period (Terenzio Alciati, Joachim Camerarius, Nicolas Caussin) and link his work with the broad European Baroque tradition of the seventeenth century.

No records have survived concerning Simeon's activities in Polotsk after 1660. He moved to Moscow in 1663 or 1664, but why and precisely when are not entirely clear. Tatarsky speculates that he came of his own accord as early as July of 1663 and, taking advantage of his superior knowledge of Latin, found employment as a translator for Paisios Ligarides, metropolitan of Gaza, a Western-educated cleric who had come to Moscow in 1662 and insinuated himself into the highest ecclesiastical and political circles of Moscow, but whose Russian and Slavonic were still rudimentary. Others have speculated that Simeon came to Moscow at the czar's behest. In any case, by August 1664 Simeon had definitely taken up residence at the Zaikonospassky Monastery.

His first impressions of the capital were not favorable. In a letter to Varlaam Iasyns'ky, a fellow Mohyla Collegium alumnus, he wrote, "Maybe some sycophant will recommend this as a place where heavenly ambrosia flows from the horn of Amalthaea, but we are about as free to take advantage of it as the dogs of Egypt are to drink from the waters of the Nile, or as one would be to take honey from combs surrounded by bees. The queen bee here has no sting, but the crowd is intolerant toward anyone who thinks differently than they do."

The intolerance of which Simeon speaks is related specifically to the constellation of political and ecclesiastical circumstances in Moscow at the time he settled there. In 1652 Patriarch Nikon had undertaken the correction of the Russian Orthodox Church's liturgical books and ritual practices to make them conform to those of the Greek Orthodox Church, thereby precipitating a major schism. An imperious prelate who viewed himself as the czar's equal, he had abruptly abandoned the Patriarchal throne in Moscow in 1658 and retreated to the New Jerusalem Monastery following a deliberate insult by Czar Aleksei. The church had therefore been without an active patriarch for six years. Exasperated by Nikon's behavior and concerned about the spread of the schism, Czar Aleksei had begun listening to the advice of Metropolitan Paisios Ligarides, who suggested calling a church council and inviting the other Eastern Orthodox patriarchs to Moscow to pass judgment on Nikon. Ligarides had been recommended to Czar Aleksei by Simeon's mentor, Lazar Baranovych, and shared with Simeon a strong bias in favor of Western enlightenment in its Jesuit redaction.

At the time of Simeon's arrival, there already existed a small but energetic group of clerics and boyars who supported certain basic forms of acculturation to the West, including such powerful hierarchs as Metropolitan Platon of Novgorod and

Bishop Illarion of Riazan, and also some of the czar's closest advisers, chief among them Fedor Rtishchev, Artamon Matveev, and Bogdan Khitrovo. The *latinstvuiushchie* (Latinizers), as they came to be known, were opposed by two groups. The first consisted of learned clerics who, while supporting in principle the need for education and enlightenment, insisted on a Greco-Byzantine orientation rather than a turn to the West. Their principal spokesman was Epifanii Slavinetsky, a learned monk who headed a school at the Chudov Monastery in the Moscow Kremlin that provided elementary training in Greek, patristics (primarily of the Eastern Fathers), and biblical theology. He was a supporter of the church reforms undertaken by Nikon and defended the use of Greek liturgical texts as a basis for correcting the Slavonic service books. The second group of opponents consisted of those who would come to be known as the *Starovery* (Old Believers), defenders of the ancient piety who rejected the reforms imposed by Patriarch Nikon and resisted almost all forms of accommodation to the Latin West. Their chief spokesmen were the Archpriest Avvakum, the priest Nikita (Dobrynin) of Suzdal', and the priest Lazar' of Romanov-Borisoglebsk.

The earliest evidence of Simeon's activities in Moscow is a letter written in 1664 and addressed to Mefodii, Bishop of Mstislavl' and Orsha, in which he indicates that he has established a small school at the monastery and is teaching Latin to scribes from the Privy Chancery (Tainyi prikaz), the czar's personal Bureau of Secret Affairs. Some of the other disciplines typical of the Kiev Collegium, in particular rhetoric and dialectics, were probably also part of the curriculum. Among Simeon's earliest pupils was Sil'vestr Medvedev, who in later years was to serve as his personal secretary and editor and would later assume Simeon's mantle as the foremost representative of the Latinizers in Moscow.

Simeon's knowledge of Latin also figures in his first documented audience with the Czar Aleksei. In December 1664 he was called on to serve as an interpreter (translating from Latin to Russian and vice versa) between Metropolitan Paisios Ligarides and the czar. His next documented contact with the czar occurred on 23 April 1665, when he presented the monarch with a bound copy of short sequence poems written in honor of the birth of Aleksei's third son. A panegyric oration accompanied the gift. It is not unlikely that this act of formal presentation had been preceded by other declamations. It is clear, in any case, that Simeon's poetic gifts were highly valued by the monarch, for there-

after poetic declamations were to become a regular part of court life, marking name-days, feast days, and other important events in the life of the royal family. Simeon thus established himself as Russia's first court poet, a position he would retain for life.

Given his close association both with the czar and with Metropolitan Paisios, Simeon soon found himself involved in the most critical ecclesiastical and political matters confronting the state. The most pressing issue at hand was the schism. Aleksei finally called a church council in 1666 to confirm the liturgical and ritual reforms that Nikon had introduced and at the same time to depose him officially and elect a new patriarch. The council was presented with a detailed critique of Nikon's reforms composed by Lazar' and Nikita in their respective *chelobitnye* (petitions) to the czar. Metropolitan Paisios had prepared a preliminary rebuttal in Latin, translated into Slavonic by Simeon, but it was deemed inadequate. Simeon was therefore called upon to write a full and complete refutation on behalf of the church council. In the space of eight weeks, between 18 May and 13 July 1666, he composed the *Zhezl pravleniia na pravitel'stvo myslennago stada pravoslavno-rossiiskiia tserkve* (Crozier-Staff of Governance for Directing the Spiritual Flock of the Orthodox Russian Church, 1667). Its full title conveys both the contents and the polemical sharpness of the document; it continues: *utverzhdeniia vo utverzhdenie kolebliushchikhsia vo vere, nakazaniia v nakazanie nepokorivykh ovets, kazneniia na porazhenie zhestokovyinykh i khishchnykh volkov, na stado Khristovo napadaiushchikh. Sooruzhennyi ot vsego osviashchennago sobora, sobrannago poveleniem blagochestiveishago, tishaishago i samoderzhavneishago velikago gosudaria tsaria i velikago kniazia Aleksiia Mikhailovicha, vseia Velikiia, i Malyia, i Belyia Rossii samoderzhtsa, v tsarstvuiushchem bogospasaemom i preimenitom grade Moskve. V leto 7144 mesiatsa maia 7 den'* (of Confirmation for Confirming Those Wavering in Faith, of Chastisement for Chastising Unruly Sheep, of Execution for Decimating the Cruel and Rapacious Wolves Fallen on Christ's Flock. Fashioned by the Entire Holy Council Convened by Order of the Most Pious, Most Serene, Most Autocratic Great Lord, Czar and Grand Prince Aleksei Mikhailovich, Autocrat of All Great, Little and White Russia, in the Royal, God-Preserved and Most Celebrated City of Moscow in the Year 1667, the 7th Day of May). Employing the entire arsenal of devices associated with classic forensic oratory and informed with a condescension born of superior training in theology, the book was irreproachable as an exercise in scholastic rhetoric and rigorous in its defense of Nikon's reforms. At the same time it was the sort of work that would repel those whom it sought to correct because of its reliance on an alien form of discourse. It also included statements contradicting traditional Orthodox dogma, and clearly revealed the influence of Catholic theology. As L. N. Maikov indicates in his biography of Simeon, it was designed first and foremost to assert uncompromisingly the authority of the church, including its right to chastise and, if necessary, annihilate those who pursued the path of schism. Simeon's text was formally approved and published in the name of the council in early 1667.

In the same year he was appointed royal tutor to the heir apparent, Aleksei Alekseevich, and after the latter's untimely death in 1669 to the new heir apparent, Fedor Alekseevich, whom he continued to instruct until he assumed the throne in 1676. There is also some evidence that he tutored Aleksei's daughter, Sofia, who was to occupy the throne as regent following Fedor's death. Simeon was responsible for teaching Latin, rhetoric, poetics, theology, and probably Polish. It was by virtue of this position more than any other that he influenced the cultural and spiritual life of Muscovy, insuring that the state would be officially receptive to the ideals of scholastic enlightenment as he perceived them.

Several original, translated, and edited works of a catechistic nature can be linked directly to Simeon's teaching activities. One of them is a manuscript harmony of the Gospels, "Zhitie i uchenie Khrista Gospoda i Boga nashego" (The Life and Teachings of Christ, Our Lord and God), based on Gerhardus Mercator's *Evangelicae historiae qvadripartita monas* (1592). Two other manuscript works were composed in part to serve as aids in instructing the czar's children: "Kniga kratkikh voprosov i otvetov katekhizicheskikh" (Book of Short Catechistic Questions and Answers) and "Venets very kafolicheskiia, na osnovanii simvola sviatykh apostol iz razlichnykh tsvetov bogoslovskikh i prochikh sopletennyi" (Wreath of the Catholic Faith, Woven from Flowers both Theological and Otherwise, on the Basis of the Creed of the Holy Apostles). The latter is a remarkable exposition of the Christian faith, organized according to the major articles of the Apostles' Creed. For each article the author provides a detailed and rhetorically elaborate exposition, buttressed by patristic witnesses, followed by questions and answers relating to the topic at hand. Some of the questions are clearly the product of Simeon's ingrained scholasticism, as when he asks what the fate of Adam's rib will be at the final Resurrection (it will remain a

part of Eve). Simeon's pedagogical concerns are also revealed in his excursus on the structure of the cosmos (essentially Ptolemaic) and his retelling of apocryphal legends. His primary theological sources are Western: of the Church Fathers he most frequently cites Jerome and Augustine, and he relies heavily on such medieval and Renaissance theologians as Anselm of Canterbury, Gilbert Genebrard, Gabriele Paleotti, Cesare Baronius, and Roberto Bellarmine. Most shocking from the viewpoint of an Orthodox reader is his use of the Apostles' rather than the Nicene Creed, the Orthodox standard, as the framework for his catechistic exposition. With his partiality to Western theology, his failure to defend the Orthodox view adequately on points of doctrinal contention with the Catholic West, and his occasional expression of views that are indeed un-Orthodox, Simeon had little hope of publishing his "Venets very," and it circulated only in manuscript form. Later it was to provide prima facie evidence when charges of heresy were brought against him posthumously.

In addition to his activities as court poet, pedagogue and theologian, Simeon made his influence felt in the area of homiletics. The groundwork for his activities here was laid by the Council of 1666–1667, which, in addition to confirming Nikon's liturgical and ritual reforms, reasserted the need for genuine preaching as part of a program to revitalize the life of the Church. In Belarus and Ukraine this tradition survived, supported both by the Society of Jesus and the Polish court, and Simeon had ample exposure to it in Polotsk, Kiev, and Vilnius. In seventeenth-century Muscovy, however, preaching, when practiced at all, amounted to the recitation of patristic homilies and the lives of the saints. It was this practice that the church wished to modify by promoting the composition and delivery of original sermons addressing issues of topical concern, including the schism.

Between 1668 and 1674 Simeon composed more than two hundred sermons, many of which he read at services in the presence of the czar and his family; others were written at the behest of clerics close to Simeon – Metropolitan Pavel of Sarai and the Don and Metropolitan Lavrentii of Kazan and Sviazhsk in particular – and were read by these hierarchs in their own churches. Still others were published in the name of Patriarch Ioasaf, Nikon's successor. In this way Simeon's views – in matters both of ethics and dogma – were promulgated before and by some of the most powerful ecclesiasts in Muscovy.

Between 1675 and 1676 Simeon prepared two major collections of sermons for publication: *Obed*

Title page for Polotsky's Vertograd mnogotsvetnyi *(The Many-Flowered Garden), one of the three
major manuscript collections of his poetry compiled in 1678 (Saint Petersburg, Biblioteka Akademii
Nauk, access no. P I A 54 [31.7.3])*

dushevnyi (Spiritual Dinner, 1681) and *Vecheria dushevnaia* (Spiritual Supper, 1683); the titles play on the words *Obednia* (the Mass) and *Tainaia vecheria* (the Last Supper). Both were organized according to the liturgical cycle: *Obed dushevnyi* collects sermons based on Gospel readings for Sunday services throughout the year, and *Vecheria dushevnaia* on the major feast days of the church in honor of Christ, the Virgin Mary, the saints, and thaumaturgic icons, followed by sermons unrelated to the liturgical cycle on miscellaneous themes and occasions (the dedication of a church, the burial of a soldier, the seven deadly sins, superstitions, and so on).

The compilation of these sermons was hallowed by the patristic tradition – Simeon, in fact, had translated a collection of sermons by Saint Gregory the Great in 1672 (in a manuscript titled "Kniga o pastyrskom popechenii Sv. Grigoriia Dvoeslova" [A Book on Pastoral Care of St. Gregory the Great]), and such compilations had an honorable place in medieval Russian letters. Simeon's familiarity with that tradition is clear from his citations: he frequently quotes Saint John Chrysostom, the most popular of the Greek Fathers in Russia. Not coincidentally, homiletic compilations ascribed to the latter (the "Zlatousty") are also ordered according to the liturgical calendar. From the viewpoint of Russian tradition, however, Simeon's sermons are profoundly innovative in their appeal to the Western homiletic canon. Rough drafts confirm his familiarity with Jacobus Marchantius's well-known Latin compilations (*Hortus pastorum,* 1626–1627; *Tuba sacerdotalis,* 1632) as well as with the works of such leading Western preachers and theologians as Roberto Bellarmine, Meffreth (Meffrettus), Matthias Faber, Pierre de Besse, and Alphonso Salmeron. Closer to home, he read and was influenced by such leading representatives of the Polish Catholic tradition as Piotr Skarga, Fabijan Birkowski, and Szymon Starowolski. Most evident is Simeon's close connection to the Ukrainian tradition. One of his models was Lazar Baranovych's *Mech duxovnyi* (Spiritual Sword, 1666), a collection of sermons arranged around the Sunday gospel readings. Simeon later composed four laudatory epigrams in honor of the book and its author. Even more important was Ioannikii Haliatovs'ky, who not only provided models of the homiletic art in his *Kliuch razumeniia* (Key to Understanding, 1663), but appended an instruction manual on the composition of sermons that Simeon appears to have followed rigorously.

Most of the sermons in *Obed dushevnyi* and *Vecheria dushevnaia* are didactic in nature; only eleven of the 217 focus on specifically dogmatic issues. Those that are the most striking in their topicality – attacking such vices as drunkenness, debauchery, and superstition, or dealing with the problem of the schism – represent little more than ten percent of the total, and in several instances they were composed for other hierarchs. The vast majority are far more general in nature, drawing lessons from the Scriptures, patristic works, and the lives of the saints. In preparing the sermons for publication Simeon frequently removed topical references, thereby universalizing their contents. It was clearly his intention to publish sermons that could be read verbatim from the pulpit by other priests.

The sermons are textbook studies in the use of classic rhetorical devices, from the phonetic level to the architecture of the whole. Alliteration, paronomasia, internal rhyme, neology, chiasmic inversion, anaphora, exclamations, rhetorical questions, apostrophe, frequent use of aphorisms and citations, and elaborate conceits are the devices Simeon regularly employs. Particularly striking, for a Muscovite listener, would be his allusions to Greek mythology and his stories about the philosophers of antiquity and citations from their works. Many would have been mystified by the exhortation to join Heraclitus in weeping over the inconstancy of the present world or to follow Diogenes's example in despising material comforts. It has been argued that the rhetorical density of the sermons would have rendered them ineffective as tools of moral persuasion, and such may be the case. On the other hand, in the process of applying these devices, Simeon was educating his audience, thereby addressing what he saw as the single most profound source of vice and heresy – popular ignorance.

Simeon composed two other major works in the first half of the 1670s that also deserve special mention. These verse plays were both apparently written for performance at the court theater established by Czar Aleksei. The first, "O Navkhodonosore tsare, o tele zlate i o triekh otrotsekh, v peshchi ne sozhzhennykh" (On King Nebuchadnezzar, the Golden Statue and the Three Youths Not Consumed in the Fiery Furnace; first published in Nikolai Novikov's *Drevniaia rossiiskaia vivliotika,* 1789) appears to be based on a mystery play originating in Russia during the time of Ivan the Terrible. The latter was performed on the Sunday before Christmas at hierarchical services (celebrated by a bishop) and represents a mixture of canonical liturgical song and dramatic action. Simeon's debt to the mystery play is evident in his incorporation of the liturgical hymns (*heirmoi*) in which Shadrach,

Meshach, and Abednego praise God for their deliverance from the fiery furnace. The play is more expansive than its prototype, however, and includes King Nebuchadnezzar in its *dramatis personae*.

The second play, "Komidiia pritchi o bludnem syne" (Comedy of the Parable of the Prodigal Son; published as *Istoriia ili deistvie evangelskiia pritchi o bludnom syne,* mid-eighteenth century), has no obvious antecedent in the Orthodox liturgical tradition, and if Simeon turned to any external source for inspiration other than the biblical parable, it would in all likelihood have been Wilhelm van de Voldersgroft Fullonius's *Acolastus, hoc est de filio prodigo comoedia* (1529). Simeon's play consists of six parts and expands considerably on the parable, incorporating scenes of drinking, card playing, music making, and other forms of general merriment that would have constituted an unusual spectacle before the court. In contrast to Christ's parable, which is clearly intended as a graphic allegory of God's love for the repentant sinner, Simeon seems intent on preaching a more mundane lesson concerning parental authority. In the play's epilogue he writes that the parable has a dual moral: youth should obey their elders and not rely on their own immature reasoning powers, and elders should keep a tight reign on their children. The comedy proved to be one of Simeon's most popular and enduring works. It went through at least three printings in the eighteenth century and two in the nineteenth.

The death of Czar Aleksei in 1676 did not significantly alter Simeon's position at the court. On the contrary, the fact that he had been the new czar's tutor for the previous seven years virtually guaranteed that he would retain his influence. The poet's relations with the church hierarchy, however, grew increasingly estranged. While the feeble and gentle Ioasaf, Nikon's successor, was well disposed to Simeon, his successors, Pitirim (from 1672 to 1673) and Ioakim (from 1673 to 1690), were less sanguine about Simeon's Latinized Orthodoxy. In 1673, for example, Patriarch Pitirim called on Simeon and his rival, Epifanii Slavinetsky, to engage in a public debate on the orthodoxy of Simeon's views concerning the moment of transubstantiation during the Divine Liturgy. Slavinetsky was able to demonstrate that Simeon's views on this subject were Catholic in origin and contradicted the accepted doctrine of the Eastern Church. Patriarch Ioakim, who had been the archimandrite of the Chudov Monastery, was particularly distrustful of Simeon, and only the latter's close relations with the czar prevented the patriarch from taking measures to silence him.

During Fedor's reign Simeon devoted less attention to homiletics and more attention to writing and translating theological treatises and to preparing manuscript compilations of his poetic works. The translations include excerpts from the writings of Pietro d'Alphonso and Vincent de Beauvais that touch on questions relating to Islam (relevant at the time to the war being waged against the Ottoman Empire) as well as several "besedy" (discourses) on various theological topics – the souls of the saints, the veneration of saints, the veneration of icons, church traditions – aimed at countering Protestant influence in Muscovy.

In 1678 Simeon turned to the daunting task of organizing his already considerable poetic output for possible publication. The vast majority of his poems were brought together in two manuscript collections, and in "Rifmologion" (Rhymebook), "Vertograd mnogotsvetnyi" (The Many-Flowered Garden), and *Psaltir' tsaria i proroka Davida* (Psalter of King David the Prophet, 1680). The first collection includes most of Simeon's occasional poems, which more than any others earned him the reputation of a professional versifier. The majority are composed and were delivered in the poet's own name, but many were written to be declaimed by a designated person in the presence of another (a child to a parent, a grandchild to a grandparent) or by a specific royal personage to another (the czarevich to his aunt, the czar's servants to the czar), usually on the occasion of a particular feast day. Clearly, Simeon intended his "Rifmologion" to function as a handbook from which declamations could be recited verbatim, or which could provide appropriate models for personalized addresses.

In addition to religious and secular declamations, "Rifmologion" includes five *knizhitsy* (booklets), so called because copies of these texts were originally bound separately and presented to the czar in connection with a particularly solemn or noteworthy event. Unlike the other declamations, they were not meant to be recited aloud, as may be surmised by the presence of poems written cryptographically or in various exquisite shapes (stars, hearts, crosses, columns) in the baroque tradition of the *figura poesis*. The earliest (and shortest) of these, presented to the czar in 1665, was composed in honor of the birth of his son Simeon and served as a model for later booklets. The second, "Orel rossiiskii" (The Russian Eagle, 1667), a panegyric to the czar and his son on the occasion of the latter's official presentation as heir to the throne, is constructed around an elaborate emblem that places the czar's coat of arms in the center of the sun. The muses all render homage in individual poems, and Apollo guides the young czarevich through the signs of the zodiac, explaining how each might influence his conduct as heir apparent. A third booklet, "Gusl' dobroglasnaia" (The Sweet-Sounding Psaltery) celebrates the coronation of Fedor Alekseevich in 1676 in twenty salutations on the part of the patriarch, the czar's wife, siblings, clergy, court, advisers, and "vse pravoslavnye khristiane" (all Orthodox Christians), followed by twenty-four greetings in the poet's name, accompanied by a labyrinth and a poem in the form of a three-barred Russian cross.

Two lengthy poetic sequences commemorate occasions of mourning: one on the death of Czar Aleksei's first wife and the other on the death of the czar. The former, entitled "Freny, ili Plachi vsekh sanov i chinov pravoslavno rossiiskago tsarstva o smerti . . . Marii Il'inichny" (Threnodies, or Dirges of All Ranks and Offices of the Orthodox Russian Czardom on the Death of . . . Maria Il'inichna) is the most elaborate and one of Simeon's finest creations. It is a multipartite funeral oration, with individual declamations assigned to the principal persons and institutions of the Russian state (the czar, his children, his boyars, the clergy, monasteries, visitors, the poor and orphaned, and so on), each followed by lines of comfort recited by corresponding personified virtues (Faith, Hope, Love, Piety, Wisdom). The twelve dirges are followed by a monologue by the czarina, who addresses the assembly from her open coffin: "Pride vremia v zemliu vozratikhsia, / i vo grobe sem telom polozhikhsia, / Iz nego zhe k vam imam glagolati, / tselovanie poslednee dati. / Glasa ne imam, vse glagolet telo / dukhovnym nekim glasom tikhim zelo" / (Now the time has come, I have returned to the earth, / and have been laid bodily in this coffin, / From which I shall speak to you, / and give you a last kiss. / I have no voice, but my body speaks / with a certain spiritual voice, most quietly). Her last words are followed by a labyrinth constructed around the words "Vechnaia pamiat'" (Eternal Memory), the closing hymn of the Orthodox burial service. The labyrinth serves as an appropriate bridge to the remaining poems of the sequence: two epitaphs in honor of Maria and her daughter (both she and her baby died from complications surrounding childbirth), and nine emblem poems (unfortunately, only draft sketches of the emblems themselves have survived) that focus on the themes of death, resurrection, and immortality.

The second major collection of verse that Simeon compiled in the closing years of his life was "Vertograd mnogotsvetnyi" (The Many-Flowered Garden). It stands in contrast to the "Rifmologion" in two major respects: its contents were meant to be read silently rather than orally, and its overall tone is didactic rather than panegyric. "Vertograd mnogotsvetnyi" comprises more than six hundred folia and three thousand poems. It has been described as museum-like *kunstkamera* displaying an extraordinarily wide range of genres – epigrams, fables, inscriptions, epitaphs, aphorisms, and others to which Simeon gives such names as *povesti* (stories), *uveshchaniia* (exhortations), *molitvy* (prayers), *oblicheniia* (exposés), and *tolkovaniia* (interpretations). The tradition of such "Gardens of Verse," traceable to the early Middle Ages, was particularly pronounced in the baroque period, and Simeon had several such compilations in his library. Their underlying principle is essentially emblematic: the world, both in its synchronic and diachronic dimensions, is a picture book which the poet is called on to interpret and thereby extract the lessons it contains. There is, in principle, no limit to the number of objects that may be interpreted or the number of lessons that may be drawn from them. The "Vertograd mnogotsvetnyi," then, may be viewed as an encyclopedia of morals to be drawn from the world order.

The sources Simeon used in searching out material for didactic exposition indicate both his own erudition and the extraordinary scope of his collection: they include the classics (Plutarch's *Moralia,* Livy's *Historiarum libri,* Pliny's *Historia naturalis,* Plautus's *Comoediae and Fabulae*), histories (Joseph Flavius's *Opera,* Baronius's *Annales ecclesiastici,* Severus's *Historia sacra*), collections of exempla (*Wielkie zwierciadlo, Facecye polskie*), emblem books, and assorted volumes on medicine, astronomy, and geography.

From the three known manuscript copies of "Vertograd mnogotsvetnyi" it is apparent that Simeon initially compiled the poems intuitively, grouping them in large, thematically related sequences. As the collection grew in size he began to catalogue the growing number of entries, assigning to the poems shorter titles reflecting the central theme of each text, and having them recopied in the alphabetical order of the new titles. Consulting such a collection, the reader could look up poems on a wide variety of topics: "Aaron," "Book," "Church," "Dew," and so on. While his scribes recopied and rearranged existing poems, Simeon continued to write new ones. A third, fair copy was eventually drawn up by Sil'vestr Medvedev shortly after the poet's death, incorporating the entries not previously properly alphabetized. This exquisitely prepared manuscript was presented to the czar and would probably have served as the copy text had the complete work ever been published.

The history of Simeon's third major collection is intimately bound up with that of the "Vertograd mnogotsvetnyi." Upon reaching the penultimate letter in the Slavonic alphabet, Simeon marked down two poems in his register – "Psalom" (Psalm) and "Psalmopenie" (Psalmody). It occurred to him at this point to translate several psalms and include them under the same heading. True to the encyclopedic spirit that inspired his earlier work, Simeon decided to set the entire Book of Psalms into syllabic verse, a feat accomplished astonishingly quickly, between 4 February and 28 March 1678. He also composed translations of the nine Old Testament odes that serve as the prototypes for the *hiermoi* of the Orthodox canon and appended to the whole a versified Saints Calendar, with one or two couplets devoted to each saint or feast day.

In translating the Psalms Simeon had a significant model at hand: Jan Kochanowski's *Psalsterz Dawidów* (1578), which, according to Simeon, enjoyed considerable popularity in Muscovy for its musical settings. There is strong evidence that Simeon referred regularly to Kochanowski's translation and was influenced by its phrasing and versification; in more than half the Psalms Simeon selects the same prosodic scheme as Kochanowski. In doing so he exploited most of the syllabic meters practiced in Polish poetry at the time, in part with the intention of making his Psalms amenable to a variety of musical settings. It was his stated intention to compose similarly pleasing versions of the Psalms in a language accessible to the educated reader of his day.

Simeon depended most heavily in his verse renditions on the existing Slavonic text of the Psalter. Therein lay the greatest danger from a political and ecclesiastical viewpoint. The Psalms were among the best-known liturgical texts, selections being read or sung at every service in the Orthodox liturgical cycle. Any attempt to play with the wording of the Psalms would be greeted with suspicion by the Muscovite clergy. Simeon was well aware of this danger, and in his preface he made clear that his translations were not for liturgical use, but "v domekh chasto iu chitati / ili sladkimi glasy vospevati / Vo slavu Bogu, – ibo uslazhdaet / rifm slukh i serdtse" (to be read often at home / or to sing with sweet voices / To the glory of God, for rhyme / satisfies the ear and heart). He also attempted to convince his reader that the changes in

Page from Polotsky's Istoriia ili deistvie evangelskiia pritchi o bludnom syne, *written in the 1670s but not published until the mid eighteenth century*

wording required by the verse form did not alter the texts' meaning. Such is indeed the case – Simeon remains remarkably close to the prosaic original – but the very notion that one could alter the words of a sacred text and still convey the same meaning was revolutionary for the time and evoked considerable controversy. Simeon knew that his enemies, particularly Patriarch Ioakim and others in the Grecophile camp, would react with hostility, but because of his privileged relationship with the czar he proceeded with his translations and his plans to publish them.

Two additional projects occupied Simeon in the last eighteen months of his life. The first involved the establishment of a new printing house which, unlike the Pechatnyi Dvor, could operate without patriarchal censorship. He began propagandizing this idea before Czar Fedor as early as 1676;

in the closing lines of his "Gusl' dobroglasnaia" (Sweet-Sounding Psaltery) he urges the czar to publish the work in order "da by im tsarsku slavu vozglasiti / Po vsei Rossii i gde sut' sloviane, / v chiuzhdykh daleche stranakh khristiane" (that the glory of the czar be proclaimed / throughout all Russia and wherever there are Slavs / and Christians living in distant lands), adding that it would enhance Russia's reputation if she would support her own poets in this fashion. The czar ultimately approved of Simeon's plans for a "Verkhniaia," i.e., "Royal" printing house, answerable to the czar alone, and the necessary physical plant was established in 1678. The first book was a 1679 publication of *Bukvar' iazyka slovenska* (A Primer of the Slavonic Language), revised to include some of Simeon's declamations suitable for recitation by children. It was followed in January 1680 by *Testament, ili Zavet, Vasiliia, tsaria grecheskago, k synu ego Lvu Filosofu* (The Testament or Will of Vasilii, King of Greece, to His Son Lev the Philosopher), a well-known book of moral admonitions previously published in Kiev but now supplied with a preface by Simeon. The third book, and Simeon's crowning success, was his metrical *Psaltir' tsaria i proroka Davida, khudozhestvom rifmotvornym ravnomerno slogi, i soglasnokonechno, po razlichnym stikhov rodom prelozhennaia*, published in April. Other works were also prepared under Simeon's supervision but appeared only posthumously. They include a saintly vita entitled *Istori[ia], ili povest' sviatago i prepodobnago ottsa nashego Ioanna, izhe ot damaska, o prepodobnom ottse Varlaame pustynnozhiteli: i o Ioasafe tsare Indiistem* (The History, or Story, of Our Holy Father, Saint John of Damascus, Our Father Saint Varlaam the Desert-Dweller, and Ioasaf, King of India, 1680) and Simeon's two collections of sermons, *Obed dushevnyi* (1681) and *Vecheria dushevnaia* (1683).

The second major project occupying Simeon in the last year of his life was the establishment of an institution of higher learning. In 1679 Czar Fedor gave his royal approval for the founding of a new school, attached to the Pechatnyi Dvor, which could train students from Greek Orthodox lands who would otherwise have had to study in Italy. The early success of this school prompted the czar and the patriarch to explore the possibility of a full-fledged academy. To the patriarch's dismay, however, the czar turned to Simeon to draft the necessary plans. The preliminary charter envisioned an institution on a Western European model that would teach both sacred and secular disciplines, including poetics, rhetoric, dialectics, philosophy, physics, law, and languages – including Latin, Pol-

ish, Greek, and Slavonic. It would also serve as a kind of semiofficial judicial office, assisting the authorities in determining the confessional reliability of foreigners working for the state.

Unfortunately, Simeon did not live to see these plans realized. In mid-August 1680 he fell ill and sensed that his death was imminent. On the evening of the 25th he received the last rites, heard his confessor read the Prayers at the Parting of the Soul from the Body, and died peacefully. He was given an elaborate funeral and buried in the monastery church where he had served for sixteen years.

In his lifetime Simeon had an extraordinary impact on the cultural life of Muscovy as a theologian, preacher, pedagogue, and poet. His works confirmed the spiritual and cultural rift born of the schism and made the break with the pre-Nikonian tradition of piety virtually irreversible. His homilies set a new rhetorical and aesthetic standard for the Russian Church. Largely through his efforts the liberal arts, in the broadest sense of the word, became part of the cultural fabric of the educated elite. Although he died before his plans for an academy were realized, they would be pursued actively in the years immediately following his death, leading to the establishment of the Slavonic-Greek-Latin Academy in 1687. Simeon was also the single most important purveyor of verse in the seventeenth century; in his role as court poet he made poetry integral to the ceremonial life of the state and in the process laid the foundation for a panegyric tradition that would dominate Russian verse throughout the eighteenth century. He made poetry fashionable, and after him the creation of verse would be accorded a central place in the cultural life of the nation.

The concrete influence of Simeon's works on the evolution of Russian poetry was, however, severely circumscribed due to political and ecclesiastical developments in the decade following his death. While Czar Fedor was still alive Simeon's influence was guaranteed, as manifest in the posthumous publication of his homilies. After Fedor died, however, Patriarch Ioakim became more vocal in his criticism of Simeon's legacy. He reproached Simeon for deception in indicating that the works published by the Verkhniaia printing house had been issued with the patriarch's blessing (they had not) and accused him of expressing views in these works that ran contrary to Orthodox dogma, which was far more serious and which was, indeed, the case. The ultimate result was a patriarchal decree in 1690 forbidding the reading and distribution of Simeon's works. The "Rifmologion," "Vertograd mnogotsvetnyi," and the rest of Simeon's manuscripts were consigned to a large trunk, and eventually to archival obscurity. Only those works already in circulation – the sermons, *Zhezl pravleniia,* and the *Psaltir'* – could influence the literary tradition directly. Of these, the verse translations of the Psalms were the most significant. They continued to be read and copied well into the eighteenth century, played an important role as models for syllabic versification, and inspired both Trediakovsky (who translated the Psalter in its entirety) and Lomonosov, who identified Simeon's *Psaltir'* as one of the "vrata uchenosti" (gateways of learning) through which he passed on his way to becoming a poet and scholar. At the same time, these poets elaborated a syllabo-tonic system of versification that soon rendered all syllabic verse obsolete. By the mid-eighteenth century, when Simeon's poetry could have been published with impunity, it was already viewed as a relic of the past, and to this day the greater portion remains in manuscript.

Biographies:

Ierofei Tatarsky, *Simeon Polotsky (Ego Zhizn' i deiatel'nost'): Opyt issledovaniia iz istorii prosveshcheniia i vnutrennoi tserkovnoi zhizni vo vtoruiu polovinu XVII veka* (Moscow: M. G. Volchangov, 1886);

Leonid N. Maikov, "Simeon Polotsky," in *Ocherki iz istorii russkoi literatury XVII i XVIII stoletii* (Saint Petersburg: A. S. Suvorin, 1889), pp. 1–162;

Lev Pushkarev, "Simeon Polotsky," in Pushkarev and D. Zhukov, *Russkie pisateli XVII veka,* Zhizn' zamechatel'nykh liudei, series 4, no. 511 (Moscow: Tsk VLKSM Molodaia gvardiia, 1973), pp. 199–335.

References:

Jan Baptist Bedaux, "Emblem and Emblematic Poem in the Work of Simeon Polockij," in *Miscellanea Slavica: To Honor the Memory of Jan M. Meijer,* edited by B. J. Amsenga and others (Amsterdam: Rodopi, 1983), pp. 53–72;

Aleksandr I. Beletsky, "Stikhotvoreniia Simeona Polotskogo na temy iz vseobshchei istorii," in *Sbornik statei v chest' Vladimira Petrovicha Buzeskula. Sbornik Khar'kovskogo Istoriko-Filologicheskogo obshchestva,* volume 21 (Kharkov, 1913-1914), pp. 587–668;

Jan Dewbski, *Twórczość rosyjskich sylabistów i tradycje literackie* (Wrocław: Wydawnictwo Polskiej Akademii nauk, 1983);

Anna S. Eleonskaia, *Russkaia oratorskaia proza v literaturnom protsesse XVII veke* (Moscow: Nauka, 1990);

Eleonskaia, "Tema vospitaniia 'sovershennogo cheloveka' v uchitel'no-polemicheskikh sochineniiakh Simeona Polotskogo," in *Russkaia publitsistika vtoroi poloviny XVII veka* (Moscow: Nauka, 1978), pp. 137–186;

Igor P. Eremin, "Poeticheskii stil' Simeona Polotskogo," *Trudy Otdela drevnerusskoi literatury,* 6 (1948): 125–153;

Eremin, "Simeon Polotsky – poet i dramaturg," in Polotsky's *Izbrannye sochineniia,* Literaturnye pamiatniki, edited by Igor P. Eremin (Moscow & Leningrad: Akademiia nauk, 1953), pp. 223–260;

Stefan Golubev, "Otzyv o sochinenii V. Eingorna: *Ocherki po istorii Malorossii v XVII v. I. Snosheniia malorossiiskogo dukhovenstva s moskovskim pravitel'stvom v tsarstvovanie Alekseia Mikhailovicha* [M., 1889]," *Zapiski Imp. akademii nauk po Istoriko-filologicheskomu otdeleniiu,* 6, no. 2 (1902): 379–399;

Anthony Hippisley, "The 'Emblimata' of Simeon Polotskij," in *The European Emblem: Selected Papers from the Glasgow Conference 11–14 August 1987,* edited by Bernd Scholz, Michael Bath, and David Weston, Symbola et Emblemata: Studies in Renaissance and Baroque Symbolism, 2 (Leiden & New York: Brill, 1990), pp. 117–128;

Hippisley, *The Poetic Style of Simeon Polotsky,* Birmingham Slavonic Monographs, 16 (Birmingham: Department of Russian Language and Literature, University of Birmingham, 1985);

Hippisley, "Simeon Polotsky's Library," *Oxford Slovonic Papers,* 16 (1983): 52–61;

Konstantin V. Kharlampovich, *Malorossiiskoe vliianie na velikorusskuiu tserkovnuiu zhizn',* volume 1 (Kazan, 1914);

Renate Lachmann, "Die Tradition des *ostroumie* und das *acumen* bei Simeon Polockij," in *Slavische Barockliteratur,* edited by Dmitrii Tschiżewskij, Forum Slavicum, 23 (Munich: Fink, 1970), pp. 41–59;

Johannes Langsch, *Die Predigten der 'Coena Spiritualis' von Simeon Polockij vom literarischen Standpunkt aus beurteilt* (Leipzig: Veröffentlichungen des Slavischen Instituts an der Friedrich-Wilhelms Universität Berlin, 1940);

Ryszard Luzny, *Pisarze kregu Akademii Kijowsko-mohylanskiej a literatura polska (Z dziejów zwiazków kulturalnych polsko-wschodnioslowianskich w XVII-*

XVIII w.), Zeszyty naukowe Uniwersytetu Jagiellońskiego, 142. Prace history-cznoliterackie, Zeszyt 11 (Kraków, 1966);

Luzny, "'Psalterz rifmowany' Symeona Polockiego a 'Psalterz Dawidów' Jana Kochanowskiego," *Slavia Orientalis* (Warsaw), 15 (Winter 1966): 3–27;

Aleksandr M. Panchenko, *Russkaia stikhotvornaia kul'tura XVII veka* (Leningrad: Nauka, 1973);

V. Popov, *Simeon Polotsky, kak propovednik* (Moscow: Lissner & Roman, 1886);

N. I. Prashkovich, "Iz rannikh deklamatsii Simeona Polotskogo," *Trudy Otdela drevnerusskoi literatury,* 21 (1965): 29–38;

Andrei N. Robinson, *Bor'ba idei v russkoi literature XVII veka* (Moscow: Nauka, 1974);

Robinson, "Zakonomernosti i dvizheniia literaturnogo barokko: mesto Simeona Polotskogo v russkom literaturnom protsesse (stat'ia vtoraia)," *Wiener Slavistisches Jahrbuch,* 27 (1981): 63–85;

Robinson, ed., *Russkaia staropechatnaia literatura (XVI – pervaia chetvert' XVIII v.),* volume 3: *Simeon Polotsky i ego knigoizdatel'skaia deiatel'nost'* (Moscow: Nauka, 1982);

Mikhail A. Robinson and Lidiia I. Sazonova, "Zametki k biografii i tvorchestvu Simeona Polotskogo," *Russkaia literatura,* no. 4 (April 1988): 134–141;

Peter A. Rolland, "'Dulce est et fumos videre Patriae' – Four Letters by Simiaon Polacki," *Harvard Ukrainian Studies,* 9 (June 1985): 166–181;

Rolland, "Three Early Satires by Simeon Polotsky," *Slavonic and East European Review,* 63 (January 1985): 1–20;

Sazonova, *Poeziia russkogo barokko (vtoraia polovina XVII–nachalo XVIII v.)* (Moscow: Nauka, 1991);

Il'ia Z. Serman, "Psaltyr' rifmotvornaia Simeona Polotskogo i russkaia poeziia XVIII veka," *Trudy Otdela drevnerusskoi literatury,* 18 (1962): 214–232;

Sofiia A. Shcheglova, "Russkaia pastoral' XVII veka," in *Starinnyi teatr v Rossii XVII–XVIII vv.,* edited by Vladimir N. Peretts (Saint Petersburg: Akademiia, 1923), pp. 65–92;

Bernd Uhlenbruch, "Emblematik und Ideologie: Zu einem emblematischen Text Simeon Polockijs," in *Slavische Barockliteratur,* volume 2, edited by Renate Lachmann, Forum Slavicum 54 (Munich: Fink, 1983), pp. 115–128;

Uhlenbruch, "Simeon Polockijs poetische Verfahren – 'Rifmologion' und 'Vertograd mnogocvetnyj' (Versuch einer strukturelen Beschreibung)," Ph.D. dissertation, Ruhr-Universität, Bohum, 1979;

Tadeusz Witkowski, "From *A Forest of Things* to *A Garden of Many Flowers:* Simeon Polotsky's Polish Affiliations," *Russian Literature,* 28 (July 1990): 145–154.

Papers:

The majority of Simeon's works have not been published and are accessible only in archival repositories. The Biblioteka Akademii nauk (Library of the Academy of Sciences, Saint Petersburg) houses presentation copies of *Glas poslednii ko Gospodu Bogu tsaria Aleksiia Mikhailovicha* (1676, Access No. P I A 4 [16.5.7]), *Orel rossiiskii* (1 September 1667, Access No. P I A 1 [16.5.7] and *Vertograd mnogotsvetnyi* (August 1678, Access No. P I A 54 [31.7.3]. The Sobranie rukopisei moskovskoi Sinodal'noi tipografii (Manuscript Collection of the Moscow Synodal Printing House) in the Rossiiskii gosudarstvennyi arkhiv drevnikh aktov (Russian State Archive of Ancient Documents, Moscow) houses "Kniga ritorika praktikaia latinskaia pismenaia. Praecepta Rhetoricae" (two essays on poetics entitled "Commendatio brevis Poeticae" and "Rhetorica practica de omnium trium generum, demonstrativi, deliberativi et iudicialis speciebus," dated 1646 and 1653 respectively), and various undated treatises and orations (fond 381, No. 1791); "Pandectae, seu Collectanea, albo Zebran[ie] scriptów rozmaitych y notatie," a collection of poetry in Polish, Belorussian, Latin and Church Slavic (1648–1660) by both Simeon and Filafei Utchytski, but copied out in Simeon's hand, and other conspectuses and notes by the author (fond 381, No. 1800); the fair copy of *Obed dushevnyi* (fond 381, No. 504); first and second proofs of the same (fond 381, No. 612); the fair copy of *Vecheria dushevnaia* (fond 381, No. 503) and proofs (fond 381, No. 309). The largest collection of manuscripts is housed in the Sinodal'noe sobranie (Synodal Collection) of the Gosudarstvennyi istoricheskii muzei (State Historical Museum, Moscow). It contains poems in Belorussian, Church Slavic and Polish and several prose salutations, undated (No. 731); poems in Belorussian and Church Slavic, 1659–1670 (No. 877); "Venets very kafolicheskiia, na osnovanii simvola sviatykh apostol iz razlichnykh tsvetov bogoslovskikh i prochikh sopletennyi" and "Kniga kratkikh voprosov i otvetov katekhisticheskikh," 1670 (No. 285 [rough draft], No. 664 [fair copy], and No. 286 [presentation copy]); "Kniga privetstvy na gospod'skiia i inyia prazdniki i inyia rechi raznyia," a collection of prose declamations and orations, many in rough drafts (No. 229); documents and sermons on saints' feasts, including a draft copy of the lost collection of sermons presented to Tsar' Aleksei Mikhailovich in 1675 titled "Slovesa pokhvalnaia kupno zhe i nravouchitel'naia na dvadesiat i edin prazdnik ugod-nikov bozhiikh . . . narodoveshchatel'naia pol'zy radi vsekh khristian pravoslavnykh" (No. 130); "Kniga o pastyrskom popechenii Sv. Grigoriia Dvoeslova," a collection of sermons by Saint Gregory the Great, translated from the Latin and compiled in April 1671, with a preface by Simeon (No. 663); "Kniga skazanii ob ikonakh," Simeon's retellings of icon legends (undated, No. 542); the original autograph (No. 656) and second draft (No. 655) of *Obed dushevnyi*; the original autograph (No. 658) and second draft (No.

657) of *Vecheria dushevnaia*; "Kniga o iskhozhdenii Sviatago Dukha i o inykh sviatykh veshchekh" [1678–79], "Zhitie i uchenie Khrista Gospoda i Boga nashego, ot bozhestvennykh Evangelii sobranoe i chinom raspolozhenoe" (1676, in the fair copy only), eight original discourses and four translated essays by d'Alfonso and others (No. 660 [rough draft] and No. 289 [fair copies]); "Rifmologion, ili Stikhoslov" (1678), containing most of the author's occasional verse, drafts of the "knizhitsy" and the two plays (No. 287); the first and second drafts of "Vertograd mnogotsvetnyi," (Nos. 659 and 288); and *Psaltir' tsaria i proroka Davida, khudozhestvom rifmotvornym ravnomerno slogi, i soglasnokonechno, po razlichnym stikhov rodom prelozhennaia* in the fair copy (Nos. 237) first draft (No. 661) and presentation copy (No. 847).

Mikhail Ivanovich Popov
(1742 – circa 1790)

Iurii Vladimirovich Stennik
Institute of Russian Literature (Pushkin House), Saint Petersburg

BOOKS: *Pesni* ([Saint Petersburg: Akademiia nauk, 1765]); revised, 1768);

Opisanie drevniago slavenskogo iazycheskago basnosloviia, sobrannago iz raznykh pisatelei, i snabdennago primechaniiami (Saint Petersburg: [Sukhoputnyi kadetskii korpus], 1768);

Slavenskie drevnosti, ili Prikliucheniia slavenskikh kniazei, 3 volumes (Saint Petersburg: [Morskoi kadetskii korpus, 1770–1771]); published as *Starinnye dikovinki, ili Prikliucheniia slavenskikh kniazei*, 2 volumes (Saint Petersburg: Veitbrekht i Shnor, 1778); revised as *Starinnye dikovinki, ili Udivitel'nye prikliucheniia slavenskikh kniazei . . .*, 2 volumes (Moscow: [Tipografiia Selivanovskogo], 1793);

Khor. Muzyka dlia sego khora sochinena gospodinom Traeto ([Saint Petersburg, 1771]);

Dosugi, ili Sobranie sochinenii i perevodov, 2 volumes (Saint Petersburg: [Akademiia nauk], 1772).

BOOK EDITED: *Rossiiskaia Erata, ili Vybor nailuchshikh noveishikh rossiiskikh pesen po nyne sochinennykh, liubovnykh, nezhnykh, gorodskikh, pastush'ikh, liubovnykh na starinnyi russkii vkus, prostonarodnykh, sviatoshnykh, svadebnykh, karavodnykh, maskeradnykh, malorossiiskikh, satiricheskikh, stolovykh, voennykh, teatral'nykh i nravouchitel'nykh*, 3 volumes (Saint Petersburg: Imperatorskaia tipografiia, 1792).

TRANSLATIONS: Johann Friedrich Cronegk and G. F. Saint-Foix, *Nedoverchivyi . . . ; i pri nei malaia komediia Devkalion i Pirra g. Sent'fua* (Saint Petersburg: Akademiia nauk, [1765]);

[François de la Mothe-Fénelon and Meuznier de Querlon], *Dve povesti: Aristonoevy prikliucheniia i Rozhdenie liudei Promifeevykh* (Saint Petersburg: [Akademiia nauk], 1766);

Voltaire, *Vadiny skazki, Beloi i Chernoi, Zhannot i Kolin i O prazdnikakh frantsuzkikh* (Saint Petersburg: Sukhoputnyi kadetskii korpus, 1771);

Torquato Tasso, *Osvobozhdennyi Ierusalim, iroicheskaia poema*, 2 volumes (Saint Petersburg: Akademiia nauk, 1772);

Abbé de la Chapelle, *Vypiski o chrevoveshchateliakh ili chrevobasnikakh* (Saint Petersburg: Akademiia Nauk, 1773);

John Bell, *Belevy puteshestviia chrez Rossiiu v raznyia Asiiatskie zemli; a imenno: v Ispagan, v Pekin, v Derbent i Konstantinopol'*, 3 volumes (Saint Petersburg: Akademiia nauk, 1776);

J. de la Lande, *Opisanie Rimskiia Vatikanskiia tserkvi sviatago Petra i velikolepnogo Kazertskogo dvorstsa, nakhodiashchegosia nedaleko ot Neapolia* (Saint Petersburg: Akademiia nauk, 1776);

Pétis de La Croix, *Tysiacha i odin den', persidskie skazki, perevedennye s persidskogo iazyka na frantsuzskii g. Petis de lia Krua*, 4 volumes (Saint Petersburg: Veitbrekht i Shnor, 1778–1779);

Lodovico Antonio Muratori, *Razsuzhdenie o blagodenstvii obshchenarodnom*, 2 volumes (Moscow: Novikov, 1780);

Pierre-Augustin Caron de Beaumarchais, *Sevil'skii tsiriul'nik, ili Bespoleznaia predostorozhnost', opera komicheskaia* (Saint Petersburg: Morskoi kadetskii korpus, 1782);

Charles-Simon Favart, *Soliman vtoryi ili Tri Sultanshi: Komediia v trekh deistviiakh* (Moscow: Teatral'naia tipografiia Khristofora Klaudiia, 1785);

David Augustin de Brueys and Jean Palaprat, *Nemoi, komediia v piati deistviiakh* (Moscow: Novikov, 1788).

A man of lower-class origins, Mikhail (or Mikhailo) Ivanovich Popov belongs to that group of eighteenth-century Russian authors whose creative work catered to the needs and tastes of the popular audience. Along with Mikhail Chulkov, he was the founder of a new tradition in Russian narrative prose and at the same time tirelessly promoted the enrichment of the comic repertoire of the national stage via a series of translations and adaptions. Popov also earned repute for his *Anuita* (1772), one of the first comic operas in Russian. His achievements in literary translation and popularizing love songs were no less significant.

Little information about Popov's private life has been preserved. He came from a merchant family from the city of Iaroslavl, where in the 1750s Fedor Volkov, another merchant's son, had started one of Russia's first amateur theaters, subsequently brought to Saint Petersburg to form the kernel of the new national theater that formally opened in 1756. Evidently Popov was brought to Saint Petersburg in the mid 1750s, and in 1757 he became an actor in the new theater. It is possible that, like other actors in the company from Iaroslavl, Popov had been enrolled for a time at the Sukhoputnyi Shlakhetskii Kadetskii Korpus (Noble Infantry Cadet Corps), where he would have had the opportunity to study foreign languages. Volkov undoubtedly asserted a formative influence on Popov, at least in that his introduction to the cultural life of the capital and his first attempts at literature were connected with Volkov's troupe. That these fellow countrymen maintained a close relationship is attested by verses Popov wrote in response to Volkov's death in 1763.

Popov's first literary experiments were translations of works for the theater. He translated the comedy *Der Mistrauische* (The Distrustful One, 1762) by the German playwright Johann Friedrich Cronegk and the one-act play *Deucalion et Pirrha* (Deucalion and Pyrrha, 1742) by the French dramatist G. F. Saint-Foix. The two were published in one volume as *Nedoverchivyi . . . ; i pri nei malaia komediia Devkalion i Pirra g. Sent'fua* in 1765. In the same year he published a collection of thirteen love songs under the title *Pesni* (Songs). In his songs Popov followed the example of Aleksandr Sumarokov, who had created a special genre of lyric romance by developing pastoral and elegiac motifs and combining them with attempts at stylization in the manner of folk lyrics. Some of the songs in Popov's collection were direct transpositions of well-known folk songs. At the same time, Popov tried his hand at translating prose, attested by the book *Dve povesti: Aristonoevy prikliucheniia i Rozhdenie liudei Promifeevykh* (Two

Tales: The Adventures of Ariston and the Birth of the Prometheans, 1766). The first tale was a translation of *Les aventures d'Aristonoüs* (1699), by the famous French writer and journalist François de la Mothe-Fénelon, author of the philosophical and political novel *Les Aventures de Télémaque* (The Adventures of Telemachus, 1699), a moralistic work that confirms virtue as the highest value of human existence. As an adventure story, *Aristonoevy prikliucheniia* may be seen as a continuation of *Les Aventures de Télémaque,* although it lacks the novel's political scope. Popov dedicated the work to Nikolai Novikov, and the dedication reveals that this future journalist and publisher helped the beginning author to publish the translation.

It is also evident from the dedication that at approximately this time Popov must have moved to Moscow, though this situation did not keep him from further translating. In the 1760s he translated David Augustin de Brueys and Jean Palaprat's French comedy *Le Muet* (1693) into Russian as *Nemoi* (The Mute), staged for the first time by the Russian Court Theater on 2 November 1766; an anonymous German comedy as *Burlin — sluga, otets i test'* (Burlin — Servant, Father and Father-in-Law); and *Le comédien imaginaire,* a version of Philippe Poisson's play *L'Impromptu de campagne* (1735; translated as *Pritvornyi komediant*), presented at the same theater on 18 September 1769. All three were collected in Popov's *Dosugi, ili Sobranie sochinenii i perevodov* (Leisure Time, or Collected Compositions and Translations, 1772), and in them Popov was following the practice accepted by the circle of the well-known Saint Petersburg drama lover and litterateur Ivan Elagin, who with Vladimir Lukin, Denis Fonvizin, and others set out to adapt leading examples of the European comedic repertoire for the Russian stage. Their translations were not meant to be accurate and literal but rather free recastings of European plays conforming to the Russian audience's needs and level of understanding. The characters in the plays were given Russian names, the action was usually transferred to Russia, and the speech and behavior of the characters were adapted to Russian manners and customs. The language of Popov's characters, especially the servants, is saturated with vernacular speech, proverbs, popular sayings, and dialects. During these same years Popov composed an original one-act comedy, *Otgadai i Ne skazhu* (Guess and I Will Not Tell, 1772), in which the traditional eighteenth-century comic plot of a rivalry between several suitors for the hand of one maiden is combined with motifs from the so-called tearful drama (for example, a poor orphan who is suddenly rescued by the appearance of her rich uncle at the decisive moment).

Popov's time in Moscow, during which he studied at Moscow University, coincided with the convocation of Catherine the Great's Komissiia o sochinenii novogo ulozheniia (Commission for Composing a New Law Code), which began work in Moscow in the fall of 1767. The legislative initiative required a significant secretarial staff, and Popov was hired to serve. Many important contemporary and future literary figures worked for the commission, including several members of Mikhail Kheraskov's Moscow circle and Novikov, who was the commission's main secretary. Popov's immediate superior was Prince Fedor Kozlovsky, himself a talented poet and playwright, and this acquaintance helped strengthen Popov's literary connections. Kozlovsky died soon after in the Russo-Turkish War, the outbreak of which was grounds for Catherine to cut short the commission's greatly touted public activity. However, the smaller commission for investigating the various categories of state inhabitants – to which Popov had been assigned – continued to function, and in 1769 he was rewarded for the diligent performance of his duties by being granted the rank of collegiate registrar, at the time the lowest rank in the bureaucratic hierarchy.

Service did not prevent Popov from continuing his active involvement in literature. He maintained his connections with Novikov, and when the latter began to put out his well-known satiric journal *Truten'* (The Drone) in spring 1769, Popov published a series of poems in it. Somewhat earlier he had contributed epigrams to the journal *I to i sio* (Both This and That), published by Chulkov, another Saint Petersburg litterateur of lower-class origin. Popov had become friends with this writer before his trip to Moscow, and he had written the words and music for the final chorus of Chulkov's comedy *Kak khochesh' nazovi* (Call It What You Will, staged in 1765).

Apparently with Chulkov's encouragement, Popov began work on the creation of a mythological dictionary of pagan gods of the ancient Slavs. To this end Popov began studying Mikhail Lomonosov's historical works, medieval Russian chronicles, and native folklore. In 1768 his *Opisanie drevniago slavenskogo iazycheskago basnosloviia, sobrannago iz raznykh pisatelei, i snabdennago primechaniiami* (Description of Ancient Slavic Pagan Mythology, Collected from Various Writers and Supplied with Notes) was published. The work presents, in alpha-

betical order, descriptions of all of the figures of pagan Slavic mythology known to contemporary historians and ethnographers: Dazhbog, Kupala, Lel', Lada, Perun, Volos (or Veles), and so on. Popov defined the purpose of his book as "bol'she dlia uveseleniia chitatelei, nezheli dlia vazhnykh istoricheskikh spravok, i bol'she dlia stikhotvortsev, nezheli dlia istorikov" (more for the enjoyment of the reader than as a serious historical reference work, more for poets than for historians). For this reason it is impossible to speak seriously about the value of Popov's research from the point of view of modern scholarship. But for the broad readership and for many eighteenth-century poets, Popov's book and Chulkov's *Kratkoi mifologicheskoi leksikon* (Brief Mythological Lexicon, 1767) served as basic sources of information about the pantheon of pagan Slavic gods and of classical mythology.

Related to his interest in Russian antiquity, Popov wrote an adventure novel titled *Slavenskie drevnosti, ili Prikliucheniia slavenskikh kniazei* (Slavic Antiquities, or Adventures of Slavic Princes, 1770–1771). This extensive narrative is made up of a collection of traditional stock subjects from European chivalric novels that have been given an ancient Slavic coloration and embroidered with elements of national folklore. The central characters are the valiant Slavic Prince Svetlosan and Princess Miloslava; Prince Vel'diuz' and the Indian czar Vidostan, good and evil sorcerers; and a host of secondary figures. The evil schemes of the terrible wizard Karachun, who kidnaps Miloslava, and her liberation by Svetlosan with the help of a magical sword constitute the core of the fantastic events that fill the novel. Some of its individual motifs (along with others from similar works by Chulkov and V. A. Levshin) were borrowed by authors of poems on folkloric themes from the end of the eighteenth century through the beginning of the nineteenth, including Aleksandr Pushkin in his first major work, "Ruslan i Liudmila" (1817–1820). The fact that Popov's novel was republished three times before the end of the century (the last time in 1794) suggests its widespread popularity.

However, the theater never lost its appeal for Popov. In 1772 he wrote the one-act comic opera *Aniuta,* one of the first Russian attempts at the genre. The play was produced successfully by a group of court singers on the stage of the Summer Theater at Tsarskoe Selo on 26 August and was published in the same year in the first volume of his collected works. As the basis for his play, Popov used the libretto from Charles Simon Favart's *An-*

nete et Lubin (1762), a French comic opera that had already been translated by Prince Kozlovsky. Its plot was traditional – Aniuta, a girl raised in a peasant family, is in love with a young nobleman named Viktor but is being courted by a farm laborer. The rivalry between the two men leads to a crisis, but the discovery of Aniuta's noble birth permits a happy ending. The ideological message of the opera is expressed with utmost clarity in the final chorus, performed by the entire cast:

Чем не создан ты владеть,
Не старайся то иметь;
Там бывает тьма забот,
 Где надеемся быть счастью,
Всех счастливей в свете тот,
Кто своей доволен частью.

(That which you were not created to possess
Do not attempt to gain;
We encounter a host of troubles there
Where we hope to find happiness.
Happiest of all in this world
Is the one content with his lot.)

Popov incorporated Russian folk songs into the play and explored aspects of the daily life and psychology of simple Russian peasants.

Popov seems to have summed up his creative career in 1772 when he published nearly everything he had ever written and translated in the two-volume *Dosugi, ili Sobranie sochinenii i perevodov* (Leisure Time, or Collected Compositions and Translations). The first volume included his compositions in verse (laudatory poems, epigrams, fables, elegies, love songs, and translated poems), original theatrical compositions, a reprint of the *Opisanie drevniago slavenskogo iazycheskago basnosloviia, sobrannago iz raznykh pisatelei, i snabdennago primechaniiami,* and a prose translation of the first two cantos of Claude Joseph Dorat's didactic poem *La Déclamation théâtrale* (1766; translated as "Na featral'noe vozglashenie"). In the second volume he published one German and two French comedies that he had translated in the 1760s.

After the publication of *Dosugi,* Popov's creative interests narrowed, and he turned primarily to translation. Somewhat earlier he had translated fragments from Voltaire's *Contes de Guillaume Vadé* (Tales of Guillaume Vadé, 1764), published in the collection *Vadiny skazki* (Tales of Vadin, 1771). As his next serious project Popov translated Torquato Tasso's poem *Gerusalemme Liberata* (Jerusalem Delivered, 1580–1581) into prose using a French version. The work was undertaken at the behest of the Sobranie, staraiushchegosia o perevode inostrannykh knig (Society Striving for the Translation of Foreign Books), which Catherine had organized in fall 1768, making use of the young writers who had gathered to work for the legislative commission. She set out on an ambitious program of translating important works into Russian and allotted five thousand rubles annually from her personal funds to pay for the labor of numerous translators. Popov fulfilled several orders for the society. Besides Tasso's poem, he translated a French version of the travel diary of the English traveler John Bell, which had been published in Paris in 1766 as *Voyages depuis St. Petersbourg en Russie, dans diverses contrées de l'Asie.* The book, titled *Belevy puteshestviia chrez Rossiiu v raznyia Asiiatskie zemli* (1776) in Popov's translation, describes Bell's travels with a Russian diplomatic group, first through Russia and then to Persia and China and later Turkey.

Clearly in response to an increased demand for popular entertainment literature, Popov translated Pétis de La Croix's 1712 French translation of *1001 Arabian Nights,* an extremely popular work translated into Russian many times during the eighteenth century (almost always via French intermediaries). Popov's four-volume translation was published in 1778–1779 and again in 1801. As before, however, a significant portion of Popov's time was occupied with translating plays for the theater. Over the course of the 1770s and early 1780s he translated Beaumarchais's famous comedy *Le barbier de Séville* (1775), Chamblain de Marivaux's one-act comedy *Le préjugé vaincu* (Prejudice Conquered, 1747), Charles-Simon Favart's three-act comedy *Soliman II ou Les trois sultanes* (Solomon II or The Three Sultans, 1762), and many others.

Near the end of his life Popov compiled a major collection of Russian songs in three volumes titled *Rossiiskaia Erata, ili Vybor nailuchshikh noveishikh rossiiskikh pesen* (Russian Erato, or a Selection of the Best New Russian Songs, 1792). Along with songs by contemporary authors, including some Popov had composed himself, he included a large number of folk songs. Popov organized the volumes thematically, and they were categorized both by function and by the social and cultural spheres in which they were sung. Thus there were urban songs, love songs "na starinyi Russkii lad" (in the old-fashioned Russian style), peasant songs, Little Russian (Ukrainian) songs, theatrical songs, and army songs. In the final volumes of the anthology Popov included such categories as songs for Christmas, marriage, round dance, masquerade, and drinking, as well as satiric songs. Each volume had an alphabetized index of songs. The anthology was not published until after Popov's death.

No information has been preserved regarding the later years of Popov's life or the circumstances of his death; even its exact date is unknown. Evidently he died in Saint Petersburg. Not all of Popov's creative legacy was of equal value. As with many eighteenth-century Russian writers, his professional work at times bordered on dilettantism. Nevertheless, Popov's many contributions to Russian literature of his day – in helping to develop a popular native prose tradition, in making European theatrical works accessible to a Russian audience via translation, in writing *Aniuta,* and in popularizing the folk song and other aspects of folklore and popular culture – all provide adequate justification for not forgetting his name.

References:

Viktor E. Gusev, "Mikhailo Popov – poet – pesennik," *XVIII vek,* 7 (1966): 132–137;

Vasilii V. Sipovsky, *Ocherki iz istorii russkogo romana,* volume 1, part 2 (Saint Petersburg, 1910), pp. 140–161;

Petr N. Stolpiansky, "Odin iz deiatelei Ekaterininskoi epokhi: Mikhailo Vasil'evich Popov," *Russkaia starina,* no. 5 (1905): 324–341;

Aleksandr V. Zapadov, "Literator XVIII veka: Mikhail Popov," *Uchenye zapiski Kurskogo pedagogicheskogo instituta,* 1 (1941): 110–130.

Feofan Prokopovich

(8 June 1681? – 8 September 1736)

Marcia A. Morris
Georgetown University

SELECTED BOOKS: *Slovo . . . o vlasti i chesti tsarskoi . . .*
(Saint Petersburg, 1718);

O voznoshenii imeni patriarshego v tserkovnykh molitvakh . . .
(Saint Petersburg, 1721);

Dukhovnyi reglament (Saint Petersburg, 1721);

Pervoe uchenie otrokom (Saint Petersburg, 1721); anonymously translated by J. T. Philipps as *The
Russian Catechism* (London: W. Meadows,
1725);

Rozysk istoricheskii (Saint Petersburg, 1721);

*Pravda voli monarshei vo opredelenii naslednika derzhavy
svoei . . .* (Moscow, 1722);

*Slovo o sostoiavshemsia mezhdu imperieiu Rossiiskoiu i
koronoiu Shvedskoiu mire* (Saint Petersburg,
1723);

Istinnoe opravdanie pravovernykh khristian (Moscow:
Novikov, 1724);

Slovo na pogrebenie Petra Velikogo (Saint Petersburg,
1725);

*Slovo v den' vshestviia na vserossiiskii prestol . . . imp.
Anny Ioannovny vseia Rossii. Ianuaria 19 dnia,
1733 goda. O tom, chto tsarskaia vlast' sobstvennym
promyslom bozhiim poluchaetsia. Propovedannoe
Feofanom arkhiereiskopom Novgoroskim v Sanktpeterburge v domashnei tserkvi eia velichestva*
([Saint Petersburg: Akademiia nauk, [1733]);

Slova i rechi pouchitel'nye, pokhval'nye i pozdravitel'nye, 4
volumes (Saint Petersburg: Sukhoputnyi
kadetskii korpus, 1760–1774);

*Istoriia imperatora Petra velikogo ot rozhdeniia ego do
Poltavskoi batalii, i vziatiia v plen ostalnykh
shvedskikh voisk pri Perevolochne, vkliuchitel'no*
(Saint Petersburg: [Morskoi kadetskii korpus],
1773);

Chetyre sochineniia (Moscow: Universitetskaia
tipografiia, 1773);

Rassuzhdenie o bezbozhii ([Moscow]: Moskovskii universitet, 1774);

*Rassuzhdenie o knige Solomonovoi, naritsaemoi Pesnia
pesnei . . .* (Moscow: Universitetskaia tipografiia, 1774);

Feofan Prokopovich

*Knizhitsa, v nei zhe Povest' o raspre Pavla i Varnavy s iudeistvuiushchimi, i trudnost' slova Petra apostola o
neudob'nosimom zakonnom ige prostranno predlagaetsia* (Moscow: Novikov, 1784);

*Rassuzhdenie o prisiage, ili kliatve, podobaet li khristianom
prisiagat', ili kliatisia vsemogushchim bogom* (Moscow:
Novikov, 1784);

*Veschi i dela, o kotorykh dukhovnyi uchitel' narodu
khristiianskomu propovedati dolzhen: inaia obshchaia
vsem, a inaia nekiim sobstvennaia* (Moscow:
Novikov, 1784);

*Bogoslovskoe uchenie o sostoianii nepovrezhdennogo
cheloveka, ili o tom kakov byl Adam v raiu? . . .*
(Moscow: Ponomarev, 1785);

De arte poetica (Mogilev, 1786);

*Rassuzhdeniia o netlenii moshchei sviatykh ugodnikov
bozhiikh . . .* (Moscow: Kh. Klaudiia, 1786);

O smerti Petra Velikogo kratkaia povest' (Saint Petersburg, 1819).

Editions: *Sochineniia,* edited by Igor Eremin (Moscow & Leningrad: Akademiia nauk, 1961);

De arte rhetorica libri X Kijoviae 1706, edited by Renate Lachmann, Slavistische Forschungen, 27, Rhetorica Slavica, 2 (Cologne and Vienna: Böhlau Verlag, 1982).

Poet, literary theorist, religious reformer, and educator, Feofan Prokopovich was indisputably one of the preeminent figures of Peter the Great's turbulent era of reform and modernization and an outstanding representative of the age of transition. He was active in the political sphere, both justifying and facilitating Peter's secularization of the state, thereby contributing to a drastic diminution of ecclesiastical power in Russia. He was equally involved in cultural life, acting as a mediator between Western and Russian learning. In his capacity as poet and critic, he was instrumental in bridging the gulf between seventeenth-century baroque aesthetics and eighteenth-century classicism. Prokopovich was also a man thoroughly enmeshed in contradiction and controversy. On the one hand, he filled the humane position of patron to such notable eighteenth-century figures as Mikhail Lomonosov, Antiokh Kantemir, and Vasilli Tatishchev, while on the other, he supported and rationalized Peter's execution of his son, the czarevich Aleksei, and engineered the imprisonment of more than a few of his own personal enemies.

Documentation for the first twenty-five years of Prokopovich's life is rather sparse. Christened Eleazar, he was, according to most sources, born on 8 June 1681 to a Kievan merchant and his wife. He was orphaned at an early age, and his maternal uncle, who was rector of the famous Kiev Academy, took charge of his education. In 1692 the uncle died, but a wealthy patron assumed responsibility for the boy. He remained at the academy until 1698, when the young scholar left Kiev for Poland, renounced the Orthodox faith, and joined the Catholic Uniate church, a common seventeenth-century procedure for Russians and Ukrainians seeking to further their studies in the West. He seems to have entered a Uniate monastery under the name Samuil

Tsereisky, taught for a time, and then gone on to Rome to complete his formal education.

In Rome, Prokopovich attended the College of Saint Athanasius, where he studied poetry, rhetoric, philosophy, and ancient history. Prokopovich's thirst for knowledge and his fine natural abilities served him well, and he formed close relationships with some of the most powerful and influential Jesuits in Rome. Through them he was even given access to restricted sections of the Vatican library. His career seemed assured. In 1701, however, he left Rome without explanation.

In 1702 Prokopovich reappeared in Ukraine, having renounced Catholicism and become an Orthodox monk. He seems to have taken a circuitous route home, stopping to meet a number of renowned scholars of the day and perhaps even spending some time at the great universities of Leipzig, Halle, and Jena. It is impossible to say with certainty whether this journey or the years spent in Rome were more important in forming Prokopovich's view of the West, but in any case, he arrived home thoroughly opposed to Catholicizing tendencies within Orthodoxy and inclined to regard many Protestantizing trends with favor.

A hiatus follows in the young monk's biography until 1705, when he first appears as Feofan Prokopovich (which he took in memory of his uncle of the same name). At this point he was again in Kiev, engaged in teaching in his former school, the Kiev Academy, and writing treatises on poetics and rhetoric as well as an original play of his own. Prokopovich produced the majority of his works that were strictly literary in character in this Kievan period.

The Kiev Academy operated, in large part, along the same lines as Jesuit schools in neighboring Poland and shared a similar curriculum and comparable administrative procedures. The primary language of instruction was Latin, and instructors taught the entire sequence of advanced courses, bringing a given group of students through each of the higher classes. Thus Prokopovich taught poetics in 1705, moved on to rhetoric in 1706, became prefect of the academy and taught philosophy from 1707 to 1711, and, as rector, read theology between 1711 and 1716.

Prokopovich was determined to reform and modernize the curriculum of the academy and to this end initiated the study of physics, arithmetic, and geometry. These subjects were taught under the rubric of philosophy, and Prokopovich's initiative effectively marked the introduction of formal instruction in the natural sciences to the Kiev school. Moreover, he also left his mark on the humanities, challenging the supremacy of the reigning school of Scholasticism in both his lectures and his own *De arte poetica* (1786), written in 1705, a manual designed to supply his students with practical exercises in composition.

Prokopovich conceived *De arte poetica* as a course of lectures for his poetics class, and it was certainly one of the finest such works produced in Russia. Although it was based on similar manuals produced in the West (J. C. Scaliger's *Poetices libri septem* [1561] was an important model), *De arte poetica* introduced much that was new to the Slavic East. Unfortunately, it was not published until 1786, by which time a great deal of its originality and usefulness had lost its force. It has been widely recognized, however, as a major intermediary between contemporary theories of literature in the West and classicist theories later developed in Russia.

In composing *De arte poetica*, Prokopovich set himself three goals: simplicity, brevity, and clarity; and these same goals became, in turn, precepts to be observed by aspiring writers as they crafted poetic works. That rules should be brought to bear on the creation of poetry was never in question. *De arte poetica* voiced the strong conviction that poetry was in the nature of man, that it was a skill intrinsic to him and not a gift of God. Prokopovich believed that it could, therefore, be nurtured and suggested that this should best be achieved through the development of a proper science of poetry.

In *De arte poetica* Prokopovich attempted to formulate just such a science. He defines poetry as "iskusstvo izobrazhat' chelovecheskie deistviia i khodozhestvenno iz"iasniat' ikh dlia nazidaniia v zhizni" (the art of depicting human actions and artistically expressing them for edifying purposes), and he suggests that success in composing poetic works depends primarily on sincerity and effort. Poetry is similar to history in that it takes the actual deeds of men as its subject matter, and writing poetry is like writing history in that it is a skill that can be learned. The major difference between the two disciplines lies in poetry's greater use of imagination, in its depiction of things "takimi, kakimi oni mogli i dolzhny byli byt' " (as they might and should be) rather than as they are.

Central to creating poetry is imitation, by which Prokopovich understood the ability to produce works similar to those written by the poets of antiquity. He referred to this process as "tvorcheskoe zaimstvovanie" (creative imitation) and declared it to be "dusha poezii" (the soul of poetry). The aspiring poet was asked not so much to expropriate the work of the great poets blindly as to align his way of thinking with theirs and thus to create a work in the same mold as the model text.

An important aspect of *De arte poetica* was its classification of kinds or genres of poetry. Prokopovich recognized seven major varieties: epic, dramatic, bucolic, epigrammatic, elegiac, satiric, and lyric. Of particular relevance to Prokopovich's poetic output was his treatment of dramatic forms. He identified three subcategories of this type of poetry: tragedy, which depicted the deeds of great men subjected to the vicissitudes of fate; comedy, which delineated the doings of simple folk and unmasked bad habits; and tragicomedy, a mixed form which combined the extraordinary and the petty as well as the serious and the amusing. It was while working on *De arte poetica* that Prokopovich wrote his own tragicomedy, *Vladimir,* which was staged by the students of the academy on 3 July 1705.

There was nothing particularly surprising in Prokopovich's decision to compose a dramatic work. The tradition of school drama was not new to Kiev, and it was common practice to have students act in dramatic productions, but *Vladimir* was perhaps the finest example of the type. A play about the Christianization of ancient Rus', it brought together in one imaginative work significant innovations in language, theme, and composition.

One of the most pressing scholarly issues of Prokopovich's times was the choice of an appropriate literary language. Prokopovich, who often wrote in Latin, believed that different languages diverge from each other in their forms and constructions but that they all reflect reality in similar ways and are informed by the same underlying logic; accordingly, all languages are equally able to express any given thought. At the same time, he acknowledged the preeminence of the languages in which Scripture had originally been written. He therefore gave priority to Old Church Slavonic as the language of the first translations of the Bible, although he conceded that it was no longer feasible to compose in an archaic language inaccessible to broad segments of the reading public. For his compositions not written in Latin, Prokopovich chose the variant of Church Slavonic that had evolved over many centuries in Moscow, proclaiming it the one that remained most faithful to the original language yet was fairly easily understood by the educated public. He further diluted this idiom with the vernacular, creating what has been termed a "gibridnyi variant tserkovnoslavianskogo" (hybrid Slavonic).

Prokopovich's solution to the linguistic dilemmas facing him highlights his status as innovator and intermediary between cultures and time periods. He could easily have adopted the practice of educated Ukrainians of his day; they composed in two disparate literary languages: Ukrainian, and a pure Church Slavonic that conformed narrowly to the rules formulated in grammars. He could also have accepted the Russian practice of composing solely in Moscow Church Slavonic, which had moved away from bookish norms to a notable extent and yet was significantly different from the spoken vernacular. Instead he attempted a fusion of spoken forms with written, varying the amount of vernacular in accordance with the solemnity of the work in question. Thus he fully accepted neither contemporary Ukrainian nor Russian usage but rather anticipated the pairing of stylistic level with genre later formulated more systematically by Lomonosov.

Vladimir, which was written according to Prokopovich's linguistic precepts, is a perfect example of his "hybrid Slavonic." It combines Polonicisms and Ukrainianisms with Church Slavonic in proportions that vary according to the subject matter at hand. Its form, tragicomedy, was one that Prokopovich decreed to be mixed. Critics who were insensitive to the subtleties of this form disparaged it as linguistically impure, but *Vladimir* calculated to accommodate its audience rather than to meet the prescriptions of a grammar.

Prokopovich's tragicomedy likewise broke new thematic ground. It was a historical drama whose plot revolved around the efforts of the Kievan Prince Vladimir to bring Christianity to Rus'. Dramatic interest centers on disputes with pagan priests who steadfastly, if somewhat drunkenly, defend their old gods. Earlier Ukrainian dramatists had preferred to take their subject matter from Scripture, and *Vladimir* signaled a significant departure from this practice. Although critics disagree as to whether Prince Vladimir's conflict with the pagan priests is meant to signify the Ukrainian Hetman Mazepa's struggle against the Uniate presence on Orthodox soil or Peter the Great's battle against the conservative forces of Old Russia, they allow that the choice of a Slavic theme, especially one that resonated against the political issues of its day, was new. It had also been common practice in Russian and Ukrainian dramas to separate comic elements from the tragic, relegating them to "intermedia," farcical or burlesque interludes presented between acts or after serious dramatic presentations. Prokopovich again swam against the current by

choosing to mix the two. His pagan priests were the principal vehicle for introducing the low and the ridiculous, and their activities were inseparable from the main action of the play.

In 1706 Prokopovich wrote a second textbook, in conjunction with his duties as instructor of rhetoric. *De arte rhetorica libri X Kijoviae 1706* (1982) was a manual for writing prose works. It identified three linguistic levels: the high, reserved for composing solemn speeches; the middle, to be used for panegyrical sermons and historical works; and the low, suitable for letters to friends, dialogues, and various sorts of treatises. A great deal of emphasis was accorded works in the middle style, which were further subdivided according to the goals they were expected to achieve. Prokopovich formulated rules for "iz"iasnitel'nye" (expressive) compositions meant to praise or censure, "soveshchatel'nye" (deliberative) pieces intended to inculcate Christian virtues, and "oblichitel'nye" (accusatory) works aimed at judging vice and heresy.

De arte rhetorica also had another, somewhat darker, side. Along with counseling how one should write, it expressed strong opinions about how one should not write. Prokopovich used his text as an occasion to castigate the Catholic Scholastics he had come to despise, with Polish preachers coming in for a particularly large burden of criticism. The Orthodox churchman objected to a tendency on the part of scholastic preachers to expound on what he considered to be their own personal messages to the disparagement of the more important message found in Scripture. He insisted that the basis for good writing must be a thorough knowledge of the Bible, of the early church fathers, and of the lives of the saints. He also inveighed against tricks of composition designed to create unusual or original effects, contending that sermons should approach their subjects directly and clearly. Prokopovich's assertions are relevant to his views on literature, but they also highlight two very essential aspects of his personal outlook and approach to life – his vehement deprecation of Catholic tradition in favor of Protestant practice and his proclivity for mocking and abusing anyone who disagreed with him. He was to avail himself of this latter habit to much more sinister effect as he grew more powerful.

The year 1706 was also marked by Prokopovich's first encounter with Peter the Great. In July Peter came to Kiev to inspect its military fortifications. Prokopovich delivered a welcoming sermon that seems to have made a favorable impression on the czar. Unlike most sermons preached to the autocrat, this one eschewed biblical comparisons, dwelling instead on Peter's concrete, specific achievements.

A second opportunity to gratify the czar was not long in coming. After Russia's 1709 victory over the Swedes at Poltava, Peter visited Kiev, and Prokopovich was once again selected to give the welcoming address. He took the opportunity to compare the defeated Swedish army with the vanquished forces in the Punic Wars and, characteristically, to denounce Mazepa, who had by this time rebelled against Russian power. Peter, however, came in for a fulsome share of accolades, and at his request the sermon was translated into Latin for broader dissemination.

Prokopovich found another occasion on which to be generous in apportioning praise – this time to the powerful Aleksandr Menshikov, Peter's court favorite, who in turn contacted the metropolitan of Novgorod and recommended the Kievan preacher as archimandrite of the Iur'ev Monastery. Although nothing came of this initiative, Prokopovich was invited to join the czar in 1711 during the Turkish campaign and, on his return to Kiev, was named rector of the academy and hegumen of the Brotherhood Monastery.

During his remaining years in Kiev, Prokopovich composed syllabic verse, translated a variety of texts, and taught theology. He also began what was envisioned to be a systematic theological explication. The seven sections that he managed to complete were all written in an identical pattern; each unfolded as an argument in which a question was posed, an answer was suggested and justified through reference to Scripture, and objections were raised and refuted.

Prokopovich's work did not go unnoticed. His method of relying on evidence gleaned from Scripture, his disparagement of the inductive method favored by scholasticism, and his championing of the doctrine of justification through faith in "Raspria Pavla i Varnavy" (The Dispute between Paul and Barnabus, 1712; published, 1784) earned him the animosity of Feofilakt Lopatinsky, the influential rector of the Moscow Academy. Lopatinsky charged him with preaching Protestant heresy, a charge which was to haunt Prokopovich throughout his career.

Prokopovich's Protestant bias, however, far from prejudicing him at Peter's court, was quite congenial to the Russian autocrat. In 1715 the already-controversial monk was called to Saint Petersburg and promised a bishopric. Although he protested in a letter to his good friend Markovich that "Eta pochest' menia takzhe privlekaet i prel'shchaet, kak esli by menia prigovorili brosit' na s"edenie dikim zveriam" (this honor attracts and entices me about as much as being thrown to wild beasts), he nevertheless arrived in 1716. Peter was away for the first year of Prokopovich's tenure in the new capital, but the aspiring bishop made good use of his time, compiling a genealogical table of Russian rulers and delivering a number of important sermons. In the first of these, read on Christmas, he continued to develop the doctrine of justification. In another, marking the occasion of the birth of Czarevich Peter, he turned to the political arena, urging the Russian people to subject themselves unquestionably to the authority of the czar. This thematic separation of sermons dealing with religion from sermons developing political ideas persisted in Prokopovich's work for some time before finally yielding to an almost-exclusive concern with temporal affairs. Significantly, the sermons written on religious themes continued to be strongly flavored with Protestant doctrine. Prokopovich made controversial pronouncements opposing the uncritical worship of icons and relics, contesting the efficacy of excessive asceticism on the part of monks, and forbidding Orthodox believers to seek martyrdom voluntarily in defense of their faith. Each of these positions incensed those who held to the traditional forms of faith and swelled the ranks of important members of the church hierarchy who opposed Prokopovich.

In October 1717 Peter returned to his capital to be greeted by Prokopovich's panegyrical sermon extolling the value of foreign travel and celebrating the czar as the reformer of Russia. Peter responded by initiating a search for a suitable position in the church hierarchy for his new favorite, and in the spring of 1718 the Russian bishops were called together to confirm Prokopovich's appointment to the diocese of Pskov. Lopatinsky, as well as the influential Greek Likhudi brothers and Stefan Iavorsky, the acting patriarch of the Russian church, voiced displeasure with the choice and denounced Prokopovich as a purveyor of "unclean dogmas," but the appointment nonetheless went through.

Prokopovich, new position not withstanding, remained in Saint Petersburg and was deeply aware of the debt of gratitude he owed to Peter. Two weeks after his accession to the episcopate, Czarevich Aleksei, Peter's son by his first wife, was arrested and incarcerated in the Peter and Paul Fortress. He was charged with plotting to overthrow his father and sentenced to death. Aleksei died under torture on 26 June. Peter's infant son (also named Peter) by Empress Catherine was declared heir to the throne. Several months before these grisly events Prokopovich had read his *Slovo . . . o vlasti i chesti tsarskoi . . .* (Oration on the Power and Glory of the Czar, 1718), in which he suggested, in a rather transparent allusion to the storm gathering around the czarevich, that to oppose the czar was to oppose God. He also stated that the clergy was but one of several social classes in Russia and that its power was not in any way commensurate with the czar's. Prokopovich never breathed a word of criticism against Peter's treatment of his heir, and, in fact, he later enthusiastically justified the czar's right to name his own successor.

Once Peter had dealt with the question of the dynastic succession, he proposed a new task to Prokopovich. During a trip to Europe, the czar had met with a group of theologians from the Sorbonne. They had broached an initiative to reunite the Russian church with the Roman Catholic and had prepared a proposal for such an undertaking. Peter asked both Prokopovich and Iavorsky to compose answers to this proposal. Iavorsky, who longed for the formal reinstatement of the patriarchate, possibly with himself at its head, rejected the French proposal on the grounds that no adequate response was possible until a proper patriarch was in place to make it. Prokopovich, however, took a different tack. He wrote that such a momentous undertaking would have to be ratified by the assembled patriarchs and bishops of all branches of the Orthodox church. Thus he cleverly avoided an outright refusal while indicating that the Russian church was not interested in union. Although Iavorsky was technically the more senior hierarch, Prokopovich's response was the one chosen to be forwarded to Paris.

Peter appreciated both the extent to which Prokopovich shared his own ideas and the ready intelligence he brought to his work. At the time of his death, Prokopovich owned a stone house in Saint Petersburg, a wooden one in the suburbs, a house in Moscow, and several vacation residences. He kept a number of boats and left a library of over three thousand works, one of the finest of its day. Most of these possessions were acquired in direct consequence of the czar's generosity.

In 1719 Prokopovich undertook an inspection of his diocese. References in letters to friends indicate that Prokopovich also worked on several projects, including an "Apostolic Geography" that was to identify places mentioned in Scripture for the modern reader; treatises on martyrdom and hypocrisy; a history of the patriarchate, in which he notes that the early church lived without this particular institution for hundreds of years; and his *Pervoe uchenie otrokom* (Children's First Guide, 1721), a catechism that was to know spectacular success for many years. He also

worked on the *Dukhovnyi reglament* (Ecclesiastical Regulation, 1721), which permanently abolished the patriarchate and established in its place a ruling council, the Most Holy Synod.

The *Dukhovnyi reglament* represents a milestone in the history of Russian Orthodoxy. Although Peter had failed to name a permanent successor when Patriarch Adrian died in 1700, he had appointed Iavorsky to be a kind of acting patriarch. In Peter's estimation, however, Iavorsky's performance left much to be desired. Moreover, the institution of the patriarchate was profoundly uncongenial to the czar. The existence of an independent hierarchy alongside his government structure threatened Peter's hegemony. He resolutely combatted the idea of a higher moral power that could contest his personal will, and he found an eager ally and ready apologist for his stance in Prokopovich, who saw certain similarities between the workings of the patriarchate and the papacy, an institution he despised.

The *Dukhovnyi reglament* created a council with eleven members: a president, two vice-presidents, four councillors, and four assessors. Iavorsky was appointed president, while the two vice-presidents were Prokopovich and Feodosii Ianovsky, the archbishop of Novgorod. The Most Holy Synod officially came into being in 1721 with the publication of the *Dukhovnyi reglament,* which had already been ratified by the hierarchs of the Russian church, and although the Russian bishops launched a furious attack against it after Peter's death, it survived as the governing body of the Orthodox church until the 1917 revolution.

From the beginning, Prokopovich was recognized as the synod's most powerful ecclesiastical member and the guiding force behind it. He was well aware of the clergy's hostility to the new institution, however, and devoted much time and effort in its defense. In *Rozysk istoricheskii* (Historical Investigation, 1721) and *O voznoshenii imeni patriarshego v tserkovnykh molitvakh* (On the Elevation of the Patriarch's Name in Church Prayers, 1721) written in 1721–1722, he argued that Roman and Byzantine emperors had wielded both temporal and spiritual power and were recognized as holding the right to the title of bishop. This was clearly meant to justify the recent diminution of ecclesiastical authority in Russia and the concomitant increase in the power exercised by Peter.

Prokopovich's attacks against the church and efforts on behalf of the autocrat so incensed Iavorsky that he made one final effort to neutralize his opponent. He appealed to the Senate, which promptly referred his case to the Most Holy Synod. The synod found in favor of Prokopovich and accused Iavorsky of "scandalous and divisive" behavior.

Prokopovich's high standing in the synod is further evidenced by a proclamation issued by that body decreeing his catechism, the *Pervoe uchenie otrokom,* a required church reading. The work is an explication of the Ten Commandments and the Lord's Prayer. Meant to serve the needs of two different audiences, it was one of the first books to be given to small children, but it was also a guide for the "simple folk" who made up the most unsophisticated layer of Orthodox believers. Although the book was intended to impart basic lessons of Christian doctrine, Prokopovich could not help but avail himself of the opportunity it offered to engage in polemics. In *Pervoe uchenie otrokom* he argued against unseemly veneration of icons and relics and provoked another round of attacks, one of the most severe of which came from Prince Dmitrii Kantemir, father of the famous man of letters, Antiokh Kantemir.

Another work characteristic of Prokopovich was published in 1721 — a short treatise on the admissibility of marriage between Orthodox believers and other Christians. Its immediate impetus, as was frequently the case with Prokopovich's polemical literature, was a practical difficulty encountered by the czar. Prisoners of war had been taken during the campaigns against Sweden, and many of them were employed in the mining industry. The Swedes' technical know-how and their diligence endeared them to Peter, who wanted to keep them satisfied and in good humor, but the Swedes were adamantly opposed to the requirement that they convert to Orthodoxy in order to marry Russian women. Prokopovich took a fairly liberal view of the question, allowing intermarriage between different Christian confessions. In *Istinnoe opravdanie pravovernykh khristian* (A True Apology for Orthodox Christians, 1724) he took a similarly liberal approach to the differences between mainstream Orthodox believers and Old Believers, declaring that anyone who exaggerated the differences between the two groups was guilty of heresy.

Prokopovich again came to the czar's aid in 1722 with one of his most celebrated works, *Pravda voli monarshei vo opredelenii naslednika derzhavy svoei* (The Right of the Monarch to Determine the Successor to His Power). Peter's son and heir, Czarevich Peter, had died in 1719, and in an effort to remove Aleksei's son from the line of succession, Peter the Great promulgated a decree in February of 1722 which entitled him to name whomever he chose as successor. No one could know that the czar

would die without availing himself of this right, and it was thought best at the time to quiet protests against the innovation. Prokopovich's *Pravda voli monarshei vo opredelenii naslednika derzhavy svoei* justified Peter's implicit act of disinheritance at the same time that it praised the principle of inherited monarchy. It was considered important enough to merit translation into German in 1724.

Another important work may also date to this period, the *Istoriia imperatora Petra velikogo ot rozhdeniia ego do Poltavskoi batalii* (History of the Emperor Peter the Great from his Birth through the Battle of Poltava), first published in 1773 with a note attributing it to Prokopovich. Assessments vary as to how much of the text was actually written by Prokopovich, but he almost certainly owns a major, if not exclusive, right to its authorship. Petr Morozov, a serious scholar of the question, suggests in his *Feofan Prokopovich kak pisatel'* (1880) that an unknown historian wrote a draft version that Prokopovich expanded in some places and cut in others. Many sections suggest his style so strongly that it seems reasonable to posit him as having corrected if not having written the entire text.

Prokopovich's interest in history was of long standing. In *De arte rhetorica libri X Kijoviae 1706* he discusses at some length the composition of historical works, and, besides his contributions to the history of Peter, he may have undertaken a history of the church up to the time of Constantine the Great that has not survived. The great eighteenth-century historian Tatishchev claimed that Prokopovich also wrote a book on the Amazons in which he proved that they were a Slavic tribe.

Few of Prokopovich's sermons from the last years of Peter's reign have survived. One of these, *Slovo o sostoiavshemsia mezhdu imperieiu Rossiiskoiu i koronoiu Shvedskoiu mire* (1723) was delivered on 28 January 1722 on the occasion of the conclusion of the peace of Nystadt, and in it Prokopovich sounds familiar notes. He first compares pre-Petrine Russia to its reformed, secular incarnation (that defeated Sweden) and points to the advantages enjoyed by the more modern state. He next calls on the populace to give thanks for Russia's great victory by supporting the army and navy, a somewhat controversial proposal considering the havoc that Peter's military expenditures had wrought on his treasury. The sermon sounds a new note, however, by admitting that the Russian people cannot be expected to welcome the victory properly unless they see real, material benefits in it for themselves. This was one of the rare occasions on which Prokopovich's role as communicator between the government and the people reflected a real advocacy of the people.

Peter died on 28 January 1725, and Prokopovich's personal and political ordeals began. At first things went the churchman's way. He lent his support to Menshikov, and, with like-minded allies, helped put Catherine, Peter's second wife, on the throne. Prokopovich had enthusiastically championed Catherine years before at the time of her coronation, and in token of his continued loyalty he was selected to read two funeral orations for Peter as well as a sermon on the occasion of the empress's accession to the throne. The second of the two sermons on Peter has been praised as the finest burial oration in all of eighteenth-century Russian literature. Together with Lopatinsky, Prokopovich was also entrusted with the delicate task of composing a narrative on Peter's death (*O smerti Petra Velikogo kratkaia povest'*, 1819), meant to dispel rumors about the czar's last moments.

Although Prokopovich's position seemed to have changed little in the new reign, his enemies within the church hierarchy judged the time right to settle old scores and perhaps even to restore the patriarchate. Ianovsky, who had earlier been appointed Prokopovich's fellow vice-president on the Most Holy Synod, took the occasion to declare Peter's death a punishment for his having fettered the clergy. A month later Ianovsky was arrested and sent to a remote northern monastery, while Prokopovich was selected by Catherine to fill the vacant position of archbishop of Novgorod. Significantly, however, Menshikov, once Peter's, and still Catherine's, favorite, was growing increasingly disenchanted with Prokopovich. He had supported the candidacy of Bishop Georgii Dashkov of Rostov for the important Novgorod vacancy and, unable to acquire that position for him, had him named to the ruling triumvirate of the Most Holy Synod, together with Prokopovich and Lopatinsky. This development was uncomfortable from Prokopovich's point of view, since Lopatinsky was a longtime enemy, and Dashkov, besides being embittered over the Novgorod affair, secretly hoped to reestablish the patriarchate and abolish Prokopovich's creation, the synod. Moreover, Dashkov cherished a longstanding antipathy toward intellectuals in general and toward Ukrainian intellectuals in particular.

Even more ominously, Markell Rodyshevsky, a monk who had known Prokopovich from Kiev, surfaced in Saint Petersburg in 1726 and charged Prokopovich with "indecent words and ecclesiastical offenses." In depositions against Prokopovich, Rodyshevsky claimed that the Kievan monk had

been sent to Rome as a reward for depredations against Orthodoxy and that he had feigned piety while living in Kiev in order to attract children of the wealthy and powerful into the academy and pollute them with heresy. Although Prokopovich was able to refute these charges successfully, Catherine nevertheless wavered in her support and admonished him to live a good life in accordance with religious precepts. Prokopovich rightly felt this as a slap in the face.

Catherine died in May of 1727, and Prokopovich's funeral oration, in which he extolled her as a worthy helper of the great reforming czar, was one of the last significant literary works he was to produce. Catherine was succeeded by Peter II, the son of Aleksei – a bad turn of events for Prokopovich, the apologist for what was effectively Peter the Great's act of disinheritance. Prokopovich's enemies were quick to take advantage of his fall from influence, and the beleaguered churchman subsequently spent an inordinate amount of his time answering charges against his orthodoxy made to the Secret Chancellery.

The accession of Peter II brought renewed hope to the champions of Muscovite piety for the restoration of the old order. Lopatinsky, Dashkov, and Aleksei Titov, the bishop of Kolomna, joined forces against Prokopovich, the symbol of all that was new. Menshikov, who was also implicated in the murder of Peter's father, tried to save himself by enlisting in their ranks. Their strength became evident when they succeeded in having future publication of *Pravda voli monarshei vo opredelenii naslednika derzhavy svoei* forbidden. Meanwhile, Markell Rodyshevsky renewed his attacks, denouncing Prokopovich for preaching Lutheranism and Calvinism. He demanded that other works by Prokopovich be condemned.

Prokopovich defended himself the only way he could. He ceased making theological justifications of himself and turned to political denunciation of his opponents instead. He accused Rodyshevsky of defaming the honor of Peter the Great, as well as of exhibiting ignorance exceeding even that of the Old Believers. Fortunately for Prokopovich, Baron Ostermann, then in high favor with Peter II, came to his aid. Menshikov fell from power and was banished, and Prokopovich breathed more easily.

The sermons written during this difficult period were different from Prokopovich's earlier ones. He eschewed debate on social issues and avoided political controversy at all costs. By restricting himself to questions of church dogma, he tried to ride out the storm. He was not entirely successful, however. His old enemy, Iavorsky, came back from the grave to haunt him.

Years earlier (possibly as early as 1713) Iavorsky had written *Kamen' very* (The Rock of Faith), a compilation based in large part on the writings of Catholic theologians which attacked the Lutheranizing tendencies manifest in the Orthodox church. It was clearly a stab at Prokopovich, but at the time of its composition his influence was at its pinnacle, and publication was forbidden. In 1728, however, permission to print was granted, and a new edition of two thousand copies was published in 1729. The controversy raised by the book raged in Russia for several years, with foreign theologians, including the German Protestant Johann Franz Buddeus and the Spanish Dominican Franciscus Bernardus Ribera, responding to it as well. As long as the debate continued, Prokopovich was in danger. Finally, in 1732, publication was again prohibited, putting an end to public discussion.

Meanwhile, Peter II had died in January of 1730, and the question of the succession again arose. Prokopovich, still engrossed in the *Kamen' very* controversy and pursued relentlessly by his enemies, knew that he had to act on his own behalf. He joined forces with those members of the Supreme Privy Council who urged that Anna, Peter the Great's niece, be crowned. The council, however, imposed important limitations on the actions of the future empress in the form of conditions that would have effectively required her to share power with them. Anna agreed to the conditions at first, but then, with the support of Ostermann and Prokopovich, she rejected them and reigned without further interference from the council.

Prokopovich lived the remainder of his life under the rule of Empress Anna. These last few years marked, from a political perspective, a sort of golden age for the embittered churchman. Anna recognized his services just as gratefully as had Peter the Great, and Prokopovich took the opportunity to settle scores with his enemies. It has been suggested by historians that many of his opponents had plotted for the accession of Evdokiia, Peter the Great's first wife and mother of Aleksei, who had been shut away in a convent for years. Whether this hypothesis is true or not, there was definitely some hesitation by certain churchmen to recognize Anna as the new empress and to name her in public prayers as autocrat. This was just the pretext for which Prokopovich was looking, and he made good use of it. Eventually Lopatinsky, Dashkov, and many lesser players were removed from high office and banished to remote monasteries.

Although the last years of Prokopovich's life were darkened by the controversy he had done so much to generate, they were nevertheless marked by many achievements that did not earn him the credit he perhaps deserved. Early in his association with Peter the Great, Prokopovich had joined the "Neptune Society," a private club made up of Peter's favorites. Here he had the opportunity to mix with both Russians and foreigners and to promote many of his reforming ideas. He soon created his own circle, which included some of the most important intellectuals of the time. Through informal gatherings of this group, sometimes referred to as his "uchenaia druzhina" (learned guard), Prokopovich was able to exercise a great deal of influence on such luminaries as Tatishchev and Kantemir.

Prokopovich also founded and supported a school for orphans at his suburban residence near Saint Petersburg. Over the years between its establishment in 1721 and his death in 1736, this school graduated 160 students, many of whom were sent on to the gymnasium of the Academy of Sciences. In his will the founder earmarked much of his considerable fortune for the continued maintenance of his students.

This final period of Prokopovich's life added little or nothing to his literary output. His last sermons were largely reiterations of the same idea — that under Anna Russia had returned to the ways of Peter the Great and that her people were now flourishing. Most of his time was devoted less to writing than to the affairs of the Most Holy Synod. He died on 8 September 1736.

Prokopovich's legacy to Russian culture was complex. Many church historians have lamented the loss of independence suffered by the Russian Orthodox hierarchy during his years of influence. While it can be argued that Peter would have reorganized the church with or without Prokopovich, the terrible atmosphere of dissension and confrontation that hung over the newly created synod owed much to Prokopovich's personal manner. By the same token, much of the criticism lodged against him by his contemporaries was undoubtedly exaggerated. His attacks against the worship of icons and relics were not, as was often alleged, aimed at destroying ancient Orthodox customs. Rather, Prokopovich defended icons, arguing only against a superstitious belief in the divine powers of material artifacts. In this he was attempting to cleanse the Church of abuses and to raise the level of faith of primitive believers.

As one of the leading intellectuals of his age, Prokopovich did much to promote literary culture.

And although his theoretical treatises were well thought-out and clearly written, an even greater contribution was made by his literary writings. His sermons were models of clarity and simplicity. In all genres he was equally innovative in his choice of subject matter and his use of language. He was one of the first representatives of high culture to select topics from Russian reality, and when he borrowed literary themes and forms, he turned, as often as not, to Greek and Roman antiquity rather than to the Bible. Both in this activity and in his linguistic reforms he paved the way for Lomonosov and the classicist movement in Russian letters.

Bibliography:

James Cracraft, "Feofan Prokopovich: A Bibliography of His Works," *Oxford Slavonic Papers,* 8 (1975): 1–36.

Biographies:

Ilarion Chistovich, *Feofan Prokopovich i ego vremia* (Saint Petersburg: Akademiia nauk, 1868);

Petr Morozov, *Feofan Prokopovich kak pisatel'* (Saint Petersburg, 1880);

Valeriia Nichyk, *Feofan Prokopovich* (Moscow, 1977).

References:

James Cracraft, *The Church Reform of Peter the Great* (Stanford: Stanford University Press, 1971), pp. 49–62;

Cracraft, "Feofan Prokopovich," in *The Eighteenth Century in Russia,* edited by J. G. Garrard (Oxford: Clarendon Press, 1973), pp. 75–105;

Hans Joachim Härtel, *Byzantinisches Erbe und Orthodoxie bei Feofan Prokopovič* (Würzburg: Augustinus Verlag, 1970);

N. Kochetkova, "Oratorskaia proza Feofana Prokopovicha i puti formirovaniia literatury klassitsizma," *XVIII vek,* 9 (1974), pp. 50–80;

Max J. Okenfuss, "The Jesuit Origins of Petrine Education," in *The Eighteenth Century in Russia,* edited by Garrard (Oxford: Clarendon Press, 1973), pp. 106–130;

Iurii Samarin, *Stefan Iavorskii i Feofan Prokopovich kak propovedniki* (Moscow, 1844);

George Shevelov, *Two Orthodox Ukrainian Churchmen of the Early Eighteenth Century: Teofan Prokopovych and Stefan Iavorskii* (Cambridge, Mass.: Ukrainian Studies Fund, Harvard University, 1985);

A. Smirnov, "K probleme sootnoshenii russkogo predklassitsizma i gumanisticheskoi teorii poezii. F. Prokopovich i Iu. Ts. Skaliger," in *Problemy, teorii i istorii literatury: Sbornik statei, posviashchennyi pamiati prof. A. N. Sokolova* (Moscow, 1971), pp. 67–73;

A. Sokolov, "O poetike Feofana Prokopovich" in *Problemy sovremennoi filologii* (Moscow, 1965), pp. 443–449;

Robert Stupperich, "Feofan Prokopovič in Rom," *Zeitschrift für Osteuropäische Geschichte,* 5 (1931): 327–339;

Stupperich, "Feofan Prokopovič und Johann F. Buddeus. Ein Beitrag zur Geschichte der geistigen Beziehungen Russland und Deutschland im Beginn des 18. Jahrhunderts," *Zeitschrift für Osteuropäische Geschichte,* 9 (1935): 341–362;

Joachim Tetzner, "Theophan Prokopovič und die russische Frühaufklarung," *Zeitschrift für Slawistik,* 3 (1958): 351–368;

Nikolai Tikhonravov, "Tragedokomediia Feofana Prokopovicha 'Vladimir,'" *Zhurnal Ministerstva narodnogo prosviashcheniia,* 5 (1879): 52–96;

Pavel Verkhovskoi, *Uchrezhdenie dukhvnoi kollegii i Dukhvnyi Reglament: K voprosu ob otnoshenii Tserkvi i gosurdarstva v Rossii* (Rostov-na-Donu, 1916);

Valentin Vompersky, "Stilisticheskaia teoriia Feofana Prokopovicha," in his *Stilisticheskoe uchenie M. V. Lomonosova i teoriia trekh stilei* (Moscow University, 1970), pp. 70–98;

Eduard Winter, "Zum geistigen Profil Feofan Prokopovičs," *Studien zur Geschichte der russischen Literatur des 18. Jahrhunderts,* 2 (1968): 24–28;

Viktor Zhivov, "Iazyk Feofana Prokopovicha i rol' gibridnykh variantov tserkovno-slavianskogo v istorii slavianskikh literaturnykh iazykov," *Sovetskoe slavianovedenie,* 3 (1985): 70–85.

Aleksandr Nikolaevich Radishchev
(20 August 1749 – 11 September 1802)

Igor Vladimirovich Nemirovsky
Institute of Russian Literature (Pushkin House), Saint Petersburg

BOOKS: *Zhitie Fedora Vasil'evicha Ushakova, s priobshcheniem nekotorykh ego sochinenii* (Saint Petersburg: Imperatorskaia tipografiia, 1789);

Pis'mo k drugu, zhitel'stvuiushchemu v Tobol'ske, po dolgu zvaniia svoego (Saint Petersburg: [Printed on Radishchev's own press], 1790);

Puteshestvie iz Peterburga v Moskvu (Saint Petersburg: [Radishchev,] 1790); translated by Leo Wiener as *A Journey from Saint Petersburg to Moscow* (Cambridge: Harvard University Press, 1958).

Editions: *Sobranie ostavshikhsia sochinenii pokoinogo Aleksandra Nikolaeva Radishcheva,* 6 volumes (Moscow: Platon Beketov, 1807–1811);

Sochineniia, edited by P. A. Efremov, 2 volumes (Saint Petersburg: Cherkesov, 1872);

Polnoe sobranie sochinenii, edited by V. V. Kallash, 2 volumes (Moscow: V. M. Sablin, 1907);

Polnoe sobranie sochinenii, edited by S. N. Troinitsky (Saint Petersburg: Sirius, 1907);

Polnoe sobranie sochinenii, 2 volumes, edited by A. K. Borozdin, I. I. Papshin, and P. E. Shchegolev (Saint Petersburg: M. I. Akinfiev, 1907–1909);

Polnoe sobranie sochinenii, 3 volumes, edited by I. K. Luppol, G. A. Gukovsky, V. A. Desnitsky, N. K. Piksanov, and others (Moscow & Leningrad: Akademiia nauk, 1938–1952);

Polnoe sobranie stikhotvorenii, edited by G. A. Gukovsky, Biblioteka poeta, bol'shaia seriia (Leningrad: Sovetskii pisatel', 1940);

Stikhotvoreniia, edited by L. Lekhtblau (Moscow: Pravda, 1940);

Stikhotvoreniia, edited by Gukovsky, Biblioteka poeta, malaia seriia (Moscow: Sovetskii pisatel', 1947);

Izbrannye sochineniia (Moscow: Khudozhestvennaia literatura, 1949);

Izbrannye filosofskie sochineniia, edited by I. Ia. Shchipanov and L. B. Svetlov (Moscow: Gospolitizdat, 1949);

Aleksandr Nikolaevich Radishchev

Izbrannye filosofskie i obshchestvenno-politicheskie sochineniia, edited by Shchipanov and Svetlov (Moscow: Gospolitizdat, 1952);

Stikhotvoreniia, edited by Georgii P. Makogonenko, Biblioteka poeta, malaia seriia (Moscow: Sovetskii pisatel', 1953);

Stikhotvoreniia, edited by V. A. Zapadov, Biblioteka poeta, bol'shaia seriia (Leningrad: Sovetskii pisatel', 1975);

Puteshestvie iz Peterburga v Moskvu. Vol'nost', edited by Zapadov, Literaturnye pamiatniki (Saint Petersburg: Nauka, 1992).

TRANSLATIONS: Gabriel Bonnet de Mably, *Razmyshlenie o grecheshoi istorii, ili O prichinakh blagodeistviia i neschastiia grekov,* anonymous (Saint Petersburg: Obshestvo staraiushcheesia o napechatanii knig, 1773);

Anton Leopold von Elsnitz, *Ofitserskie uprazhneniia,* 4 volumes (Saint Petersburg: Akademiia nauk, 1777);

Jean-Baptiste Barthelemy, *Lessepsovo Puteshestvie po Kamchatke i po Iuzhnoi storone Sibiri,* 3 volumes (Moscow, 1801–1802).

SELECTED PERIODICAL PUBLICATION – UNCOLLECTED: "Beseda o tom, chto est' syn otechestva," anonymous, *Beseduiushchii grazhdanin,* 3 (December 1789): 308–324.

The career of Aleksandr Nikolaevich Radishchev, whom Soviet critics christened "the first Russian revolutionary," constitutes one of the most perplexing issues in Russian literary history. The fact that his main claim to fame, the *Puteshestvie iz Peterburga v Moskvu* (Journey from Petersburg to Moscow, 1790) – a sharp denunciation of serfdom and autocratic rule in Russia – was banned and its author exiled to Siberia accorded Radishchev the status of a martyr in later tradition. Yet why should this writer – who took almost no part in Russian literary life and whose main work, which Aleksandr Pushkin and others have declared to be mediocre, was almost completely unknown to the reading public – occupy one of the highest places in the pantheon of Russian letters? The question is whether Radishchev's actual place in Russian literature really corresponds to this estimate, or whether it merely reflects his reputation as a revolutionary and the Russian tendency to equate political correctness with literary value.

Aleksandr Nikolaevich Radishchev was born on 20 August 1749 in the village of Verkhnee Abliazovo in the Saratov region, where his father owned his largest estate. Here the future writer spent the first eight years of his life. By the time of his birth the Radishchev family had acquired fame and wealth, and Radishchev's father, Nikolai Afanasievich, spared nothing to give his children a good education. (Radishchev was one of seven brothers and four sisters.) Radishchev studied at home until the age of eight; his first teachers were a serf named Petr Mamontov and a fugitive soldier of French extraction whose name has not been preserved; but it may be assumed that Radishchev studied French as a child. In 1757 Radishchev went to Moscow to continue his education. He lived at the home of M. F. Argamakov, a relative on his mother's side, and studied science, for the most part with professors from the newly opened Moscow University who gave him private lessons. In November 1762, at age thirteen, Radishchev entered into civil service as a page at the court of the new empress Catherine II, who was spending the first year of her reign in Moscow, and in 1764 he left Moscow with the imperial court and moved to Saint Petersburg.

Two years later, on 23 September 1766, an event occurred that shaped the course of Radishchev's entire life: he and nine other young noblemen were sent to study at Leipzig University in Germany on the personal command of Catherine. Like many later Russian dissidents, during the course of his study abroad Radishchev developed a powerful animosity toward conditions in Russia. Furthermore, his time at Leipzig University gave the future writer a broad and systematic education, which distinguished him from the majority of his contemporaries in Russia, where, notwithstanding the opening of Moscow University in 1755, the basic form of education was still home schooling. Radishchev studied at the law faculty and attended classes taught by some of the best professors of Europe, including Christof Schmidt, professor of philosophy and follower of the French Encyclopedists, who lectured on civil law; Karl Ferdinand Hommel, expert on canon law; and Ernst Platner, probably the most celebrated professor at the university at the time, who lectured on mathematics, psychology, and aesthetics. Many years later that other famous Russian traveler Nikolai Karamzin met with Platner, and it is remarkable that the aged professor still remembered Radishchev, his inquisitive student from Russia.

Radishchev also spent much time reading on his own, especially the works of Claude-Adrien Helvétius, the French philosophe and Encyclopedist. Radishchev later recalled what a strong impression Helvétius's *De l'Esprit* (Essays on the Mind, 1758) made on him. He was also enthralled by the works of Gabriel Mably and Jean-Jacques Rousseau, and French social thought of the Enlightenment became an integral part of Radishchev's worldview. Rousseau's idea of a social contract, and his conviction of the inalienable right of the people to call its sovereign to account if he (or she) violates that contract, became central to Radishchev's thinking.

Life in Leipzig was marked by an event that reinforced Radishchev's hatred of despotism. Indignant at the tyrannical acts of their ignorant supervisor, Maj. Gerhard von Alten Bokum, the Russian students organized a revolt against him. It is clear from Radishchev's *Zhitie Fedora Vasil'evicha Ushakova* (Life of Fedor Vasil'evich Ushakov, 1789), in which Radishchev recounts the event, that he and the other Russian students consciously based their actions on Rousseau's theory of natural rights. Defending those rights, the students decided that the student whom Bokum had insulted, Prince Nasakin, should answer Bokum's insult in kind and slap the major in the face. He did so, and the revolt against the cruel major cost the Russian students their freedom – they were arrested and put in jail. It almost cost them their careers as well; the empress considered recalling them to Russia. There is no doubt, however, that Radishchev saw the experience as a moral victory in that the students were able to stand up for their injured dignity. One of Radishchev's dominant convictions was taking shape: his insistence on the unity of theory and practice. Like Rousseau, and the later Russian sentimentalists, he strove to realize the high goals of moral philosophy in his own life.

The young Radishchev found a model for imitation and even worship in the person of his friend Fedor Ushakov. The *Zhitie Fedora Vasil'evicha Ushakova* outwardly suggests a work of old Russian hagiography and indeed was structured like a traditional saint's life, chronicling the sinner's life, fall, repentance, act of moral heroism, and martyr's death. To Radishchev's thinking, Ushakov's greatness consisted in his constant attempt to live in accordance with moral law, although this was something which Ushakov was far from being able to do at all times. Radishchev even emphasizes his hero's sinning and suggests the source of his final illness – syphilis. Yet on the whole the *Zhitie Fedora Vasil'evicha Ushakova* had an undoubtedly apologetic character. The last pages, which describe the protagonist's death, achieve a sublimely heroic pathos. Ushakov's life is crowned by his ability to overcome the fear of death, an ability Radishchev admired and that subsequently played a crucial role in his own life.

The *Zhitie Fedora Vasil'evicha Ushakova* is one of the first works of sentimentalism in Russian literature. Yet it was not simply a literary experiment but rather a model of moral behavior which Radishchev wanted to share with the reader. On the whole Radishchev's first works are remarkably close in spirit to those of the young Leo Tolstoy. Like Tolstoy, Radishchev is convinced of the primacy of the moral over the aesthetic and constantly strives toward Truth. In his unfinished "Istoriia

vcherashnego dnia" (A History of Yesterday), written in 1851, Tolstoy set himself the task of honestly describing his life, if only for the period of one day. Radishchev had already set himself a similar goal in his short and experimental "Dnevnik odnoi nedeli" (Diary of a Week, 1811). Scholars have traced its sources to Laurence Sterne's *A Sentimental Journey* (1768), but while Sterne's work may have been influential, Rousseau's confessional narrative and his insistence on "pure truth" – stripped of all of the parody and playfulness of Sterne's text – was paramount.

At the end of 1771 Radishchev returned to Russia and on 9 December was made *protokolist* (secretary) for the first department of the Senate. Among his duties was to write short surveys of the juridical matters reviewed in the department, including cases concerning peasant uprisings. From 1773 to 1775 Radishchev served as *ober-auditor* or military prosecutor and took direct part in legal proceedings. Little is known about this period in Radishchev's life beyond the fact that, soon after the suppression of the Pugachev peasant rebellion in 1775, he retired from the service.

In 1772, in Nikolai Novikov's satirical journal *Zhivopisets* (The Painter), an article titled "Otryvok. Puteshestvie v *** I*** T***" (Fragment of a Journey to *** by I*** T***) was published anonymously. In an article published in 1858, Radishchev's son Pavel remarked that selections from his father's masterwork *Puteshestvie iz Peterburga v Moskvu* had been published in Novikov's *Zhivopisets* (although he indicated the date as 1781), and on this basis many scholars have attributed "Otryvok" to Radishchev (Vladimir Semennikov defended this position in detail; A. I. Nezelenov argued that I. P. Turgenev was a more likely candidate; and, more recently, Georgii P. Makogonenko tried to nominate Novikov as the author).

The remarkably harsh comments about serfdom in the "Otryvok" provide circumstantial evidence of Radishchev's authorship. Like the other works of the 1770s that are definitely attributed to him, it was unsigned. His translation of Gabriel Bonnet de Mably's *Observations sur l'histoire de la Grèce* (1766), for example, was published anonymously in 1773. In this instance Radishchev's authorship was conclusively established by the Russian bibliographer V. S. Sopikov and by Semennikov, who located a receipt showing that Radishchev had been paid for it.

Radishchev's decision to translate Mably may have been prompted by the Obshchestvo staraiushcheesia o napechatanii knig (Society Striving to Publish

Books), which Novikov had founded. Since Radishchev did not make his living from literature and did not work as a translator on a regular basis, he probably undertook this work because it interested him – as suggested by Radishchev's notes to the translation, which debate the author's ideas. While Radishchev disagreed with certain of Mably's judgments – for instance, that the Macedonian monarchy was absolutist and despotic and necessarily led to the annihilation of the Greek sense of morality – Mably's equation of political freedom and moral standards, and the notion that in conditions of despotism a person loses all virtue, was extremely close to the position Radishchev later advocated in his *Puteshestvie iz Peterburga v Moskvu*.

Radishchev's participation in the Society Striving to Publish Books as well as his possible contribution to *Zhivopisets* also suggest his links to Novikov's literary circle, although Radishchev scarcely considered himself a professional literary man. Literature was certainly not more important to him than his new position in the service, which began at the end of 1777. As noted earlier, Radishchev's retirement from the service in 1775 may have been connected to the suppression of the Pugachev peasant rebellion. The tragic circumstances of the uprising were well known to Radishchev, both through his earlier work in the Senate and the fact that his father and younger brothers and sisters had almost become victims of the rebels (they were saved only through the intercession of their serfs). Radishchev had also been an eyewitness to the severe punishments meted out to Pugachev and his men in Moscow in spring 1775. However, his retirement might just as well have been because of his marriage to Anna Vasil'evna Rubanovskaia in 1775.

For a time family life consumed all of Radishchev's time and energy, but on 22 December 1777 he accepted a position as an official in the *kommerts-kollegiia* (Board of Commerce). His unusual abilities, personal integrity, and education attracted the attention of the president of the board, Count A. R. Vorontsov, who became more than a patron to Radishchev. In 1780 the writer was appointed to the post of deputy manager of the Saint Petersburg Customs House; all of the activities of the Customs House came under his control, insofar as the manager was not involved in its actual day-to-day activities. Radishchev continued to receive promotions and by 1790 became *gubernskii sekretar'* (provincial secretary) and director of the Customs House. Some scholars hold that Radishchev did not take his governmental service seriously, but his success-

ПУТЕШЕСТВІЕ,

изъ

ПЕТЕРБУРГА ВЪ МОСКВУ.

„Чудище обло, озорно, огромно, стозѣвно, и лаяй„

Тилемахида, ТомЪ II. КН: XVIII. сти: 514.

1790.

ВЪ САНКТПЕТЕРБУРГѢ.

Title page for Radishchev's indictment against serfdom. Catherine II ordered the edition to be destroyed and exiled its author to Siberia.

ful rise on the career ladder and Vorontsov's patronage suggest the reverse.

In the 1780s Radishchev produced few literary works, probably because he was consumed with his duties. The most important were the *Pis'mo k drugu, zhitel'stvuiushchemu v Tobol'ske* (Letter to a Friend who Resides in Tobol'sk, 1790), written in 1782, and his ode "Vol'nost'" (Freedom, circa 1781–1783). Radishchev's other poetry of the 1780s includes songs, orations, and epitaphs. His first poems, fashionable love songs modeled on those of Aleksandr Sumarokov, were not an auspicious debut. His "cantata" or "pesnoslovie" (oration), "Tvorenie mira" (The Creation of the World), employed polymetry (mixed meters) and was also in a traditional mold.

The *Pis'mo k drugu* reflects all of the complexities associated with the figure of Peter the Great that had accumulated over the course of the eighteenth century in the Russian and European traditions. The occasion that prompted the work was the unveiling of the monument to the czar-reformer by the French sculptor Etienne Falconet in 1782. By the end of the eighteenth century attitudes toward Peter and the Petrine reforms had become a point of contention, dividing Russian society into an early version of nineteenth-century "Westernizers" and "Slavophiles" – into *gosudarstvenniki* (supporters of the government) and those who proclaimed the primacy of the individual over society and the state. Obviously, the official attitude toward Peter was unabashedly positive. In the monument's inscription, written by Catherine ("To Peter the First from Catherine the Second"), the empress underscored the continuity from Peter's reign to her own. At the same time Russian writers were forming their own, more skeptical view of Peter, as in Prince M. Shcherbatov's celebrated essay "O povrezhdenii nravov v Rossii" (On the Decline of Morals in Russia), written at about the same time as Radishchev's *Pis'mo,* in 1786–1789. Shcherbatov argued that the Petrine reform was the basic reason for the decline in morals because the czar had imported European institutions that ran counter to the special features of Russian national development. Rousseau directed a similar reproach at Peter in his *Social Contract,* in which he wrote that the czar had wanted to create Germans and Englishmen out of Russians, when, Rousseau asserted, it was most important to create Russians.

Radishchev's *Pis'mo* is unquestionably sympathetic to the Petrine reforms and is, at least in part, a polemic directed against Rousseau and his denial that Peter was a genius. At the same time, however, Radishchev did not accept the totally optimistic conclusions of Voltaire, who had ended his *Histoire de l'empire de Russie sous Pierre-le-Grand* (1759–1763) with praise that seemed to Radishchev excessively filled with faith in Enlightenment: "If, in the frosty darkness of ancient Scythia a man, driven by the force of his genius alone, had accomplished such great deeds [as Peter did in Russia], what then will we be able to accomplish in states where the combined efforts of many centuries has made everything so much easier?" In light of Radishchev's insistent declarations about the primacy of private life, the reproach which he directed at the czar-reformer is not unexpected: "I ia skazhu chto mog by Petr slavnee byt', voznosia otechestvo svoe, utverzhdaia vol'nost' chastnuiu" (And so I say that Peter could have been even more glorious if in raising his country up he had affirmed individual freedom).

Radishchev posed the issue in the spirit of Pushkin's narrative poem "Mednyi vsadnik" (The

Bronze Horseman), written in 1833, the title of which refers to Falconet's monument. Radishchev's criticism is not as pointed as that in Pushkin's tale. If for Pushkin the opposition between the protagonist Evgenii, a "little man," and Peter, who represents the power of the state, was fatally and fundamentally irresolvable, for Radishchev compromise was still possible. A government founded on the principles of the social contract, he believed, can and must take into account the interests of the individual; otherwise the state does not have the right to exist.

It is just this point of view which Radishchev expresses in his programmatic works of the 1780s, specifically in the ode "Vol'nost'," which was later published as an appendix to the *Puteshestvie.* The work is a finely constructed philosophical treatise that examines world history through the prism of Rousseau's *Social Contract.* It is an abstract expression of Radishchev's cardinal belief in the sovereignty of the people, understood in terms of a natural equilibrium between individual will and the interests of the government, represented in the person of the sovereign.

Radishchev's ode shows the influence of Russian didactic poetry, especially the works of Sumarokov, the moralizing odes of Mikhail Kheraskov and Vasilii Maikov, and Vasilii Kapnist's "Oda na rabstvo" (Ode to Slavery, 1783); the poetry of French classicism, especially that of Rousseau, was no less important. Radishchev employs the traditional Russian odic stanza established by Mikhail Lomonosov, but his style greatly differs. On the whole "Vol'nost' " is deliberately ponderous; in the discussion of the ode in the *Puteshestvie,* Radishchev notes its purposeful "negladkost' stikha" (roughness of verse), meant to express the difficulty of the action depicted in the poem. By making his language hard to read (via high-style archaic diction and convoluted syntax), and in opposition to much of sentimentalist "sladostnyi" (smooth and sweet) verse, Radishchev forces his reader not merely to peruse but to confront and comprehend his poetry. The notion of "rough verse which expresses the difficulty of the action" applies to much of Radishchev's later poetry as well.

Simultaneous with "Vol'nost' " Radishchev labored over the work that became the main product of his career as a writer and thinker, the *Puteshestvie iz Peterburga v Moskvu.* The most recent textual study, by Vladimir Zapadov (1992), identifies two basic versions of the *Puteshestvie,* the first completed in 1788 and the second immediately before the book's publication in 1790. Scholars disagree on how long Radishchev worked on this book, but the most persistent opinion is that it was the result of almost twenty years' labor. Semennikov and others have considered the "Otryvok" a kind of rehearsal for the book, and on this basis the majority of scholars accept 1772 as the starting date of Radishchev's work on the *Puteshestvie*.

Be that as it may, Radishchev's main efforts on the *Puteshestvie* came during the second half of the 1780s, when he wrote the "Slovo o Lomonosove" (Oration on Lomonosov), which eventually became its closing piece. During the later 1780s the names of Edmund Burke, Charles James Fox, Honoré-Gabriel Riqueti, Comte de Mirabeau, and other political figures whose names are mentioned in the *Puteshestvie* became widely known in Russia, and contemporary events mentioned in the work also provide clues as to the dates of composition of its various parts. The chapter titled "Podberez'e" (a place name, which like most of the chapter titles designates a stop on the journey), for example, could not have been written any earlier than 1782 since Denis Fonvizin's comedy *Nedorosl'* (The Minor) is mentioned, and the chapter called "Tosno" could not have been written any earlier than 1785, as it discusses Catherine II's journey there, which took place in that year.

The different sections of the *Puteshestvie iz Peterburga v Moskvu* were, in fact, written over such a long period of time that it is exceedingly difficult to determine whether Radishchev actually had a unifying plan for the work when he began. Nezelenov argues that the work was a series of publicistic articles on various subjects. On the other side, G. A. Gukovsky insists on the work's unity of design and on the fundamental originality of the genre Radishchev had chosen. The fact that there were two disparate versions of this work – the first written before 1788 and the second dated 1788–1789 – indicates that, at least in the beginning, the *Puteshestvie* was not meant as a unified work but rather as a special kind of publicistic writer's diary. As selections accumulated, it began to coalesce into a single work, which Radishchev chose to organize as a journey, a widespread convention in contemporary European literature. It seems likely that Radishchev came to this decision during work on the second version, that is, after 1788.

The center of Radishchev's *Puteshestvie* is its attack on serfdom. Radishchev's fundamental arguments against this monstrous social institution are based on ethics, as in the section "Proekt v budushchee" (Project for the Future), where serfdom is condemned as a violation of natural rights.

It asserts, first of all, that "poraboshchennost' est' prestuplenie" (enslavement is a crime) and, second, that slavery corrupts both master and slave equally. By presenting an entire gallery of attractive and virtuous peasants and contrasting them to corrupt landowners (especially in the chapters titled "Edrovo" and "Zaitsevo"), Radishchev rebuts those who believe that peasants need to be under the guardianship of landowners because of their inadequate moral development.

In "Proekt v budushchee" Radishchev warns his fellow citizens that oppression of the serfs will inevitably lead to rebellion, but it is a mistake to assume, as have Soviet critics, that Radishchev approved of peasant revolts, especially against the Russian nobility. Those who support this position usually cite the chapter called "Mednoe," in which Radishchev condones peasants who murder their evil owners. However, it should be noted that the serf owner it depicts is not noble by birth but a former *istopnik* (court janitor) who had reached gentry status by intrigue and cunning; it does not, therefore, necessarily constitute an attack on the Russian nobility as a class.

Radishchev proposes a plan for the gradual dismantling of serfdom by the state and insists on immediate action only with regard to the abolition of household slaves and the granting of personal inviolability to all peasants. He further argues that land allotted to them should become their private property. This proposal was radical; even the emancipation of 1861 did not go so far, and it was only the Stolypin reforms at the start of the twentieth century that allowed Russian peasants land as personal property.

In the chapter titled "Spasskaia polest'" Radishchev considers the evils of absolutism. The abuses it depicts are not meant as isolated incidents but as inevitable, rooted in the nature of autocracy. Radishchev's condemnation of unlimited czarist power is especially sharp in the section entitled "Son" (Dream), which Catherine II took as a personal attack on her. Radishchev contrasts autocratic rule with a government of the people in the chapter titled "Novgorod," in which he recounts the tragic events surrounding the dissolution of the republic of Novgorod in the fifteenth century. Contrary to the official version of events, Radishchev was convinced that Ivan III had unlawfully annexed Novgorod to the kingdom of Muscovy by the use of force. The chapter also demonstrates Radishchev's anticentrist views, and in the chapter named "Tver" he was one of the first in Russia to speak out for a federative organization.

Questions concerning Radishchev's political allegiances and political views as presented in the *Puteshestvie* are hard to answer. Was Radishchev on the side of republican government, or was he more sympathetic to the ideal of an enlightened monarchy? While such questions are valid, they ignore the fact that the *Puteshestvie* is written from a broadly humanist perspective and that Radishchev considered himself a champion of all oppressed people; put simply, it is misleading to portray Radishchev's *Puteshestvie* exclusively as a political treatise, although Radishchev's humanism in no way excluded concrete political activism. Radishchev's introduction to the *Puteshestvie,* addressed to his friend and sympathizer A. M. Kutuzov, defines the guiding spirit of the work: "Ia vzglianul okrest menia – dusha moia stradaniiami chelovechestva uiazvlenna stala" (I looked all around me – and my soul was wounded by the sufferings of humanity).

These words also encapsulate the work's highly emotional approach to Russia's social ills. Work on the *Puteshestvie* coincided with the rise of sentimentalism in Russia, and many modern scholars have seen it as a sentimentalist work, although in some respects it was the opposite of Nikolai Karamzin's sentimentalism both in literary and political terms. Other scholars, however (notably the American scholar Tanya Page), have taken the *Puteshestvie* to be an attack on and parody of sentimentalism as a philosophical and ethical system. However, if sentimentalism is defined as a championing of individualism in the broadest sense, including the demand that an author reveal his own personality in his writing, then it could not have coincided more closely with Radishchev's own brand of social non-conformism and an individual moral protest in the name of humanity. Radishchev's sentimentalist concern with the life of the soul was a major determining factor both in the content of the *Puteshestvie,* in which almost every page contains a description of a character's inner emotional life, and in its "tearful" narrative and style.

The *Puteshestvie iz Peterburga v Moskvu* was basically completed by the middle of 1789; on 22 July Radishchev submitted his manuscript to the police (who in the later eighteenth century fulfilled the function of censors). After the book had been approved, however, Radishchev rewrote and added material to several chapters (most important, "Podberez'e") and then, during the first half of 1790, printed up 650 copies of the book on his home printing press. Radishchev distributed 7 (including a copy given to Gavriil Derzhavin), and 25 were turned over for sale at G. K. Zotov's bookshop.

The public immediately identified the book as seditious. Radishchev prepared for the worst and destroyed all of his papers; he burned the remaining copies of the book in his possession, refusing a request by the bookseller Shnor for 100 copies as payment of a debt. On 25 June 1790 Radishchev's book came into Catherine's possession; after reading the first thirty pages she ordered Zotov's arrest, and shortly thereafter, on 30 June, Radishchev joined the bookseller in the Peter Paul Fortress.

Much of what was written in the *Puteshestvie* was perceived by Catherine as a personal insult, especially the chapter titled "Spasskaia Polest'," and the *Puteshestvie* clearly amplified the panic Catherine was feeling due to the recently begun French Revolution, whose influence she rightly perceived in Radishchev's book. Catherine was also undoubtedly suspicious of Radishchev's connections to the Freemasons, especially to those of Novikov's circle. Only one year later Novikov was imprisoned and several of his colleagues were sent into exile.

The investigation was entrusted to "domashnemu palachu krotkoi Ekateriny" (humble Catherine's personal executioner – Pushkin's words), S. Sheshkovsky. The empress compiled questions to ask the prisoner; she was most interested in the intentions of the writer and in finding out who his accomplices were. Sheshkovsky was known to use torture on those under investigation, but he did not resort to it in Radishchev's case. The psychological pressure on Radishchev was so great, however, and the investigation so precipitate and threatening that he suffered serious nervous trauma while in the fortress. He confessed that "kniga napolena stol' gnusnymi, derzkimi i razvratnymi vyrazheniiami, chto ia pochitaiu sebia dostoineishim vsiakogo ot pravosudiia istiazaniia" (the book is filled with such vile, disrespectful and depraved expressions that I consider myself most worthy of any castigation given in the name of justice).

Castigation was not delayed for long: on 24 July 1790 the Criminal Court pronounced Radishchev guilty on all counts and sentenced him to death; two days later it was confirmed by the Senate. After that the matter was turned over to the Council, at which point Catherine added a new charge to the existing ones: breaking an oath. The Council confirmed the death sentence, but it was understood that room was left for the empress's "mercy," and indeed on 4 September 1791, at her personal command, the death sentence was commuted to a ten-year exile to the fortress town of

Radishchev's house in Saint Petersburg in which he printed his Puteshestvie iz Peterburga v Moskvu *(1790)*

Ilimsk, in the far reaches of Siberia, 500 *versts* (approximately 330 miles) to the north of Irkutsk.

Vorontsov's intercession and aid eased Radishchev's situation. Thanks to letters Vorontsov sent ahead to the governors of Nizhny Novgorod, Perm, and Irkutsk, warm welcomes awaited the author along his route into exile. Vorontsov also furnished the exile with money and undertook the care of his children. Even in Ilimsk, Vorontsov did not forget Radishchev, sending him books. Through Vorontsov's efforts, Radishchev's future second wife, Elizaveta Rubanovskaia, was able to come to him there.

During his exile Radishchev returned to his literary pursuits, which he had never entirely abandoned even during his imprisonment. In fact, he wrote the "Povest' o Filarete Milostivom" (The Story of Merciful Filaret) while in the Peter Paul Fortress in 1790. On the way to Siberia the writer began a diary, titled in manuscript "Dnevnik, vedennyi na puti v Sibir' i obratno" (A Diary, Kept on the Road to Siberia and Back). While in exile in Ilimsk in 1792, Radishchev worked on the main labor of his last years, the philosophical treatise "O cheloveke, o ego smertnosti i bessmertii" (On Man, on his Mortality and Immortality).

In this work, as Pushkin put it, "Radishchev, khotia i vyrazhaetsia protiv materializma, no v nem vse eshche viden uchenik Gel'vetsiia. On okhotnee izlagaet, nezheli oprovergaet dovody chistogo afeizma" (although Radishchev argues against materialism, one can still see in him the student of Helvétius. He more willingly demonstrates than refutes the conclusions of pure atheism). It has been traditionally accepted that in "O cheloveke" Radishchev's ideas are closest to those of Helvétius and Leibnitz, and, to be sure, the treatise contains extensive borrowings from Helvétius's *De l'Esprit*. It is also generally thought that in this work Radishchev rejects the extremes of German metaphysics. However, in refuting Helvétius's position that all actions of reason are merely simple sensation, and in differentiating between what can and cannot be known by experience, Radishchev willingly or unwillingly approaches the position of his famous contemporary, Immanuel Kant, not only on gnosiological questions but in matters of moral philosophy. The issue of Radishchev's possible interest in Kant has not been researched, so one can as yet only speak of typological similarities between Radishchev's ideas and those of the Kantian system, but like Kant's idealism, Radishchev's work has a strong objective character. This treatise remained unfinished, however, and the extant text is to a certain extent a scholarly reconstruction.

Radishchev continued to write poetry in the 1790s and struck out in new directions. Starting in the late 1780s Radishchev's poetry had begun to demonstrate more and more pre-Romantic traits, including an interest in folk culture and a search for a correlation between national content and forms of expression. In fact, Pushkin saw in Radishchev not so much an original social thinker (still the dominant view on Radishchev) as a formal innovator and experimenter in verse. In the chapter titled "Tver" in the *Puteshestvie,* Radishchev criticizes existing Russian versification, charging that neither syllabic nor syllabo-tonic poetry (poetry based on the number of syllables in a line, and poetry based on feet) corresponds to the spirit of genuine Russian verse. Radishchev proposed a system that he considered closer to folk versification, and as often happened in such cases, Radishchev's orientation on ancient meters basically boiled down to the creation of a new tonic (accentual) system. Such a system had already been suggested by Nikolai L'vov and by Karamzin, although while Karamzin's Russian verse tended toward trochaic meters (with a dactyllic clausula), Radishchev avoided syllabo-tonics altogether. Radishchev read Karamzin's *bogatyrskaia skazka* (heroic tale) "Il'ia Muromets" in 1795, and it evidently inspired Radishchev to try his own hand at a longer work of the new type: thus appeared his "Pesn' istoricheskaia" (Historical Song) and the "poema-skazka" (fairy-tale poem) "Bova." The "Pesn' istoricheskaia" with its monumental subject – a retelling of ancient history – recalls his earlier "Tvorenie mira," and in some respects is its continuation. "Bova," Radishchev's last larger work, is a bawdy satirical poem on the subject of the popular chivalric tale *Bova Korolevich,* which ultimately derived from the thirteenth-century French romance about Beuve d'Antone and which had become a favorite Russian chapbook. Only the introduction and first canto of "Bova" survive, together with a prose summary of the entire work.

Radishchev spent six years in Ilimsk, where he actively pursued his interests in literature, natural science, and economics. Then, on 23 November 1796 Emperor Paul I, who had just ascended to the throne, put an end to Radishchev's exile. Radishchev was permitted to live on his estates, at first in the village of Nemtsovo in the Kaluga province and then at Preobrazhenskoe, his father's estate in the province of Saratov. His return turned out to be joyless, however, since his financial affairs were in disarray and his relations with his father strained.

Radishchev returned to real freedom only when Alexander I became czar in 1801, at which time his exile was not only completely ended but he was appointed to the important commission to work out a new law code. In the course of his first year on the throne Alexander I bestowed many marks of favor on the formerly disgraced writer, including the return of his order of Saint Vladimir, increases in salary and financial help, and an invitation to the coronation ceremony in Moscow. Some of these marks of favor may have been due again to the efforts of Vorontsov, whom the new emperor had put in charge of his so-called reform government.

Given this situation, Radishchev's death seems tragic and inexplicable. On 11 September 1802 the writer died after having poisoned himself with sulfuric acid. The traditional explanation for his death (as related by Pushkin) is that after the emperor appointed Radishchev to his commission for establishing the new law code he ordered him to set forth his views concerning several points of civil law. The unfortunate Radishchev was allegedly carried away with enthusiasm for the subject. He recalled many of his earlier ideas about reform and in the memorandum he presented to the authorities threw caution to the wind. Count Zavadovsky was surprised at the youthful fervor of the gray-haired old man and exclaimed with a friendly reproach: "Oh, Aleksandr Nikolaevich, haven't you had enough of all that empty prattle? Or wasn't Siberia sufficient?" Radishchev took this as a threat and hurried home in distress. He recalled Fedor Ushakov, the friend of his youth who had first stimulated his thoughts about suicide, and drank the acid.

This account includes many inaccuracies but reflects an important feature of Radishchev's moral outlook: despite Christian prohibitions against suicide, Radishchev considered it not only a possible but a necessary response to life's hardships, something which raises humans above mute animals. Radishchev's suicide provoked an angry rebuke from Karamzin, who published an article in *Vestnik Evropy* (European Herald) objecting to suicide on ethical grounds.

It is doubtful, however, that the reason for Radishchev's decision to commit suicide rested solely on the friendly rebuke of Zavadovsky, someone by no means tyrannical and whose attitude toward the author had never been harsh. Radishchev's sons noted in their memoirs that at that time the writer was going through a severe depression, probably over the equivocal position in which Radishchev found himself at the beginning of Alexander I's reign. This dissident writer, one of the ideologues of the "Russian fronde" during Catherine's time, suddenly found himself in the center of the government camp. Today it is also hard to imagine the extent of the hostility with which the

Russian nobility received Alexander's innovations. Those who were ideologically opposed to the young emperor included not only reactionaries but even people like Derzhavin and Karamzin. Only the small circle of young people who made up Alexander's "unofficial committee" and Vorontsov, last of the important figures from Catherine's reign, shared Alexander's views.

At his death the majority of Radishchev's works remained unpublished. This gap was only partly filled when in 1807–1811 a six-volume collection of his writings was published. *Puteshestvie iz Peterburga v Moskvu,* which almost no one had read but everyone had heard about, was not included, nor were "Povest' o Filarete Milostivom," "Dnevnik, vedennyi na puti v Sibir' i obratno," the ode "Vol'nost'," or other important works.

However, Radishchev continued to assert an important influence on the younger generation. The heroic example of his life and certain aspects of his social thought, especially his stand against serfdom, made a strong impression on the young generation of Decembrist poets and thinkers (named for the unsuccessful December 1825 rebellion). His ideas about Russian poetry also attracted followers. During his later life Radishchev had been closely associated with a group of young writers and literary men including Semen Bobrov, V. V. Popugaev, and I. N. Pnin, who founded the Vol'noe obshchestvo liubitelei slovesnosti, nauk i khudozhestv (Free Society of Lovers of Literature, the Sciences and Arts), which helped to promulgate Radishchev's theories about Russian verse. In the 1810s Radishchev's ideas about Russian verse were debated between those who interpreted Radishchev's dactyllic-trochaic meter as an approximation of classical hexameter and those who saw Radishchev's versification as a tonic system in imitation of Russian folk verse.

However, from the second half of Alexander's reign, the censors almost never allowed Radishchev's name to be mentioned in print. Pushkin's attempt to break the silence in 1836 with his article "Aleksandr Radishchev" in his journal *Sovremennik* (The Contemporary) was vetoed, even though the article was by no means an apology for the writer. Metropolitan Evgenii Bolkhovitinov published a short biography of Radishchev in his *Slovar' russkikh svetskikh pisatelei, sootvechestvennikov i chuzhestrantsev, pisavshikh v Rossii* (Dictionary of Secular Writers, Native and Foreign, Who Wrote in Russia, 1845), but this was virtually the only thing published about the writer before the late 1850s.

The fate of the publication of *Puteshestvie iz Peterburga v Moskvu* was also dramatic. It remained a

СОБРАНІЕ
ОСТАВШИХСЯ СОЧИНЕНІЙ

ПОКОЙНАГО

АЛЕКСАНДРЪ НИКОЛАЕВИЧА
РАДИЩЕВА.

ЧАСТЬ ПЕРВАЯ.

МОСКВА,
ВЪ ТИПОГРАФІИ ПЛАТОНА БЕКЕТОВА.
Иждивеніемъ Издателей.

1807.

Title page for Radishchev's collected works

forbidden work throughout the nineteenth century, although it circulated in manuscript copies. A few copies of the original 1790 printed version also escaped destruction, including the one on which Catherine II wrote her comments (Pushkin purchased this copy, and it has been preserved in his library). The censors gave permission to publish the *Puteshestvie* in 1868 but then twice ordered editions which had already been printed to be destroyed. The exiled Aleksandr Herzen published an edition in London in 1858, but the first true full edition of *Puteshestvie* was published in 1905 by N. P. Pavlov-Sil'vansky and P. E. Shchegolev. In contrast to this long period of mostly enforced silence, interest in Radishchev in the twentieth century has been enormous.

Letters:

Polnoe sobranie sochinenii, volume 3 (Moscow & Leningrad: Akademiia nauk, 1952), pp. 307–536.

Bibliographies:

Roza Mandel'shtam, "Bibliografiia Radishcheva," *Vestnik kommunisticheskoi akademii,* no. 13 (1925): 282–301; no. 14 (1925): 312–334; no. 15 (1925): 339–352;

I. D. Smolianov, "Bibliografiia A. N. Radishcheva," *Sovetskii Bibliograf,* 1 (1941): 118–133;

T. A. Karpenko and S. K. Simkina, "Iubileinaia literatura 1949 goda ob A. N. Radishcheve," in *A. N. Radishchev: Stat'i i materialy,* edited by M. P. Alekseev (Leningrad: Leningradskii universitet, 1950), pp. 305–324;

Georgii Galin, *Pervenets svobody (Radishchev. Dekabristy): Rekomendatel'nyi ukazatel' literatury* (Moscow, 1971);

G. S. Smith, "Radishchev: A Concise Bibliography of Works Published Outside the Soviet Union," *Study Group on Eighteenth-Century Russia Newsletter,* 2 (1973): 53–61;

Il'ia Serman, "A. N. Radishchev - pisatel' v issledovaniiakh poslednego desiatiletiia, 1965–1975," *Russkaia literatura,* 18, no. 4 (1975): 180–191.

Biographies:

Boris S. Evgen'ev, *Alexander Radishchev: A Russian Humanist of the Eighteenth Century* (London & New York: Hutchinson, 1946);

Georgii P. Makogonenko, *Radishchev i ego vremia* (Moscow: Khudozhestvennaia literatura, 1956);

David M. Lang, *The First Russian Radical: Alexander Radishchev, 1749–1802* (London: Unwin, 1959);

Nikolai Radishchev, *Biografiia A. N. Radishcheva, napisannaia ego synov'iami,* edited by Dimitrii Babkin (Leningrad: Akademiia nauk, 1959);

Allen McConnell, *A Russian Philosophe: Alexander Radishchev, 1749–1802* (The Hague: M. Nijhoff, 1964).

References:

A. N. Radishchev i literatura ego vremeni, XVIII vek, 12, special issue (1977);

M. P. Alekseev, ed., *A. N. Radishchev: Stat'i i materialy* (Leningrad: Leningradskii universitet, 1950);

Dimitrii Babkin, *Protsess A. N. Radishcheva* (Moscow: Akademiia nauk, 1952);

Iakov Barskov and M. V. Zhizhka, *Materialy k izucheniiu "Puteshtviia iz Peterburga v Moskvu"* (Moscow: Akademia, 1935);

Pavel Berkov, "Nekotorye spornye voprosy sovremennogo izucheniia zhizni i tvorchestva A. N. Radishcheva," *XVIII vek,* 4 (1959): 170–205;

Evgenii Bolkhovitinov, "A. N. Radishchev," in his *Slovar' russkikh svetskikh pisatelei, sootvechestvennikov i chuzhestrantsev, pisavshikh v Rossii,* volume 2 (Moscow, 1845);

Jesse V. Clardy, *The Philosophical Ideas of Alexander Radishchev* (New York: Astra Books, 1964);

Iurii Kariakin and Eugenii Plimak, *Zapretnaia mysl' obretaet svobodu* (Moscow: Nauka, 1966);

David M. Lang, "Radishchev and Sterne: An Episode in Russian Sentimentalism," *Revue de litterature comparée,* 21 (1947): 254–260;

Lang, "Some Western Sources of Radishchev's Political Thought," *Revue des études slaves,* 25 (1949): 73–86;

Iurii Lotman, "Istochniki svedenii Pushkina o Radishcheve (1819–1822)," *Pushkin i ego vremia,* 1 (1962): 45–66;

Aleksandr Orlov, ed., *A. N. Radishchev: Materialy i issledovaniia* (Moscow: Akademiia nauk, 1936);

Tanya Page, "Helvetianism as Allegory in the 'Dream' and the 'Peasant Rebellion' in Radishchev's 'Journey from Petersburg to Moscow'," in *Russia and the West in the Eighteenth Century* (Newtonville, Mass.: Slavica, 1983), pp. 135–143;

Page, "A Radishchev Monstrology: The *Journey from Petersburg to Moscow* and Later Writings in Light of French Sources," in *American Contributions to the Eighth International Congress of Slavists* (Columbus, Ohio: Slavic, 1978), pp. 605–629;

Page, "Radishchev's Polemic Against Sentimentalism in the Cause of Eighteenth-Century Utilitarianism," in *Russian Literature in the Age of Catherine the Great,* edited by Anthony Cross (Oxford: Meeuws, 1976), pp. 141–172;

V. V. Pugachev, *A. N. Radishchev: Evoliutsiia obshchestvenno-politicheskikh vzgliadov* (Gorky: Gorkovskii universitet, 1960);

Vladimir Semennikov, *Radishchev: Ocherki i issledovaniia* (Moscow, 1923);

Vladimir Zapadov, "Istoriia sozdaniia 'Puteshestviia iz Peterburga v Moskvu' i 'Vol'nost,'" in Radishchev's *Puteshestviia iz Peterburga v Moskvu. Vol'nost',* edited by V. A. Zapadov (Leningrad: Nauka, 1992), pp. 624–643.

Dimitrii Rostovsky
(Daniil Savvich Tuptalo)
(11 December 1651 – 28 October 1709)

Sergei Nikolaev
Institute of Russian Literature (Pushkin House), Saint Petersburg

BOOKS: *Runo oroshennoe, prechistaia i preblagoslovennaia Deva Mariia, ot eia zhe chudotvornogo Chernegovskogo obraza slezami inogda v monastiru Troitsi zhivonachalnoi rosivshago chudodeistvennuiu blagodati rosu* (Chernigov: Tipografiia Troitskaia, 1680);

Kniga zhitii sviatykh v slavu sviatyia zhivotvoriashchiia Troitsy Boga khvalimago v sviatykh svoikh. Na tri mesiatsy pervyia: septemvrii, oktovrii i novemvrii (Kiev: Kievo-Pecherskaia lavra, 1689);

Kniga zhitii sviatykh . . . Na tri mesiatsy vtoryia: dekemvrii, ianuarii i fevruarii (Kiev: Kievo-Pecherskaia lavra, 1695);

Kniga zhitii sviatykh . . . Na tri mesiatsy tretii, mart, april', mai (Kiev: Kievo-Pecherskaia lavra, 1695);

Apologiia v utolenie pechali cheloveka sushchago v bede, gonenii i ozloblenii (Chernigov: Tipografiia Troitskaia, 1700);

Kniga zhitii sviatykh . . . Na tri mesiatsy chetvertyi: iun', iiul', avgust (Kiev: Kievo-Pecherskaia lavra, 1705);

Razsuzhdenie o obraze Bozhii i podobii v chelovetse (Moscow: Synod, 1714);

Rozysk o raskolnicheskoi brynskoi vere, o uchenii ikh, o delakh ikh i iz"iavlenie, iako vera ikh neprava, uchenie ikh dushevredno i dela ikh nebogougodna (Moscow: Synod, 1745).

Editions: *Zhitiia sviatykh,* 4 volumes (Moscow: Synod, 1759);

Dnevnyia zapiski sviatogo chudotvortsa Dimitriia mitropolita Rostovskago, izdannyia s sobstvennoruchno pisanoi im knigi, nakhodiashcheisia v kievopecherskoi biblioteke (Moscow: Novikov, 1781);

Letopis' izhe vo sviatykh ottsa nashego Dimitriia, mitropolita Rostovskago, novoiavlennogo chudotvortsa, skazuiushchaia vkratse deianiia ot nachala mirobytiia do rozhdestva Kristova, sobrannaia iz bozhestvennykh pisanii, iz razlichnykh khronografov i istorikov, grecheskikh, slavenskikh, rimskikh, pol'skikh, evreiskikh i inykh . . . ([Moscow]: I. Lopukhin, 1784; revised, 2 volumes, edited by Vasilii Sopikov, Saint Petersburg: Akademiia

Dimitrii Rostovsky (late-eighteenth-century portrait; Gosudarstvennaia Tret'iakov Gallery)

khudozhestv, 1796; revised again, 2 volumes, edited by F. Rozanov, Moscow: Ridiger i Klaudii,1799–1800);

Sobranie raznykh pouchitel'nykh slov i drugikh sochinenii, 6 volumes (Moscow: Synod, 1786);

Ostal'nyia sochineniia sviatogo Dimitriia, mitropolita Rostovskago (Moscow, 1804);

Sochineniia, 4 volumes (Moscow, 1805–1807);

Stikhi na strasti Gospodni, sochinennyia sviatym Dimitriem mitropolitom Rostovskim, edited by Arkhimandrit Amfilokhii (Iaroslavl', 1889);

Psalmy ili dukhovnye kanty sviatitelia Dimitriia Rostovskogo, perelozhennye na chetyre golosa, edited by A. Izrailev (Moscow, 1891);

Propovedi sviatitelia Dimitriia, mitropolita Rostovskogo na ukrainskom narechii, edited by Andrei Titov (Moscow, 1909).

OTHER: "Uspenskaia drama (Komediia na uspenie Bogoroditsy)," edited by O. A. Derzhavina, in *Russkaia dramaturgiia poslednei cherverti XVII i nachala XVIII v.,* edited by A. O. Derzhavina (Moscow: Nauka, 1972), pp. 172–219, 329–332;

"Rozhdestvenskaia drama" (Komediia na rozhdestvo Khristova)," edited by O. A. Derzhavina, in *Russkaia dramaturgiia poslednei cherverti XVII i nachala XVIII v.,* pp. 220–274, 333–334;

"Intermedii (Mezhdorechie)," edited by A. S. Demin, in *Russkaia dramaturgiia poslednei cherverti XVII i nachala XVIII v.,* pp. 275–292, 339–344.

Saint Dimitrii Rostovsky — a monk, theologian, and preacher; a poet and playwright — was in many ways a typical figure of Russian literary life of the late seventeenth and early eighteenth centuries. But his fame as a writer was not for his theological treatises or his baroque sermons, but rather for his collection of saints' lives, which has been read and appreciated for centuries by generations of Eastern Orthodox faithful not only in Russia but in Ukraine, Belarus, Moldova, Bulgaria, Serbia, and Romania. Dimitrii Rostovsky's *Zhitiia sviatykh* (Lives of the Saints, 1689–1705) was an ascetic labor of love by an Orthodox writer who united in his work the hagiographic achievements of Eastern and Western branches of Christianity.

Saint Dimitrii, metropolitan of Rostov, was born Daniil Savvich Tuptalo in December 1651 in the small town of Makarov, not far from Kiev, into the family of the *sotnik* (Cossack lieutenant) Savva Grigor'evich Tuptalo. In 1660 the family relocated to Kiev to escape unrest over frequent local military clashes with the Poles. By the age of eleven Daniil had already learned to read and write Church Slavonic at home, and in 1662 he was placed in the only institute of higher learning in Ukraine, the Kiev Mohyla Collegium. Here Daniil spent only three years, as the school was destroyed in 1665 during an invasion; classes did not resume until the

end of the 1660s. Nevertheless, Daniil received a nearly complete academic education. He studied grammar, dialectics, and rhetoric; mastered Latin; and apparently learned some rudiments of Greek. By the age of seventeen Daniil's poor health, his inclination toward literary and scholarly pursuits, and his profound piety led him to consider life as a monk. In July 1668 Daniil took monastic vows at the Kirillov Monastery in Kiev and received the name Dimitrii, under which he entered the history of Russian culture.

In 1675 the bishop of Chernigov, Lazar' Baranovych, took Dimitrii under his wing, and until 1677 Dimitrii was a preacher in the Chernigov diocese, where he gained fame as a church orator. The first of Dimitrii's works that has survived, the *Runo oroshennoe* (The Tear-Washed Fleece, 1680) dates to this period. It describes miracles performed by the miracle-working icon of Our Lady from the Trinity-Il'insky Monastery, followed by a series of *besedy* (conversations) on spiritual themes and *nravoucheniia* (moral admonitions). Dimitrii spent 1677–1679 in Lithuania, at the time part of Poland. Confronted by the difficult plight of Eastern Orthodox Christians in this Catholic environment, Dimitrii spent much of his time preaching in various cities (Vilnius, Novogrudok, Sluttsk) but also found time for a thorough study of Polish language and literature.

After returning to Ukraine Dimitrii became hegumen of various smaller monasteries, and in 1682 he became prior of the Nikol'sky Monastery in the city of Baturin. At the end of 1683 Dimitrii returned to Kiev and became the preacher at the Kievan Crypt *Lavra* (Laura, or principal monastery). Apparently, it was at this time that he conceived of the idea of compiling a full yearly cycle of saints' lives. This idea was not new and had long occupied the minds of Ukrainian churchmen; because of Catholic inroads into the Orthodox East it was essential to furnish the Eastern Orthodox church in Ukraine with the major texts of Christian dogma and ethics. The absence of an accessible collection of Eastern Orthodox hagiography facilitated the spread of Catholic writings in the Ukraine, especially the *Zywoty swietych* (Lives of the Saints, 1579) of the Polish Jesuit Piotr Skarga.

Dimitrii began the major work of his life by taking a monastic vow on 6 May 1684; he would devote almost twenty years of unceasing, pious labor to the hagiographic enterprise. As the basis for his *Zhitiia sviatykh* Dimitrii used the *Chet'i-Minei* (Reading Menaea), a manuscript compiled in the sixteenth century by Makarii, metropolitan of Moscow, whose papers were stored in that city. Dimitrii supplemented this source with the Russian *Prolog,* an ancient miscellany of saints' lives and other didactic writings, as well as with Western works, chiefly those of Simeon Metafrast, Laurentius Surius, Piotr Skarga, and the publications of the Bollandists, a Roman Catholic society dedicated to collecting and disseminating saints' lives. Dimitrii became so immersed in hagiographic writings and so absorbed in his work that he began to see saints in his sleep. Dimitrii claimed that after he had finished his hagiography of the martyr Orest, the saint appeared to him in a dream and complained, "Ia bol'she preterpel za Khrista, chem ty napisal" (I suffered more for Christ than you wrote) – so Dimitrii went back and enlarged his entry.

Dimitrii looked upon his labor not only as the fulfillment of a personal monastic vow but also as a work of penance assigned to him by the entire "Little Russian" (Ukrainian) church. By 1688 the printing press at the Kievan Crypt *Lavra* began preparations to publish the first voluminous tome of a planned four; it was finished early in 1689 and immediately enjoyed success among readers.

It was not Dimitrii's fate to be confined to a monastic cell and to pursue literary endeavors, however. Important church matters increasingly occupied his time and energy. He participated in the famous debate between Ukrainian and Russian theologians over the precise time of transubstantiation of the holy gifts in the Eucharist. In 1689 he traveled to Moscow in the retinue of Hetman (a local ruler) Ivan Mazepa and at the capital was presented to the coczars Ivan V and Peter I. There he also witnessed the execution of the supporters of the fallen Czarevna Sofia, which marked the start of Peter's independent rule. Dimitrii avoided highchurch positions, although in the 1690s he was compelled several times to serve as prior of various monasteries. Dimitrii also regularly preached, in keeping with his credo that "Moemu sanu (ego zhe ia nedostoin) nadlezhit slovo Bozhie propovedati ne tol'ko iazykom, no i pishushcheiu rukoiu. To moe delo, to moe zvanie, to moia dolzhnost'" (To my office [of which I am not worthy] belongs the responsibility of preaching the word of God not only with the tongue, but with the hand that writes. That is my work, that is my calling, that is my duty).

Despite all interference Dimitrii continued to work on the saints' lives. In 1695 the second volume appeared, followed by the third in 1700. Dimitrii also wrote theological compositions, religious songs, and spiritual poetry. But an abrupt

turning point in his life came at the end of 1700, when it became necessary to name a new metropolitan for Tobol'sk and Siberia, and Peter's choice fell upon Dimitrii. In February 1701 Dimitrii came to Moscow and was immediately appointed to the position. Most likely Stefan Iavorsky – at that time fulfilling the duties of the empty patriarchal throne, and Dimitrii's friend and fellow Ukrainian – had probably pushed for his candidacy. Dimitrii took no joy in the promotion, for he presumed that, torn from the libraries of Moscow and Kiev, he would be unable to complete his life's work. He fell ill, and his departure for Tobol'sk was postponed. The czar came to visit the ailing metropolitan, and Dimitrii confessed that the reason for his illness lay not only in physical weakness but in his fear of not fulfilling his monastic vow. Peter released Dimitrii from the appointment but did not allow him to return to Ukraine. Later that year the metropolitan of Rostov died, and Dimitrii was appointed in his place.

In March 1702 Dimitrii arrived in that small, ancient Russian city. According to Il'ia Shliapkin's 1891 biography of Dimitrii, soon after his arrival he preached a sermon before parishioners and clergy in which he declared: "Ia prishel ne dlia togo, chtoby vy mne posluzhili, no chtoby ia posluzhil vam" (I have come not so that you will serve me, but that I might serve you). During the sermon he is said to have also indicated the place in the cathedral where he said he would be buried – one of the many elements of Dimitrii's biography that were later declared to establish his sainthood.

Confronted with the ignorance of the local clergymen, Dimitrii became indignant and actively took up his pastoral duties. Soon after his arrival in Rostov he established Russia's first provincial ecclesiastical school, which served approximately two hundred children of all social classes. Although the school did not last long, owing to lack of funds, during the time it was open Dimitrii accomplished much, including his institution of a school theater after the example of the Kiev Mohyla Academy and the Moscow Slavonic-Greek-Latin Academy.

The first plays the pupils performed were dramas written by Dimitrii. Dimitrii's legacy as a dramatist has not been fully established – from three to six plays are ascribed to him – but it is generally accepted that he wrote the *Komediia na Rozhdestvo Khristovo* (Comedy for Christmas), *Uspenskaia drama* (Drama of the Assumption), and *Greshnik kaiushchimsia* (The Repentant Sinner), whose text has not survived. The *Komediia na Rozhdestvo Khristovo* was performed as early as 27 December 1702. The play was based upon episodes from the Gospels and included elements of Polish school theater and Ukrainian puppet show Nativity plays. Drama staged in religious schools served not only the ends of moral education but also fulfilled the purely pedagogical functions of teaching language, oratory, and the development of imagination, good diction, and memory. It preserved many features of medieval European religious dramaturgy. The mystery play and Miracle play were sources for the abundant allegorical, biblical, and mythological characters appearing in Dimitrii's works. Before Dimitrii's school closed in 1705 its students also performed the play *Venets Dimitriiu* (A Crown for Dimitrii), written by one of the teachers in honor of the name day of the founder of the school; it was therefore dedicated to the metropolitan's divine patron, the martyr Saint Dimitrii Solunsky.

On 9 February 1705 Dimitrii fulfilled his monastic vow: the *Zhitiia sviatykh* was finished, and later that year the final volume was published in Kiev. He had created a national pantheon of Christian saints and a grandiose monument of Eastern Orthodox hagiography. But the tireless Dimitrii immediately took on new tasks. In Russia he had encountered Old Believers (schismatics from the official Orthodox Church) for the first time. Dimitrii was unable to appreciate the historical and intellectual roots of this movement, and from the heights of his erudition took it for common ignorance, which he denounced in an enormous composition, *Rozysk o raskolnicheskoi brynskoi vere* (Investigation of the Schismatic Faith, 1745), published posthumously. Dimitrii simultaneously began work on a textbook for the local clergy which he was not able to complete, his *Letopis', skazuiushchaia vkrattse deianiia ot nachala mirobytiia do Rozhdestva Khrista* (A Short Chronicle Telling of Events from the Beginning of the World Until the Birth of Christ, 1784).

The responsibility of running the diocese and his diverse literary pursuits undermined Dimitrii's health, and his ascetic way of life further weakened him. In his final years his relationship with the czar soured because Dimitrii, like Stefan Iavorsky, did not approve of Peter I's church reforms, which made the church subservient to the state. Dimitrii began early to prepare for death. In 1707 he wrote a last will and testament, in which he noted among other things that "S vosemnadtsatiletnego vozrasta do priblizheniia moego do groba ia ne sobiral nichego, krome knig, u menia ne bylo ni zolota, ni serebra, ni izlishnikh odezhd . . . Pust' nikto ne truditsia iskat' posle menia kakikh nibud' skladov" (from the age of eighteen until my approach to the grave I collected nothing except books, neither gold, nor silver, nor unnecessary clothing . . .

[So] let no one start searching for hidden treasures after I am gone).

In the summer of 1709 Dimitrii fell ill, and he died early in the morning on 28 October. On the eve of his death Dimitrii called the church choristers into his cell to sing *kanty* (songs) that he had composed — "Iisuse moi preliubeznyi" (Christ My Most Beloved) and "Nadezhdu moiu v Boze polagaiu" (I Place My Faith in God). The scene is beautifully portrayed in Ivan Bunin's short story "Sviatitel'" (The Prelate, 1924). Dimitrii wished to present his literary works to God, and at his request the drafts for his saints' lives were placed in his coffin. Dimitrii was laid to rest by Iavorsky, his closest friend, who composed a magnificent verse epitaph in his honor.

In 1752, during reconstruction of the cathedral where Dimitrii was buried, his grave was opened, and although his manuscripts were found beside him, reduced to dust, his body was miraculously found to be whole and uncorrupted, a mark of divine favor in the Orthodox hagiographic tradition that Dimitrii had so assiduously chronicled. Five years later he was canonized as Saint Dimitrii Rostovsky. Such an event was extremely rare — in the eighteenth and nineteenth centuries only four saints were canonized in the Russian Orthodox church. Dimitrii's *Zhitiya sviatykh* continued to enjoy immense popularity and was published approximately a dozen times in both the eighteenth and nineteenth centuries.

Biographies:

Vasilii Nechaev, *Sviatyi Dimitrii, mitropolit Rostovsky* (Moscow: Got'e, 1849);

Il'ia A. Shliapkin, *Sv. Dimitrii Rostovsky i ego vremia (1651–1709 g.)* (Saint Petersburg: A. Transhel', 1891);

M. S. Popov, *Sviatitel' Dimitrii Rostovsky i ego trudy* (Saint Petersburg: Transhel', 1910);

R. Dabrowski, *Dymitr Rostowski jako obronca prawd wiary nieuznawanych dzis przez prawostawie* (Warsaw, 1936);

Michael Berndt, *Die Predigt Dimitrij Tuptalos. Studien zur ukrainischen und russichen Barockpredigt* (Frankfurt am Main: Herbert Lang / Bern: Peter Lang, 1975).

References:

Aleksandr Derzhavin, "Chetii-Minei sviatitelia Dimitriia, mitropolita Rostovskogo, kak tserkovnoistoricheskii i literaturnyi pamiatnik," *Bogoslovskie trudy,* 15 (1976): 61–145; 16 (1976): 46–141;

Marina A. Fedotova, "Tuptalo Dimitrii (Issledovatel'skie materialy dlia 'Slovaria

knizhnikov i knizhnosti Drevnei Rusi'),"
Trudy Otdela drevnerusskoi literatury, 45 (1992):
133–143;

Liudmila A. Jankovska, "K issledovaniiu
pisatel'skogo masterstva Dimitriia Rostovskogo (Literaturnaia obrabotka 'Zhitiia
Avraamiia Smolenskogo')," *Slavia Orientalis,* 3–
4 (1984): 383–396;

Viktor Kalugin, "Avtograf 'Uspenskoi dramy'
Dimitriia Rostovskogo," in *Pamiatniki kul'tury.
Novye otkrytiia. Ezhegodnik 1985* (Moscow:
Nauka, 1987), pp. 99–101;

Kalugin, "Keleinyi letopisets Dmitriia Rostovskogo," *Al'manakh bibliofila,* 15 (1983): 160–174;

Kalugin, "Pedagogicheskaia deiatel'nost' Dimitriia
Rostovskogo," in *Prosveshchenie i pedagogicheskaia
mysl' Drevnei Rusi,* edited by E. D. Dneprov
and others (Moscow: Akademiia pedagogiche-
skikh nauk, 1983), pp. 76–84;

Iurii A. Labyntsev, *Poslednii obshcheslavianskii pisatel'
Dimitrii Savich Tuptalo i glavnaia kniga ego zhizni:
Katalog vystavki* (Kiev: Tsentral'naia nauchnaia
biblioteka, 1989);

Liudmila A. Sofronova, " 'Rozhdestvenskaia
drama' Dimitriia Rostovskogo," in *Dukhovnaia
kul'tura slavianskikh narodov,* edited by M. P.
Alekseev and others (Leningrad: Nauka,
1983), pp. 97–108;

Andrei A. Titov, *Novye dannye o sviatitele Dimitrii
Rostovskom* (Moscow, 1881).

Vasilii Grigor'evich Ruban

(14 March 1742 – 24 September 1795)

Irwin R. Titunik
University of Michigan

SELECTED BOOKS: *Oda na den' vseradostneishego torzhestva za predpriiatyi i blagopoluchno sovershivshiisia, k ne opisannomu schastiiu vseia Rossii, ee imp. velichestva i ego imp. velichestva v privitii ospy podvig, 22 noiabria 1768 goda* (Saint Petersburg: Akademiia nauk, 1768);

Nadpisi k kamniu, naznachennomu dlia podnozhiia statui imperatora Petra Velikogo ([Saint Petersburg: Sukhoputnyi kadetskii korpus, 1770]);

Sochinennye i perevodnye nadpisi, na pobedy rossiian nad turkami (Saint Petersburg: Morskoi kadetskii korpus, 1771);

Kratkie geograficheskie, politicheskie i istoricheskie izvestiia o Maloi Rossii (Saint Petersburg: Morskoi kadetskii korpus, 1773);

Kratkaia letopis' Maloi Rossii s 1507 po 1776 god (Saint Petersburg: Artilleriiskii kadetskii korpus, 1776);

Opisanie imperatorskogo, stolichnogo goroda Moskvy (Saint Petersburg: Artilleriiskii kadetskii korpus, 1782);

Blagodarstvennye stikhi ego svetlosti sviashchennoi Rimskoi imperii kniaziu Grigor'iu Aleksandrovichu Potemkinu . . . za okazannuiu milost' sochiniteliu sego, novopriniatiem onago v vysokoe ego svetlosti nachal'stvo i pokrovitel'stvo (Saint Petersburg: [Ovchinnikov], 1784);

Vseobshchii i sovershennyi gonets i puteukazatel' . . . , 2 volumes (Saint Petersburg: Sytin, 1791); revised as *Novyi Vseobshchii i sovershennyi gonets i puteukazatel',* 3 volumes (Saint Petersburg: Imperatorskaia tipografiia, 1793);

Rossiiskoi muzy ob uchrezhdenii i otkrytii Voznesenskoi gubernii, v iuzhnoi polose, Rossiiskoi imperii, poslanie k Ovidiiu . . . (Saint Petersburg, 1795).

OTHER: Antoine François Prévost [incorrectly attributed to Jean Baptiste de Boyer d'Argens], *Nastoiatel' Kilerinskoi,* 6 volumes, edited by and translation attributed to Ruban (Saint Petersburg: Kadetskii korpus, 1765–1781);

Vasilii Grigor'evich Ruban

Ni to ni sio v proze i stikhakh, nos. 1–20 (21 February–11 July 1769), edited by Ruban;

Saint John Damascene, *Kanon Paskhi prelozhennyi stikhami,* translated by Ruban (Saint Petersburg, 1769);

Marc-Antoine Muret, *Presvit: iuriskonsul'ta i Grazhdanina Rimskogo, Otrocheskoe nastavlenie, Dannoe Plemianniku Ego . . . ,* translated by Ruban (Saint Petersburg: Morskoi kadetskii korpus, 1770);

Trudoliubivyi muravei, nos. 1–26 (1771), edited by Ruban;

Starina i novizna, sostoiashchaia iz sochinenii i perevodov prozaicheskikh i stikhotvornykh, volumes 1 (1772) and 2 (1773), edited by Ruban;

Pseudo Homer, *Omirova Vatrakhomiomakhiia, To Est' Voina Myshei i Liagushek; Zabavnaia Poema Na Russkii iazyk Perevedena Vasiliem Rubanom,* translated by Ruban (Saint Petersburg: Akademiia nauk, 1772);

Kitaiskii mudrets, ili nauka zhit' blagopoluchno v obshestve . . . , edited by Ruban, translated by S. P. Kozlov (Saint Petersburg: Akademiia nauk, 1773);

Ovid, *Dve iroidy, ili Dva pis'ma drevnikh iroin', Sochinenie Publiia Ovidiia Nasona, S Priobshcheniem Avtorovoi Zhizni, Soderzhannii i Nuzhneishikh Na Kazhdoe Pis'mo iziasnenii,* translated by Ruban (Saint Petersburg: Akademiia nauk, 1774);

Virgil, *Eneidy kniga 1–3,* edited by Ruban, translated by Vasilii Sankovsky (Saint Petersburg: Akademiia nauk, 1775);

Liubopytnyi mesiatseslov na 1775 god, edited by Ruban (Saint Petersburg: Akademiia nauk, 1775);

Moskovskii liubopytnyi mesiatseslov na 1776 god, edited by Ruban (Moscow: Moskovskii universitet, 1776);

Virgil, *Virgilieva ekloga Titir,* translated by Ruban (Saint Petersburg: Artilleriiskii i inzhenernyi kadetskii korpus, 1777);

Nachertanie, podaiushchee poniatie o dostoslavnom tsarstvovanii Petra Velikogo, edited by Ruban (Saint Petersburg: Artilleriiskii kadetskii korpus, 1778);

Istoricheskoe geograficheskoe i topograficheskoe opisanie Sanktpeterburga Ot Nachala Zavedeniia Ego, S 1703 Po 1751 God, sochinennoe Bogdanovym . . . , edited by Ruban (Saint Petersburg, 1779);

Rossiiskii tsarskii pamiatnik, soderzhashchii po poriadku alfavita kratkoe opisanie zhizni rossiiskikh gosudarei, ikh suprug i chad . . . , edited by Ruban (Saint Petersburg: Gos. voennaia kollegiia, 1783; revised edition, Saint Petersburg: Sukhoputnyi kadetskii korpus, 1783; revised again, Saint Petersburg: [Breitkopf], 1783; revised again, Saint Petersburg: Sukhoputnyi kadetskii korpus, 1784);

Trifona Korobeinikova, moskovskogo kuptsa, s tovarishchi, puteshestvie vo Ierusalim, Egipet i k Sinaiskoi gore v 1573 god, edited by Ruban (Saint Petersburg: Artilleriiskii i inzhenernyi kadetskii korpus, 1783);

Zerno istorii pervykh trekh monarkhii sveta Assiriiskoi, Persidskoi i Grecheskoi . . . , edited by Ruban, translated by Vasilii Filippovich (Saint Petersburg: Sytin, 1791);

Ovid, *Iroida, ili Pis'mo v stikhakh Ot Vrisendi K Akhillu Publiem Ovidiem Nasonem Sochinennoe,* translated by Ruban (Saint Petersburg: Artilleriiskii i inzhenernyi kadetskii korpus, 1791);

Martin von Baumgarten, *Posetitel' i opisatel' sviatykh mest . . . ili Puteshestvie Martyna Baumgartena . . . v Egipet, Araviiu, Palestinu i Siriiu . . . ,* 3 volumes, translated by Ruban (Saint Petersburg: Korpus chuzhestrannykh edinovertsev, 1794).

Vasilii Grigor'evich Ruban was an enterprising and prolific participant in eighteenth-century Russia's equivalent of Grub Street — a host of professional literary men willing and able to undertake any writing task, equally adept at producing manuals on agriculture or card playing, at composing panegyric odes to the high and mighty or Russifying the works of Homer or Horace, and at performing as compilers, editors, and publishers. Such hackwork was by no means necessarily of poor quality; on the contrary, many respectable compositions by reputable writers were produced in this way. In Ruban's case there were works compiled, edited, published, and also translated by him that received wide approval and appreciation. However, Ruban was notorious among his contemporaries for producing great quantities of occasional poems, especially those written for or to patrons whose protection, gifts, and monetary support he solicited and often gained. Ruban's more distinguished and independent fellow writers reviled and mocked these "obsequious" verses, and he was subsequently condemned as a sycophant whose name was emblematic of vilely motivated and shamelessly produced poetry. Although that reputation has survived into the twentieth century, an unbiased assessment, without denying his reprehensible traits, must also acknowledge Ruban not only as a literary entrepreneur of extraordinary energy and versatility (not to speak of productivity) but also a competent writer typical of eighteenth-century Russia and of interest in his own right, especially as a poet.

Vasilii Grigor'evich Ruban was of Ukrainian origin, possibly from Cossack stock. He was born in the small town of Belgorod, not far from Kiev, on 14 March 1742. He began his formal education at the venerable Kiev Academy, then flourishing under the rectorship of Georgii Konissky, but in 1754 transferred to the Moscow Academy and a year later enrolled at a gymnasium attached to the newly founded (1755) University of Moscow. In 1759 he was admitted as a student to the university, where he won medals for scholastic excellence and became the protégé of Mikhail Lomonosov's former protégé, Nikolai Popovsky, who was then the university's lecturer in rhetoric and poetics.

Upon completion of his university studies in 1761, Ruban began a lifelong career in the government civil service. He entered the Department of Foreign Affairs, his first assignment returning him to Ukraine, specifically Zaporozhie, where he was employed as a Turkish-language translator. The circumstances in which Ruban had acquired a knowledge of Turkish (some claim it was Tatar) remain a mystery. He held the position for approximately two years, then moved to Saint Petersburg in 1764, his official duties still with the Department of Foreign Affairs. In 1773 he was transferred to the Mezhevaia ekspeditsiia (Land Survey Office) of the senate, where he served under the first (presumably) of his many patrician patrons, Prince Aleksandr Viazemsky.

The list of Ruban's patrons included several powerful figures, but the most eminent and, for Ruban, by far the most important of those patrons was Count (later Prince) Grigorii Potemkin, whose acquaintance he is believed to have made during his tour of duty in Zaporozhie. When Potemkin was appointed governor-general of three southeastern provinces of the empire in 1775, Ruban accepted the opportunity to accompany him as secretary, and in the course of the ensuing experience Ruban found himself, among his other duties, serving as the temporary superintendent of schools of Novorossiisk, one of Potemkin's provinces. Ruban returned to Saint Petersburg with Potemkin in 1784, when the latter was made head of the War Department. Ruban was given a post in that department as administrator in charge of foreign correspondence and as Polish translator. He remained in that capacity more or less until the end of his life, achieving his highest civil service rank, collegiate counselor, in 1786. Earlier, in 1777, presumably in recognition of his governmental service, he had been elected a member of the Vol'noe Ekonomicheskoe Obshchestvo (Free Economic Society). He had also been elected one of the first members of the Vol'noe Rossiiskoe Sobranie (Free Russian Assembly) in 1774, in recognition of his labors in the field of letters.

As was common in eighteenth-century Russia, Ruban managed to combine with his official civil service career a second, lifelong career as a writer, engaging in a variety of professional literary endeavors: the writing, editing, and publishing of journals and almanacs; the compilation, annotation, and publication of historical materials of various kinds; the translation of literary and other kinds of works in both prose and verse from classical and modern languages; and the composition of original poetry, mainly of the type called "epideictic" (that is, occasional verse).

Ruban's literary ambitions, evidence of which goes back to 1761, began in earnest in 1769, the year of the first flowering of Russian satiric journals under the stimulus of Catherine II's *Vsiakaia Vsiachina* (All Sorts and Sundries). On 21 February Ruban came out with his contribution, the weekly *Ni to ni sio v proze i stikhakh* (Neither This Nor That in Prose and Verse), a takeoff on *I to i sio* (Both This and That), a satiric journal being published by his old schoolmate Mikhail Chulkov. Ruban's journal was less specifically a satiric work than the others; it was, rather, a humor magazine not without certain serious intellectual pretensions (translations, for example, of ancient authors and of modern ones, such as Voltaire). The fact that it ceased publication on 11 July 1769 is usually taken as a sign of its lack of success with the public. Whatever the actual opinion of the time, scholarly opinion since has tended to disparage Ruban's 1769 journal, failing to see any satire in it or any value in humor other than the satiric kind. But unbiased reading shows that Ruban had deliberately plied the tongue-in-cheek, making the journal's title into a pervasive editorial leitmotiv – "Maxima de Nihilo nascitur historia" (The Greatest Tale Is Born Out of Nothing) was the journal's epigraph. The editor's patently ironic and mock-self-deprecatory statements that the journal's publication was prompted "okhotoiu pokazat'sia gramotnymi" (by the desire to show that we are literate) or that "mezhdu mnozhestvom oslov i my visloukhimi byt' ne pokrasneem" (in a crowd of asses our being lop-eared will not cause embarrassment) were later read by historians as evidence of Ruban's cynicism and even nihilism.

Ni to ni sio was followed in mid 1771 by Ruban's second effort at a "satiric" journal, the weekly *Trudoliubivyi muravei* (The Industrious Ant), which ran for twenty-six issues and basically repeated its predecessor in kind. Both journals were largely Ruban's work in all aspects (contributions in prose and verse, editing, and publishing), but items were also supplied by others, among whom were Mikhail Popov, Vasilii Petrov, and Vasilii Maikov. In turn, Ruban amply contributed to other people's journals, including those edited by Mikhail Kheraskov, Chulkov, and Nikolai Novikov.

Not long after ceasing his first two journals, Ruban, partly because he had so much unused material on hand, brought out a literary and historical compendium (usually cited as a journal) under the title *Starina i novizna, sostoiashchaia iz sochinenii i perevodov prozaicheskikh i stikhotvornykh* (Old Times and New, consisting of Original Compositions and Translations in Prose and Verse, 1772 and 1773), in two parts. Many of Ruban's compositions and translations, especially works in verse, appeared in this compendium, but it also included works by other authors and historical-documentary material, mostly relating to Russia. Among the items it published are such notable curiosities as Gavriil Derzhavin's first printed work, "Iroida ili Pis'mo Vivlidy k Kavnu" (Heroide or Letter of Byblis to Caunas), a translation from a German version of Ovid's *Metamorphoses*; translations of five so-called Homeric hymns by Ruban (presumably from Greek); Ivan Barkov's "Oda v pokhvalu liubvi" (Ode in Praise of Love), "ispravlennaia i dopolnennaia pozvolitel'nymi vyrazheniiami V. Rubanom" (emended and expanded in more permissible locutions by Vasilii Ruban); verses by Kheraskov; and publication from manuscripts of homilies by several distinguished Ukrainian and Russian churchmen of past and present, including Feofan Prokopovich and Ruban's first mentor, Georgii Konissky.

Both during and after the publication of *Starina i novizna,* Ruban devoted energy to publishing activities involving either materials that he compiled or works by others that he edited or otherwise prepared for publication. These numerous works vary widely in nature – almanacs; compendia of brief lives of Russian rulers and their families; books and brochures of information and statistics about Ukraine and Russia; travelogues, especially accounts of pilgrimages to the Holy Land; compilations of books of information for travel in Russia and Europe; a history of philosophy; a schoolbook history of ancient civilizations; Vasilii Sankovsky's translation of the first three books of Virgil's *Aeneid* with Ruban's corrections and annotations; and various Russian historical documents.

Translation of one kind or another was de rigueur for Russian eighteenth-century literary men, and Ruban did not fail to make a substantial contribution in this area as well. Many of Ruban's translations consist of historical-informational or didactic works such as Martin von Baumgarten's *Peregrinatio in AEgyptum, Arabiam, Palaestinam & Syriam* (1594) or Marc-Antoine Muret's *Insitutio puerilis* (1585). As for translations of more strictly literary works, the biggest of Ruban's efforts is his translation of Antoine François Prévost's *Doyen de Killerine* (1739–1740) (in its Russian version, mistakenly attributed to Jean Baptiste de Boyer d'Argens), which was published in six volumes over the years 1765–1781; however, there is some question as to whether Ruban actually did the translation or merely edited it. Otherwise, Ruban concentrated on the ancient classics, especially the poetry of Pseudo-

Homer, Virgil, and Ovid. In addition to the already mentioned pseudo-Homeric hymns, Ruban translated the pseudo-Homeric mock epic *Batrachomyomachia* into Russian prose in 1772. It is not known whether Ruban translated directly from Greek; he had studied it at the University of Moscow, but his translation of one of Lucian's "Dialogues of the Dead" claims to be "translated from Latin." He translated selections from Virgil's *Eclogues* and from Ovid's *Amores, Metamorphoses, Heroides, Tristia,* and *Ex Ponto.* Clearly, Ovid was his favorite, as evidenced not only by the quantitative tilt in Ovid's favor but also by Ruban's verse tribute to Ovid, *Rossiiskoi muzy . . . poslanie k Ovidiiu . . .* (The Russian Muse's Epistle to Ovid, 1795). Ruban's translations display certain hallmarks of contemporary Russian translation practice, in particular, occasional alterations and expansions of the received text. His talent as a verse translator was perhaps not remarkable, but the results were competent and apparently were appreciated by his contemporaries. Ruban also adapted into Russian verse parts of the Russian Orthodox liturgy – for example, the Easter service of Saint John Damascene.

Among all his literary activities Ruban's real passion was the writing of original verse. An anecdote has it that so rampant was this passion that Ruban was even moved to write official reports for Potemkin in verse. From at least the mid 1760s to the end of his life he composed a steady stream of occasional poetry – inscriptions, epitaphs, elegies, choruses, hymns, paeans, odes, and songs – which commemorated birthdays, namedays, weddings, deaths and burials, promotions, departures and returns, military victories of Russian forces over the Turks, and many other events; he even composed an ode on the inoculation of Catherine II against smallpox. The poetic imagery employed is erudite, based on classical and biblical allusion, and the poetic form is usually Alexandrine couplets. The single most popular item in this flood of verses was a *nadpis'* (inscription) on the so-called "Grom-kamen'" (Thunder-Stone), the foundation of Etienne-Maurice Falconet's equestrian statue of Peter I (the "Bronze Horseman"), written in 1770. The poem underwent at least six printings and was translated into several languages, including English.

Aside from that particular specimen, however, Ruban's poetry generally elicited negative reaction from the Russian literary community. One of the leading poets of the time, Mikhail Murav'ev, who managed to remain on good personal terms with Ruban, wrote of him in a private letter: "Ne mozhno voobrazit' podlee lesti i glupee stikhov ego . . . so vsiakogo stikha nadobno razorvat'sia ot smekha i negodovanii" (It is impossible to imagine viler flattery or stupider poetry than his [Ruban's]. . . . With any line you read you cannot help but burst out in laughter and scorn). Ruban figured prominently in several verse satires on bad poets where inevitably a play on the Russian verb *rubit'* (to chop, to rough-hew) identified the intended target. He also served as a model for the ode writer burlesqued in Ivan Dmitriev's well-known poem "Chuzhoi tolk" (Other Folk's Chatter, 1794). Ruban's ill-repute as a poet has survived and even grown since his own time. Grigorii Gukovsky, the leading and most brilliant authority on eighteenth-century Russian literature in modern times, expressed utter contempt for Ruban and his poetry.

However, the question of whether Ruban deserves such a reputation is an open one. There can be no doubt that merely by writing unfailingly loyalist or, in the pejorative key, "servile" poetry, Ruban laid himself open to the contempt of his own and future generations, regardless of the quality in his work. But unstinting homage and even shameless flattery do not automatically exclude skillful use of versification, sonority, imagery, or thematic organization. Perhaps the most important and at the same time most misunderstood aspect of Ruban's reputation has to do specifically with the poems he wrote during the last several years of his life (unpublished in his lifetime). These are addressed to various patrons and typically include prominent mention of the gifts or the money Ruban received or expected to receive for them, a frankness which Gukovsky and other literary historians regarded as despicable. An unprejudiced reading of those poems will reveal, however, that they are largely about the poet himself, including, besides his relationship with his patron, his reminiscences about his own trials and triumphs, his present needs and troubles, and his view of life at a time when, chronically ill and nearly blind, he had to struggle incessantly, bringing to bear all his strengths and talents in order to survive. From this point of view these poems take on an unusual and engaging refraction that throws into relief not flattery and importunity but the myriad details of the poet's predicament, told with undeniable dignity and often wry humor,

sometimes even at the poet's own expense. The poems in question are not great poetry, but neither are they unworthy of the name *poetry*.

The efforts Ruban made during the last years of his life to obtain comfort and security did not bear fruit. Despite embellishing his relationships with his patrons in terms that made them to him as Maecenas was to Virgil or Horace; despite Potemkin's promise of property that would have become Ruban's Sabine farm but of which the poet wrote, "na pis'me . . . lish' zriatsia vidy" (the vistas can be viewed only on paper); despite appeals to such favorites of Catherine II as Semen Zorich and Platon Zubov to intercede with the empress about providing him a pension; and despite his own continuing official and mercenary labors, no tack seemed to work for him, and both his means and his health seriously deteriorated. On 24 September 1795 in Saint Petersburg, Vasilii Grigor'evich Ruban, the Russian eighteenth-century writer most denigrated for his actual or putative obsequiousness and servility, died in circumstances close to poverty.

Bibliography:

Aleksandr Neustroev, *Literaturnye deiateli XVIII veka*, volume 1: *Vasilii Grigor'evich Ruban* (Saint Petersburg: Leshtokovskaia Skoropechatnia P. O. Iablonskago [*sic*], 1896).

References:

Anthony G. Cross, "An English Version (1791) of a Poem by Vasilii Ruban," *Study Group for Eighteenth Century Russia Newsletter*, 7 (1979): 38–40;

Lidiia Ginzburg, "Neizdannye stikhotvoreniia Rubana," *XVIII vek*, 1 (1935): 413–430;

B. L. Modzalevsky, "Vasilii Grigor'evich Ruban (Istoriko-literaturnyi ocherk)," *Russkaia starina*, 8 (1897): 393–415;

Semen Vengerov, ed., *Russkaia poeziia, Sobranie proizvedenii russkikh poetov*, volume 1, *XVIII vek, Epokha klassitsizma* (Saint Petersburg: A. E. Vineke, 1897), section 3, pp. 337–345;

Vladimir Zapadov, "Problema literaturnogo servilizma i diletantizma i poeticheskaia pozitsiia G. R. Derzhavina," *XVIII vek*, 16 (1989): 56–75.

Aleksei Andreevich Rzhevsky
(1737–1804)

Alexander Levitsky
Brown University

BOOKS: *Oda e. i. v. vsepresvetleishei derzhavneishei velikoi gosudaryne Ekaterine Alekseevne . . . na vseradostneishee vosshestvie na prestol* (Moscow: Moskovskii universitet, 1762);

Oda e. i. v. gosudaryne Ekaterine Alekseevne . . . na den' rozhdeniia eia, aprelia 21 dnia, 1763 godu (Moscow: Moskovskii universitet, 1763);

Oda vsepresvetleishei derzhavneishei velikoi, i istinnu liubivoi materi svoego narode, gosudaryne Ekaterine Alekseevne . . . podnesennaia v novyi 1764 god, ianvaria 1 dnia (Moscow: Moskovskii universitet, 1764);

Oda vseprestvetleishei i vseavgusteishei . . . gosudaryne vserossiiskoi imperatritse Ekaterine Vtoroi na vsevozhdelennoe pribytie eia velichestva iz Sanktpeterburga v Moskvu 1767 goda, fevralia 13 dnia (Moscow: Moskovskii universitet, 1767);

Oda Ego Velichestvu . . . Aleksandru Pavlovichu . . . na den' vosshestviia na vserossiiskii prestol (Saint Petersburg, 1801).

OTHER: Ippolit Bogdanovich, *Dushin'ka Drevniaia povest' v vol'nykh stikhakh,* edited by Rzhevsky (Saint Petersburg: Veitbrekht, 1783); revised as *Dushen'ka. Drevniaia povest' v vol'nykh stikhakh* (Saint Petersburg: Korpus chuzhestrannykh edinovertsov, 1794);

"Podlozhnyi Smerdii. Tragediia," in *Tetral'noe nasledstvo,* edited by Pavel N. Berkov (Moscow: Iskusstvo, 1956), pp. 143–188;

"A. A. Rzhevsky," in *Poety XVIII veka,* volume 1, edited by Georgii P. Makogonenko and Il'ia Z. Serman, Biblioteka poeta, malaia seriia (Leningrad: Sovetskii pisatel', 1958), pp. 323–350;

"A. A. Rzhevsky," in *Poety XVIII veka,* volume 1, edited by Makogonenko and Serman, Biblioteka poeta, bol'shaia seriia (Leningrad: Sovetskii pisatel', 1972), pp. 189–298;

"A. A. Rzhevsky," in *Russkaia literatura vek XVIII: Lirika,* edited by N. D. Kochetkova and others (Moscow: Khudozhestvennaia literatura, 1990), pp. 158–173.

Aleksei Andreevich Rzhevsky's brief but productive career as a poet was for a time almost completely forgotten in the annals of Russian literary history, and his legacy was measured (if at all) in terms of his achievements in the civil service rather than in literature. This situation was largely a result of Rzhevsky's choice to devote most of his adult life to career advancement. After his rather abrupt exit from the literary scene at age twenty-seven, awareness of Rzhevsky's role in Russian literature diminished to the point that his name was only recognized in conjunction with a poem by Gavriil Derzhavin addressed to him. Rzhevsky's obscurity finally came to an end in the 1920s with the work of the pioneer of eighteenth-century Russian literary studies, Grigorii A. Gukovsky, and modern scholars have begun to appreciate Rzhevsky's place in the development of Russian literary culture. Still, biographical data on this interesting and facile poet is sparse, and no monograph-length study of his life and works is likely to appear in the near future.

Of ancient and distinguished Russian noble lineage from the Smolensk region, Rzhevsky was apparently able to receive a well-rounded education at home. His studies included a solid grounding in literature, and he began experimenting with poetry as a young man. Some poems from his juvenilia were noted and praised by Aleksandr Sumarokov; how the elder poet got hold of them is uncertain, but Sumarokov's appreciation of Rzhevsky's work had a profound effect on the young man. It forever confirmed his ardent admiration of Sumarokov, whom he recognized as a teacher and mentor. Feelings of admiration were apparently reciprocated, and their friendship lasted until Sumarokov's death.

It is, then, no accident that at the age of twenty-two, when he already held a minor officer's rank in the army, Rzhevsky published his first elegy, "Svershilosia teper' serdechno predskazanie" (My Heart's Prophecy Has Now Been Fulfilled), in the February 1759 issue of Sumarokov's newly founded literary journal, *Trudoliubivaia pchela* (The

Industrious Bee). Rzhevsky's elegy was published with four other elegies (two by Sumarokov, one by A. Nartov, and one by S. Naryshkin) under the general rubric *Elegii* (Elegies) – reflecting Sumarokov's idea of having literary culture evolve by competitions. Rzhevsky belonged to the generation of Russian poets that was trying to establish the syllabotonic system of Russian verse (which combines stressed and unstressed syllables into regular feet), and such contests not only enlarged the repertoire of Russian poetry but were also meant to create lasting models for treating specific themes and genres. Rzhevsky's entry into the world of literature was thus shaped by his tacit acceptance of Sumarokov's aesthetic views subordinating an author's role to the idea of the immanence of the genre, in this case the elegy. What was crucial was not the author's individual contribution but the striving to create a universal example of the given genre.

A separate incident might have given Rzhevsky reason to hide his authorship altogether. Rzhevsky had prepared a selection of eleven poems for inclusion in the February issue of *Ezhemesiachnyia sochineniia* (Monthly Compositions), the only Saint Petersburg journal that printed poetry prior to the appearance of Sumarokov's *Trudoliubivaia pchela*. The last poem, a sonnet titled "Sonet ili Madrigal Libere Sake, Aktritse Italianskago vol'nago teatra" (A Sonnet or Madrigal to Libera Sacco, Actress of the Italian Free Theater), created such a stir among women readers in high society (perhaps reaching as high as Empress Elizabeth) that it and all the other poems were physically cut from the issue, which had already been printed. In fact, the journal ceased publishing any poetry for the remainder of the year, for the first time since its inception in 1755, and continued the policy into the next year. The censorship apparently arose over Rzhevsky's seemingly innocuous assertion that the beauty of Sacco, then the leading ballerina from Locatelli's Italian theatrical troupe, was incomparably superior to that of "nekikh dam" (certain noble ladies) who slandered her out of feelings of envy.

Despite this mishap, Rzhevsky succeeded in publishing these poems at a later date, and the negative influence of the *nekikh dam* seems to have been short-lived as far as his personal fortunes were concerned. Yet the connoisseurs of Russian poetry in 1759 missed the opportunity of becoming acquainted with what may be seen as an outline of the poet's future literary activity. The eleven poems, which exhibited Rzhevsky's versatility as a poet, consisted of one elegy, one set of stanzas, two riddles, six madrigals, and one sonnet. Notably,

Rzhevsky did not include any odes, on which aspiring poets would usually have staked their claim for recognition. Rather, he exhibited a preference for smaller varieties of lyric, such as riddles and madrigals, suggesting a playful, rococo orientation.

Indeed, most of Rzhevsky's poems published over the four years following this abortive publication are short lyric genres with the addition of fables, idylls, rondeaux, and epigrams, and a view of literature as a game became a major component of his craft. Most of Rzhevsky's nearly 250 works published during these years, primarily in the journals *Poleznoe Uveselenie* (Useful Amusement, 1760–1762) and *Svobodnye Chasy* (Idle Hours, 1763), display considerable technical skill, often surpassing that of Sumarokov. If Rzhevsky, like Sumarokov, was concerned with expanding the variety of genres available to Russian literature, he clearly preferred small, often technically demanding, poetic forms, such as the sonnet, of which he composed twice as many as his mentor. Rzhevsky's minimalist orientation often led him away from Sumarokov's brand of classicism to the more mannered forms of poetry favored by baroque and rococo sensibilities, such as poems written in peculiar shapes, riddles, acrostics, poems made up of words of one syllable, poems that could be read in multiple ways, and poems composed on preselected rhymes. Moreover, his reintroduction of Mikhail Lomonosov's favorite trope, the oxymoron, which Sumarokov had ridiculed, signaled Rzhevsky's independent literary stance, allowing a peculiar symbiotic mixture of baroque, rococo, and classicist elements. In this sense Rzhevsky's poetry may typify the contradictory nature of Russian literature of the early 1760s better than the streamlined version of classicism that Sumarokov advocated.

Most of Rzhevsky's literary activity was connected with Moscow's first Russian literary weekly, *Poleznoe uveselenie* (Useful Amusement), published by Mikhail Kheraskov. For approximately six months the journal was in competition with the first Russian literary weekly, *Prazdnoe vremia v pol'zu upotreblennoe* (Idle Time Spent Usefully), which had been published in Saint Petersburg since 1759, but after its demise in mid 1760, *Poleznoe uveselenie* became virtually the only venue for noteworthy developments in Russian literature for the next two years. The journal, while it paid tribute to some of Sumarokov's rationalist views on literature, began rather early to cultivate topics of mystical significance, resurrecting the baroque topos of *vanitas vanitatum* ("vanity of vanities," from Ecclesiastes 1:2), which found productive treatments in Rzhevsky's poetry. This contradicts the image suggested by some historians of Rzhevsky as a slavish imitator of Sumarokov. The journal was also one of the first Russian literary publications providing impetus for the subsequently prominent *kul't druzhby* (cult of friendship) in Russian letters, publishing such works as Rzhevsky's "Pis'mo k A. N." (A Letter to A. N[aryshkin]) and "Stans sochinen 1761 goda iiulia 19 dnia po vyezde iz derevni g. Kh." (Stanzas Composed on 19 July 1761, upon Departing Mr. Kh(eraskov)'s Village).

In 1761 Rzhevsky published ninety-one poems in *Poleznoe uveselenie,* and some issues were entirely his work; he thus became its main contributor after Kheraskov. Rzhevsky continued to participate in literary competitions with Kheraskov, A. Naryshkin, A. Karin, and later Ippolit Bogdanovich; they composed transpositions of the same text, wrote variants of one genre, or wrote poems on preselected rhymes. In addition to the specific sonnets, odes, and elegies written for these competitions, Rzhevsky continued to develop an independent approach to these genres.

Rzhevsky's contributions to these competitions concerned not only genre but also theme and metrical realization. One of the particularly exotic meters for this period, dactylic dimeter, had been advanced for the first time in print by Sumarokov's "Chasy" (The Clock), in the August 1759 issue of *Trudoliubivaia pchela;* the poem attempted through the uninterrupted rhythm of its two-foot dactyls to reproduce the movement of a clock, thereby underscoring the uselessness of human endeavor before the relentless passage of time. While Sumarokov hesitated to assign any generic label to the poem, Rzhevsky's variant of the theme, rendered in the same meter and published two years later in *Poleznoe uveselenie,* was written in seven miniquatrains and designated as an ode ("Oda I"). Sumarokov's text of approximately the same length could not have been considered an ode in any traditional sense, if only due to the fact that it was not divided into stanzas, yet Rzhevsky was not being facetious or disrespectful toward his model; rather, the poem demonstrated his concern with establishing a minimal unit of what could be called an ode. The fact that this was his concern was made evident by its companion, "Ode II," which appeared on the next page; it was accurately subtitled "sobrannaia iz odnoslozhnykh slov" (composed of one-syllable words).

In this way Rzhevsky's odes testified to some of the major contemporary changes in Russian literary aesthetics aimed at reducing the lofty pathos of Lomonosov's odes. Yet in Rzhevsky's mind this did not entail rejecting Lomonosov's legacy; he seems to have only wished for an expansion of the functional use of the genre. Indeed, in the same year Rzhevsky also composed his "Oda Blazhennyia i Vechno Dostoinyia Pamiati Istinnomu Ottsu Otechestva, Imperatoru Pervomu, Gosudariu Petru Velikomu" (An Ode to the Blessed and Eternally Worthy Memory of the True Father of Our Fatherland, the First Emperor and Sovereign Peter the Great), which can be considered not only one of the most splendid odes written in the memory of Peter the Great but also Rzhevsky's testimonial to Lomonosov's poetics.

Despite Rzhevsky's varied contributions to Russian literature, none of his works left a lasting mark on the development of Russian poetry, nor was one chosen by succeeding generations as a necessary part of their cultural heritage. This situation is undoubtedly due to his flourishing career in state service after Catherine II came to power, which deflected his energies from literature to government administration. But even before his career began to take off around 1767, when he became a deputy to the Legislative Commission, followed in 1768 by his appointment in an advisory capacity to the director of the State Bank, Rzhevsky seems to have exhausted some of his creative energy. If in 1763 he was able to publish ninety-two poems in *Svobodnye chasy,* he managed only one in 1764. It is true that in the mid 1760s Rzhevsky was turning from small lyrics to the large-scale genre of tragedy, having finished two in verse, *Prelesta* (Charming, 1765) and *Podlozhnyi Smerdii* (The False Smerdis), first staged in 1769, and these must have taken a great deal more time than his clever poetic "games" of the early 1760s. Neither of these tragedies had much success or lasted long on the stage.

In 1769, after the death of his first wife, Aleksandra (née Kamenskaia), Rzhevsky left the literary scene for good. He gradually rose in the ranks to higher and more responsible positions, which included the vice-directorship of the Academy of Sciences in 1771, the presidency of the Medical College in 1775, and the posts of privy councillor and senator in 1783. Many of these promotions paralleled his rise in degrees in Masonic lodges during the 1770s. He was a member of the Arestea lodge in 1775–1776 and the Latona lodge in 1776–1779, the latter of which was headed by Novikov. At some point during his advancement to the highest posts in government in the early 1780s, he befriended the rising star of Russian poetry, Derzhavin. Derzhavin's poem, "Schastlivoe semeistvo" (Happy Family, 1783), immortalized Rzhevsky in Russian literature, not for his accomplishments in poetry, but for his ability to achieve marital bliss with his second wife (née Alymova), whom he had married in 1773. Ironically, it may have been the security of marital bliss, together with his career, that had drawn Rzhevsky away from Russian letters. In several respects Rzhevsky had a lot in common with Derzhavin, including his provincial education, his unmistakable talent, his penchant for exploring metaphysical and baroque topics, his involvement in domestic life, and his distinguished service career. But as opposed to that of the great poet, Rzhevsky's career was not characterized by squabbles with his superiors, which in Derzhavin's case often resulted in demotions and periods of unemployment (and often provided him with opportunities for writing poetry).

Rzhevsky did Russian literature an inestimable service by becoming patron publisher to what was arguably one of the greatest achievements of Russian eighteenth-century literary culture: Ippolit Bogdanovich's humorous and erotic narrative poem *Dushen'ka* (Little Soul, 1783). Bogdanovich, one of Rzhevsky's friends from the days of their collaboration on *Poleznoe uveselenie,* was nearly penniless at the time, and Rzhevsky took it upon himself to publish the revised and completed version of what had originally been called *Dushin'kiny pokhozhdeniia, skaska v stikhakh* (Dushin'ka's Adventures: A Tale in Verse, 1778). There were profound changes between the 1778 and 1783 versions of *Dushen'ka,* but the extent of Rzhevsky's editorial efforts in bringing it to its final form is unclear. In any case, his alert aesthetic eye in identifying a masterpiece of Russian eighteenth-century literature and his assistance in its creation and dissemination are significant. Rzhevsky's pioneering experimentation with lighthearted and playful poetic diction in the late 1750s and early 1760s was also important, as it paved the way for Bogdanovich's masterpiece.

References:

Iakov L. Barskov, *Perepiska moskovskikh masonov XVIII veka* (Petrograd: Akademiia nauk, 1915);

Pavel N. Berkov, "Tragediia A. A. Rzhevskogo 'Podlozhnyi Smerdii,'" in *Tetral'noe nasledstvo* (Moscow: Iskusstvo, 1956), pp. 139–143;

William Edward Brown, "A. A. Rzhevsky and the Elegy," in his *A History of 18th Century Russian Literature* (Ann Arbor: Ardis, 1980), pp. 292–301;

Grigorii A. Gukovsky, *Ocherki po istorii russkoi literatury XVIII veka: Dvorianskaia fronda v literature 1750–1760–kh godov* (Moscow & Leningrad: Akademiia nauk, 1936);

Gukovsky, "Rzhevsky," in his *Russkaia Poeziia XVIII v.* (Leningrad: Academia, 1927), pp. 151–182;

Mikhail N. Longinov, "Biographicheskie svedeniia o nekotorykh russkikh pisateliakh XVIII veka i bibliographicheskie izvestiia ob ikh proizvedeniiakh: Suprugi Rzhevskie," *Russkia starina,* 7 (1870): 78–80;

Il'ia Z. Serman, "Biograficheskaia spravka," in *Poety XVIII veka,* volume 1, edited by Serman and Georgii P. Makogonenko (Leningrad: Sovetskii pisatel', 1972), pp. 189–194.

Aleksandr Aleksandrovich Shakhovskoi

(24 April 1777 – 22 January 1846)

Vadim Dmitrievich Rak
Institute of Russian Literature (Pushkin House), Saint Petersburg

BOOKS: *Novyi Stern: Komediia v I deistvii* (Saint Petersburg: Imperatorskii teatr, 1807); translated by J. Eyre as "The New Sterne: A Comedy in One Act," *American Slavic and East European Review,* 4 (August 1945): 80–92;

Rusalka: Komicheskaia opera v 3 deistviiakh. Chast' 4 (Saint Petersburg: Imperatorskii teatr, 1807);

Debora, ili Torzhestvo very: Tragediia v 5 deistviiakh, by Shakhovskoi and Lev N. Nevakhovich (Saint Petersburg: F. Drekhsler, 1811);

Kozak-stikhotvorets: Anekdoticheskaia opera-vodevil' v 1 deistvii (Saint Petersburg: Imperatorskii teatr, 1815);

Ivan Susanin: Opera v 2 deistviiakh (Saint Petersburg: Imperatorskii teatr, 1815);

Krest'iane, ili Vstrecha nezvanykh: Novaia opera-vodevil' v 2 deistviiakh (Saint Petersburg: Imperatorskii teatr, 1815);

Urok koketkam, ili Lipetskie vody: Komediia v 5 deistviiakh v stikhakh (Saint Petersburg: Imperatorskii teatr, 1815);

Lomonosov, ili Rekrut-stikhotvorets: Opera-vodevil' v 3 deistviiakh. Muzyka sobrannaia iz raznorodnykh pesen, marshei i val'sov, aranzhirovannaia dlia orkestra g. [F.] Antonolini (Saint Petersburg: Imperatorskii teatr, 1816);

Pribavlenie novogo iavleniia k opere Krest'iane, ili Vstrecha nezvanykh (Saint Petersburg: Imperatorskii teatr, 1817);

Svoia sem'ia, ili Zamuzhniaia nevesta: Komediia v 3 deistviiakh v stikhakh, by Shakhovskoi, Aleksandr S. Griboedov, and Nikolai I. Khmel'nitsky (Saint Petersburg: Imperatorskii teatr, 1818);

Ne liubo – ne slushai, a lgat' ne meshai: Komediia v 1 deistvii, v vol'nykh stikhakh (Saint Petersburg: Imperatorskii teatr, 1818);

Pustodomy: Komediia v 5 deistviiakh v stikhakh (Saint Petersburg: Imperatorskie teatry, 1820);

Kakadu, ili Sledstvie uroka koketkam: Komediia v 1 deistvii v stikhakh (Saint Petersburg: Imperatorskie teatry, 1820);

Aleksandr Aleksandrovich Shakhovskoi

Liubovnaia pochta: Komicheskaia opera v 1 deistvii (Saint Petersburg: Imperatorskie teatry, 1821);

Ssora, ili Dva soseda: Komediia v 1 deistvii (Saint Petersburg: Imperatorskie teatry, 1821);

Akter na rodine, ili Prervannaia svad'ba: Opera-vodevil' v 1 deistvii (Saint Petersburg: Imperatorskie teatry, 1822);

Urok zhenatym: Komediia v 1 deistvii vol'nymi stikhami (Saint Petersburg: Imperatorskie teatry, 1823);

Sokol kniazia Iaroslava Tverskogo, ili Suzhenyi na belom kone: Russkaia byl' v 4 deistviiakh s pesniami, khorami, voinskimi potekhami, tantsami, igrami, bor'boi i bol'shim spektaklem, muzyka sochineniia g. [K. A.] Kavosa (Saint Petersburg: Imperatorskie teatry, 1823);

Aristofan, ili Predstavlenie komedii "Vsadniki": Istoricheskaia komediia v drevnem rode i v raznomernykh stikhakh grecheskogo stoposlozheniia, v 3 deistviiakh, s prologom, intermediiami, peniem i khorami . . . S pomeshcheniem mnogikh myslei i izrechenii iz Aristifanova teatra (Moscow: N. Stepanov, 1828);

Moskva i Parizh v 1812 i 1814 godakh: Vospominaniia v raznostopnykh stikhakh (Saint Petersburg: A. Smirdin, 1830);

Svat Gavrilych, ili Sgovor na iamu: Kartina russkogo narodnogo byta v 1 deistvii, s pesniami, pliaskami i igrami (Saint Petersburg: K. Krai, 1833);

Dvumuzhnitsa, ili Za chem poidesh, to i naidesh: Romanticheskaia drama v 2 chastiakh, v 5 sutkakh, s prinadlezhashchimi k nei protiazhnymi, pliasovymi, khorovodnymi, podbliudnymi i razboinich'imi pesniami, pliaskami, khorovodnymi igrami (Saint Petersburg: I. Vorob'ev, 1836);

Churova dolina, ili Son naiavu: Volshebnaia opera v 3 deistviiakh, s prevrashcheniiami, khorami i baletami. Muzyka A. N. Verstovskogo (Moscow: I. Smirnov, 1844).

Editions: *Sochineniia,* Deshevaia biblioteka, 207 (Saint Petersburg: A. S. Suvorin, 1898);

Komedii, stikhotvoreniia, edited by Abram A. Gozenpud, Biblioteka poeta, bol'shaia seriia (Leningrad: Sovetskii pisatel', 1961).

OTHER: "Tetushka, ili Ona ne tak glupa: Komediia v 1 deistvii," in *Buket: Karmannaia knizhka dlia liubitelei i liubitel'nits teatra na 1829 god,* edited by Egor V. Alad'in (Saint Petersburg: Meditsinskii departament Ministerstva vnutrennikh, 1829), pp. 141–227;

"Pradedushkina zhenit'ba," *Novosel'e,* volume 2 (Saint Petersburg: A. Pliushar, 1834), pp. 117–127;

"Marusia, Malorosiiskaia Safo," in *Sto russkikh literatorov,* volume 1, edited by Aleksandr F. Smirdin (Saint Petersburg: A. Smirdin, 1839), pp. 769–830;

"Dva uchitelia, ili Asinus asinum fricat," in *Staryi russkii vodevil', 1819–1849,* edited by Mikhail Polushkin (Moscow: Goslitizdat, 1937), pp. 51–94.

SELECTED PERIODICAL PUBLICATIONS – UNCOLLECTED: "Razgovor tsenzora i ego druga," *Dramaticheskii vestnik,* 65 (1808): 89;

"Raskhishchennye shuby: Iroi-komicheskaia poema" and "Pesn' I," *Chtenie v Besede liubitelei russkogo slova,* 3 (1811): 42–64;

"Pesn' II," *Chtenie v Besede liubitelei russkogo slova,* 7 (1812): 69–83;

"Pesn' III," *Chtenie v Besede liubitelei russkogo slova,* 19 (1815): 66–81;

"Merkurii na chasakh, ili Parnasskaia zastava," *Atenei,* 10 (May 1829): 354–386;

"Nechaiannaia svad'ba: Moskovskaia byl': Rasskaz molodogo polkovnika K . . . D . . . ," *Biblioteka dlia chteniia,* 2, section 1 (1834): 32–48;

"Fin: Volshebnaia trilogiia, v 3 chastiakh, s prologom i intermedieiu: Zaimstvovana iz poemy Pushkina 'Ruslan i Liudmila,' " *Panteon russkogo i vsekh evropeiskikh teatrov,* 2, no. 5 (1840): 1–35;

"Fedor Grigor'evich Volkov, ili Den' rozhdeniia russkogo teatra: Anekdoticheskaia komediia-vodevil' v 3 deistviiakh," *Repertuar russkogo teatra,* 6 (1840): 1–29;

"Vstuplenie v moe nazemnoe poprishche (Pis'mo k P. M. B.)," *Maiak sovremennogo prosveshcheniia i obrazovaniia,* 6 (1840): 41–44;

"Kerim-Girei: Romanticheskaia trilogiia v 5 deistviiakh, v stikhakh: Soderzhanie vziato iz 'Bakhchisaraiskogo fontana', poemy A. Pushkina, i mnogie ego stikhi sokhraneny tselikom," *Panteon russkogo i vsekh evropeiskikh teatrov,* 4, nos. 11–12 (1841): 1–50;

"Teatral'nye vospominaniia," *Repertuar i panteon,* 5, section 1 (1842): 16–25;

"Lomonosov i Sumarokov: Glava iz romana 'Zhizn' Aleksandra Pronskogo'," *Moskvitianin,* 1, no. 4 (1846): 60–73;

"Pritchi, ili Ezop u Ksanfa: Komediia s kupletami, v 2 deistviiakh," *Panteon i repertuar russkoi stseny,* 10–11 (1848): 1–50;

"Dvenadtsatyi god: Vospominaniia," *Russkii arkhiv,* 3, no. 11 (1886): 372–401; revised as "Pervye dni v sozhzhennoi Moskve: Sentiabr' i oktiabr' 1812 goda," *Russkaia starina,* 64, no. 10 (1889): 31–65.

During the four decades of his creative life Aleksandr Aleksandrovich Shakhovskoi wrote, translated, and adapted more than 110 plays. Sensitive to the interests and disposition of his audience, he worked in the most varied of genres, from classical tragedy to romantic drama, from high comedy in verse to vaudeville, from the "volshebno-romanticheskoe zrelishche" (romantic-fairy-tale spectacle) to scenes from Russian peasant life. His experiments and quests in the sphere of language and verse prepared the ground for Aleksandr Griboedov's masterpiece, the comedy *Gore ot uma* (Woe from Wit, 1833). Shakhovskoi's oeuvre reflects nearly all of the major developments in the evolution of Russian drama in the first third of the nineteenth century, especially its first twenty years. Fanatically devoted to the theater, Shakhovskoi labored in its service not only as a playwright: as an official of the Directorate of Imperial Theaters, he determined their repertoire for almost two decades. As theatrical director and trainer of actors, he discovered and promoted a whole pleiad of remarkable talents. From the 1800s through the 1810s Shakhovskoi was at the center of the ideological and literary struggle against "zapadnichestvo" (Westernism), a striking example of the Russian cultural nationalist who opposes Western culture and thought, yet who has been profoundly influenced by it; indeed it was the adoption of Western culture that paradoxically provided the foundation for its opposition.

Prince Aleksandr Aleksandrovich Shakhovskoi was born on 24 April 1777 into an impoverished branch of the ancient Shakhovskoi clan, which had been reduced to leading the life of the middling provincial gentry. The future playwright's father, Aleksandr Ivanovich Shakhovskoi, had served for a time as chamberlain (*kamerger*) to the Polish King Stanislav II Augustus and then retired to his estate of Bezzaboty in Smolensk province, where his wife Anastasiia Fedorovna (née Passek) gave birth to Aleksandr.

When the boy was seven he was enrolled in the Moscow *Blagorodnyi pansion* (Noble Boarding School). At ten, according to practice of the day, he was registered as a sergeant in the Royal Guard (*leibgvardiia*) of the Preobrazhensky Regiment, and at sixteen, after graduating school, the young man went to Saint Petersburg to begin his actual service. The noisy, variegated life of high society attracted the young guardsman, but being financially restricted and without social connections (since the support from rich relatives he had hoped for was not forthcoming), he became close with those in his regiment who, lacking funds, turned to the theater and literature for entertainment and as an outlet for their creative energy. This choice was natural for Shakhovskoi, who had been attracted to the theater since childhood. Praise from the writer N. F. Emin for Shakhovskoi's early experiments in verse (epistles and madrigals) also pushed Shakhovskoi in the direction of a literary career.

Shakhovskoi's comedy *Zhenskaya shutka* (A Woman's Jest) successfully premiered on 31 October 1795 at the Hermitage Court Theater and opened doors for the author to the aristocratic salons of Saint Petersburg, where, as he reports in his memoir "Vstuplenie v moe nazemnoe poprishche (Pismo k P. M. B.)" (1840), "promyshliaia obez'ianstvom i popugaistvom" (getting on by aping and parroting), he "popal v stolichnye liubezniki" (became a darling of capital society). His madrigals "krasovalis' v bogatykh al'bomakh" (adorned rich albums), his romances "pelis' milymi golosami za dorogimi fortepianami" (were sung by sweet voices [to the music of] expensive pianos), and, knowing all the fashionable salon games, he was an entertaining conversationalist. He was so good at this that he was invited to all the fashionable households and practically became a professional entertainer. Nature may have predisposed the prince to such a role by endowing him with an appearance so ugly as to be comical, as well as a shrill voice. Society wits were ready to outdo themselves mocking Shakhovskoi's deficiencies, but he took the poisoned quills out of their hands by mocking himself for his "telesnuiu pukhlost' i karmannuiu sukhost' " (corporeal stoutness and arid pockets), first in his satirical "Epître à ma laideur" (Epistle to My Ugliness) and then in a comic opera also written in French.

Nevertheless, Shakhovskoi did not sink to the humiliating role of high-society jester. In 1798 he was attached to a corps of French immigrants to teach them the Russian ways of handling arms, and the French émigré author Xavier de Maistre helped turn his attentions to more serious things. Still captivated by the theater, Shakovskoi took part in amateur performances and became involved in life behind the stage. He made friends with the director of the Imperial Theaters, Aleksandr Naryshkin, who offered Shakhovskoi a position in his service. After retiring from the guards, on 22 April 1802 Shakhovskoi was appointed a member of the repertory department and soon after was sent to Paris to hire actors for Saint Petersburg's French troupe. He successfully completed this task and returned home in 1803 to become deeply immersed in official activities on behalf of the theater.

From 1802 to 1804 Shakhovskoi submitted poems to the journal *Vestnik Evropy* (The Herald of Europe), but they were rejected — according to contemporaries, because of his hostility to the journal's editor, Nikolai Karamzin. Shakhovskoi's comedy *Kovarny* (The Crafty One), adapted from Jean-Baptiste-Louis de Gresset's *Le méchant* (1747), premiered on 16 December 1804 but had no success. The work is nevertheless significant as it takes the side of conservatives (known in modern scholarship by Iury Tynianov's term as the *arkhaisty*, or "archaists") who believed foreign influence to be pernicious and who opposed the changes proposed by Alexander I and his reformist ministers. *Kovarny* reveals the chain of associations being forged in the author's imagination: *chuzhebesie* ("foreignomania," or blind imitation of the latest foreign trends) leads to the assimilation of sentimental thinking and behavior contrary to the national temper and finally to an estrangement from the native soil and the loss of common sense and moral grounding.

In his next comedy, *Novyi Stern* (1807; translated as "The New Sterne," 1945), which opened on 31 May 1805, Shakhovskoi caricatured the sensitive hero of sentimental literature, thereby joining forces with Admiral Aleksandr Shishkov – author of the *Rassuzhdenie o starom i novom sloge* (Discourse on the Old and New Style, 1803), the manifesto of the archaists – and his partisans in their struggle against Karamzin and his followers. The play parodies the clichés of sentimental style (first and foremost, those of Vladimir Izmailov and Petr Shalikov) and mocks the favorite sentimentalist plot of a love affair between a nobleman and a peasant girl, as well as the sensitive traveler who admires the beauty of nature untouched by civilization and the unspoiled moral purity of the simple country girl. The play enjoyed a huge success and generated vigorous debate.

Shakhovskoi considered all new ideas from abroad to be carriers of sedition and a threat to Russia's peace and prosperity, and his hostility to things foreign affected every aspect of his writings and activities, both literary and theatrical. In 1807, commenting on the fierce ideological resistance to attempts to modernize farming, Shakhovskoi wrote an aphorism that expresses the essence of the conservative position: "Da na chuzhoi maner khleb russkii ne roditsia" (Even Russian bread won't grow in the foreign manner). He rejected contemporary Western European drama, including Denis Diderot, Pierre-Augustin Beaumarchais, and Louis Sebastien Mercier, preferring the French classicist drama of Jean Racine, Voltaire, and Molière. He was also an admirer of the classicist style in acting and found his ideal in the French prerevolutionary theater. Shakhovskoi's views found expression in 1808 in the journal *Dramaticheskii vestnik* (Drama Herald), which was founded on his initiative. Its goal was "izyskivat' v drevnikh sochineniiakh vse, kasaiushcheesia khudozhestv, i tem sodeistvovat' otvrashcheniiu durnogo vkusa, kotoryi, gospodstvuia v novykh inostrannykh sochineniiakh, razvrashchaiushchikh i um, i serdtse, ugrozhaet zarazit' i nashu slovesnost'" (to seek out in ancient works everything concerning the arts that will help countermand the bad taste which now reigns in new foreign writings and which corrupts the mind as well as the heart and threatens to poison our literature too). His verse satire "Razgovor tsensora i ego druga"

КОЗАКЪ

СТИХОТВОРЕЦЪ,

Анекдотическая опера водевиль
въ одномъ дѣйствіи,

Сочиненіе Князя А. А. Шаховскаго.

Печатано съ дозволенія Особенной Канцеляріи Министра Полиціи.
25 Маія 1814 года.

САНКТПЕТЕРБУРГЪ,

въ Типографіи Императорскаго Театра
1815 года.

Title page for Shakhovskoi's Kozak-stikhotvorets, *the first original Russian vaudeville*

(Conversation Between the Censor and His Friend, 1808) was published in this journal. In it Shakhovskoi again ridiculed sentimentalism in all its manifestations. Earlier, in 1807, he had begun work on the *iroi-komicheskaia poema* (mock epic) "Raskhishchennye shuby" (The Purloined Fur Coats, 1811–1815), the plot of which was based on a funny incident at the Saint Petersburg German Club, in which a drunken porter had confused the coats and furs of its patrons, causing great confusion at the end of a ball. The work was aimed at Shakhovskoi's literary and theatrical opponents and is saturated with polemical barbs and topical allusions. Work on this poem continued intermittently until 1815, when the third canto was published. The fourth and final canto has not survived.

Meanwhile, the demands of life sometimes forced Shakhovskoi to retreat from the direct application of his theoretical principles. Although he strongly disliked German drama, Shakhovskoi in his position in the repertory department could not impede production of plays by August von Kotzebue (to which he objected but which were public favorites); in fact, he even translated Kotzebue's drama *Die Vermläuder* as *Klevetniki* (Slanderers, 1808) and his *Des Teufels Lustschloß* (1801) as *Chertov uveselitelnyi zamok* (The Devil's Funhouse, 1810). Neither could Shakhovskoi halt French vaudevilles, though he thought them trivial and foolish.

Audiences no longer accepted acting in the pure classicist style, which was perceived as dry and stilted, but even the compromise solution combining it with the sentimentalist manner – introduced to the Saint Petersburg stage by the French actor Aufresne (Jean Rival) and advocated and taught by Shakhovskoi – was already perceived as archaic in light of the general trend toward Romanticism. As a result of Shakhovskoi's conservatism in this area, the tragic actress Ekaterina Semenova, who had studied declamation with Shakhovskoi, deserted him and began to work with Nikolai Gnedich, under whose tutelage her talent blossomed. Shakhovskoi's other disciple, Maria Ivanovna Val'berkhova, could not compete with Semenova in Saint Petersburg and was transferred to Moscow, but even there she had to stop performing tragic roles, returning to the stage later only in dramas and comedies.

During these years Shakhovskoi wrote one play after another. In his best comedy of manners, *Polubarskie zatei, ili Domashnii teatr* (Semi-Gentlemanly Projects, or the Home Theatre, 1808), written in prose, he created the character type of the Russian *bourgeois gentilhomme,* the former tax farmer Tranzhirin ("Spendthrift"), who has bought an estate and, in imitation of the nobility, organizes a domestic serf theater. The play opened on 22 April 1808 and remained in the theater's repertoire until 1837, influencing several playwrights of the next generation. Its main character reappeared in two more comedies: *Chvanstvo Tranzhirina, ili Sledstvie polubarskikh zatei* (Tranzhirin's Arrogance, or The Consequences of Semi-Gentlemanly Projects, 1822) and *Bedovyi maskarad, ili Evropeistvo Tranzhirina* (The Mischievous Masquerade, or the Tranzhirin's Europeanism, 1832).

Shakhovskoi's tragedy *Debora, ili Torzhestvo very* (Debora, or The Triumph of Faith, 1811) opened on 24 January 1810. Modeled on Racine's *Athalie* (1691), the play promoted monarchism and illustrated the idea that people do not understand their own interests and goals and are incapable of great deeds unless ruled by "zhezl edinoi vlasti" (the rod of a single power), which can suppress discontent, defend the authority of religion, and force people to obey. Shakhovskoi's politics earned him many enemies, who spread all sorts of evil rumors about him. Spurred on by his common-law wife, Ekaterina Ivanovna Ezhova, Shakhovskoi also took an active part in backstage intrigues and squabbles. The most dismal such episode occurred when the directorate of the Imperial Theaters canceled Vladislav Ozerov's tragedy *Poliksena* after only two performances (14 and 23 May 1809) and refused to issue the author the promised payment. This episode occurred not long before the opening of *Debora, ili Torzhestvo very,* which was clearly directed against Ozerov. Shakhovskoi, a former friend and devotee of the young playwright, played an unseemly role in the intrigue, although there is evidence to suggest that his was not the main part, which may have belonged to Gavriil Derzhavin and Aleksandr Shishkov, both bitter critics of Ozerov.

Shakhovskoi's career was closely connected with these latter writers, key figures in the movement opposed to Karamzin's literary reforms. With the goal of rallying like-minded literary men, he attended the literary meetings they initiated in 1807, was elected a member of the Rossiiskaia akademiia (Russian Academy) on Derzhavin's nomination in 1810, and took part in founding the society Beseda luibitelei russkogo slova (Society of Lovers of the Russian Word) in 1811. At its meetings Shakhovskoi read his mock-epic "Raskhishchennye shuby," making significant changes in the text and saturating it with new topical allusions.

At the beginning of the War of 1812, Shakhovskoi took on the command of a regiment of the Tver militia. His was the first regiment into the Kremlin on the heels of the retreating Napoleon; soon after, he formed a reserve division in Riga and redeployed it to Warsaw. On 1 July 1813 he was back in Saint Petersburg, where he again immersed himself in his favorite activity.

Shakhovskoi turned to writing vaudeville plays, loading them with patriotic content and contemporary allusions in accord with the prevailing mood. Even before the war he had written an opera-vaudeville, *Kozak-stikhotvorets* (The Poet Cossack, 1815), which had had one performance at the court theater on 15 May 1812. This first original Russian vaudeville was staged again on 28 May 1814 and met with resounding success; it remained in the repertoire until 1852. *Kozak-stikhotvorets* was followed by other works in the same spirit: *Krest'iane, ili Vstrecha nezvanykh* (The Peasants, or The Meeting of the Uninvited, 1815) opened on 23 November 1814, with scenes of partisan battles and monologues hailing loyalty to the czar and fatherland; *Lomonosov, ili Rekrut-stikhotvorets* (Lomonosov, or the Poet-Recruit, 1816) opened on 31 December 1814;

and *Ivan Susanin,* an historical opera based on the story of a peasant who lured a detatchment of Polish interventionists deep into the forest, opened on 19 October 1815.

In 1815 Shakhovskoi returned to his favorite theme of *chuzhebesie,* choosing as his arena the genre of high comedy, which had long been in decline and into which he breathed new life. On 23 September his most biting comedy, *Urok koketkam, ili Lipetskie vody* (A Lesson to Coquettes, or the Lipetsk Spa), had its premiere. In it Shakhovskoi presents his vision of the postwar life of noble society. Adherents of fundamental Russian values emerge as intelligent and positive people, whose deeply rooted beliefs form the basis for their healthy morality, patriotic turn of thought, and rejection of alien fashions. Shakhovskoi opposes these characters to those who adopt foreign "vol'nodumnyi vzdor" (freethinking nonsense) — amoral, scheming people (at best, frivolous dolts) who had proved themselves cowards during the war against Napoleon. Contemporaries detected malicious caricatures of real people in some of the minor characters, including the poet Vasilii Zhukovsky, depicted as the sentimental rhymer Fialkin ("Violet"), who writes fashionable ballads. This character generated a furious and extended polemic, which came to be known as the "Lipetskii potop" (Lipetsk flood) and which largely determined the one-sided reception of the play so that its literary merits passed unnoticed. At court, where Zhukovsky was much respected, the comedy was performed with the role of Fialkin cut. While Shakhovskoi was being crowned with a laurel garland at the home of Pavel Golenishchev-Kutuzov — the greatest of Karamzin's enemies — the archaists' opponents rallied into the new literary society Arzamas and showered the "briukhastyi stikhodei" (paunchy rhymster) and Beseda with satires, epigrams, and invectives. Shakhovskoi was dubbed "Shutovskoi" (jester, or buffoon) and was attacked as an envious slanderer; the episode with *Poliksena* was recalled, and Shakhovskoi was blamed for Ozerov's subsequent mental illness and death.

With time the debate lost its sting. In 1816 Beseda ceased to exist, and in 1818 Arzamas disintegrated. Gradually, Shakhovskoi established links with Arzamas through his association with Pavel Katenin and Aleksandr Griboedov. These young authors were drawn to the author of *Novyi Stern* and *Urok koketkam* by their critical attitude to the Karamzin-Zhukovsky school, their interest in Russian history and folklore, and their quest to enrich the literary language by introducing elements both from the language of the people and from high-style

Slavonic (for heroic themes). However, unlike Shakhovskoi, their position was not based on a categorical rejection of everything new or foreign but on the freedom-loving, patriotic spirit of the new generation that came just before the Decembrist rebellion. When the future Decembrist Nikolai Turgenev, who joined Arzamas in 1817, decided to publish a political journal, he invited Shakhovskoi to participate. In the beginning of December 1818 Katenin brought Pushkin to meet Shakhovskoi; Pushkin regretted his attacks on the prince and sought his acquaintance. Shakhovskoi welcomed the young poet, who became a frequent guest at his house and read his first major work, "Ruslan and Liudmila" (1820) there.

Shakhovskoi's *cherdak* (loft), as his apartment was called, became a gathering place for theatrical and bohemian circles of the capital. Even the pupils from the theatrical school made appearances. New plays were read and discussed, literary and theatrical debates held, and opinions about productions and actors voiced. But Shakhovskoi's apartment was also a place of intrigue, malicious gossip, and rumor, actively aided by the mistress of the house, Shakhovskoi's companion, Ekaterina Ivanovna Ezhova. Shakhovskoi was involved in spreading the slander that Pushkin had been flogged, a piece of gossip that understandably chilled his relations with the poet. The salon itself was also the subject of much gossip.

In July 1818 Shakhovskoi retired, the official reason being differences of opinion about financial matters between Shakhovskoi and the current Director of Imperial Theaters Prince Petr Tiufiakin. The more likely reason was that Tiufiakin considered himself insulted by a line from Shakhovskoi's comedy *Svoia sem'ia* (Within the Family, 1818), which everyone read as a parody on him. In 1821, with the appointment of Apollon Maikov as director, Shakhovskoi was invited back to the theater, but, with the administrative changes in the theater board after the Decembrist uprising of 1825 and the ascension of Nicolas I, Shakhovskoi was definitively dismissed on 23 January 1826.

During these years, whether in active service or in retirement, Shakhovskoi never stopped teaching acting. He achieved particular success teaching comedy, in which he demanded from actors mastery of a style that was somewhat conventionalized but nevertheless true to life. This approach was a response to the main theatrical trend of the age and the transition from the character mask to the depiction of a real human personality. In 1821 Shakhovskoi organized a "Molodaia truppa" (Young Troupe) from imminent graduates of the theatrical school and other beginning actors. It played small comedies and vaudevilles and produced several remarkable actors.

This was the background upon which Shakhovskoi's dramaturgy developed in the period after *Urok koketkam,* one marked by various new explorations. He wrote a few more plays in the genre of comedy of manners in verse. In two of them – *Pustodomy* (The Prodigal Landowners, 1820), written in 1817 and premiered on 19 October 1819, and *Kakadu, ili Sledstvie uroka koketkam* (The Cockatoo, or The Consequences of the Lesson to Coquettes, 1820), which opened on 16 January 1820 – Shakhovskoi continued his struggle against foreign influence, although in the second work the outrageously negative characters of *Urok Koketkam* seem to have been toned down. In working toward creating lifelike characters for the stage, Shakhovskoi often wrote with specific actors – especially Ezhova – in mind. Shakhovskoi made abundant use of colloquial language, prosaisms, dialectisms, and vulgar speech (he was criticized because his countesses speak like servants). He used inexact rhyme and was the first to write a comedy in free iambic verse, *Ne liubo – ne slushai, a lgat' ne meshai* (Do Not Listen If You Want, but Do Not Stop Me from Lying, 1818). After 1823 and the appearance of Griboedov's masterpiece *Gore ot uma,* however, he abandoned this genre.

Shakhovskoi continued writing vaudevilles and comic and fairy-tale operas, and in 1817 he participated with other authors in the translation of Pierre Corneille's *Horace* (1640), initiated by Pavel Katenin. At the same time, he explored new paths by turning to romantic dramatic genres. On 21 January 1821 his five-act romantic comedy with "turnirom, srazheniem, balladami i tantsami" (a tournament, a battle, ballads and dances) titled *Ivanoi, ili Vozvrashchenie Richarda L'vinoe Serdtse* (Ivanhoe, or the Return of Richard the Lionhearted) premiered. It was followed by reworkings of other Sir Walter Scott novels for the stage, as well as of works by William Shakespeare, Ossian, and Pushkin and plays on topics from Russian history. He conducted an intensive search for new subjects and forms and for synthetic genres, such as the "volshebno-romanticheskoe zrelishche" (fairy-tale romantic spectacle) and the "romanticheskaia komediia balet" (romantic comic ballet). He even made use of elements of classical tragedy, attempting to revive the tradition of Aeschylus for the Russian stage. Nevertheless, though Shakhovskoi made broad use of the elements of "velikolepnyi spektakl' " (grand

УРОКЪ КОКЕТКАМЪ

и л и

ЛИПЕЦКІЯ ВОДЫ,

КОМЕДІЯ ВЪ ПЯТИ ДѢЙСТВІЯХЪ,

въ стихахъ.

Сочиненіе Князя А. А. Шаховскаго.

Представлена въ первый разъ въ Санктпетербургѣ, на Маломъ Театрѣ, 1815 года Сентября 23 дня.

САНКТПЕТЕРБУРГЪ,

въ Типографіи Императорскаго Театра 1815 года.

Title page for Shakhovskoi's satire on the negative influences of foreign ideas on fashionable Russian nobility

spectacle) – dances, processions, frequent changes of scenery, and various special effects – he mastered only the external manner of theatrical Romanticism.

After retiring Shakhovskoi worked intensively for several more years in the theater, composing two and three plays per year. In 1832, in which he wrote six plays, he began to turn to prose. He published several stories and planned a cycle called "Russkii Dekameron" (The Russian Decameron) – two plots from which he used in the plays *Dvumuzhnitsa* (The Bigamous Wife, 1836) and *Suzhenyi ne riazhenyi* (The Unprepared Groom, 1834) – and a novel in the style of Scott. Shakhovskoi also wrote articles on the history of the theater and on poetry, fragments of memoirs, and in his last years translated Jacques-Bénigne Bossuet's *Discours sur l'histoire universelle* (1681).

Shakhovskoi became reconciled with his former opponents and even maintained contacts with them; however, after one evening at the Zhukovsky home on 7 January 1830, he recalled feeling that behind their cordial manners lurked the old resentments. During the unfolding polemic between the members of the Pushkin circle and Faddei Bulgarin and Nikolai Polevoi, who had declared war on the "literaturnaia aristokratiia" (literary aristocracy), Shakhovskoi, who hated journalism and the mercenary spirit in literature, took Pushkin's part. All the while, he continued to oppose the latest Western influences (the "raving" of French Romanticism under the influence of George Gordon, Lord Byron's "fiery storm"). Shakhovskoi also befriended the Slavophiles, who were grouped around the historian and author Mikhail Pogodin.

Shakhovskoi lived alternatively in Moscow and Saint Petersburg and during his last years spent more time on his estate in the province of Kharkov. Toward the end of his life, ill and weak, he still found strength enough to help organize the Kharkov theater. Shakhovskoi died on 22 January 1846 and was buried in Moscow. He was still a bachelor. He had proposed twice to his longtime companion Ekaterina Ezhova, but she had refused, reportedly claiming that she preferred "byt' liubimoi Ezhovoi, a ne smeshnoi kiaginei" (to be the beloved Ezhova rather than a laughable princess); she died in 1836.

Despite his many contributions to the Russian stage over the course of several decades and the leading role he played in Russian theatrical life, Shakhovskoi's extreme politics and the various scandals and gossip that surrounded much of his career obscured his achievements for later generations. Indeed the greater part of Shakhovskoi's works for the theater has still not been published, and the majority of his short writings that appeared in various early-nineteenth-century journals and almanacs – including fragments of plays, couplets, poems, and essays – have never been collected and republished. Manuscripts of his plays are preserved in the Saint Petersburg Theatrical Library and in the library of the Maly Theater in Moscow, and, like many aspects of Shakhovskoi's legacy, they have not yet received serious study.

Bibliographies:

"Dramaticheskie proizvedenia i perevody A. A. Shakhovskogo," in Shakhovskoi's *Komedii, stikhotvorenia,* edited by Abram A. Gozenpud, Biblioteka poeta, bol'shaia seriia (Leningrad: Sovetskii pisatel', 1961), pp. 817–825;

T. M. El'nitskaia, "Repertuar dramaticheskikh trupp Peterburga i Moskvy, 1801–1825," in *Istoria russkogo dramaticheskogo teatra,* edited by Efim G. Kholodov and others (Moscow: Iskusstvo, 1977), volume 2, pp. 449–542; volume 3, pp. 218–338.

References:

Evgenii Garshin, "Odin iz zabytykh pisatelei," *Istoricheskii vestnik,* 13, no. 7 (1883): 136–173;

Aleksei A. Iartsev, "Kniaz' Aleksandr Aleksandrovich Shakhovskoi (Opyt biographii)," *Ezhegodnik Imperatorskikh teatrov, Sezon 1894–1895gg.,* supplement, no. 2 (1896): 102–144; supplement, no. 3 (1896): 1–46;

Simon Karlinsky, *Russian Drama From its Beginnings to the Age of Pushkin* (Berkeley: University of California, 1985), pp. 228–249;

Bertha Malnick, "A. A. Shakhovskoy," *Slavonic and East European Review,* 32 (December 1953): 29–51;

Rafail M. Zotov, "Kniaz' A. A. Shakhovskoi," *Repertuar i panteon,* 14, no. 4 (1846): 4–40.

Sergii Aleksandrovich Shirinsky-Shikhmatov

(1783 – 7 June 1837)

Mark G. Altshuller
University of Pittsburgh

BOOKS: *Pozharskoi, Minin, Germogen, ili spasennaia Rossiia* (Saint Petersburg, 1807);

Pesn' rossiiskomu slovu: Sochinil i chital v Imperatorskoi Rossiiskoi Akademii chlen onyia kniaz' Sergii Shikhmatov po sluchaiu priniatiia ego v chleny onoi Akademii (Saint Petersburg, 1809);

Petr Velikii. Liricheskoe pesnopenie v os'mi pesniakh (Saint Petersburg, 1810);

Vozvrashchenie v otechestvo liubeznogo moego brata kniazia Pavla Aleksandrovicha iz piatiletnego morskogo pokhoda, v techenie kotorogo plaval on na mnogikh moriakh, nachinaia s Baltiki do Arkhipelaga, videl mnogie Evropeiskie zemli i nakonets iz Tulona sukhim putem cherez Parizh vozvratilsia v Rossiiu 1810 goda maiia 30 dnia (Saint Petersburg, 1810);

Pesn' Rossu porazivshemu Galla i vsekh ego soiuznikov vo mnogikh krovoprolitnykh bitvakh, a naipache 26 avgusta 1812-ogo goda pri sele Borodine pod predvoditel'stvom generala-fel'dmarshala kniazia Mikhaila Larionovicha Golenishcheva-Kutuzova (Saint Petersburg, 1812);

Noch' na grobakh: Podrazhanie Iungu (Saint Petersburg, 1812);

Noch' na razmyshleniia (Saint Petersburg, 1814);

Iisus v Vetkhom i Novom Zavetakh, ili nochi u kresta (Saint Petersburg, 1824).

TRANSLATION: Alexander Pope, *Opyt o kritike* (Saint Petersburg, 1806).

Sergii Aleksandrovich Shirinsky-Shikhmatov is remembered in Russian literary history primarily because the most renowned writers of the early nineteenth century (including Aleksandr Pushkin and Konstantin Batiushkov) wrote malicious and witty epigrams about him. However, there was a brief period when he was at the center of literary life, when he had not only enemies and deriders but also devoted admirers, some of whom saw in him the hope of Russian poetry. Those times are long past, but his subsequent oblivion is far from justi-

fied. This talented author undoubtedly deserves a place in the history of Russian poetry.

Prince Sergii Aleksandrovich Shirinsky-Shikhmatov (later Hieromonk, or monastic priest, Anikita) was born in 1783 in the village of Dernovo in the Viazemsky district of Smolensk province. The day and month of his birth are unknown. His father was a retired lieutenant of modest means, though a well-educated man. At home the future poet studied Russian letters, as well as the German and French languages. The family was religious and strict in the fulfillment of church rituals, and Sergii, just as his brothers, observed the rules and rituals of the Orthodox religion throughout his life.

In 1795 Shikhmatov entered the Morskoi Kadetskii Korpus (Naval Corps of Cadets), which he completed in 1800 with the title of *michman* (midshipman). He left the corps with an inclination toward literary activity and a good knowledge of modern and ancient languages, including English, which was rare among Russians at the time. Most probably this knowledge influenced his first appointment. After graduation from the corps Shikhmatov was assigned to the Morskoi uchenyi komitet (Naval Committee of Learning) at the Admiralty. The chairman of this committee was Aleksandr Shishkov, the famous publicist, philologist, and one of the forerunners of Russian Slavophilism. Shikhmatov completely assimilated Shishkov's ideas and remained his most devoted and consistent disciple.

In May 1804 Shikhmatov was assigned as a teacher with the rank of sublieutenant to his alma mater, the Naval Corps of Cadets. This position was probably to his liking, since he served in this capacity until his retirement in 1827. He was made a full lieutenant in 1808 and in 1813 received the rank of lieutenant captain. Based on the testimony of his students, Shikhmatov was a good teacher, learned and kind. He was one of a few who did not resort to physical punishment. When a prestigious lyceum opened in 1811 in Tsarkoe selo, on the initiative of Alexander I, Shikhmatov was offered the position of *inspektor*. He declined the flattering offer, not wanting to part with his pupils.

In 1806 Shikhmatov published a translation of Alexander Pope's *An Essay on Criticism* (1711), which made his name famous in literary circles. At about this time the poet Gavriil Derzhavin and other writers who adhered to conservative political and literary views began to gather at Shishkov's home in Saint Petersburg. They did not approve of the liberal initiatives of Emperor Alexander I, were dissatisfied with the rapprochement with the French after the Peace at Tilsit (1807), and advocated an "archaic" style and national traditions in literature. By the beginning of 1807 these gatherings had become regular.

Naturally, Shishkov brought his favorite disciple Shikhmatov to these meetings. A contemporary memoirist, S. Zhikharev, has left a description of Shikhmatov: "Moriak Shikhmatov neobyknovenno blagoobraznyi molodoi chelovek, rostom mal i vovse ne krasavets, no imeet takuiu krotkuiu i svetluiu fizionomiiu, chto, kazhetsia, ni odno nechistoe pomyshlenie nikogda ne zabiralos' k nemu v golovu" ("The sailor Shikhmatov is an unusually good looking young man, small in stature and not at all handsome, but he possesses such a meek and radiant physiognomy, that it seems that not a single impure thought ever entered his head").

The year 1807 marked the start of the most fruitful period of Shikhmatov's creative activity. He wrote the long poem *Pozharskoi, Minin, Germogen, ili spasennaia Rossiia* (Pozharsky, Minin, Germogen, or Russia Saved). In complete harmony with the views of the Shishkov circle, the poem took as its subject a heroic moment of national history. Shikhmatov turned to the Time of Troubles, when Prince Pozharsky and the Novgorod merchant Kuz'ma Minin became leaders of the struggle against the Poles who had captured Moscow. Patriarch Germogen, a supporter of Minin and Pozharsky, was captured by the Poles and starved to death in prison.

However, Shikhmatov was scarcely interested in narrating historical events. His work is subtitled "Liricheskaia poema v trekh pesniakh" (A Lyrical Poem in Three Cantos), and its poetics are precisely lyrical rather than epic. The work is basically an impassioned authorial monologue, relating the poet's feelings in connection with great and tragic events. The many speeches by its characters (Germogen, Minin, Pozharsky) are indistinguishable from those of the author in their passionate excitation. A narrative poem was thus turned into what was in essence

ПОЖАРСКОЙ, МИНИНЪ, ГЕРМОГЕНЪ,

или

СПАСЕННАЯ РОССІЯ,

Лирическая Поэма въ трехъ пѣсняхъ.

*сочинилъ
Князь Сергій Шихматовъ.*

Въ Санктпетербургѣ,
печатано въ Императорской Типографіи,
1807 года.

Title page for Sergii Aleksandrovich Shirinsky-Shikhmatov's 1807 narrative poem, in which he first experimented with fusing epic and lyric principles

a long solemn ode, whose lyrical nature was emphasized by the many rhetorical questions and exclamations characteristic of odes. In this way the most important principle of classicism, requiring the strict separation of genres, was destroyed.

The poem's "gromkii stil' " (loud style) and maximal internal tension are achieved by the frequent use of verbs, which become the predominant part of speech in the poem. While lacking in events, the poem is rich in action, although Shikhmatov never uses verbs in his rhymes. In Russian, verbs in the present tense have different endings for each person (whereas in English only the third person gains an "s"), and verbs in the past tense have endings which mark gender (masculine, feminine, and neuter); this situation presents the Russian poet numerous opportunities to rhyme with verbs. Shikhmatov, however, rejected this easy path and always used verbs in the middle of the line, which serves to increase the internal tension of his verse. Shishkov was delighted with the poem and at one of his literary gatherings, on 9 February 1807, recited the work. Shishkov was particularly enraptured by the poem's style, which was in complete harmony with his ideas. It is rich in archaic forms and Slavonicisms, and hence from Shishkov's point of view, "[slog] vazhen i krasnorechiv, mnogie izobrazheniia i opisaniia velikolepny, iazyk bogat i silen" (dignified and eloquent, [with] many magnificent images and descriptions, its language rich and powerful).

However, that which was worthwhile for the archaist Shishkov and his circle was a shortcoming for their opponents, the pro-Western supporters of the new style. Several years later Pushkin wrote a clever epigram on Shikhmatov's poem. Repeating the title of the poem in the first two lines, he pithily characterized its style from the point of view of Shishkov's opponents, giving it an evaluation directly opposite from that of the archaists:

Пожарсий, Мнин, Гермоген,
Или Спасенная Россия.
Слог дурен, темен, насыщен--
П тяжки словеса пустые.

(Pozharsky, Minin, Gergomen,
Or Russia Saved.
A nasty style, obscure, pompous--
And serious words all hollow.)

In spite of his opponents' derision, Shikhmatov's poem was recognized as a serious event in Russian cultural life. Shikhmatov presented a copy to Alexander I (preserved in the Public Library in Saint Petersburg, with Shikhmatov's dedicatory inscription) and was rewarded with a diamond signet ring.

On 13 March 1809 Shikhmatov was elected a member of the Russian Academy, and at his induction on 3 April he recited his composition *Pesn' rossiiskomu slovu* (Song to the Russian Word), in which he praises Russian writers of the eighteenth century, including Antiokh Kantemir, Mikhail Lomonosov, Aleksandr Sumarokov, and Mikhail Kheraskov. At the end of the poem he also recalls his guide and patron Shishkov. His programmatic "Priglashenie druzei na vecherniuiu besedu" (An Invitation to My Friends to an Evening Conversation, 1810) bears the date 9 December 1809; its central portion consists of conversations between the author and his confederates on literary themes. Their love for Russia's native culture and language is emphasized. They are not among those who:

. . . любит без ума чужую красоту,
Презрев несметные отцов своих богатства.

Прогоним от себя языки чуждых царств,
Но с русской простотой своим родным словом
Беседовать начнем о старом и новом.
Друг другу подтвердим, что истый русский дух
Как огнь у нас в груди, не токмо не потух,
Но пламенем горит.

(. . . madly love foreign beauty,
Despising the countless riches of their fathers.

Let us rid ourselves of the languages of alien kingdoms,
But with Russian simplicity and in our native tongue
Begin to converse about what is old and new.
We will affirm to each other, that the true Russian spirit
Like a fire in our breast, has not only not faded,
But blazes brightly.)

For Shikhmatov, as for Shishkov, the old is always preferable to the new: "Vernee v sii dni derzhat'sia stariny" (In these days it is better to adhere to the old ways), he asserts.

Shikhmatov wrote a long poem (dated 30 May 1810), which is interesting from an artistic point of view and bore the deliberately archaicized and cumbersome title *Vozvrashchenie v otechestvo liubeznogo moego brata kniazia Pavla Aleksandrovicha iz piatiletnego morskogo pokhoda, v techenie kotorogo plaval on na mnogikh moriakh, nachinaia s Baltiki do Arkhipelaga, videl mnogie Evropeiskie zemli i nakonets iz Tulona sukhim putem cherez Parizh vozvratilsia v Rossiiu* (The Return to the Fatherland of My Dear Brother Pavel Aleksandrovich from a Five-Year Naval Sojourn, in the Course of Which He Sailed on Many Seas, from the Baltic to the Archipelago, Saw Many European Lands and Finally from Toulon Returned Over Land by Way of Paris to Russia). In aphoristic verses he formulates a patriotism so extreme that it could not help but provoke mockery among readers not infected by xenophobia:

. . . более себя
Свое отечество любя . . .
На все природы южной неги
Не променяем наши снеги
И наш отечественный лед.

(. . . loving our fatherland
More than ourselves . . .
We will not exchange our snows
And our native ice
For all the comforts of southern climes.)

In *Vozvrashchenie v otechestvo* Shikhmatov continues breaking down the generic hierarchy of

Russian classicism. He extends high odic principles to a poem with an intimate lyric character, in the first place in his title, which imitates the long, lavish titles of classic odes. Shikhmatov follows the Lomonosovian odic system both in meter (iambic tetrameter) and stanza (there are twenty-two twelve-line strophes). He saturates his verse with archaic lexicon to an even greater degree than Lomonosov. Criticism of the time noted Shikhmatov's practice but was far from approving.

In the same year Shikhmatov composed his second huge poem, *Petr Velikii. Liricheskoe pesnopenie v os'mi pesniakh* (Peter the Great. A Lyrical Hymn in Eight Cantos, 1810). The desire for merging and mixing genres to create a unified literary system founded on the high style and engendering a constant lyrical tension is apparent even in the poem's self-appointed genre, "A Lyrical Hymn." Shikhmatov devised this new literary genre as an attempt to fuse the epic and lyric principles (hymns and lyrical poetry).

Shikhmatov's new poem was more strictly grounded in epic traditions than *Pozharskoi, Minin, Germogen* had been. The narration develops over time. The author includes most of Peter's biography in the poem, from the creation of the Russian navy to his death, but in the full sense, Shikhmatov accomplishes neither an epic poem nor Peter's poetic biography. The work is broken up into a series of separate episodes or cantos, each of which may be considered independently: the battle at Poltava, the naval engagement with the Swedes, and so on. In each of them the lyrical voice of the author prevails over the description of events. Everything that he had been able to do successfully in the comparatively brief first poem was missing in his huge second epic work, which disintegrated into a series of self-sufficient odes. The seventh canto, for example, seems to be almost entirely unconnected with the poem's subject. In it the author beseeches Raphael to describe the magnificence and prosperity of Russia that has resulted from Peter's activities. Addressing painters, including Raphael, was a common device in Lomonosov's and Derzhavin's odes, and that is clearly why Shikhmatov made use of it, yet in this context it seems unnecessary and strained, and poorly integrated into the work's whole composition.

Petr Velikii describes the victories of Russian arms. Written when a new war with the Napoleonic coalition was about to begin, it ended with a bellicose address to Russia's potential opponents:

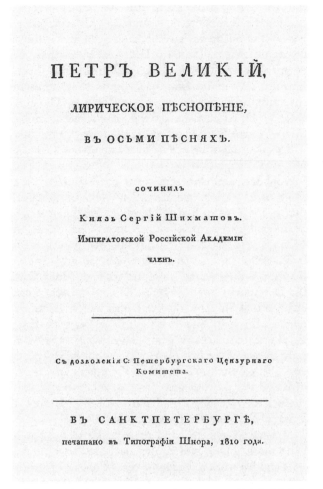

Title page for Shikhmatov's second epic poem, which he labeled a "liricheskoe pesnopenie" (lyrical hymn)

Бойтесь дерзкие соседы,
Его [Петра] воинственная тень
Сильна еще стяжать победы,
Создать другой Полтавский день,
И в персть низвергнуть ваши воиска.

(Beware impudent neighbors,
His [Peter's] martial shadow
Is yet strong enough to win victories,
To make another day like Poltava,
And to turn your battalions into dust.)

Thus the poem expressed the opinion of Shishkov's patriotic party, for which Russia's previous military defeats had been a national disgrace and the alliance with Napoleon a betrayal of the national interest. In such a setting, *Petr Velikii*, possessing unquestionable artistic merit, seemed destined to become a major ideological document for the conservative patriots, but this situation never occurred. Shikhmatov's supporters, confused by the cumbrousness of the poem, reviewed it cautiously and without assurance. Even Shishkov later remarked that the poem, although "izobiluet mnogimi krasotami" (overflowing with many beauties), also has an unusual structure, being neither an epic nor an ode. The poet was also reproached for paying insufficient attention to pre-Petrine Russia and underestimating its culture. The evaluation of Peter's role became one of the basic points of contention between the Westernizers and Slavophiles, and these criticisms of Shikhmatov are some of its earliest manifestations. It is paradoxical that in the eyes of Slavophile critics Shikhmatov appeared to be an inconsistent defender of their ideas. In 1825, fifteen years after the poem was published, a long article was written about Shikhmatov by one of the most influential critics of the younger generation, the Decembrist poet Vil'gel'm K. Kiukhel'beker. He claimed that Shikhmatov was a poet with uncommon talent who had "pravo na odno iz pervykh mest mezdu nashimi lirikami i poetami-zhivopistsami" (the right to one of the first places among our lyrical poets and poet-painters). He admired the potent lyrical nature of *Petr Velikii* but was forced to acknowledge that the ordinary reader would not be able to endure a hymn of four thousand lines.

Such were the friendly reviews. Shishkov's opponents mocked him, glad for the chance to drag both the poet and his work through the dirt. The lack of strong structure and the intermingling of lyric and epic principles in the poem were immediately targeted. In an epistle to Vasilii Zhukovsky, the poet Vasilii Pushkin, a fierce polemicist and follower of Nikolai Karamzin (and Aleksandr Pushkin's uncle), wrote:

Поэма громкая, в которой плана нет,
Не песнопение, но сущий только бред.

(A loud poem, in which there is no plan,
No lyric hymn this, but only utter raving.)

Dozens of witty epigrams were addressed at Shikhmatov. The best of them by the poet K. N. Batiushkov is entitled "Sovet epicheskomu stikhotvortsu" (Advice to the Epic Poet):

Какое хочешь имя дай
Твоей поэме полудикой
Петр длинный, Петр большой, но только Петр Великий--
Её не называй.

(Give whatever name you want
To your half-savage poem:

Peter the Long, Peter the Large, only do not call it--
Peter the Great.)

Even after seventeen years the 1810 printing had not sold out. In need of money after his retirement, on 10 December 1827 Shikhmatov petitioned the Russian Academy to buy one hundred copies of *Petr Velikii* from him for 250 rubles. The poem's publication had turned out to be a major literary setback for Shikhmatov. The sensitive poet keenly endured the failure of his beloved creation, and the constant mockery intensified his hypochondria.

In 1811 the official opening of the literary society Beseda liubitelei rossiiskogo slova (Colloquium of Lovers of the Russian Word) took place. This was the most influential literary association in Saint Petersburg of the day. At its meetings, held once a month in Derzhavin's home, up to two hundred people gathered, practically the whole Saint Petersburg intelligentsia of that time. The main initiator of the founding of Beseda was Shishkov, who naturally invited Shikhmatov to participate, and he became a member of the first division, over which Shishkov presided. Shikhmatov regularly attended meetings and actively participated in the journal the society published, *Chteniia v Besede liubitelei rossiiskogo slova* (Readings in the Colloquium of Lovers of the Russian Word). In 1812 he was awarded by the czar a pension of fifteen hundred rubles a year for his literary endeavors. On 12 May 1817, at Shishkov's suggestion, the poet received the Russian Academy's large gold medal for the "otlichnuiu pol'zu rossiiskomu slovu prinesshemu" (outstanding benefit [he] brought to the Russian word).

Such outward successes did little to console Shikhmatov, however, and allusions to the attacks of his literary opponents and to the unpleasantness of literary life may be seen in his verse of the 1810s. His brother and biographer, Platon, remarked that the poet's honorable celebrity was not without a touch of bitterness. Shikhmatov searched for comfort in religion, and after 1810 religious motifs noticeably increase in his works. In 1812 his poem *Noch' na grobakh: Podrazhanie Iungu* (A Night in the Graveyard: An Imitation of Young) was published. It is an imitation of one of the gloomiest books of European preromanticism: Edward Young's *Night Thoughts on Life, Death, and Immortality* (1742–1746). The basic motifs of Shikhmatov's poem are night, death, the immortality of the soul, and the Last Judgment. The earth is envisioned as full of corpses and the skulls of the deceased, and the whole of creation is enveloped by death: "Grobami nashimi

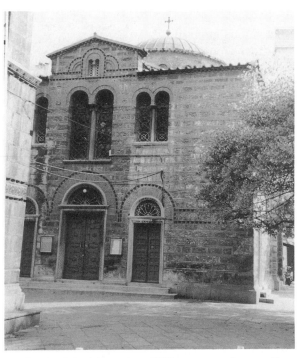

The church in Athens where Shikhmatov served as an abbot
in 1836–1837

vselennaia polna" (The universe is full of our graves).

These sinister motifs were already well-known to the Russian reader both through translations of Young and the lyric poetry of such poets as Derzhavin and Semen Bobrov. In spite of often masterful verses, Shikhmatov's poem represented a stage in Russian poetry that had already passed. Members of the Beseda liubitelei rossiiskogo slova praised the poem, but other critics did not pay any attention to it. The same lot befell another of Shikhmatov's Youngian poems, *Noch' na razmyshleniia* (A Night of Meditation, 1814), with its characteristically pre-Romantic deliberations over the fateful march of time, whose symbol was a clock striking the hours.

In the following years Shikhmatov published little. In 1824 the last book published in his lifetime was issued, *Iisus v Vetkhom i Novom Zavetakh, ili nochi u kresta* (Jesus in the Old and New Testaments, or Nights by the Cross). Written in blank verse, the work presents a romantic recounting of episodes from the Bible. On 31 May 1824 Shikhmatov read its conclusion at a meeting of the Russian Academy. It met with approval, and the academy resolved to print twelve hundred copies, a large run for the time, and to put them at Shikhmatov's disposal. However, for Russian literature of the day, preoccu-

pied with political problems and on the eve of the Decembrist uprising, this interesting book was felt to be an obvious anachronism.

Shikhmatov was never interested in civic or political activity. At an official inquiry on 12 May 1826, when asked whether he was a member of any secret society, Shikhmatov answered: "Ni k kakomu tainomu obshchestvu ni vnutri gosudarstva, ni za granitsami onogo ne prinadlezhal, ne prinadlezhu i prinadlezat' ne budu" (I have not belonged, do not belong, and will not belong to any sort of secret society whether within the state or beyond its borders). He lived a humble and solitary life, ate little, drank nothing but water, slept five or six hours a night, and gave a large part of his seven-thousand-ruble salary to charity.

On 9 November 1827 Shikhmatov retired, allegedly because of illness (the usual form for such petitions). He gave his serfs their freedom, as *vol'nye klebopashtsy* (free ploughmen), and granted them land. Early in 1828 Shikhmatov settled in the Iur'ev monastery on the outskirts of Novgorod. The abbot there was Archimandrite Fotii, known for his extreme fanaticism. Shikhmatov found himself under his strong influence. Shikhmatov was hot-tempered but aware of this shortcoming and fought with it. Once when Fotii slapped Shikhmatov in the face for being slow to respond to a summons, the novice humbly accepted the punishment and meekly withdrew, as Fotii demanded.

On 25 March 1830 Shikhmatov took monastic vows under the name Anikita, in order to mark the angel's day simultaneous with that of Fotii (12 August, day of the saint's holy martyrs Fotii and Anikita). In the monastery he led a severe life, denying himself necessary things. In 1834 he left on a long-contemplated journey to Jerusalem, although Fotii did not want to let him go. From Constantinople he traveled to Mount Athos, and on 10 September 1835 he arrived in Jerusalem. He spent seven months in the Holy Land, although travel in Palestine in those years was difficult and dangerous. Shikhmatov described his travels, or more accurately, his inner state and his religious meditations, in diaries written in a heavy, archaic style. They were published in the journal *Khristianskoe chtenie* (Christian Reading) in 1891.

In April 1836 Shikhmatov arrived in Athens, where he was appointed by the Russian Synod as abbot of the church attached to the Russian embassy. In Athens his health suffered greatly, though he continued to perform his church duties assiduously. In April 1837 he took to bed. On 7 June, repeating the words "Pora, pora v Ierusalim" (It is time, it is time to go to Jerusalem), Father Anikita passed away. He is buried in the Archangel Monastery near Athens.

Letters:

"K istorii russkoi bogoslovskoi mysli tridtsatykh godov tekushchego stoletiia: iz perepiski brat'ev kniazei Shirinskikh-Shikhmatovykh," edited by Vasilii Zhmakin, in *Khristianskoe chtenie* (Leningrad: Dukhovnaiu akademia, 1889–1890).

Biography:

Platon A. Shirinsky-Shikhmatov, *O zhizni i trudakh ieromonakha Anikity, v mire kniazia Sergiia Aleksandrovicha Shirinskogo-Shikhmatova* (Saint Petersburg: Akademii Rossiiskoi, 1838).

References:

Mark Altshuller, *Predtechi slavianofil'stva v russkoi literature: Obshchestvo "Beseda liubitelei russkogo slova"* (Ann Arbor: Ardis, 1984);

Vil'gel'm K. Kiukhel'beker, "Razbor poemy kniazia Shikhmatova *Petr Velikii*," in *Puteshestvie. Dnevnik. Stat'i*, edited by V. D. Rak (Altshuller) and N. V. Koroleva, Literaturnye pamiatniki (Leningrad: Nauka, 1979), pp. 468–492;

Stepan P. Zhikharev, *Zapiski sovremennika*, edited by Boris M. Eikhenbaum, Literaturnye pamiatniki (Moscow & Leningrad: Akademiia nauk, 1955).

Aleksandr Semenovich Shishkov
(16 March 1753 – 9 April 1841)

Mark G. Altshuller
University of Pittsburgh

BOOKS: *Nevol'nichestvo dramma v odnom deistvii* ([Saint Petersburg: Morskoi kadetskii korpus, 1780]);

Stikhi na vziat'e Ochakova ([Saint Petersburg: Morskoi kadetskii korpus, 1788]);

Treiazychnyi morskoi slovar' na angliiskom, frantsuzskom i rossiiskom iazykakh, 3 volumes ([Saint Petersburg]: Morskoi kadetskii korpus, 1795);

Zhurnal kompanii 1797 goda, vo vremia vysochaishago prisutstsviia i komandovaniia flotom gosudaria imp. i samoderzhtsa vserossiiskago Pavla Petrovicha, vedennyi na fregate Emmanuile (Saint Petersburg: Imperatorskaia tipografiia, 1797);

Spisok korabliam i prochim sudam vsego rossiiskago flota ot nachala zavedeniia onago do nyneshnikh vremen, s istoricheskimi, voobshche o deistviiakh flotov i o kazhdom sudne, primechaniiami, volume 1 ([Saint Petersburg]: Morskoi shliakhetnyi kadetskii korpus, 1799);

Sobranie morskikh zhurnalov ili ezhednevnykh zapisok, soderzhashchikh v sebe plavaniia flotov, eskadr i sudov rossiiskikh, nachinaia s 1797 goda, 2 volumes ([Saint Petersburg]: Morskoi shliakhetnyi kadetskii korpus, 1800 [–1801]);

Rassuzhdenie o starom i novom sloge rossiiskogo iazyka (Saint Petersburg, 1803);

Pribavlenie k rassuzhdeniiu o starom i novom sloge rossiiskogo iazyka (Saint Petersburg, 1804);

Rassuzhdenie o krasnorechii Sviashchenogo Pisaniia i o tom, v chem sostoit bogatstvo, obilie, krasota i sila Rossiiskogo iazyka i kakimi sredstvami onyi eshche bol'she rasprostranit', obogatit' i usovershenstvovat' mozhno (Saint Petersburg, 1811);

Razgovory o slovesnosti mezhdu Az i Buki (Saint Petersburg, 1811);

Sobranie vysochaishikh manifestov, gramot, ukazov, reskriptov, prikazov voiskam i raznye izveshcheniia, posledovavshie v techenie 1812, 1813, 1814, 1815 i 1816 godov (Saint Petersburg, 1816);

Sobranie sochinenii i perevodov, 17 volumes (Saint Petersburg: Rossiiskaia Akademiia, 1818–1839);

Zapiski, mneniia i perepiska Admirala Shishkova, 2 volumes, edited by N. Kiselev and Iu. Samarin (Berlin & Prague, 1870);

Pesnia nekotorago morekhodtsa iz" iasniaiushchago liubov' svoiu temi slovami i mysliami, kakimi po privychke k moreplavaniiu voobrazhenie ego napolneno ([Saint Petersburg: Morskoi shliakhetnyi kadetskii korpus], n.d.).

TRANSLATIONS: Joachim Heinrich Campe, *Detskaia biblioteka,* 2 volumes (Saint Petersburg: Akademiia nauk, 1783–1785);

Charles Romme, *Morskoe iskusstvo, ili Glavnyia nachala i pravila nauchaiushchiia iskustvu stroeniia, vooruzheniia i vozhdeniia korablei . . . ,* 2 volumes ([Saint Petersburg]: Morskoi shliakhetnyi kadetskii korpus, 1793–1795).

Aleksandr Semenovich Shishkov, known in Russian literary history as Admiral Shishkov, was a man of various talents: a brilliant, temperamental polemicist; a poet, translator, and linguist; and an outstanding government official. He may also be considered an early Slavophile. All of his literary activity was aimed at the defense of native Russian culture and its preservation from foreign influences. In politics he was a fierce opponent of Enlightenment philosophy and the French Revolution, and during the first third of the nineteenth century he successfully opposed attempts at reform in Russia. Shishkov remained faithful to his conservative and monarchist convictions throughout his life.

Aleksandr Semenovich Shishkov was born on 16 March 1753. Little is known about his childhood. His father was a prosperous Russian nobleman, but there were no great riches evident in Shishkov's home, and later he lived only on his salary. Shishkov probably gained from his parents his deep Orthodox religiosity (which did not, however, keep him from marrying outside of his faith), his love of old church books written in Slavonic, and his outstanding knowledge of this language.

Aleksandr Semenovich Shishkov

Shishkov had three brothers: Nikolai, Ardalion, and Dmitrii. He was married twice. The first time was to Dar'ia Alekseevna Shelting, a Dutch Lutheran. After her death in 1825, Shishkov, by then an elderly man, married Iulia Osipovna Narbut, a Polish Catholic. Shishkov did not have any children, although several of his nephews and nieces were brought up in his home. One of Shishkov's favorites was Aleksandr Ardalionovich Shishkov, later a poet who belonged to Aleksandr Pushkin's circle.

Shishkov received his education in the Morskoi kadetskii korpus (Naval Cadet Corps), where he was one of the best students. In fall 1771, already a senior cadet, he made a dangerous journey on a military ship from Archangel through the White Sea and around Europe to Saint Petersburg. Near the island of Bornholm the ship was seriously damaged and almost wrecked. The young naval cadet turned out to be the only person aboard who knew German and was capable of communicating with the local inhabitants. He took an active part in organizing rescue efforts and care for the wounded, although he nearly died of a se-

rious cold. In 1771 Shishkov finished the naval corps near the top of his class and received the title of midshipman.

After this, Shishkov sailed on military ships in the White, Baltic, and North seas. In 1776 he was appointed to the frigate *Severnyi Orel* (Northern Eagle), which sailed from Kronstadt (the naval fortress at Saint Petersburg) to the Black Sea through the Mediterranean Sea and the Dardanelles. This journey lasted three years. Shishkov visited Athens, Constantinople, and the shore of Anatolia in Turkey where Troy once stood. Italy, where he spent several months, made a special impression on him. Good at languages, Shishkov learned Italian and maintained a love for Italian literature throughout his life. Later he translated Torquato Tasso's *Gerusalemme Liberata* (1581) as "Osvobozhdennyi Ierusalem" (published in his *Sobranie sochinennii i perevodov,* volumes eight and nine, 1826–1827).

Soon after his return in 1779 Shishkov received the rank of lieutenant and became professor of tactics at the Naval Cadet Corps. The beginning of

Shishkov's literary activity dates to this time. In 1780 he wrote a drama in one act, *Nevol'nichestvo* (Slavery), which praised Catherine II, who had sacrificed a considerable sum to ransom Christian slaves in Algiers. The play was staged in the court theater with success, more for its plot than any other merits.

Shishkov soon published the first book in Russian intended for young readers, *Detskaia biblioteka* (The Children's Library, 1783–1785), a translation and adaption of Joachim Heinrich Campe's *Kleine Kinderbibliothek* (circa 1782). Shishkov's book was reissued several times and, according to the testimony of contemporaries, was for many decades standard children's reading.

In 1784 the journal *Sobesednik liubitelei rossiiskogo slova* (Interlocutor of Lovers of the Russian Word) published Shishkov's programmatic though humorous poem "Pesnia staroe i novoe vremia" (The Song of Old and New Times), which was republished three more times. "Pesnia staroe i novoe vremia" outlines a binary opposition between old and new, past and present. For Shishkov the past was always better than the present. He imagined a utopia of Russia's ideal, harmonious past, which he contrasted with its present, turned rotten under the influence of the West. Shishkov's career may be seen as an attempt to reconstruct this utopian, nonexistent past.

Shishkov's literary and pedagogical pursuits were interrupted in 1790 by the war with Sweden. As a captain of the second rank he commanded the frigate *Nikolai* and for his services received a gold saber with an inscription honoring his bravery and a gold snuffbox covered with diamonds.

After the war Shishkov returned to his scholarly and literary activities. He translated Charles Romme's *L'Art de la marine* (1787) as *Morskoe iskusstvo* (1793–1795). In 1795 Shishkov published another serious work that testified to his linguistic interests: *Treiazychnyi morskoi slovar' na angliiskom, frantsuzskom i rossiiskom iazykakh* (A Trilingual Dictionary in English, French and Russian).

Shishkov was elected a member of the Russian Academy in 1796. At the same time, while continuing to live in Saint Petersburg, he became the head chancellor under Count Platon Zubov, the commander of the Black Sea fleet and one of Catherine II's favorites. He maintained good relations with the heir to the throne, Pavel Petrovich (the future Paul I), who was at odds with his mother, and thus Catherine II's sudden death on 5 November 1796 had no effect on Shishkov's career. Shortly afterward he was promoted to captain of the first rank (colonel) and received an estate with 250 serfs in the Kashin district. Before long

he was appointed *eskadr-major* (major of a squadron) and was assigned to the emperor, whom he accompanied on his sea travels. For ten days he sailed with Paul on the frigate *Emmanuil* and was rewarded with the title adjutant general. Service with the hypochondriac and suspicious emperor, with his difficult and volatile temperament, was oppressive. Shishkov especially disliked and feared horseback riding, which his service for the emperor occasionally necessitated. He attempted as much as possible to avoid visits to the palace.

Having gone to Austria on official business, Shishkov requested permission to stay for treatment at the famous German spa at Karlsbad. Paul allowed him this leave but ordered him to observe the behavior of several Russians there who had been close to Catherine. It was an onerous and unpleasant assignment for Shishkov, and he tried to ignore it.

Shishkov returned to Russia and continued to serve under Paul I. Once he brought on himself the emperor's ire by falling asleep while on duty at the palace; Paul removed him from service at court and transferred him to the admiralty. Nevertheless, he was shortly thereafter awarded a decoration and promoted to vice admiral.

On the night of 11 March 1801 Paul was murdered in a palace coup, and Alexander I became the new emperor. Shishkov did not react with much sadness, as it had been difficult to serve under the capricious emperor. Every day people fell into disgrace, were exiled, or were arrested. Like many of his peers, Shishkov joyfully welcomed the new emperor's promise to rule according to the law and the spirit of Catherine the Great. Shishkov wrote "Stikhi . . . pri vosshestvii na prestol Imperatora Aleksandra Pervogo" (Verses . . . on the Ascension to the Throne of Emperor Alexander I), in which he described the exultation of the people and how he saw in the new czar, "velikuiu dushu Ekateriny" (Catherine's great soul).

The new czar, however, dreamed of large-scale reforms in education and land ownership and even contemplated the abolition of serfdom. These reforms were meant to lead Russia closer to the West, to make it a true European power. Such ideas were profoundly alien and repugnant to Shishkov. Like the majority of old grandees of Catherine's court, he did not get along with Alexander. He even wrote some satiric verses that were circulated in manuscript, in which he made fun of the young courtiers of the emperor's most intimate circle and of the emperor himself, whom he called Miroprav ("He Who Rules the World").

Alexander similarly felt encumbered by the conservative admiral, who protested against any innovation. Gradually, Shishkov quit the court and concentrated on literature and scholarship. In 1805 he became the head of the admiralty's department of science, which well suited his tastes.

In 1803 Shishkov's *Rassuzhdenie o starom i novom sloge rossiiskogo iazyka* (A Discourse on the Old and New Style in the Russian Language) was published; it was followed by *Pribavlenie k rassuzhdeniiu o starom i novom sloge rossiiskogo iazyka* (Supplement to the Discourse on the Old and New Style in the Russian Language) in 1804. In this book Shishkov spoke out as a defender of Russian antiquity and traditional Russian culture. He fought against what he saw as the perversion the Russian language was undergoing at the hands of writers with a Western orientation, primarily Nikolai Karamzin and his followers. Shishkov considered Slavonic and Russian to be not separate but two stages of the same language, with the first being "the root and basis" of the latter. He argued that for the successful development of Russian culture and the Russian state it was necessary to return to tradition, to that time when the Russian nobility did not stand apart from the people but shared with them a common set of morals, customs, and way of life. Modern writers and political figures led by the czar, he felt, were deepening this chasm. Shishkov's book immediately marked him as the head of the Conservative Party (what the scholar Iury Tynianov later called the *arkhaisty,* "archaists"), at least in matters concerning culture.

In 1807, on Shishkov's initiative, regular, informal literary gatherings began, in which supporters of Shishkov and adherents of the Russophile ideology participated. Here Gavriil Derzhavin, Ivan Krylov, and Shishkov read their poems; younger members included Sergii Shikhmatov and Nikolai Gnedich. In 1810 the idea of turning these gatherings into an official literary society arose. The emperor did not hurry to grant permission for the regular meetings of dignitaries from the opposition, and he delayed the final approval on the opening of the society. When permission was finally given, he did all he could to avoid attending any of the meetings. The society was finally formed under the name "Beseda liubitelei russkogo slova" (Colloquy of Lovers of the Russian Word), and its official opening took place on 14 March 1811 at a large public gathering. Shishkov began the session with a programmatic "Rech' pri otkrytii Besedy" (Speech on the Opening of the Colloquium), dedicated to Russian literature and its importance to the development of a patriotic consciousness. Shishkov identified three sources that made up this literature: church books, folklore, and the new belles lettres formed under the influence of the West. The last, in

Shishkov's opinion, was decidedly harmful, as it destroyed the Russian national identity.

Shishkov developed these ideas in two books, beginning with *Rassuzhdenie o krasnorechii Sviashchenogo Pisaniia i o tom, v chem sostoit bogatstvo, obilie, krasota i sila Rossiiskogo iazyka i kakimi sredstvami onyi eshche bol'she rasprostranit', obogatit' i usovershenstvovat' mozhno* (Discourse on the Eloquence of Holy Scripture, and on What Constitutes the Wealth, Abundance, Beauty and Strength of the Russian Language and by What Means It Is Possible to Further Propagate, Enrich and Perfect It, 1811). In this short book, which contends that there is a complete genetic link between Slavonic and Russian, Shishkov demands that in serious, important works the Russian literary language conform to the language of the Bible and so essentially distinguish itself from conversational usage. On the other hand Shishkov writes that in fictional, romantic books that depict the inner world of men, writers should orient themselves to the language of the simple people as preserved in folklore. In 1811 the second book appeared. It was the first work on the poetics of Russian folklore, *Razgovory o slovesnosti mezhdu Az i Buki* (Conversations on Literature Between A and B). The book claims that the poetry of the simple folk preserved the idyllic pre-Petrine world of Old Rus', devoid of social contradictions and united in its culture.

The year 1812 was approaching. War with France was drawing nearer. Conservative patriotic portions of society were increasingly dissatisfied with the humiliating Peace of Tilsit, the rapprochement with Napoleon, and the liberal views of the czar. On 15 December 1811 at a meeting of Beseda, Shishkov read his "Rassuzhdenie o liubvi k otechestvu" (Discourse on Love for the Fatherland), in which he developed his favorite ideas on the harm of foreign upbringing and the connection of language with the spirit of the people. He compared Russian heroes with such patriots of ancient Rome as Regulus and Epaminondas. On every page Shishkov cited examples of the exploits of Russian arms. His enmity was primarily directed against the French, with whom Russia was formally at peace. Shishkov was wary of reading the work publicly in light of the political situation and did so only after securing the approval of his colleagues.

However, the czar's politics had also begun to change. Alexander was forced to make concessions to public opinion, and Shishkov's fears were not confirmed. On 17 March 1812 State Secretary Mikhail Speransky, the czar's closest adviser and an initiator of reforms, was suddenly sent into exile.

The next day Alexander summoned Shishkov and told him that he had read the "Rassuzhdenie o liubvi k otechestvu" and was impressed by Shishkov's patriotism. He asked the writer to compose a manifesto aimed at recruiting soldiers for a probable war with France.

Thus Shishkov finally received the audience about which he had long dreamed – the Russian people. Shishkov had always thought that the simple people knew, understood, and loved the old church books better than did the post-Petrine Russian nobility. He wrote his manifestos in an inspired, high oratorical Slavonicized language, with an abundance of lexical, syntactic, and stylistic archaisms, supposing that such a language would not only be accessible to the simple people but would also inspire patriotic enthusiasm. Shishkov turned out to be right. At public readings of this work his audiences reportedly reacted with strong emotion: individuals pulled their hair, wrung their hands, wept, even gnashed their teeth.

Alexander did not have any special liking for Shishkov and would have preferred to see in the conservative admiral's place the profound and highly educated Karamzin, with whom he was linked by cordial personal relations. However, his first manifesto had shown that Shishkov knew how to talk to the people. His patriotic feelings and hatred for the French and the French Revolution were known to all. Alexander was able to appreciate the persuasive and inspired language of Shishkov's manifestos and to suppress his personal enmity. On 9 April 1812 a directive was signed commanding Shishkov to attend to the person of the emperor as state secretary, with a salary of twelve thousand rubles per year. Shishkov's conservative patriotic faction had triumphed. He accompanied the emperor on all his movements during the war and in December 1812 was awarded one of Russia's highest orders, the Order of Aleksandr Nevsky, "za primernuiu liubov' k otechestvu" (for exemplary love for the fatherland).

The manifestos, written in the name of the czar and the government, gave Shishkov the opportunity to set forth his political program. He condemns the French for their unbelief and depravity and calls the French nation (following Voltaire) "sliiane tigra s obez'ianoi" (the combination of a tiger and a monkey), whose capital, Paris, was a "gnezdo miatezha, razvrata i paguby narodnoi" (nest of mutiny, dissipation, and national ruin). He accuses the nobility and the czar of blind affection for the French language and culture: "My liubovalis' i prizhimali k grudi nashei zmeiu,

kotoraia, terzaia sobstvennuiu utrobu svoiu, prolivala k nam iad svoi i nakonets za nashu k nei priznatel'nost' i liubov' vsezlobnym zhalom svoim uiazvliaet" (We loved and held to our breast a serpent, which, tearing its own womb to pieces [an allusion to the revolution], poured out its poison on us and, finally, in return for our gratitude and love, is now wounding us with its evil sting). Shishkov contrasts the depraved French to the Russians with their chastity, meekness, and good behavior.

The concept of historical development and the irreversibility of change was entirely alien to Shishkov. He thought that, having defeated Napoleon, it was necessary to restore all kingdoms to their former condition and thus to establish truth and good behavior. As regards Russia, Shishkov believed that her people as a mass were untouched by the depraved European ideas. Therefore, the blessing of Russia consisted in preserving her in her former condition. Nothing needed to be changed; nothing new should be introduced. The basic governmental institutions, including autocracy and serfdom, should remain inviolable.

In this spirit Shishkov wrote a manifesto summing up the victorious war and outlining his plans for the further development of the country. After some arguments and wavering the czar signed this manifesto. Governmental reform and the abolition of serfdom were put off for many years (the serfs were finally freed in 1861). From Shishkov's point of view, one of the foundations on which Russian national self-consciousness rested was the long-existing tie between the landowners and the serfs, "established for their mutual benefit" and "distinctive to Russian morals and virtues." An unselfish man, Shishkov did not receive a kopeck from his serfs, nor did he force them to work for him. He conceived of the relationship between landowners and serfs idyllically. Characteristically, he thought in utopian terms, sweeping aside social and economic problems.

Shishkov was relieved of his responsibilities as state secretary in 1814 and appointed a member of the state council. He devoted his new free time wholly to literary pursuits. His creation, the "Beseda liubitelei rossiiskogo slova," had continued its activities during the war, and after the war's end its gatherings attracted the same large crowds as before, among which high governmental officials and generals dominated. The czar, however, as before, avoided the meetings. Shishkov, busy with other matters, had cooled toward the group's activities. Derzhavin, in whose home the meetings were held, died in 1816, after which meetings of the Beseda ceased.

In 1813 the president of the Russian Academy died, and Shishkov petitioned the emperor to entrust the academy to him, "po userdiiu i liubvi k russkomu iazyku i slovesnosti" (because of his diligence and love for the Russian language and philology). He was appointed its president on 29 May 1813. The Russian Academy, founded in 1783, concerned itself with language and literature, which could not have suited Shishkov better. He plunged into the work of the academy with enthusiasm. On Shishkov's suggestion, the yearly budget of the academy was increased from nine thousand rubles to sixty thousand rubles. He put together a new charter, in which a wide field of activities was envisioned (compiling dictionaries, the codification of Russian versification, the creation of a scientific grammar of the Russian language, translations, and publishing).

Shishkov's serious interest in Slavic linguistics dates from this time. While in Prague, Shishkov became acquainted with the outstanding Slavist Abott Josef Dobrovsky. Shishkov had several Czech and Polish Slavists (Dobrovsky, Vaclav Hanka, Samuel Bogumil Linde) elected as honorary members of the academy. He kept up an active correspondence with well-known scholars and Slavists: Pavel Safarik and Vuk Karadjic. He agitated for the creation of Slavic faculties in Russian universities and did much to awaken interest in Slavic philology in Russia. Not possessing any specialized training, Shishkov began to study comparative linguistics. He tried to demonstrate the relationship between European and Slavic languages by means of amateurish etymological "proofs."

On 15 May 1824 Shishkov was appointed minister of education. In this post he tried by any means possible to prevent the penetration into Russia of liberal Western ideas and to regulate and limit the freedom of teaching, fearing that teachers trained to approach all subjects openly and critically would teach their pupils to do the same. Any change was bad as far as Shishkov was concerned. Therefore, he was against the spread of literacy and strove to restrict education, believing that it led to the dissemination of liberal and revolutionary ideas. Teaching rhetoric to a peasant, for example, would only make him "khudym i bespoleznym ili eshche i vrednym grazhdaninom" (bad and useless, or worse, a harmful citizen).

The most important result of Shishkov's work as minister of education was a new statute on censorship, approved in 1826 after the death of Alexander I, which introduced severe limitations on practically all historical, philosophical, and scientific writ-

ings and restricted the right of Russian writers to their own independent ideas. Under this statute, practically all the works of Rousseau, Voltaire, Montesquieu, Helvétius, and other foreign writers were forbidden. The censor and journalist Sergei Glinka commented that under such a statute one could even read the "Our Father" as the work of Jacobins. Contemporaries nicknamed this statute "chugunnym" (cast iron). Fortunately, it lasted only until 1828, when Nicholas I ordered it abolished and replaced by a more liberal policy.

In 1826 Nicholas appointed Shishkov a member of the High Court judging the Decembrists, noblemen who had tried to stage a coup after Alexander's death in December 1825. Naturally, he was a confirmed enemy of anyone who would take arms against the monarch and state system of Russia. However, he not only demanded the strictest observance of the law in the investigation and determination of punishment but also attempted to soften the fate of the accused. Some Decembrist writings mention Shishkov's courageous behavior and protests in court, and although these stories do not necessarily relate facts, they testify to Shishkov's reputation. Nevertheless, even Shishkov's most ardent opponents never doubted his high moral character. "Dobryi Shishkov" (Kind Shishkov), Karamzin called him. Even his opponent, the sharp polemicist Vasilii Pushkin, admitted during the height of literary polemics that Shishkov was "dushoiu dobr, no avtor on durnoi" (a good soul, although he is a bad writer).

In 1828, having abolished the 1826 statute on censorship, Nicholas I sent Shishkov into retirement due to old age and poor health. Although he lived for many years afterward and remained the president of the Russian Academy and a member of the state council until his death, Shishkov no longer actively participated in public affairs. In the 1830s he began to go blind, and toward the end of his life he lost his sight entirely. In 1840 the writer Sergei Aksakov, who had become friends with Shishkov at the beginning of the century, saw his older friend for the last time. He described Shishkov as "uzhe trup chelovecheskii, nedvizhimyi i bezglasnyi. Tol'ko blizko naklonias' k nemu mozhno bylo zametit', chto slaboe dykhanie eshche ne prekratilos' " (already a human corpse, immovable and mute. Only by bending over close to him was it possible to tell that his weak breathing had not ceased). Shishkov died on 9 April 1841.

References:

S. T. Aksakov, "Vospominanie ob Aleksandre Semenoviche Shishkove," in his *Sobranie sochinenii,* volume 2 (Moscow: Khudozhest-vennaia literatura, 1955), pp. 266–313;

Mark Altshuller, "A. S. Shishkov o frantsuzskoi revoliutsii," *Russkaia literatura,* 1 (1991): 144–149;

Altshuller, *Predtechi slavianofil'stva v russkoi literature: Obshchestvo "Beseda liubitelei russkogo slova"* (Ann Arbor, Mich.: Ardis, 1984);

Altshuller, "Rassuzhdenie o starom i novom sloge rossisskogo iazyka kak politicheskii dokument (A. S. Shishkov i N. M. Karamzin)," in *Russian and the West in the Eighteenth Century,* edited by A. G. Cross (Newtonville, Mass.: Oriental Research Partners, 1983), pp. 214–222;

Michele Colucci, "Il pensiero linguistico e critico di A. S. Shishkov," in *Studi sulla questione della lingua presso gli slavi* (Rome, 1972), pp. 225–274;

P. Garde, "A propos du premier mouvement slavophile," *Cahiers du Monde Russe et Soviétique,* 5 (1964): 261–269;

M. I. Gillel'son, "Literaturnaia politika tsarizma posle 14 dekabria 1825 g.," *Pushkin: Issledovaniia i materialy,* 8 (1978): 195–218;

V. V. Kolominov and M. Sh. Fainshtein, *Khram muz slovesnykh: Iz istorii Rossiiskoi Akademii* (Leningrad: Nauka, 1986), pp. 41–64;

N. I. Mordovchenko, "Polemika o starom i novom sloge," in his *Russkaia kritika pervoi chetverti XIX veka* (Moscow & Leningrad: Akademiia nauk, 1959), pp. 77–98;

Sergei Nekrasov, *Rossiiskaia Akademiia* (Moscow: Sovremennik, 1984), pp. 88–106;

V. A. Stoiunin, "A. S. Shishkov. Biografiia," in his *Istoricheskie sochineniia,* volume 1 (Saint Petersburg, 1880), pp. 1–271.

Papers:

Aleksandr Semenovich Shishkov's papers are located in the Central State Historical Archive in Saint Petersburg (Tsentral'nyi gosudarstvennyi istoricheskii arkhiv v Peterburge), f. 1673, Shishkov.

Aleksandr Petrovich Sumarokov
(14 November 1717 – 1 October 1777)

Marcus C. Levitt
University of Southern California

SELECTED BOOKS: *Eia imp. velichestvu vsemilosti-veishei gosudaryne imp. Anne Ioannovne . . . pozdra-vitel'nyia ody v pervyi den' novago goda 1740 ot Kadetskago korpusa sochinennyia chrez Aleksandra Sumarokova* (Saint Petersburg: Akademiia nauk, 1740);

Tri ody parafrasticheskie psalma 143, sochinennye chrez trekh stikhotvortsev, iz kotorykh kazhdyi odnu slozhil osoblivo, by Sumarokov, Vasilii Trediakovsky, and Mikhail Lomonosov (Saint Petersburg: Akademiia nauk, 1744);

Khorev tragediia (Saint Petersburg: Akademiia nauk, 1747; revised, 1768);

Dve epistoly. V pervoi predlagaetsia o ruskom iazyke, a vo vtoroi o stikhotvorstve (Saint Petersburg: Akademiia nauk, 1748); revised as *Nastavlenie khotiashchim byti pisateliami* (Saint Petersburg: Akademiia nauk, 1774);

Gamlet tragediia (Saint Petersburg: Akademiia nauk, 1748);

Artistona tragediia (Saint Petersburg: Akademiia nauk, 1751);

Sinav i Truvor tragediia (Saint Petersburg: Akademiia nauk, 1751; revised, 1768);

Tsefal i Prokris opera (Saint Petersburg: Akademiia nauk, 1755);

Al'tsesta opera (Saint Petersburg: Akademiia nauk, 1759);

Novye lavry. Prolog dlia predstavleniia na Imperatorskom teatre, pri torzhestvovanii tezoimenitstva e.i.v. po pre-slavnoi pobede oderzhannoi rossiiskim voiskom nad korolem prusskim 1759 goda avgusta v 1 den' pri Frankfurte (Saint Petersburg: Akademiia nauk, 1759);

Pribezhishche dobrodeteli. Balet (Saint Petersburg: Akademiia nauk, 1759);

Opisanie ognennogo predstavlenie v pervyi vecher novogo goda 1760 ([Saint Petersburg: Akademiia nauk, 1760]);

Rech' idilliia i epistola e. i. v. gosudariu velikomu kniaziu Pavlu Petrovichu v den' rozhdeniia ego 1761 goda

Aleksandr Petrovich Sumarokov

sentiabria 20 chisla (Saint Petersburg: Akademiia nauk, 1761);

Oda e. i. v. . . . Ekaterine Alekseevne . . . na den' vozshestviia eia na vserossiiskii prestol iiunia 28 dnia 1762 goda (Saint Petersburg: Akademiia nauk, 1762);

Prichti, 3 volumes (Saint Petersburg: [Akademiia nauk], 1762–1769);

Difiramb e. i. e. gosudaryne Ekaterine Alekseevne . . . na den' tezoimenitstva eia noiabria 24 dnia 1763 godu (Saint Petersburg: Akademiia nauk, 1763);

Oda e. i. v. . . . Ekaterine Alekseevne . . . na den' koronovaniia eia sentiabria 22 dnia 1763 goda (Saint Petersburg: Akademiia nauk, [1763]);

Novaia i zabavnaia lotereinaia igra sostoiashchaia iz 60 emblem s 60 devizami, razdelennaia na chetyre klassa (Moscow: [Moskovskii universitet, 1764]);

Opekun komediia (Saint Petersburg: Akademiia nauk, 1765);

Slovo pri osveshchenii Sanktpeterburgskoi imp. Akademii khudozhestv vo prisutstvii e.i.v. Ekateriny Vtoryia pred sonmom pochtennykh liudei rechennoe gospodinom Sumarokovym onyia Akademii pochetnym chlenom v leto 1765 iiunia 28 dnia ([Saint Petersburg]: Akademiia nauk, 1765);

Difiramb Pegasu (Saint Petersburg: Akademiia nauk, 1766);

Ot avtora tragedii Sinava i Truvora Tat'iane Mikhailovne aktrise Rossiiskago imperatorskago teiatra na predstavlenie Il'meny noiabria 16 dnia 1766 goda. ([Saint Petersburg: Akademiia nauk, 1766]);

Elegiia ([Saint Petersburg: Akademiia nauk, 1768]);

Slovo e. i. v. gosudaryne Ekaterine Alekseevne . . . na 1769 god ianvaria 1 dnia (Saint Petersburg: Akademiia nauk, 1768);

Iadovityi komediia (Saint Petersburg: Akademiia nauk, 1768);

Iaropolk i Dimiza tragediia (Saint Petersburg: Akademiia nauk, 1768);

Likhoimets komediia (Saint Petersburg: Akademiia nauk, 1768);

Pervyi i glavnyi streletskii bunt, byvshii v Moskve v 1682 godu v mesiatse maii ([Saint Petersburg]: Akademiia nauk, 1768);

Semira tragediia ([Saint Petersburg]: Akademiia nauk, 1768);

Tri brata sovmestniki komediia (Saint Petersburg: Akademiia nauk, 1768);

Vysheslav tragediia (Saint Petersburg: Akademiia nauk, 1768);

Nartsiss komediia (Saint Petersburg: Akademiia nauk, 1769);

Oda e. i. v. . . . Ekaterine Alekseevne . . . na vziatie Khotina i na pokorenie Moldavii (Saint Petersburg: Akademiia nauk, 1769);

Pridannoe obmanomn komediia (Saint Petersburg: Akademiia nauk, 1769);

Pustynnik drama (Saint Petersburg: Akademiia nauk, 1769);

Raznyia stikhotvoreniia (Saint Petersburg: Akademiia nauk, 1769);

Dimitrii Samozvanets tragediia ([Saint Petersburg]: Akademiia nauk, [1771]);

Madrigaly ([Saint Petersburg: Akademiia nauk, 1773]);

Dvadtsat' dve rifmy. Pesnia, podrazhennaia Goratsiiu: kn. 3, oda 9 ([Saint Petersburg: Akademiia nauk, 1774]);

Elegiia na smert' Marii Ivanovny Elaginoi . . . (Saint Petersburg: Akademiia nauk, 1774);

Gospodinu Paseku vot nash byvshii razgovor ([Saint Petersburg: Akademiia nauk, 1774]);

Na strel'tsov ([Saint Petersburg: Akademiia nauk, 1774]);

Nastavlenie mladentsam. Moral', istoriia i geografiia (Saint Petersburg: [Akademiia nauk], 1774);

Nekotorye strofy dvukh avtorov ([Saint Petersburg: Akademiia nauk, 1774]);

O kazni ([Saint Petersburg: Akademiia nauk, 1774]);

Oda e. i. v. . . . Ekaterine Alekseevne na zakliuchenie mira s Portoiu Otomanskoiu (Saint Petersburg: Akademiia nauk, [1774]);

Oda Grigoriiu Aleksandrovichu Potemkinu. 1774 ([Saint Petersburg: Akademiia nauk, 1774]);

Oda na Pugacheva (Saint Petersburg: Akademiia nauk, 1774); revised as *Stikhi na Pugacheva* ([Saint Petersburg: Akademiia nauk, 1774]);

Pis'mo k devitsam g. Nelidovoi i g. Barshchovoi ([Saint Petersburg: Akademiia nauk, 1774]);

Pis'mo ko priiateliu v Moskvu ([Saint Petersburg: Akademiia nauk, 1774]);

Prichta na nesmyslennykh pistsov ([Saint Petersburg: Akademiia nauk, 1774]);

Stans gradu Simbirsku na Pugacheva (Saint Petersburg: Akademiia nauk, 1774);

Uvedomlenie – Epigramma – Uvedomlenie – Diuku Bragantsy ([Saint Petersburg: Akademiia nauk, 1774]);

Eklogi (Saint Petersburg: Akademiia nauk, 1774);

Elegii liubovnyia (Saint Petersburg: Akademiia nauk, 1774);

Kratkaia moskovskaia letopis' (Saint Petersburg: Akademiia nauk, 1774),

Liubovnaia gadatel'naia knizhka ([Saint Petersburg: Akademiia nauk, 1774]);

Mstislav (Saint Petersburg: Akademiia nauk, 1774);

Ody torzhestvennye (Saint Petersburg: Akademiia nauk, 1774);

Satiry, volume 1 ([Saint Petersburg: Akademiia nauk, 1774]);

Sokrashchennaia povest' o Sten'ke Razine (Saint Petersburg: Akademiia nauk, 1774);

Stikhotvoreniia dukhovnyia (Saint Petersburg: Akademiia nauk, 1774);

Oda e. i. v. . . . Ekaterine Alekseevne . . . na torzhestvo mira s Portoiu Otomanskoiu 1775 goda iiulia dnia

(Moscow: Gosudarstvennaia voennaia kollegiia, [1775]);

Sion Moskovskii ozarilsia . . . ([Moscow: Universitetskaia tipografiia, 1776]);

Polnoe sobranie vsekh sochinenii, v stikhakh i proze, 10 volumes, edited by N. I. Novikov (Moscow: Universitetskaia tipografiia, 1781–1782; revised,
1787);

Chudovishchi komediia (Moscow: Universitetskaia tipografiia, 1786);

Mat' sovmestnitsa docheri (Moscow: Universitetskaia
tipografiia, 1786);

Pustaia ssora, komediia (Moscow: Universitetskaia tipografiia, 1786);

Rogonosets po voobrazheniiu, komediia (Moscow: Universitetskaia tipografiia, 1786);

Tresotinius komediia (Moscow: Universitetskaia tipografiia, 1786);

Vzdorshchitsa komediia (Moscow: Universitetskaia tipografiia, 1786);

Desiat' otbornykh basen' g. Sumarokova ([Saint Peters-
burg]: Shlakhetnyi sukhoputnyi kadetskii korpus, 1789);

Rodoslovie kniazei rossiiskikh ([Moscow: Universitetskaia tipografiia], n.d.);

*Sumarokova Liubovnaia gadetel'naia knizhka chrez metanie
dvukh kostochek* ([Saint Petersburg], n.d.).

Editions: *Izbrannye dramaticheskie proizvedeniia,* edited
by A. N. Chudinov, Russkaia klassnaia biblio-
teka, 14 (Saint Petersburg: I. Glazunov, 1893);

Stikhotvoreniia, edited by A. S. Orlov, Biblioteka poeta, Bol'shaia seriia (Leningrad: Sovetskii
pisatel', 1935);

Izbrannye proizvedeniia, edited by Pavel N. Berkov, Biblioteka poeta, Bol'shaia seriia (Leningrad:
Sovetskii pisatel', 1957);

Dramaticheskie sochineniia, edited by Iu. V. Stennik,
Biblioteka russkoi dramaturgii (Leningrad:
Iskusstvo, 1990).

Editions in English: *Selected Tragedies of A. P.
Sumarokov,* translated by Richard and Ray-
mond Fortune (Evanston, Ill.: Northwestern
University Press, 1970);

Selected Aesthetic Works of Sumarokov and Karamzin,
translated by Henry M. Nebel, Jr. (Washington, D.C.: University Press of America, 1981).

OTHER: *Trudoliubivaia pchela* (January 1759–
December 1759), edited by Sumarokov.

The Russian Boileau, the Russian Racine, the
Russian Molière, the Russian Lafontaine, the Russian Voltaire – these are some of the titles contemporaries accorded Aleksandr Petrovich Sumarokov.

The foremost representative of Russian classicism,
Sumarokov aspired to be the founder of a new,
modern European literature in Russia. He founded
and directed the Russian national theater (for which
he supplied most of its early repertory), published
the first private literary journal in Russia, helped establish the norms of the new literary language, and
provided models of virtually every current European poetic and dramatic genre, including fable,
song, sonnet, elegy, satire, eclogue, idyll, epigram,
ballad, madrigal, rondeau, folktale, and a wide variety of odes – panegyric, spiritual, philosophical, An-
ancreontic, Horatian, and Sapphic – as well as the
first Russian tragedies, comedies, operas, and ballets. While his reputation declined in the early nineteenth century when a new Romantic generation repudiated the tradition Sumarokov had tried to establish, Sumarokov was arguably the first professional writer in Russia, in that (at least after 1756)
he was the first to dedicate himself to literary pursuits full-time. He was also arguably the first to
fashion of his career a modern literary biography.

Aleksandr Petrovich Sumarokov was born on
14 November 1717, the second of three brothers.
According to one of his poems he was born near the
town of Vil'mandstrand (Lappeenranta) in present-
day Finland, where his father, Peter Pankrat'evich
Sumarokov, was probably serving against the
Swedes in the Great Northern War. Sumarokov
took great pride in his noble lineage and his family's
loyal service to the state. His grandfather Pankratii
Bogdanovich Sumarokov had served Czar Fedor
and was rewarded for faithful service by Peter, who
reportedly became godfather to his son,
Sumarokov's father. In the unfinished "Vtoryi
Streletskii bunt" Sumarokov told the story of his
great-uncle Ivan Bogdanov. Nicknamed "the Eagle"
for saving Czar Aleksei Mikhailovich from a bear
while on a hunt, he later refused, despite prolonged
torture, to bear false witness against Czarina Sofia's
enemies. The story is indicative of Sumarokov's
moral and political convictions and also reflects his
self-image as a writer and truth sayer.

Almost nothing is known of Sumarokov's
early years. He ascribed his "first groundings in the
Russian language" to his father, who had been educated by the Serb I. A. Zeikan, a man whom the
czar had appointed as tutor to the Naryshkin family
and who later tutored Peter II. On 30 May 1732
Sumarokov entered the newly opened Sukhoputnyi
Shlakhetskii Kadetskii Korpus (Noble Infantry
Cadet Corps), established by Empress Anna to prepare noblemen for service as officers in the army.
At the so-called rytsarskaia akademiia (chivalric

academy) courses on military science took second place to a secular and humanistic curriculum — unique for Russian schools of that day — which included history, geography, jurisprudence, Latin, modern languages (German, French, Italian), as well as fencing, drawing, horsemanship, music, and dancing, which helped cadets develop the special skills and new Europeanized manners needed to participate in aristocratic court life, as they were often called upon to do.

Literature was clearly a major pursuit at the corps, which produced many eighteenth-century literary figures (including Ivan Elagin, Mikhail Kheraskov, Andrei Nartov, Sergei Poroshin) and which in the late 1750s opened its own press; according to some accounts there was even a literary society among the cadets in Sumarokov's day. Sumarokov's first published work was an ode to Empress Anna in the name of the corps in 1740, written in accord with Vasilii Trediakovsky's verse reform of 1735; he later disclaimed this ode and advised young poets to burn their immature works, as he said he had done to his first nine years' production.

Sumarokov graduated from the corps on 14 April 1740. He was made an adjutant to Count M. G. Golovkin, who was arrested and sent into exile soon after Empress Anna's death in the fall of that year. Sumarokov was then appointed to the suite of Count A. G. Razumovsky, Empress Elizabeth's morganatic husband and brother of K. G. Razumovsky, president of the Academy of Sciences. Sumarokov was appointed Razumovsky's adjutant on 7 June 1743; from late in 1745 he was put in charge of the administration of the *leib-kompaniia,* a military body created by Elizabeth as a reward to the troops that had supported her ascension to the throne. Sumarokov found in Razumovsky a continuing supportive patron as well as entry into high court circles. Sumarokov's presence at court led to his marriage on 10 November 1746 to Johanna Khristiforovna Balk (or perhaps Balior), lady-in-waiting to Princess Sofia of Anhalt-Zerbst, the future Catherine the Great, with whom Sumarokov's literary fortunes were to be intimately linked. Sumarokov's first marriage, which ended in divorce in 1766, produced two daughters, Ekaterina and Praskov'ia. Ekaterina, long thought to be a poet because of some verses Sumarokov signed with her name, married Sumarokov's protégé, the tragedian Iakov Kniazhnin, sometime before 1769.

Sumarokov first attracted general attention by writing fashionable songs that became the rage at court. In contrast to Trediakovsky's syllabic songs,

СЕМИРА

ТРАГЕДІЯ

АЛЕКСАНДРА СУМАРОКОВА.

Представлена въ перьвый разъ въ Санктпетербургѣ на Императорскомъ театрѣ въ исходѣ 1751 года.

ПЕЧАТАНО

при Императорской Академіи Наукъ 1768 года.

Title page for the first publication of Sumarokov's tragedy Semira

Sumarokov created the first examples of the modern Russian (syllabo-tonic) romance, in his day often put to the music of minuets or other fashionable European dances and accompanied by a lute; some were put to music by the court musician T. Belogradsky and others by Grigorii Teplov in his popular collection *Mezhdu delom bezdel'e* (Idleness Betweentimes, circa 1745–1751), the first published anthology to include both songs and notes. The love song, a relatively insignificant genre for European classicists, became an important vehicle through which Sumarokov developed the language and rhythms of his new lyric poetry. As opposed to Trediakovsky's songs, which reflected the flirtatious affectation of Parisian salons, Sumarokov's songs are closer in theme to the more serious songs of the Russian folk tradition. As the scholar Il'ia Z. Serman has noted, Sumarokov's songs pointed the way to his later tragedies, in which the psychological torments his protagonists undergo may be seen as an extension of those experienced by the lyric personae of his songs. Furthermore, as

Sumarokov asserts in his "Epistola o stikhotvorstve" (Epistle on Versification, 1748): "Slog pesen dolzhen byt' priiaten, prost i iasen, / Vitiistv ne nadobno; on sam soboi prekrasen" (A song's style should be pleasant, simple and clear, / Orations are not needed; it's beautiful all by itself). This couplet expresses a central plank of Sumarokov's classicism, which stressed precision, simplicity, and clarity of expression – as opposed both to Trediakovsky's clumsy and convoluted style and to the ornate, quasi-baroque poetics of Mikhail Lomonosov's odes.

Sumarokov's notorious and often bitter rivalry with Trediakovsky and Lomonosov may be counted as one of the major literary facts of the middle of the century, as all three strove for preeminence in establishing the rules and norms for the fledgling literature. Their competition dates to the early 1740s; in 1744 they jointly published three verse paraphrases of Psalm 143 (Psalm 144 in English Psalters) for public judgment. Various perspectives on their rivalry have been asserted. Some scholars have stressed Sumarokov's extraordinarily cantankerous and argumentative personality, although in this respect Lomonosov was surely a close second; their rude behavior should be seen within the context of the blunt and often coarse manners of the day, when the polite society of salons existed more in theoretical pronouncements than in actuality. Various poetic polemics reveal minutia such as that Sumarokov was a redhead and may have had a nervous tic and stutter.

Unlike Trediakovsky, who was primarily a literary scholar, and Lomonosov, who was first and foremost a scientist and who viewed poetry as a sideline, Sumarokov dedicated himself to Russian letters, and what has appeared to many readers to be unseemly self-promotion was due at least in part to the great resistance he met in trying to establish the profession of writer in Russia as something worthy of respect. Further, the view of the time that equated public glory with virtue made an overriding concern with public image natural and even expected (Catherine the Great, who was a champion self-promoter, is a case in point). Others have argued that deeper class antagonisms were at work – that Sumarokov represented the interests of the hereditary nobility, as opposed to Trediakovsky, son of a priest, and Lomonosov, son of a peasant fisherman who was patronized by newly risen grandees close to Elizabeth's throne. In the later 1750s the hostility of antagonistic court factions, each of which adopted its poet and egged him on against the others, also clearly played a role

in Sumarokov's feud with Lomonosov. Finally, not the least significant factor in this hostility was the legacy of medieval Russian patterns of thinking, which assumed that there was only one right and immutable way to do things. This was eminently amenable to classicism, which assumed the existence of perfect, fixed, impersonal laws, one consequence of which was to elevate minor personal disagreements into battles over absolute truths.

While Sumarokov was clearly indebted to Trediakovsky's and Lomonosov's reforms of Russian versification, he arguably did far more than they in putting it into practice and creating a modern poetic system of genres and a tradition of actual poetic practice. Disclaiming apprenticeship from his rivals, Sumarokov asserted in his "K nesmyslennym rifmotvortsam" (To Witless Poetasters, 1759) that at the time when he made his literary debut "Stikhotvortsev u nas eshche ne bylo i nauchit'sia bylo ne u kogo. Ia budto skvoz' dremuchii les sokryvaiushchii ot oche moikh zhilishche Muz bez provodnika prokhodil, i khotia ia mnogo dolzhen Rasinu, no evo uvidel ia uzhe togda, kak vyshel iz sego lesa, i kogda uzhe Parnasskaia gora pred"iavilasia vzoru moemu. No Rasin Frantsuz i v Russkom iazyke mne dat' nastavleniia ne mog. Russkim iazykom i chistotoiu sklada, ni Stikhov, ni Prozy, ne dolzhen ia ni komu krome sebia" (there were no Poets, and no one to learn from. It was as if I went without a guide through a dark forest which screened the dwelling of the Muses from my eyes. Although I am much indebted to Racine, I only espied him once I was out of the woods, when Mount Parnassus had already presented itself to my gaze. But Racine is a Frenchman and could not instruct me in Russian. For the Russian language and purity of style I am indebted to no one but myself, both in Poetry and Prose).

In 1747–1748 Sumarokov published his first major works, at his own cost, at the Academy of Sciences typography. These included the tragedies *Khorev* (1747) and *Gamlet* (Hamlet, 1748) and *Dve epistoly* (Two Epistles, 1748), one epistle on the Russian language and the other on the art of poetry. They established Sumarokov as a major figure in Russian letters and helped to galvanize support of other young poets, mostly graduates of the corps, around him. The epistles, a "manifesto of Russian classicism," were based on Boileau's *Art poétique* (1674) – which was in turn based on Horace – and set forth Sumarokov's Russianized version of the classicist hierarchy of genres. The author triumphantly concluded:

Все хвально: драма ли, эклога или ода--
Слагай, к чему тебя влечет твоя природа;
Лишь просвещение писатель дай уму:
Прекасный наш язык способен ко всему.

(All are laudable: the drama, eclogue, or ode--
Compose that to which your nature draws you;
Only, writer, let your mind be enlightened:
Our beautiful tongue is capable of anything!)

Sumarokov's tragedies, written in the Russian equivalent of French Alexandrine verse (iambic hexameter with caesura after the third foot, with paired rhymes), employed a minimum of means — few characters, little action or plot, abstract settings (mostly labeled as ancient Russia), and no props except a dagger (traditional symbol of tragic theater) — to maximum emotional and emotive effect. All share a classical (mostly five-act) structure and observe the three unities of space, time, and action. The crisis usually involves two lovers' struggle between love and duty on the one hand and their conflict with the throne (a jealous, evil, or badly advised monarch) on the other. Sumarokov's tragedies have been called "shkola grazhdanskoi dobrodeteli" (a school of civic virtue), embodying an enlightened ideal of the Russian nobility's new corporate sense of honor and admonitions to the autocracy to rule justly under law.

Perhaps in response to Trediakovsky's criticism that tragedy should be "an imitation of God's actions on earth," with evil defeated and good triumphant, Sumarokov gave *Gamlet* and most of his later tragedies happy endings (hence Hamlet lives to marry Ophelia and ascend the Danish throne). For his basic acquaintance with William Shakespeare's play Sumarokov was indebted to Pierre Antoine de La Place's 1745 French translation, although records in the Academy of Sciences library indicate that Sumarokov, who did not know English, borrowed the fourth folio version of Shakespeare's plays from the Academy of Sciences library. However, apart from the famous "To be, or not to be" monologue — for which Sumarokov consulted (and borrowed from) Voltaire's version in the *Lettres anglois* (1733–1734) — Sumarokov himself noted that his version hardly resembled Shakespeare's tragedy. While the later tradition tended to see Sumarokov's play as a travesty of Shakespeare, several modern critics have been more charitable toward Sumarokov's attempt to create a unique play.

Sumarokov's tragedies, staged by cadets at the corps with all-male casts, were brought to Elizabeth's attention by Razumovsky. The empress invited the cadets to perform at court in early 1750 and took a personal hand in dressing up the handsome young cadets in lavish regalia and even lent the leading "lady" her crown diamonds. The performances were a great success, and in 1750–1751 Sumarokov added *Sinav i Truvor* (Sinav and Truvor, 1751), *Artistona* (1751), and *Semira* (1768) to his tragedic repertoire; Sumarokov was doubtless pleased when the tragedies commissioned from his rivals Trediakovsky and Lomonosov proved unworthy of the stage. Sumarokov also wrote the first Russian comedies, in prose, the one-act *Tresotinius* (1786) and *Chudovishchi* (Monster, 1786), which Sumarokov later renamed "Treteinoi sud" (Court of Arbitration); posthumous editions of the play mistakenly retained the discarded title. These were transparently satiric burlesques, closer to the old *intermedia* — brief comical interludes that came in between acts of the often interminably long school dramas — or to Russian *igrishchi* (folk farces) which Sumarokov theoretically repudiated, rather than to classical comedy.

On 30 August 1756 Elizabeth brought a national Russian theater into being by official proclamation. The kernel of the troupe was formed by actors from Fedor Volkov's private Iaroslavl troupe, which had been brought to the capital to perform at court in 1750; several actors had been subsequently sent to the corps for further training. Sumarokov was named director and assigned a yearly salary of one thousand rubles beyond what he received according to his rank of brigadier, although from that date Sumarokov was freed from his other official responsibilities.

During the later 1750s Sumarokov also regularly contributed poetry to the Academy of Sciences miscellany *Ezhemesiachnye sochineniia* (Monthly Compositions), actively experimenting in a variety of verse forms and genres. In 1759 he published his own journal, *Trudoliubivaia pchela* (The Industrious Bee), the first private literary journal in Russia, although precedence is sometimes accorded to *Prazdnoe vremia, v pol'zu upotreblennoe* (Idle Time Used Well), begun the same year by former cadets and to which Sumarokov also contributed. Sumarokov dedicated *Trudoliubivaia pchela* to Catherine, an act of considerable boldness considering that the Grand Princess was in disgrace following a failed court intrigue in 1758. The episode had resulted in Aleksei Bestuzhev-Riumin's arrest; according to one source Sumarokov himself was subjected to interrogation during the investigation.

Trudoliubivaia pchela included essays on history, philosophy, and literature, as well as original poetry (mostly Sumarokov's) and translations from classical and modern authors (including Voltaire and Jonathan Swift). Particularly notable were Sumarokov's satiric essays, which served as prototypes for the later Russian satiric journals. Among his targets were the abuse of serfs by landowners, bribe-taking, favoritism, and other bureaucratic and social ills — themes that informed many of Sumarokov's works (especially his fables) throughout his later career. Increasing difficulties with censors at the academy typography, some of them instigated by his archenemy Lomonosov, forced Sumarokov to cease publication of the journal after a year. The final issue included the poem "Rasstavanie s muzami" (Farewell to the Muses), in which Sumarokov vowed never to write again, a vow the author was to make and break repeatedly in future years.

Sumarokov met with even greater frustrations organizing the new Russian theater. Although it became an official "court" (rather than "free") theater in 1759 and hence presumably eligible for greater state support, Sumarokov was burdened by constant financial hardships — his salary withheld; no money to pay the actors or his own rent; lack of costumes, which forced cancellation of performances; no stagehands or other assistants; and at times not even enough to eat. On top of this there were endless bureaucratic obstacles put in his way by the officials on whom he had to rely, especially K. I. Sivers (Sumarokov had his revenge by ridiculing Sivers in a memorable article in *Trudoliubivaia pchela*). Among other problems with which Sumarokov was forced to contend were the lack of a fixed venue for the theater, competition with French and Italian troupes (which were far better paid) and other court activities, performances canceled due to a prematurely thawed Neva River (preventing its crossing by travelers), and his own illnesses. Sumarokov struggled heroically to improve conditions for his troupe; for instance, he fought to get them decent medical care and the privilege for his male actors to wear swords (a sign of noble prerogative). After repeated threats to resign from the theater, Sumarokov was finally taken at his word and forced out of the directorship against his will in 1761. Apart from his writing, Sumarokov laid the institutional groundwork for the later Imperial Russian Theater and helped establish a tradition of distinguished Russian acting that lasted well into the nineteenth century.

Sumarokov complained of having little time to write, but in the later 1750s he managed to compose a sixth tragedy, *Dimiza* (1758), later revised as *Iaropolk i Dimiza tragediia* (1768); a drama, *Pustynnik*

Title page for the first volume of Sumarokov's fables, which were among his most popular works during his lifetime

(The Hermit, 1769), written in 1757; the first Russian operas, *Tsefal i Prokris* (Cephalus and Procris, 1755) and *Al'tsesta* (Alceste, 1759), both with music by the Italian composer Francesco Arai; the ballet *Pribezhishche dobrodeteli* (Sanctuary for Virtue, 1759); and an allegorical prologue, *Novye lavry* (New Laurels, 1759), to celebrate the Russian army's victory over the Prussians near Frankfurt. In the early 1760s he also contributed to the new Moscow journals *Poleznoe uveselenie* (Useful Amusement, 1760–1762) and *Svobodnye chasy* (Free Hours, 1763), around which a new generation of young poets had arisen, including Kheraskov, A. A. Rzhevsky, and Vasilii Maikov, commonly referred to as the "Sumarokov school."

Catherine the Great's coup of 28 June 1762, which put an end to her husband Peter III's brief reign, promised Sumarokov good fortune. He was promoted in rank, and his debts to the academy typography (which had vexed him since 1748) were annulled, although he spent many years trying to collect money that he felt had been wrongly withheld during his tenure at the theater. Catherine also granted Sumarokov the unique lifetime privilege of having all of his works printed at her cost, which may help explain Sumarokov's prodigious list of publications. Their popularity, given the nebulous nature of the Russian reading public in the eighteenth century, is hard to gauge, although many of his contemporaries unquestionably considered Sumarokov's work to be classic. Catherine's ascension must have seemed to Sumarokov like a triumph for his own political ideals, and he celebrated the empress in a series of laudatory odes (notably, in the later 1750s he had largely disdained writing such works to Elizabeth). The longest of these, an ode printed on 8 July 1762 and reprinted three weeks later, has been called a poeticized version of the famous manifesto that Catherine had published on coming to the throne, in which she echoed Montesquieu's condemnation of despotism and praise of monarchy based on law.

At the same time Sumarokov found himself in a somewhat unusual position professionally, since he continued to receive a salary but had no official position or duties; in 1764 he even proposed that Catherine finance a trip to France and Italy so that he could write travel notes for the edification of his countrymen. Committed both to the political program of enlightened monarchy which Catherine espoused and to the prestige and independence of Russian letters, Sumarokov increasingly found himself in a quandary, as his personal and political impertinences often threatened to alienate the empress, on whose goodwill he relied both as writer and ideologue. The first indications of a problem may have been that Sumarokov did not publish his outspoken coronation speech of 22 September 1762 and that a portion of his "Khor ko prevratnomu svetu" (Chorus to a Perverted World) was cut from the published verses he had written for the elaborate three-day celebration titled "Torzhestvuiushchaia Minerva" (Minerva Triumphant), which he helped organize together with Volkov and Kheraskov and which was held in Moscow in early 1763 to honor Catherine's coronation; both works were first published in the posthumous complete works. Other, more certain grounds for Catherine's discontent were an ode Sumarokov dedicated to her former lover, the Polish king Stanislav Augustus, in 1765 (she ordered the academy to burn the work, and no copies have survived) and the satiric fable "Dva povara" (Two Cooks), published the same year, which she had confiscated. Sumarokov's letters to Catherine with which he often "bombarded" her (as she put it) are remarkable for their frank and outspoken tone and as expressions of Sumarokov's marked self-regard as a poet.

Sumarokov's father died in 1766, and a scandal ensued when Sumarokov went to Moscow to claim his inheritance; Catherine intervened on his mother's behalf after she appealed to the empress for protection against her son, who had terrified her household and threatened her with physical violence. Sumarokov was enraged at the thought that his mother was taking sides against him with his hated brother-in-law A. I. Buturlin (whom the poet lampooned in several of his comedies). The situation was probably complicated by the fact that by this time Sumarokov's wife had left him and he had taken up with a serf woman, Vera Prokhorovna, whom he officially married in 1774; some have speculated that this relationship may have brought the poet some measure of social ostracism. Prokhorovna bore Sumarokov two more children, Anastasiia and Pavel, who received gentry status at the time of their parents' marriage.

In response to the essay contest Catherine suggested to the Free Economic Society in 1766 the desirability of granting property rights to peasants and in his notes on the draft of the empress's *Nakaz* (Instruction, 1767), Sumarokov staunchly defended the institution of serfdom. Catherine was apparently not pleased with his response and wrote that "gospodin Sumarokov khoroshii poet, no . . . chtob byt' khoroshim zakonodavtsem, on sviazi dovol'noi v mysliakh ne imeet" (Mr. Sumarokov is a good poet but . . . he does not have sufficient clarity of mind to be a good lawgiver). Be that as it may, Sumarokov was an outspoken defender of serfs' human and legal rights and sharply attacked such practices as selling serfs "like cattle," that is, apart from their land. While asserting fundamental human equality according to nature, Sumarokov also defended the necessity of social hierarchy. The essential point was that each social order fulfill its duty appropriately. Some of his most memorable attacks were against *pod'iachie* (bureaucrats), in which category he sometimes included those granted noble status by appointment, and against *otkupshchiki* (concessionaires), notorious in the eighteenth century for extorting high prices for vodka after obtaining the right to sell it under the state liquor monopoly. But the main target as well as audience for Sumarokov's admonitions was his own class, the hereditary Russian nobility. As he wrote in his programmatic satire "O blagorodstve" (On Nobility, 1774);

Дворяне без меня свой долг довольно знают,
Но многие одно дворянство воспоминают,
Не помня, что от баб рожденных и от дам

Без исключения всем праотец Адам.
На что ль дворяне мы, чтоб люди работали,
А мы бы их труды по знатности глотали? . . .
Не в титле-- в действии быть должен дворянином.

(The nobles know their duty quite well without me,
But many only recall their nobility,
Forgetting that all people, born of country gals
    or ladies
Without exception have Adam as progenitor.
Are we nobles so that people should work,
So that we exalted ones swallow up their labor? . . .
One should be noble not in title but in action.)

The failure to keep to one's proper station is repeatedly ridiculed in Sumarokov's fables, published in three volumes between 1762 and 1769 (three more books of fables were published in his collected works, bringing the total number of fables to about 380). Among Sumarokov's most popular works during his lifetime, the fables were full of coarse humor and sharp, mocking invective and were often directed at contemporary political targets or literary enemies. They were also among his most innovative works, written mostly in iambic lines of varied length and capturing the dynamic intonations of popular and folk speech. While such things were permissible in a "low" genre such as the fable, Sumarokov resolutely rejected those new bourgeois literary phenomena that he felt threatened the classical hierarchy. He was disdainful of the flood of translated novels that hit Russia in the 1760s (and scornful of their Russian imitations by such writers as Fedor Emin and Mikhail Chulkov) and resolutely opposed the new dramas that combined comic and tragic elements. In the preface to *Dimitrii Samozvanets* (Dimitrii the Pretender, 1771) Sumarokov triumphantly published a letter written to him by Voltaire dated 26 February 1769 (new style) in which Voltaire praised Sumarokov and approved his rejection of "comédies larmoyantes" (tearful comedies).

On 26 January 1767 Catherine awarded Sumarokov the Order of Anna, possibly in part for several more odes he had written to her. He was in Moscow during the summer of that year while Catherine was organizing the Commission for a New Law Code. He spent 1768 and early 1769 in Saint Petersburg, where he published a prodigious number of old, new, and revised works, including the comedies *Likhoimets* (The Extortioner, 1768), *Iadovityi* (The Poisonous One, 1768), *Tri brata sovmestniki* (Three Brother Rivals, 1768), *Nartsiss* (Narcissus, 1769), and *Pridannoe obmanom* (Dowry by Deceit, 1769); the popular but heretofore unpub-

lished tragedy *Semira*, written in 1751; revised versions of *Khorev, Sinav i Truvor, Iaropolk i Dimiza*, and *Pustynnik;* and his seventh tragedy, *Vysheslav* (1768). In addition he published his historical essay *Pervyi i glavnyi streletskii bunt* (The First and Main Streltsy Rebellion, 1768) and the collection *Raznyia stikhotvoreniia* (Various Poems, 1769), as well as the third volume of his fables.

In March 1769 Sumarokov moved to Moscow, where he became involved in complicated negotiations to establish a permanent theater there. He managed to quarrel with many people in the theatrical world, which led to a conspiracy to embarrass the extraordinarily vain author publicly. At the center was Moscow's commander in chief Count P. S. Saltykov. Saltykov forced Belmonti's troupe to stage *Sinav i Truvor* on 31 January 1770, despite the fact that the actors were not ready or willing and despite Sumarokov's contract with Belmonti explicitly forbidding him to put on any of Sumarokov's plays without the author's permission. Two days before the performance Sumarokov took to his bed in grief and from there wrote a series of desperate letters to Catherine imploring her help. In one he included an autobiographical elegy – "Vse mery prevoshla teper' moia dosada" (Now My Vexation Has Exceeded All Bounds), and in another he appealed to her, citing lines adapted from his recent tragedy *Vysheslav:* "Ne emliu sil vel'mozh vokrug stoiashchikh trona, / I ot predpisanna rukoi tvoei zakona" (I have neither the power of grandees who surround the throne, / Nor that of the law prescribed by your hand). In answer Catherine wrote caustically that "mne vsegda priiatnee budet vidit predstavlenii strastei v vashi drammy, nezheli chitat ikh v pis'makh" (it will always be more pleasant for me to see presentations of passion in your plays than to read them in your letters). It was a remarkable exchange over the proper limits of literature between the classicist poet and the enlightened despot. On the accompanying letter Sumarokov had written to her secretary, Catherine noted to herself with a pun, "Sumarokov bez uma est' i budet" (Sumarokov is and will be brainless). The scandal continued as Saltykov circulated copies of Catherine's letter to the poet, and mocking epigrams proliferated, including one against Sumarokov by the young Derzhavin.

Catherine's refusal to intervene dramatically demonstrated the limits of her patronage and possibly also her impatience with Russian writers in general (although it should be noted that her intervention would have been against a trusted senior official). This was the period (1769–1774) of the short-

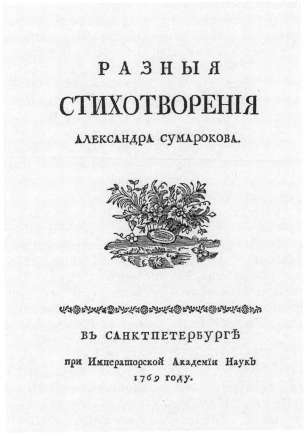

РАЗНЫЯ

СТИХОТВОРЕНІЯ

АЛЕКСАНДРА СУМАРОКОВА.

ВЪ САНКТПЕТЕРБУРГѢ

при Императорской Академіи Наукъ
1769 году.

Title page for a collection of Sumarokov's poetry

lived satiric journals that Catherine's *Vsiakaia vsiachina* (All Sorts and Sundries) had initiated. Sumarokov contributed little to them, but his works were held up as the prime example of "satira na litso" (personal satire), which Novikov in particular advocated, as opposed to the generalized "satira na porok" (satire of vices), which the empress tried to promote. Catherine's political liberalism was wearing thin, and she tried increasingly to regulate Russian letters, either through her own efforts or by turning to such truly subservient court poets as Vasilii Petrov. Characteristically, two years earlier Catherine had again played the role of Sumarokov's personal censor and, despite Sumarokov's protests, had supported theater director Ivan Elagin's excision of several lines from *Likhoimets* that referred to religion and to the Commission on the New Law Code in a flippant manner.

Despite the debacle in Moscow, Sumarokov completed his next and by general consensus his greatest tragedy, *Dimitrii Samozvanets,* which opened in Saint Petersburg on 1 February 1771. In the foreword to the play Sumarokov lambasted Pierre-

Augustin Beaumarchais's tearful drama *Eugénie* (1767) and the Moscow audiences that had recently applauded a Russian version of it; he appended Voltaire's letter, which had become a kind of talisman for the beleaguered author. *Dimitrii Samozvanets,* set during the time of troubles of the early seventeenth century, was the most contemporary, most truly historical, and most patriotic of Sumarokov's tragedies, which the author said would "show Russia Shakespeare." Dimitrii was Sumarokov's most shocking anti-utopian tyrant, and the play balances between a staunch defense of the hierarchical and autocratic principle, on the one hand, and legitimacy based on merit rather than birth, on the other — "Kol' on dostoinyi tsar', dostoin tsarska sana" (He who is a worthy czar is worthy of the czar's station). At the end of the play nobles and people alike rise up to oust Dimitrii, to the chiming of Kremlin bells. *Dimitrii Samozvanets* remained in the repertory through 1812 and was the prototype for many later plays on the theme, most notably Aleksandr Pushkin's *Boris Godunov* (1831). Scholars have tried, not too successfully, to see this and other of

Sumarokov's tragedies as covert commentaries on specific contemporary issues (that is, as criticisms of Elizabeth's or Catherine's despotism), but their fundamental political message – a defense of lawful monarchy and an attack on the abuses of despotism – is clear. Nevertheless, Sumarokov's eloquent denunciations of tyranny were a starting point for the republican trend in later Russian literature, most notably Iakov Kniazhnin's *Vadim Novgorodsky* (Vadim of Novgorod, 1793), which Catherine had burned and which was in turn a link to the Decembrists.

Dimitrii Samozvanets also presented a defense of Russian Orthodoxy, which was juxtaposed to Catholicism's "false doctrine" that demanded blind obedience. Characteristically, Sumarokov advocated a rationalistic view of Orthodoxy that did not see any necessary or apparent contradiction between reason and divine revelation. Sumarokov's religious thought was in the quasi-Protestant tradition of Feofan Prokopovich, main architect of Peter I's church reform, a stance characteristic of eighteenth-century Russian religious thought. The harmonizing of faith and reason also corresponded to the mid-century attempt to create a new literary language based on both Church Slavonic and vulgar Russian, so-called "Slavenorossiiskii" (Slaveno-Russian), and to the blurring of boundaries between religious and secular literature (secular poets writing psalm paraphrases, as well as clerics writing sermons and catechisms in the vernacular). While Sumarokov was an advocate of such a literary, linguistic, and philosophical rapprochement between secular and religious traditions, in subsequent literary consciousness he was largely associated with Karamzin's reforms, which were oriented to the secular spoken language of the salon; this association occurred partially by negative analogy with Trediakovsky, who was identified with the camp of the politically and religiously conservative *arkhaisty* (archaists).

On 29 March 1771 Sumarokov renewed his agreement with Belmonti, paving the way to present his works on the Moscow stage, but all plans were postponed when the black plague began to ravage the city. Sumarokov left Moscow on account of the epidemic and did not return until April 1772, to find Belmonti dead and most of the actors scattered. Again Sumarokov involved himself in the politics of theatrical plans and proposals. Despite chronic medical problems, he also continued to write. On Metropolitan Platon's advice he finished his poetic paraphrase of the Psalter, which he published in 1774. The same year saw publication of collections of his

Eklogi (Eclogues); *Elegiia liubovnyia* (Love Elegies); *Ody torzhestvennye* (Triumphal Odes); *Satiry* (Satires); his last tragedy, *Mstislav;* and several shorter works, including poems decrying the Pugachev rebellion. He also continued to write comedies; his last three – *Rogonosets po voobrazheniiu* (The Imaginary Cuckold, 1786), *Mat' sovmestnitsa docheri* (Mother-Daughter Rivalry, 1786), *Vzdorshchitsa* (The Argumentative One, 1786) – manifest the influence of Denis Fonvizin's *Brigadir* (1792?, written in 1766) in their depiction of Russian types and their earthy language. Many readers consider *Rogonosets* a minor masterpiece.

While he continued to publish through 1775, Sumarokov was afflicted in his final years by sickness, poverty, and probably alcoholism. He spent part of 1773 and 1774 in Saint Petersburg, where with the help of his new patron, Grigorii Potemkin, he arranged for his son Pavel's entry into the Preobrazhensky Regiment and attended the presentation of *Mstislav.* In Moscow accumulated unpaid debts threatened to deprive the poet and his family of their home, and he was further insulted when refused the customary free entrance to performances of his own work. He published his last ode to Catherine in July 1775, celebrating the peace of Kuchuk-Kainardji, but financial relief was not forthcoming from the empress. A final crisis occurred after the death of Sumarokov's wife Vera in May 1777, as Sumarokov's mother unsuccessfully attempted to prevent her son's third marriage to another serf, his second wife's niece Elena Gavrilova. The details are obscure, but Sumarokov may have desired the marriage to protect his daughter or perhaps simply to have someone to take care of him. He died on 1 October 1777, approximately four months after this marriage and just a few days after his Moscow home had been sold at auction for debts.

Legend has it that almost no one attended the funeral of the destitute poet, apart from several Moscow actors who had carried his coffin to the Donskoi Monastery, where he was buried in an unmarked grave. A lasting monument to the writer was the exemplary ten-volume *Polnoe sobranie vsekh sochinenii, v stikhakh i proze* (Complete Works in Verse and Prose) published by Novikov in 1781–1782 and revised in 1787. Unfortunately, the poet's papers, which Novikov had rescued after Sumarokov's death and used for the complete works, were lost after Novikov's arrest in 1792. Although in the nineteenth century Sumarokov's name became synonymous with Russian *lzhe-* (false)- or *psevdo-klassitsizm* (pseudo-classicism), terms that denied to most eighteenth-century writing the right to be considered as literature, in 1772 Novikov expressed the prevailing view of Sumarokov's contemporaries when he wrote that the poet had "Razlichnykh rodov stikhotvornymi i prozaicheskimi sochineniiami priobrel on sebe velikuiu i bezsmertnuiu slavu netol'ko ot Rossiian; no i ot chuzhestrannykh Akademii i slavneishikh Evropeiskikh pisatelei" (achieved great and immortal fame for himself via works in a variety of poetic and prose genres, not only from Russians but from foreign Academies and from the most famous European writers).

Letters:

"A. P. Sumarokov," edited by V. P. Stepanov, in *Pis'-ma russkikh pisatelei XVIII veka,* edited by G. P. Makagonenko (Leningrad: Nauka, 1980), pp. 68–223.

Biographies:

N. N. Bulich, *Sumarokov i sovremennaia emu kritiki* (Saint Petersburg: Eduarda Pratsa, 1854);

V. Ia. Stoiunin, *A. P. Sumarokov* (Saint Petersburg, 1856);

M. V. Longinov, "Poslednie gody zhizni Aleksandr Petrovicha Sumarokova (1766–1777)," *Russkii arkhiv* (1871): cols. 1637–1717, 1955–1960;

Pavel N. Berkov, *A. P. Sumarokov, 1717–1777,* Russkie dramaturgi, nauchnopopuliarnye ocherki (Moscow & Leningrad: Iskusstvo, 1949).

References:

Pavel N. Berkov, *Lomonosov i literaturnaia polemika ego vremeni, 1750–1765* (Moscow & Leningrad: Akademiia nauk, 1936);

Berkov, "Neskol'ko spravok dlia biografii A. P. Sumarokova," *XVIII vek,* 5 (1962): 364–375;

Berkov, "Zhisnennyi i literaturnyi put' A. P. Sumarokova," in Sumarokov's, *Izbrannye proizvedeniia,* edited by Berkov, Biblioteka poeta, Bol'shaia seriia (Leningrad: Sovetskii pisatel', 1957), pp. 5–46;

M. S. Grinberg and B. A. Uspensky, *Literaturnaia bor'ba Trediakovskogo i Sumarokova v 1740-kh-nachale 1750-x godov,* special issue on Sumarokov, *Russian Literature,* 31, no. 2 (1992): 133–272;

G. A. Gukovsky, "Lomonosov, Sumarokov, shkola Sumarokova," in his *Russkaia poeziia XVIII veka.* Voprosy poetiki, 10 (Leningrad: Academia, 1927), pp. 9–47;

Gukovsky, "O sumarokovskoi tragedii," *Poetika,* 1 (1926): 67–80;

Gukovsky, *Ocherki po istorii russkoi literatury XVIII veka: Dvorianskaia fronda v literature 1750-kh-1760-kh godov* (Moscow & Leningrad: Akademiia nauk, 1936);

David M. Lang, "Boileau and Sumarokov. The Manifesto of Russian Classicism," *Modern Language Review,* 43 (October 1948): 500–506;

Lang, "Sumarokov's 'Hamlet': A Misjudged Russian Tragedy of the Eighteenth Century," *Modern Language Review,* 43 (January 1948): 67–72;

Marcus C. Levitt, "Drama Sumarokova 'Pustynnik': k voprosu ob ideologicheskikh istochnikakh russkogo klassitsizma," *XVIII vek,* 18 (1993): 59–74;

Levitt, "Sumarokov's Russianized 'Hamlet': Texts and Contexts," *Slavic and East European Journal,* 38 (Summer 1994): 319–341;

Tamara Livanova, *Russkaia muzykal'naia kul'tura XVIII veka, v sviazi s literaturoi, teatrom i bytom,* volume 1 (Moscow: Muzgiz, 1952), pp. 65–92;

Il'ia Z. Serman, *Russkii klassitsizm: Poeziia, drama, satira* (Leningrad: Nauka, 1973);

Iu. V. Stennik, *Zhanr tragedii v russkoi literature: epokha klassitsizma* (Leningrad: Nauka, 1981);

L. Vindt, "Basnia sumarokovskoi shkoly," *Poetika,* 1 (1926): 81–92;

V. M. Zhivov, *Kulk'turnye konflikty v istorii russkogo literaturnogo iazyka XVIII - nachala XIX veka* (Moscow: Institut russkogo iazyka, 1990).

Vasilii Kirillovich Trediakovsky

(22 February 1703 – 6 August 1769)

Irina Reyfman
Columbia University

BOOKS: *Pesn'. Sochinena v Gamburge k torzhestvennomu prazdnovaniiu koronatsii eia velichestva gosudaryni imp. Anny Ioannovny samoderzhitsy vserossisskiia, byvshemu tamo avgusta 10 (po novomu chislveniiu) 1730* ([Saint Petersburg: Akademiia nauk, 1730]);

Panegirik ili Slovo pokhval'noe vsemilostiveishei gosudaryne imp. samoderzhitse vserossiiskoi Anne Ioannovne chrez vsepodanneishego eia velichestva raba Vasil'ia Trediakovskago sochinennoe, i eia imp. velichestvu v den' tezoimenitstva eia podnessennoe fevralia v 3 den' 732 goda (Saint Petersburg: Akademiia nauk, 1732);

Oda privetstvennaia vsemilostiveishei gosudaryne imp. samoderzhitse vserossiiskoi Anne Ioannovne v den' otpravlisiushchagosia torzhestva toest' 19 genvaria dlia radostnago vsem nam vozshestviia eia na vserossiiskii prestol (Saint Petersburg: Akademiia nauk, 1733);

Novoiu dostoino ukrashennomu chestiiu prevoskholditel'neishemu gospodinu gospodinu Ioannu Albrekhtu baronu fon Korff eia imp. velichestva samoderzhitsy vserossiiskiia. Deistvitel'nomu kamergeru nyne zhe v Sanktpeterburgskoi Akademii nauk glavnuiu imeiushchemu kommandu pokorneishee pozdravlenie ([Saint Petersburg]: Akademiia nauk, 1734);

Oda torzhestvennaia o sdache goroda Gdan'ska, sochinennaia v viashchuiu slavu imeni . . . velikiia gosudaryni Anny Ioannovny imp. i samoderzhitsy vserossiiskiia (Saint Petersburg: Akademiia nauk, 1734);

Novyi i kratkii sposob k slozheniiu rossiiskikh stikhov s opredeleniiami do sego nadlezhashchikh zvanii (Saint Petersburg: Akademiia nauk, 1735); revised as "Sposob k slozheniiu rossiiskikh stikhov . . . ," in his *Sochineniia i perevody kak stikhami tak i prozoiu*, volume 1 (Saint Petersburg: Akademiia nauk, 1752), pp. 99–155; translated by Rimvydas Silbajoris as "New and Brief Method for Composing Russian Verse" and "Method for Composing Russian Verse," in *Russian Versification: The Theories of Trediakovskij, Lomonosov, and*

Vasilii Kirillovich Trediakovsky; frontispiece from his Deidamiia tragediia *(1775)*

Kantemir (New York: Columbia University Press, 1968), pp. 36–67, 100–127;

Rech, kotoruiu v Sanktpeterburgskoi Imperatorskoi Akademii nauk, k chlenam Rossiiskogo sobraniia, vo vremia pervago onykh sobraniia, marta 14 dnia, 1735 goda (Saint Petersburg: Akademiia nauk, 1735);

Vsepresvetleishei derzhavneishei velikoi gosudaryne imp. Elizavete Petrovne samoderzhitse vserossiiskoi gosudaryne vsemilostiveishei vsepodanneishee pozdravlenie v vysochaishii den' eia koronovaniia v tsarstvuiushchem i stolichnom gorode Moskve aprelia dnia 1742 goda v privetstvennoi ode izobrazhennoe i eiia sviashchenneishemu velichestvu userdneishe posviashchennoe (Saint Petersburg: Akademiia nauk, [1742]);

Tri ody parafrasticheskie psalma 143, sochinennye chrez trekh stikhotvortsev, iz kotorykh kazhdyi odnu slozhil osoblivo, by Trediakovsky, A. S. Sumarokov, and M. V. Lomonosov (Saint Petersburg: Akademiia nauk, 1744);

Slovo o bogatom, razlichnom, iskusnom i neskhotstvennom vitiistve (Saint Petersburg: Akademiia nauk, [1745]);

Razgovor mezhdu chuzhestrannym chelovekom i Rossiiskim ob ortografii starinnoi i novoi i o vsem chto prinadlezhit k sei materii (Saint Petersburg: Akademiia nauk, 1748);

Socheneniia i perevody kak stikhami tak i prozoiu, 2 volumes (Saint Petersburg: Akademiia nauk, 1752);

Tilemakhida ili Stranstvovanie Tilemakha syna Odysseeva opisannoe v sostave iroicheskoi piimy, 2 volumes (Saint Petersburg: [Akademiia nauk], 1766);

Tri rassuzhedeniia o trekh glavneishikh drevnostiakh rossiiskikh (Saint Petersburg: [Sukhoputnyi kadetskii korpus], 1773);

Deidamiia tragediia (Moscow: [Gosudarstvennaia voennaia kollegiia], 1775).

Editions: *Izbrannye sochineniia* ([Moscow]: P. Perevlessky, 1849);

Sochineniia, 3 volumes (Saint Petersburg: A. Smirdin, 1849);

Stikhotvoreniia, edited by A. S. Orlov, Biblioteka poeta, Bol'shaia seriia (Leningrad: Sovetskii pisatel', 1935);

Izbrannye proizvedeniia, edited by L. I. Timofeev and Ia. M. Strochkov, Biblioteka poeta, Bol'shaia seriia (Moscow & Leningrad: Sovetskii pisatel', 1963);

Psaltir' ili Kniga psalmov blazhennogo proroka i tsaria Davida prelozhennykh liricheskimi stikihami i umnozhennykh liricheskimi pes'mi, edited by Alexander Levitsky, Biblia Slavica, series 3, volume 4b (Paderborn, Germany: Ferdinand Schoningh, 1989).

TRANSLATIONS: Paul Tallemant (Tal'man), *Ezda v ostrov liubvi* (Saint Petersburg: Akademiia nauk, 1730) – includes original poems by Trediakovsky;

Pierre Surirey de Saint-Remy (Sen-Remi), *Memorii ili Zapiski artilleriiskiia,* 2 volumes (Saint Petersburg: Akademiia nauk, 1732–1733);

F. Prata, *Sila liubvi i nenavisti: Dramma na muzyke . . .* (Saint Petersburg: Akademiia nauk, 1736);

Luigi Ferdinando Marsigli (Marsil'i), *Voennoe sostoianiie Ottomanskoi imperii, s ee prirashcheniem i upadkom,* 4 volumes (Saint Petersburg: Akademiia nauk, 1737);

Istinnaia politika znatnykh i blagorodnykh osob (Saint Petersburg: Akademiia nauk, 1737);

Izvestie o dvukh vozmushcheniiakh sluchivshikhsia v Konstantinopole 1730 i 1731 goda pri nizlozhenii Akhmeta III i vozvedenii na prestol Magometa V (Saint Petersburg: Akademiia nauk, 1738);

Charles Rollin, *Drevniaia istoriia ob egiptianakh, o karfagenianakh, ob assirianakh, o midianakh, persakh, o makedonianakh i o grekakh,* 10 volumes (Saint Petersburg: Akademiia nauk, 1749–1764);

John Barclay (Dzhon [or Ioann] Barkli), *Argenida povest' geroicheskaia . . . ,* 2 volumes (Saint Petersburg: Akademiia nauk, 1751);

David Mallet, *Zhitie kantslera Frantsiska Bakona* ([Moscow]: Moskovskii universitet, 1760);

Alexander Deleyre (Deler), *Sokrashchenie filosofii kantslera Frantsiska Bakona,* volume 1 ([Moscow]: Moskovskii universitet, 1760);

Rollin and Jean Baptist Louis Crévier, (Krev'e) *Rimskaia istoriia ot sozdaniia Rima do bitvy Aktiiskiia, to est' po okonchanie Respubliki,* 16 volumes (Saint Petersburg: [Akademiia nauk], 1761–1767);

Crévier, *Istoriia o rimskikh imperatorakh s Avgusta po Konstantina,* 4 volumes (Saint Petersburg: Morskoi shliakhetnyi kadetskii korpus, 1767–1769);

Abu-l-Gazi, *Rodoslovnaia istoriia o tatarakh, perevedennaia na frantsuzskoi iazyk s rukopisnoi tatarskoi knigi,* 2 volumes (Saint Petersburg: Akademiia nauk, [1768]);

Joseph Bourdillon Voltaire (Vol'ter), *Opyt istoricheskii i kriticheskii o razglasiiakh tser'kvei v Pol'she* (Saint Petersburg: Morskoi shliakhetnyi kadetskii korpus, 1768).

OTHER: "Pis'mo, v kotorom soderzhitsia rassuzhdenie o stikhotvorenii, ponyne v svet izdannom ot avtora dvukh od, dvukh tragedii i dvukh epistol, pisannoe ot priiatelia k priiateliu," in *Sbornik materialov dlia istorii imperatorskoi Akademii Nauk v XVIII veke,* volume 2, edited by A. Kunik (Saint Petersburg: Akademiia nauk, 1865), pp. 435–500.

Vasilii Kirillovich Trediakovsky, one of the three leading Russian writers of the mid eighteenth century, was in many respects a product of the Petrine reforms: energetic, adventurous, socially mobile, and eager to work for the benefit of Russia in the field for which his talents and education prepared him best. An able philologist, skillful translator, and devoted poet, he was the first Russian writer to gain a direct knowledge of European literary life and to attempt to transplant its forms onto Russian soil, as well as the first to draw attention, later in his life, to the importance of the Russian national tradition. During his long career as a writer he produced works in virtually all meters and genres. However, his significant contributions to poetry, versification, literary theory, criticism, linguistics, and the development of the Russian literary language were overshadowed by his reputation as the most tasteless and giftless of all poetasters, the pedantic author of worthless poems written in ludicrous language and meter. His negative image became a tool in literary polemics and thus survived long past the polemical exchanges of the mid eighteenth century in which it had originated. Trediakovsky's place in the history of Russian literature is determined by his negative image as much as by the impact his works had on subsequent literary development.

Vasilii Kirillovich Trediakovsky was born on 22 February 1703 in Astrakhan, on the Volga Delta near the Caspian Sea. In the beginning of the eighteenth century, Astrakhan, situated on the road to Persia, was a busy trading town with a large cosmopolitan population. Trediakovsky's father, Kirilla Iakovlevich, a priest whose father had been a priest, had at least two other children, Iakov and Maria. The entire family, except for Maria and her son, subsequently perished in a plague that struck Astrakhan in 1727–1728.

As the firstborn son, Vasilii was expected to follow his father into the priesthood, but his early education in a school run by Italian Capuchins was likely instrumental in opening up his horizons and turning him away from a church career. During his years in the school (which he probably entered in 1712 or 1715 and left in 1722 or 1723), Trediakovsky studied the basics of rhetoric, philosophy, and geography, as well as Greek, Latin, and Italian. His interest in Western culture probably dates from this time. Having completed his studies at the school, Trediakovsky wished to continue his education. His first choice was the Kiev Mohyla Academy (a religious school on the Jesuit model with a distinct Western orientation), and in February 1722 he asked the vice-governor of Astrakhan for a passport to go there to study Latin. Trediakovsky apparently changed his mind and went to Moscow, where he enrolled in the Slavonic-Greek-Latin Academy, modeled after and staffed with graduates of the Kiev Academy. The circumstances and the precise date of Trediakovsky's departure for Moscow remain unclear. It is known, however, that he left behind his young bride, Fedosiia Fadeeva, to whom Kirilla Trediakovsky had married his son in order to prepare him for the priesthood. Fedosiia also died during the plague of 1728; the marriage produced no children.

In September of 1723 Trediakovsky was accepted into the poetics (or intermediate) class at the academy. He spent two years at the school, studying Russian and Latin poetics during the first year and rhetoric during the second. In 1726 Trediakovsky left the school without having finished the course and went to western Europe, probably with the help of Catholic missionaries in Moscow. He spent about two years in The Hague, in the house of the Russian ambassador to Holland, Ivan Golovkin, studying French and familiarizing himself with European cultural life. In late 1727 Trediakovsky proceeded to Paris, where he remained until 1730, living in the house of the Russian ambassador to France, Aleksandr Kurakin. Both Golovkin and Kurakin were involved in an attempt to unify the Russian Orthodox and Catholic churches that was being undertaken around that time by the Jansenists, and Trediakovsky apparently took part in their ecumenical activities. Trediakovsky used his time in France well: not only did he study theology, mathematics, philosophy, history, and philology at the Université de Paris and the Collège de France, but he also was able to partake in French literary life of the late 1720s. He gained access to the Paris salon life and began writing French poetry.

By this time Trediakovsky was a writer with some experience. The Slavonic-Greek-Latin Academy's curriculum had included literary exercises, and several of Trediakovsky's surviving syllabic poems date from this time, including "Elegiia o smerti Petra Velikogo" (Elegy on the Death of Peter the Great, 1725) and "Pesenka, kotoruiu ia sochinil, eshche buduchi v moskovskikh shkolakh, na moi vyezd v chuzhie krai" (The Song That I Composed, While Still at the Moscow School, on My Departure to Foreign Lands, 1726), although two dramas he composed (*Jason* and *Titus, the Son of Vespasian*) have perished. In the elegy Russia, accompanied by various allegorical characters (Universe, Glory, Peace, Pallas, Mars), laments the death of Peter, "svoego gosudarstva novyi sotvoritel'" (the new creator of his state). Trediakovsky later rewrote the elegy in syllabo-tonic meter and published it in his *Sochineniia i perevody* (Compositions and Translations, 1752). The "pesenka," which was very popular among contemporaries, later became one of the poems cited to prove Trediakovsky's abysmal lack of talent. The dramas were produced at the academy's theater, a sure sign of their high quality, since normally only professors' dramas were considered worthy of staging. At the academy Trediakovsky also translated John Barclay's *Argenis* (1621), though this translation was never published.

While abroad, Trediakovsky began to compose love poetry and occasional verse. In The Hague he composed "Opisanie grozy, byvshiia v Gage" (Description of a Thunderstorm that Happened in The Hague, 1726 or 1727), which combines a traditional interpretation of a thunderstorm (as God's punishment) and Greco-Roman mythology. In Paris Trediakovsky wrote love songs, both in Russian and French, sometimes giving parallel versions (the Symbolist poet Mikhail Kuzmin translated the French poems into Russian for a 1935 collection of Trediakovsky's poetry), and he also experimented with the genres of epigram, ballad, pastoral, and meditative ode. His models were French libertine poets of the Regency period whose sensual Epicurean poetry was coming into vogue after the death of Louis XIV in 1715 (the first collection of their leader, Guillaume Amfrye de Chaulier, and his friend the Marquis de la Fare had been published in 1724). Trediakovsky's love poetry, playful and often erotic, introduced the Russian audience to the ideas of gallantry and laid the foundations of Russian love discourse. His songs enjoyed significant success up to the time when Aleksandr Sumarokov replaced him as the leading writer of love songs. Trediakovsky's interest in light poetry remained unmatched until the turn of the century, when Nikolai Karamzin proclaimed the value of poetic "trifles" with his 1794 collection *Moi bezdelki* (My Trifles).

Trediakovsky's poem, "Stikhi pokhval'nye Rossii" (Laudatory Verses to Russia, 1728), written in Paris, is one of the first examples of Russian patriotic poetry. The lyrical hero, away from his motherland, is struck by nostalgia and takes stock of Russia's excellent qualities. Mother Russia is described in superlatives: she is "solntse iasno" (the bright sun), "Bozhie ... izvodstvo" (God's creation), and "sokrovishche vsekh dobr" (the repository of everything good). Its inhabitants are pious and courageous, always ready to defend their coun-

try. Happiness in Russia reaches truly cosmic proportions in this poem. Trediakovsky chose to supplement this poem with another one, "Stikhi pokhval'nye Parizhu" (Laudatory Verses to Paris, probably dating from 1728). The parallel titles signal that the poems are meant to comprise a diptych and that the poet deliberately juxtaposes two points of view that were traditionally viewed as mutually exclusive. The poem favorably compares the banks of the Seine to the Elysian fields, where eternal spring reigns and Apollo and the Muses play their lyres, Russian *gusli,* and flutes. Another comparison is made to the promised land, whose main attributes of milk and honey Trediakovsky ascribes to Paris: "Tochish' mleko, med i vesel'e milo, / Kakogo nigde istinno ne bylo" (You flow with milk, honey, and pleasant merriment, / Of the kind that nowhere else have yet appeared). The utopian image of a foreign land as the blissful other world, the promised land, and the future eternal home for all humankind is thus contrasted to the nationalistic vision of Russia in the first poem.

Upon returning to Russia (via Hamburg, where he remained from November 1729 to August 1730), Trediakovsky affiliated himself with the Academy of Sciences in Saint Petersburg. He became a student at the academy, and in 1732 he began to work there as a translator; finally, in 1733 he was hired as acting secretary.

By that time Trediakovsky had acquired a reputation as a leading figure in Russian literary and scholarly circles. While in Europe, he translated Paul Tallemant's novel *Voyage à l'île d'Amour* (1663) and published it soon after his return under the title *Ezda v ostrov liubvi* (A Journey to the Island of Love, 1730). Tallemant's work, still popular in France in the first quarter of the eighteenth century, was an allegorical description of a love affair between Tirsis and Aminta (in Trediakovsky's spelling). With Cupid as his guide, Tirsis travels around the Island of Love, visiting such allegorical locations as the city of Hope, the cave of Cruelty, the castle of Sincerity, and finally the castle of True Luxury, where his love is consummated. Aminta, however, soon becomes unfaithful, and Tirsis courts different women to find consolation, until he meets the beautiful Glory, who commands him to leave the Island of Love. The novel is epistolary, comprising Tirsis's letters to his friend Litsida, and combines prose narrative with short poems. Trediakovsky contributed an introduction to the translation in which he set forth his linguistic views, and an appendix in which he published original poems under the title "Stikhi na raznye sluchai" (Poems for Various Occasions).

Ezda v ostrov liubvi displeased members of conservative circles and some in the clergy with its frivolous contents but enjoyed considerable success among the liberal-minded aristocracy and church officials, including Feofan Prokopovich.

Trediakovsky also became a familiar figure in court circles. Empress Anna's sister, the Duchess of Mecklenburg, was his patroness, and in early 1732 he received an audience with the empress. He was invited to the court several times and was well on the road to becoming a court poet. His services included writing poetry to order, translating French and Italian comedies and operas for the court theater (between 1733 and 1735 he translated nearly forty such pieces), and teaching Russian to Antony Ulrich of Brunswick, father of the future emperor, Ivan VI.

Trediakovsky's duties at the Academy of Sciences involved writing ceremonial poems, translating from German, French, and Latin, and preparing a Russian grammar and a dictionary. In the 1730s he was also productive as a linguist. Vernacular Russian was in disarray in the first third of the century and required consolidation and codification. Trediakovsky was well qualified for the job – he had arrived from France armed with new linguistic ideas and a plan of action. Already, in the introduction to *Ezda v ostrov liubvi,* he advocated the use of Russian instead of traditional Church Slavonic in works of secular literature. He asserted that "ochiun' temnyi" (very obscure) and "zhestokii" (harsh) Church Slavonic was inappropriate for a book about "sladkiia" (sweet) love and that colloquial Russian – "kakovym my mezh soboi govorim" (the kind that we use to converse among ourselves) – was the language to use. In 1735 Trediakovsky established the Russian Assembly at the Academy of Sciences, a body of linguists whose goal would be, as Trediakovsky indicated in his opening speech, "chistota nashego iazyka" (the purity of our language). Following the ideas of the French linguist Claude Favre de Vaugelas, Trediakovsky proclaimed the usage of the cultural elite as a model for the language of literature. A grammar and a dictionary were to aid in the endeavor.

Ezda v ostrov liubvi and the Russian Assembly represented Trediakovsky's effort to transplant European cultural life to Russia. The former attempted to introduce salon culture with its love for refined conversation and elegant play, while the assembly was meant to imitate the Académie Française and its effort a century earlier to codify French literary language. The novel ultimately

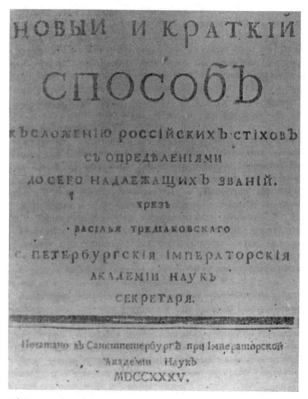

Title page for Trediakovsky's treatise on Russian prosody, the most influential of his works on literary theory

failed because Trediakovsky's translation, removed from the environment that had provided a context for its allegories and supplied a key to their meaning, could not effectively function as a work of literature. It was, after all, the single novel existing in Russian. It turned into a kind of manual on love, similar to other works produced by the Petrine epoch, such as *Priklady kako pishutsia komplementy* (Examples for Writing Complements, 1708). Russian literature lost interest in salon culture until Karamzin's effort to reintroduce it at the turn of the century. The Russian Assembly was more successful. By the end of the 1740s its members had compiled a seventeen-volume handwritten dictionary that included sixty thousand words. It served as a starting point for the formidable *Slovar' Akademii Rossiiskoi* (Dictionary of Russian Academy, six volumes, 1789–1794), which is still a useful reference work. In addition, the first Russian grammar to be written in Russian was composed by another assembly member, Vasilii Adodurov, around 1738–1741. It survives only in excerpts and in M. Groening's translation, *Thet är Grammatica Russica* (1750), but its influence can be seen in Mikhailo Lomonosov's *Rossiiskaia grammatika* (Russian Grammar, 1755), a pinnacle of Russian eighteenth-century linguistic thought.

Another result of the Russian Assembly's activity was the reform of Russian versification. In his opening speech to the assembly, Trediakovsky mentioned "slozheniia stikhov nepravil'nost" (irregular versification) as one of the obstacles to the beautification of Russian but reassured his audience that there were means to surmount the obstacle, some of which he had already worked out. This statement was a preview of his book *Novyi i kratkii sposob k slozheniiu rossiiskikh stikhov* (A New and Brief Method for Composing Russian Verse, 1735), the most influential of Trediakovsky's works in the field of literary theory. The book calls the syllabic system of versification, which had been dominant in Russia since the 1660s, "nedostatocha" (inadequate) and inappropriate for the Russian language and suggests adopting the Greek and Latin idea of feet, which, in the case of Russian, meant regular alternation of stressed and unstressed syllables. It proposes keeping the same foot (preferably the trochee) throughout the line in eleven- and thirteen-syllable verses, using a caesura after the fifth or seventh syllable; shorter verses were to remain syllabic. The innovation resulted in a kind of verse that Trediakovsky called "tonicheskii" (tonic) and that served as a starting point for the sweeping reform of versification undertaken in 1739 by Lomonosov. Trediakovsky's and Lomonosov's collective effort created the syllabo-tonic verse that continues to predominate Russian poetry.

The *Novyi i kratkii sposob* also includes a comprehensive discussion of such other aspects of versification as rhyming, cadence, and enjambment – with Trediakovsky's poems illustrating the new meter – and an overview of genres with examples. Among the poems, "Epistola ot Rossiiskiia poezii k Apollinu" (Epistle from Russian Poetry to Apollo) was the most important. It presents Trediakovsky's version of the history of world literature, beginning with Homer and ending with German poets, including Martin Opitz, the creator of German syllabotonics. The list of writers presented by Trediakovsky was meant to prescribe appropriate models for imitation. It demonstrates his preference for the Latin and the French, as well as his exceptional knowledge of the Germans, most likely gained in discussions with German colleagues at the Academy of Sciences.

Trediakovsky revised *Novyi i kratkii sposob* for his collection, *Sochineniia i perevody kak stikhami tak i prozoiu* (Compositions and Translations in Verse and Prose, 1752). The new version, "Sposob k slozheniiu Rossiiskikh stikhov" (Method for Composing Russian Verse), incorporated the results of a decade of experimentation in the field of syllabotonics by Lomonosov, Sumarokov, and Trediakovsky. It provided several generations of Russian poets with a comprehensive theory of versification.

In 1742 Trediakovsky married his second wife, Maria Filippovna Sibileva. Around 1745 their only son, Lev, was born. Trediakovsky's intimate life was not reflected in his poetry, as was typical for Russian poets until the late eighteenth century. However, several events of Trediakovsky's life had a profound impact on his psychological makeup, as well as on the way his contemporaries and descendants perceived him. One such set of events was a string of fires in his household and in the Academy of Sciences between 1736 and 1749 that destroyed many of his possessions and manuscripts, as well as copies of his freshly printed books in the academy warehouses. Future literary generations found Trediakovsky's vulnerability to fires extremely amusing, especially the fact that after each disaster he would set out with great diligence and patience to restore his lost work. Another episode that had a lasting effect on Trediakovsky's life and helped to shape his negative reputation was his confrontation in February 1740 with Artemii Volynsky, the cabinet minister at Empress Anna's court. Volynsky commanded Trediakovsky to write a poem for a wedding of jesters organized to entertain the empress. The poet refused, and Volynsky ordered him to be beaten and locked up in the guardhouse. Trediakovsky finally wrote the ill-fated poem, "Privetstvie, skazannoe na shutovskoi svad'be" (Salutation Said During the Jesters' Wedding) and was brought to the wedding to recite it. His injuries were so severe that for a while he claimed to be near death, but he survived and even received monetary compensation after Volynsky was accused of treason and executed that summer. This episode amused Russian writers and the reading public for the next hundred years, contributing a commedia dell'arte flavor to Trediakovsky's image as a pedant. In addition, in the 1830s and 1840s Slavophiles declared Volynsky a national hero who had been condemned to death because he opposed Empress Anna's German favorite, the infamous Ernst Johann Biron. Trediakovsky, then, was blamed for allegedly being an accomplice of Biron and thus Russia's enemy.

Despite his misfortunes, the 1740s were professionally productive years for Trediakovsky, marked by many achievements and friendly relations with future rivals Lomonosov and Sumarokov. The monument of their collaboration was the book *Tri ody parafrasticheskie psalma 143, sochinennye chrez trekh stikhotvortsev, iz kotorykh kazhdoi odnu slozhil osoblivo* (Three Paraphrases of the 143rd Psalm Composed by Three Poets, Each One Composing One Independently, 1744), the product of a 1743 dispute over whether poetic meters should correspond to thematic matter or be semantically neutral. Lomonosov and Sumarokov defended the former point of view, arguing that since the iamb was an "ascending" meter (moved from an unstressed syllable to a stressed one) it was more suitable for the heroic diction of solemn ode. The trochee, as a "descending" meter, was better for "tender" genres, such as songs. Trediakovsky asserted the equality of meters. To resolve their argument, each of them translated Psalm 143 – Lomonosov and Sumarokov used iambic tetrameter; and Trediakovsky, trochaic tetrameter. The translations were published anonymously with an anonymous introduction by Trediakovsky. The attempt to settle the dispute in a public competition was characteristic of the normative aesthetic mentality shared by Russian writers of the mid eighteenth century. It reflected their belief in the possibility of only one valid artistic decision based on eternal and rationally defined aesthetic norms. The value of individual artistic approaches was not even contemplated.

In 1745 Trediakovsky received the rank of Professor of Latin and Russian Eloquence, thus becoming (simultaneously with Lomonosov, who received the rank of Professor of Chemistry) the first Russian professor in the predominantly German academy. A Latin oration on "Rich, Diverse, Artful, and Distinctive Eloquence" served as his inaugural.

Trediakovsky's major linguistic work, *Razgovor mezhdu chuzhestrannym chelovekom i rossiiskim ob ortografii starinnoi i novoi i vsem, chto prinadlezhit k sei materii* (Conversation Between a Foreigner and a Russian About Orthography, Ancient and New, and About Everything That Belongs to This Matter) was published in 1748. In this work the author takes stock of the orthographic reform of 1708 which had replaced the Old Church Slavonic orthography and script with a new system. Trediakovsky found the new system still excessively dependent on church tradition and proposed to end this dependence by making spelling strictly phonetic. He also eliminated certain inconsistences in the alphabet, created by tradition, such as the existence of two letters for the same sound, and urged adoption of a more Latinized shape of letters (S rather than 3, for example) to reinforce the secular spirit of the 1708 reform. To demonstrate the valid-

ity of his new orthography, Trediakovsky employs it throughout the book. Although his proposed orthography did not take root, it influenced Lomonosov's *Russkaia grammatika* and, through Anton Barsov, a student of Trediakovsky's and later a professor at Moscow University, the linguistic views of Karamzin.

Friendly relations between Trediakovsky, Lomonosov, and Sumarokov began to deteriorate around 1747, after Trediakovsky, at the request of the academy, evaluated Sumarokov's first tragedy, *Khorev*. His evaluation was unfavorable, and in response Sumarokov included in his "Epistola o stikhotvorstve" (Epistle on Poetry, 1747) a nasty comparison of Lomonosov (cast as Malherbe) and Trediakovsky (presented as Shtivelius): "On nashikh stran Mal'gerb, on Pindaru podoben; / A ty, Shtivelius, lish tol'ko vrat' sposoben" (He is the Malherbe of our land, akin to Pindar, / But you, Shtivelius, can only talk nonsense). The name of the pedant Shtivelius, modeled after the name of a German mathematician, Michael Stifel, who had loved complicated operations with numbers and predicted the end of the world in 1533, probably hinted at Trediakovsky's manuscript "Matematicheskie i istoricheskie nabliudeniia o syskanii Paskhi" (Mathematical and Historical Observations on the Calculation of Easter, 1737–1758). The inane Shtivelius began a gallery of Sumarokov's portrayals of Trediakovsky as a pedantic fool. The pedants Tresotinius in the 1750 comedy of the same name and Krititsiondius in the comedy *Chudovishchi* (The Monsters, 1750) followed. Trediakovsky responded to *Tresotinius* with a lengthy critical essay, "Pis'mo, v kotorom soderzhitsia rassuzhdenie o stikhotvorenii, ponyne v svet izdannom ot avtora dvukh od, dvukh tragedii i dvukh epistol, pisannoe ot priiiatelia k priiateliu" (Letter Containing a Discussion of a Poem That Has Now Been Published by the Author of Two Odes, Two Tragedies, and Two Epistles, Written from a Friend to a Friend, 1865). In it Trediakovsky discusses in minute detail everything that Sumarokov had written to date and portrays Sumarokov as an incompetent and conceited author. He concludes the essay with a parody of Sumarokov's comedy, insinuating that the play was no better than a crude folk farce.

Trediakovsky's and Sumarokov's relations further deteriorated after Empress Elizabeth in September of 1750 ordered the former to compose a tragedy. He wrote *Deidamiia* (1775), based on the plot of Pietro Metastasio's *Achille in Sciro* (1737). Fetis, in order to spare her son Achilles from taking part in the Trojan War, hides him on the island Sciro in the disguise of a girl, Pirra. A daughter of a local king falls in love with him. Eventually Odysseus appears, tricks Achilles into revealing his true identity, and convinces him to sail to Troy. Trediakovsky's tragedy received a reputation as the most hilarious ever written in Russian. Legend maintains that it could never be staged because no actor could recite it without laughing. In 1752, for the sake of symmetry, Trediakovsky translated Terence's comedy *Eunuchus* as *Evnukh,* (The Eunuch) purging it first of its "merskikh samykh svamoslovii" (most loathsome foul language).

Around the same time Trediakovsky's and Lomonosov's relations also became hostile. Trediakovsky was offended by Lomonosov's lack of support in his quarrel with Sumarokov. Lomonosov, in turn, was vexed by Trediakovsky's reluctance to acknowledge his contributions to the reform of versification. Thus, in the introduction to his translation of John Barclay's *Argenis* (1621), which he published under the title *Argenida povest' geroicheskaia* (Argenida, a Heroic Tale, 1751), Trediakovsky asserted his priority in introducing syllabo-tonics. Lomonosov insisted that this honor belonged to him and tried to stop the publication of *Argenida.* The translation was published only after Trediakovsky toned down his claims that he was the first to introduce syllabo-tonics in Russia. The second round of their quarrel concerned Trediakovsky's revised "Sposob k slozheniiu Rossiiskikh stikhov," published in the *Sochineniia i perevody.* The author tried to prevent Lomonosov from evaluating the publication for the academy press but did not succeed. The fierce struggle for acknowledgment reflected the crucial importance of the idea of models for the mid-eighteenth-century Russian writers: whoever was acknowledged as the first and best would assure the everlasting exemplary value of his legacy.

Trediakovsky's *Sochineniia i perevody* was the product of more than twenty years of work. The collection opens with works on literary theory: a verse translation of Nicholas Boileau's *L'art poétique* (1674) and a prose version of Horace's *De arte poetica,* followed by Trediakovsky's original essays, including "Mnenie o nachale poezii stikhov voobshche" (An Opinion on the Origin of Poetry and Verse in General) and "Pis'mo k priiateliu o nyneshnei pol'ze grazhdanstvu ot poezii" (A Letter to a Friend on the Present Benefit to Society of Poetry). In "Mnenie," Trediakovsky makes a distinction between poetry as subject matter and poetry as form and points out that the latter's power of per-suasion lies in its rhythm. He emphasizes the importance of verse for the emergence of civilization and organized society: in his opinion, social contract required persuasion achieved through rhythmical speech. In "Pis'mo," Trediakovsky laments the diminished importance of poetry, which had once functioned as philosophy, ethics, law, and religion, but he argues that poetry is still useful as entertainment – as "frukty i konfekty" (fruits and candies) – and thus continues to be a civilizing force in contemporary society.

Other important prose works in the collection include the 1735 speech to the Russian Assembly, his "Rassuzhdenie o komedii voobshche" (A Discourse on Comedy in General), written as an introduction to his translation of Terence's *Eunuchus,* and the "Slovo o premudrosti, blagorazumii, i dobrodeteli" (Oration on Wisdom, Prudence, and Virtue), with a glossary of philosophical terminology. Poetry in the collection includes solemn odes, paraphrases of psalms, fables composed "dlia opytka," (on an experimental basis), and some translations. Among solemn odes Trediakovsky included a revised, trochaic version of his "Oda o sdache goroda Granska" (Ode on the Surrender of the City of Gdansk). Its syllabic original, which was the first regular solemn ode in the Russian language, was written in July 1734 and modeled after Boileau's "Ode sur la prise de Namur" (1694). A theoretical essay, "Rassuzhdenie ob ode voobshche" (A Discourse on the Ode in General), based on Boileau's "Discours sur l'ode," accompanied both the 1734 and 1752 publications. Another ode, "Pokhvala Izherskoi zemle, i tsarstvuiushchemu gradu Sanktpeterburgu" (A Praise to the Land of Izhora and the Reigning City of Saint Petersburg), written to celebrate the fiftieth anniversary of the new Russian capital, marks the emergence of the "Petersburg myth," a prominent feature in Russian literature of the nineteenth and twentieth centuries. The narrator looks fifty years back in time and sees only a marshy wilderness where Saint Petersburg would come to stand. He looks one hundred years ahead and sees a Russian capital that has eclipsed Venice, Rome, Amsterdam, London, and Paris with its beauty. The idea of the miraculous emergence of a beautiful city as a result of Peter the Great's civilizing effort is echoed in Aleksandr Pushkin's *Mednyi vsadnik* (The Bronze Horseman, 1837). Unlike his successors, Trediakovsky was optimistic about the idea of progress and the Westernization of Russia: his Saint Petersburg is miraculous but not unnatural or hostile to its inhabitants as it became in later tradition. A poem, "Strofy pokhval'nye poselianskomu

ДЕИДАМІЯ

ТРАГЕДІЯ,

Покойнымъ Надворнымъ Совѣт-
никомъ и Императорской Санктпетербургской Академіи наукъ красnorѣчія Профессоромъ;
Васильемъ Кириловичемъ Тре-
діаковскимъ, сочиненная въ
1750 году.

печатана первымъ тисненіемъ.

въ Москвѣ, 1775 года.

*Title page for Trediakovsky's tragedy about Achilles, written in
1750 at the behest of Empress Elizabeth*

zhitiiu" (Laudatory Stanzas to Country Life), contributed to the development of another recurrent
theme in Russian poetry from Antiokh Kantemir to
Pushkin: the assertion of the value of private life as
opposed to one of public service. Following
Trediakovsky, later Russian writers adopted
Horace's Second Epode "Beatus ille" for this purpose but omitted the ironic conclusion of the original, turning Horace's sarcastic poem into a utopian
vision of a sheltered and independent life on one's
estate.

From 1750 to 1754 Trediakovsky worked on a
long philosophical poem, "Feoptiia" (Theoptia).
The impetus came from Alexander Pope's *Essay on
Man* (1733–1734), which Trediakovsky had read in
a French translation. The poet felt an urge to supplement Pope's examination with an examination of
man's Creator and adopted François Fénelon's *De
l'Existence de Dieu* (On the Existence of God, 1713)
into Russian verse for that purpose. In six epistles
addressed to a fictional Evsevii ("Pious One"),
Trediakovsky examines the question of God's existence in the light of contemporary philosophy and
science. The poem did not get into print in

Trediakovsky's lifetime, was lost, and was finally
rediscovered and published in 1963 in *Izbrannye
proizvedeniia* (Selected Works). Trediakovsky's introduction to the poem was first published in 1989.

Simultaneously with "Feoptiia," Trediakovsky
worked on a complete translation of the Psalter,
which he finished in 1753 but which remained unpublished until Alexander Levitsky's edition of
1989. The genre of psalm paraphrases was popular
both in Europe and Russia, and virtually every
eighteenth-century Russian writer tried his hand at
it – Trediakovsky's *Psaltir' ili kniga psalmov blazhennogo proroka i tsaria Davida prelozhennykh liricheskimi
stikahami i umnozhennykh liricheskimi pes'mi* (Psalter, or
The Book of Psalms of the Blessed Prophet and
King David Paraphrased in Lyric Verse and Supplemented with Lyric Songs) was the second complete
translation of the Psalter into Russian, following
Simeon Polotsky's *Psaltir' rifmotvornaia* (Rhymed
Psalter, 1680). Trediakovsky approached the task
as a scholar, using available translations of psalms
into Latin, French, and Greek in order to figure out
obscure passages in the Church Slavonic version.
His paraphrases are precise and clear, and they

could have provided corrective to Trediakovsky's reputation as an author with an obscure and convoluted style had his *Psaltir'* been published at the time.

"Feoptiia" and *Psaltir'* reflected crucial changes in Trediakovsky's views that had occurred in the 1750s, when he discovered the value of national tradition. The Russian Orthodox Psalter represented for him both Christian values and the Russian tradition as embodied in Church Slavonic. Trediakovsky's linguistic and literary views changed accordingly. He acknowledged the importance of pre-Petrine culture, whose value he had denied in the 1730s and 1740s. In his 1755 essay, "O drevnem, novom i srednem stikhotvorenii rossiiskom" (On Ancient, Middle, and New Russian Poetry), Trediakovsky unfolds a three-stage outline of Russian literary development: the ancient period, the time of the highest status for poetry; the medieval, pictured as a deviation from original values; and the new, presented as a return to tradition. Only Christian poetry and Church Slavonic carried the tradition from the first stage to the third. Church Slavonic thus regained its value for Trediakovsky and became noticeable in his style. Trediakovsky's new views on Russian language and history are reflected in his *Tri rassuzhdeniia o trekh glavneishikh drevnostiakh rossiiskikh* (Three Discourses on the Three Most Important Russian Antiquities, 1773), written in 1758. In the first discourse, concerning linguistics, Trediakovsky argues that Church Slavonic actually is an early stage of Russian and thus a legitimate source of stylistic enrichment for literary Russian. These views anticipated the ideas of Aleksandr Shishkov, an early-nineteenth-century proponent of national tradition, and later, of the Slavophiles.

By the second half of the 1750s Trediakovsky felt isolated and mistreated by his colleagues at the academy. He believed that his access to the academy press was unfairly restricted. He conducted an experiment, submitting one of his poems, "Veshnee teplo" (Spring Warmth, 1756), under another person's name, in order to prove that the academy refused to publish his works out of personal animosity rather than because of their poor quality. The poem, whose title included a cryptogram of Trediakovsky's initials, was promptly published, to Trediakovsky's bitter triumph. The victory did not change his isolation, however, and in August 1757 he ceased to attend the academy. A year later the academy stopped paying his salary, and on 30 March 1759 he was dismissed. He concluded his service at the rank of court councillor but without a pension. In the last decade of his life he earned his living with private lessons and continued his work as a translator and poet.

Trediakovsky's central work in the 1760s was *Tilemakhida ili Stranstvovanie Tilemakha syna Odysseeva opisannoe v sostave iroicheskoi piimy* (Tilemakhida, or The Wandering of Telemachus, the Son of Odysseus Described in the Form of a Heroic Poem, 1766), an adaptation into verse of Fénelon's popular political novel, *Télémaque* (1699). This was also Trediakovsky's most notorious work, upon which his negative reputation was largely based. Using the myth of Telemachus as presented by Fénelon, Trediakovsky attempted to create a Russian epic, the only classical genre that had not yet been mastered by eighteenth-century Russian poets. He rejected both Roman and modern European models of versification and aimed at the reconstruction of the ancient Greek original. To complete this task, he developed a unique verse, an unrhymed dactylotrochaic hexameter, which he proposed as an imitation of classical hexameters. He had begun his experiments in *Argenida* and eventually developed a meter that was a combination of six trochaic and dactylic feet, with an occasional spondee. It was thus an accentual meter rather than syllabo-tonic — in fact, the first example of such meter in Russian literature. The hexameter Trediakovsky developed proved to be an apt imitation of the Greek and was used, together with a similarly constructed pentameter, by Nikolai Gnedich and Vasilii Zhukovsky in their respective translations of the *Iliad* (1829) and the *Odyssey* (1849), as well as in other nineteenth-century imitations of classical verse. In *Tilemakhida* Trediakovsky also perfected his new poetic style. To create a poetic language distinct from everyday parlance, he employed unusual stylistic elements (such as obsolete Church Slavonic words and compound adjectives that imitated the compound epithets of the Greek original) and experimented with word order and intonation. His effort resulted in an intense and embellished style, which he called in the introduction to the poem "bakharskoe techenie slova" (oratorical flow of discourse — *bakhar'* being a professional storyteller, a fibber, or someone who heals with the help of incantations). This idiosyncratic style, together with the innovative meter, greatly contributed to the work's negative reputation.

Throughout his life Trediakovsky incessantly worked as a translator. A large part of this work was official business, such as ceremonial odes by his German colleagues at the academy, explanations of court fireworks, or papers by fellow academicians. Other translations were labors of love, such as his versions of *L'art poétique, De arte poetica,* and *Argenida.* The most important enterprise of this sort, which took Trediakovsky thirty years to complete, was his translation of the historical works of Charles Rollin, his teacher at the Collège de France. Trediakovsky began translating his thirteen-volume *Histoire ancienne* (1730–1741) in 1738. The ten-volume *Drevniia istoriia ob egiptianakh, o karfagenianakh, ob assirianakh, o midianakh, persakh, o makedonianakh, i o grekakh* (Ancient History of Egyptians, of Carthaginians, of Assyrians, of Midianites, Persians, of Macedonians, and of Greeks), a translation of the first nine and a half volumes of the original, was published in 1749–1762; his sixteen-volume translation of *Histoire romaine* (1738–1741; volumes 10–16 were written by Rollin's disciple Jean Baptist Louis Crévier), *Rimskaia istoriia ot sozdaniia Rima do bitvy Aktiiskiia, to est' po okonchanie Respubliki* (Roman History from the Creation of Rome to the Battle of Actium, That Is, to the End of Republic) appeared in 1761–1767; and the four-volume translation of Crévier's *Histoire des empereurs jusqu'à Constantine* (1750–1756), titled *Istoriia o rimskikh imperatorakh s Avgusta po Konstantina* (History of Roman Emperors from Augustus to Constantine) was published in 1767–1769. Trediakovsky's translations presented Greek and Roman history to the Russian reader in a systematic way for the first time. They were still in use at the beginning of the nineteenth century. These publications served an additional function. Since Trediakovsky's access to the press had become restricted, he used introductions to his translations of Rollin as a forum for his own ideas.

Trediakovsky died in poverty and isolation on 6 August 1769, and his grave in the Smolensk Cemetery in Saint Petersburg is lost. However, Trediakovsky has by no means been forgotten. For almost a century after his death he survived in Russian cultural memory as a ridiculous pedant, the originator of everything bad in Russian literature. This comical image was useful in literary polemics, but it also ensured the survival of the very ideas for which Trediakovsky was ridiculed. His works on literary theory, his linguistic views, his experiments with nontraditional meters (especially hexameters and blank verse), and his experiments with ornate style were all useful to Russian writers looking for fresh ideas and innovative poetic forms. Even the comical image proved useful: for the twentieth-century Russian modernists it symbolized their own contempt for conventional success. By the present time scholarly investigation of Trediakovsky's legacy has left little doubt about the significance of his contributions. The comical image of Trediakovsky as a giftless and hapless poet survives, but it no longer obscures the outstanding part the writer played in the introduction and cultivation of a variety of important traditions in Russian literature.

Letters:

"Pis'ma V. K. Trediakovskogo," in *Pis'ma russkikh pisatelei XVIII veka,* edited by Grigorii Makagonenko (Leningrad: Nauka, 1980), pp. 44–67.

Biography:

P. P. Pekarsky, "Zhizneopisanie V. K. Trediakovskogo," in his *Istoriia Imperatorskoi Akademii Nauk v Peterburge,* volume 2 (Saint Petersburg: Akademiia nauk, 1873), pp. 1–258.

References:

W. Breitshuh, *Die Feoptia V. K. Trediakovskijs: Ein physikotheologisches Lehrgedicht im Russland des 18. Jahrhunderts* (Munich: Sagner, 1979);

Simon Karlinsky, "Tallemant and the Beginning of the Novel in Russia," *Comparative Literature,* 15, no. 3 (Summer 1963): 226–233;

Alexander Levitsky, "Literaturnoe znachenie 'Psaltiri' Trediakovskogo," in Vasilii Trediakovsky, *Psaltir' ili Kniga psalmov blazhennogo proroka i tsaria Davida prelozhennykh liricheskimi stikahami i umnozhennykh liricheskimi pes'mi,* edited by Alexander Levitsky Biblia Slavica, Series III, Band 4b (Paderborn, Germany: Ferdinand Schoningh, 1989), pp. xi-lxxviii;

Levitsky, "Russian Sacred Verse from Simeon of Polock to the Epoch of Derzhavin," in Trediakovsky, *Psaltir',* pp. 566–575, 589–605;

Iurii Lotman, " 'Ezda v ostrov liubvi' Trediakovskogo i funktsiia perevodnoi literatury v russkoi kul'ture pervoi pol. XVIII v.," in *Problemy izucheniia kul'turnogo naslediia* (Moscow: Nauka, 1985), pp. 222–230;

N. I. Nevskaia, "Rabota Trediakovskogo po istorii kalendaria," in her *Peterburgskaia astronomicheskaia shkola XVIII veka* (Moscow: Nauka, 1984), pp. 195–196;

S. I. Nikolaev, "Rannii Trediakovsky (Pervyi perevod 'Argenidy' D. Barklaia)," *Russkaia literatura,* no. 2 (1987): 93–99;

A. S. Orlov, " 'Tilemakhida' V. K. Trediakovskogo," *XVIII vek,* [1] (1935): 5–60;

Irina Reyfman, *Vasilii Trediakovsky: The Fool of the 'New' Russian Literature* (Stanford, Cal.: Stanford University Press, 1991);

James L. Rice, "V. K. Trediakovsky and the Russian Poetic Genres, 1730–1760: Studies in the History of Eighteenth Century Russian Literature," Ph.D disseration, University of Chicago, 1965;

Karen Rosenberg, "Between Ancients and Moderns: V. K. Trediakovskij on the Theory of Language and Literature," Ph.D dissertation, Yale University, 1980;

A. B. Shishkin, "Sud'ba 'Psaltiri' Trediakovskogo," in Vasilii Trediakovsky, *Psaltir'*, pp. 519–535;

Rimvydas Silbajoris, *Russian Versification: The Theories of Trediakovskij, Lomonosov, and Kantemir* (New York: Columbia University Press, 1968);

M. Sokhranenkova, "Trediakovsky kak kompozitor," in *Pamiatniki kul'tury: Novye otkrytiia 1986* (Leningrad: Nauka, 1987), pp. 210–221;

N. S. Travushkin, I. I. Nakhimov, and V. P. Samarenko, eds., *Venok Trediakovskomu* (Volgograd: Volgogradskii pedinstitut, 1976);

Boris Uspensky, *Iz istorii russkogo literaturnogo iazyka XVIII - nachala XIX veka: Iazykovaia programma Karamzina i ee istoricheskie korni* ([Moscow]: Moskovskii universitet, 1985);

Uspensky, "The Language Program of N. M. Karamzin and Its Historical Antecedents," *Aspects of the Slavic Language Question,* volume 2, *East Slavic,* edited by Riccardo Picchio and Harvey Goldblatt, Yale Russian and East European Publications, 4-b (New Haven: Yale University Press, 1984), pp. 250–274;

Uspensky and Shishkin, *Trediakovsky i iansenisty* (Paris: Bibliothèque Slave, 1990);

G. O. Vinokur, "Orfograficheskaia teoriia Trediakovskogo," in his *Izbrannye raboty po russkomu iazyku* (Moscow: Gos. uch.-ped. izdat., 1959), pp. 468–489.

Checklist of Further Readings

Al'tshuller, Mark. *Predtechi slavianofil'stva v russkoi literature (Obshchestvo "Beseda liubitelei russkogo slova")*. Ann Arbor, Mich.: Ardis, 1984.

Baehr, Stephen L. *The Paradise Myth in Eighteenth-Century Russia: Utopian Patterns in Early Secular Russian Literature and Culture*. Stanford, Cal.: Stanford University Press, 1991.

Berkov, Pavel N. *Istoriia russkoi komedii XVIII veka*. Leningrad: Nauka, 1977.

Berkov. *Istoriia russkoi zhurnalistiki XVIII veka*. Moscow & Leningrad: Akademiia nauk, 1952.

Berkov. *Lomonosov i literaturnaia polemika ego vremeni, 1750–1765*. Moscow & Leningrad: Akademiia nauk, 1936.

Berkov, V. P. Stepanov, and Iurii V. Stennik, eds. *Istoriia russkoi literatury XVIII veka: Bibliograficheskii ukazatel'*. Leningrad: Nauka, 1968.

Billington, James. *The Icon and the Axe: An Interpretive History of Russian Culture*. New York: Vintage, 1966.

Blagoi, D. D. *Istoriia russkoi literatury XVIII veka*, fourth revised edition. Moscow: Gos. Uchebno-Pedagogicheskoe Izdatel'stvo, 1960.

Brown, William Edward. *A History of 18th Century Russian Literature*. Ann Arbor, Mich.: Ardis, 1980.

Brown. *A History of 17th Century Russian Literature*. Ann Arbor, Mich.: Ardis, 1980.

Burgi, Richard. *A History of the Russian Hexameter*. Hamden, Conn.: Shoe String Press, 1954.

Čiževskij, D. *History of Russian Literature: from the Eleventh Century to the End of the Baroque*. The Hague: Mouton, 1962.

Cross, A. G., ed. *Russian Literature in the Age of Catherine the Great*. Oxford: Oxford University Press, 1976.

Cross and G. S. Smith, *Eighteenth Century Russian Literature Culture and Thought: A Bibiliography of English-Language Scholarship and Translations*. Newtonville, Mass.: Oriental Research Partners, 1984.

De Madariaga, Isabella. *Russia in the Age of Catherine the Great*. London: Weidenfeld & Nicolson, 1981.

Drage, C. L. *Russian Literature in the Eighteenth Century: The Solemn Ode, The Epic, Other Poetic Genres, The Story, The Novel, Drama*. London: Drage, 1978.

Etkind, Efim, Georges Nivat, Ilya Serman, and Vittorio Strada, eds. *Histoire de la littérature russe: Des origines aux Lumières*. Paris: Fayard, 1992.

Fennell, John and Anthony Stokes, eds. *Early Russian Literature*. Berkeley: University of California Press, 1974.

Garrard, J. G., ed. *The Eighteenth Century in Russia*. Oxford: Clarendon Press, 1973.

Gleason, Walter J. *Moral Idealists, Bureaucracy, and Catherine the Great.* Brunswick, N.J.: Rutgers University Press, 1981.

Gukovsky, G. A. *Ocherki po istorii russkoi literatury XVIII veka: Dvorianskaia fronda v literature 1750-kh–1760-kh godov.* Moscow & Leningrad: Akademiia nauk, 1936.

Gukovsky. "O russkom klassitsizme," *Poetika,* 5 (1929): pp. 21–65; partially translated in *Russian Literature Triquarterly,* no. 21, section 2 (1988): 7–13.

Gukovsky. *Russkaia literatura XVIII veka: Uchebnik dlia vysshikh uchebnykh zavedenii.* Moscow: Gos. Uchebno-Pedagogicheskoe Izdatel'stvo, 1939.

Gukovsky. *Russkaia poeziia XVIII veka.* Leningrad: Academia, 1927.

Hammarberg, Gitta. *From the Idyll to the Novel: Karamzin's Sentimentalist Prose.* Cambridge: Cambridge University Press, 1991.

Istoriia russkoi literatury, 10 volumes. Moscow & Leningrad: Akademiia nauk, 1941–1956.

Karlinsky, Simon. *Russian Drama from Its Beginnings to the Age of Pushkin.* Berkeley: University of California, 1985.

Likhachev, D. S. "The Petrine Reforms and the Development of Russian Culture," *Canadian American Slavic Studies,* 13, no. 1–2 (1979): 230–234.

Lotman, Iurii M. *Besedy o russkoi kul'ture: Byt i traditsii russkogo dvorianstva (XVIII – XIX veka).* Saint Petersburg: Iskusstvo–SPB, 1994.

Lotman, "Literaturnaia biografiia v istoriko-kul'turnom kontekste (k tipologicheskomu sootnosheniiu teksta i lichnosti avtora)," *Uchenye zapiski Tartuskogo Gos. Universiteta, 683, Trudy po russkoi i slavianskoi filologii* (1986): 106–121.

Lotman and B. A. Uspensky. *The Semiotics of Russian Culture,* edited by Ann Shukman. Michigan Slavic Contributions, number 11. Ann Arbor: University of Michigan Press, 1984.

Marker, Gary. *Publishing, Printing, and the Origins of Intellectual Life in Russia, 1700–1800.* Princeton: Princeton University Press, 1985.

Mirsky, D. S. *A History of Russian Literature,* edited by Francis J. Whitfield. New York: Knopf, 1949.

Moser, Charles A., ed. *The Cambridge History of Russian Literature.* Cambridge: Cambridge University Press, 1989.

Muratova, K. D. *Istoriia russkoi literatury XIX veka: Bibliograficheskii ukazatel'.* Moscow & Leningrad: Nauka, 1962.

Neustroev, A. N. *Istoricheskoe rozyskanie o russkikh povremennykh izdaniiakh i sbornikakh za 1703–1802 gg. bibliograficheski i v khronologicheskom poriadke opisannykh.* Saint Petersburg: Tovarishchestva "Obshchestvennaia pol'za," 1874.

Neustroev. *Ukazatel' k russkim povremennym izdaniiam i sbornikam za 1703–1802 gg. i k istoricheskomu rozyskaniiu o nikh.* Saint Petersburg: N. O. Iablonsky, 1898; reprinted, Vaduz: Kraus, 1963.

Orlov, O. V. and V. I. Fedorov. *Russkaia literatura XVIII veka.* Moscow: Prosveshchenie, 1973.

Panchenko, A. M. "O smene pisatel'skogo tipa v Petrovskuiu epokhu," *XVIII vek,* 9 (1974): 112–128.

Panchenko. *Russkaia stikhotvornaia kul'tura XVII veka.* Leningrad: Nauka, 1973.

Papmehl, K. A. *Freedom of Expression in Eighteenth Century Russia.* The Hague: Martinus Nijhoff, 1971.

Raeff, Marc. *Origins of the Russian Intelligentsia: The Eighteenth-Century Nobility.* New York: Harcourt, Brace & World, 1966.

Reyfman, Irina. *Vasilii Trediakovsky: The Fool of the 'New' Russian Literature.* Stanford, Cal.: Stanford University Press, 1990.

Riasanovsky, Nicholas V. *The Image of Peter the Great in Russian History and Thought.* New York: Oxford University Press, 1985.

Riasanovsky. *A Parting of Ways: Government and the Educated Public in Russia, 1801–1855.* Oxford: Clarendon Press, 1976.

Rogger, Hans. *National Consciousness in Eighteenth-Century Russia.* Cambridge, Mass.: Harvard University Press, 1960.

Russian Literature Triquarterly, special issues on eighteenth-century Russian literature, nos. 20–21 (1988).

Sazonova, L. I. *Poeziia russkogo barokko (vtoraia polovina VXII - nachalo XVIII v.).* Moscow: Nauka, 1991.

Segel, Harold B. *The Literature of Eighteenth-Century Russia,* 2 volumes. New York: Dutton, 1967.

Serman, Il'ia. *Russkii klassitsizm: Poeziia, Drama, Satira.* Leningrad: Nauka, 1973.

Silbajoris, Rimvydas. *Russian Versification: The Theories of Trediakovskij, Lomonosov, and Kantemir.* New York: Columbia University Press, 1968.

Slovar russkikh pisatelei XVIII veka, 1 volume to date. Leningrad: Nauka, 1988– .

Stennik, Iurii V.. *Russkaia satira XVIII veka.* Leningrad: Nauka, 1985.

Stennik. *Zhanr tragedii v russkoi literature: Epokha klassitsizma.* Leningrad: Nauka, 1981.

Stepanov, V. P. "K voprosu o reputatsii literatury v seredine XVIII v.," *XVIII vek,* 14 (1983): 105–120.

Svodnyi katalog russkoj knigi XVIII veka: 1725–1800, 5 volumes. Moscow: Gos. Biblioteka imeni Lenina-Kniga, 1962–1975.

Uspensky, B. A.. *Iz istorii russkogo literaturnogo iazyka: XVIII – nachala XIX veka.* Moscow: Moskovskii Universitet, 1985.

Welsh, David J. *Russian Comedy 1765–1823.* The Hague: Mouton, 1966.

Zhivov, V. M. *Kulk'turnye konflikty v istorii russkogo literaturnogo iazyka XVIII–nachala XIX veka.* Moscow: Institut russkogo iazyka, 1990.

Zhivov and Uspensky. "Tsar i Bog: Semioticheskie aspekty sakralizatsii monarkha v Rossii," in *Iazyki kul'tury i problemy perevodimosti,* edited by Uspensky. Moscow: Nauka, 1987, pp. 47–152.

Contributors

Nadezhda Iur'evna Alekseeva.................*Institute of Russian Literature, Saint Petersburg*
John T. Alexander...*University of Kansas*
Mark G. Altshuller...*University of Pittsburgh*
Thomas Barran.................................*Brooklyn College, City University of New York*
Charles L. Byrd ....*Indiana University*
David Gasperetti...*University of Notre Dame*
Gitta Hammarberg ....*Macalester College*
Natal'ia Dmitrievna Kochetkova...........*Institute of Russian Literature, Saint Petersburg*
Elena Dmitrievna Kukushkina................*Institute of Russian Literature, Saint Petersburg*
Konstantin Iur'evich Lappo-Danilevsky ....*Institute of Russian Literature, Saint Petersburg*
Alexander Levitsky ....*Brown University*
Marcus C. Levitt ....*University of Southern California*
Gary Marker ....*State University of New York at Stony Brook*
Galina Nikolaevna Moiseeva ....*Institute of Russian Literature, Saint Petersburg*
Marcia A. Morris...*Georgetown University*
Igor Vladimirovich Nemirovsky ....*Institute of Russian Literature, Saint Petersburg*
Thomas Newlin ....*Oberlin College*
Sergei Nikolaev.................................*Institute of Russian Literature, Saint Petersburg*
K. A. Papmehl..*University of Western Ontario*
Vadim Dmitrievich Rak......................*Institute of Russian Literature, Saint Petersburg*
Irina Reyfman ....*Columbia University*
Iurii Vladimirovich Stennik...................*Institute of Russian Literature, Saint Petersburg*
Irwin R. Titunik ....*University of Michigan*
Ronald Vroon ....*University of California, Los Angeles*
A. Woronzoff-Dashkoff..*Smith College*
Viktor M. Zhivov......................................*Institute of the Russian Language, Moscow*
Andrei Zorin ....*Russian State Humanitarian University, Moscow*

399

Cumulative Index

Dictionary of Literary Biography, Volumes 1-150
Dictionary of Literary Biography Yearbook, 1980-1993
Dictionary of Literary Biography Documentary Series, Volumes 1-12

Cumulative Index

DLB before number: *Dictionary of Literary Biography*, Volumes 1-150
Y before number: *Dictionary of Literary Biography Yearbook*, 1980-1993
DS before number: *Dictionary of Literary Biography Documentary Series*, Volumes 1-12

Q

S

ISBN 0-8103-5711-9

90000

9 780810 357112

(Continued from front endsheets)

Documentary Series